Inside a Service Trade

HARVARD-YENCHING INSTITUTE MONOGRAPH SERIES
34

INSIDE A SERVICE TRADE
Studies in Contemporary Chinese Prose

RUDOLF G. WAGNER

Published by COUNCIL ON EAST ASIAN STUDIES, HARVARD UNI-
VERSITY and distributed by HARVARD UNIVERSITY PRESS, Cambridge (Massachusetts) and London   1992

The Harvard-Yenching Institute, founded in 1928 and headquartered at Harvard University, is a foundation dedicated to the advancement of higher education in the humanities and social sciences in East and Southeast Asia. The Institute supports advanced research at Harvard by faculty members of certain Asian universities, and doctoral studies at Harvard and other universities by junior faculty at the same universities. It also supports East Asian studies at Harvard through contributions to the Harvard-Yenching Library and publication of the *Harvard Journal of Asiatic Studies* and books on pre-modern East Asian history and literature.

Library of Congress Cataloging in Publication Data

Wagner, Rudolf G.
Inside a service trade : studies in contemporary Chinese prose /
Rudolf G. Wagner.
p. cm. – (Harvard-Yenching Institute monograph series ; 34)
Includes bibliographical references and index.
ISBN 0-674-45536-3 : $35.00
1. Chinese prose literature—20th century—Political aspects.
I. Title. II. Series.
PL2413.W34   1991
895.1′8520809358—dc20   91-43239
CIP

Acknowledgments

This study was begun while I was a research scholar at the Fairbank Center for East Asian Research, Harvard University, and finished when I was a Research Linguist at the Center for Chinese Studies, University of California, Berkeley. To both institutions I owe much gratitude for offering me the possibility of extended scholarly research, and to the scholars and librarians there I am greatly indebted for their patient advice and help. I have in particular benefited from the critical advice of Merle Goldman and Cyril Birch. David Zweig was kind enough to make many helpful suggestions for improving the chapter on Gao Xiaosheng. Nancy Hearst has given me much help in compiling the record for the chapter on Jiang Zilong. A shortened version of the second part of this study has appeared in *Modern Chinese Literature* 2.1 (1986). Howard Goldblatt took it upon himself to render my feeble attempts at English into something at least compatible with that language. I am exceedingly grateful to him for shouldering this thankless burden. Dieter Plempe has been of great help in checking the manuscript. And Florence Trefethen has gracefully weeded out many of the more obscure and recondite passages, allusions, and terms from the manuscript in the process of editing it. Without this advice, help, and criticism, the book would never have seen the light of day. As is customary and correct, I reserve for myself the privilege of being responsible for all errors.

R. W.

Preface

Wei zhengzhi fuwu, to serve politics, has been the bane and duty of Chinese literature at least since 1949, and the literary world is described as a *fuwu hangye,* a service trade in a story by Wang Meng analyzed in this volume.

This functionalization of literature has led authors to exercise great skill and care in respect to politics, while deflecting their attention from such "extraneous" problems as the craft of writing, and the structuring of plot. Scholars have been puzzled about how to treat this amphibious material. It is evident, and generally recognized, that literary texts play a key role in the political setup of the People's Republic of China as both instruments and battlegrounds of social and political contention. Political historians, political scientists, sociologists, and economists, however, feel uneasy with literary material, since it would require literary analysis before being integrated into their studies, an analysis they see as outside their area of competence. Literary scholars, on the other hand, find themselves confronted often with fairly crude pieces which bluntly refuse to react to the refined methodological devices of literary scholarship and cry out for political analysis; these scholars deem such analysis to be outside their area of expertise.

The effect of this curious dichotomy has been that PRC literature has been largely neglected, with unanimous assertions that it would be very important to study it. The studies assembled in this book do not purport to give a "history of PRC fiction"; they are methodological explorations of prose texts written during the Hundred Flowers period in the mid-1950s, and, often by the same writers, after the beginning of economic reforms in 1979. They are a segment of a wider enterprise, other parts of which have appeared elsewhere, or will do so.

The texts have not been submitted to some unified theoretical standard; rather, the attempt was made, to let them decide on their own to what method of exploration they would react best. Within the limits of my capacities, I have tried to treat them "philologically," as though they were texts from some long-forgotten time, the environment, the editions, and the allusions of which we have to restore by painstaking labor so as to understand the context in which they operated, and to which they reacted. Both the cultural distance and the inaccessibility of many areas of experience in modern China have suggested this approach. The result again is not a unified set of methods to "decode" their hidden messages. They are all short prose pieces and share the features encoded in these genres; they use a series of very similar devices like the clues in characters' names, but each text has to be studied in its own light.

The following studies are thus suggestions of possible ways of handling these materials rather than attempts to set up the one and only way to treat PRC literature or even these texts. I have not spent enough time in tracing the various stylistic devices, and probably the harvest would be great if they were pursued in the manner I tried in the chapter on *texie*. A handbook on the standard literary devices of PRC literature could well be written, and should be written; this book contains only suggestions of how to do it.

Contents

ONE

Introduction

This study focuses on the role of literature and literary criticism within the political ecology of China during the mid-1950s, up to and including the Hundred Flowers period, 1956–1957. Texts of literature and literary criticism will be tested for their potential to yield information otherwise unavailable about the social history and social contention of the time. I hypothesize that it was here, in literature and criticism, that new assessments of society's problems and conflicts were postulated, new role models for social behavior were tested, and deferred battles about various policies were waged. Being scrutinized with a nearly obsessive and certainly not wholesome care by both the highest political authorities and the mostly youthful and city-bred intelligentsia for hints and indications, the texts were bound to show the signs of this stress in contortions of their inner structure and in bulges and dents of their outer form.

Happily, some research has been done on the period. Merle Goldman's pathbreaking study, *Literary Dissent in Communist China*, details the Party's cultural policies and conflicts from the Yan'an period through the Hundred Flowers period;[1] Roderick MacFarquhar's first volume of his study on the origins of the Cultural Revolution traces the

---

1. Merle Goldman, *Literary Dissent in Communist China* (Cambridge: Harvard University Press, 1967).

conflicts among top political leaders during the Hundred Flowers period.[2] And the first volume of the *Cambridge History of China* dealing with the People's Republic gives an overview of the different aspects of this period.[3] In the few attempts at a history of PRC fiction from the hands of scholars like Minoru Takeuchi, Lin Manshu, or the various writing collectives publishing recently in the PRC itself, some works are mentioned and briefly characterized.[4] To this must be added some more specialized studies like Douwe Fokkema's work on Soviet influence on Chinese literary doctrines,[5] Lars Ragvald's treatment of Yao Wenyuan,[6] or David Arkush's lengthy treatment of Wang Meng's "A Newcomer in the Organization Department."[7] These studies and others have established a fair body of knowledge and insight, and only by standing on the shoulders of their authors may we be able to see some broader vistas.

The literary texts at the center of the public controversy during the period have been mentioned, summarized, and judged, but not really studied and analyzed in their own right. Goldman deals with literary policies, not with the works; Fokkema handles theory but not the role of soviet literary works in China. Thus it would seem that a legitimate field of study remains to be explored.

As evident from the controversy arising around these texts, they are

2. Roderick MacFarquhar, *The Hundred Flowers Campaign and the Chinese Intellectuals* (New York: Columbia University Press, 1960); also MacFarquhar, *The Origins of the Cultural Revolution I, Contradictions Among the People* (New York: Columbia University Press, 1974).

3. Roderick MacFarquhar and John Fairbank, eds., *The Cambridge History of China, Vol. XIV, The People's Republic of China, Part I: The Emergence of Revolutionary China 1949–1965* (Cambridge: Cambridge University Press, 1987).

4. Lin Manshu, Hai Feng, Cheng Hai, *Zhongguo dangdai wenxueshi gao* (A draft history of modern Chinese literature; Paris, Hong Kong: Université de Paris VII, Centre de publication Asie Orientale, 1978); Minoru Takeuchi, *Gendai Chūgoku no bungaku* (Modern Chinese literature; Tokyo: Kenkyusha, 1972); Lu Shiqing, ed., *Zhongguo dangdai wenxueshi*, (A history of contemporary Chinese literature, 3 vols.; Fuzhou: Fujian Renmin Press, 1985); Zhang Zhong et al., *Dangdai wenxue gaiguan* (A survey of contemporary literature; Beijing: Beijing Daxue Press, 1980); *Zhongguo dangdai wenxueshi chugao* (A draft history of contemporary Chinese literature; Beijing: Renmin Press, 1981).

5. D. W. Fokkema, *Literary Doctrine in China and Soviet Influence 1956–1960* (The Hague: Mouton, 1965).

6. Lars Ragvald, "Yao Wenyuan as a Literary Critic and Theorist, The Emergence of Chinese Zhdanovism" (PhD dissertation, University of Stockholm, 1978).

7. David Arkush, "One of the Hundred Flowers: Wang Meng's 'Young Newcomer,'" *Papers on China* 18 (1964).

operating within a highly charged environment. According to the official socialist doctrine, the purpose of fiction is to "educate" the laboring masses, providing them with role models of proper behavior. Its official publication is the stamp of approval, and thus an important legitimation of a behavior modeled on that of the hero. Affirming certain values of behavior and attitude, the texts at the same time reject others, frequently in the form of negative figures. To understand the impact of a text (and the stress under which it is operating) it is necessary to reconstruct the environment in which it emerges on the day of its publication, the reading techniques, experiences, and expectations of the various segments of readers, as well as the way in which the author projects his own role.

While it would be most pleasant to be able to start right away with the analysis of these texts and reconstruct the various segments of their horizon as needed, I feel that too much detailed work has to be done in this process to prevent the analysis from becoming unwieldy and hard to follow. With eyes firmly set on what will be necessary for the understanding of the texts, I shall therefore start with the reconstruction of the environment. The eventual gratification for the reader should come with the economy then possible in the analysis of the texts themselves.

Environment is a vague term for a holistic ensemble of interrelated factors. Because of this vagueness, the depiction of the component factors has to be as specific as possible. In the case of recent Chinese history, the case is complicated by the extreme selectiveness and high unification of published and accessible material. This is counterbalanced to a certain degree by the curious phenomenon that some of the unspoken and unprinted objections to the policies of any given time will be expressed when policies take a turn towards the other side. Objections to and bitter memories of the Sufan Campaign to purge counterrevolutionaries (since the second half of 1955) were printed in 1956–1957, and the mute opponents of the Hundred Flowers had their say after the summer of 1957. Some tentative rules can thus be established for the reading of these materials.

(1) Each statement must be read against the background of another. Often the "other" statement is not publicly available at the time, but the text at hand reveals the force of the opposition. The publication of such opposing statements during the next phase of the political controversy,

or the later publication of memoirs of such muted opposition, can serve as a control to prevent wanton application of the rule. In terms of evaluation, the later pronouncements will of course oppose the earlier ones, but in terms of fact they refer to the same phenomenon. An example: an "honest fellow who faithfully follows the Party's directions" of one period is the "yes-man" in the next. It will be stressed in the first period that the Party needs precisely this kind of person, while in the second, the Party will be criticized for recruiting only yes-men. We are then permitted to assume that, in the earlier period, strict obedience was stressed as a key qualifying criterion for Party membership. In this manner we are able to restore some of the non-text against which our available texts have been written.

(2) There is a consistency and logic to policy articulations in China in that period. We can assume that a policy that stresses "collective spirit" would not encourage great variety in individual clothing styles. Thus we can describe policies at a time with a certain consistency. The control again comes with the change in line. If these things cohere, the change in one element, for example, stress on individual creativity, would have to be accompanied by a change in the other, encouragement of people to wear a greater variety of clothing styles. In terms of analysis, this permits a certain amount of inference from accessible to inaccessible information. The latter method was popularized during the Vietnam War. Counterinsurgency experts would, for example, infer from the absence of the elaborate ceremonies traditionally accompanying marriages in a Vietnamese village the presence of otherwise invisible strong Communist influence; the Communists were known to oppose elaborate marriage ceremonies.

(3) There is no linear relationship between the purpose of a proposition maintained in a text and the role the proposition will play in social life. The reading habits of the public might completely deform the intention of a text; the complex interest structure of people affected by a policy leads them to pursue all kinds of strategies to bend the text to their purpose, and the proposition itself may be a complex compromise which provides a platform for contention rather than sets an end to it. In the period with which we are dealing here, China may be described as having passed from the high temperature of the revolutionary period

to the lower temperatures of economic development, although rapid and great changes occurred even in these two years. The New Physics argues that most physical laws are low-temperature phenomena. The closer things get to the Big Bang, the smaller the number of different types of particles and of operative laws. This looks like a fairly apt model for the description of the validity of patterns of social behavior. The lower the social temperature gets, the more complex and diverse become motives and relationships among people, while many of the concerns, constraints, considerations, and interests give way when the social temperature rises, to the point that people are willing to sacrifice their own lives or victimize their own mothers. Clues for the actual social impact of a text or policy will again come from contemporary interpretations, later charges, and again later recharges, according to the first rule developed above.

In terms of intellectual ecology, the People's Republic of China, in its published opinion, has been very much a monoculture during the first thirty years of its existence, and its leaders have time and again asserted that only the unification of the thoughts of the nation could galvanize the country into a single force capable of the most astonishing feats. Lin Biao's dream about the spiritual atomic bomb constituted by a China unified in Maoist thinking was only the grandest and most feverish expression of a shared belief. The necessity of and the possible benefits from intellectual niches and complete ecotopes within an environment dominated by quite different values and structures have never been recognized. This frenzied apotheosis of intellectual homogeneity, this "dream of unity" as John Fairbank called it, is the heirloom of a past where the cohesion of the vast country depended more on the unified orientation of the officials than on the circulation of goods. This heirloom has received new life and legitimacy from Leninist theory with its emphasis on the unified hierarchy of the Party as the prerequisite of an effective bid for power.

The vitality of a social system, however, depends on its capacity to change, to innovate and accommodate. By subjecting society to a strong pressure for homogeneity, the political leadership threatens the very niches in which alternative options can be developed, on which it may draw when changes are imperative. In traditional China, such niches were de facto present in the form of illegal associations, secret societies, scholarly circles, and religious groups. But they led a precarious existence and were, as a rule, not recognized for their positive contribution, but rather seen as holes in the dikes of unity. Later, the foreign enclaves unwittingly became such niches on Chinese soil, offering alternative options ranging from Christianity to Marxism, from steam engines to opium, from labor laws to colonial submission. Ironically, with the victory of their Revolution in 1949 and the return of these enclaves to Chinese control, the Chinese Communists also blocked the main source for innovation and alternative options.

The idea of change and innovation is not alien to Marxist-Leninist thinking, but forms its very core. The Chinese Communist leadership thus became a victim of its own assumptions by simultaneously maintaining the necessity for unity and for change, and eliminating the options for the latter by insisting on the former.

By the end of 1955, forces in the leadership like Mao Zedong and Deng Xiaoping concluded that the "socialist transformation" was over and that a shift from "class struggle" to economic construction was the order of the day. This switch had vast implications for the status of intellectual specialists, for the definition of the main obstacle for progress, and for the structure of the country's institutions, which were to shift from a model of military command of a combat army to the civilian administration of a modernizing society. It involved a radical change in the relative values of subordination and independent thinking, and concomitantly in the lifestyle and attitude of the activists of modernization. Where would the leadership and the activists get their models, and how could these be legitimately implanted on Chinese soil where hitherto they had not been allowed even a small niche?

Literature, both actual fiction and literary theory, played an exceedingly important role in the public exploration of this dramatic change, and it is by a few literary texts that the period of the Hundred Flowers is mostly remembered. This period started in late 1955, well before Mao's speech on "Letting a Hundred Flowers Bloom and Letting a Hundred Schools Contend" (February 1956), and ended abruptly in June 1957. Some of the political leaders of the time, like Deng Xiaoping and Hu Yaobang, have been the engineers of the dramatic changes in China since early 1979, and the most prominent writers of the Hundred Flowers period like Wang Meng and Liu Binyan have returned to the literary stage since 1979. Surprisingly, the intervening years, which for some of them were bitter, have changed very little in their basic assumptions; they took off right where they left off in 1957. Given the short duration of the earlier experiment, the policies followed after 1979 might serve as a magnifying glass for that earlier period, making visible many features which, in 1956 or 1957, were at best potential derivations from the most daring thoughts of the main protagonists. In this sense, the present study is also an investigation into the origins of the post-1978 reform policies. It will focus on the problems, strategies, and tactics involved in the public exercise of a literature which in the early 1950s set out to redefine the problems of the country, to identify the characters capable of addressing them, and to operate as the harbinger of a new and necessary kind of publicized opinion.

Part One
The Challenge of the "Young Man"—
Literature and the Social History of Youth
in the Early 1950s

TWO

The Backdrop: Socialist Realism

The texts to be studied here constituted a challenge to the hitherto unquestionable assumptions, and were read in this manner. We are thus forced into a short description and analysis of the backdrop against which they were written, since the weight of an argument or pattern is determined by its position within the internal logic of the text, and the intensity of rejection of or support for a (usually unmentioned) background "text," which may be a political line or even an unwritten assumption. This "text" may, in the present case, be called "socialist realism" including this literary theory, the works written in its framework, and the ideals maintained by these works.

The doctrine of socialist realism was codified at the Soviet Writers' Congress in 1934. Originally suggested by Stalin and Gorki,[1] it was then greeted by many writers as a liberation from the dogmatic controls arrogated by the RAPP, the Association of Proletarian Writers. The Congress's definition of socialist realism ran:

> Socialist realism, the basic method of Soviet literature and literary criticism, demands of the artist a true and historically concrete expression of reality in its revolutionary development.[2]

1. A. Medvedev, *Let History Judge: The Origins and Consequences of Stalinism* (New York: Knopf, 1971), p. 511.
2. Cf. Statut des Verbands de Sowjetschriftsteller, in H. J. Schmitt and G. Schramm, eds., *Sozialistische Realismuskonzeptionen, Dokumente zum 1. Allunionskongress der Sowjetschriftsteller* (Frankfurt/M: Suhrkamp, 1974), pp. 389f. See also Herman Ermolaev, *Soviet Literary The-*

The emphasis on a "true and historically concrete" expression rejected purely propagandistic writing. It referred back to a statement by Marx who had praised Balzac's *Comédie Humaine* for giving a realistic picture of the decline of the French aristocracy. Although, Marx claimed, Balzac had been a royalist himself, the writing method of realism had forced him to show reality in its own development. The claim that things had to be described in their "revolutionary development" countered the then popular documentary writing with its claim for authenticity which Gorki had decried as "factography." The definition went on:

> At the same time, the truthfulness and historical concreteness of artistic expression have to be combined with the task of remolding and educating the working people in the spirit of socialism.

The task of remolding and educating the working classes was handled by the Party, and literature was thus integrated into the propaganda machinery of the Party. Institutionally, it came under the leadership of the Party's Propaganda Committee, and has remained there in most socialist states.

The third mandate called for the typicality of both characters and circumstances, a formula culled from a private letter of Friedrich Engels to Margaret Harkness. As the Party was expected to give an assessment of the status and merits of each class at any given time, typicality was understood as reflecting such assessments.

The most important element in this definition, however, is one of omission. In 1905, Lenin had demanded, in a note "On Party Organization and Party Literature," that literature was to be a "cog and screw in the revolutionary machinery."[3] The note was written against members of Lenin's Party who in this time of a relaxation of censorship laws in Russia (1905) failed to integrate their work fully into the immediate and urgent tasks of the Party. They could publish elsewhere, Lenin argued.

---

ories 1917–1934: The Genesis of Socialist Realism (Berkeley: University of California Press, 1963), pp. 139ff.

3. W. I. Lenin, "Parteiorganisation und Parteiliteratur," in W. I. Lenin, *Ausgewählte Werke* (Berlin [GDR]: Dietz Verlag, 1970), p. 184.

The term *literatura* used by Lenin covers journalistic articles but not belles lettres, the latter being *khudozhestvennaia literatura* in Russian, but Communist authorities have always interpreted the note as referring to fiction as well. By not quoting the statement, the 1934 Soviet Congress intended to reduce the writer's subjection to institutional controls. The collectivization of agriculture had been nearly completed; a little over a year later Stalin was to claim the abolition of the bourgeoisie as a class in the Soviet Union; literature was to enter the vast field of socialist construction and turn away from "class struggle." However, soon after the promulgation of the new constitution, inner-Party "class struggle" broke out, culminating in the terror of the late 1930s; then came World War II.

The definition of socialist realism, which originally was understood as a replacement of Lenin's harsh dictum, was now combined with it in the fever of renewed "class struggle" and war. In operating according to the prescriptions of socialist realism, the writer was to function as the cog and screw of the Party. Being thus saddled with the worst of both worlds, Soviet writing took a dramatic turn downhill. In his "Talks on Literature and Art" in Yan'an in 1942, Mao Zedong quite logically took up the combined formula, being at the time very much in a war situation which for him required full unity among his followers under his unified command.[4] Arguing against writers like Ding Ling, Xiao Jun, and Wang Shiwei, who insisted that "even the sun had dark spots," and that even the Communist areas had problems that had to be described, he quoted Lenin's demand that literature should be the "cog and screw in the revolutionary machinery" and focus on attacking the enemy. He added that writers were to serve with their writing the workers, peasants, and soldiers and not people of their own class and background—which effectively eliminated intellectuals from the ranks of potential heroes in fiction. By expanding statements made by Mao Zedong in 1940 and

---

4. Mao Zedong, "Zai Yan'an wenyi zuotanhui shang de jianghua" (Talks at the Yan'an Forum on Literature and the Arts), in *Mao Zedong xuanji* (Beijing: Renmin Press, 1969), III, 822. For the original text and the history of its becoming the literary standard, cf. B. MacDougall, *Mao Zedong's "Talks at the Yan'an Conference on Literature and Art": a Translation of the 1943 Text with Commentary* (Ann Arbor: Michigan Papers in Chinese Studies 39, 1980). The original "screw in the whole machine" was later changed to the verbatim Lenin quotation "'cog and screw' in the whole revolutionary machinery"; cf. ibid., p. 75 and note 173.

1942, a unique Chinese formula for the functions of literature was created which had no precedent in Marxist-Leninist theory, although it might have at times guided earlier practice, namely, that literature and the arts were "to serve politics." Since the very early 1950s, this formula was used in important pronouncements on cultural matters by such leaders as Zhou Yang, Lu Dingyi, Shao Quanlin, Mao Dun, Lin Mohan, and Ding Ling as the line followed in Yan'an, and to be followed ever after. It became the general line for literature for the next decades, gradually realizing its full potential during the Anti-Rightist Campaign and eventually during the Cultural Revolution.[5] Its specific content becomes clear from the terms used by Deng Xiaoping in September 1979, when he abrogated it in his address to the Writers' Congress: "In leading the work in literature and the arts, the Party is not [anymore] issuing orders, and does not [anymore] demand that literature and the arts subordinate themselves to short-term, specific, and direct political assignments (*zhengzhi renwu*)."[6] To "serve politics" accordingly meant subordination to "short-term, specific, and direct political assignments."

The formula marked the elimination of literary and artistic creation as an exploration of alternatives in form, behavior, and values. The Chinese Communists thus radicalized the most extreme Soviet positions into a general line for literature. Originally, much of the authority of this line had come from Stalin's Soviet Union. Eventually, after Stalin's star had dimmed in the Soviet Union, the Yan'an talks became the guiding light, and the theory of socialist realism was restated on Mao's authority in early 1958 as the art to "combine revolutionary realism with revolutionary romanticism."

Better than many theoretical digressions, the simile adopted by Mao from Lenin, that of literature as "cog and screw" in the revolutionary machinery, gives a precise functional model for the role assigned to lit-

---

5. The history of the slogan is traced in Li Shiwen, "'Wenyi wei zhengzhi fuwu' kouhao de xingcheng pingshu" (How the slogan "Literature is to serve politics" · me about), *Anhui Wenxue* 12:88ff (1980).

6. Deng Xiaoping, "Zai Zhongguo wenxue yishu gongzuozhe disici dahui de zhuci" (Congratulatory speech at the 4th Congress of Chinese Literary and Art Workers), *Wenyibao* 11–12:5 (1979).

erature in Maoist thinking. The model implies the full integration of artistic creation in every aspect into the Party's revolutionary machinery which, by definition, confronts a formidable enemy, and therefore has to be under unified command. The misadjustment, malfunctioning, or independent operation of a single "cog and screw" can stall the entire machine, make it ineffective for its revolutionary purposes, and cause its eventual destruction. The logic of the simile requires the immediate removal of dysfunctional parts, and sets a premium on the fulfillment of assigned functions with minimal friction. A machine, of course, might very well be described as functioning only through the regulated interaction of quite contradictory forces—including controls and safety valves for moments of malfunctioning—but Mao as much as Lenin chose to stress operativeness of the machinery in confronting an enemy. The behavioral values associated with the optimal functioning of the cog are upheld not only for literature but also for the writers themselves. Their personal behavior had often been, both in the West and in China during the May Fourth period, a role model for alternatives, as an example in their attitude towards love and the institution of arranged marriages. Within the "cog-and-screw" model, the process was to be reversed, the writer had to strive to make himself as inconspicuous as possible.

Finally, the values extolled through the heroes of the texts were to be those of complete obedience and devotion to the Party's goals and assignments as a role model for the readers to follow, thus fulfilling the "educative" purpose of literature. A literary example for the model in action is Zhou Libo's *Baofeng zouyu* (Hurricane, 1949), studied elsewhere in more detail.[7] The text was written with the assignment of showing and propagating the Party's ongoing land-reform drive; the writer's persona is completely obliterated, and he operates as a camera held by the land-reform team coming into the village; the members of the land-reform team have barely more than their names to individualize them, and they certainly have no opinions of their own—beyond the Party's assessments—concerning land reform; even the peasant who eventually can

7. Zhou Libo, *Baofeng zouyu* (Hurricane; Tianjin: 1949). See my "The Chinese Writer in His Own Mirror," in Merle Goldman et al., eds., *Chinese Intellectuals and the State; In Search of a New Relationship* (Cambridge: Council on East Asian Studies, Harvard University, 1987).

take over as village leader qualifies himself for this position by the gradual elimination of any distinctive trait until he looks as much a cog as the members of the land-reform team. He volunteers to leave his young wife and the piece of land he got through land reform, and to join the army in the final push against the Guomindang. With this act he shows his willingness to proceed to the natural extreme of self-obliteration—death. The group to which literature at the time was addressed, people with access to books, the capacity to read them, and interest in literature, that is, by and large educated city-dwellers, was also seen as the most volatile part in the "machinery." As persons with a public voice, they would form public or at least publicized opinion, and be the educators to instill these values into the general populace.

For this very reason, this class was the target of ever renewed efforts by the Party in the early years of the People's Republic. It tried to convince them, educate them, reeducate them, force them, and, of course, organize them into accepting the Party's values.

THREE

Gao Gang, Rao Shushi, and the New Master Text

During the first years of the PRC and well into 1955, the Party unanimously dealt with this group as "bourgeois intellectuals," who by definition had to submit to reeducation. Their leeway in terms of frank speech, actual discretionary power, and lifestyle was ever more restricted through the easy charge that these were "bourgeois," a charge quickly carrying over to the more serious "counterrevolutionary" when criticisms were interpreted as but thinly veiled attempts at "bourgeois restoration." During the Three-Anti and the Five-Anti Campaigns of the years 1951–1953, directed against ("anti") various forms of "bourgeois" corruption, this happened all too often with the effect of silencing many members of this group altogether. Already late in 1953, when the leadership tried to harness the intelligentsia into the fulfillment of the 1st Five-Year Plan with his heavy reliance on technological specialists, a distinct "lack of enthusiasm" was discovered among this group. While these campaigns, however, were mostly directed against people who were not members of the Party, the next campaign took on the first classes of "new" intellectuals who had received part or all of their professional training after 1949 and were members of Communist mass organizations. This campaign was the Sufan Movement, the Movement to Purge Counterrevolutionaries.

It is accepted wisdom that two members of the Politburo, Gao Gang and Rao Shushi, were ousted after a prolonged inner-Party campaign at the National Party Conference of 21–31 March 1955. (Gao committed suicide.) It is also accepted knowledge that, at about the same time, the public press campaign against Hu Feng and his associates was in progress. It seems, however, that the academic division of labor has prevented scholars from exploring the connection between the two beyond a short remark by Merle Goldman.[1] At a Politburo meeting on 24 December 1953, Mao gave the first indication that things were amiss in the top leadership by stressing that "the cohesion of the Party should be strengthened," which meant he felt individual leaders were emphasizing their independence of action too much. The 4th Plenum of the Central Committee, meeting from 6 through 10 February 1954, decided—Mao himself was on sick leave—to make this suggestion into a "Resolution on Strengthening Party Unity." It argued that the first stage of the revolution had been completed, and that the second, the stage of "socialist revolution," was "even broader and more far-reaching than the revolution against imperialism, feudalism, and bureaucratic capitalism." Consequently, it had to be expected that "counterrevolutionary elements will conspire with foreign imperialism and take every opportunity to sabotage the cause of the Party and the people." It would be most effective for them to draw high Party leaders over to their side, and corrupt them ideologically to the point of their becoming willing to split the Party. "No member of the Party should therefore think it strange if the imperialists who are trying hard to stage a comeback and those bourgeois elements who are resolutely resisting a socialist transformation create divisions and look for agents inside our Party." Vigilance "has to be raised." It is a rule in socialist political culture that each political power struggle has to be lifted from the triviality of individuals fighting for power to the level of an "ideological struggle" between classes.

Stalin's *History of the Communist Party, Bolsheviks (Short Course)* had been instilled into the head of each Party member over many sessions with this lesson. Thus the Resolution gives the underlying reasons why such corruption of high-level Party leaders is possible. The revolution is still young, and the Party presently has a coalition with the bourgeoisie.

1. Merle Goldman, *Literary Dissent* (note 1), p. 124. Frederick Teiwes does not mention Hu Feng in his *Politics at Mao's Court: Gao Gang and Party Factionalism in the early 1950s* (Armonk: M. E. Sharpe, 1990).

"Since the victory of China's new-democratic revolution, among some cadres within the Party a most dangerous kind of self-conceit has arisen. They become swellheaded over certain achievements in their work, forgetting the modest attitude and spirit of self-criticism that should animate a Communist Party member. They exaggerate the role of the individual and emphasize individual prestige. They think there is no equal to them in the whole wide world. They listen only to flattery and praise from others, but cannot accept others' criticism and supervision; they suppress and take revenge on those who criticize them. They even regard the region or department under their leadership as their personal property or independent kingdom."[2]

In a very long editorial, *Renmin ribao* elaborated on the Resolution on 13 April, calling on Party members to "Safeguard the High Moral Fibre of Communist Party Members, and Oppose Despicable Bourgeois Individualism," introducing the catchword of "bourgeois individualism" as the common denominator for the ills described in the Resolution, which were said to be "the obstacle on the way to progress of our people" and thus the main target of combat. Bourgeois individualism, the editorial said, was "presently spreading within the Party" and it was in no way restricted to a handful of top leaders. It fed on a complacency (*zhanzhan zixi*) with the success of the revolution that was "already relatively widespread among a part of the comrades. To tell the truth, a part of the cadres today have in very fact already become arrogant (*jiaoao*)." Thus a broad movement was called for. To the list of bourgeois individualist activities was added an important ingredient—"engaging in small-clique activities," that is, forming networks of communication outside Party channels. Proletarian ideology was "collectivism," and thus the ideology of bourgeois individualism with its offspring of bureaucratic conceit "is altogether bourgeois in its sources"; the new society does not engender such things.[3] The names of Gao Gang and

2. "Zhongguo gongchandang diqijie zhongyang weiyuanhui juxing disici quanti huiyi de baogao" (Communiqué of the 4th Plenum of the 7th Central Committee of the Chinese Communist Party), *Renmin ribao*, 28 February 1954.

3. "Baochi gongchandangyuande gaogui pinzhi, fandui beibi de zichanjieji gerenzhuyi" (Safeguard the high moral fibre of Communist Party members, oppose despicable bourgeois individualism), *Renmin ribao*, 13 April 1954.

Rao Shushi, the two Politburo members who were the target of this attack, were not mentioned, but they disappeared from public view.

The framers of the Resolution were aware that this extreme emphasis on unity and the depiction of individualistic attitudes as potentially counterrevolutionary could and might be used for an onslaught against critics of bureaucratic obstruction. In a helpless attempt at preventive damage control, the Resolution had added: "It is not permissible to restrict democracy or criticism and self-criticism within the Party [under the pretense] of strengthening the unity of the Party; on the contrary the full development of criticism and self-criticism within the Party must be safeguarded. . . . In criticizing shortcomings or errors of Party members, different approaches should be adopted." Against people carrying on and persisting in factional activities, "strict disciplinary action" must be taken, while those repenting should be treated according to the principle "treating the sickness and helping the patient." Especially it was warned that "unimportant shortcomings" should not be "exaggerated into systemic serious ones." The sequence of the two points made it clear that unity was the primary goal, and thus the appended warning was but a pious wish if not simply the result of a compromise within the Center.

In 1953, Mao and others had begun to attack what they saw as a quickly rising tide of bureaucratism among the leaders. The Resolution inserted itself into this context. Stressing simultaneously the need for greater control from the Center and for greater democracy and criticism within the Party, it was ambivalent enough to permit exploration in quite different ways, and, as we shall see, it was explored in quite different ways. In hindsight it would seem that the stress on the abolishment of diversity and "bourgeois individualism" was so pronounced that, with the inner-Party investigation about the two top leaders and their associates drawing to a close, a major purge could have been expected. While power politics crude and simple was certainly an important element in this campaign, it should be remembered that all factions shared many assumptions, and were as much victims of the bizarre dynamics resulting from the interaction of these assumptions and the social phenomena themselves as they were actors shaping these assumptions and adapting them to reality.

The leadership had difficulties in formulating an ideological criticism of Gao Gang and Rao Shushi as well as the forces they were by necessity spearheading. In the desperate words of the National Party Conference of 31 March 1955, which expelled the surviving Rao Shushi, "They never openly put forward any program."[4] Persistent rumors in the PRC have it that the entire affair hinged on Mao's appetite for a young woman protégé of Zhou Enlai and the resulting conflict with the Premier. This rumor might very well be true. Should it be true, the great record of Marxism in de-trivializing history would have been topped by the Sufan Movement which is to be outlined below.

In the February 1954 Resolution quoted above, the fostering of a split was identified as a policy to be expected from hardened imperialists, but it was not described as something that had already happened, which would have been a public announcement that an investigation was under way. As the investigation progressed and the need for an ideological conflict grew which could substantiate the charges, the Center decided to match the internal investigation with a public scenario. For this purpose, I contend, it chose intellectuals as targets whose published or accessible writings could prove that Gao and Rao were the silent moles of an otherwise articulate counterrevolutionary conspiracy. In rapid succession and with shifting targets, this public exercise matched the pitch then achieved internally with the purge of Gao Gang and Rao Shushi.

In September 1954, the scholar Yu Pingbo, a specialist on the novel *Dream of the Red Chamber*, came under attack for his refusal to accept

---

4. "Resolution on the Kao Kang-Jao Shu-Shih Anti-Party Alliance, 31 March 1955," original in *Renmin ribao*, tr. in Harold C. Hinton, ed., *Government and Politics in Revolutionary China, Selected Documents 1949–1979* (Wilmington: Scholarly Resources, 1982), p. 22. Rumors circulating among well-informed PRC scholars impute the conflict to an argument between Mao Zedong and Zhou Enlai. Mao is said to have set his eyes on the daughter of two Communists who were with Zhou Enlai in France. Both had died during the Revolution, and Zhou took their daughter under his wing. He opposed the Chairman's desires. Mao is then said to have prodded Rao Shushi to make a bid for the job of prime minister based on the fact that Rao ruled the industrially most developed area of China, namely Manchuria, and that this area had been the starting point for the southward drive of the Liberation Army. Support for Zhou Enlai, however, was too formidable, and Mao dropped Rao Shushi to the latter's considerable confusion. Frederick Teiwes, *Policies at Mao's Court* (Armonk: M. E. Sharpe, 1990) does not mention this version.

Party guidance in his research; this implied sporting a public behavior which could only estrange the students from the Party if they followed him as a role model. Well in line with the February Resolution, he "did not accept criticism" and set up his own kingdom of opinion. Yu Pingbo and his mentor, Hu Shi, were said to pursue their scholarship in order to satisfy their own interests but "not the needs of the country and the people," another charge from the Resolution.

After many meetings from October to early December 1955, the target was shifted to the next higher level. Feng Xuefeng, a Communist intellectual as opposed to the "bourgeois" Yu, was attacked in December 1955 in a campaign which, as Merle Goldman has written, "appears to have been planned at the very top of the party hierarchy."[5] Feng headed the editorial board of the main journal of literary criticism, *Wenyibao*, the Chinese *Literaturnaya Gazeta*. He had at first refused to publish an article critical of Yu Pingbo but eventually carried it in September 1955. Feng, who otherwise toed the Party line in most of his articles, was accused of setting up *Wenyibao* according to his own principles instead of following the Party line. "The editors regard *Wenyibao* as their personal achievement, have become vain, and have indulged in decadent authoritarian thought"; they were "intolerant of countercriticisms,"[6] and Zhou Yang echoed this "independent-kingdom" theme in his final remarks on the meeting to struggle against Feng: "Individual authority, friendship, and the power of their journal were more important to them than the interests of the people and the country."[7] No disciplinary action had been taken against Yu. Feng Xuefeng, however, was a step ahead on the road to bourgeois corruption by having an actual institution under his control. After a self-criticism, he was relieved of the editorship, but, in another conciliatory move, was retained on the board. We still don't know what went on inside the Party at the time; this might very well have been a public demonstration for the benefit of the "Gao-Rao Clique"—that they be spared, and even retain office, if they confessed and recanted, even if there had been more than an ideological drift towards independence from Party controls. In a next move, the focus now shifted to Hu Feng.

5. Merle Goldman, *Literary Dissent*, (Introduction note 1) p. 124.
6. Ibid., p. 125.
7. Ibid., p. 126.

Hu Feng had a small coterie of friends with whom he maintained an extensive correspondence. Politically he was as close as possible to general Communist goals, but he felt the functionalization of the intellectual and literary endeavor to "serve" politics (or the workers, peasants and soldiers) killed the creative impulse. He stood in the way of Zhou Yang, who managed the service trade. He misread the February 1954 Resolution as an appeal by the leadership to denounce arrogance and conceit of cadres and even leading cadres as a corruption by bourgeois thought. In his eyes, nothing could better describe Zhou Yang's autocratic and pompous handling of the literary realm than the very words of the Resolution, and he decided to use the leeway created by the Resolution and the perfectly legal form of a letter to the Central Committee to attack Zhou Yang's rule. As he said in this letter, "Recently, having read the Resolution of the 4th Plenum and afterwards the *Renmin ribao* editorial 'Study the Resolution of the 4th Plenum, Correctly Unfold Criticism and Self-Criticism,'[8] I pondered for a while"; eventually he decided to send his memorial.[9] This editorial quoted Malenkov, then the Soviet Party Secretary, with the words: "Each leader, especially each Party worker, has the responsibility to create a climate in which each honest Soviet citizen can frankly and without fear criticize deficiencies in our organization and work." It agreed with Malenkov that people who suppressed criticism were "our mortal enemies" and denounced those who took revenge on their critics.

Indeed, at the time it still seemed undecided whether the Resolution would open the way for a more outspoken criticism of the Party's "deficiencies" or become the instrument with which these very critics would be purged. Hu Feng was to be the loser in this interpretive battle. It was not that he lacked arguments, but the leadership around Mao sensed in Gao Gang and Rao Shushi a challenge to their supreme command, and the chips fell in favor of strengthening the top leaders' control over the Party, and not in favor of "opening up." With the historical

---

8. "Xuexi sizhong quanhui jueyi, zhengquedi kaizhan piping he ziwopiping" (Study the resolution of the 4th Plenum, correctly unfold criticism and self-criticism), *Renmin ribao*, 22 March 1954.

9. "Hu Feng dui wenyi wenti de yijian" (Hu Feng's critical opinions on problems of literature and the arts), *Wenyibao* 1.2 (1955), appendix, p. 2.

example of Hu Shi, the leadership proceeded to prove, from October 1954 on, how Hu Shi's "bourgeois idealism" and concomitant individualism led him straight towards opposition to the anti-Japanese struggle, and eventually towards becoming the ambassador of the "counterrevolutionary" Guomindang in "imperialist" America—truly a model career. Yu Pingbo had started on this road by keeping, against Party advice, his own counsel. Feng had gone one step further in opposing the leadership in general, and Zhou Yang in particular, by setting up a little "independent kingdom."

Yu Pingbo and Feng Xuefeng were individuals with "bourgeois" leanings opposing themselves to unified "Party" control which in their case meant the control of Zhou Yang's fraternity. In the "parking orbit" of possible targets of attack there was one single *jituan*, group, clique, or coterie which presented something like an organized opposition to the unity of the Party. In January 1953, the editorial note accompanying the *Renmin ribao* reprint of a *Wenyibao* article by Lin Mohan criticizing Hu Feng for "anti-Marxist literary views" mentioned "Hu Feng and his clique" as a group of people sharing the same ideas.[10] Having earned the wrath of Zhou Yang and his associates with his letter to the Central Committee, Hu Feng and his "clique" were retrieved from the parking orbit as the nearest public equivalent of what was internally discussed as the "Gao/Rao clique" with their "independent kingdom(s)" in Manchuria and Shandong.

On 31 March 1955, a National Conference of the Party determined that Gao Gang and Rao Shushi had formed an "Anti-Party-Clique." Gao was dead by then; Rao, said to be unrepentant, was expelled; and most of the people accused as their associates, like An Ziwen, received disciplinary punishments but stayed in office. No links between Gao/Rao and the imperialist countries or the Guomindang were established. Thus they were "anti-Party" but not "counterrevolutionary." The same terms were applied to Hu Feng and his friends at the time.

This ideological construct was highly unsatisfactory. Two Politburo

---

10. Editor's preface to Lin Mohan, "Hu Feng de fan Makesizhuyi de wenyi sixiang" (Hu Feng's anti-Marxist thinking on literature and the arts), *Renmin ribao*, 31 January 1953. The preface was carried on the following days in reprints of the article in *Jiefang ribao* and *Tianjin ribao*. See "Hu Feng's Critical Opinions" (note 9 above), p. 2.

members had succumbed to bourgeois individualism, which by definition cannot originate within a proletarian Party. They must have been
led astray by a consciously "counterrevolutionary" bourgeois group
which attempted to turn the weaknesses of Communist cadres into a willingness to become tools for counterrevolutionary forces. Otherwise no
convincing campaign against the grave dangers presented by bourgeois
corruption could be mounted, and the Gao/Rao affair could not be
accounted for.

The honor of playing the role of the conscious counterrevolutionary
fell on Hu Feng. On 13 May 1955 and on 24 May 1955, *Renmin ribao*
published the first two installments of "Materials on the Anti-Party Hu
Feng Clique" with Mao's unsigned but greatly publicized comments. In
an article on 24 May, Mao switched from anti-Party to "counterrevolutionary."[11] This implied not only prosecution for criminal offense (Hu
Feng was arrested in June), but above all the creation of the threat from
a consciously counterrevolutionary group hidden in the Party itself. In
a second specification, the target group was enlarged to include all other
"hidden counterrevolutionaries" of the Hu Feng type.

Under the imperative of defining the leadership struggle in terms of
class struggle with its ideological overtones, Mao Zedong now reordered
things in a major way. He restructured events and personalities, which
at the outset were quite unconnected, into a unified scenario of counterrevolution and initiated the Movement to Purge the Counterrevolutionaries (*suqing fangeming yundong*), a movement that now affected society
at large, and the intelligentsia in particular.

11. Editor's preface to "Guanyu Hu Feng fandang jituan de yixie cailiao" (Some materials
concerning the Hu Feng Anti-Party Clique), *Renmin ribao*, 13 May 1955; editor's preface to
"Guanyu Hu Feng fandang jituan di erpi cailiao" (A second batch of materials concerning the
Hu Feng Anti-Party Clique), *Renmin ribao*, 24 May 1955. The editorial on 24 May, "Bixu cong
Hu Feng shijian xiqu jiaoxun" (We must draw lessons from the Hu Feng affair), uses the term
counterrevolutionary for the first time. The term was retained in the third installment, which
appeared on 10 June 1955 in *Renmin ribao* under the title "Guanyu Hu Feng fangeming jituan
de disanpi cailiao" (A third batch of materials concerning the Hu Feng Counterrevolutionary
Clique).

FOUR

The Sufan Campaign, the Orthodox Personality, and the Political Climate

In July 1955, Peng Zhen declared in his "Report on the Work of the Standing Committee of the National People's Congress" that two NPC deputies, Hu Feng and Pan Hannian, had been arrested "for their counterrevolutionary activities."[1] A few days later, Luo Ruiqing, the Minister for Public Security, declared: "Hu Feng's counterrevolutionary clique has disguised itself as a group of progressive writers. A number of them have infiltrated into Communist Party organizations. A few counterrevolutionaries have even succeeded in worming their way into the governing bodies of the Party and the departments of the Public Security Agency. Pan Hannian, former Deputy Mayor of Shanghai, was in close contact, for a long period of time, with enemy espionage organizations. Working under the orders of Rao Shushi, a Communist Party renegade, and of Pan Hannian, Yang Fan, former head of the Public Security Bureau of Shanghai, sheltered and made use of a number of counterrevolutionaries and espionage agents."[2] Although no direct link between the two groups is claimed here, they clearly are of the same ilk. The merit of having most elaborately documented and studied these joint political campaigns at the very time when they occurred goes to

1. "Report on the Work of the Standing Committee of the National Congress of Representatives of the People," Xinhua News Agency, Beijing, 27 July 1955.
2. Xinhua News Agency, Beijing, 27 July 1955.

Léon Trivière writing in the journal *Saturn,* a contribution entirely overlooked by the scholarly community until recently.[3]

Hu Feng and his friends wrote things in dark language, had theories, and even dared to appeal to the Central Committee; the Hu Feng Clique was set up as the embodiment of the expected vile onslaught on the socialist transformation. Neither the collectivization of agriculture nor the development of state industries in the 1st Five-Year Plan could get ahead if this army was not wiped out.

In the new scenario, the "counterrevolutionary" ideologues with their secret organizations and "underground kingdom" (Mao) of the Hu Feng type were feasting on the weaknesses of individualism developed by some Party people, including highest leaders like Gao and Rao. These two were reinforced in their weakness to become "anti-Party" and eventually "counterrevolutionary." But Gao and Rao were not said to have conspired with imperialism, while Hu Feng was. For the purpose of a general political campaign, both protagonist groups were generalized: Gao/Rao into a self-complacent and individualistic attitude prevailing among "many" Party cadres, leaders included; Hu Feng into the general onslaught by "the bourgeoisie" managed by "the Hu Feng Clique and all hidden counterrevolutionaries." The interaction between the two is best illustrated by a cartoon. Within socialist publicized opinion, the cartoon serves the didactic purpose of publicly ridiculing certain forms of behavior deemed inappropriate at the time and thus creating a climate where they can be criticized and perhaps controlled. The cartoon "exaggerates," but it exaggerates what is considered typical, and thus shows the "essence" of actions and relationships that, on the surface, might seem quite innocuous. The persuasive power of cartoons is strong, since it implies the matter attacked does not even deserve an argument, and is just vile or ridiculous. Control therefore is tight. They

3. L. Trivière, "The Fall of Kao Kang, Deputy Chairman of the Central Government of the PRC and 'Dictator of the North-East,'" in International Commission against Concentration Camp Practices, *Monthly Information Bulletin* 2:33ff (1955). Id., "Hu Feng, the Dream of the Red Chamber and the Quarrel of the Peking Intellectuals," 3:38ff (1955). Id. "A Nation-Wide Campaign of Repression in the PRC," ibid. 4:36ff (1955). In January 1956, the *Monthly Information Bulletin* changed its name to *Saturn.* It continued to publish extensive reports on political and social developments in China. Recently, Siwitt Aray made extensive use of this documentation in his *Les Cent Fleurs, Chine 1956–1957* (Paris: Flammarion, 1973).

can be read as the most trenchant expression of opinion of the leaders of a publication at a given time. In the following pages I shall therefore make ample use of them. The general interaction between counterrevolution and inner-Party weakness is shown in the following cartoon by Wei Qimei:

"Bagging"

From *Wenyibao* 14:21 (30 July 1955).

In the first picture we have a pompous cadre in a cadre suit, probably someone in the cultural sphere, as indicated by the books. The papers on the ground are inscribed "criticism," and he completely disregards them. This weakness is observed by two men, the fat one being inscribed "Hu Feng Clique and Counterrevolutionary Elements." They tell the cadre he is great and "number one" to further blow up his ego. The inscription on the bag reads "Winning people over," a quotation from the "Materials." In the third picture he is bagged and is carried along their path of counterrevolution.

Merle Goldman has explained the Sufan Movement as an attempt to whip up some public fervor for the collectivization of agriculture. Since this movement was mainly directed against members of the intelligentsia and cadres, it could be argued with as much justification that the Party, which made the decision on the 1st Five-Year Plan at the same meeting where Gao and Rao were expelled, needed the specialists of the intelligentsia and would feel inclined to placate them. The implied assumption about the primordial importance of the economic base might have its merits for traditional "capitalist" states, but it certainly has not proved its worth for the analysis of socialist states where the "relative independence of the superstructure," which Marx himself had admitted, is much stronger because of the impediments in the translation of economic contradictions into public contention for social, political, and ideological change.

In the present case, it would seem that three factors interact: political contention for power in the center; a wish to create a high pitch of public fervor for the rapid "socialist transformation," with seats among the "counterrevolutionaries" reserved for those who opposed the move as too rash; the status of the Chairman as the chief theoretician for the new period, the problems of which he had "correctly anticipated."

The enterprise to make Hu Feng the public scapegoat for the internal corrosion of the Party's leadership had something artificial, and even wanton, about it, it being more a deduction from the Chairman's presumed infallibility than a result of any sort of factual investigation. The Chairman had announced, shortly before the People's Republic was set up in 1949, that, as a consequence of this success, a feeling of pride and arrogance might arise and grow" (*jiao'ao qingxu keneng shengzhang*). The 4th Plenum confirmed in 1954 the Chairman's remarkable insight, that this very feeling was now widespread and evolving to a degree of endangering the unity of the Party. Quoting from a Resolution on Strengthening the Party Spirit passed in 1941, the important *Renmin ribao* editorial of 22 March 1954 linked this feeling to "bourgeois individualism," "an undisciplined attitude," and "anticentralistic dispersalism."[4] The mold for Gao/Rao and Hu Feng was precast. Their being subsumed under these categories is indicative of the Chairman's status at the time as well as the degree to which deduction had replaced investigation. The same was true for the second basic assumption, which dealt with the way in which class struggle in socialism would "by necessity" develop. The Resolution of the 4th Plenum had said in February 1954: "Presently, China is in the process of socialist revolution [as opposed to the 'new-democratic' 1949 revolution], that is, the stage of socialist transformation; we realize step by step socialist industrialization as well as the gradual socialist transformation of agriculture, handicrafts, and capitalist industry and trade, and build our land into a grand socialist country. This is an even more penetrating and more encompassing revolution than the revolution against imperialism, feudalism, and bureaucratic capital and involves an exceedingly complex and sharp struggle. In this struggle, foreign imperialism, on the one hand, will absolutely not stand idly by, and the already overthrown classes within the country, on the other hand, will certainly not resign themselves to their demise; it *is absolutely impossible that these classes to be eliminated will not resist,* and the hardened counterrevolutionary elements among them will by necessity link up with the foreign imperialists,"[5] in order to destroy the Revolution. The drive of the Revolution had come from a clearly defined and broadly accepted "enemy," first Japan and then the Guomindang. It had provided cohesion for the Party and popular support. With immaculately logical thinking, a new "enemy" was now conjured up *because* neither did the United States invade China nor did "the bourgeoisie" show much resistance after 1949. A year later, after the bourgeoisie and imperialism still failed to oblige, the theory reached its natural extreme of both logic and radicalism. In his notes to the third installment of Hu Feng's materials, Mao quoted a letter by Zhang Zhongxiao to Hu Feng dated 25 May 1951, where he referred to the "wild killings" going on at the time in the *Zhenfan* Movement to "suppress counterrevolutionaries." Zhang ended the letter with the words,

4. "Study the resolution," (page 23 note 8). Mao had made the remark at the 2nd Plenum of the 7th Central Committee.

5. "Resolution on the Kao Kang-Jao Shu-Shi" (p. 21 note 4).

"The struggle will necessarily become deeper."[6] In his comments on this announcement from a "counterrevolutionary," Mao asserted "That's quite true." This line confirmed what logic said *must* come. The "new democratic" revolution still operated in a "coalition with the bourgeoisie"; therefore the resistance was not too desperate. The socialist transformation would mean the *elimination* of the bourgeoisie as a class, and therefore their resistance must by necessity be stronger, "deeper." The *Renmin ribao* editorial on the day these materials were published spelled out the new theory of the *necessary exacerbation* of class struggle in socialism. If it was not written by Mao himself, it was at least handled with the same degree of deference, and reprinted together with the annotated Hu Feng materials in periodicals like *Zhongguo qingnian*. It said: "During the gigantic movement for the socialist industrialization of the state and the establishment of a socialist [as opposed to new-democratic] society, class struggle will become even more acute, and the counterrevolutionary elements will by necessity (*biran*) increase their sabotage activities."[7]

What was, in terms of political theory, a logical and, within the logic of the basic assumptions, a convincing construct, was in terms of political strategy an astute maneuver. There was, and Mao said so repeatedly, substantial opposition to rapid collectivization among the cadres. As might be expected, the memory of this opposition was refreshed after 1980, when the new leadership proceeded to dismantle much of the collective structure in the countryside. By managing a campaign against the devious bourgeois corrosion of the cadres side by side with the campaign to collectivize agriculture, the avenues for legitimate dissent were effectively closed, because any dissenter invited the charge that he, too, was under the influence of a bourgeoisie desperately trying to prevent the collectivization of agriculture and the nationalization of industry, and therewith its own demise as a class. Inversely, however, this combination of two campaigns developed its own quite unpredictable dynamics. It forced the cadres to prove that they were

6. "A third batch of materials" (p. 25 note 11) item no. 66. This letter concludes the "materials" with this quotation.

7. Editorial, "Bixu cong Hu Feng shijian xiqu jiaoxun" (We have to continue to draw the lessons from the Hu Feng incident), *Renmin ribao*, 10 June 1955. Reprinted in *Zhongguo qingnian* 12:17 (1955).

not influenced by bourgeois thought, and they did so by outbidding each other in the ever-greater acceleration of the drive, charging the critics among the peasantry of this frenzied speed to be in their turn under the influence, or even the tools of the desperate bourgeoisie's opposition. The pattern was repeated, in a grander dimension, during the Great Leap Forward.

The conflict between the postulate that "by necessity" the bourgeoisie would resist, and the fact that it did not, was solved with the argument that it did so in a "hidden" fashion, masking itself. It would be a facile solution to discount these ideological ruminations and impute a hearty cynicism to the Communist leadership. These leaders were quite confident that their ideology served them in good stead; they had just won the Revolution and assumed this was due to their correct analysis of the development of class struggle, and their own appropriate strategy. That in fact the causes may have been quite different, and that they won although they misread essential features of Chinese society, is irrelevant here, since we are dealing with their beliefs and their credibility. There is, however, little in Marxist theory to help one understand the dynamics of a political structure of a Leninist cast of characters on Chinese soil. They went by the only precedent they had, the Soviet Union directly after the Revolution and during the collectivization of agriculture a decade later, as depicted in the *Short Course*. The fact that the "bourgeois counterattack" was a phantom did not prevent the leadership from pushing their lower levels to come up with warm bodies to make this phantom concrete, and to kick loose a social avalanche over the course of which they had only little control.

Whatever specific motives and ideologies the people might have had who were accused of being linked to these "cliques," they were called upon to provide public testimony for the analytical powers of the leadership, and fuel for the campaign against a logical phantom, the hidden, the masked bourgeoisie. True, this bourgeoisie "looked like a group of revolutionaries operating in broad daylight," but in fact "most of them have a very shady background. The main force of the clique consists of imperialist and Guomindang secret agents, Trotskyites, reactionary army officers, or renegades from the Communist Party." They were not only in the field of letters, Mao continued, but "have wormed their way into political, military, economic, cultural, and educational departments," forming an "underground independent kingdom" there.[8] The *Renmin ribao* editorial elaborated on this point. If Hu Feng and his clique could stay hidden in these organs, "why cannot other counterrevolutionary elements use similar double-dealing tactics to hide themselves in our political, military, etc. departments?" "One has to say," it continued, "they must by necessity have wormed their way in there." How many were "they"? The editorial generously admitted that "about 90 percent (*baifen zhi jiushi ji*) of the people in our revolutionary contingent are good," which left a substantial 10 percent in the category of "hidden counterrevolutionaries and bad elements."[9] Chinese readers are accustomed to read in such numbers a quota of people to be identified in each unit. A few days later, the slogan of the campaign was changed from "Unmask and Denounce the Crimes of the Hu Feng Counterrevolutionary Clique" to "Decidedly Purge the Hu Feng Clique and All Hidden Counterrevolutionary Elements." What had started out ambivalent enough to encourage criticism of Party bureaucrats had now turned into a full-scale persecution of any possible critic, a pattern repeated in ever greater dimensions in later developments, that is, the Hundred Flowers/Anti-Rightist Campaign sequence, the Second Hundred Flowers/Cultural Revolution sequence, and, within the Cultural Revolution itself, the Red Guard/Revolutionary Rebels sequence.

The next months were spent in frenzied search for people to fill the quota. Zhou Yang claimed in May 1957 that the critics of the enormous proportions this movement had taken failed to acknowledge the moderating influence of the Center. "Some people express their dissatisfaction with the quota of 5 percent set for [counterrevolutionaries in the Party to be eliminated in] the Sufan Movement, but they don't know that very many regions at the time went as high as 30 percent, and that the quota of 5 percent set by the Center had the function of restricting this."[10]

It was hard to identify the hidden counterrevolutionaries and the people "bagged" by them on the basis that they "looked revolutionary."

8. Mao Zedong, "Preface and Editor's Notes to 'Materials on the Counterrevolutionary Hu Feng Clique,'" in Mao Zedong, *Selected Works* (Beijing: Foreign Languages Press, 1977), V, 179.

9. "We have to continue" (ch. 3 note 11). The number 90% (i.e. or 10% bad elements) comes from Mao's comments to the third batch of Hu Feng Materials, (ch. 3 note 11), item 33.

10. Zhou Yang, "Jieda guanyu 'baihua qifang, baijia zhengming' fangzhen de jige wenti" (Answering some questions concerning the line of 'Letting a Hundred Flowers Bloom and a Hundred Schools Contend'), in *Zhou Yang wenji* (Beijing: Renmin Wenxue Press, 1985), II, 513.

They were to be found "in government organs, Army units, schools, factories, mass organizations, and democratic parties," that is, they were cadres with a more or less substantial education. Their "shady background" referred to by Mao, was specified to ease the difficulties in recognition. Candidates for the quota were

- *you cuowu de ren*, "people who had made [ideological] mistakes";
- *dui gongchandang buman de ren*, "people dissatisfied with the Communist Party";
- *lishishang youwenti de ren*, "people with a problematic past [like bad class background, earlier cooperation with Guomindang government, residence in 'imperialist' states]";
- *sangshi jingtixing de ren*, "people who have lost their vigilance."[11]

On the basis of this list, but liberally expanded, an ideal negative personality was constructed, and particular traits were depicted for easy identification of counterrevolutionaries. This ideal negative personality embodied the attitudes officially rejected, and was the negative image of the ideal positive personality.

A cartoon from *Wenyibao* illustrates the list from the *Renmin ribao* editorial:

"Hu Feng's 'Literary Salon,'" by Zhang Wenyuan

From *Wenyibao* 13:19 (15 July 1955).

11. "We Have to Continue" (note 9).

Hu's "old bar of twenty years" has Hu Feng himself behind the bar pouring "*wei (xinzhuyi),*" idealism, into glasses to drink. The sign on the left announces that "especially welcome are friends who lost their vigilance, have problems with their past, are dissatisfied with the Communist Party and have ideological mistakes," that is, the very groups mentioned in the *Renmin ribao* editorial. Lured by the foamy idealistic beverage, and the promise on the glasses to be "lavishly praised" (those who lost vigilance), "comforted" (those with the troubled past), "sympathized with" (those dissatisfied with the CP), and "treated with warmth" (those with ideological mistakes), the Party's weaklings go into the trap with Hu's gang members hidden behind the counter to pull the straps.

The sequence of indicators given in the *Renmin ribao* editorial is retained here, but in inverse order. This would seem to indicate that the editorial put the greatest problem last (which is unusual), and the cartoon reestablished the standard order in Chinese series with the most important first. In fact, the pompous cadre comes in for the greatest attention in the cartoons.

From *Wenyibao* 12:12 (13 June 1955).

The snake with Hu Feng's head coils around a pompous cadre's neck, inscribed "Scarf brand 'warm and cosy.'" The inscription refers to Hu

Feng's demand for a more congenial atmosphere among literary intellectuals, which was seen as an opposition to class struggle and reeducation campaigns.

The Youth League came out with similar warnings:

"High Hat," by Ding Cong

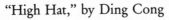

From *Zhongguo qingnian* 16:10 (16 August 1955)

A counterrevolutionary element, now in the general image of the disguised tiger, leads a young man down the wrong road. The young man is blinded by the high hat of praise put on his head by the tiger, inscribed "active, pure youth, capable." Under his arm he carries a "recommendation" from the tiger. The leather shoes, cadre suit, and briefcase mark him as a young office cadre.

These cartoons are less social criticisms of certain public attitudes than justifications for selecting certain types of people to fill the quota. The older military cadres were both appalled at and threatened by younger cadres with higher qualifications and a more purist idea of how society should be run. By identifying these qualities ("active, pure, capable") as indicators of bourgeois conceit, senior cadres could eliminate potential competitors and challengers. In this way they also evaded the possible charge of "lacking vigilance," since their purging of others was contrary evidence. By way of self-protection, cadres thus continuously expanded the range of possible quota candidates. This had the effect of ostracizing types of behavior seen as threats to bureaucratic stagnation. I shall shortly document the attitudes most severely attacked.

One of the expressions of "individualism" was the urge of young members of the intelligentsia to see their names in print. This by defini-tion was a weakness. If they managed to get printed, the counterrevolu-tion would make use of their big airs:

"You Truly Are a Genius, I Hug You," by Ding Cong

"你真是天才,我擁抱你!"   丁聰作

From *Wenyibao* 12:14 (30 June 1955).

The young man has been published in a book "Gifted Young Authors" with a preface by Hu Feng. Elated, he does not notice how he is made into a Guomindang agent by Hu Feng who holds the stamp with the Guomindang emblem, while pulling "secrets" out of the young man's pockets, which indicates that he is a member of either the Party or the Youth League. If getting published bloated people's ego with the concomitant dangers, not getting published was much worse, because then "dissatisfaction with the Communist Party" could be assumed to occur as an additional affliction.

The Youth League periodical alone received several thousand manuscripts per month at times, and this for a space of 32 pages. It can be assumed that many of the more active, articulate, and outspoken youths would have been among the people sending in manuscripts. The harvest for the campaign to be gathered here was thus better both in terms of quality and of quantity:

"Empathy," by Ding Cong

From *Zhongguo qingnian* 14:8 (16 July 1955).

A young writer holds what is probably his first manuscript. It has been rejected; he is distressed. A "Hu Feng element" discerns in the individualistic drive to get published, and in the frustration over being turned down, an inroad for his dark purpose. The rest does not need comment.

To concentrate on scholarly or technical work became evidence for being "not concerned with politics," that is, with the campaign to weed out counterrevolutionaries, and made one an easy victim of counterrevolutionary lures. Instead of quoting Guo Moruo's long diatribe calling upon his colleagues in the Academy of Sciences to join the campaign, some cartoons may illustrate the point:

"The Ears Don't Hear What is Going On Outside the Window,"
by Huang Zhuanmou

From *Zhongguo qingnian* 15:10 (1 August 1955).

A student, a book of "cartography" on his desk and the words "Professional work comes first" written across his calendar, broods over a design in his study, while behind him the Marxist-Leninist classics are rotting unread behind spider webs, and the rats are gnawing away at the book "Basic Knowledge of Politics." Outside, the loudspeaker blares "Fundamentally purge all hidden reactionary elements." The student's concentration on his professional studies renders him deaf to this din, and the counterrevolutionary element can be identified as a person who would encourage students in their studies instead of focusing on the political campaign, which of course would be directed against them. Encouraging people in their professional work and study, as well as focusing oneself on such matters, became a valuable clue for the identification of further counterrevolutionaries.

"Somebody to Get," by Shen Tongheng

From *Zhongguo qingnian* 16:11 (16 August 1955).

A student is engrossed in his work. On the backs of all of his books is the word "technology" and he says in the blurb, "Read, read, read; in the books you find technology, make a name for yourself, and become rich." His study is closed off from the world by a curtain inscribed "Engrossing oneself only in technology, no interest in politics," and that is where Hu Feng enters with vampire teeth, Guomindang emblem, and a rope to capture the student.

Being a theoretical construct, the campaign against Hu Feng and the hidden counterrevolutionaries lacked credibility. So did the purge of the Gao/Rao alliance, if ever it was one. Mao admitted in the final remarks after Deng Xiaoping had made his report on this "Clique" and earned himself one of their vacant seats in the Politburo, that there were people in the Center who still were uncertain "whether there was such an alliance or not."[12] In the public sphere, people argued that Hu Feng and his friends were just a small group of literati and hardly a threat to the revolution. Mao's charge in the editorial notes to the Hu Feng material, that Hu Feng and his friends were a "counterrevolutionary faction" with a veritable "underground kingdom" bent on overthrowing the Communist government, carried little conviction. A mouse showed up in a program where a veritable lion had been announced. This weakness of the campaign accounted for the eventual frenzy with which it was conducted. As the enemy was masked, the pressure was on people who knew each other in the private sphere, like friends and family members, to report on each other, as masks are taken off for the night. Students, of whom more than 80 percent were from "bourgeois or petty bourgeois" backgrounds at the time, were particularly vulnerable and were thus under strong pressure to denounce the "enemy at their side" in order to exonerate themselves. This poisoned private relationships. Friendships furthermore were automatically under suspicion, since they constituted a latent *jituan*, "Clique," with all its implications, and went against the principle of collectivism with equally official and close (or distant) relationships among all. Given the arbitrariness of the criteria, it was more a question of good will than of hard facts if denunciations were made. It became a social habit for many to make detailed notes of statements made by others, since the campaign showed what superb material they might make at a later occasion. In 1957, many remembered that the habit had started during the Sufan Campaign, and could occasionally write so publicly. An example may be given from the very personal and moving "Between One Human Being and Another" by Wang Ti, who talked about the slowly "growing wall" separating people from each other, and his own "loneliness." All this happened "in the last three years":

> Gradually I came to see that it was people "made of a special stuff" who were building this wall there. They were not using steel rods and concrete, neither wood nor bricks; the material they used was also special. In normal days, these people had not much to do with people made of normal stuff. They

12. Mao Zedong, "Speeches at the National Conference of the Communist Party of China, March 1955, Concluding Speech," in Mao Zedong, *Selected Works*, V, 161.

were, however, much interested in the sayings and doings of these normal people. In the depths of their memory they engraved the words and deeds of some people and reported them to the Party branch. These materials are stored, and come in handy for the next campaign. Sometimes these people communicate with you and other common people with the purpose of understanding the ideological stance. When eventually these secrets are exposed, people feel their hearts freeze and are frightened. A number of such special bricks make a fine fundament for this wall. Once a movement comes, these people are all a-shuffle day and night, not in order to sincerely help people who may have committed some errors or just one; no, they wield an invisible club in their hands and with frowning brows and staring eyes they hurl invectives.

The trust necessary for personal friendships cannot develop under such circumstances. "Because of this high and thick wall, the distance between one human being and another becomes ever greater. People who were friends in the past see ever less of each other; new friendships are just regular relations among comrades."[13] Liu Binyan described the movement, also in 1957, as an "attack on human ethics." "Human rights," he went on, "were trampled under foot, and the dignity of human beings was insulted."[14]

The invisibility of the "enemy" set in motion another, and classical mechanism of radical politics. The campaign's lack of credibility was seen as evidence for the extreme danger the bourgeois attack posed. Thus, in a dramatic enlargement of the campaign's scope, a person's willingness or unwillingness to join in the hunt became the key criterion for judging whether or not he or she belonged to the camp of the revolution or that of counterrevolution. This made the campaign into a *perpetuum mobile* which generated more fuel than it consumed at any stage, and thus made it run ever faster.

The cadre who claimed that in his office there were no counterrevolutionaries proved with this statement that he was one himself:

13. Wang Ti, "Ren yu ren zhi jian" (Human relations), *Harbin ribao*, 13 June 1957. In mid-1956, *Zhongguo qingnian* carried an extensive discussion among its readers about the question of whether private friendship should be permitted, which indicates that in fact in many places it was not; see "Zai jitili ke bukeyi you jige tebie zhixin de pengyou?" (Is it permitted to have particularly close friends within a collective?), *Zhongguo qingnian* 17:37ff (1958).

14. Huang Sha, "Jielu Liu Binyan zai Shanghai renmin diantai sanbu de fandong kuangyan" (Expose the reactionary blabber spread by Liu Binyan at the Shanghai People's Broadcasting Station), *Zhongguo qingnianbao*, 19 July 1957, sec. 3.

From *Wenyibao* 16:17 (30 August 1955).

The head of the office here proclaims with authoritative gesture, "In our office there can't be any counterrevolutionary elements," while a Guomindang agent glues a sign to his back "The fellow himself is the counterrevolutionary element." The poem to which the cartoon was attached spelled out the message in detail. It was written by the writers' group "Ma Tieding," Ma Iron-Nail, which included the poet Guo Xiaochuan, one of the warped souls of this period, who joined with equal poise and vigor every movement, whether Hu Feng criticism, Hundred Flower liberalization, or Anti-Rightist drive.

The threat of being branded a counterrevolutionary if the quota was not filled increased the pressure on officials to exceed the quota rather than fall short.

Hitherto we have dealt with reject definition and redefinition. The strongest evidence for the social climate of 1954–1955, however, comes from the positive formulation of the criteria for correct behavior from that period. Hero and reject definition are, of course, interrelated, and together give a fairly precise picture of the policies pursued at the time, and their social outcome.

In terms of class analysis, the intelligentsia were considered "bourgeois" in that period, and therefore had to submit to *gaizao*, reeducation. They thus not only lacked the status to challenge existing policies; the key criterion for their acceptability into "socialism" was willingness to submit meekly to the *gaizao* efforts of the "masses," which were administered by the cadres in charge of their work units.

Accompanying the campaign against "individualism" and its dangerous outgrowths was thus, from October 1954 to the middle of 1955 a "movement to foster a Communist ethical caliber and to ward off the corrosion by bourgeois ideology" among youths.[15] The core value stressed in this campaign was *jitizhuyi*—collectivism or collective spirit—a socialist virtue as opposed to "bourgeois individualism." Hu Yaobang spelled out the criteria for a youth with "high consciousness." He would (in this order):

- "Fervently love the Communist Party," which would take the form of "closely uniting around the Party, consciously accepting the Party's leadership, decidedly adhering to Party policies, faithfully protecting Party interests," etc.
- "Fervently love labor"; youths were not to strive for "official position" and "individual wealth" but labor for the "collective interest. It is an important criterion to assess the level of the political consciousness of a Communist Party member, a Youth League member, and a revolutionary student whether he/she has the habit of working or not, loves work or not, keeps labor discipline or not, and cherishes the working people or not."
- "Fervently love the masses of workers and peasants," since the future for the intelligentsia could be assured only in their "closely uniting with the workers and peasants."
- "Fervently love all the laboring people in the world."
- "Constantly pay attention to politics, contemporary affairs, and Party policies. For each and any of our labors, political theory is of the greatest importance."
- "Hate and despise all our enemies in the world," specifically the "imperialist elements," "Chiang Kai-shek's traitorous clique," and the "hidden counterrevolutionaries."[16]

15. "Wei jiaqiang qingniande gongchanzhuyi jiaoyu er douzheng" (Fight for the strengthening of Communist education of youths), *Zhongguo qingnian* 7:1f (1955).

16. Hu Yaobang, "Tigao jingti tigao juewu" (Increase vigilance, raise consciousness), *Zhongguo qingnian* 17:13f (1955).

There is no word about the necessity to develop diversified special qualifications in order better to serve "socialist construction" or the like; all six criteria stress the complete subordination to the Party's directives as the proof of a completed reeducation and a high political consciousness. The working-class heroes held up for emulation were described as fully corresponding to this ideal of the revolutionary cog and screw. In terms of public policy, any articulation of individual diversity was unpublishable; fictional heroes always did their thing by following orders, never by defying them; independent thinking was reduced to an expression of bourgeois individualism; love was a non-theme in the literary realm and reduced to the most unemotional political practicalities in social life. On the basis of the political-reeducation drive, there was legitimacy in subjecting the lives of young intelligentsia members to extremely tight controls. Formal courses for university students ran to 30 hours a week; the remainder went to meetings of a political nature with mandatory attendance. Nearly every evening there was a meeting, and there were several on weekends. Afterhours were regulated in the spirit of collectivism. Pursuit of individual interests during this time was deemed and denounced as individualism. The reading of unassigned matter, even from the official periodicals, was seen as a breach of discipline involving some secret political motive.

These ideals, which informed the educational purpose of the nation's schools, universities, and mass organizations, had been in operation for quite a while. They combined the worst of three worlds: the ideas about education the middle-level leaders had received in their own youth in village schools, where subordination both in terms of formal discipline and content (rote learning) was stressed; cadres' military experience, where much of the fighting power and persuasiveness of the Communist armies had depended on the very high degree of discipline and subordination they had been able to maintain; and finally these cadres' enlightened self-interest, which necessitated a strict enforcement of control over a population which both in terms of its youth and its qualification presented a threat to them. The combination of the general, "class-analysis"-based, reeducation effort with an ill-defined political campaign, which made it possible to class even minute deviations from Party-line or collectivism as potentially or actually counterrevolutionary, put a well-stacked "hat factory" at the disposal of these cadres, greatly enhancing the persuasiveness and effectiveness of the Sufan Campaign in terms of manifest behavior.

Perhaps the most visible, and stunning, indicator of the effectiveness of these policies to regulate public behavior was the dramatic change in clothing styles which emerged in China after 1949 and had become all pervasive in the cities by 1955. In the words of a critic writing in the Youth League journal in March 1956:

> The clothing of our people at present is not beautiful at all. Especially in the cities you can see wherever you go that about everybody, whether man or woman, worker or peasant, adult or child, government cadre or member of the common masses, wears blue, grey, or black uniforms. There is no difference in men's and women's [clothing], no variation of styles. The colors are drab. It looks everywhere uniformly blackish and greyish.[17]

This uniformity, quite different from the picture prevailing before 1949, was not enforced by government policy as had been the queue by the Manchu government. In a soothing vein, the above quoted author continued:

> In the past we never suggested that people should wear uniforms ... That so many people wear uniforms today is mainly the result of people voluntarily learning from the personnel (now) running our state.

Wearing this kind of clothes signaled cooperation with the new authorities and successfully completed reeducation on the part of intellectuals who were now visibly one with the workers and peasants. From the amount of ink spilled in 1956 to establish some legitimacy for more diversified clothing styles and to take the stigma of bourgeois individualism from them, we can safely infer that cadres tended to regard collectivist clothing as an important feature of a well-adapted member of the intelligentsia, and there is much evidence that they actively discouraged even modest signs of diversity in this respect.

A 1956 cartoon may illustrate the point:

17. Sun Yiqing, "Rang women de fuzhuang fengfu duocai" (Let our dresses be varied and colorful), *Zhongguo qingnian* 6:20 (1956).

From *Zhongguo qingnianbao*, 22 March 1956, by Ge Yi
The secretary of the Youth League branch: Have you considered that? What does it
contribute to you ideologically to wear this bow?

As implied in the harsh depiction of the woman cadre in the above caricature, the wind had changed by 1956, and the very attitudes promoted
in 1955 were now publicly denounced.

Moving to the higher level of role models for public emulation, the
old guard had a complete kit at its disposal. The character held up for
the emulation of the young, and Youth Leaguers in particular, was a Russian, Pavel from Nikolai Ostrovski's novel *How the Steel was Tempered*,
probably the text most widely read by Youth League members in the
entire socialist camp.[18]

Pavel Korchagin is a working class youth. Living through the October Revolution and the first decade of the Soviet Union, he gradually
overcomes his youthful individualist urges and becomes a loyal and honest servant of the Party, sacrificing on the way his love (Rita), his limbs,

18. Nikolai Ostrovski, *How the Steel was Tempered*, tr. R. Prokofieva (Moscow: Progress Publishing Company, n.d.). P. Link, "Fiction and the Reading Public in Guangzhou and Other Chinese Cities 1979–1980," in J. Kinkley, ed., *After Mao: Chinese Literature and Society 1978–1981*
(Cambridge: Council on East Asian Studies, Harvard University, 1985), pp. 230ff, gives some
statistical data on book publishing.

his eyesight, and, in the unwritten prolongation of the story, his very life, all this without much hesitation, and with the single ambition to stay active in Party work. The text provides much guidance for Youth League cadres about how to evaluate things. Dancing parties are as much a sign of bourgeois decadence as are beautiful clothes and stylish hair. Only Trotskyites can find fault with the Party leadership, and they are shown to be hysterical intellectuals, who otherwise whore around. Private happiness, as a matter of principle, has to be sacrificed to the "interests of the Revolution." When Pavel meets Rita again after many years, and learns that she is now married, he states what has since been quoted myriad times in China both as a demand on youths and in heroic declarations of youths themselves: "I stand for the type of revolutionary whose personal life is nothing as compared with the life of society as a whole." When Pavel is together with others they talk about the Party or their life during the Revolution. When, shortly before his limbs refuse to serve him altogether, he moves in with a young woman hardly known to him, this is an exceedingly practical affair to help her out of the narrow confines of her backward family and into the Party; there certainly is no flirting and carousing, and in fact the success of his political education is such that she becomes a delegate to all sorts of meetings and conferences and hardly sees anything of Pavel, who is now immobile and blind, and in the last sacrifice tears himself away from her so as not to impede her advance. The book had been elevated to be the model after which members of the Soviet Komsomol were to pattern themselves, and with this authority it became a catalogue of orthodox values and behavior in China.

The book thus became not only reading matter for youths but a weapon in the hands of Youth League administrators who would discipline the youths under their control by referring to the way Pavel and Rita had behaved. Pavel himself had not invented his own personality but lived it as a quotation of another revolutionary life, that of the Gadfly from the novel of the same name by the American author Ethel Voynich, whose book as a consequence became equally well known in Russia and China. Pavel Korchagin, however, learns to overcome the longing for romantic grandeur and suffering in the Gadfly (which is set during the Italian revolution) and to become the cog and screw in the Party's revolutionary machinery until he is worn out and discarded.[19] Ostrovski was mandatory reading matter, and Pavel was a mandatory role model for Youth Leaguers, fleshing out what otherwise might have remained too abstract for young people.

Moving still one level higher to the general values used as yardsticks for Youth League and Party recruiters, we find that, in the most general terms, a candidate would have to be *zhongcheng laoshi,* true, honest, and obedient. This was already a polemical notion in 1955. An article in the Youth League journal in January 1955 spelled this out. It admonished youths to be *laoshi.* It argued that youths were *yonggan* (daring) but without experience, and thus *mangmuxing* (blindly rushing about). They had to become *wenzhong* (steady) and *jinshen* (prudent). This would in fact be progress for them, not a regression. They needed to learn to distrust their own subjective opinions and accept the collective wisdom of the Party. Youths had *lixiang* (ideals) but these were unmediated by *shishi qiushi* (seeking truth in facts) which the Party performed. What was requested was a *laoshi taidu* (a *laoshi* attitude), which consisted in "respecting the masses, learning from the masses, emphasizing the strength of the collective, and making oneself into a servant of the people."[20] That one was to be *zhongcheng laoshi* towards the Party was a universally enforced *daoli* (principle) in 1955.

A young man describing how much his wife, who was then "discovered" to be a counterrevolutionary, seemed devoted to state and Party, used these words: "She also read a lot of Marxist-Leninist books and not only did she perfectly understand the *principle that one has to be loyal, obedient, and well behaved (zhongcheng laoshi) towards the organization,* but constantly made use of this principle to educate others."[21] Writing in December 1955, the young man described this principle as being

19. Ethel Voynich, *The Gadfly* (New York: Grosset & Dunlap, 1893). A Chinese edition is Ai.Li. Funiqie, *Niumang,* tr. Li Liangmin (Beijing: Qingnian Chubanshe, 1953). By 1988, the book had gone through 16 printings with a total circulation of 1.763 million copies.

20. Lai Ruyu, "Yao laoshi he qianxu, buyao xukua he jiaoao" (Be honest and self-effacing. Don't be boastful and arrogant), *Zhongguo qingnianbao* 1:4f (1955). The title of this article is in bold print in the table of contents.

21. Ai Nan, "Wo shi zenyang duidai ziji de fangeming airen de" (How I handled my counterrevolutionary wife), *Zhongguo qingnian* 1:5 (1955).

generally familiar. By implication the emphasis on this principle discouraged daring, outspokenness, and willingness to innovate as products of youthful immaturity.

In the next stage of development, beginning early in 1956, the Youth League leadership under Hu Yaobang switched its basic attitude and stressed as positive the very values that had been rejected a few months earlier. From the scathing satires about the recruits and the recruiting criteria of the Sufan Movement of 1955, we get reject definitions of the *zhongcheng laoshi* heroes. Stripped of their polemical bent, these writings can help us flesh out the personality type fostered for elite membership in the period preceding 1956. In fact, the Sufan Campaign was designed to last for two years so that the 1956 polemics were not only directed against past practices but against a present threat.

Already during the first months of the Sufan Campaign itself, there had been signs of uneasiness about the way in which it was run. Hu Yaobang not only spelled out, as quoted above, the ideal personality of the reeducated intelligentsia member, but also warned against exaggerations. Speaking early in August 1955 at the 16th National Delegates Conference of the Chinese Student Association on "Rise Vigilance, Rise Consciousness," the head of the Youth League first spoke with fervor about the hot class struggle just under way: "The struggle presently going on is nothing other than an acute and complex class struggle such as there never was before in history." The students were among the natural targets. "Students today are for the most part still from bourgeois and petty-bourgeois families and have received manifold influences from the old society and old education; consequently their thinking has an enduring propensity towards individualism and idealism." They could escape this inclination only by greatly "raising their consciousness." However, he felt it necessary to warn that prosecutors should not forget the "differences between three kinds of people and counterrevolutionaries." "First, make a difference between normal people who complain and are dissatisfied on the one hand, and counterrevolutionaries on the other. Second, differentiate between normal people with historical problems and counterrevolutionaries. Third, differentiate between general backward elements, like people who have stolen a couple of times and have some hooligan habits, and counterrevolutionaries."[22] The most widespread abuse was again listed first, so that the most common charge was that someone had made *guaihua*, complained, or was "dissatisfied with the Communist Party," one of the official criteria for quota selection.

From early 1956 on, however, there were open polemics. The following cartoon illustrates to what extent political "hats" were put on personal behavior:

"To Be a Human Under These Hats Is Hard," by Ding Cong

From *Zhongguo qingnianbao*, 13 February 1956.

22. Hu Yaobang, "Increase Vigilance" (note 16 above), pp. 11ff.

For studying together, the two young people earn the hat "setting up small circles" (the forerunner of "cliques"); for studying independently, the hat is "not helping each other." In the second pair, the young man wears a worn-out uniform and is awarded the hat "liberalistic sloppiness," while the nattily dressed one to his right gets the hat "corrupt lifestyle." Dancing, in the third group, receives the hat "not eagerly studying," studying at the desk is "having thoughts about fame and wealth." Giving a solo at a social gathering of the Youth League earns the hat "separating oneself from the masses, pushing one's personality to the fore." The last hat signals the apprehensions about dangers that might still come. It might be pointed out that the cartoonist Ding Cong, who here attacks the stifling of youths, also drew the cartoon "High Hat" reproduced above, on which a Hu Feng tiger leads a pompous young author down the road to counterrevolution.

Those political ideas that could be expressed publicly were narrowed to the reiteration of current Party policies. The language in which they were to be uttered was equally stylized. In public behavior utmost suppression of individualistic urges in lifestyle and clothing was advocated as an expression of the seriousness of one's devotion to the great cause of socialism and the Party. Even bodily movements were to be subdued, a behavior inculcated through political pressure. We know what great importance physical exercise and freedom of bodily movement play for the mental development of young people. Time and again, political restlessness of youths found its first expression in a frenzy of physical culture, doing sports, climbing mountains, enduring hardships with no other support but one's own body strength and will power. Turnvater Jahn in nineteenth-century Germany was not the only example of the close interaction between exercise and student rebellion. Mao Zedong himself wrote his first major tract precisely on sports and detailed in his talks with Edgar Snow the role physical exercise and daring played for his own development. But in the new China of the early 1950s, rigorous physical control and subdued behavior were part of the reeducation process to create the new socialist intelligentsia. This was especially true for those who aspired to Youth League membership and therewith to be part of the recruiting pool for the Party and for leadership positions. A cartoon from February 1956 gives a summary of this situation:

"Demands on Youth League Members," by Ge Defu

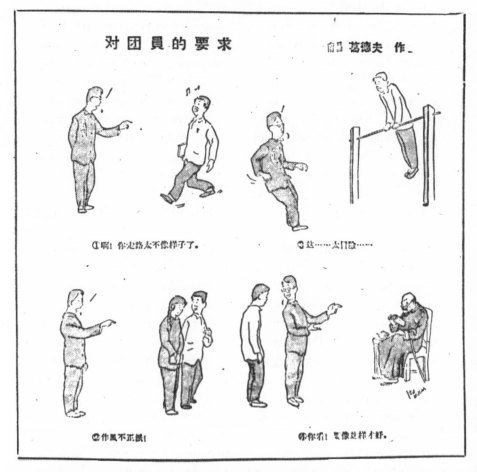

From *Zhongguo qingnian* 5:23 (1 March 1956).

The Youth League member walks with a song on his lips and a bounce in his step, to be admonished by the Youth League branch secretary, whose physical stance is well controlled, "Hey, the way you walk around is unbecoming!" Taking a swing alone on the horizontal bar, he finds the secretary scolding him, "That . . . that's too adventurous!" Walking with a girl, he is told, "This is indecent behavior!" Eventually the secretary shows him how he should comport himself. "See, this is how you should be." This type of physically controlled behavior and subduing of one's personality was an odd blend of traditional educational ideals, and high-powered political "reeducation."

This historical continuity guaranteed that the cadres could rely heavily on public opinion, even among the young themselves, for chastising anyone who made him- or herself conspicuous in deed, word, gesture, or habit. When the readers' letters columns opened some public channel for the expression of the grievances of those who had been disciplined and cowed after having shown some sprightliness and independence, their complaints were directed not only against the cadres, but as much against their peers who ostracized them with the cadres' encouragement and support. Indeed, in the Youth League the lower-level cadres themselves were often quite young. The interaction of power, tradition, and peer pressure guaranteed a fairly heavy enforcement of behavioral standards.

The enormous leverage of cadres over the fate of the members of the intelligentsia naturally led to many outright abuses. Even rapes (forced marriages) were so frequent that a public issue was raised. In each reported case, abuse of political and ideological powers was involved.

"Forced Marriage," by Chen Jinyan

强　迫　婚　姻　　　　陈今言作

From *Zhongguo qingnian* 10:37 (16 May 1956).
"According to the letter from a reader, the leading comrade in a base-level unit set his eyes on a woman comrade, and, without bothering to ask whether she consented or not, was dead set on her marrying him; the Office of Personnel Affairs and the Youth League branch exerted pressure from the sidelines and they organized a forced marriage."

The happy bridegroom is leading the procession. The weeping woman in the sedan inscribed "happiness" is carried to her new home by the

Youth League branch and the personnel office in front, while the representative of the women's organization and a gentleman with a club inscribed "choosing a partner (according to one's liking) is indecent behavior" share the weight in the back.

The various positive and negative values detailed in the preceding pages combine to form a general educational ideal which was publicly uncontested until the end of 1955. Deviance was threatened with political ostracism and persecution. Adaptation was rewarded with high social esteem, and perhaps a career.

Those who set the public climate for such an educational ideal did not mean ill, and certainly most of them were not self-serving cynics. They acted according to their experience and ideology and felt they were doing a good thing in educating people to operate as they themselves did; and they would, as a consequence, achieve successes similar to their own—the victory of the Revolution. Theirs were not bad consciences, although the campaign in its wanton abandonment had certainly sharpened their political skills and their wits in dealing with challenges. The polemical cartoons of their educational ideal, which started to appear in late 1955, were quite accurate if the polemical stance is for once discounted.

"How To Make Good Youths," by Jiang Yousheng

怎 样 作 个 好 青 年　　　　江有生畫

From *Zhongguo qingnian* 13:9 (1 July 1956).
Leader of school X: We bring up a bunch of good youths. They have absolutely no individual thoughts, and one need not have the slightest concern when putting them into operation.

The title of the book through which the leader guides the youths towards the fulfillment of the education ideal reads "How to Make Good

Youths (regulations and taboos)," with the bracket linking these two special means. The term employed there, *qinggui jielü*, originally referred to the monastic rules for Buddhists and Taoists. The diversity of youthful interests, clothing styles, and physical stances on the left is transformed to a uniform code of behavior on the right after the youths have successfully gone through their education. "Putting them into operation" (*shiyong*) is the term used for putting a machine into operation.

In another metaphor, the functionality of youths as preferred by the leaders is again ironically stressed:

"Men Are Not Marionettes," by Wu Yun

From *Zhongguo qingnian* 22:19 (16 November 1955).
Member of Youth League Committee X: That would be nice if youths would obediently do whatever they are told.

The reader should maintain here the mental discipline of not being too easily swayed by the ironical attitude towards this typical, rather aged Youth League cadre whose fingers are twitching with the thought of being able to manipulate youths like marionettes with regard to the

"Ideological Situation of the Youth League Branch," the report on which he holds under his arm. The cadre might feel perfectly justified in educating youths to negate any personal urge or drive other than to serve the Party, and in developing the necessary educational devices for this purpose.

The instilling of these behavioral values was not restricted to young adults but was even more important in the education of small children. There was a theory of "malleability" of children (*kesuxing*), which guaranteed that they could be made to correspond to the same pattern. A cartoon from the Youth League *Zhongguo qingnianbao,* 27 May 1956, depicts this assumption common among educators:

"The Cake Mold," by Hua Junwu

糕　餅　模　子

華君武　作

The inscription on the mold reads "Dragon Breeds Dragon, Phoenix Breeds Phoenix." The implication is, it would seem, that people tend to try to replicate themselves in their educational objectives, and thus confine the growth of youths to narrowly defined "molds."

The methods through which respect for the rules and limits are enforced, are depicted in the following piece by Zhang Tailai in the same paper, which also illustrates a point made in an accompanying text.

From *Zhongguo qingnianbao*, 27 May 1956.

The children in the first picture, the text says, would like to jump around, smell flowers, and look at the stone elephant, but the nurse lectures them: "When going out one has to keep to the rules. Don't stretch to the east and gaze to the west! Don't make such a tumultuous noise! Hold hands, go in rows, the collective spirit must be strengthened!" Arriving at a playground, the children are not allowed to enter it and play there. In the third picture, the child Mingming comes home with a hat denouncing her "individualism, arrogance, and complacency," and her "separation from the masses."

The unquestioned and well-authenticated validity of this educational ideal meant that its adherents would certainly not abandon it at the next turn of the wind, first because their own personality corresponded to and accepted the values inscribed therein, and, second, and perhaps unconsciously so, it served their own survival interests very well.

There is no question that these policies had a strong impact on the behavior of young city intelligentsia throughout the Sufan Movement and later, and that this impact was further reinforced by the fact that Youth League and Party recruitment relied mostly on the criteria presented above.

From many accounts we know that it was exceedingly difficult in 1954–1955 to get into the Party and even the Youth League.[23] Even after the beginning of 1956, things eased only gradually. The standards for the recruitment of intelligentsia members hardened as cadres tried to avoid charges of "lack of vigilance" towards possible agents of the bourgeoisie and recruited people on whose malleability and willingness to obey they could rely. A cartoon by Shi Bing from March 1956 attacked this prevalent type of elite recruitment. It shows a Youth League cadre handling new applications:

23. Zhou Enlai, "On the Question of the Intellectuals" (January 1956), in R. Bowie and J. Fairbank, eds., *Communist China 1956–1959, Policy Documents with Analysis* (Cambridge: Harvard University Press, 1962), p. 139: "But in the past few years we have seldom admitted in the Party members of their [the intellectuals'] ranks and this is a tendency of isolationism." "During the Sufan Movement . . . a number of regions stopped recruiting new [Youth] League members," wrote Lu Jindong, "Kefu baoshou sixiang jijidi zhuangda tuande zuzhi" (Suppress conservative thinking. Actively expand the League's organization), *Zhongguo qingnian* 3:27 (1956).

"She loves wearing flowered dresses, a downright manifestation of bourgeois thinking."

"This one does not talk much; by and large he has no mass viewpoint."

"This one loves dancing, absolutely indecent behavior."

"This one loves to read novels, but the arts separate him from politics."

"No question . . ."

From *Zhongguo qingnianbao*, 10 March 1956.

The secretary writes on all applications "not admitted." This combination of pressure to conform and promise for advancement produced in the eyes of critics an extremely homogeneous body of cadres, and the satire heaped on their heads beginning in early 1956 reflected the frustration among critics that these people remained in power without fundamentally changing their attitudes and values.

Open and explicit polemics against the ideal of the *zhongcheng laoshi* cadre began in December 1955 in the Youth League journal *Zhongguo qingnian* with an article by Lin Wei entitled "What Kind of People Do We Want the Youths Whom We Educate to Become?" This article provided the title for a regular column discussing this question in later months.[24]

According to the article, Youth League cadres and educators upholding the earlier values wanted to educate people who were self-effacing (*qianxu*), realistic (*shiji*), reliable (*wendang*), [looking at things from] all angles (*quanmian*), and without shortcomings (*meiyou quedian*), which can be translated into having no ideals (*meiyou lixiang*), no courage (*meiyou yongqi*), no creative spirit (*meiyou chuangzao jingshen*), no interest in digging themselves into things on their own impulse (*bu xihuan*

24. Lin Wei, "Peiyang qingnian zuo shenmeyang de ren" (What kind of people do we want the youths whom we eduate to become?), *Zhongguo qingnianbao* 24:26ff (1955). See also "Qingnian yinggai chengwei shenmeyang de ren" (What kind of people should youths become?), *Zhongguo qingnian* 11–15 (1956).

zhudong zuanyan) and thinking on their own (*duli sikao*), and not actively battling against irrational phenomena and harmful tendencies (*dui bu heli xianxiang he buliang qingxiang ye bu jiji douzheng*). The situation produced a "Mr. Yes-sir" (*hao hao xiansheng*), who was neither very good nor very bad at things (*bu gao bu di*), had neither hatred nor love for things (*bu zeng bu ai*), did not strive for achievements (*bu qiu chenggong*), but tried only to avoid mistakes (*dan qiu wuguo*), was worldly wise and played it safe (*ming zhe bao shen*), and generally retreated (*fanshi houtui*), in short, mediocre and unambitious (*yongyong lulu*) people who were timid and afraid of getting themselves into trouble (*danxiao pashi*).[25] Ground down by criticisms of being naive (*youzhi*), not sufficiently realistic (*bugou shiji*), not comprehensive in their perception of problems (*kan wenti bu quanmian*), and furthermore having a bad attitude (*taidu buhao*), and even ideological problems (*sixiang you wenti*), epitomized by the charge that they defied the organization (*wu zuzhi*) and were undisciplined (*wu jilü*), youths would eventually accommodate the routine (*laolian*) in political behavior, and would stick to the old rules (*mo shou chenggui*).[26]

The ideal of the educational leaders for the public comportment of youths was said to be that they should act like adults while still young (*shaonian laocheng*) with lowered brows and submissive eyes (*dimei shunmu*), should listen when addressed, make no move without observing propriety (*feili wudong*), and never say a word without observing propriety (*feili wuyan*); in short, they wanted them as subdued as the Confucian gentlemen (*siwenren*) of old.[27] In polemical language this meant they had to learn to restrain themselves (*rennai*), not to "quarrel" with people (*bu he ren chaojia*), to observe their leaders' mien when speaking and adapting the content accordingly (*kan yanse shuohua*), and guide their ship according to the winds (*jianfeng shichuan*).[28] The blocking of their youthful drive and energy, it was claimed, made them into

---

25. Lin Wei, "What kind of people?" (note 24 above), p. 26. In this first pathbreaking article most of the core terms and arguments already appear.

26. Zhi Guang, "Bu yao moguangle tamen de lengjiao" (Don't polish off their edges), *Zhongguo qingnian* 7:28f (1956).

27. "Laigao congshu" (Summary of letters received), *Zhongguo qingnianbao* 13:34f (1956).

28. Zhi Guang, "Don't polish off their edges" (note 26 above), p. 28.

people who were cautious even in small things and circumspect even with trifles (*jinxiao shenwei*), restrained and awkward (*juju shushu*), meticulously acting on orders received (*fengming weijin*).[29] They eventually became people with a vision both narrow and shallow (*yanguang duanxiao*), limited knowledge (*zhishi xia'ai*), dried up and uninteresting (*kuzao wuwei*), repeating only what their leaders said (*ren yun yi yun*),[30] sensing dangers at both head and tail (*weishou weiwei*), with bound hands and feet (*shushou shujiao*), uttering only "Yes, yes, whatever you say, whatever you say" (*weiwei nuonuo*).[31] A student who had been sent to the Soviet Union was allowed to comment critically on his Chinese co-students there. They were working hard, he said in January 1956, but "they and their lives are too tight (*guoyu jinzhang*); very little attention is paid to cultural activities and rest, our lives' interests are not broad, and our sphere of life is very small. There are some co-students who don't know very well what to do with their free time and waste it with idle chatter or sleep." He quoted the Soviet students whom he described as a lively crowd, as not wanting to become a Byelinkov, which seemed to be more what the Chinese students were. The allusion was not lost on his Chinese readers. Byelinkov is a character from a Chekhov story well known in China. He is the "man in a case," a teacher of Greek, who encases his body with all sorts of wrappings quite independently of the weather, and his mind with a set of fixed and firm principles. "Only bulletins and newspaper articles in which something was prohibited were clear to him. If he saw a bulletin forbidding the scholars to go out on the street after nine o'clock, or if he read an article enjoining him from carnal love, that was fixed and clear to him—and basta. For him there was always an element of doubt, something unspoken and confused, concealed in licence and liberty of action." He keeps a check on the other teachers and without doing much manages, with the best of possible intentions, to "hold the whole school in the hollow of his hand for

29. Wu Yuzhang, "Rang qingnian fahui gengduo de duli jingshen" (Let youths develop a still stronger spirit of independence), *Zhongguo qingnian* 15:2 (1956).

30. Editorial note for the series "What kind of youths?" (note 24 above), *Zhongguo qingnian* 11:38 (1956).

31. Yu Guo, "Qingnianren bu yinggai fuyou lixiang he baofu ma" (Should youths not be richly endowed with ideals and aspirations?), *Zhongguo qingnian* 11:12 (1956).

fifteen years. The whole school, did I say? The whole town!"[32] The aesthetic feelings of his Chinese co-students, the author continued, were stunted. On a beautiful night, when they had a walk by the sea with Soviet friends, the latter recited Pushkin verses with soft voices, while the Chinese students did not get beyond *mei ya, taimeile* (beautiful, ah, how beautiful).[33]

In the minds of responsible cadres of schools, universities, and Youth League branches, it was said, young people's spontaneous urges belonged to the category *luan*, chaos, and bourgeois chaos at that. The very purpose of education was to eliminate such chaotic elements. The criteria of these cadres for recruitment into the future elite of the land were in decreasing order of importance:

• *laoshi* — well-behaved
• *wenzhong* — steady
• *guigui juju* — well disciplined

These terms would reappear in the personnel files of young people selected for political promotion. In polemical language this reads as "atrophic and over-cautious (*weisuo jujin*), timid and cautious (*danxiao pashi*),"[34] or "living corpses of clay and wood (*nisu mudiao de huo siren*) with heads bent and ears clogged (*fushou tie'er*) saying 'Yes yes, whatever you wish, whatever you wish'" (*weiwei nuonuo*).[35]

The consequence was, in the eyes of people able to publish their opinions during the 1956–1957 period, that a substantial part of the cadres were now "not striving ahead (*bu qiu shangjin*), unambitious and mediocre (*yongyong lulu*), content with the status quo (*an yu xianzhuang*), and some of them are rigid in their ways (*zuofeng shengying*)";[36] Liu Binyan went so far as to state in public that "some people are dull-witted

32. Anton Tchekoff (Chekhov), "The Man in a Case," in *Stories of Russian Life*, tr. M. Fell (New York: Charles Scribner, 1914), pp. 78ff.

33. Luo Yuanzheng, "Wo suo kan de Sulian qingnian de wenhua shenghuo" (The cultural life of Soviet youths as I saw it), *Zhongguo qingnian* 13:19 (1956).

34. Zeng Delin, "Gaijin he jiaqiang tuan zai daxuesheng zhong de zhengzhi sixiang jiaoyu gongzuo" (Improve and strengthen the Youth League's educational work, politics, and ideology among university students), *Zhongguo qingnian* 13:7 (1956).

35. Mei Zu, "Yinggai zunzhong bieren de ziyou" (One has to respect other people's freedom), *Zhongguo qingnian* 12:31 (1956).

36. "Daodi yinggai zhongyong shenmeyang de ren?" (What kind of people should one really put into important positions?), *Zhongguo qingnian* 16:28 (1957). This is an article in the

(*yuchun*), cling to the old rules (*shoujiu*), have neither learning nor skill (*buxue wushu*), and block life's progress. Others have lost their political enthusiasm (*zhengzhi reqing shuaitui*), have become slack and negligent (*pipi tata*), give no serious thought to anything (*wu suo yongxin*), or are planning only their pleasures (*qitu xiangle*). Still others are selfish and timid (*zisi qieruo*) and don't dare to speak out (*bu gan shuohua*), afraid they might lose their official's hat." The cadres upholding these values were *baichi* (ignoramuses) and *mangcongzhe* (people blindly obeying their superiors' orders); they repeated their superiors' words like parrots (*yingwu xueshe*). In short they could be described with terms like cynics (*quanru zhuyi*), crawlers (*paxing zhuyi*), sharp dealers (*shikuai*), politicos (*zhengke*), and revolutionary guardians of their self-interest (*geming zishen baoweizhe*).[37] *Yingshengchong* (echo insect) or *liushengji* (phonograph) were other flattering epithets for their attitude towards their superiors. Liu Binyan and others charged that, owing to these recruitment standards, "the quality of Party and Youth League members has gone down."[38]

Polemics notwithstanding, both sides were largely on common ground when it came to describing the prevailing Party and League recruitment ideal. The core term, on which both sides agreed, albeit with a radically different value attached to it, was that someone had to be *laoshi*, obedient and well-behaved, had to be a *laoshi ren*, such a person. A much read article in June 1957 claimed under the subheading "One-sided Preference for *Laoshi Ren*," that "for quite some time one hears that what a number of Party and Youth League base-level organizations most appreciate are *laoshi ren*, well-behaved and obedient people, as under any circumstances they will not make any trouble (*bu da hui chu shenme maobing*). It is said they always rely on the 'correct standpoint,' very rarely have 'ideological problems,' and are very tractable. People of this kind are the first to be selected to become members of the

Anti-Rightist Campaign summarizing the "rightist" opinion about the characteristics of the "old cadres" in office in 1956.

37. Liu Binyan, as quoted in He Fei, "'Fa ziji de guang'" (Letting one's own light shine), *Zhongguo qingnian* 15:5 (1957).

38. The source for this quotation has been lost. Liu Binyan confirmed its accuracy in a telephone interview on 13 May 1991.

Party and Youth League. This is paramount to giving people a hint: You have to be *laoshi*, you have to be well-disciplined (*guiju*)." This quality is then defined as "Party spirit" (*dangxing*).[39] The negative image of the *laoshi* cadre became so familiar that a cartoon (of which, sadly, I have only a description) appeared in 1957 depicting the "Winner of the *Laoshi* Cadre Award" who achieved this honor because he lacked the instrument of outspokenness, a tongue.[40] Another variant was to read the word *laoshi* with the appendix *-tou* as *laoshitou*, simpleton.

For the revolutionary guardians of the inherited values, *laoshi* was a time-tested quality; they confirmed our assumptions about these polemics on taking over the media after the beginning of the Anti-Rightist Campaign in June 1957. They rejected all invectives published during the Hundred Flowers period, and asserted that *laoshi* embodied revolutionary obedience and devotion. In late 1957, to be *laoshi* became a key criterion for *de*, or moral fibre, which eventually was considered "basic" in recruitment decisions compared to *cai*, professional skill. On 1 October 1957, National Day, a programmatic article came out in *Zhongguo qingnian* entitled "Forever Be *Laoshi Ren* Loyal to the Party."

The "rightists" had attacked the well-behaved followers of the Party, the article charged, because they wanted to oppose the Party and topple it:

> We young people have always prided ourselves on the fact that we "listened to the Party's words." Being true and loyal *laoshi ren* of the Party is nothing we have to be in the least defensive about; it is not in the least disgraceful for us, but is our glory. The Party and the people's basic interests correspond, and that is why the Party needs innumerable *laoshi ren* who are honest and loyal to both Party and people, needs innumerable . . . docile instruments. The Communist Party and the Youth League have to be made up of exactly such people. It is perfectly normal that, in the close unity of our Party and Youth League, the Party members should follow and obey the Party leadership and that they should be united on the basis of Marxist-Leninist ideology. And it is also absolutely necessary that Youth League members, who generally lack experience in

39. Hu Bowei, "Jiaotiaozhuyi dui daxuesheng de yingxiang" (The influence of dogmatism on university students), *Zhongguo qingnian* 11:34 (1957).

40. Quoted in Yao Yuanfang, "Yongyuan zuoge zhongcheng yu dang de laoshiren" (Eternally be an honest fellow loyal to the Party), *Zhongguo qingnian* 19:21 (1957). The cartoonist was Li Binsheng.

political struggles, should in the great winds and waves of political struggles trust the organization and rely on the organization, and at all times accept the leadership of the Party organization. This conscious organization viewpoint is what our young people have to be educated in, and it is in no way something of the sort of "some people saying 'Yes, yes, whatever you wish, whatever you wish' to some other people.

The article concludes that

the rightist elements are most averse to our loyal, true, and well-behaved attitude towards the Party, and it is precisely this that proves that we must love the Party even more passionately, follow the Party's leadership, forever stand at the Party's side, and that we must make a commitment and set our minds on forever being true, honest, and obedient (*zhongcheng laoshi*) towards the Party and the people.[41]

Using 1955 criteria for heroes and rejects, their inversion in the years 1956 and 1957, and their reinversion during the time after the beginning of the Anti-Rightist Campaign, we can affirm with some confidence that the *zhongcheng laoshi* ideal of an extremely authoritarian personality type dominated Party and Youth League recruitment, and continued to do so even when this criterion was challenged in 1956–1957. The *zhongcheng laoshi* ideal embodied in its first part the "loyalty" and "sincerity" of Confucian state servants, and in the second—*laoshi*—a popular ideal of an honest, down-to-earth fellow. With the specification that such people would today follow the Party's directives instead of relying on their own scattered and individualistic thoughts, the *zhongcheng laoshi* ideal corresponded to both the experience of the Party cadres from their revolutionary past and the educational ideal of Chinese parents with regard to their children, apart from being the very ideal of the village school system under which these cadres themselves had studied. On the negative side, the grim experiences of the city intelligentsia with political outspokenness and nonconformist behavior under imperial, Guomindang, Japanese, and Communist rule, together with the weak status of the bourgeois intellectuals at the time, combined to form a mighty deterrent to such behavior. Both promise and threat were greatly increased when the Sufan Campaign relegated nonconformist

41. Ibid., pp. 21f.

behavior to the counterrevolutionary category, while offering promotion for those who adapted and joined the hunt. Under these conditions the Sufan Campaign, which had originated with a logical necessity, namely the necessary exacerbation of class struggle after the Revolution, could and did flourish. The effect was that a substantial part of the younger new recruits for the League and the Party replicated the personality features of the old middle-level cadres without sharing their experience. Manifest behavior became rigidly uniform. In Summer 1955, Mao had said that the Sufan Campaign was to last for two years, and so it did. The challenge to "bureaucratic" behavior during 1955–1957, which eventually became known as the "Hundred Flowers Period," was thus mounted against a well-armed opponent who had at his disposal not only an unchallenged institutional position but also the legitimacy that comes from being part of a successful movement and from having a theory spelled out by the Chairman himself.

In the still very high temperature of Chinese society of the time, otherwise discrete phenomena like power struggles, ideological controversies, political events, literary policies and writings, and finally the life of the common people commingled in one cauldron, so that what might have started with a trivial controversy between the Chairman and the Prime Minister over a young woman ended up by determining the personality composition of the Party for decades to come, along with the fate of the country in this one-Party system. In the same process, the sources lost much of their distinctiveness. Politburo documents had to be studied as closely as a line from a poem; a novel emerged as an administrative handbook; and hundreds of tons of clothes were stacked away or dug up again as the political climate changed.

FIVE

The Challenge: Strategies and Tactics

We shall now study the techniques used in mounting a challenge to this dominant line under conditions as inimical as those described in the preceding pages.

The press in China is defined as a "political weapon" of the leadership. Open contention around fundamental issues has therefore not been possible. This was also true for the post-1978 period where it would have been impossible to publish an article praising, say, the Cultural Revolution. However, like any general political theory with some history of application, Marxism-Leninism operates rather as the general language and code in which policies of the most diverse kinds are expressed than as an unequivocal guide for actual policies. The writings of the classics and the actual policies pursued in Communist political organizations and Communist-ruled states are ambivalent enough to offer appropriate quotations for any variant of policy. A faction or line dominating at a given moment will try to impose a unified reading on that diverse body, eliminating the options for contention. The attempts to cut off from the "classics," as an example, the writings of the young Marx, are evidence of a certain strain and stress. The guardians of the dominant lines are aware that in the "parking orbit" of possible Marxisms there are arguments and precedents which would justify policies directly opposed to those pursued at the time. Furthermore, the "line" documents themselves are frequently ambivalent enough rather to organize than to conclude the battle for the political line to be followed. An example was the 4th Plenum's resolution in 1954 which called forth both Hu Feng's letter to the Central Committee and his being ruthlessly persecuted as anti-Party and counterrevolutionary.

While in theory this parking orbit may have infinite dimensions, Communist history has in fact settled for two basic strategies, each with its complete package of supporting arguments, quotations, and precedents. To simplify crassly, the first defines the class enemy as the main obstacle to progress, and class struggle as the correct road to take. It requires full subordination in thought and action under the Center's commands, has limited use for and great distrust of the intelligentsia, and operates with military or other mass movements and campaigns. The second sees the development of the productive forces as the main problem to be solved. This may be true even before a revolution, where it is argued that this development will end in "state monopoly capitalism," and at the same time create a powerful coalition of working class and intelligentsia which will be strong enough to take over by peaceful means and change the name to "state monopoly socialism." After the revolution, this strategy abandons class struggle, tries to enlist the intelligentsia as specialists in the organization of production, advocates gradual and planned progress with no tumultuous mass participation, and defines bureaucratism as the social obstacle to be overcome, making sure however to define it as a "contradiction among the people" and not an antagonistic one. Evidently, the time at the eve of the Hundred Flowers period with its theory of the sharpening of class struggle under socialism was dominated by the first strategy, while the policies gaining ascendance for a few months (until mid-1957) at the 8th Party Congress in September 1957 corresponded to the second strategy. The later changes in the PRC, like the Cultural Revolution/post-1978 reform period, involved a similar change. This change implied a very substantial redefinition of the role of the "bourgeoisie" (which had no say in the matter), the intelligentsia, and the bureaucracy, and we can presume that the change involved substantial contention. Our question is thus how this change in 1956 was engineered, and which strategies were used to bring it about.

It is established wisdom that Zhou Enlai's "important" talk "On the

Question of the Intellectuals" on 14 January 1956 "set the stage"[1] for the new policies which were named after Mao's remarks on a "Hundred Flowers" on 2 May 1956.[2] While there can be no question that these statements represented clear and explicit formulations of the new direction, coming as they did from the top leaders, a closer study would seem to indicate that they stood rather at the end than at the beginning of a longer contention, and it is the earlier part, and the role of literature in it, in which we are interested here. We shall first sketch the orthodox options for contention, the theoretical parking orbit, then detail the specific elements of which it was composed in this case, and eventually study the avenues over which its elements were brought "down" into the public sphere to exercise their function.

Within Marxist-Leninist categories, the sciences and technology are a part of the economic base, and not a part of the superstructure of ideas and institutions tied to class. It could thus be argued that the professionals plying these trades would, in the simple exercise of their profession, develop the productive forces and be socially useful, even if their class point of view and ideas were not proletarian and Marxist-Leninist. Historical precedents for a treatment based on this assumption were found during the first years after the October Revolution, when even American specialists were hired by the Soviet Union.

Marx had maintained concerning Balzac, and Lenin concerning Tolstoy, that both writers, although royalist and bourgeois respectively in their ideologies, had accurately depicted the social realm and its development in their realist fiction. The method of realism forced upon them a truthful depiction of trends they abhorred. Strictly adhering to the method of realism, a writer may thus write the truth even if his ideology is backward. These arguments were a standard defense against the "cog-and-screw" theory, and had informed the 1st Soviet Writers' Con-

---

1. Zhou Enlai, "On the Question of the Intellectuals" (p. 60, note 23).

2. Mao's talk on the "Hundred Flowers" policy, if ever there was one, has not been made available. Scholars like Roderick MacFarquhar assume that there was no such speech, but rather just a short note or reference, on which Lu Dingyi elaborated in his well-known talk. In a later event, the formulation of the literary program of "combining revolutionary realism with revolutionary romanticism," we may see a similar process. Mao Zedong's few remarks in his speech in Chengdu (*Mao Zedong sixiang wansui*, 1969, p. 180) were developed into a full "theory" by Zhou Yang and Guo Moruo and led to the folksong movement accompanying the Great Leap.

gress's definition of socialist realism. It could justify the exemption of literature from rigorous Party control and ideological indoctrination. The same argument could be made for other workers in the superstructure, like philosophers and historians. As long as they adhered to the equivalent of realism, here historical and dialectical materialism as a method, they could operate independently. In his late years, Stalin had given a prop to this argument with his book on linguistics, which suddenly transferred language from the superstructure to the base and thus made the study of language into a politically neutral science. Other branches like education, management, and administration all had edged towards the hard sciences in the Soviet Union (using Pavlov, Fordism/Taylorism, and the mathematics of planned economy as props) in order to increase their legitimate leeway.

There were thus arguments and precedents for exempting the intelligentsia from direct Party supervision and control as long as they remained within the confines of "scientific socialism." There was, however, no sound theoretical base for shifting from the bourgeoisie to the bureaucrats the blame of being the main obstacle to progress. Ever since Trotsky had been branded a counterrevolutionary by Stalin, the theory that bureaucrats might be a class was anathema among orthodox Communists. Only Lenin's post-revolutionary diary entries with their violent attacks against the Soviet bureaucrats provided a precedent. As far as the Chinese side was concerned, things were easier because the Soviet Union with its high authority had already broken the ice. The 23rd Congress of the Soviet Party, held in 1951, had unequivocally stated that bureaucratism was the main obstacle to the rapid development of production. The intelligentsia, which is supposed to base itself on "scientific" truth, became, by definition, the main force opposing bureaucratism, which is defined as adhering to old rules and forms even if they are "not rational" any more, and deciding things on the basis of ulterior, and not very pure, motives. The implied glorification of the intelligentsia's commitment to truth suggests that this line of argument has its own ulterior motive of lobbying for the intelligentsia. The concomitant shift from a war economy to rapid economic development further enhanced the status of the specialists and decreased that of the generalist political bureaucrats.

As socialist society, by definition is not in fact set up for rapid development, which means constant change, the ideal personality type to constantly question the existing situation and drive ahead would be a fairly creative personality with a sharp critical eye and a commitment to abolish rotten old structures for the benefit of "the people." Precedents for this personality were found in Marx's description of socialism in *German Ideology*, and in figures like Vera Pavlovna in Chernyshevky's novel *What's To Be Done*. More specifically, there were personalities within the Communist movement (or who were regarded as within this movement) who had already developed the core traits of this new personality, like Mayakovsky and his Chinese counterpart, Lu Xun, both of whom had a strongly independent and critical stance while remaining committed to revolution. Both had obtained the support of the top leaders, namely Lenin and Mao Zedong. They were potential models of intelligentsia behavior within socialism.

In practical terms, these were abstract options, and there was no way for a Chinese text to find a niche where such options could be articulated on Chinese soil. In fact, Hu Feng had tried to do exactly that in his letter to the Central Committee. There he had argued with the Balzac material that the definition of socialist realism had in fact been developed *against* an overpolitization of literature as advocated by the Association of Proletarian Revolutionary Writers in the Soviet Union (RAPP), Germany, and elsewhere, and that cultural leaders like Lin Mohan and He Qifang, who had attacked him, were in fact following the RAPP line, which said that all literature is and must be propaganda.[3] While he quoted earlier and very recent Soviet texts to support his argument, trying to muster some of their authority for himself, it was much too early to come out with a Chinese text challenging the dominant line and personalities, quite apart from the fact that Hu had a feud of long standing with the cultural leadership around Zhou Yang, which eventually sealed his fate. But Hu Feng had been quite right in assuming that the only way to protect his assumptions was to base them on Soviet authority. Thus we see, from 1954 on, Soviet texts, theories, films, discussions, and even personalities appearing in Chinese officially printed matter, interacting there to form an alternative niche of conflict

3. "Hu Feng's Critical Opinions," (p. 23 note 9), pp. 8ff.

definition, strategies for conflict handling, and personality traits required for the new period. Within a fairly homogeneous official press, these materials could appear because of the Soviet prestige, and, under the general implication that one was to "learn from the Soviet Union," they could command considerable authority. To Chinese sympathizing with the views contained in these texts, their publication provided an avenue to get these materials to the Chinese public and to express their own views through translations, interviews, and reportages on things going on in the Soviet Union. There, Stalin had died, bureaucratism had officially become the main obstacle, educated youth were called upon to help with the rapid development of agriculture, and the first flowers of a literature of the "Thaw" were out with intelligentsia heroes (young ones at that) valiantly battling against the bureaucrats in the name of reason, progress, and Khrushchev.

On 15 April 1954, *Renmin ribao* devoted a full page to the translation of a literary reportage (*očerk*) by Valentin Ovechkin, which had been carried by *Pravda* late in February, "At a Meeting. . . ." The inordinate length signaled importance, and so did the Chinese editor's introduction: "'At a Meeting' penetratingly exposes bureaucratic leadership style. Bureaucratism of this brand, viz. holding endless meetings, reading off reports while not going deeply among the masses and not understanding what is actually going on, and not solving the problems, are also in our country not of rare occurrence. We especially print this text in order to alert everybody, so that bureaucratism may be better suppressed and our leadership work may be improved."[4] Ovechkin was the mentor of a group of young and very outspoken Soviet writers, including people like Tendriakov and Troepolski, who promoted the *očerk* (*texie* in Chinese), treated elsewhere in this volume, as documentary, fact–biased literary reportage against the writers of fiction, whom they chose to call "varnishers" (who glossed over the gloomier aspects of Soviet society and the bitter conflicts prevailing with a "literature of no-conflict"), a criticism originally made by Stalin himself in 1950. In the wake of the Soviet Party's new definition of bureaucratism as the main

4. Walianjin Aoweiqijin (V. Ovechkin), "Zai yige huiyishang" (At a meeting), *Renmin ribao*, 15 April 1954, and the editor's preface there.

obstacle to progress and "enemy of the people," and Khrushchev's policies of sending "the 30,000" technically qualified people from the cities to prop up technology and leadership in the countryside, these writers, together with Sholochov, whose *Virgin Soil Upturned* Part 2 came out in 1954, dominated the literary scene of the early Thaw. In Soviet literary history, this period is often referred to as the "period of Ovechkin," and Ovechkin created in the bureaucrat Borzov what became the proverbially typical character of this type. The fact that *Pravda* would publish Ovechkin's "At a Meeting" over a full page testifies to his standing in the Soviet Union at the time.

"At a Meeting" is an *očerk* giving a factual and satirical account of a Party activist meeting at the district (rayon) level; all factual and concrete experiences of the workers have been dissolved into the general verbiage of "glorious success," "great importance," and "further strenuous efforts" with the successful diary activist painfully stuttering through a text written for her by the kolkhoz chairman, and the representative of the province level pompously maintaining "Comrades! Fodder—fodder is the basis for feeding cattle." Martynov, set up by Ovechkin in many stories as the new matter-of-fact, efficient, hard-hitting, and combative rural leader, eventually intervenes and, after having silenced his bureaucratic colleagues, manages to get the meeting to discuss real facts and issues, and come up with specific plans for the future. He does this at great risk to his career, but finds support from the highest leader at the province level.

Published a few weeks after the 4th Plenum of the 7th CC of the CPC with its denunciation of arrogance and "individualism" as possible inroads for bourgeois subversion, the text showed that there were efforts to read this resolution as an appeal to shift to the anti-bureaucratic struggle in the manner of the Soviets at that time. Evidence for this is the important editorial in *Renmin ribao* "Learn from the Resolution of the 4th Plenum, Correctly Unfold Criticism and Self-Criticism" (22 March), which had encouraged Hu Feng to write his letter to the Central Committee. Using the same strategy as in the case of the publication of "At a Meeting," that is, Soviet texts and quotations to make a Chinese point, this editorial had quoted Malenkov, then still the head of the Soviet Party, with his attacks against bureaucratism, and, while generally mentioning influence from "bourgeois ideology," had not referred to a new attack from the "bourgeoisie" as a class, which would have necessitated class struggle. Read against the resolution as well as against this editorial, "At a Meeting," again seen as a *Chinese* text comes out as a forceful, if implied, reevaluation of the key conflict and the proper methods for its solution.

First, the editorial note reiterates the term *bureaucratism* as against the vague *bourgeois individualism,* and the text unequivocally portrays bureaucratism as the main obstacle to the coalition for progress. This coalition consisted of the "activists" at base levels and the top leader in both rayon and province, reflecting the ascension of the reformist highest leader in the Center, Khrushchev. The meeting, designed for the communication between these two parts of the coalition, cannot achieve its purpose because, in the bureaucratic ritual, the activists read reports written for them by the cadres who know nothing about their experiences, and the cadres babble general phrases. The main obstacle here is bureaucratism. Furthermore, the bureaucrats in the text don't form a *jituan,* an anti-Party clique or the like, but they form a complete stratum at the middle levels of administration linked by horizontal *guanxi* (connections), with the result that telephones from as far away as Moscow ring if an attempt is made to push one of them out. The notion of "the bureaucracy" as a stratum of officials linked by common interests and connections, and willing as well as able to edge out the Martynovs, appears here for the first time in a Chinese text.

Second, the bourgeoisie is absent in fact and argument. Consequently, the notion of class struggle as a way to solve conflicts does not appear. The method employed at this meeting is to "unfold democracy." The coalition of enlightened top leaders, base-level activists, and the writer who publishes the news of their struggle takes on the bureaucrats by criticizing them openly. The initiative for this comes from Martynov at the top. This coalition brushes aside the charge that this constitutes "lack of discipline," "lack of Party spirit," and "opposing the leadership"; now Stalin and Beria are gone, and such charges don't carry the same threat as before.

Third, the solution comes because Martynov manages to open the channels of criticism from below, not because some Central Discipline

Commission intervenes. This is in tune with the words of Malenkov quoted in the said *Renmin ribao* editorial: "Experience proves that even the best administrators (*gongzuozhe*) will degenerate and become bureaucratic if they are not checked and if their work is not inspected." Originally, this referred to some sort of popular check and inspection, especially the "inspection groups" and "stations" set up by Komsomol activists.

The 4th Plenum Resolution saw the solution clearly in a strengthening of the control exercised by the Center, and, anticipating that this might lead to a deterioration of inner-Party democracy, lamely added that it should not. The editorial, however, takes up exactly this appendix, and stresses the need for open criticism from below of bureaucratic abuses, the very position of "At a Meeting." "At a Meeting" addresses two issues which remained hidden to the Chinese reader until more stories by Ovechkin about Martynov were translated. The rayon leader had originally been Borzov, the bureaucrat. He had been dismissed by the provincial leader after many struggles, and Martynov had become his successor. This signaled an important power shift in the Center. The reformists around Khrushchev were seen by Ovechkin to be strong enough actually to replace the bureaucrats and to be depicted as the top leaders at each level, a rank and station their Chinese literary equivalents never even came close to. Second, Martynov originally was kolkhoz chairman, then a journalist and intellectual, and later was assigned work here. By inversion, the writer Ovechkin had been a kolkhoz chairman for many years, and Troepolsky was an agricultural engineer. The literary hero Martynov thus combines the daring outspokenness of a city intellectual with rural expertise, with the evident purpose of serving as a guiding light for "the 30,000." It was the first time in PRC literature that an "intellectual" played the role of hero. Although the editors of *Renmin ribao* probably knew this, they did not make the point explicitly. "At a Meeting" thus puts a complete alternative scenario into the Chinese parking orbit, albeit in a literary, implied form hidden within the translation of a Soviet text.

If our assumption about the role of the Soviet Thaw writings is correct, there are chances that the journal that printed most of the new Soviet literary texts in translation, namely *Yiwen* (Literature in translation), would become the place where these texts would be on hold in the Chinese orbit. Indeed, *Yiwen*, the only literary window to the outside socialist world, quickly developed into a storehouse of alternative socialist options in literary form, quite apart from the often superior quality of the works translated. In a survey in early 1956, the editorial board claimed that the "majority of the readers of *Yiwen* are between 20 and 30 years of age,"[5] and we can safely assume that this was a rather well-educated crowd of city intellectuals. It may be that *Yiwen* attracted this group of readers exactly because Soviet Thaw texts were published there. *Yiwen* was edited jointly by the Chinese Writers' Association and was under the nominal editorship of Mao Dun.

In May 1954, *Yiwen* printed the next Chinese Ovechkin text, "Days in the Rayon," together with a 20-page study of Ovechkin and his writing by A. Petrosian.[6] "Days in the Rayon" had been published even before Stalin's death in September 1952. The text confronts Martynov with Borzov. The grain deliveries from the kolkhozes are coming in irregularly. Borzov, interested only in fulfilling the overall delivery quota set by higher levels, sends threatening dispatches asking for immediate delivery, although endless rain stalls the harvest. Finally, he decides to fleece the one kolkhoz that is well organized and has all the grain in the bins by increasing its quota. Martynov wants to leave the fruits of their labor with the members of this kolkhoz and to punish with lower income those others who have been slack. Borzov claims to follow the "proletarian way" of putting the "collective interests" first, and charges Martynov with catering to the "peasant way" of parochial interests. In the shouting match between the two, Borzov recommends Martynov's transfer. Martynov persists and manages to get the rayon committee to postpone a decision on raising quotas, using the time to get the backward units to build drying sheds for the grain and shelter for the threshers. The gods reward him by bringing good weather, so that the problem is solved.

5. Editorial Board of *Yiwen*, "Benkan duzhe yijian zongshu" (A summary of the comments of our readers), *Yiwen* 4:193 (1956).
6. W. Aoweiqijin (V. Ovechkin), "Quli de richang shenghuo" (Everyday life in the rayon, a translation of "Raionnye budni"), *Yiwen* 5:1ff (1954). A. Bideluoxiang (A. Petrosian), "Cong shenghuo chufa" (Taking life as the starting point), *Yiwen* 5:39ff (1954).

In a conversation with Borzov's wife, a former Stakhanov production enthusiast, Martynov expands on other symptoms of bureaucratism. The core assumptions are similar to those in "At a Meeting." The bureaucrats are the main obstacle, blocking the potential enthusiasm of the agricultural laborers, and clogging their channels of communication with the enlightened top leadership. The reformers are not now the chairmen, but they put up a valiant battle, and already get their way here and there at great risk. The writer operates as a propagandist for the coalition for progress, and class struggle is nonexistent. Petrosian deftly puts Ovechkin into the context of Malenkov's appeal at the 19th Party Congress that "we need Soviet Gogols and Shchedrins who with their satire like a fire burn down all negative, rotten, and dead things in life and all things that block progress."

The great Chinese discovery about the connection between individualism/bureaucratism and the bourgeois attack is brushed aside, by implication, as irrelevant. True, bureaucratism, embezzlement, careerism, and so on are "all an inheritance handed down to us from the times of the system of exploitation. But it is our duty to recognize these old dregs in the midst of the sprightly movement of our new life, to observe the specific forms of existence of these old dregs under the new social conditions [underlined in original]."

In talking about the specific nature of deficiencies under the Soviet system, there is very little use for all-encompassing technical terms and definitions. What about Borzov's character? Does he belong to the old dregs? One could say he does, and one could say he doesn't. He does because his character is based on remains of the old non-Soviet psychology—arrogance and conceit, self-aggrandizement, striving for fame and wealth, negligence, and a formalistic bureaucratic attitude towards the interests of the people's enterprises. And one may say that he doesn't [underlined in original], because Borzov's character in its particular appearance is a product of our time and is even linked to a specific time and to particular typical circumstances."[7] "Days in the Rayon" ends abruptly with a remark by the author that life had not developed further by the time the story was written, an indication that the struggle

---

7. A. Petrosian, "Taking Life," (note 6 above), p. 50.

with Borzov had but begun. This formal element was seen in the Soviet Union as "unconventional," emphasizing the documentary nature of the text; in China it operated as a shock, because both in the press and in literature things would only be reported once the problem had been solved, assuring a positive ending; this announcement of an ongoing struggle in the party questioned the very principle of the unified guidance of the Party, at least in public presentation. The story also revealed Martynov's "intellectual" past, and Petrosian stated simply that "Martynov embodies the healthy spirit of the Party."

The *Yiwen* editors added further information in their customary introduction of the author in the "postface." Borzov is merely transferred, not dismissed, we learn from later stories, but his wife does not join him; she returns to tractor driving. As a contrast, Martynov's happy and cultured family life is depicted in another story.[8]

Yiwen was not entirely alone in retaining the anti-bureaucratic potential of the resolution; this option remained an undercurrent during the subsequent year, and *Renmin ribao* ran a regular column denouncing waste in industrial enterprises. In terms of political line, however, its main thrust was not against "the bourgeoisie."

In the winter of 1954, Ovechkin came to China as a member of a journalists' delegation. He traveled for a month through the country, accompanied by a young journalist from the Youth League paper whose Russian was impeccable—Liu Binyan. Much later, in April 1956, Liu Binyan described in his "Days with Ovechkin" the deep impression this man made on him as a model of public behavior, which he set out to emulate. "Observe, study, generalize life's contradictions and conflicts without a second of relaxation, this is Ovechkin's characteristic," he wrote, and then described the public role Ovechkin played in the Soviet Union as the person to turn to when all other channels were clogged, as the nimble and independent "scout" of the Party in its antibureaucratic endeavor.[9]

As we have seen, the public behavioral ideal especially for young intel-

---

8. Aoweiqijin (V. Ovechkin), "Renlei linghun de gongchengshi" (The engineer of human souls), in *Aoweiqijin texie ji*, tr. Jun Qiang et al. (Beijing: Zuojia chubanshe, 7 September 1955), pp. 71ff.

9. Liu Binyan, "He Aoweiqijin zai yiqi de rizi" (Days with Ovechkin), *Wenyibao* 8:80f (1956).

lectual cadres at the time of this encounter was one of obedience and "not making waves." Here came a man, a devoted Communist, who saw it as his duty to make trouble, whose heroes were making nothing but trouble, and who claimed that, if nobody got into a rage when reading one of his stories, he must have written it wrong. For young Chinese intellectuals with the independence potential of a Liu Binyan, the Soviet Union seemed the distant land of spring and daring free talk, where one could even talk back to bureaucratic superiors and be supported by the top leaders. At the time, Liu Binyan put his own dream of becoming a Chinese Ovechkin into the parking orbit. He did not write his "Days with Ovechkin" then; this was not possible, because it would have been a "Chinese" text. The anti-bureaucratic stance was not only a question of political assessments, which were at variance with the way the 4th Plenum's Resolution was read in late 1954; it became with Ovechkin's personality a much more visceral affair, a lifestyle rejecting bureaucratic torpor in speech and thinking, acting, and dress, though for the moment held in reserve as a daydream.

Ovechkin gave a talk in Beijing "On Očerk" ("Lun *texie*"), in which he spelled out the political assumptions implied in this genre. He spoke at a time when the public campaign had switched from Yu Pingbo and Feng Xuefeng to Hu Feng, who had ceased to be a "comrade," and when class struggle was being unfolded against a group of left-wing literati of long standing. Completely oblivious of these conditions, and possibly encouraged by his Chinese interlocutors, Ovechkin laid down his program of what literature was to do at that moment. The other and longer literary forms were slow to react to the rapid changes, and loath to take on such a heady subject as the battle against bureaucratism and backward things. "But our time is a time of such hot and lively struggles, things around us change with such a speed and grow so fast that before our very eyes many new processes unfold and develop. This leads quite naturally to a request put to us, namely to shape our artistic language in order to directly intervene in life (*ganyu shenghuo*), intervene in these changes. And this request on the očerk (*texie*) has been growing." It should be a "militant" genre, and "well researched," and play in the literary army the role of a scout.

The core slogan of the literature of 1956–1957 was thus slipped into

China in the midst of the Hu Feng campaign, namely, that literature should "intervene in life" in a militant, independent, and daring manner. But it was not a class-struggle genre. The very use of this kind of *očerk* was a political program. Ovechkin spoke without manuscript, and Liu Binyan unobtrusively assisted by making a transcript, translating it, and getting it published in the most important journal of literary criticism, *Wenyibao*, in April 1955, amidst copious denunciations of Hu Feng. True, it was printed as the last text in both issues, but the editors appended a rare note: "The incisive analysis in this article of the importance of the *texie*, its characteristics, and the problems of the author's deeply penetrating life deserve the utmost attention from the literary workers of our country."[10] By this time, Qin Zhaoyang had become one of the editors of *Wenyibao* and had given his unequivocal support to the *texie* and its implied political assessment and point of view; it is reasonable to assume that he had a hand in this publication.

The impact of Ovechkin's text and speech was reinforced in December 1954 with *Yiwen*'s publication of his associate Tendriakov's *texie*, "The Fall of Ivan Chuprov," as the lead story.[11] The link with Ovechkin was made in the editor's biographical information. The story deals with a kolkhoz chairman, a veritable rotten egg. Instead of being thrown out and handled in class-struggle fashion, even this man is saved in the story, a point stressed in the postface by the *Yiwen* editors. To underscore the importance of the story, they quote the Soviet author Chakovsky with an appreciation: "I think this work of only a few pages is for our literature of principal (*yuanzexing*) importance . . . Life's truth is not only beautiful, but sometimes grim. To depict this truth is the duty of the Soviet author." To reassure the readers that they were not trading in literary contraband, the *Yiwen* editors added that Ovechkin's and Tendriakov's works "were regarded as good works in Soviet literary circles."[12]

By the time the Hu Feng campaign went into its heated phase, an alternative political assessment in literary form, a literary genre encod-

10. W. Aoweiqijin (V. Ovechkin), "Tan texie" (On *očerk*), *Wenyibao* 6:37ff (1955), and 7:45ff (1955). The quotation from Ovechkin is on p. 37 in the first part, the editorial note on p. 39.
11. F. Tiandeliyakefu (F. Tendriakov), "Yifan Chupuluofu de duoluo" (The fall of Ivan Chuprov), *Yiwen* 15:1ff (1954). Originally in *Novy Mir*.
12. Editor's postface on Tendriakov, *Yiwen* 12:241 (1954).

ing it, and a personality type maintaining it were present in the Chinese orbit, with *Yiwen* and *Wenyibao* sharing the risk and the fun. On 30 May 1955, the same *Wenyibao* ran an editorial entitled "Conscientiously study the Resolution of the National Delegates Conference of the Chinese Communist Party, struggle for a strengthening of Party spirit in literature and the arts."[13] The preceding issue had carried, by way of preparation, two texts by Lenin. In the first, he praised the "party spirit" of Eugene Pottier, the poet from the Paris Commune who wrote "The International" for the International Workers Association; in the second he wrote on German workers' choruses and the relationship between proletarian culture and the Social Democratic Party. The two conflicting paradigms for the relationship of the party to the intelligentsia in general and for literature and the arts in particular stood next to each other in the same journal, without editorial comment.

13. "Renzhen xuexi Zhongguo Gongchandang quanguo daibiaohuiyi de jueyi wei zeng-qiang wenxue yishu shiye de dangxing er douzheng" (Conscientiously study the resolution of the National Delegates Conference of the Communist Party, struggle for a strengthening of Party spirit in literature and the arts), *Wenyibao* 9/10:5ff (1955).

SIX

Shaping the New Personality

Meanwhile, two rather unrelated changes began to alter the overall climate in China's political ecosystem. First, early in January 1955, Khrushchev gave a talk in Moscow at a Conference of Young Volunteers for the Opening Up of New Lands. In his attempts to find a social basis for his agricultural policies, and for his battles against cadres who were unwilling to go along with his reforms, Khrushchev strongly relied on educated youth. They provided the volunteers for his plans, and the steam for his campaign against "bureaucratism." The status of Chinese educated youths at the time was different. They were still considered "bourgeois" and in dire need of Communist reeducation. If it could be argued, however, that they were the real activists of the Five-Year Plan, their status would change dramatically from bourgeois intellectuals to shock troops and the avant-garde.

Preparing the ground with a reprint of Khrushchev's speech,[1] the Youth League Central Committee decided in February 1955 to call a conference in September of young "activists of socialist construction," a decision made public in May.[2] In the same month, the Youth League

1. "Zai Mosike qingnian zhiyuan kaikenzhe de huiyishang Heluxiaofu tongzhi de yanshuo" (Talk of Comrade Krushchev at the Moscow Conference of Young Volunteers for the Opening Up of New Lands), *Zhongguo qingnian* 2:2ff (1955).
2. "Guanyu zhaokai quanguo qingnian shehuizhuyi jianshe jijifenzi dahui de jueding (26 February 1955)" (Resolution on the convening of a national grand meeting of young activists for the building of socialism), *Zhongguo qingnian* 9:1ff (1955).

papers started to print articles showing how "activist" and "progressive" youths like engineers overcame obstructions put in their way by their leaders, and made improvements in production. The emphasis in the stories as well as in the projected conference was on industry, not agriculture. The Youth League leadership began to claim that "every youth" should become a "newborn force of the Revolution," and warned young people that they had to overcome the scorn and envy of conservative public opinion, and the obstructions of their leaders. Evidently, the personality type that disappeared within the anonymity of the collective and that loyally and sincerely followed all orders did not fit this new role, which was gradually carved out through the depiction of activist labor heroes. The first cartoon of a bureaucrat appeared in May 1955 without the Hu Feng Clique's playing any role:

The man sits on a rocking-horse by the name of "conservative thinking," proclaiming, "I, too, am progressing."[3] Even more definitely than the articles starting in this issue, this cartoon indicates a decision by the

3. Zhang Zhengti, "I, too, am progressing," *Zhongguo qingnian* 9:10 (1 May 1955). It illustrates an article about a young man who perseveres in pushing through a technical innovation against leadership obstruction.

Youth League leadership to publicly attack bureaucratic obstacles with both argument and satire, and this in May 1955, well before Mao's Hundred Flowers speech.

From the memoirs of members of the editorial board of *Zhongguo qingnian* and *Zhongguo qingnianbao* we learn that the head of the Youth League, Hu Yaobang, took a direct interest in these publications. Every Sunday night he would convene the editors and the members of the Youth League's propaganda department to directly guide the content and emphasis in Youth League propaganda. The new orientations of the Youth League press as well as new reporting techniques, emphasizing direct reportage and readers' letters as well as contributions by nationally renowned figures, seem to have originated with Hu Yaobang's interventions, or at least had his consent.[4]

The second change was initiated by Mao himself. A bare six weeks after his notes on Hu Feng and the editorial on the sharpening of class struggle during the socialist transition, Mao began his speech "On the Cooperative Transformation of Agriculture" with the following words: "An upsurge in the new, socialist mass movement is imminent throughout the countryside. But some of our comrades, tottering along like a woman with bound feet, are complaining all the time, 'You're going too fast, much too fast.' Too much carping, unwarranted complaints, boundless anxiety, and countless taboos—all this they take as the right policy to guide the socialist mass movement in the rural areas." In short, the leadership "lagged behind the mass movement." Conspicuously, there was no word about class struggle in the entire talk. A part of the rural leadership was bluntly accused of "conservative thinking" but "the bourgeoisie" did not seem to be behind this, nor did conservative thinking seem to lead to "counterrevolution." In the same manner, the papers had attacked "conservative thinking" in industry during the preceding months. To be sure, Mao repeated his theory of increased class struggle in socialism as late as October 1955, but this speech was not published, and the 31 July speech "On the Question of Agricultural Cooperatives"

4. Cf. Yang Zhongmei, *Hu Yaobang, a Biography* (Armonk: M. E. Sharpe, 1987), Chapter 7, sec. 3: "Taking Control Over the Youth League Press." Yang's source is Xing Fangqun (Editor-in-Chief of *Zhongguo qingnian* in the first half of the 1950s), reminiscing in *Xinwen yanjiu ziliao* 21:3 (1983).

was read by the later activists as the actual beginning of the "Hundred Flowers" period.[5]

The Youth League was instantly alert to the potential of this campaign. It sent large numbers of youth activists to the countryside in the second half of 1955 to help with the establishment of agricultural cooperatives and to reduce illiteracy; there were also efforts to open up new lands in the Krushchev style.[6] These youths were "newborn forces" and activists who legitimized a slowly expanding freedom of action and thought with the necessities of developing production and socialism, not with the individualist fancies of bourgeois youths.

The young educated labor hero who with a high degree of socialist idealism blows away the obstacles on the way to progress became the model in which the Youth League described itself. For this character a new word and a new environment was offered from Soviet materials. The word was *yonggan* (courageous, or bold). Vera Ketlinskaya's novel with that title had come out in February 1955 in Chinese, and, showing the growth of *yonggan* features in a group of Komsomol members who volunteer to build a city near the frosty borders of Heilongjiang, it was quickly reviewed in the Chinese Youth League press.[7] *Yonggan* was defined there as the capacity to face difficulties fearlessly, take them on, and overcome them. Within the novel those difficulties are mostly the harsh climate, inadequate accommodations, and flagging spirits, not obstruction by bureaucratism. However, these young people move in a new environment, the wilderness, where they have to rely on their own wits, energy, and mutual support without a senior pontificator guiding and controlling their steps. They were on their own out there, and the thrill for the Chinese readers was less in the political orthodoxy of this

---

5. Mao Zedong, "On the Cooperative Transformation of Agriculture," in his *Selected Works* (Beijing: Foreign Languages Publishing House, 1977), V, 184ff. The theory of increased class struggle is upheld in Mao Zedong, "The Debate on the Cooperative Transformation of Agriculture and the Current Class Struggle," in ibid., V, 215. This talk was given on 11 October 1955.

6. Programmatically, *Zhongguo qingnian* 13 (1955) in July carried a cover depicting Youth Leaguers from the city moving to the countryside.

7. V. Ketlinskaya, *Fortitude* (Moscow: Progress Publishers, 1975). Cf. Lin Liu, "Tan Sulian gongqingtuanyuan de yonggan jingshen" (On the daring spirit of Soviet Komsomol members, a review of Ketlinskaya's book), *Zhongguo qingnian* 5:22ff (1955).

all-time classic (reprinted in the Soviet Union since 1938 to this very day whatever way the wind blew) than in the daring independence and freedom coming with this challenge, a far cry from their own regulated lives. *Yonggan* had figured among youthful features before, but as something inherently chaotic and rash, which had to be tempered to become *wenzhong* (moderate, steady, and sedate).

The title of a Soviet film shown in October 1955, *Fostering a Bold Spirit (Peiyang yonggan jingshen)*, also much discussed,[8] elevated the development of such a spirit into a program, although Chinese commentators stressed that both a more disciplined *and* a bolder behavior were essential for Chinese youths. Both book and film had Youth League heroes, and thus the model of a Youth League literature promoting the new personality and the new values, and replacing the values encoded in Ostrovski's *Pavel Korchagin*, took shape on Chinese soil.

Mao's Cooperatives talk of June 1955 was published in October. The Sufan Campaign went on and on endangering ever broader sections of the younger cadres, Hu Yaobang's warnings notwithstanding. In this climate, heavy reliance on Soviet materials had to continue to keep alive and flesh out the bare bones of the alternative personality. In August, *Yiwen*, although by design a translation journal, felt pressed to print, for the first time, some articles against Hu Feng. In the same issue, however, it carried the first part of the text which was to play a key role in redefining the framework of human values and human behavior in a way congenial to the "newborn socialist forces" of youth. It was Galina Nikolayeva's novella *The Director of the Machine Tractor Station and the (Woman) Chief Agronomist*.[9]

Published originally in the Soviet Union in October 1954, the work was exceedingly successful, hailed by Smirnov in May 1955 as one of only two works "directly reflecting the great events presently happen-

8. Zhang Zhangmu, "Yonggan chansheng zai douzheng zhong—yingpian 'Peiyang yonggan jingshen' guanshou" (Fortitude grows in battle—after seeing the film *Fostering a bold spirit*), *Beijing ribao*, 12 November 1955.

9. Jialinna Nigulayewa (Galina Nikolayeva), *Tuolajizhan zhanzhang he zongnongyishi* (The director of the Machine Tractor Station and the [woman] chief agronomist), *Yiwen* 8, 9, 10 (1955). There is an English translation, G. Nikolayeva, *The Newcomer* (Moscow: Foreign Languages Publishing House, n.d.).

ing in the life of the kolkhozes" after the 3rd Plenum had ratified Khrushchev's agricultural plans in September 1953.[10] Although these plans did not call for the "socialist transformation" then promoted in China but for technical and managerial improvements, the theme of educated youth being sent to the countryside resonated loud enough with the Chinese situation to make the actual development of the story's theme less dangerously conspicuous.

The story was dedicated by the author to the "young men and women, you who have chosen Nastya's [the heroine's] path," and, more specifically, to the "Komsomol members of the Altai and Kazakhstan regions," where the story is set. Nastya herself is a "rank-and-file member of the Komsomol" (the Soviet Communist Youth organization), and set up as an object of emulation for other young people in the text itself. Within socialist argumentative ecology, there always is a lobby element to literature; the texts are seen as propaganda for the social segment to which the hero or heroes belong. In this sense the text is a Youth League novel. Nastya's impact is reinforced by secondary characters: The young mechanics and peasants, who become the activists in the drive for rational organization and higher production organized by Nastya, are Komsomol members. And the Director of the MTS, who originally opposed her and eventually is converted, is still young enough to be just beyond Komsomol age.

The story starts with a meeting of advanced agricultural workers in the Kremlin somewhere in late 1953. Chalikov, the director of a Machine-Tractor Station (MTS) where Nastya works, is called upon to report on how the success in his unit came about; overpowered by the grand occasion and some inner trouble, he stalls. A few days later, the writer meets Chalikov in the night train back to his MTS in Siberia. In the anonymity of this nighttime encounter, Chalikov tells the story of Nastya's struggle and success while out of the dark night the sun slowly rises. Throughout the text runs his direct speech, a narrow frame being provided by the writer's recording the circumstances of the interview in the beginning, and taking leave of Chalikov in the end. Using this

10. Ximengnuofu (Smirnov), "Women wenxue de zhandou duiwu" (Our literary battle contingent), *Yiwen* 7:124 (1955).

presentation technique, the writer claims complete authenticity, and the earthy colloquialisms of the narrative are to seem like the language of real life. The author confines herself to the role of secretary. This form responds to the apprehension of readers (who have long been fed "varnishing" literature) by promising them unembellished truth. Ovechkin had set up the *očerk* as *the* literary form for the depiction of truth, and Nikolayeva reacted by absorbing some of the *očerk* techniques into her novella.

The direct-speech narrator, Chalikov, was a young man of high aspirations when in college. "I was quite self-confident at the time and felt that, once my studies were finished, I would immediately perform all sorts of labor feats and heroic actions." He loved to recite Mayakovsky's poem "At the Top of My Voice, First Prelude to a Poem on the Five-Year Plan," where the poet addresses the later born "Hi, listen! Comrades, heirs, and descendants . . ." claiming fame for his achievements. The reader is warned, however, by an ambivalence in Chalikov's physiognomy that the latter's straight course will be obstructed: "The upper part of his face had large pensive eyes with long eyelashes which were like a young girl's, yes, all too soft and effeminate," while the lower part sported *gangyi*, resoluteness, with a "chin full of will power, a firm and big mouth" with a nice grin only to be found in "intelligent, daring (*yonggan*), and cheerful" people.

Assigned the directorship of a Siberian MTS, Chalikov is helped by the chief engineer, Arkady, an older, experienced, and imposing man who had contracted a chronic disease during the war, and had taken the advice of doctors to retire to a "calm life" in the steppe. The third man in the MTS leadership, the Party secretary, is also young and under Arkady's wing.

Arkady turns out to be the villain of the story; by making the details of his biography specific, the text strives to limit his typicality for his generation of leaders. He is an individual case, we are told, but such cases exist and such people do play important roles. The three men manage to stay "shoulder to shoulder" with the other MTS, learn from Arkady "the charms of life in the steppe," and go out to hunt and flirt. The steppe "lulls" Chalikov "like a cradle," things take on their slow routine, and the dust of the steppe settles on his mind. The steppe becomes a metaphor for the eventless drag of bureaucratic routine, as dust became the very emblem of bureaucratism both in the Soviet Union and in China:

Arkady and I often went to the stand by the train station to drink a beer, stay a while, and look around. I have to tell you, this earth of ours is all chestnut and clay. The earth is yellow all over and the dust rising from it is like a yellow column. The huts, too, are made from clay and they are not even whitewashed so that they retain their natural color. . . . There's a camel looking at the train from behind the low walls around the Agricultural Supply Office, and its head too has that color as if it was made of clay . . . Worse still, the beer stand is greyish yellow, and even that dog Shelma that runs out of the Supply Office for every train that comes and waits for a sausage skin, has the color of camel hair. You drink your beer (and damn it, even the beer has that color!) and think "To hell with this yellow color!"

The one train passing the station each day comes from Moscow, but for the moment nothing dramatic is happening there. Chalikov's past is not as specifically described as Arkady's, and thus his slow succumbing to the rhythm and yellow dullness of bureaucratic routine is a more typical process for the younger new leaders, which is further repeated in the young Party secretary.

Borrowing a grand scene from Serafimovich's *Iron Flood,* Nikolaeva introduced a grotesque blare of sound into this dull scene as a means of foreshadowing. Whenever the Moscow train would pull up, "Kostya, our wireless man, played records for the train with the loudspeaker turned on full blast. His favorite record was 'Mid the Noisy Stir of the Ball.'" And thus, as the two men stood there, over the yellow landscape "wafted this voice, so out of place at our little station and in such discord with everything about us: 'Mid the noisy stir of the ball / I glimpsed you by chance / But a secret . . .' And these words seemed to come flying from some other planet. Mysterious and ringing, they at once drowned out all other noise, the voice trembled and tore as though overwhelmed by unendurable emotions. And suddenly you'd find yourself thirsting . . . for this kind of unendurable emotion . . . for this secret which lies deeply hidden in the heart. . . ." The young man's hidden longing for some great deed, and for love, resonates with that song. When the train finally arrives at Chalikov's home and the story is all told, we know that the deed is done and he loves Nastya; the writer assures us that the music is not "out of place" anymore.

The Chinese translators cut the second line from the Russian text which reads "Mid the noisy stir of the ball / in the flurry of worldly vanity / I glimpsed you . . ." "As the noisy stir of the ball" here stands for the deafening routine in which Chalikov lives, longing for the grand emotion, the Chinese translators felt it would be exaggerating to describe the routine activities of a MTS director as a "flurry of worldly vanity."

The song is one of the four romantic waltzes Tchaikovsky composed in 1878 to texts by A. K. Tolstoy.[11] To Russian readers the other stanzas were known. In the love song the young woman is described amidst this flurry of vanity, "eyes gazing sadly" with a "slender figure" and a "pensive air whilst she laughs." The young man who voices his feelings in the song ponders her "sad eyes" and "merry speech" and "pensive thus, melancholy, I fall to sleep, and drowse in unknown dreams . . . / I am not sure if I love you," he ends, "but it seems to me that I do!" The unquoted text thus suggests the kind of woman who will appear, and how Chalikov, after much pondering, will eventually conclude that he loves her. In terms of craft, a well-wrought scene.

When Nastya arrives "fresh from college" as the new chief agronomist, she is a disappointment to the three men, who had hoped for a beauty and not a girl with unkempt hair. Amid the din of their party and bragging about keeping up with the others, she keeps her "sad eyes" when finding out that the MTS is not run according to the books, and that there is great penury in the kolkhozes "behind the salt marshes."

The MTS leaders are interested in their good standing with the higher levels, and anxious not to fall behind other MTS. Thus they shrug off their sloppy machine repair and low harvests as "normal" in the area, and "unavoidable" in the development of socialism.

Nastya, on the other hand, goes by what is "scientific" and "rational," what should be. She establishes the proper class base by making friends with the young mechanics from the MTS who come in for the "working class," and with the peasants from the poorest villages. With the peasant and worker Komsomol members she even talks openly about the qualities and shortcomings of the MTS leaders. Arkady

11. A. K. Tolstoy, "Shred shumnovo bala," music by P. Tchaikovsky, op. 38.3. For a performance and the texts, see *Songs by Tchaikovsky and Britten*, Galina Vishnevskaya (soprano), Mstilav Rostropovich (piano), London, stereo OS 26141. Actually, the voice should be male as the text is written from a male perspective.

quickly discovers that she is a threat and a nuisance, charges her with "lack of experience" and "naiveté," and eventually determines that she is an "enemy." A "life-and-death struggle" ensues. As the author gives no class background for Arkady, we are not witnessing a class struggle, but the new type of rather ill-defined conflict between the bureaucrats and the young production enthusiasts with their high ideals. When Nastya fights back by publicly charging that Arkady is "irresponsible" in his work, the narrator, Chalikov, tries to get her out of the way by assigning her the duty of compiling voluminous, meaningless statistics. Nastya refuses to obey:

> "By what right are you disobeying my instructions and withholding the reports?" I demanded.
> "The questions in the forms are very silly," she said.
> "I have an order from the regional center. How can I ignore the region's instructions?"
> "Very simply," she said. "You can do the same thing that I am doing about your instructions."

This was quite a conversation, even for a Soviet reader; in the Chinese context of late 1955, young readers must have stared in disbelief at this behavior of a Soviet Youth League heroine. Nastya gets a written warning in her file. Against the explicit orders of Arkady, she uses an occasion when he is absent and trains the tractor drivers for several days in a new seeding technique. She receives a reprimand in her file. Eventually, she puts her body in front of the seeders which have been sloppily repaired to prevent them from starting work. The leaders decide to have her fired for "disobedience" and for daring to overrule the orders of the manager. When the regional Party secretary asks her whether she is familiar with the principles of one-man management in Soviet enterprises, and why nonetheless she "dared to defy openly the orders of the MTS director," she answers without lifting her head, "I . . . did dare . . ."

However, we are in the year 1953, Stalin is dead, and Khrushchev is on the rise, the time is early spring, both in politics and in nature. While Nastya is desperately battling below, the regional Party secretary, a man of great merit in the prewar years, who has, however, acquired some bureaucratic habits and has become estranged from the laboring masses, is criticized at Party meetings and in the press. He quickly reforms, and this gives Nastya her chance. She openly challenges him that he has been "lying" for years to the peasants by promising them good harvests. She produces a bottle with water and ground sunflower seeds, a mixture used by women in the poorest villages as a milk substitute and demands a radical change in the crop-rotation plans at this moment, just a few days before seeding is to start. Taken aback by the harsh accusation, the secretary first balks, but his superb class background eventually gets the better of him. In fact, he himself had grown up in one of the poorest villages under the MTS. Nastya's plans are examined and eventually approved.

The secretary refuses the MTS leaders' wish to have her fired. He concedes that her behavior was "rash, intolerable, yes (*zuofeng shi culu . . . bu neng rongxudi*), but . . . her fighting spirit is very strong . . . and in a struggle the main thing is not work style but . . . but what the purpose of the struggle is and who the opponent is." In this polarization, the middle has to get moving, since the "opponent" is Arkady. As we have seen, Chalikov had felt some uneasiness with his life even before Nastya arrived: "Here the best years of my life were passing and I had nothing to show for them." He witnessed Nastya's confrontation with the Party secretary, and had a spurt of sympathy with her childlike naiveté and openness. Eventually, he was impressed by her close links with people of excellent class background, and, most of all, with the fact that this young nuisance, once she had her way, produced results that landed the MTS within a few months in the nation's papers as a model unit, and procured for him an invitation to attend the "Advanced Agricultural Workers' Conference" in Moscow. Chalikov finds his youth back, reassesses his work, and falls in love with Nastya, getting ever more estranged from Arkady in the process. The MTS Party secretary understands his superior's hint that he should create a "normal environment for normal demands" and that Nastya's demands are indeed reasonable and normal. The story is saved from dissolving into syrup through Arkady, who arrogates all of Nastya's merits for himself, blocks her invitation to the Moscow conference, and rides on her merits to a job in a Moscow office, once he notices that he has lost control over the other two men.

Nastya, the well-trained specialist and young heroine from the Komsomol, has indeed developed a type of behavior and list of priorities that anticipated those ratified at the Communist Party Plenum in September 1953, a plenum that marked Khrushchev's ascent to power, as much a rupture with past policies as was the Chinese CC's 3rd Plenum in December 1978. In fact, the author claims, the September Plenum only transformed into a general line what had been spontaneously developed in obscure Siberian villages by activist and educated Youth League members. Chalikov rejoices:

> Then, in September, a most happy event occurred, the Central Committee's September Plenum! And what was so remarkable about that? What gave us such a jolt? Well, we looked in the papers, and they talked about us . . . our concerns and troubles, and what we had done. . . . The most amazing thing in truth was . . . well you are just groping for something, and your mind just comes up with some vague idea, but there [in the Plenum's documents] it had already been systematically thought out and spelled out! Through the September Plenum, it became ever clearer to us that the line we had followed was correct, that the line to which Nastya had daringly adhered was correct.

Nastya eases this conversion by apologizing for one instance when she wrongly disobeyed orders, and, after Chalikov in turn apologizes for his blunders, she accepts him as a leader, without softening her basic political principles.

To minimize typicality, Nastya is equipped with a uniquely favorable class background (her father being a model miner), much patriotic devotion (her brother died a hero in the war), and a superb education at "the best schools"; thus she is enabled to become a perfect emblem for the best qualities of "the Russian woman," being "courageous, selfless, fearless, and noble in deed," and thus an ideal and idealized role model for Komsomol members. Chalikov himself is still young enough to understand that only by imitating Nastya's "straightforwardness (*zhishuai*), sincerity (*kenzhi*), and frankness (*tanbai*)" can he win her confidence and contribute something himself.

The story idealizes the "best forces" from the Youth League, and depicts a coalition of progress consisting at base levels of Nastya, the best young workers at the MTS, and the most enlightened peasants, both young and old; and at the top the number-one regional leader (a reflection of the new number-one man in the Center, Khrushchev), and the enlightened Center itself, which takes up the best initiatives from the young activists. The coalition's success hinges on the existence of "Nastyas" and their willingness to risk their heads and their happiness for reforms.

The purpose of the coalition is the improvement of people's living standards, not the fulfillment of some plan for heavy industry. Thus the daily necessities in people's lives receive much attention from the positive figures. This reflects the shift to agriculture and raising living standards marked by the September Plenum. The novel is written after this Plenum as a kind of *post festum* prediction. This shift involves a profound change in standpoint, attitude, and lifestyle among the leaders, and it eventually gives Chalikov access to the common people and to Nastya's heart. A subordinate theme in the novel is love. It was then still too early for love stories to appear; love could gain legitimacy only through its close association with politics. Once Chalikov accepts Nastya's politics, her looks don't matter anymore and he loves her for her correct line.

In the middle of the hierarchy are the bureaucrats. Their hard-core members (Arkady) cannot be changed, but they are exceptions. The younger leaders will be spurred on to remember their lofty aspirations by the Nastyas below and the enlightened leaders above. The story strikes a conciliatory note by being recounted as a conversion narrative of a sinner who came to see his mistakes and returned to the true path. This imputes a basic good will to the younger bureaucrats and assures the young Nastyas that, after many tribulations, they will eventually be supported by their leaders.

Communications between the top and the bottom of the coalition of progress are impeded. Nastya's merits are unknown in the Center due to Arkady's obstruction. But the MTS is in fact successful, and Nastya may rest assured of that. Chalikov will try to get her invited to the conference next time. Literature joins the coalition of progress by articulating at base levels those experiences that are too complex and difficult to articulate on such grand occasions as the Kremlin conference. The novel becomes the meeting ground of the top and bottom of the coalition, literature taking on the role of writing the protocol of life as it is, with all its stuttering and awkward expressions, all its ups and downs, in utmost truthfulness and authenticity. Needless to say, I am not arguing that the novel does any of these things; I am trying to extrapolate the message implied in the articulated and silent elements of the text.

A few features of relevance for the Chinese discussion should be noted. In Nikolayeva's story, the bureaucrat has replaced natural conditions as the great obstacle to progress. There is no class enemy. The battle is led by a "weak" person, a youth, a newcomer, a female, against the older experienced males. Nastya belongs to the "intelligentsia" but is of proletarian origin. She is leading the proletarian and peasant Komsomol youths, and under her guidance they provide the social, political, and production shock troops for the reformist assault. Her daring is expressed in her outspokenness, obstinacy, and willingness to accept responsibility, and not restricted to a capacity to endure natural hardships. Her eventual success and vindication is possible only through her *direct refusal to obey those orders of her superiors that she feels to be unacceptable;* she is willing to *zhenglun,* to get into a dispute with them. At the time of that refusal she is on her own, there is no Party document on which she can base her action, as the story is set before the September Plenum. Thus it is she and people like her who develop the new line. Bluntly speaking, the educated and technically qualified Komsomol members unite the working-class Komsomol members, and lead, both in the fields of production and of political orientation, the battle for the eventual shift in the Party's policies. Nastya achieves this without any "collective" around her into which she could submerge herself. The standard arguments against a leading role for youths—lack of experience, rashness, and a tendency to exaggerate—are negated by being proffered from the mouth of Arkady. Her naiveté is praised as a quality that makes her expect things to be as they should; her lack of experience appears only as an unwillingness to accommodate to things that are "unscientific." Her rashness and exaggerations are the very conditions for her having an impact.

Among the people infected with bureaucratism, some have built up connections with others of the same kind for purposes of mutual support and protection. Arkady is not fired, but promoted to Moscow, unchanged, even hardened in his attitude. The provincial Party secretary, on the other hand, is saved by criticism. The young cadres, the director and the Party secretary, can both be saved through Nastya's activities. Among all the numerous young people in the novel, only two are "bad eggs," and they side with Arkady. Proportions in numbers and ranks of the protagonists of the different groups in a story are the standard devices to denote the typicality of a character or a problem. They can be translated into statistical assessments and have been thus translated by literary and political critics. The story makes use of these statistical devices.

The heroic grandeur of Nastya is very consciously subdued and made tolerable through emphasis on her pitiful looks, a sympathetic depiction of her shedding tears alone in her room when the leading males all gang up against her, and the fact that, on one occasion, she exaggerates her unruliness and apologizes. The frame of the story and the narration through the mouth of one of her early opponents also works in the same direction. Being directly geared to the young and the Youth League, this story mapped out the pioneer role for intelligentsia Youth Leaguers equipped with a new personality, and the brazen assumption that they would eventually cure the Party of its conservatism in the middle layers, and lay the foundations for a new progressive political line in which the interests of the people would be the dominant factor. It should be kept in mind that the Chinese Youth League was officially described as the Party's loyal handmaid. To put Nastya and the politics of this novel into the parking orbit of Chinese daydreams as a possible alternative to Ostrovsky's Pavel was no small feat.

The text could, of course, claim that, with the emphasis on the dangers of arrogance and conceit about past successes, it was in the mainstream of the line developed in China since the 4th Plenum. The editor's postface in *Yiwen* softened the impact of the story by not treating the question of Arkady's "class nature," but it made clear that it saw Nastya as the replacement of Ostrovsky's Pavel in the role of the model for youths to emulate. The author "proves forcefully with artistic means that to lead a heroic battle for new things is not only within the purview of persons with exceptional talent and exceptional heroism; every single person can lead this battle."[12] While breaking new ground in terms of independent thinking, outspokenness, and combativeness, the

---

12. Editor's postface to the Chinese translations of Nikolayeva's novel, *Yiwen* 9:249 (1955).

story remained conservative on the cultural side. Nastya's clothing and hairdo show no bourgeois corruption, while the men's hope that a dashing beauty might arrive is depicted as backward. Nastya never flirts or talks of love; no dancing distracts her from her single-minded pursuit of the great goal of improving the life of the poorest kolkhozes.

For the moment, the text stayed on hold to find its readers. In the September issue of *Yiwen,* the second installment of Nikolayeva's novel was printed. The issue contained an article by Kalinin on the importance of the "agricultural theme" and the great contribution made by Ovechkin and his associates in penetrating the disguises of bureaucratism. Kalinin, who worked as a journalist for the Soviet Komsomol paper, went into some detail describing these disguises. The bureaucrat "is an expert in adapting to new circumstances and situations. In order to avoid detection, he will masquerade with progressive slogans and quotations as well as gestures and tricks that fool people. . . . Although not concerned with life and people, he will time and again pose as a progressive, and that is why one has to use the method of cracking a nut if one is to show its kernel."[13]

Technically, the article helped situate the texts by Ovechkin, Nikolaeva, Tendriakov, and others into the context of "kolkhoz literature," which fitted into the conflict between "conservative thinking" and socialist upsurge perceived in the Chinese countryside by Mao. The Soviet texts, however, depicted a conflict between technical and managerial innovators and the bureaucrats, while Mao stressed the political backwardness of the rural cadres compared to the progressive "masses," that is, non-Party-members. In September 1955, a Chinese edition of Ovechkin's *texie* came out, including the two already printed, and several others operating with the same political assumptions.[14] In October, Tendriakov's *The Fall of Ivan Chuprov* came out as a book.[15] These texts were now moving from the more esoteric journal *Yiwen* to the general reading public.

13. Annatuoli Kalining (Anatoli Kalinin), "Dangqian de zhongda zhuti" (An important theme of our time), *Yiwen* 9:190 (1955).

14. *Aoweiqijin texie ji* (Oçerki by Ovechkin). Cf. ch. 5 note 8.

15. "Nigulayewa de yibu youxiu xinzuo" (An excellent new work by Nikolayeva), *Beijing ribao,* 1 November 1955.

The first texts in the new vein written by Chinese on things Chinese also made their appearance in the month of October. With the decision to publish Mao's July text and the edition of the *Upsurge*, the conditions were ripe to start bringing some of the options to earth which were in the parking orbit.

The general theme of combating "conservative thinking" was linked directly to a specific change in the position of youth by the discovery of a quotation in Mao's comments in *Upsurge*. In September 1955, Mao included a report in this compilation about a youth shock brigade (*qingnian tujidui*) in Zhongshan county in Heilongjiang which had made a great contribution to the socialist transformation. He added his editorial comment: "Among all social forces, youths are the most active and the most lively. They are most willing to learn, are least conservative, and this even more so in the socialist period."[16]

As a general pronouncement, this quotation could justify a claim that, in the current struggle against "conservative thinking" which had been started with Mao's talk late in July, the Youth League and youth in general would take the lead, and that, in the ongoing rapid technical and social transformation of the country, theirs would remain the decisive role in preventing the system from stagnating. They would be the force that "battled to clear the way for new things" against bureaucratic obstruction. With relish the first Chinese texts pointed out what that implied.

On 1 October, *Zhongguo qingnian* printed a story entitled "The Doctor in the Forest." It reported the deeds of a Youth League member, Dr. Jin Zhendu, dispatched to become a doctor in the wilderness of the northeast.[17] Under these harsh circumstances, independent thinking and acting are developed. His ultimate opportunity arises when the leadership sends him a message to hurry to save a young member of their team who has fallen ill. As he is new in the area, the leaders order him to go by the bigger, safer roads, a distance of 200 li. Defying the orders of his leaders, he takes a little-known small path, which leads there

---

16. Mao Zedong, ed., *Socialist Upsurge in China's Countryside*, Editor's notes excerpted from his *Selected Works*, V, 264.

17. Lu Fei, "Senlin de daifu" (The forest doctor), *Zhongguo qingnian* 19:25ff (1955).

directly through 80 li of virgin forest, with bandits and bears roaming about. Driven by his desire to help the Youth League member, he arrives two days early, and saves a life. In addition, he shows his valor by willingly forfeiting an academic career, and by helping to solve the conflict between an activist, outspoken young man and the leader who was persecuting this young man after receiving harsh criticisms from him. Nastya performed her great deeds in explicit defiance of her superiors' orders. Dr. Jin follows in her steps.

The symbolic juxtaposition of the easy, broad road recommended by the leaders, which safely but slowly would bring him to the destination with the risk that on arrival the patient might have expired, and the narrow, unmapped, direct road to the ill patient, which one walks, however, at the substantial risk of being eaten by bears or shot by bandits, was not lost on Chinese readers. In the standard language of the time, this was "undisciplined" behavior, "lack of organization spirit," "opposition to the leadership," and, of course, youthful rashness. The young man, however, was depicted as an "activist for socialist construction," a participant in the national conference of such activists just going on in Beijing with the highest leaders attending, and as a man who had been accepted into the Communist Party. Most important, all this glory was awarded to a member of the intelligentsia, someone with a university degree, a far cry from the self-effacing bourgeois youth who represented the intelligentsia earlier. The story of Dr. Jin had been written up in *Renmin ribao* on 7 June 1955, but no mention was there made of the fact that he did his greatest deed by defying the orders of his leaders. The geographical ambiance is reminiscent of the wilderness of freedom of Ketliskaya's *Yonggan*, while Nastya might have been the inspiration for the depiction of his daring independence, although he does not *zhenglun*, does not get into an argument with the leaders. Altogether, the text is noncommittal when it comes to the leaders, and makes its points implicitly through the depiction of the hero's deeds, and the symbolism of the two roads. At this same time, a Chinese film was begun, where, sure enough, the young hero does his thing by defying an order from his officer.[18] The idea of defiance was now in fashion.

18. The film is *Dong Cunrui*; it is discussed in this context of non-obedience to irrational orders in Fang Qun, "Yinggai gaibian luan koumaozi de fengqi" (This habit of putting hats on people at random must be changed), *Zhongguo qingnian* 11 (1956).

The same issue of *Zhongguo qingnian* that carried Dr. Jin's story, printed the speech made by the highest Party operator in the Youth League and effective leader of that body, Hu Yaobang, to the Conference of Activists of Socialist Construction. Hu Yaobang maps out an entirely new framework of reference for youth under the title "The Task of China's Youth in the Struggle for the Realization of the 1st Five-Year Plan." "Our party," he says "sees the young generation as huge shock forces (*tuji liliang*) for the realization of the Five-Year Plan and the building of socialism. Why is the young generation a huge shock force? Because Chinese youth [between the ages of 14 and 24] comprise 120 million people, about a fifth of the entire population, and more than a third of the nation's labor force; because young people are not only physically strong and full of mental vigor, but, having grown up under the education of the Chinese Communist Party, they have an acute instinct for fresh and new things, have high hopes and superb courage, and strive for the glorious future of socialism in their fatherland." The general paradigm for youths was that the Communist Party had reared them, and their positive energies could be brought to bear by their becoming the shock troops of socialist industrialization and of the socialist transformation of the countryside. They had two advantages: their labor energy; and their feeling for the new. Their "creativity" in developing and furthering that feeling was positively stressed. "Our state has always greatly nurtured creative labor. Creative labor can smash people's old and conservative thoughts and can greatly enhance labor productivity."[19]

At the same conference, Deng Xiaoping spoke for the Party Politburo. He said, in a statement which reads like a close re-statement of the words the provincial Party secretary had for Nastya's rash manner: "As long as your orientation is correct, your enthusiasm must be welcomed and treasured in every way, and has to be supported by Party and state. No force whatsoever is permitted to obstruct your advance."[20] This con-

19. Hu Yaobang, "Zhongguo qingnian wei shixian diyige wunianjihua er douzheng de renwu" (The task of China's youth in the struggle for the realization of the 1st Five-Year Plan), *Zhongguo qingnian* 19:2ff (1955).

20. Deng Xiaoping, quoted in Zhi Guang, "Don't Polish Off Their Edges," (ch. 4 note 26), *Zhongguo qingnian* 7:29 (1956).

ference marked the turning point in the assessment of youths in the Party's Center. This eventually created the climate in which a new ideal for educated youth could be advocated.

For the leadership, there was no "liberal" or "democratic" motivation in this new emphasis. A greater leeway for young people was to help them unfold their potential as creative labor enthusiasts, and this was exactly the way in which Nastya and Dr. Jin were being portrayed. As far as the leadership was concerned, the new personality was a means, not an end.

That this conference was a turning point was also sensed by those few figures whose personality features most strongly resonated with the Martynovs and Nastyas. Liu Binyan published a salute to the young activist conference in *Wenyibao*, extolling their "shock-troop spirit" surpassing the norms set by the Five-Year Plan; their common features were *zhudong jingshen*, a spirit of initiative coming from their own impulses, and *shouchuang jingshen*, pioneering spirit:

> They are no ticklers for any fixed and settled methods, but mobilize all their own intellectual capacities to search for the best methods in order to fulfill their assignment excellently; at any time they are the first to understand the intentions of the Party, and lead a determined battle against all backward phenomena that are detrimental to the people's interests. . . . On their own initiative they come up with methods, they proffer criticism, and protect the interests of the state.

Liu Binyan is here referring to the role of Youth League teams in fighting waste in state enterprises, an adaptation of the Komsomol inspection stations. These youths, he concludes in a very daring metaphor taken from Ovechkin's "scout" image, "observe like the eyes of the state clear-sightedly the problems in all the workshops and building sites." Liu chose his words carefully. These youths don't "follow at any time the directives of the Party"; they are the first to *linghui* (to sense or understand) the Party's *yitu* (intentions), which might be more implied than spelled out in official statements. True, the eye is an organic part of the body, and in a general manner directed by the brain. However, it is bound by the reality it sees, and thus may transmit impressions that are not necessarily pleasing to the brain.[21]

21. Liu Binyan, "Xiang genggaofeng qianjin" (Forward to still higher peaks), *Wenyibao* 18:8ff (1955).

For the reconstruction of the recommended personality type in the years preceding 1956, we had to read many 1956 texts backwards, extracting positive information from their negative comments. Now we can read the very same texts forward to learn about the new type of personality they advocated.

By the end of October, Ovechkin found his first Chinese actual writing pupil in Qin Zhaoyang, whose "Two District Committee Secretaries" was serialized in the capital's *Beijing ribao* from 30 October on.[22] The transition to fiction is important. The story about Dr. Jin was a reportage, although it made use of more imaginative literary symbols. The general features of this model man were to be emulated, but the narrative portions and the anecdotes did not have to match the typicality mandate in the same way in which fiction had to match it. Qin had followed Soviet developments closely. When the Soviets started to attack "formulism" and "generalism" in literature, as well as the absence of true conflict, and started, by 1952, to shift to specific documentary unveilings of bureaucratic styles with Ovechkin leading the onslaught, Qin was de facto editor of *Renmin wenxue* (People's literature), the journal set up to guide the nation's short fiction by publishing exemplary works. The literary situation in China was desperate, he recalled later. "Because, during the first years after Liberation there were few manuscripts coming in from the old writers and only a handful of good new writers appeared, we had many manuscripts but only few which could be used, and the journal was constantly in danger of not being able to come out."[23] The main problem with the manuscripts landing on his table was that they were written by immature writers trying to toe the line. With the authority of the Soviet attacks on formulism, empty generalizations, and absence of conflict as support, Qin wrote many letters of criticism and advice to these new authors, and had them published in 1953 as a book.[24] The time, however, was not yet ripe in China. These were still the years of laying down rules for intellectuals through

22. Qin Zhaoyang, "Liangwei xianwei shuji" (Two district secretaries), *Beijing ribao*, 30 October 1955 and following, later contained in his book *Zai tianyeshang qianjin* (On the fields, forward; Beijing: Zuojia Press, 1956).

23. "Jiaqiang bianjibu tong zuojia de tuanjie" (Strengthen the cooperation between editors and writers), *Renmin ribao*, 8 May 1957.

24. Qin Zhaoyang, *Lun gongshihua gainianhua* (On the tendency towards formulism and

massive criticisms of scholars like Yu Pingbo, and the eventual incarceration of the Communist Hu Feng, whose letter to the Central Committee had maintained that literature after Liberation was in shambles.

Qin Zhaoyang's criticisms were all too close to Hu Feng's; he exonerated himself with a vituperous attack against Hu Feng,[25] and, being apparently associated with Zhou Yang, was rewarded with an editorial post in the reorganized *Wenyibao* early in 1955. Between January 1953 and May 1954, he had been in a village in Hebei, and had taken an active part there in the setting up of an agricultural cooperative. Mao Zedong drew on attempts like this in his July 1955 speech, arguing that the masses demanded such higher and more socialist forms of cooperation. "Encouraged" by Mao's speech, Qin set out to write the story of the two district committee secretaries.

The story is set in 1953, and thus argues that the suggestions made by Mao in 1955 were but the summary of experiences in the countryside; in the same manner, Nikolayeva had invested Nastya with the glory to have staked out the road eventually approved by the 3rd Plenum. The struggle between the two secretaries in Qin's novel echoes the struggle between Borzov and Martynov, who also operate at the rayon (district) level. The dominant line is invested by Wang Zekun, the first secretary; his name, *Zekun*, means, with one change in character, "tied down by the rules." Although only 40, he looks 50, and, with his slow speech and slow movements, is generally called "the old secretary Wang." The head of the district government as well as the provincial leadership support his position. The latter coined the slogan "slow and steady advance," and consequently he stressed the need to consolidate the Mutual Aid Teams before even talking about cooperatives. The challenger is a vice-secretary called Zhang Jun, the *jun* being a fine and fast horse. Although he is over 30, he looks "like a youth," and 10 months in a Party school have given him theoretical knowledge and intellectual agility. Also, he has a fresh and loving relationship with his wife. In his

abstract concepts; Beijing: Renmin Wenxue Press, 1953), reprinted in his *Wenxue tansuoji* (Beijing: Renmin Wenxue Press, 1984).

25. Qin Zhaoyang, "Lun Hu Feng de 'yige jiben wenti'" (On Hu Feng's "Basic problem"), *Wenyibao* 4:4ff (1955).

thinking and appearance he is as much of a member of the intelligentsia as might be credible under such circumstances.

One village had applied for permission to set up a cooperative. The district committee members are concerned only with their own departments and do not care about the long-term perspectives of the road to socialism. Wang Zekun is clearly opposed to the formation of the cooperative, but Zhang Jun gets into an argument with him. As such *zhenglun* (heated arguments) are anathema to the atmosphere of harmonious stagnation advocated by Wang, he grants permission to set up the cooperative when Zhang takes personal responsibility. After his return from the Party school, Zhang Jun goes to the village to prop up the shaky cooperative, which has been left without any guidance. The split between the secretaries is repeated in the split between the district government head, who never commits himself (and is again taken from an Ovechkin character) and his wife who pushes for socialist transformation. After having, without effect, criticized Wang Zekun in personal encounters, she eventually uses the occasion of a meeting of the district leaders to attack him openly for bureaucratic neglect, something "she had never done before, and which had altogether hardly ever happened before," and falls out with her husband on the same occasion. Coming down, for the first time in many years, to the village, Wang Zekun seeks confirmation for his theory that "the masses are backward" and discourages an expansion of the cooperative for which Zhang Jun had been campaigning. "The great problem is not in the peasants themselves . . . but in the leadership of the Party," wrote Qin in the preface.

Zhang Jun had managed to get the cooperative going by taking the responsibility on himself. Without asking for higher-level approval, he calls several conferences of the Communists and Youth Leaguers of the area in order to spread the idea of the coop. This is not forbidden, but not really allowed either. As it turns out, the leader of a Party branch in a neighboring village was so put off by the troubles with the approval of the first coop that he and several other families *secretly* set up a coop, which is already operating for a year. For Wang Zekun this spontaneous upsurge is "rash and adventurous," "undisciplined," and violating "collective spirit." Zhang Jun, who promised to "protect" the secret coop, frankly and explicitly disagrees, and argues that innovative niches in which new socialist things are tried do not need leadership approval as long as they are pro-socialist. The frank and outspoken way in which the three heroes, Zhang Jun, the woman leader, and the Party secretary with his secret coop oppose the highest leader of the district and are justified in the context of the story was unheard of in Chinese literature at the time. Qin took care to show that they maintained Party unity externally, and abided by all the reasonable rules.

Needless to say, Wang Zekun is not bourgeois or a landlord, although there is an indication that his family became "middle-peasants" with the land reform, thus influencing his backward attitude. The long excerpts printed in *Beijing ribao* deal only with the two secretaries. Other parts dealing with earlier class struggle and inner-Party dispute were left out, although they appeared in the book eventually published in 1956. The selection as well as the introduction to it made it clear that this confrontation of young and old, progressive and backward, bureaucratic formulism and daring innovation, in short, of two types of personalities and policies within the Party was at the center of attention. By putting the standard charges against the socialist enthusiasts (rash, undisciplined, trying to excel among others, no spirit of organization, opposition to the leadership, damaging relations between Party levels by too outspoken criticism, and so on) into Wang Zekun's mouth they are negated as self-serving arguments. They reflect, and get their legitimacy from, the Sufan Movement with its emphasis on disciplined subordination under the leadership's commands. Zhang the racehorse is not asking freedom to do anything he thinks fit; there is no "liberalism" in him. He strives only for a faster advance to "socialism." Borrowing another device from Ovechkin, Qin broke off the story before the conflict between the two men was resolved, indicating that in social fact dominance was still with the Wang Zekuns, who were, however, forced to make some accommodations. In a postface, Qin sketched what might be the ending, expressing his hopes about further developments. A man from the Center will come and read Zhang Jun's report. He will call Wang Zekun and give him a dressing down. The two opponents will reestablish harmony on their way back to the district. The man from the Center obviously collects materials for Mao's speech and collection. Politically the text tried to explore what was in store in Mao's new assessment of the main contradiction.

The importance of the reportages or literary texts was emphasized by frequent references and reviews. The Soviet texts by Nikolayeva and Ovechkin reappeared in the speeches of Soviet cultural leaders like Fadeev and Sarkov as the best examples of recent Soviet writing, and care was taken that these speeches were quickly translated into Chinese.[26] The core point of the story of Dr. Jin was brought out by a review two issues later entitled "To Progress or to Regress," which focused exclusively on Jin's defying orders and taking the short and dangerous way.[27] "That a person can so conscientiously go about his work is a manifestation of high Communist consciousness. Such people are not in need of others' supervision and urging on (*ducu*) as far as the interests of the Revolution are concerned; they can act on their own initiative." The review bluntly set up Jin as a hero to imitate. "Each and every youth must learn from models like Jin Zhendu . . . and become a conscious (*zijue*) and daring (*yonggan*) master of new China."

A review in *Beijing ribao* of Nikolayeva's book on 1 November indicated how influential the *Yiwen* translations were. The review stressed Nastya's uncompromising battle with "old things" and the "individualism" of Arkady, and mentioned that a separate edition of the book was prepared for January 1956 by the Youth League.[28] In November, *Zhongguo qingnian* published a review of Nikolayeva's book which was announced as "important" by its boldface title in the table of contents. Entitled "Let's Peel Off the Horn from Our Hearts,"[29] the text stresses the immediate positive response Nastya got from young Chinese readers. She confronted the "conservative" leaders and was *dan'gan*, outspoken and daring, in her actions. "Normal" people now are characterized by "looking ahead and taking into account what is behind" (*zhanqian guhou*), "anxiously reacting to small things and cautiously handling even trifles" (*jinxiao shenwei*), "having hands and feet bound"

26. Cf. A. A. Suerkefu (A. A. Surkov), "Sulian wenxue de xianzhuang he renwu" (The present state and tasks of Soviet literature), *Wenyibao* 1–2 (1955).

27. Zhong Qun, "Qianjin ne, haishi houtui?" (To progress or to regress?), *Zhongguo qingnian* 21:27ff (1955).

28. "Nigulayewa de yibu youxiu xinzuo" (An excellent new work by Nikolayeva), *Beijing ribao*, 1 November 1955.

29. Zi Gang, "Boqu women xin shang de houjian" (Let's peel off the horn from our hearts), *Zhongguo qingnian* 22:25ff (1955).

(*suoshou suojiao*), and "resigning themselves to mediocrity" (*zigan ping-yong*). Not so Nastya; her model should help "us" to get rid of the "horns thickly covering our hearts," [that is, to overcome insensitive and routinized bureaucratic behavior] and to develop her "spirit of valiantly battling for the collective." The review evinced the irritation coming with the presence of two simultaneous campaigns at cross purposes, and tried to harmonize the conflict by giving to Arkady the name of an "individualist" in Sufan Campaign language, and to Nastya the purpose of "strengthening the collective," both against the better evidence of the text.

On 22 November 1955, things again reached a new stage. The Propaganda Department of the Youth League Central Committee decided to set up Nastya as the new heroine to emulate for educated Youth League members, and thus officially replaced Pavel. The decision was immediately made public, and prefixed to the reprint of Nikolayeva's novel in the *Zhongguo qingnian* journal, even prior to the book's publication. The communiqué said:

> Communiqué of the Propaganda Department of the Youth League Central Committee about the recommendation of the Soviet novella, *The Director of the Machine Tractor Station and the (Woman) Chief Agronomist.*
> To the Propaganda Departments of the Youth League Committees of the provinces (autonomous regions), and cities:
>
> The novella *The Director*... by the Soviet author (Galina) Nikolayeva is a work of very great educational significance for young people. The Propaganda Department of the League Central Committee resolves to promote this novel to the end of February next year (1956) among students beyond upper-middle school as well as among young administrative cadres and young workers and employees with a relatively high cultural level. Propaganda Departments of League Committees at all levels are to coordinate with the respective departments that serious propaganda is made for the novel among young people, with the emphasis of the propaganda being on the principled spirit with which the novel's heroine, Nastya, daringly battles to blast open the way for new things, as well as the high caliber of her serving the people and uniting with all her body and heart with the laboring people.
>
> In order to do a good job in guiding the reading, the Propaganda Departments of the Youth League Committees are to arouse the concerned units to study the matter, lay out plans and requirements (the plan of the Propaganda

Department of the League Central Committee will be published separately), ask these units to provide assistance, and together do a good job in propagandizing and organizing the promotion of this work.[30]

The fact that this internal document was published in the Youth League paper suggests, as much as the text of the communiqué itself, what troubles the leader expected. There would be no support for such a move, and thus the common members had to get both the text of the novel and the resolution, so that they would be ready for discussions with their Youth League officials.

The model youth, pushed by Hu Yaobang and the closely knit group of young cadres he had assembled around himself in the preceding years, from now on were to have a "principled spirit of daringly (*yonggan*) battling to clear the way for new things," the concluding clause of another quotation from Mao Zedong. As might be expected, things would start to move on other fronts as well. After a long article had pointed out how in the Soviet Komsomol the "inspection stations" would use cartoons, public criticism, bulletins, and other genres to combat waste and low-quality production, their satirical bulletins having programmatic names like "Hedgehog," "Hornet," or "Crocodile," the stage was set for a similar development in China.[31] Bureaucratic cadres became a favorite butt of cartoons, from which the Hu Feng-type class enemy had disappeared, while their opponent, the enthusiastic youth, has entered the picture.

30. "Qingniantuan zhongyang xuanchuanbu guanyu tuijian Sulian zhongpian xiaoshuo *Tuolajizhan zhanzhang he zongnongyishi* de tongzhi" (Communiqué of the Central Propaganda Department of the Youth League concerning the propagation of the Soviet novella *The Director of the MTS and the Chief Agronomist*), *Zhongguo qingnian* 23:13 (1955); the first part of the novel was printed immediately thereafter.

31. Cao Lifu, "Gongqingtuan jiandugang he qingnian jianchadui" (The Komsomol inspection stations and the youth investigation brigades), *Zhongguo qingnian* 18:28ff (1955).

"Please look out of the window!" by Xiao Li

From *Zhongguo qingnian* 121:34 (1 November 1955).

The peasants outside hold requests to be admitted into the cooperative, while the cadre writes "The development of the cooperatives is far beyond the level of consciousness of the masses. The Youth League members must be the first to withdraw from the cooperative." The book on his table carries the title "Restrictions and Taboos." The Youth League journal had established a new small column "Xinyu lin" (Forest of new sayings) in August 1955. It contained little satires on current events in the new line, and eventually sheltered a critical small satire form popular in the 1930s, the *xiaopinwen*, a short gloss relating to one minor incident to which some broader comments are attached. The *Wenyibao* did the same with the "Xinyu si" (Thread of new sayings) and the "Wenyi suibi" (Jotted notes on literature and the arts). By December, these forms had developed to accommodate quite biting satire.

A "Sequel to 'The Foolish Old Man Who Removed a Mountain'" by Liu Zheng took up this grand myth evoked by Mao as a symbol of the Chinese Revolution. The old man has now removed the big mountains of imperialism and feudalism, and in an accompanying picture is shown resting exhausted in the grass, before him a manuscript entitled "Final Report on Removal of Mountains." The story tells that the neighbors come to alert him to weeds growing where the mountains had been, and to a mud slide that has blocked the street. They ask him to take charge. He, however, only groans "Eee Eee" and falls asleep again. The others thereupon take things into their own hands and make a broad new street. Fate wills that its path goes straight through the place where the old man is lying. As they can not wake him nor get him to move, they lift him onto a cart and, together with the stones, cart him away. The story ends with the words: "It would be fine if all this was only make believe. Aren't there in life, though, people who are being 'removed' [because they obstruct further progress]?"[32] The revolutionary cadres who victoriously fought the war have gone to sleep. Their final report has been delivered, and they don't care about things that happen now, after the mountains have been removed. In fact they become an obstacle in the way, and now *they* have to be "removed."

In tune with the development of the new personality ideal propagated by the leadership, there was leeway to attack the old ideal. Some of the attacks have been documented earlier in cartoons denouncing an authoritarian educational style, and the sweet dream of cadres to have youths who perform like marionettes.

In the field of literary theory, cautious attempts were made in December to revive the Balzac/Tolstoy debate. The credit goes to Lin Xiling, a personality much like Liu Binyan in terms of her independence and outspokenness. She felt called upon by the new voices in the group of periodicals linked to the Youth League. She was the fiancée of Hu Yaobang's private secretary, and a few months later she was to become one of the most controversial and famous of the Hundred Flowers activists. In an article in *Wenyibao* in December, she argued that Hu Feng

32. Liu Zheng, "Xu 'Yugong yishan' ji qita" (A continuation of "The Foolish Old Man Removed the Mountain," etc.), *Wenyibao* 24:41 (1955).

had been wrong when he separated the world view of a writer completely from realistic content, and that his critics had been exaggerating by maintaining there was complete correspondence between the political views and the "real" content of a literary work. It should be remembered that, when this article appeared, Hu Feng was in jail. Consequently, all his opinions carried a counterrevolutionary connotation. To deal, in the midst of the Sufan Campaign, with Hu Feng's ideas, and even to defend them, was a political challenge of sorts, as was the decision of *Wenyibao* to print this article.

In fact, Lin Xiling argued, writers like Balzac and Tolstoy were self-contradictory; they certainly were influenced by contemporary class struggles and at the same time maintained old-fashioned ideas. She supported the need for a writer to immerse himself in the real struggles around him in order to become a more "realist" writer and to develop his theoretical insights. In stating this point she managed to leave out another point altogether, the "Party spirit" of the writer.[33] She was operating on good authority, since some weeks earlier Surkov had visited China and given a talk on "The Party Spirit of Literature and the Work of the Writer." Surkov had bluntly rejected the notion of a direct control of the Party over literature as an expression of Party spirit. "The more truthful a novel is in its 'historical quality,' the stronger the Party spirit will be. A writer with Party spirit will be good at seeing the sprouts of tomorrow in the society of today." The spirit of his talk becomes clearer when we see his advocacy of satirical literature, and his scorn for the Soviet critics who did not dare to write a review of Ehrenburg's "Thaw" before the Party paper had indicated how things were to be seen.[34] The relative independence of the socialist enthusiast writer vis-à-vis a conservative leadership at the middle levels was beginning to be established. His commitment was more to realism than to Party mandate.

These sprouts of new thoughts, words, and values by no means

33. Lin Xiling, "Shilun Baerzhake he Tuoersitai de shijieguan he chuangzuo" (An exploration of the world-view and creative work of Balzac and Tolstoy), *Wenyibao* 21:32ff (1955).

34. Suerkefu (Surkov), "Wenxue de dangxing he zuojia de laodong" (The Party spirit of literature and the work of the writer), talk originally given on 4 October, printed in *Wenyibao* 22:33ff (1955).

saturated the field. In the same issues in late 1955 where these new elements appeared, we find long articles by Lin Mohan[35] and Zhang Chunqiao[36] praising Lenin's "On Party and Party Literature" as the "fundament" of literary theory, repeating the "cog-and-screw" model time and again, explicit and hard in their demands for a complete submission of the literary endeavor to Party controls. Articles advocated close inspection of one's spouse's political background, lest one love a counterrevolutionary;[37] warned friends against getting together because this association was easily turned by the class enemy into a "clique";[38] and criticized Xiao Jun's book on the Tangshan mines as "poisonous."[39] The early attempts to harmonize the two incompatible campaigns by distorted definition were not further pursued. The texts in the "anti-bureaucratic" current denied the legitimacy of the Sufan Movement, and the supporters of the Sufan Movement denied the orthodoxy of the critics. Both movements managed to find their own social base in that segment of officialdom to which the slogans were best suited, and the two segments opposed each other openly and frankly. By the end of the year the "anti-bureaucrats" dominated a number of periodicals, most of them linked to Hu's Youth League, and their opponents had ever fewer opportunities to see their opinion in print. But beyond their enforced public silence, there remained the huge tenacious block of reality with millions of Party and League members recruited under the old standards, and holding out. The attitude now characterized as "conservative" was in no way absent from the League. The desperation of the top leaders of the League with their inferiors' unwillingness to admit into the League and to support active and strong-willed young people, and with their persistent efforts to exert tight political pressure and control on such young people is evident from many articles in the League press in late 1955.

35. Lin Mohan, "Dangxing shi women de wenxue yishu de linghun" (Party spirit is the soul of our literature and our arts), *Wenyibao* 21:3ff (1955).
36. Zhang Chunqiao, "Zai xin de gaochao mianqian" (In the face of a new upsurge), *Wenyibao* 22:4ff (1955).
37. Ai Nan, "How I Handled" (p. 50 note 21), p. 5.
38. Zeng Xisan, "Qingnianmen yinggai jujue canjia fandong de xiaojituan huodong" (Young people must refuse to take part in reactionary clique activities), *Zhongguo qingnian* 24 (1955).
39. Yan Xue and Zhou Peitong, "Xiao Jun de *Wuyuede kuangshan* wei shenme shi youdu?" (Why is Xiao Jun's *The Mine in May* a poisonous weed?), *Wenyibao* 24:43f (1955).

A leading official of the League, Hu Keshi, followed a muted acknowledgment of some recent improvements with a resounding *however:* "In many places and in many kinds of work there manifests itself a harmful, passive, conservative thinking [in the Youth League] and a lack of spirit of activist initiative."[40] The confrontation was not young against old, but, instead, the few young people with the newly appreciated personality traits, supported to a degree by some top politicians, against the rest.

The last weeks of the year signaled that leaders like Hu Yaobang and Deng Xiaoping were using their influence to push for more dramatic changes. This support might also have been prompted by the fact that these two leaders themselves had personality traits close to those advocated since late 1955. The last issue of *Zhongguo qingnian* in 1955 had a programmatic cover. Three caterpillar tractors, driven abreast by young drivers, are "removing a mountain," the title of the illustration. The old rubbish they set out to remove is not just earth. After some class-struggle articles came the last installment of Nikolayeva's novel, and then an article that attempted the first systematic exposition of the qualities to be fostered in a leader. "What kind of people do we want the youth whom we educate to become?"[41] This title headed a regular column in 1956 where young activists found a place to air their grievances with the entrenched bureaucracy. The style was set with the first article, which in fact answered a letter from a student. This itself is of importance. The initiative for change, as evident in this choice of form, was not coming from leaders but from the young themselves. The leaders would discuss matters with them but not lecture them.

The author of the letter this article answered had straight 5s (= As), but had written a long letter with criticisms to his professor. This had been judged to be "self-aggrandizement" by the Youth League. A Soviet specialist had told them that a graduate student who did not aspire to the Academy of Sciences was no good, but the enforced habit among his

40. Hu Keshi, "Fahui jiji zhudong jingshen, touru nongye hezuohua gaochao" (Unfold the spirit of being activist and enterprising, throw yourselves into the upsurge of agricultural collectivization), *Zhongguo qingnian* 23:8 (1955).
41. Lin Wei, "What Kind of People?" (p. 62 note 24).

Chinese peers, the student continued, was self-deprecation. The student felt the leadership's appeals to the "newborn forces" were addressed to him, but he was alone. People who read non-assigned materials were reported to the Youth League and the teachers. Lin Wei, the author of the answering article, said it was easy indeed to spell out an ideal of young people's behavior. They should have far-reaching aspirations, lively spirits, should be unafraid of difficulties in their scientific and professional work, should be bold and creative, and dare to confront any difficulty. But for the realization of this ideal "the [appropriate] public opinion and climate is necessary." In many units the climate was not receptive to such personalities; in others "exactly the opposite climate prevails." There, "people who don't have ideals, have no guts, no creative spirit, don't enjoy pursuing things on their own initiative, don't think independently (*duli sikao*), and don't battle actively against irrational things and unhealthy tendencies, rarely receive stern criticism, and are even wrongly judged modest, practical, steady, well-balanced, and without deficiencies." People have inherited these criteria, Lin maintained, from the old society, where "the reactionaries" did not permit independent thinking, and parents had to warn their children to keep their mouths shut to avoid running into trouble. He was wise enough not to mention that the experience after 1949 was not much different on this count. Lin then appealed to the Youth League cadres to change this "climate," which he claimed was entirely out of harmony with the new society.

Apart from establishing some new words like "independent thinking" (*duli sikao*), and "pursuing things on one's own initiative" (*zhudong zuanjiu*), this text marks the first explicit confrontation of two personality types, and states the fact that "public opinion" in both the political leadership and among the parents, and as a consequence among many youths is opposed to the individualistic values encoded in the new ideal. The minimal condition for such independent development of one's faculties and interests would have been a substantial reduction in Youth League activities with mandatory participation. The discussion had already begun in August 1955 with an article by "Ma Tieding," who claimed the authority of Ketlinskaya's *Yonggan* for his assertion that each person should be permitted and encouraged to develop his or her own interests and preferences.[42] Since individual pursuits had been attacked as "individualism," many letters reached the journal. In December, "Ma" came back with another article which extended the field of legitimate personal interests to food, sports, and cultural entertainments. "Individual preferences and interests . . . must be respected, provided they don't run counter to the interests of the collective," was the principle he established. Obviously, there was a clear hint of which restraints were blocking the development of characters with "their own initiative" and "independent thinking."[43]

The second journal catering to the segment of young intelligentsia, the *Wenyibao*, also closed the year with indications of more important changes to come. "Ma Tieding" got a boldface title for his "Courageously Break the Rigid Rules" in December.[44] Writers should have more time to write, and more space; attendance at meetings should be reduced, and housing conditions improved. But there were not only external obstacles to be overcome. "There are quite a few obstacles which we create ourselves. There are people among us who spend a lot of their mental energy fussing about their personal advantages and disadvantages to the point of getting lax in their work; or they are over-cautious with exaggerated and unnecessary concerns; or they just while away their time in repose, afraid that otherwise an additional white hair might grow on their heads; in short, they follow an established routine to the point of passing their days grumbling, sighing, and half asleep." The surprise is not that this was the intellectual climate after the hard months of 1955, and even the years before, but that this could be enunciated so bluntly. Ma ended with a personal pledge: "[I will] more frequently and in a more outspoken manner intervene in our lives, and

42. Ma Tieding was in fact a group of three writers: the poet Guo Xiaochuan, head of the Propaganda Department of the Southeastern Office, and since 1955 head of the Secretariat of the Chinese Writers' Union; Zhang Tiefu, since 1954 in the Central Committee's Rural Work Department, later in the Beijing City Committee; and Chen Xiaoyu, since 1954 in the literature and arts division of *Renmin ribao*. Information provided by Shao Yanxiang, December 1986. The article is Ma Tieding, "Shenghuozhong de aihao, xingqu ji qita" (Love, personal interests, and other things in life), *Zhongguo qingnian* 15:22 (1955).
43. Ma Tieding, "Zai tan shenghuozhong de aihao he xingqu" (More on love and interests in life), *Zhongguo qingnian* 24:29 (1955).
44. Ma Tieding, "Yonggandi tupo changgui" (Courageously break the rigid rules), *Wenyibao* 23:8ff (1955).

more often contribute my own work." Ovechkin's phrase about literature's "intervening in life" had now become a program possible for a Chinese essayist and poet. Ma had been instrumental in opening the discussion on many issues in *Zhongguo qingnian* and in *Wenyibao*. His pledge transferred the words until then used for the "activists of socialist construction," that is the heroes of works of literature, to the writer's trade.

In the same issue, an address by Ovechkin appeared in translation. "Our main problem today—it's not in the objective realm [nature, technology] but in the subjective [management methods]," he said. "Presently the cadre question is the most important question," and literature, "including satirical literature," was to "help in creating a climate in society" where bureaucratic obstruction would become as shameful as desertion in the army. He advocated the "researched *oçerk*" as a very useful form at present, which he said had achieved much prominence, and he reaffirmed the image of the *texie* as a "scout" operating independently ahead of the bulk of the literary forces.[45] By now the first novel had appeared which was in tune with the new policies, Sholochov's *Virgin Soil Upturned*, Part Two; although it dealt with the collectivization of agriculture in the late 1920s, the figure of Davidov, a worker sent to the countryside to support the drive, resonates with "the 30,000" sent down under Khrushchev's plan. We shall return later to Ovechkin's criticism of Nikolayeva. Ovechkin was now a familiar name among the reform crowd, and his speeches were treated on the same level with those by Fadeev or Surkov.

The last issue of *Wenyibao* carried an editorial deploring the sorry state of literature and literary criticism in China. "In our opinion, the development of criticism, much as living people need air, needs above all a climate of free discussion. It seems that this climate is patently absent among us. Our fear of a debate is sometimes greater than our fear of tigers. . . . From now on the great topic of our work will be to eliminate decisively that climate [where people are afraid to offend the 'gods']. The *Wenyibao* has an important responsibility here. The journals

---

45. Aoweiqijin (V. Ovechkin), "Jitihua nongcun zhong de xin shiwu he wenxue de renwu" (New phenomena in the kolkhozes and the duties of literature), *Wenyibao* 23:38ff (1955).

edited by the Writers' Association have already aired appropriate discussions of this problem and have passed a plan for reform. They will make efforts to intervene in life in an outspoken manner (*dadandi ganyu shenghuo*), intervene in all sorts of phenomena in literary work, and violently attack this climate of keeping on good terms with everybody (*yituan heqi*) in literary life."[46] Ovechkin's phrase by then had become a program for all the journals coming out from the Writers' Association. They also committed themselves to support "young writers," since they would be the "least conservative."

Also with a boldface title, the senior dramatist and film-script writer Xia Yan spoke up for the older generation. Literature had not lived up to the expectations of the people, expectations he defined mainly in terms of the "socialist upsurge":

> Our generation grew up mostly during the struggle against imperialism and feudalism, and, if we think back for once, at that time our feelings of love and hate were so clear and so strong; each victory or defeat in this struggle, each advance and retreat was of absorbing interest to us. . . . But are we today in this socialist period, in this sharp and hot class struggle, as much concerned as in the past about each victory and defeat, advance and retreat? . . . One has to admit, our enthusiasm seems already to have waned. When people from literature and the arts meet, they rarely talk at any length about contemporary affairs or study them; they "go through the motions with the campaigns" (*zao yundong*), listen to reports, and many people already regard that a "burden."

Xia attributed the attrition of enthusiasm to "habit" or "inertia." At the time of the founding of the PRC there were no rules; now there were always more, and they became more and more complex, and started to "obstruct the new." If people clung to them and didn't adapt, the new things would combat them and they "might even become the object of the Revolution [so that they would have to be overthrown]." Chen Boda, Xia Yan said, argued quite rightly that, during the long revolutionary years, the cadres had become familiar with the Party's "minimal program," but they had not learned of its "maximal program," which was socialism.[47] During the Cultural Revolution, this argument was used

---

46. "Xianqi wenxue yishu chuangzuo de gaochao" (Set off an upsurge of literature and artistic creation), *Wenyibao* 24:3f (1955).

47. Xia Yan, "Dapo changgui, zouxiang xinlu" (Break down the rigid rules, walk in new ways), *Wenyibao* 24:8 (1955); the title is set in boldface.

against the older generation of cadres, among them Xia Yan himself.

With this autobiographical and fairly personal statement, Xia Yan provided the first depiction of the revolutionary cadre who loses energy and enthusiasm and turns into a bureaucrat. There is no bad class background, no deep "counterrevolutionary" ambition, just inertia, a natural, nearly physical process. This was an important addition to the Chinese arsenal from which young writers could get their materials in 1956.

The third journal in our group, *Yiwen*, started to print Sholochov's *Virgin Soil Upturned*, Part Two, in December; with Ovechkin and Nikolayeva, this text had provided the core pieces of the orthodox current in the Soviet Thaw, which in the Chinese context, however, were rather like an officially arranged earthquake.

By January 1956, it became clear that the forces advocating the new propaganda line had had their way. There was no longer an open competition. A high-level decision had obviously been made late in 1955, and opponents of the new line were hard put to find an outlet thereafter for publicly articulating their grievances. There was no purge and no cultural revolution against the opponents, so that they were silenced but not deprived of their discretionary powers. During the next eighteen months there arose a curious situation in which the media tried to establish a climate and to establish values which were clearly anathema to most administrators of public affairs in government, Party, and League, trying to convert them with arguments, satire, public exposure, and face-to-face challenges by the few young people who dared live up to the new ideal. The implied assumption was that these people, the "bureaucrats," were in substance revolutionaries who need not be overthrown but could be converted. They needed constant pushing and needling to be aroused from their natural torpor, inertia, and lassitude. For this purpose active and highly legitimized youths were needed, and they had the press to print the experiences of their battles and publicly expose the culprits. It was an attempt to use two weak forces—educated youth and publicized opinion—to get and keep a big boulder moving, which above all, had weight, and time.

SEVEN

Policy Change in Published Opinion

By January, two new publications were directly integrated into the effort to create a "new public climate" and to support the new personality. First, *Renmin wenxue* (People's literature); it was taken over by Qin Zhaoyang who moved there from *Wenyibao* which had already joined the reform group. As *Renmin wenxue* was supposed to set the pace nationally for shorter fiction, Qin's transfer signaled that the efforts started with the publications of Ovechkin, Nikolayeva, and others were to be followed by domestic Chinese products in this journal, which would light the way for the rest. The change implied that young writers would be published with works about the battles between the socialist activists and the bureaucrats, and that the irregular smaller forms like the *xiaopinwen*, the *texie*, *zawen*, and others with their anti-bureaucratic tradition would be promoted here. *Renmin wenxue* basically catered to the same stratum as *Yiwen*, *Wenyibao*, and *Zhongguo qingnian*. But it extended the propaganda instruments to include strictly fictional works and included young writers among the possible socialist activists. The second addition, however, *Zhongguo qingnianbao* (The China youth daily), which also partly switched its stance in January 1956, began to offer some of the new gratifications to literate youth in general. In January it introduced a weekly half-page series called "Lajiao" (Hot pepper). The cover illustration made it clear that hottest *dadan* language was to be used here, and the texts proceeded straightway to "intervene in life."

Title illustration of *Hot Pepper*

Within "Lajiao," *xiaopinwen* (satire) found its place, symbolized by the prickly hedgehog, which had been mentioned among the "critical" animals used in the titles of Komsomol papers:

The distinctions among the various journals, however, were maintained in the Youth League. The discussion about Nastya was among Youth League members and young government cadres at a relatively "high cultural level," and thus was handled by *Zhongguo qingnian*, and not *Zhongguo qingnianbao*. With an editorial in its first issue of the new year, the bi-weekly *Xin guancha* (New observer), which also catered to this educated group, announced it would now criticize "more outspokenly" (*dadan*).[1]

In the older core group of journals, things they had touched on earlier with an article here and a cartoon there moved up to the rank of regular discussion topics or even regular columns. *Yiwen* had in fact printed many *oçerki* or *texie* in Chinese, but now it took a headline from *Nowy mir*, which had started to promote Ovechkin's form of *oçerk* since July 1955 under the heading "*Oçerki* of Our Time," and intro-

---

1. "Yiding yao ba kanwu banhao" (Periodicals have definitely to be improved), *Xin guancha* 1:3 (1 January 1956).

duced a fixed category "*Texie* of Our Time" in January 1956, which announced that this was the most appropriate genre "for our time," as Ovechkin had indeed claimed.

Zhongguo qingnian started with its second issue to publish small selections of the thousands of letters streaming in from young people who tried to "learn from Nastya" as they were told; the letters were printed under the heading "The Image of Nastya Spurs Us to Progress," and expanded this theme later on with a long series of letters and answers to letters under a heading from the title of the article by Lin Wei referred to above: "What Kind of People Do We Want the Youth Whom We Educate to Become?" evidently a platform for the discussion of the core problem plaguing both leaders and socialist enthusiasts. Before we return to these discussions and the literary works they generated, I wish briefly to study the fringe of this discussion, questions that might seem trivial on occasion but in fact might contribute to a much clearer overall picture.

A striking new topic was introduced into the discussion in January— the question of clothing. *Zhongguo qingnian* had printed an article early in 1955 advocating the right of women to prefer flowered cloth for their dresses,[2] and had followed in August with a stunning cover showing six young women in various hairdos, each wearing a blouse of different cut and color. They were reading a newspaper and were thus shown as educated city youths. This had then been an isolated item; now the advocacy of individual taste in clothing became an official indicator for the leeway granted to the educated segment as a whole. In January 1956, the editors prefaced two letters about flowered dresses and the obstacles they met in public opinion and among cadres with a bold appeal: "Now the new year has come, and soon we are going to enjoy the spring festival; girls (*guniangmen*), from now on put on your flowered dresses!"[3] The impact of young women daring to sport a variety of flowered patterns and cuts in public was probably equivalent to that of Lu Dingyi's Hundred Flowers speech a few weeks later. And both were dealing with

2. Wei Junyi, "Cong huayifu de wenti tanqi" (Talking about the problem of flowered blouses), *Zhongguo qingnian* 5:21 (1 March 1955); the title is set in boldface.

3. "Guniangmen, chuanqi huayifu laiba" (Girls, wear flowered blouses), *Zhongguo qingnian* 1:38 (1 January 1956).

the same problem, the encouragement of a greater variety of individual preferences in matters of personal taste, be it fabrics or literary styles. In a society with such a degree of homogeneity (if not homogenization), people are accustomed to adapt their dress to the political climate, and continued to do so with two basic styles fitting the "two lines."

In times of "class struggle," when Pavel is the model, the army outfit prevails. In times of mild encouragement for criticisms of the "bureaucracy," flowered dresses are dug out from the depths of the closets. Clothes are thus a public statement, and the simplest way to tell a cadre in military baggy green that he is a bureaucrat is to put on a flowered blouse and cut off one's pigtails. This was well understood by all sides, and the accusations against the pioneers were deftly political. By February 1956, *Zhongguo qingnianbao* printed suggestions of different styles not just for women but for men too. Needless to say, they were adapted from Soviet models:

From *Zhongguo qingnianbao*, 22 February 1956

In March, the Youth League coined the promotional slogan "Let Our Dresses be Variegated and Colorful,"[4] and a veritable "dress-elegantly campaign" began, which explicitly included men. There seems to have been a similar campaign by the Youth Leagues in the Soviet Union as well as in East European states.

On another front, January brought higher status for love. As with clothes, this was mostly a theme for educated city youth. Until the end of 1955, the discussion about love had focused on warnings about the class enemy sneaking into revolutionary beds and the need for much vigilance. Now, the journal took the line that, within certain limits, contacts between the sexes were legitimate and not inherently lascivious or decadent. It will be recalled that Pavel and Rita sacrifice their private lives for the Revolution. In Nikolayeva's story, on the other hand, a bond of love grows between Nastya and Chalikov as he comes over to the "right" side. Love became one of the two great themes of the stories by young authors for the next eighteen months.

In early March, *Zhongguo qingnianbao* carried instructions for group

4. "Rang women de fuzhuang fengfu duocai" (Let our dresses be variegated and colorful) became the slogan over a series of articles dealing with this matter, *Zhongguo qingnian* 6:20 (16 March 1956).

dances, although not even hands touched. But a cartoon shortly thereafter satirized the banning of dancing in heterosexual pairs:

鋼鉄厂的团委書記：　"这样限制点，免得出 '乱子' 。"
紡織厂的团委書記：　"是啊，我也是怕当丈母娘。"　　王乐天　作

From *Zhongguo qingnianbao,* 11 March 1956. By Wang Letian.
The Youth League Committee secretary of the steel plant: If kept a bit under control like this, they won't become "rowdies." The Youth League Committee secretary of the textile plant (where the women work): Yeah, I'm also afraid of becoming a "mother in law."

Both committee secretaries are evidently beyond the age of Youth League members. The "senility" of Youth League cadres was often referred to.

"The Distance Is Too Far," by Zhang Tailai

相差 太远　　　　　　張胎來　作

遼寧省錦縣的十一个区，61个鄉団总支書記中，30 歲到 49
歲的有31名，最大的是十一区金城鄉団总支書記孟声久，已經59
歲了。　　　　　　　　　団遼寧省委　刁迺淑

From *Zhongguo qingnianbao*, 8 March 1956

In the eleven precincts of Mian district, Liaoning province, 31 of the 61 township
Youth League general secretaries are between 30 and 49 years of age, the oldest . . . is
already 59 years old.
The insignia on their jackets designate their rank.

A series of articles from January on advocated greater independence
for educated youths in their spare time which before had been fully organized and controlled by the League. Diversity of interests now was described not as "opposition to the collective" and "separation from the
masses" but as a positive thing to be encouraged. Eventually, a decision
was made for a curricular reform for students from September 1956 on,
which cut their classes with mandatory attendance from 30 to 24 hours
a week and advocated the principle of voluntarism for political and
social activities. This institutional change created the flexibility for the
more active phase of the Hundred Flowers period. To advocate unorganized spare time for educated youths was a supreme show of confidence
in their newly acquired socialist qualifications.

Xin guancha and *Zhongguo qingnian* set out to restore friendship as a legitimate relationship.[5] Until the end of 1955, *Zhongguo qingnian* had called on students to stay out of such *jituan* clique activities (then the designation for friendships), since they invited corrosion by counter-revolutionaries with anti-Party purposes. In Ostrovski's novel, these private links are associated either with debauchery, or Trotskyism, or both. In Nikolayeva's novel, Nastya privately befriends some Komsomol members and chats with them outside branch meetings. They also talk about their assessments of the MTS leadership, which in China-1955 terms was a clear anti-Party activity. In the novel, this is the way Chalikov perceives it—before he is converted. What could be discussed in friendships was still narrowly defined. However, in January the students of bourgeois or landlord background were soothed in their apprehensions and assured that there was a future for them.[6] Thus the number of potentially "wrong" friends was greatly reduced.

There was thus a general purpose observable most clearly at the fringes to create a space in which the new type that was envisioned could exist, develop, and be secure. The discussions, which also started in January, about the experiences of young people in emulating Nastya dealt not with the two concepts neatly separated, as we have presented them here, but with the battle between the two. The socialist activists dominated the pages, the opponents the institutions.

When the Youth League made its decision to promote Nastya, it did so with the knowledge that the novel and Nastya as a character were far from uncontroversial in the Soviet Union. The main critic was none other than Ovechkin. In October, *Literaturnaya Gazeta* had carried an exchange between a reader and Nikolayeva. The reader said he had heard for the first time of the novel when, at a conference on advanced repair methods for tractors, an engineer argued that the low harvests after the September Plenum were due to the "weakness" of the young women sent as chief agronomists. The Soviet Minister for Agriculture

5. "Zhengzhishang de youyi yu shenghuo shang de youyi" (Friendship in politics and friendship in life), *Xin guancha* 1:27 (1 January 1956); "Youyi yinggai jianli zai shenme jichu shang?" (On what basis does friendship have to be built?), *Xin guancha* 4:23ff (16 February 1956).

6. Qin Chuan, "Shehuizhuyi shi yiqie qingnian de meihao qiantu—xie gei zichanjieji jiating chushen de qingnian" (Socialism is the glorious future of all youths—a letter to a youth of bourgeois descent), *Zhongguo qingnian* 2:12ff (16 January 1956) as well as the subsequent articles.

thereupon pulled Nikolayeva's book out of his pocket and pointed to Nastya as proof of the opposite. Having read the work subsequently, the reader found things went much too "easy" for Nastya; she was glorified, and did not correspond to real life. There were many people who had been sent to the MTS stations with the "30,000" who had tried their best, but given up and "returned to the cities." The reader was among those who held out, but felt that it was unjustified to denounce those who left as "labor contractors" in the figure of Arkady.

Nikolayeva answered that there were only "two roads," the "Communist" road of Nastya, and the "road of (Arkady) Furzanov." She had set out to describe Nastya as a heroine in order to give greater educative powers to her and to encourage people to emulate her example. A "middle" character would not have done as well, as the letters showed which she received from readers.[7]

On 17 November 1955, Ovechkin came out against Nikolayeva in a speech at a conference on the kolkhoz theme:

> This novel by Nikolayeva is built, in terms of plot, around an important and very acute conflict. The problem is exactly that. True, the conflict is very acute, but, if one examines this novel carefully against the background of life itself, one will see that there is something farfetched and strained about it. It proceeds from the imagination and not from the real truth of life. According to this novel, Nastya <u>all on her own</u> [underlined in original] pushed the three most backward kolkhozes onto the proper road, and this not only without any support from the rayon committee and the MTS leadership, but even against their opposition. Generally, she pushes them all too easily and simply — namely with proposals of correct agricultural technique — onto the proper road. But this in no way corresponds to the logic of life! Why are these kolkhozes backward? Obviously because the (MTS) chairmen are all laggards without education and technical knowledge; the kolkhoz chairmen are drunkards and embezzlers; and there is chaos in the Party organization. A chief agronomist would meet in such a kolkhoz with the most obstinate resistance against any new method. Without severe disciplinary measures and at times even police measures, and without yelling at those leaders you will not get anything done in such kolkhozes.[8]

---

7. "Guanyu *Tuolajizhan zhanzhang he zongnongyishi* de taolun" (Discussion about *The Director of the MTS and the Chief Agronomist*), *Yiwen* 1:139ff (1 January 1956).
8. Ovechkin's talk in ibid., p. 144.

We have here a confrontation of two different political assessments, and two literary strategies. Ovechkin tried to restore the credibility of literature by emphasizing its documentary responsibility, abandoning fictional devices like plots and educative heroes and villains, proclaiming the *oçerk* (*texie*) as the proper genre "in our time." Nikolayeva adopted some of the *oçerk* claim to authenticity, but as a fictional device, and wrote a novel (*xiaoshuo*) with a developed plot and exploration of character, including the theme of love, which was not handled in *oçerk*. In her response she charged that Ovechkin wrote "in protocol fashion" but his characters "lacked soul," and that there was cause for concern because "a big crowd of young writers run after him," who "might leave aside the great duties of literature and pursue reportage."[9] She claimed that Ovechkin made the *oçerk* into the only acceptable literary form for the present. "Each genre has its own rules, and one cannot reduce an entire literature to the single genre of *oçerk*," she said.[10]

It should be mentioned that Ovechkin and Nikolayeva also had many friendly things to say about each other, since their texts addressed similar problems, and they moved politically in a similar direction. Ovechkin focused on the conflict among "progressive" and "retrograde" leaders in the middle level of the rural administration, while Nikolayeva saw the main conflict as between the educated Youth League activists and the bureaucratic stagnation common in middle-level leadership.

These discussions were quickly translated into Chinese, and known to the people concerned. The Soviet public debate was not about the legitimacy of Nastya's independent actions; no charges of promoting disregard for discipline were leveled against the novel. The Chinese Youth League thus opted for Nikolayeva's novel not because of the "truthfulness" of its portrayal, but because it presented in Nastya an educated Youth Leaguer who seemed to embody the personality traits and attitudes the Chinese Youth League leaders set out to promote, and because she seemed, being Soviet, best able to cope with Pavel on a fictional

9. Ibid., pp. 146f.
10. Quoted in "Sulian zhaokai zuojia huiyi taolun jitinongzhuang ticai wenti" (The Soviet Union convened a writers' conference to discuss problems of the theme of the collective villages [in literature]), *Yiwen* 12:236 (1 December 1955).

level. However, the differences between Nikolayeva and Ovechkin in terms of political attitude, literary approach, and genre were not lost in China; they were to surface in China in the difference between Wang Meng, who opted for Nikolayeva's approach, and Liu Binyan, who cast his lot with Ovechkin.

In December 1955, Surkov had argued in essence that "Party spirit" in literature was best expressed through literature's adherence to "truth" (and not to orders from cultural officials). In the first article on Nastya in January 1956, Lin Wei, who had started the discussion about educational goals a month before, quoted the MTS Party secretary in the novel approvingly: "Her (Nastya's) line is to obediently (*laolao shishi*) serve the people. Adhering to that line means adhering to the Party's line."[11] By defining the Party's line as service to the people, Nastya took a position apart from the party officials if their actions did not correspond to the people's interests. He saw Nastya "without a shadow of the past," symbolizing "a new generation raised by the Party and the League."

In all elements, the definition of the main conflict, the protagonists, and the proper ways of handling the conflict, Lin Wei saw coincidence between Soviet and Chinese realities, and thus felt justified in addressing his Chinese readers in exclamatory exhortations: "All you youths who want to serve the fatherland and the people [not "the Party"], all you youths who want the socialist endeavor to proceed even faster, Nastya's way is your way! The things Nastya strives for are the things you should strive for! And what Nastya rejects and opposes you should reject and oppose!" The prolific literary scholar Ba Ren reiterated that the novel "seemed to have been written about our own affairs," so well did it correspond with Chinese reality.[12]

Li Helin came out in support of the novel against Ovechkin's criticisms, and extracted five teachings from the novel: Believe in and hold on to truth; hate evil like an enemy and fight it to the end; be full of daring, without arrogance and uninterested in individual weaknesses; go

11. Lin Wei, "Zhuiqiu shenme?" (To strive for what?), *Zhongguo qingnian* 1:7f (1 January 1956).
12. Ba Ren, "Yibu fandui baoshouzhuyi de zuopin" (A work opposing conservatism), *Wenyi xuexi* 1:5ff (1 January 1956).

deeply among the masses, and serve the masses; have faith in the Party, rely on the Party, and follow the Party's line. The five points, as always, presented a hierarchy with the lowest priority last.[13]

These articles at the beginning of the "learn-from-Nastya" campaign were to guide the reading of the novel. They were still hesitant to deal with Arkady in terms of categories. The "bureaucrat" was still not an official personage, and they opted for leaving the message about the new main conflict in its encoded form. A month later, in February, the Youth League came out with 400,000 copies of a booklet written by Wang Ruowang, *Learn from Nastya.* This was the authoritative guide.[14]

One should not mechanically copy Nastya, Wang argued, but "grasp the 'core of the matter,' so that we can differentiate right and wrong in our own work, dare to struggle against all people and things detrimental to the people's interests, educate ourselves to serve the people with all our hearts, and labor selflessly and creatively; so that we are people with a daring (*yonggan*) innovative (*gexin*) spirit who clear the way for new things." The opponents were, however, "bureaucrats" supporting the "old and backward," who pursued fame and the good life. Arkady's superb technical qualifications were not denied, but he did not use them "in the service of the people." Nastya was—a metaphor used in the novel itself—like a "dentist" who finds the decayed spots. In China, however,

there are among us very many people who also see in their own unit persisting deficiencies which should be corrected; not that they don't have some criticisms stored up in their guts, but they don't dare to bring them up. They first ponder like this: "Is it appropriate for me to bring it up? How embarrassing if I were to be rebuffed!" Or "What's the use of bringing up all sorts of criticism? The leadership must not get a bad impression of me. Forget it, you should not meddle in too many affairs, this deficiency is not unheard of; which unit after all does not have it?" Against this opportunistic behavior Nastya stands out in contrast. She is in a sorry situation, but she doesn't care. The moment she discovers a boil, she pricks it without formalities; she does

13. Li Helin, "Du 'Tuolajizhan zhanzhang he zongnongyishi'" (Reading *The Director of the MTS and the Chief Agronomist*), *Zhongguo qingnian* 2:17ff (16 January 1956).
14. Wang Ruowang, *Xiang Nasijia xuexi* (Learn from Nastya; Shanghai: Shanghai Renmin Press, 1956).

not at all consider what consequences she might incur; what she considers above all are the highest interests of the socialist state."[15]

In the third section, Wang dealt with the apprehensions of young people that the vengeance of their elders might descend on them. "If in a leadership position there is someone of Arkady's type who enjoys only hearing flattery and takes a hostile attitude towards anyone coming up with criticisms, we should not be discouraged but continue the struggle, even if the result of our proffering criticism time and again is to be beaten down and treated with contempt. We have the Party and Chairman Mao, and both support us forever."[16] This evokes the constellation in Nikolayeva's novel where the Khruschevian top leaders interact with the activists of the Nastya type, and eventually vindicate Nastya's struggle even on the political level by adopting her line as the government line.

The Constitution, Wang argued, gives citizens the right to air and voice their grievances. In fact, however, his readers had little confidence in its guarantees. "Some people think criticizing the weak spots of leaders and pointing out mistakes in work is just 'asking for trouble,' and hold that the 'arm can't twist the thigh,' but this kind of thinking is only appropriate for the era of Guomindang rule." Having made this strong statement, he reported on a Youth League meeting about Nastya, where a young worker pointed out that the leaders in China didn't openly oppose their critics in Arkady's manner, but feigned a very "democratic attitude" when hearing the criticisms, and then changed nothing. But they would make use of other means to get back at their critics, defining them as "individualist," "unruly devils" (*tiaopi gui*), putting them on the list of "backward elements" (*luohou fenzi*), lowering them one rank in the cadre evaluation, or sending them away first when people were to be transferred.[17] Nastya's refusal to fill out the forms would be seen in China as counter to the spirit of obedience to the leadership. Wang argued that one should not learn opposition to the leader-

15. Ibid., p. 12.
16. Ibid., p. 13.
17. Ibid., pp. 14f.

ship from Nastya, but that leaders who suppress criticism must be given help to "overcome their incorrect working style." Democratic centralism provided an avenue for proffering criticisms, and Nastya's refusal to fill out the forms was wrong and undisciplined. The words used for Nastya in the editorial of the *Literaturnaya Gazeta* in late 1955, "full of creativity, daring to do and daring to act, with bold thoughts (*dadandi sixiang*) and strong feelings" were allowed to remain, however, as an ideal for china. The Chinese Nastyas would be "a bit older, probably men not women, and not as mature as Nastya," but "this type of personality must receive the attention and the nurture from Party and League."

The booklet ends with the words "Learning from Nastya also means to make this cherished 'Russian character' [ascribed to Nastya in the novel] into a common feature of our Chinese youths."[18] Evidently, it was unimaginable at the time that the youths could develop some specific Chinese trait. The "modern" behavior required was outlandish; here it was Russian, and from the Russian Thaw. The personality type encoded in Nastya again has many traits which in Russia itself were imports from the United States, made during the late 1920s when Taylorism and Fordism became catchwords of scientific production management.

From mid-January on, the slogan "The image of Nastya spurs us to progress" (*Nasijia de xingxiang guwu women qianjin*) was coined in *Zhongguo qingnian*,[19] and the journal printed letters from youths about their experiences in becoming Chinese Nastyas. The letters often described personal failures to live up to Nastya's high calibre.

Here, a young man would tell how he failed to push for the publication of a manuscript in which he uncovered the corruption of the leaders of a factory.[20] There, another would narrate how he failed to prevent the perfectly unnecessary demolition of a little bridge, although the local peasants had been desperately trying to keep it.[21] Here, a construc-

18. Ibid., pp. 29f.

19. "Nasijia de xingxiang guwu women qianjin" (The image of Nastya spurs us to progress) became the slogan heading a series of readers' letters on the matter in *Zhongguo qingnian* 2:22 (16 January 1955).

20. Quoted in Jiang Meng, "Dapo zhongzhong gulü, jianchi yuanze douzheng" (Do away with all considerations, maintain a principled struggle), *Zhongguo qingnian* 4:23 (16 February 1956).

21. Li Shengliang, "Shike guanxin qunzhong liyi" (Constantly keep in mind the interest of the masses), *Zhongguo qingnian* 2:23 (16 January 1956).

tion engineer would report how his peers started to put pressure on him to conform to a nonsensical order by the leadership, because they did not want to become known collectively for "unorganized, undisciplined behavior," and so he acceded.[22] There, an agricultural engineer would tell the story of his failure to wage a principled struggle for the introduction of a new crop, and thus did damage to the people.[23] There was not a single published report from someone who actually managed to live up to Nastya.

After having received floods of letters, the editors of *Zhongguo qingnian* started in February summarily to answer them. First, in February, they argued that the conditions "in our country have fundamentally changed since Chairman Mao published his 'On the Cooperative Transformation of Agriculture.'" Since then, an upsurge had swept city and countryside, and thus the conditions for imitating Nastya were good, because the Party called for a struggle against "laxness, corruption, and bureaucratism."[24] Quite correctly, this editorial saw the beginning of what eventually evolved into the Hundred Flowers line with this speech of July 1955, and not with Zhou Enlai's speech on the intellectuals in January 1956, or Mao's remarks on "Letting a Hundred Flowers Bloom and a Hundred Schools Contend."

In the next issue in late February, the column with readers' letters about Nastya was abruptly canceled. The editorial board inserted an article demanding "Break through those heavy concerns, maintain a principled struggle," which acknowledged with some alarm that the letters that kept streaming in were all enthusiastic about Nastya, but all ended with their authors admitting that they had not matched her principled attitude. There was no lack of occasions in China for principled struggle; factory directors squandered money, engineers disregarded rationalization proposals, leaders showed no concern for the suffering of the masses. The reasons why the young people resigned themselves to the

22. Hong Yiping, "Zhengque de yinggai jianchi" (What is correct must be upheld), *Zhongguo qingnian* 3:3 (1 February 1956).
23. Ye Yuming, "Jianchi yuanze biding shengli" (Keeping to principle definitely will be victorious), *Zhongguo qingnian* 3:24 (16 February 1956).
24. "Jiujing wei shenme yao tuijian *'Tuolajizhan zhanzhang he zongnongyishi'*—ta duzhe wen" (Why after all "The Director of the MTS and the Chief Agronomist" has to be promoted—answering readers' letters), *Zhongguo qingnian* 3:22 (16 February 1956).

status quo were to be found in their own concerns; they were "afraid of offending people and leaving a bad impression; afraid of blocking their own chances for admission into the Party and the Youth League; afraid of vengeance and of isolating themselves among the masses; afraid of the criticism by others that they were showing off and of being considered unorganized and undisciplined; afraid that their criticism might not be correct and would, instead, expose their own weakness; and afraid that others might be induced to expose in turn their own weaknesses."[25] As the Party was supporting and encouraging their criticisms, however, "one cannot find objective reasons [for their resignation], but has to look for the reason in the youths themselves."

The author then claimed that all these concerns were perfectly unfounded, which might be understandable as encouraging propaganda for youths, but certainly did not correspond to the youths' experiences. The idea of criticizing superiors, and even bluntly disregarding orders in certain cases, seemed to be so directly opposite to model behavior in China that readers asked in disbelief why such a novel could be recommended, since Nastya was evidently *wu zuzhi wu jilü* (lacking organization spirit and discipline).

In March, the Youth League leadership withdrew core parts of Nastya's activities from the model to be emulated. These things were just too much for China, even in fiction. For the purpose of this reevaluation, the first Chinese emulator of Nastya, the doctor from Heilongjiang mentioned earlier, was also dug up again. It was now said in an article that Nastya's refusal to accept orders after her suggestions and criticisms had not been heeded "cannot be condoned by organization discipline." True, there might be extreme situations where one had to go by one's own judgment and do what was necessary, but normally "the organizations of the Communist Party and the Youth League demanded that their members obey the organization's directives and decisions." The line advocated late in 1955 in the article "To Progress or to Regress?" which praised the young doctor's independent decision, was wrong. One should not mechanically copy Nastya and Dr. Jin. An editorial note attached to the article stated that the editors of *Zhongguo*

25. Jiang Meng, "Do Away with All Considerations" (note 20 above), p. 23.

qingnian agreed with this reasoning and retracted their statements in "To Progress or to Regress?"[26]

The opponents of the new personality type obviously had gained an important battle; the internal and better-documented discussions in late 1986 and early 1987 among about the same protagonists (Hu Yaobang, Deng Xiaoping, Peng Zhen) read like a replay of the early months of 1956. When some scholars, writers, and students began publicly clamoring for greater personal leeway as a necessary accompaniment to China's intellectual and industrial diversification, the blame was put on Hu Yaobang, and in a much harder crackdown he was dismissed as head of the Party.

With the articles backtracking from the original Nastya enthusiasm, her model shrank to more amenable size, but the thrill and temptation of really doing something brave and new was gone. Given the original impetus of the Nastya campaign, Zhou Enlai's speech in late January "On the Question of the Intellectuals" was not an encouragement for the freer spirits, but rather a damper. There is not the slightest indication in the talk that a new kind of daring personality was called for; and the young were mentioned only as helpers to the senior scholars in mineral exploration and the like. In the opinions of readers' letters, however, the old academic teachers shared with the cadres the responsibility for the intellectual stupor of the schools, both of them stressing docility as the core virtue for intellectual learning and lifestyle. Quickly, the teachers and cadres used Zhou's talk to subdue and discipline the students, some of whom probably behaved with what was seen as unbearable arrogance, self-righteousness and obstinacy, donning the big names of Chinese Nastyas. They were to honor and follow their teachers, it was now said, and do what they were told.

Nonetheless, the same article that shrank Nastya's size put forth Dr. Jin as a "model to follow," adducing the proof that one could become a Nastya on Chinese soil and one could even become a recognized "activist of socialist construction." The basic thrust of the campaign was kept up. The concluding summary of the "several thousands of letters from

26. Dan Tong, "Guanyu Nasijia he Jin Zhendu de zuzhixing jiluxing wenti" (Concerning the problems of Nastya's and Jin Zhendu's attitude towards organization and discipline), *Zhongguo qingnian* 6:16f (16 March 1956).

young people" about their impressions after reading Nikolayeva's novel was entitled "Don't polish off their edges (*lengjiao*)."[27] The latter term referred to the irregular bumps and edges in young people's behavior. A *lengjiao* is a person difficult to get along with, and thus the strict opposite to the *laolao shishi* character. The later student leader Lin Xiling was to claim proudly that she was a *lengjiao*, which certainly was true. The article argued that indeed youths had been singularly unsuccessful in transplanting Nastya's features to Chinese soil; after some failure they had given up, their *lengjiao* had been polished off, they had become *laolian*, routineers, and "not just in a few units." Cadres continued to prefer young people who talked as the wind blew, were polished to blandness, didn't argue and had learned to read in their (cadres') faces what was proper to say; to achieve this educational goal, senior cadres ridiculed critics, and took their vengeance. The main reason for this attitude among senior cadres was that "they are afraid their deficiencies might be uncovered by daring, restless, creative young cadres." The legitimacy of the opposing educational concept was in doubt, as it was maintained by rather crude self-interest, according to this argument. The Youth League then shifted the emphasis. The discussion about learning from Nastya flowed into the broader discussion about what kind of people "we" wanted to educate, a discussion as much directed to Youth League and other leaders as to the youths themselves.

Meanwhile, a new group was recruited into the effort to promote the new personality. It should be recalled that this personality was an "activist of socialist construction." The writers in the environs of the Youth League felt motivated and were called upon to come to the support of this sparse crowd of heroes. The mentors of these writers would be people in powerful positions like Qin Zhaoyang (*Renmin wenxue*) and Ma Feng from the editorial board of the *Wenyi xuexi*. Liu Binyan had done more than most others to prepare the ground for the new policies by introducing Ovechkin's writings and theories of the *texie* with its "intervention in life," as well as the satirical poems of another Soviet writer. He had direct links with the activists of socialist construction, as he had eulogized their feats for *Wenyibao*, and, as the head of the industry

27. Zhi Guang, "Don't Polish Off Their Edges" (p. 63 note 26).

section of *Zhongguo qingnianbao*, he was in daily contact with young intelligentsia in the big plants and building sites through their letters and the reportages coming to his desk. Qin Zhaoyang claimed that there was no shortage of manuscripts from young writers; "over 90 percent" of the manuscripts came from them, but little was publishable. Qin was waiting for the Chinese Ovechkin, who, like his Russian counterpart, would gather the best young minds around him and set the standard for an entire generation of writers. The writers of the older generation had fallen silent, and, with the emphasis on youth in the new constellation, there was little hope that they would be able to handle such themes. To encourage the younger writers, and pave a way for them, a meeting of "Young Literary Creators" was held in late March in conjunction with the Writers' Congress. "Young" meant that they were under 30, and "literary creators" was chosen as a term to include many part-time writers, among whom there was a particularly high percentage of the young. Most of the speeches were published in *Wenyi xuexi*, the Youth League literary journal, evidence that this meeting was held under Youth League auspices.[28]

The young writers were summarily referred to as "newborn forces" who should be fostered and not suppressed by the older writers who controlled the editorial boards. The link to the "activists of socialist construction" was explicitly made. The old/young technical cadre controversy from industry and the old/young administrative cadre controversy from the countryside were thus transferred to the literary realm. Liu Binyan had made his contribution by reporting from Moscow about the Congress of Young Soviet Writers in January. There, he said, Aleyev, the leading pontificator, had been publicly assailed by men like Sholokhov and Ovechkin for uttering empty phrases. Liu Binyan noticed a tendency among young Soviet writers to turn away in their irritation from labor themes to introspection.[29]

In the speeches by leading cultural officials and older writers at the Chinese meeting, there was no exhiliaration; voices were subdued, since

28. *Wenyi xuexi* 3:3f (18 March 1956).
29. Liu Binyan, "Disanci Quan Su Qingnian Zuojia Huiyi de qingkuang" (The situation at the Third All-Soviet Youth Writers' Conference), *Wenyi xuexi* 2:13ff (8 February 1956); the title is set in boldface.

the work of the young suffered much from general sloganeering. A collection of prose pieces by young writers published on the occasion drew sober comments.[30] Ma Feng, an older rural writer with a record of some independent opinion since the Yan'an days, felt compelled to entitle his speech about these works "One Must Deeply Enter Into Life, and Intervene In Life," which implied that these short works suffered from a lack of knowledge of life, as well as from a harmonizing attitude towards the conflicts.[31] The education of the preceding years had had its impact, and there were few personalities around who had the knowledge and the guts to bring the Soviet options from the parking orbit of *Yiwen* and other esoteric niches onto Chinese soil. The young writers who achieved prominence during the subsequent months—Liu Binyan, Wang Meng, Liu Shaotang, Deng Youmei, Gao Xiaosheng, and others—had been involved with this conference of young writers; they were themselves Youth League members or just beyond the age; they worked in the context of the Youth League, and their heroes, as a rule, were Youth Leaguers.

Given the direct interest Hu Yaobang took in the propaganda for the new personality, it may be surmised that these writers, whether consciously or not, were "Youth League writers" supporting Hu's position at the time; support for this hypothesis is the fact that all these writers came back to the literary scene and started publishing again in 1979, days after Hu Yaobang had become head of Party Propaganda. During the subsequent years, these writers have by and large kept their allegiance and are among the strongest literary supporters of Hu Yaobang's policies, which testifies both to the obstinacy of their political commitment and to their loyalty to the leadership personalities with a similar commitment.

In the search for quotable Soviet sources, *Wenyibao* had already made use of any material that was a bit more open, salvaging Soviet speeches from broken-down tape recorders and disorganized notes, and rushing them into print without ever contacting the original authors, a clear

---

30. *Qingnian wenxue chuangzuo xuanji* (A selection of works by young writers; Beijing: Zhongguo Qingnian Press, 1956).

31. Ma Feng, "Bixu shenru shenghuo ganyu shenghuo" (One must deeply enter into life and intervene in life), *Wenyi xuexi* 4:31f (8 April 1956).

evidence of *Wenyibao*'s eagerness.[32] Now, it adopted the same methods for Chinese texts. Informal discussions were taped, flashy titles were added, and the results were thrown into the market as long as they supported the new "intervene-in-life" line. An informal discussion of the Short Story Group of the Committee on Creative Writing of the Chinese Writers' Association on 21 January 1956, which dealt with the recently available works by Ovechkin, Nikolayeva, and Sholokhov, was thus printed under the title "Daringly Unveil the Contradictions and Conflicts in Life." The publication of the discussion, the editors commented, was "to help readers in China understand these works and learn from the spirit of the Soviet authors of courageously intervening in life." In the discussion, Kang Zhuo explicitly transferred the function associated with the socialist-construction activists, namely, to courageously "intervene in life" to literature depicting such heroes. Literature had to be like Nastya who "while being simply a Soviet youth still takes part in life and intervenes in life."[33]

Given the speed of the changes and the importance of intervention, the short forms of *texie* and the short story were most appropriate at the moment, said Ma Feng. From February on, Qin Zhaoyang created the proper slot for the *texie* by grouping them together as a separate genre in *Renmin wenxue*, claiming that many readers had explicitly demanded this. All the periodicals in the group studied here carried strongly worded articles that literature "must" intervene in life, but the few short stories and *texie* that made the first attempt were still meek and exceedingly schematic. A critic observed about these early *texie* that they were supposed to be close-ups, as in films, but authors lacked lenses and focus, were simplistic, showed no sharp conflicts, and were unfamiliar with the actual processes they described. "But these are just views of things past," he concluded, because, "after reading Liu Binyan's 'At the Building Sites of the Bridges' I was newly encouraged."[34]

32. This was the case with Ovechkin's speech on *očerki* as well as with Surkov's speech mentioned above (p. 116 note 35). In both cases, editorial notes were attached absolving the original authors from responsibility.

33. "Yonggan de jielu shenghuozhong de maodun he chongtu" (Courageously unveil the contradictions and conflicts in life), *Wenyibao* 3:21f (15 February 1956).

34. Luo Ren, "Zhongyaode shi bixu ganyu shenghuo" (The most important thing is to intervene in life), *Wenyibao* 9:16 (15 May 1956).

EIGHT

Fiction Enters the Contest: Liu Binyan's "At the Building Sites of the Bridges"

Liu's story was written in February, and *Renmin wenxue*, the national leader in short fiction, carried it in April. The *texie* genre was described as best adapted to dealing with present-day problems; the piece appeared first in the journal; the title was set in boldface in the table of contents, indicating particular importance; the editor prefaced the text itself with a most extraordinary statement: "We have already been waiting a very long time for this kind of *texie* which sharply identifies problems, and is critical as well as satirical; we hope that, after the publication of "At the Building Sites of the Bridges," many more such works may appear"; the editor returned to the same theme in the postface at the end of the issue, praising the piece again.[1] Readers were informed in no uncertain terms that this was a national event. Liu was singularly qualified, due to his close link to Ovechkin, his earlier efforts to establish an alternative parking orbit, his cosmopolitan behavior, and his direct experience with industrial work sites in his job as head of the industry section of the Youth League paper *Zhongguo qingnianbao*, which also gave him access to the flood of letters coming in from the "Learn-from-Nastya campaign."

Immediately after the publication of the story, periodicals pushing

1. Liu Binyan, "Zai qiaoliang gongdi shang" (At the building sites of the bridges), *Renmin wenxue* 4 (April 1956).

the same line came out with reviews, a highly unusual response to a piece of short fiction. *Wenyibao* asserted in a headline, countering people who might think otherwise, that this was "an excellent *texie*," and furthermore published a series of short essays on the text by different authors.[2] *Xin guancha* stated on 1 May, even before Mao's comments on the Hundred Flowers, that "May is the season when the hundred flowers blossom together" and then started to heap praise on Liu Binyan's story.[3] The text became popular enough that an "Open Letter to Luo Lizheng" could be published in *Xin guancha* a year later in June 1957 with the assumption that every reader would recognize the name as that of the head of the building sites in the story.[4] Ovechkin's Borzov had had a similar if more elevated career. He became the "Borzovian man," the archetype of the Soviet bureaucrat, the literary father of Luo Lizheng.

The story is set at the building sites of two bridges over the Yellow River in Gansu province. The northwest, with its combination of mineral wealth and inaccessibility, was the great area of investment and development in these years, and a key to the opening of the area was the development of trunk transport routes. North of Lanzhou in Gansu province an old steel bridge, built in 1909, crossed the Yellow River, providing the "hub of communication between Lanzhou and Xinjiang, Qinghai, Ningxia, and the Gansu corridor." The pillars and girders of this bridge had served their term and were certainly unable to support heavy traffic with the weighty modern engines and fully loaded oil and mineral trains. In April 1954, work began to replace the most important support elements.[5] At the same time, construction of another bridge was undertaken near Lanzhou over which the projected Baotou-Lanzhou railway was to pass, linking up the remote northwest with the

2. Su Ping, "'Zai qiaoliang gongdi shang' shi yipian chuse de texie" ("At the Building Sites of the Bridges" is an excellent *texie*), *Wenyibao* 8:24ff (1 May 1956). "Texie 'Zai qiaoliang gongdi shang' bitan" (Notes on the *texie* "At the Building Sites of the Bridges"), *Wenyibao* 9:16ff (15 May 1956), contains articles by Luo Ren, Li Yang, and Lin Yuan.

3. Two articles to greet the "advanced producers" appear on the first page of *Xin guancha* 9 (1956) on 1 May, "Xiang xianjin shengchanzhe zhijing" (Greetings to the advanced producers) with the quotation, and "Tan Luo Lizheng shi de renwu" (On the personality of Luo Lizheng), Luo Lizheng being the bureaucrat in the "At the Building Sites."

4. Shen Yan, "Gei Luo Lizheng de xin" (A letter to Luo Lizheng), *Xin guancha* 12:15 (16 June 1957).

5. New China News Agency, Lanchow 22 June 1954, quoted in *Survey of China Mainland Press* 834.

rest of China. This was to be "one of the biggest arch-span bridges" of China, an important, costly, and technically daring enterprise.[6] In the framework of China's 1st Five-Year Plan we are thus dealing with two key projects of top national priority where the best human and technical resources were concentrated.

Institutionally, the bridges were built by the central government, not by the province or the city. According to Liu Binyan's story, the responsible managers reported directly to the Ministry. By selecting these highly publicized projects for his story, Liu Binyan argued by implication that his story did not depict problems moldering in some remote backwater. The problems described in the text existed at the very forefront of the industrial advance in a project of top national priority, managed directly by the Center. Elsewhere, it followed, problems must have been much more serious than here where the best resources were pooled.

The work on the two building sites, which are a few miles apart, is under the direction of Luo Lizheng. The geographical distance gives the repair team for the old bridge under the young engineer Zeng Gang much independence, as Luo's office is near the arch-span bridge where technical matters are handled by engineer Zhou Weiben. The two sites confront the same problems in terms of climate, matériel deliveries, and organization, and they deal with the same river. The setup is a near-perfect social "experiment" where two attitudes and management styles can be compared and measured.

The authorial voice is that of a journalist visiting the site. He is an old friend of Luo Lizheng's, since they had been building and repairing bridges together in the last days of the war. Proudly, Luo tells of the recent achievements, but his mood changes when the journalist announces his intention to interview engineer Zeng Gang. Luo suggests Zhou Weiben instead, head of the technical office. From telephone conversations accidentally overheard by the journalist from next door, he gathers that Zhou Weiben is unwilling to shoulder responsibilities and to state his own opinions. If he does venture an opinion, he does so on the authority of others, "This is the opinion of the Soviet specialists,"

6. New China News Agency, 2 June 1954, cf. *Survey of China Mainland Press* 825, p. 38. Information that it was an "arch-span" bridge is confirmed by New China News Agency, 16 November 1954; cf. *Survey of China Mainland Press* 929, p. 27.

"Head engineer Zhang from the Bureau said this," and so on. A worker who also hears these statements is exasperated; he charges that the project lost eight work days owing to Zhou's incessant referral to and waiting for directives from above. "We crane operators would love to work with an engineer such as this [engineer Zeng]. He dares to make decisions and always says "That's the way we do it, and I take the responsibility."

Many conflicting rumors have been circulating about Zeng. He cares about the personal life of the workers, is interested in "the international political situation," and made many proposals for important savings at the building site. In crisis situations, Zeng is said to personally take the lead, and to have been successful. Opinions are divided. Some admire his "bold spirit" (*dadan jingshen*), others feel "this man is taking chances (*maoxian*), is immature (*youzhi*), and does not pay attention to science." The latter opinion prevails among people in the construction office of the Ministry, while the former prevails among the workers. From the terms used to describe Zeng it is evident that Liu Binyan is presenting a specimen of the "new personality" in social operation. What will happen to this foreign character on Chinese soil? Who will be his friends and who his enemies? What will be his fate?

The journalist visits the site under Zeng's command and finds it well organized with every man knowing his place and duties. At the other building site where Luo Lizheng and engineer Zhou hold sway, general chaos reigns. The first part of the month is wasted and, in the second half, extra hours are required to fulfill the plan by month's end. It seems that there is more *maoxian* (adventurism) here than at Zeng's site. On closer inspection, the journalist discovers that higher technical know-how and better management skills are insufficient to explain Zeng's success. The problem is one of attitude and personality. Some people just give up, saying "It's impossible," their "minds are covered with dust." Zeng cultivates close relationships with the workers, not by playing poker with them, but by taking their suggestions seriously. The journalist discovers, however, that things are not that easy. "After having talked (with Zeng) for two nights, it suddenly dawned on me that his [Zeng's technical and managerial methods] was not the most important thing for me to understand." These methods were all well known, but nonetheless many people did not apply them, and even obstructed their application, so that conflicts were inevitable. Zeng sighs: "Something might evidently be good, and experience might evidently be successful, but, when you think about applying it in great style, there are troubles." Zeng's group of Youth League activists intends to double the norms in the "spirit of Stachanov," but Luo Lizheng objects with an urgent message that they should not mobilize the workers for this drive as this would be "adventurous" (*maoxian*). Zeng concludes, "In order for everyone to be able [underlined in original] to work in the spirit of [the Soviet norm-tripling miner] Stakhanov, those people who do the planning, organizing, and projecting must first have this spirit." In the naïveté of his demand for the rational progressive process to prevail, Zeng is "something of a child," a feature familiar from Nastya. Why does Luo Lizheng charge his successful engineer with being *maoxian* (adventurous) while considering as *wendang* (reliable) people who in fact risk the danger of failure (*maozhe shibai de weixian*)?

It has been Luo who made Zeng into both team leader and responsible engineer of his group, and he has often praised Zeng's role in reversing the trend of the bridge-building brigade's not fulfilling the state plan. But, as the years have gone by, Luo has shifted his sympathies to Zhou Weiben who is so "careful" (*xixin*) and "cautious" (*jinshen*) that he has gradually stopped making plans of his own, it being so much easier (*qingsong*) to approve or revise the plans of others. When Zeng recommended late in 1953 increasing the plan norms instead of reducing them for easier fulfillment and overfulfillment, Luo noticed that "this man is changing." The day before, he had privately explained his strategy of easy plan fulfillment to Zeng, and today Zeng has decided to bring up this question publicly. In 1954, Zeng and his group formed a "Youth Team for Economizing," as many others did. But, while the other youth teams collected scrap material, which was uncontroversial, Zeng planned an "exhibition against the waste of material," which was not within his responsibilities. In June 1954, Zeng wrote a long proposal for reducing the amount of raw materials needed, which implied some criticism of the bridge-building brigade, and, when he got no answer from the engineering office after three weeks, the letter turned up in the Ministry. When some years ago other people said scornfully that Zeng was *dadan* (bold), Luo had defended Zeng. But now he began to understand Zeng's boldness as a source of acute discomfort. When the other groups called Luo, they gave reports or asked for instructions. Zeng's team went further; it "loved to point out problems, and generally pressed for speed and started nagging (*zheng*)." To "prevent this boldness from doing damage," Luo put the brakes on Zeng by imposing all sorts of difficult conditions on his team, which of course could all be defended on the basis of some regulation or other, so that the ultimate purpose was not immediately evident. In consequence Zeng has tried to run things as much as possible in his own manner.

Through the changing relationship between these two men, Liu Binyan described the political history of the past few years with the evolving conflict between two generations and two types of personalities. Zeng bases his anti-waste stance on the "anti-bureaucratic" aspect of the Resolution of the 3rd Plenum of March 1954. By trying to run things in a more efficient way and to reduce interference from Luo, he ends up in the slot reserved for those who "set up an independent kingdom" and refuse close supervision by the Party, that is in the trap of the other half of the same Resolution.

Sure enough, he is charged by Luo with the crime of "lack of discipline" (*wu jilü*), and, when he refuses to accept norms set too moderately, the head of the dispatcher's office asks "whether this is not anti-Party behavior." Clearly, Zeng is on the road to becoming one of the quota of "counterrevolutionaries" to be weeded out in the Sufan Movement a year later.

At this time, however, the Party secretary "personally" intervenes to stop this line of attacking Zeng. "The criticism, however, has already exerted its influence, and some people see Zeng Gang as a dangerous person, while those who understand him and sympathize with him can only silently worry and feel anxious for him." "Public opinion among a part of the brigade cadres" now thinks that Zeng's group is difficult to handle because Zeng is *tai dadan*, (too bold). The pressure becomes such that Zeng himself claims he is not *dadan* at all. "Later I learned that, in the bridge-building brigade, the underlying meaning of *dadan* was a composite of *maoshi* (rash), *kuangwang* (presumptuous), *lumang* (crude and unreflecting), and *bufu zeren* (irresponsible), and sometimes *dadan* and *maoxian* (bold and adventurous) had the same meaning."

In spring 1955, at the time of the journalist's visit, the conflict reaches a new level. This was the time when "youth shock teams" *qing-nian tujidui* were springing up in the factories and building sites of China. A worker correspondent from Zeng's group writes an article for a paper entitled "The Youth Shock Team of the Third Group of the Bridge-Building Brigade (Zeng's group) Starts a Movement to Double the Norms." The article claims that the leadership of the brigade is "conservative," *baoshou* (keeping norms artificially low).

Readers in 1956 knew of course that this was the very word used by Mao Zedong in his talk on the agricultural cooperatives in July 1955 to characterize cadres opposed to rapid collectivization. But both protagonists of the story itself cannot know that the Chairman will intervene in this manner. They operate without the protection of an official pronouncement.

Luo intends to prevent the publication of the piece. The norms have been approved by the Construction Bureau, and thus the article implies, he argues, that his high-level office, too, is conservative. Furthermore, there are other brigades who don't even fulfill the present norms. "And what would happen if this suggestion became known in the Ministry? They would order the Construction Bureau to follow it in each brigade. This would give the director of the Construction Bureau much trouble. Evidently, it cannot be done. But, in the Ministry they will say, if the bridge-building brigade can do it, why cannot other brigades do it? All this is expectable. And what if the responsible comrade from the Center would learn of this matter? Then perhaps the leadership of the Ministry itself would be in trouble—and the entire country would have to proceed in this way."

Historically, the Stakhanov movement and its Chinese imitation were quite ambivalent. At the beginning, and in the eyes of many participants, they may have appeared as an outburst of "socialist labor enthusiasm." The conditions, however, under which these feats of labor were being performed were often rigged, and later the new norms set by these "heroes of labor" were made into the new standards, with extreme pressure exerted on the workers to fulfill them under radically different circumstances, and regularly so. Among many workers, animosity against the labor heroes ran high. Ovechkin himself had depicted and denounced this animosity,[7] and, more recently, Wajda's "Man of Marble" took a new and critical look at such a labor hero in Poland, with much sympathy for the animosity among his peers. By having Luo Lizheng articulate the objections to Zeng's proposal, Liu denounced these objections as bureaucratic foot-dragging.

In a fine satirical passage, Liu Binyan had Luo Lizheng spell out the difference between the Soviet Union with its political Thaw, Youth League inspection teams against waste, and Youth League shock brigades on the one hand, and Chinese "peculiar characteristics" on the other.

> "No," Luo Lizheng stretched out a hand as if he wanted to close his opposite's mouth. "The problem is that this [body overfulfilling the norms] cannot be realized. The ten fingers are never equal. I know the Soviet Union once had such a movement—called "doubling the norms," but that was the Soviet Union. No, it does not work: one just cannot mechanically apply these Soviet fancies (*wanyir*) to China. China has Chinese peculiarities (*tedian*). As an example, in the Soviet Union you can criticize the leadership; in China that's not done. When there is a big movement like the Three Antis or the Five Antis, there is a directive from the Center, and then you may criticize. In normal times when there is no such directive, we cannot criticize the Bureau; if you want to criticize you have to have the approval of the Bureau. The Soviets go about things really violently; we in China do it really sedately (*wen*), and that's a peculiarity. Generally, one has to keep to Chinese peculiarities in everything. Then one does not commit mistakes. Understand?"

When Zeng Gang strenuously objects and mentions that the intention of the workers to double the norms is also a "Chinese peculiarity," Luo veers off to trivial topics. "In this moment a flock of crows made off with big clamor from the roof of the house." Their hoarse *guagua* echoes Luo's talk, and as they relish dead and putrid matter they are appropriately assembled on Luo's roof. Luo ends the conversation with the suggestion to withhold the article, and with a threat:

> We are old comrades, and I should tell you that there are comrades in the brigades who say you are too one-sided, only seeing the defects and not the achievements. Some comrades in responsible positions even brought up the

7. Cf. Liu Binyan, "Days with Ovechkin" (p. 82 note 9), p. 30.

question whether this was not an anti-Party attitude because otherwise why should you do everything to find defects in the leadership?

The intervention of the Party secretary notwithstanding, the political threat of being branded an "anti-Party element" still loomed. For readers in April 1956 who were aware of the frenzy of "class struggle" dominating the second half of 1955 this threat was clearer than to either Luo or Zeng in spring 1955. Nature obliges with the appropriate climate after this threat. "The sky was already quite dark, and from the river blew a wind that made it hard to breathe."

The *texie* of the Ovechkin variant includes elements of the political essay. After this exchange between Luo and Zeng, Liu Binyan generalized his observations, and introduced a new catch-word, *zhudongxing* (one's own initiative). The plans, he argues, are abstract; to translate them into reality and to adapt them to the particular conditions of a project many problems have to be overcome, and here the contributions of the workers, of the "masses," are of greatest value. Not only can they find methods of using their own hands more effectively; they also can help the leadership to organize these thousands and ten thousands of hands better and to recognize dangers earlier. Needless to say, Zeng fosters this *zhudongxing* (initiative), which is said to be "one of the most precious qualities in human beings" in which they can show *du chu xin-cai* (the capacity to "come up on one's own with new ideas.")

Both independent thinking and individual initiative are among the new values advocated in the story as opposed to the humdrum pace of the "normal" (*pingchang*) so cherished by Luo. The box for suggestions in front of his office has never been used, and the lock is rusted. Suggestions from below are considered irritating nuisances by this man who "only recognizes the decisions, directives, rules, and regulations coming from the Bureau" and follows them with all his strength, even if they are absurd. "For us, the most important thing is to understand the intentions of the leadership," says Luo. He is well in tune with the current emphasis on "Party unity," derived from the same resolution on which Zeng bases his action. His obedience to the decisions of the leadership is bluntly defined by Liu Binyan as *sishi er fei* (seemingly correct but in fact false), because he fulfills the directives in form only and not in substance. But within the Bureau it earns Luo the reputation of being "extremely strong in organization spirit and discipline" as opposed to Zeng.

As the Party secretary of the brigade explains, Luo follows the directives of the Bureau and disregards the "editorials in the papers." The latter are the instruments by which the (enlightened) top leaders try to address the political class and even the populace in general, bypassing the bureaucracy. Zeng thus reads the editorials, and follows their appeals. Luo, on the other hand, "does not study the policies of the Center; he does not understand the decisions and directives of the Center if they are not accompanied by orders from the Bureau; he never reads the editorials in the Party paper, saying that "these deal with the 'general situation' while in our brigade there is a 'specific situation' which is quite different." His line is: "If someone does not run things according to the editorials he will never be reprimanded for that. That does not count as a mistake. If one runs the things according to the administration's orders, the lower levels cannot be held responsible even it [their actions] deviate from Party policies."

With his "sociological" investigation, Liu Binyan thus discovered two chains of command. One within the administration's hierarchy; this one has stability and the power to punish deviations. The other came directly from the Center through editorials, but carried no institutional power. It fanned the fire of the production enthusiasts on the base level, but they again had no power. As long as the two "progressive" sectors stayed divided and apart, their strength was merely the thin air of an argument, and the base-level critics could be dealt with in traditional administrative fashion. Each chain of command accompanied a different type of personality, military obedience being the chief value of one group, independent initiative that of the other, and both spared neither word nor metaphor to denounce each other as "adventurers" or croaking crows feeding on dead matter.

The Party does not come in for much leadership on the local level in the story. The Party secretary is "meager" and "anemic," and so are his actions. True, he supports Zeng Gang and his Youth League activists, but he is no match for Luo Lizheng's sophistication in handling social relations. Luo does not "fight back," but rather follows official directives and distorts them in the process to fit his own purposes. When the Youth League under Zeng sets up Youth-Control Posts (following the Soviet model), the other groups are advised to imitate this. But then the secretary general of the brigade's Youth League, who is of the same stamp as Luo Lizheng, gives out the directive that these posts "should not turn their spearhead against the leadership" but that they should "handle problems among the workers"; this transforms the critical potential of this drive into a further instrument to discipline the workers.

Luo's sophisticated strategy of joining the pack, and redirecting its course is not only engineer Zeng's main problem. It is also the main obstacle the Party secretary has to face. Class struggle is not the orthodox method for handling bureaucrats. But how is one to handle a bureaucrat who bends to every wind, and even takes the "lead" in the struggle against bureaucratism?

Luo is not a hidden class enemy who eventually shows his colors but a revolutionary in good standing. In a flashback, Liu Binyan describes Luo's earlier enthusiasm and great dreams for a new China. But gradually this enthusiasm has subsided. The language used for the description here recalls Xia Yan's admission quoted above: "This Luo Lizheng had by now built more than one bridge over the Yellow River, and now China's first big arch bridge rose under his hands. Strangely, however, Luo Lizheng now did not feel any enthusiasm anymore [about the final realization of his old dreams]. Of course, looking back on the achievements of the past years, he unwittingly felt some pride and a faint smile lit up on his weary face, but a moment later it was gone." Now, his hobbies are hunting and repairing watches. He lacks culture, too, while Zeng becomes the first *kultur'nost* Chinese cadre in literature. He reads, to Luo's great scorn, *Dream of the Red Chamber.*

This literary reference is packed with allusions. First, it was discussed in the political campaign against Yu Pingbo, and the reading shows that Zeng follows the campaign and even takes care to read the original in order to form his own judgment. Second, Zeng does not read a contemporary novel of revolutionary activity, but a classical novel, which shows that he has a balanced and reasonable attitude towards the past. Third, his reading contrasts with Luo's lack of cultural interest, his ignorance, and emphasizes that a "rich cultural life" is an important ingredient in the new personality. Borzov in Ovechkin's text also has no interest in reading, and Liu Binyan's later bureaucrats epitomize this trait of Luo's. Before the "facts will prove" in the story whose line is right and whose wrong, Liu contributed his own telling detail about the suffocating atmosphere of bureaucratism.

The journalist and Luo drive on a dirt road along the Yellow River. "It was a stormy day, and the car slowly went ahead in a huge cloud of dust. The little standard in front of the car was pushed right and left by the gusts of wind. Through each fissure of the jeep grains of sand blew in. I could nearly feel how the sand gradually penetrated to the very roots of my hair." This storm is the natural metaphor for the meeting at Zeng's bridge site, where Luo has been confronted with manifold criticisms and suggestions by the workers instead of a docile crowd listening to his report. "To lead workers is much more difficult than leading soldiers," Luo complains, incensed. Soldiers are not supposed to present their opinions and criticisms about the plans worked out by their leaders. As long as there are directives from the Center, Luo feels things cannot go wrong. "I often think what else do we need as long as we have the correct leadership of the Party?" Certainly not criticisms and suggestions from below. "There is only one rule: not to make mistakes! Not to make mistakes is victory! But this rule is difficult to follow." While Luo develops his philosophy in this manner, the dust gets ever thicker. "It was now completely dark. In the car's headlights there was a sea of dust. On our clothes and our skin a yellow layer of dust had gradually settled. The dust clogged the nose, breathing was made difficult by acrid dryness."

This is reminiscent of the scene in Nikolayeva's novel where Chalikov describes the yellow landscape where the dust of Arkady's philosophy slowly settled on his mind and eventually nearly suffocated it. In a story by Alexander Yashin, "The Levers," which came out in the Soviet Union at about the same time, the room where the local Party committee, which in the story is described as infested with bureaucratism, meets and discusses is eventually so devoid of oxygen that the candle simply dies.[8] Bureaucratism is suffocating the mind, we are told

---

8. Alexander Yashin, "The Levers," in Patricia Blake and Max Hayward, eds., *Dissonant Voices in Soviet Literature* (New York: Pantheon, 1961).

through these metaphors, which became part of the metaphorical canon of the reformers.

The test of practice eventually comes with the river's factual and metaphorical spring tide. Liu Binyan changed the time schedule of reality here to fit his political intentions. He redated developments of 1954 to 1955. In fact, the old bridge (here repaired by Zeng's team) survived what was probably the worst flood in decades in early 1954, and was finished prematurely in June, while the arch bridge's second pillar went under, and construction was resumed only in November; eventually it was finished in June 1955. In Liu's story, the crisis occurs in spring 1955; then, the youth-shock-brigade movement was in full swing. In some rural areas people "spontaneously" formed cooperatives. The Yellow River is an old metaphor for China in its historical development. Now, there is a feeling of spring, the "thaw" brings much water, and the test.

Liu used the water metaphor in his later 1956 work, where the river stands for life in all its turmoil, and swimming for a physical contact with life. The "downsurge" of the river here evokes the *gaochao* high tide of socialism proclaimed by Mao in his collection of reports about the cooperatives. On a symbolic level, the tide, we may expect, will wash away such persons as Luo and, indeed, the pillar that is just being built as his bridge collapses, while Zeng organizes his workers to keep up with the water's rising tide, and they finish their work ahead of time.

The two levels of metaphoric action are not well integrated. The allusion to the spring tide of the river must have evoked in the reader's mind the general devastation wreaked by overflowing rivers in China, and by the dreadful floods of 1954 and 1955. This threatening aspect of the "high tide" of socialist and collectivist enthusiasm of the people carries the metaphoric load of much hostility towards the bureaucrats in the mind of Liu Binyan. Their network is to be washed away. The high tide as used by Mao, however, was more benign. It mostly referred to enthusiasm. Liu Binyan did not clear up this ambivalence in his language, and in fact we have two layers of text here. On the surface layer, the metaphor is orthodox with spring as the season, and high tide of political and labor enthusiasm swelling all hearts. By tying the story to the big flood and the destruction of the bridge pillar, there is a subliminal threat and hope that the bureaucrats and their structures might be washed away, and violently so. Liu Binyan took issue, metaphorically and perhaps unintentionally, with the essentially benign form of the anti-conservatism drive which never threatened the bureaucrats with a loss of their jobs and positions. The aggressive pitch of the high tide metaphor in his story is that of class struggle, although the theoretical environment is not.

In the final confrontation, Luo desperately phones the Bureau in Beijing for directives while his support bridge and first installations for the pillar are washed away in the floods. He calls Zeng with orders to evacuate the site of his bridge, but there everybody is at work in a well-prepared and well-planned battle to stay above the water level with the new pillar; the telephone remains unanswered. Zeng is able to finish his bridge, we learn from the papers, ahead of time in mid-June, while work on Luo's bridge has to be interrupted until November when the water is again low enough to permit resumption of work after a huge loss in labor, materials, time, and machinery. Luo is content to have asked for directives in time so that "no mistake" was committed, and is proud that no one was hurt or killed.

In October 1955, Mao's July talk on agricultural cooperatives was published, and another much higher *gaochao* (high tide) swept the country: "The labor enthusiasm of the masses was like a tide (*chaoshui*) breaking through the dikes erected by the conservatives." "There had been," continued Liu Binyan, "such high tides of labor enthusiasm in the past, and there had been movements for technical reforms with mass character, but none of them were ever as vast, and as fast. This was the first time the spearhead of the mass drive was primarily directed against conservatism and bureaucratism." Liu Binyan was well aware of the importance of Mao's change of direction. This was the first time the inner-Party bureaucrats were targeted instead of some "class enemy." The workers were quoted by Liu with the exultant words "Chairman Mao backs us."

It would seem that Zeng's line is vindicated both by his success with his bridge, and by the Chairman's call for a battle against the "conservatism" of the leadership where even Mao's term is "taken from" the earlier report by the worker correspondent in Zeng's bridge team. When the reporter returns in February 1956, he finds that Luo has faithfully followed the most recent directive and organized criticisms of bureaucratism and conservatism "from the base to the top" so that the workers are supposed to criticize their own conservatism first, then come the middle levels, and, in the end, comes Luo, too; earlier he could not act much differently "because there was no directive." As it turns out, Luo Lizheng had already managed to transfer and demote his young challenger engineer Zeng to work in a cement factory in May 1955, even before work on the old bridge was finished. The Party secretary, the third in a single year, had again been unable to prevent this.

In the realities of China, Zeng's mass appeal, technical competence, and success, even his top-level political vindication through the movement against conservatism, have one simple consequence, we are told by Liu Binyan: Zeng Gang is removed from the scene by the bureaucrat in power, who always adapts to the newest line, but never forgets to remove the irritants that disturb his peace. It is a Chinese peculiarity that the "invisible machine," as Liu was to call it twenty-five years later, manages to increase its own power in each movement, even in those directed against its very parts and members, while the young activists are doomed even if their suggestions eventually make it to the top and become policy.

The text ends with the sigh of the journalist:

Unbounded despair suddenly welled up in my heart. I also felt distress and anger. I had thought that today, in the midst of such a nationwide high tide, it should not be too difficult to combat and topple (*fan diao*) the conservatives, or at least make them regain consciousness. I have been wrong. The trouble is exactly that men like Luo Lizheng don't make a stand against this tidal wave; the trouble is that the problem is not just one of conservative thinking. . . .

Outside, the storm hollered from the nightly Yellow River. It seemed as if one could hear the breath of spring filled with life through the window. The spring from the north sent this wild wind to clear the way for spring. And my friend [Luo] still sat there, his eyes filled with drowsiness. Spring wind, when finally will you blow into this office?

Beyond being a part of the social contention of the time and thus a source for its social history, the text presents a reasoned history of the events leading up to the "spring" at the end, which was to be the climate in which the "hundred flowers" were to blossom. The two chief protagonists, Luo and Zeng, as well as the cohorts for whom they stand as "typical" examples, part ways in the same rhythm as the two aspects of the 4th Plenum Resolution evolved into different directions. Zeng throws himself into the Five-Year Plan, and his critical attitude is powered by his desire for a faster pace of advance. He develops ever closer links with the young workers, and combines, in the idealizing features of the text, mass line with technical know-how and personal engagement. Luo takes the line of "strengthening the unity of the Party" and strengthening the leadership of the Center, that is, himself and the immediate administrative hierarchy to which he is attached, to ward off the threat to his comfort coming from the young activists. He and his peers use the Sufan charges of "undisciplined" and eventually "anti-Party" against Zeng Gang, while Zeng attacks Luo for being a bureaucrat.

In the context of the story, the two possible prongs of the Resolution are thus appropriated by two different sections of the political class: The administrators go for Party unity against critics whom they would eventually cast in the role of anti-Party elements and class enemies; the activists, on the other hand, take the encouragement to criticize shortcomings of their superiors. In the subtext of the story, Liu Binyan argued that this very Resolution and the political activity following it forced the activists, who based themselves on the second part of the Resolution that encouraged criticism, into the mistake outlined in its first part. In order to evade bureaucratic interference, Zeng has to set up an "independent kingdom" at his bridge and ask as seldom as possible for directives, becoming *wu jilü* (undisciplined) in the process. As his successes have given him some confidence, he indeed is somewhat *jiaoao* (proud), the very core negative attitude outlined in the first section of the Resolution as the cause of anti-Party individualism. As for the Chairman, Liu Binyan's statements in the story were less an analytical attempt to depict his position than a *captatio benevolentiae*, an attempt to win him over for the coalition of progress.

In fact, it had been Mao Zedong who had emphasized Party unity; it had been he who had enunciated the vague terms *pride, individualism,* and *conceit* as features indicating anti-Party elements and even the hidden counterrevolutionaries; finally, it had been he who had edited the Hu Feng materials and spelled out the theory of the exacerbation of class struggle under socialism, which provided a solid ground for the administration to increase its political control over every aspect of life. Nothing of this is mentioned in the story, but, when Mao came out with his criticism of "conservative thinking" in the speech published in October 1955, Liu reported that "the workers" said that Mao supported them, and that this was the "first time that the spearhead of a mass drive was primarily directed against conservativism and bureaucratism."

In the context of the story, the Chairman is merely taking up the slogans developed by "the workers" and articulated by *their* intellectual, Zeng. While admitting the importance of Mao's "support," the movement itself develops independently in the story, which implies that it cannot be stopped by leadership fiat either. Mao's support furthermore does not change much; the brunt of the anti-bureaucratic resistance is to be carried by the activists, and the bizarre "specifically Chinese" result is that the instigator of the drive against conservative thinking is transferred to a lower post and remains there as the "conservatives" take over the leadership of the anti-conservatism drive.

Liu Binyan was not interested in writing the history of factional struggles but in analyzing the social dynamics of the new republic, and its guiding political lines. The text was written in full knowledge of the relevant works of both Ovechkin and Nikolayeva, and of their polemics, and it took a stand on the issue. Nikolayeva's bureaucrats disappear or are convinced on the strength of Nastya's technical rigor and eventual success. In Ovechkin's "Daily Rounds . . ." the "soft" leadership qualities of Martynov create the human and social conditions for the application of better technology, and Borzov has to be toppled and transferred before a substantial change becomes possible. In Liu's text, the polemics against Nikolayeva are continued. Zeng is technically excellent and successful, like Nastya, and he has as close links with the laboring masses as she does. But, as opposed to Nastya's fictional fate, Zeng experiences the more realistic Ovechkinian fate: "Sometimes I envy you journalists and writers. Whereever something good occurs or an experience is completed, you go and write it up, it is published in the paper, and your duty is done. . . . But how does it go in reality? Something might quite evidently be good, and an experience might quite evidently be successful, but once you want to apply it in grand style, troubles arise."

This is what actually happens in Liu Binyan's story; Nikolayeva's solution is implicitly denounced as being (at best) the naive fancy of a fiction writer. What, then, is the structure of the obstacles engineer Zeng is confronting?

Luo is only one of a number of administrators in the story. According to the rules of typicality, it is possible to infer Liu's assessment of the danger of bureaucratism quantitatively from the number of representatives of this affliction in the story, and qualitatively from their relative rank. Within the bridge-team leadership and the Bureau under which it is operating, there is not a single "Martynov," not a single person supporting Zeng actively. "Public opinion" on both levels is strongly against this rash young man, and the administrative leaders are immediately willing to use political criteria to put an "anti-Party" hat on their opponent, already a very heavy charge. There is much loyalty and mutual understanding among these people, who share basic values and attitudes. From Luo himself we hear about the extent of this homogeneous group and network with its inward-directed loyalty. In the eyes of this group, at the level of the Minister understanding for administrative constraints already becomes weak, and he is likely to put grand demands on the administration to get in tune with a "mass movement." For the Minister this is still "trouble," political accommodation out of fear of negative consequences should he not promote the mass movement. Beyond that, in the Center, the Politburo and the State Council, things look bad. Leaders there are likely to make reckless demands on the administrators because they believe in the claims of the mass movement (here, to double the norms) and have little knowledge of real life.

This homogeneous group of bureaucrats in the middle reaches of the body politic finds a positive echo among a part of the intelligentsia, represented here by the engineer with the telling name Zhou Weiben, the *weiben* standing for *weihu benshen*, protecting one's own interests. This part of the intelligentsia is qualified enough to assume technical responsibilities, and weak enough to stand in for the better protected administrators as all-purpose targets when some campaign is under way. When the movement to criticize conservative ideas comes, Luo suggests Zhou Weiben as a good representative of such ideas. The negative strategies of these bureaucratic administrators center around the notion of trouble avoidance. They are not only content with the status quo; they actively defend it. Their positive strategies focus on administrative and political control over the base-level activists, and on preventing the establishment of any direct link between the two sources of their troubles, the enlightened leaders in the Center, and the base-level activists.

Luo prevents the publication of Zeng's experiences, and is incensed at his sending up suggestions, bypassing the clogged channels of communication. The behavioral ideal and strategy of Luo and his peers is indicated by his name *lizheng,* a military term meaning "stand at attention" when facing a superior and receiving orders. The officer is not supposed to *ti yijian,* come up with criticisms when receiving orders from the general, and he can expect the noncoms to have the same attitude towards his orders, and so on down the line. As long as the order is executed verbatim the lower levels carry no responsibility and make no mistakes. Luo confides to the journalist: "There is a saying 'Leading soldiers is like leading a tiger.' I think leading workers is even more difficult than leading soldiers. I really envy the army cadres. In the army there's no need to call on the soldiers to discuss strategic plans, and it is completely out of the question for soldiers to criticize their commander . . . But here in our place . . ." The military-command structure had been the environment in which these cadres had been groomed, and they could claim that it had proven its effectiveness by the fact that the Communists won the contest. Finally, the common strategy of the group is to avoid openly opposing a movement supported by the Center, but to take over the leadership of the movement, thwart its intent, and possibly use its momentum to eliminate its activists as possible opponents. Liu Binyan made this point most radically many years later, when the "invisible machine" in one locality actually uses the rectification movement of 1985 which is directed exactly against the members of this "machine," to eliminate its critics. Borzov does make a stand and asks for the transfer of Martynov. Arkady ditto; he comes out openly against Nastya, and wants to have her dismissed. As the Center comes out in support of the Nastyas and Martynovs, the unrepentant bureaucrats can be removed from the scene, although not from the administration.

This, too, had been the purpose of the reformers in Liu's story, to "oppose and replace" the "conservatives," wash them away in the "high tide" of the mass movement as the Yellow River had metaphorically washed away the structures erected by Luo Lizheng. But, although the "high tide" is there, and the political climate of "spring" with which it customarily comes, the Chinese administrators are more skilled than their Soviet counterparts. "The trouble is exactly that men like Luo Lizheng don't make a stand against this tidal wave"; the structures he had erected were washed away but he had asked for directives in time, and thus had committed "no mistake." Liu Binyan then added the ominous line "The trouble is that the problem is not just one of conservative thinking. . . ." an open-ended thought where the reader is to fill in the ellipsis. Liu Binyan took issue with the target definition of the movement coming from the Center. The Center had defined "conservative thinking" among cadres with otherwise good standing as the problem. The story seems to indicate that, as long as no institutional measures are taken (removal), these people stay in power and manage to thwart any effort by the young activists. Obviously, they are not just people with "conservative thinking" but have evolved into a solid body of well-entrenched, politically conscious, and skilled operators, defending their prerogatives and preferences against even the most obviously rational innovations, as well as the climatic pressures of this spring. As opposed to the Soviet stories, even those by Ovechkin, which strike an optimistic note, the journalist ends his investigation with "unbounded despair," "distress and anger," at the hopeless task of the two weak forces—the editorials and the young activists—in making any headway against that strong force, the administration, with its great assets of power, skill, and time.

Opposing Luo and his crowd is a coalition of progress, the main protagonist of which is Zeng Gang. As a member of the intelligentsia, Zeng Gang has the honor of being the first intellectual hero in Chinese literature since Mao established the "worker-peasant-soldier" orientation of literature, with its straightforward consequence of reducing the ranks of possible heroes to these three segments. Taking a hint from Ovechkin, Qin Zhaoyang had grafted his second district secretary on Martynov, by letting him go for some time to the Party school to get an education. But Zeng Gang is the first real intellectual hero.

In the text, the enormous environmental pressure relating to this issue is felt in great stress and a number of deformations. First, Liu used the instrument of typicality to express that he was not dealing with a heroic class of intellectuals. Two of them appear in the story. Traditionally in leftist writing, the intellectuals are not a "class" but an intermediate buffer between the antagonistic classes, and some will side with the revolution, some others with the counterrevolution. The ambivalence might be expressed through a class division in the parent generation (father: landlord, mother: poor peasant concubine), opposite types (revolutionary versus Guomindang spy), or other devices. Here, one half of the intelligentsia, the Zhou Wenbens, side with the bureaucrats, the other half with the progressives.

In order to have a progressive intelligentsia hero in the inimical environment of these years, Liu had to put much padding around him. The workers love him; he cares for their private happiness as well as for labor organization; he takes the lead in work; he is scientific and takes up the suggestions from the workers on how to integrate general scientific truths with the specific conditions of the site; he is interested in the great questions of the nation and the world; and is even *kultur'nost*, reading the *Honglou meng*. In his disputes with Luo, he is exclusively motivated by the wish to promote the public welfare, and there is no trace of careerism or private interest in him. His complete devotion is epitomized by the absence of a partner for his private happiness. This portrayal in its fantastic exaggeration confronts all the charges leveled against the "bourgeois intellectuals" in the preceding years, and Liu felt all this was necessary to establish the legitimacy of the new-style hero.

Zeng is in charge of the managerial and the technical aspects of his building site, and he is a member of the Youth League Committee, and thus a part of the political leadership, indicating in one person the three core realms where the young intelligentsia activists were to challenge the established leadership. The text does not set the Youth League against "the Party" or "the bureaucrats." True to the constant laments in the Youth League papers, where articles and editorials blasted away at the middle-level leaders of the Youth League for obstructing the activists, the general secretary of the Youth League for this brigade under Luo cooperates with Luo in thwarting the direction of the Youth League "control stations." However, while not all Youth League cadres share the Stakhanovite spirit, the Stakhanovites all seem to come from the young generation, the Youth League in particular. The working class enters the story early in the text in one single unified personality, the worker who declares that Zeng Gang is the kind of engineer under whom his colleagues want to work. There are no lax or backward workers in the text; they are a unified progressive group. Their effectiveness, however, depends on whether or not they have leaders like Zeng Gang. They may be, and are, dismayed at Luo Lizheng's and Zhou Weiben's proceedings, but there is nothing they themselves can do in terms of improving their labor. Engineer Zeng's role in the plot corresponds to the line then advocated in Youth League articles, "The young technical personnel have to march in the forefront of this movement [of advanced producers for the early fulfillment of the Five-Year Plan], and have to become the organizers of this movement."[9]

In fact, the powers of the base-level activists are nil; all they can do to express their protest is to keep the memory of the date of Zeng's dismissal. In terms of values and appreciation, the worker and intelligentsia base-level activists are thus fairly unified, but they lack discretionary power. They find eventually that their aspirations are "supported" by the top leaders through Mao's speeches and the "editorials." To make it quite clear that this support does not carry institutional weight, Liu Binyan had the "editorial" line of the Center materialize in the "anemic" Party secretary of the brigade. He supports the editorial line, and understands quite well the problem of Luo; he comes out against branding Zeng Gang an "anti-Party" element and tries to prevent Zeng's transfer elsewhere, but in neither endeavor is he successful. After his first intervention, Luo continues to threaten Zeng with the "anti-Party" hat, and, after the second intervention, Zeng is transferred.

In terms of tactical sophistication and actual power, the representative of the Center is weak and anemic compared with Luo and his associates; the name Zhang Zhihua might indicate this weakness with *zhihua* probably being the short form for *zhiqi, zhiyuan,* or *zhixiang* (aspiration), and *huafei* (spent), making him Zhang With-the-Spent-Aspirations.

9. Dong Xin, (Secretary, All China Federation of Trade Unions), "Qingnian gongcheng jishurenyuan yao zhandao xianjin shengchanzhe de hanglie lilai" (Young engineers and technicians must accede to the ranks of advanced producers), *Zhongguo qingnian* 8:8 (16 April 1956).

There was a tradition of not contradicting another cadre in public. "Zhang Zhihua of course could not be entirely free from the fetters of this tradition. Furthermore, the trouble was that, if you made up your mind to put the problem on the table and everybody delightedly chipped in to struggle for the clarification of the truth, things still did not go according to hopes, since the opponent dodged your spearhead and was unwilling to accept battle." The top and the bottom of the coalition of progress thus had some knowledge of each other, cooperating with public-opinion appeals and exemplary actions, but both failed to impress their opponents, who did not read the editorials and were uninterested in the activists' successes. Needless to say, in the polemical tone of the text there never is a question who is wrong and who is right. That there might be some wisdom in the "bureaucrats'" obstruction of the rapid collectivization of agriculture or campaign-like industrial development, or that both sides might be wrong in their assessments, is never considered a possibility.

The authorial voice of the journalist shares the character features of Zeng. First, he comes to the site without assignment; his paper did not send him. Being advised to interview Zhou Weiben, the journalist takes his own stand, and, after careful investigation, comes out in support of Zeng and his approach. Both go into uncharted land, explore new possibilities and problems. Although the position of the authorial voice is very clear, no mention is made of an article about Zeng written by the journalist, nor, of course, of the consequences of such an article. In fact, Liu wrote the story which was this article, but he did not make it a topic of the text itself. Such fictional anticipation would have been quite possible, even in a *texie*. However, it would seem that such a described publication would have lacked "typicality." In fact, texts mentioning such problems as the ones prevailing at the bridge sites were an extreme rarity at the time in China. Liu's text was among the first.

Literature and journalistic writing were as weak as the other parts of the coalition. The *texie* could help members of the coalition understand each other and their opponent better. The focus of the text thus is on Luo Lizheng; with a device borrowed from Nikolayeva, Zeng is introduced through the opinions and attitudes of others towards him. Once informed of the actual situation, the authorial voice shifts its unfocused view, and observes Luo from the perspective of Zeng and his supporters, situating the authorial voice among them. It is an investigative *texie*. The Center misinterprets the problem as being merely "conservative thinking." Zeng in turn is unable to understand the obstacles into which his effort is heading. The authorial voice shares the features of Zeng, but, while he advances into the uncharted lands of organizational and technical innovation, the text proceeds, endowed with the same virtues as Zeng, to explore the social dynamics, and find out about the moves and motives of the "other side," Luo and his people.

Ovechkin had defined the *texie* as the "scout" of the literary army. Liu Binyan operated in exactly this tradition. The simile interacted with and rejected the "cog-and-screw" simile used by Lenin and Mao, and might deserve some attention. The scout (*zhenchabing*) is a military figure, sent ahead of the main body of the army to explore what obstacles lie in the way of advancement. He has a general mandate, but has to operate independently and to make his own decisions once out in the open. His own people cannot give him specific guidelines. They have to rely on his unswerving commitment to their cause and trust him in his independent investigations. This makes for a uniquely complex relationship in a military environment. The scout is a common soldier, not an officer or a general. However, he is required to report the facts on the "other side," and these reports might contradict the assessments of his own leaders, and reflect on weaknesses in the ranks of his own people in terms of understanding the situation. There is a tradition of blaming the scout for the facts he reports, charging him with having changed sides and supporting the other side. But there is also a tradition that an enlightened leader would never blame the scout for his reports. Given the critical potential of his job, and the independence of his operation, the scout is in a structurally unstable position with regard to his own leaders. And of course there is the danger of his misreporting. However, the factuality, immediacy, speed, and analytical penetration of his reporting on the basis of a fundamental commitment to serve the cause operate excellently as a behavioral model of the *texie*-writer, with his "Party conscience" and the fast, hard-hitting and analytical *texie* as his instrument.

The *texie* as a genre is thus defined as the scout of the literary army. The *texie* writer embodies the virtues of this scout with his independence and loyalty, devotion to facts and critical poise, outspokenness, individual initiative, and daring.[10] The military simile used for the "activists of socialist construction" in the Youth League shock brigades is that of fighters "in the forefront"; the image of the "avant-garde" had already been used by the Party for itself. From the personality traits now emphasized for Zeng Gang and his people it is quite clear that they share the features, in the realm of labor organization and technology, which the text and its writer claim for this literary genre of the scout-*texie*. There is a division of labor: The scout does the investigating; the activists do the fighting and producing. The journalist's endeavor is closely linked to the activity of the activists. The legitimacy of his investigation and his harsh criticism and eventual frustration with Luo are based on the close link with the productive endeavor.

Questions beyond this narrow realm like human rights, general freedom, and the like cannot now be articulated. The most immediate political criticism of a general nature is vaguely indicated in the terminology used to denounce Zeng Gang, which implies that the victims of the Sufan Movement were generally the most valuable people around, as well as the proof offered by the story that the problem was *not* just one of bureaucratism. But, in both places, the awareness of the political risks is evident from the measures taken to hide these criticisms, while they are made, in ellipses and slight changes of time (in the case of Zeng's transfer).

The relationship of the text to Soviet texts and the Soviet Union in general was very close. This was true for the genre, which was that preferred by Ovechkin and his group, and was used within the categorical framework mapped out by Ovechkin; it was true for the role of the journalist/*texie* writer, taken from the visiting journalist in Ovechkin's "Collective Farm Sidelights," who, just because he is an outsider, discovers problems there that remain hidden to the local leaders. Most important, however, Zeng Gang and his team take their orientation from the early Soviet Thaw. Their plan to "double the norms" originates there; their labor hero Stakhanov is Russian; the inspection stations of the Youth Leaguers and their "shock brigades" have been pioneered by the

10. Cf. Part 2 of this book.

Komsomol as well as the techniques of making "exhibitions" about waste of material with much criticism of the local leaders. With their preference for *zhenglun*, for "disputes" with Luo, and their habit of *ti yi-jian* (proffering criticism), they imitate Soviet habits, at least as far as they are described in journalistic and literary works. The greatest praise of the progressiveness of the Soviet Union in this period of the Thaw comes through the denunciation of the Soviet "gimmicks" (*wanyir*) by Luo Lizheng. There, people can criticize their leaders, even if not invited to do so, these things take a bold (in Luo's terms, a rash) course, and don't proceed in the "measured steps," which Luo considers typically Chinese.

In the last lines of the text, Liu Binyan had the mighty spring wind come from the "north," from the Soviet Union. While this might be considered climatically bizarre, it reflects his political assessment. The Soviet Union is the land of spring; the ice is thawing, while in China, around Luo's office, the political ice is still on the ground, preventing the "hundred flowers" from budding. The stage was thus set by early 1956 for a conflict; the protagonists were in place, and had settled for their fields of action.

The movement to suppress counterrevolutionaries went on throughout 1956 together with other harsh measures; 60,000 *liumang* (rowdies) were reported arrested and sent to labor reform in 1956 in the Shanghai region alone, many of them unemployed youths.[11] The papers reported a flood of arrests of "counterrevolutionaries" throughout the year, and did not fail to point out that events like the Poznan riots in Poland proved that the bourgeoisie and the agents of imperialism were hidden in the ranks of the Revolution, and that more vigilance was necessary.[12] The cooperative movement was forced ahead by cadres eager to meet their quota with methods soothingly called "commandism,"[13] but which in many areas were outright coercion. Although not comparable

11. *Guangming ribao*, 14 April 1957, quoted by S. Aray *Les Cent Fleurs* (p. 28, note 3), p. 56.
12. Editorial, *Renmin ribao*, 12 July 1956, quoted in "Political Developments in China from March 1956 to the 8th Congress," in *Saturn* 2.4:112f (August-November, 1958).
13. The *Renmin ribao* editorial on 27 June 1956 gives a seasoned account: "Before collectivization, when peasants still worked on their own, the tyranny of cadres could assume only the form of political pressure. Now, they can terrorize people by economic means. They say, since the land belongs to the collective farm, the peasants are in their hands and they can do whatever

to the Soviet collectivization of agriculture in the late 1920s, cattle slaughter was widespread, and many peasants absconded to the cities. Shanghai grew by half a million people in 1956; 300,000 people sneaked into Guangzhou between autumn 1956 and spring 1957.[14] The Sufan Movement to suppress counterrevolutionaries provided ongoing legitimacy for the use of denunciatory vocabulary and the advocacy of stern measures against young critics.

A few months into 1956, many of the young intelligentsia moved on to flesh out their roles in their fantasies, words, and actions. Literary texts that reflected their aspirations better than Nikolayeva's Nastya gradually became the fashion, namely Goethe's *The Sufferings of Young Werther*, and Romain Rolland's *Jean Christophe*.[15] Young Werther enters a suffocating world of feudal officialdom with all its pompousness, conceit, and cunning, and is depressed. In his private life, his love for Lotte is frustrated by her narrow circumstances which do not permit her to break her engagement to a man both nice and boring, and follow her own passion. The helplessness of young Werther in these subjective and objective structures leads him to the only grand emotional deed at his hands, suicide. Jean Christophe is modeled upon Beethoven and depicted as the genius breaking out of the narrow confines of tradition and society, and setting up his own art and emotions as the standard by which he lives. Both novels echo the emotional pitch of Nastya's Chinese disciples in their gloomy realization that they were no real match for the prevailing attitudes and powers, and echoed their aspirations, born of the frustrations of a minutely regulated existence, for the grand deeds and emotions in both their public and private lives.

Throughout spring and summer, the Youth League papers did not spare strong language to support them, publishing letter after letter on

---

they want. Whoever does not obey will see his income reduced or his right to work suspended." Cf. Aray, *Les Cent Fleurs* (p. 28 note 3), p. 54.

14. *Laodong bao*, Shanghai, 14 March 1957; *Nanfang ribao*, Canton, 16 March 1957, quoted in Aray *Les Cent Fleurs*, (p. 28, note 3), p. 56; see also "Political Trends in the People's Republic of China from January to March 1957," in *Saturn* 3.3:203ff (1957), for these and other sources.

15. Zhu Gùangqian, "Wei shenme yao fang? Zenyang fang?" (Why blooming? And how?), *Zhongguo qingnian* 13:17 (1 July 1957). The article includes a unique glimpse of the changes in preferred reading matter among young intelligentsia.

the obstacles put in the way of the Nastyas, attacking Youth League and other cadres with scathing words in editorials for obstructing the "newborn forces," and headlining articles in boldface with such titles as "Absolutely Don't Bend to Elements Who Disregard the Laws and Throw the Rules into Disorder,"[16] "Don't Criticize Indiscriminately and Don't Suppress the Legitimate Zeal of Young People."[17] Following the abortive Nastya debate, the Youth League opened a broader discussion on the "kinds of people we should educate," with the same method advocated by Hu Yaobang for Youth League periodicals in general, that is, readers' letters, and articles by nationally renowned intellectuals.[18] On 1 April, *Zhongguo qingnian* published, with boldfaced title, the article signed Zhi Guang "Don't Polish Off Their Edges (*lengjiao*),"[19] which started:

> If you cooperate with many young comrades in your work unit, please answer this question: What kind of young people would you enjoy having? This is not a question invented out of the blue; in fact it has been posed by the young people themselves. This is the situation: Several thousand youths have written to *Zhongguo qingnian* detailing their feelings after having read *The Director of the MTS and the Chief Agronomist* by the Soviet writer Nikolayeva. Among them there are those who say that, when they had just graduated and moved into life, they had been "full of enthusiasm and full of confidence." Once they saw weak spots or mistakes at their work sites, they actively came forth with their criticism in the style of Nastya, and made suggestions. However, some of the comrades there did not appreciate this at all, declaring they were inexperienced, had insufficient practice, did not see all aspects of a problem, and they even said [the young people's] attitude was bad, and they had ideological problems. Having gone through this several times, some youths beat the drums of retreat. But others still persevered, and wrote to the papers or to higher levels. And what was the result? They were criticized and incriminated for this as "lacking organization spirit, and lacking discipline," "aggrandizing themselves and loving to show off," etc. In this manner, the drive of these

16. "Jue bu xiang weifa luanji fenzi qufu" (Absolutely refuse to bend to elements who disregard the laws and throw the rule into disorder), *Zhongguo qingnian* 9:10 (1 May 1956).

17. Jiang Ming, "Buyao lanshi piping, sufu qingnian de zhengdang jijixing" (Don't criticize indiscriminately and don't suppress the legitimate zeal of young people), *Zhongguo qingnian* 10:2f (16 May 1956).

18. It became an established category in *Zhongguo qingnian* 11:38ff (1 June 1956), which came out on 1 June 1956 and remained so through issue no. 15, moving in the last issues to the very top of the table of contents.

19. Zhi Guang, "Don't Polish Off Their Edges" (p. 63 note 26), pp. 28ff.

youths gradually petered out, their "edges" were polished to roundness. Step by step they became "routineers" (*laolian*), failed to see fresh things, and got used to regarding defects and faults as normal. This situation does seem to prevail in more than only some scattered units.

The article gathers from the perusal of many readers' letters that this unequal confrontation between the young challengers and their elders leaves the former depressed in spirit (*qingxu kunao*) and deprives them of their energy for work (*gongzuo bu qijin*). Some are even *qingxu xiaochen* (altogether dejected). The author rejects the arguments proffered by the cadres disciplining these youths as but self-serving fabrications. "In fact they fear that their own weak spots will be pointed out by daring, 'edgy,' creative youths, and they fear that they will not be able to prevent their losing face."

The methods of criticism were detailed in a later issue under the title (boldface) "The Habit of Putting Hats on People at Random Must Be Changed."[20] Especially young Youth League cadres were quick to denounce contacts among good friends as "small clique activity," read criticisms of irrational practices in the assignment of jobs as general dissatisfaction with work, and the like. In August, the Youth League published an investigation of how cadres had constructed a complete conspiracy out of a group of friends. The article with the (satirical) title "A Scandalous 'Small Clique,'" reported how these young people in a school in Sichuan province were charged with "being like the Gao Gang Rao Shushi alliance," with "attempts to split the organization, . . . attempts to usurp the leadership of the League, . . . private criticism of the leadership and sabotage of the leaders' prestige, . . . provoking and disseminating disagreements." In fact, the accused were but young critics of their leaders' bureaucratic airs, and, after two Youth League reporters investigated the case, the Party leadership intervened to save the "clique." The young critics found no sympathy among their peers who cheerfully joined in the move against them, contributing eponyms like *tufei* (bandit) to the already long list.[21]

---

20. Fang Qun, "Yinggai gaibian luan kou maozi de fengqi" (The habit of putting hats on people at random must be changed), *Zhongguo qingnian* 11:7f (1 June 1956).

21. Ding Panshi and Yu Kun, "Yige hai ren tingwen de 'xiao jituan'" (A scandalous "small clique"), *Zhongguo qingnian* 15:10ff (1 August 1956).

Friendship thus was a place where young people would discuss "defects of the organization (League or Party), the leaders, or other comrades," which could be read either as secret opposition to "the leadership" or as a source of strength for more indomitable criticisms, the latter being the reporters' attitude. Other articles established the new values of a "straightforward character (*zhishuai de xingge*), lively work style (*shengdong huopo de zuofeng*), independent thinking (*duli de jianjie*), broad ideals (*yuanda de lixiang*), revolutionary drive (*geming de jinquxin*), and spirit of daringly battling for truth," which characterized the "socialist new man";[22] in more general terms, Feng Xuefeng argued that "the main problem is (how) to develop in young people the strength and creativity of a democratic spirit and independent thinking."[23] Authors advised young people not to be intimidated, and, if bad came to worse, to adopt Dante's motto and "go their own way without concern for the talk of others;"[24] to illustrate the point, a story called "Experiment" was published[25] in which a young engineer, obstructed in his innovative drive by both the chief engineer and the manager, does his experiments secretly and successfully with worker support, and eventually gets his way after many appeals to the top leaders.

This story, however, was fiction, and the upbeat note was didactic. Most young people bent to the wind. After having been charged with sticking their noses into things that were not their concern (*duoguan xianshi*) in order to aggrandize themselves (*zigao zida*) and to stick out their necks (*chu fengtou*)[26] and in general corroding the unity of the collective (*ba jiti tuanjie fushi*), they started to close their mouths (*guanshangle zuiba*), drop their pens (*fangxiale bigan*), and turn into weaklings (*nuoruo de ren*)[27] with a strategy of keeping on the right side of everybody (*baochi yituan heqi*), not caring about other things (*shi buguan ji*),

22. The terms are used in the editorial note introducing the column "What Kinds of People Should Young People Become?" *Zhongguo qingnian* 11:38 (1 June 1956).
23. Feng Xuefeng, "Qingnianmen de fazhan ye yao 'baihua qifang'" (In the development of young people, "Hundred Flowers" have to bloom, too), *Zhongguo qingnian* 14:3f (16 July 1956).
24. Yu Guo, "Should Youths Not Be Richly Endowed?" (p. 64 note 31), *Zhongguo qingnian* 11:12 (1 June 1956).
25. Su Hui, "Shiyan" (Experiment), *Zhongguo qingnian* 13:28ff (1 July 1956).
26. Zhi Guang, "Don't Polish Off Their Edges" (p. 63 note 26), p. 29.
27. Dan Tong, "Concerning the Problem of Nastya" (p. 141 note 26), p. 17. Cf. also Hu Bowei, "The Influence of Dogmatism" (p. 67 note 39), p. 29.

keeping themselves out of trouble (*gaogao guaqi*), and following the time-honored principles "Knowledge does no good" (*mingzhi bu dui*) and "The best is to talk less" (*shaoshuo weijia*).[28] This transformation was described in many letters published in 1956. In the face of their earlier aspirations, present transformation, and bleak prospects for dramatic improvement, given the situation of both League and Party at the base level, the word most frequently used to describe their mood was "depressed" (*qingxu kunao*) or even *qingxu xiaochen*, mixed with a feeling of shame, (*cankui*),[29] for having adapted. Liu Binyan's alter ego with its frustrated sigh in the end of the story reflects this feeling.

This mood notwithstanding, efforts continued to carve out, at least in the only area where this was possible, in print, some legitimate leeway for the new personality in other realms beyond work, such as clothing, hairdos, evening entertainment, private relations, and private hobbies. Even a first article on sex appeared which declared that sex was not harmful to young people but would lead to blindness and other ills if enjoyed too early and beyond measure.[30]

Young people started to make extensive use of the option to write to the press. In August, *Zhongguo qingnian* received 50,000 letters, twice the number from July, which again had been up sharply from June.[31] An open challenge was mounted to Mao's theory of the necessary exacerbation of class struggle in June and July 1956 in the periodical *Xuexi*, which, prior to the founding of *Hongqi*, operated as the Party's theoretical organ. The authors bluntly stated that this theory was wrong, which implied that the Sufan Movement, the basis of this theory, had to be reconsidered. Nevertheless, this was but a challenge, not a reversal.[32]

The literary texts of the period by some of the young Youth League

28. Fang Qun, "This Habit" (note 20 above), p. 7.

29. Zhi Guang, "Don't Polish Off Their Edges," (ch. 4 n 26), p. 29.

30. "Guanyu xing zhishi de jige wenti" (Some problems of sexual knowledge), *Zhongguo qingnian* 13:27 (1 July 1956).

31. "Jingao laigao tongzhi" (A sincere word to comrades who have sent manuscripts), *Zhongguo qingnian* 13:24 (1 July 1956); "Benkan zhongyao qishi" (An important communication from our journal), *Zhongguo qingnian* 19:29 (1 October 1956).

32. Zou Shumin, "Guodu shiqi de jieji douzheng shifou hui riyi jinruihua?" (Can class struggle get ever more acute during the transition period?), *Xuexi* 7:22ff (1 July 1956). Zhang Jing, "Guodu shiqi nongcunzhong de jieji douzheng ye bushi riyi jianruihua" (Class struggle in the villages will also not get ever more acute during the transition period), *Xuexi* 7:42 (1 July 1956).

writers reflected, generalized, and intensified the conflict and the characters operating on both sides. Being literature, they aspired to broader generalization than newspaper reports, and, using the specific code of fictional language, they were able to deal with issues and concepts long before they made their way into the language of officially approved political documents. This was already true for the first story of Liu Binyan analyzed above, and we shall find more evidence in the subsequent pages.

NINE

The Challenge in the Press:
Liu Binyan's "Inside News"

Liu Binyan's "Inside News of our Paper" (first part) was published in June 1956, the title printed in boldface in the table of contents, and heading the list of the long pieces; again, a *texie* ranked first.[1] In the editor's comment at the end of the issue, Qin Zhaoyang further emphasized the importance of the piece. At a time where "everybody has already become used to literary works opposing rightist conservative thinking, this *texie* brings up a new problem; In life there still persist manifold networks which fetter people's initiative, creativity, and labor enthusiasm and hinder life's development. But how complex are the causes for the formation and development of such networks!"[2] Through the depiction of various characters in this piece, Liu explored this formation and development. In this first part, the top bureaucrat, the editor of the paper, Chen Lidong, is described only through other people's eyes and experiences, and not in his own right.

Qin Zhaoyang encouraged Liu to write a sequel, and this intention is mentioned in the postface. Given the structure of the political system at the time as well as the forms of political contention, the "reformers" could focus on the press to create some public opinion, and they could focus on Party recruitment because there the composition of the Party

1. Liu Binyan, "Benbao neibu xiaoxi" (Inside news of our paper), *Renmin wenxue* 6 (June 1956).
2. "Bianzhe an" (Note from the Editor), *Renmin wenxue* 6:125 (June 1956).

in the future was decided. The most controversial stories of 1956, Liu's "Inside News" and Wang Meng's "Newcomer" focused on exactly these two realms. Early in 1956, when "At the Building Sites" was written, contention was still impossible. No article wrote up engineer Zeng's experience, and the personnel office transfers him without further ado. "Inside News" is set in spring and early summer 1956, and now both the Party-controlled press and Party recruitment criteria were being challenged.

The story provides again a chronology of change. Things began to move in fall 1955 (after the publication of Mao's speech) when "times worked themselves up into ever higher waves, . . . the pace of life accelerated, and the layers of protective walls built up long since from old habit and blind belief were broken through in greater measure. A great many people whose progress had been very slow started to free themselves from ossified thinking."

One of the characters of the story who had gone into bureaucratic stupor is shaken up enough to go for a trip to the countryside to see the "upsurge of socialism" with his own eyes. Two articles written by another journalist on rightist conservative thinking among cadres in the countryside, however, were not published then. Since the beginning of 1956, things moved further. "The criticisms made in the papers still lagged behind the development of the objective situation" (which Mao had said about the cadres in general). "Although now those cadres who were criticized were all below the level of the rural and city districts (the *xian* and *qu*), criticism had started at least, and quite pointed forms of criticism like the short satire (*xiaopinwen*) had made their appearance. . . . Most recently, a new atmosphere had gradually come about in the newspaper offices: People from the highest to the lowest ranks seemed to become ever more inclined towards thinking things over, and they started to show an interest in debating problems. . . . When spring came this year, the situation changed still more. The Propaganda Department of the Provincial Party Committee criticized the papers for being too monotonous (*dandiao*) and dry (*kuzao*), and some editors also asked: How should papers be run? . . ."

Elated by the new developments, one journalist in the story breaks into a paean on spring 1956:

What a spring is this spring of 1956! A spring full of good things, brimming with joy! The grand victory of the socialist transformation of industry and trade, the advance towards science [a movement started in January calling for greater scientific achievements], the reform of salaries [salaries were increased in February], the movement of advanced producers [the sequel to the "activists of socialist production" movement, which had held a great congress in March 1956], the work done with regard to the top-ranking intellectuals [subsequent to Zhou Enlai's speech "On the Question of the Intellectuals," conditions for such intellectuals improved]. . . . how should we call this? . . . What general term should be given? . . . Ai, yes, excellent—the ever greater unfolding of people's initiative, yes?

Political changes, production movements, and improvements for the intelligentsia all came together, and in this glorious list the only thing missing is what is usually considered the beginning of this new phase, Mao's remarks about a "hundred flowers" being allowed to flourish, and Lu Dingyi's speech elaborating on this. In the perspective of the activists at the time, these came at the end, not at the beginning, and were not even mentioned as important in this June 1956 text which, as a note by Liu claims, had been written in February. The dramatic changes in outlook and attitude among a public that a year before made resentful murmurs against the paper and now asked for definite changes; the new leadership, which after the replacement of the provincial Party secretary called the paper monotonous and dry; and the journalists, mostly in their twenties, who used daring and free words and thoughts— nothing of this did lead to significant changes in the paper. The articles describing problems in the province still remained "inside news" for limited distribution, and were not printed. The title of Liu Binyan's story played on this, insinuating that this very story depicting the inside ruminations and conflicts in a provincial Party paper might in turn become "inside news" for limited circulation, since few of the literary journals were willing to print such hot matter.

"Inside News" starts with a literary criticism, and a literary program. The young heroine, Huang Jiaying (Huang-the-Beautiful-Heroine), is recalled from a mine in Heilongjiang province where she had been investigating workers' complaints. In the train, she reads one of the early PRC industrial novels, *Tieshui benliu* (Molten iron flows) by none other than Zhou Libo (who remains unnamed), the author of the *Baifeng zouyu* (Hurricane). After her fourth attempt to read on, she muses: "Why was it that life and characters in so many novels were depicted as so commonplace, so trite, and so simplistic as if after Liberation people had lost all strong emotions and had at once become polite and eternally smiling people who held their meetings at the fixed times, and traveled only between work and home. Some of these books really read like a factory log. And some people even said that this was called 'recording life.' Does life really look like that? No, absolutely not!"

The genre *xiaoshuo* (novel and short story) could not hold the attention of those members of the intelligentsia really investigating the conflicts in society; being fiction, this genre embellished reality, and failed to expose the problems and conflicts prevailing "after Liberation" among those who might have supported the Revolution. That a young writer would take on such an opponent like Zhou Libo who was furthermore heralded as China's greatest contemporary author by Zhou Yang himself, the man in charge of literature in the Propaganda Department of the Party, was quite a feat.

Zhou Libo himself wrote much *baogao wenxue* (reportage literature) and had, as will be shown elsewhere in this volume, translated Kisch's pathbreaking *Secret China* into Chinese. Liu Binyan thus took issue with that brand of socialist realism that claimed to describe real events and persons in slightly fictionalized form ending up with bland "factory logs" without conflicts. Huang Jiaying, like Liu Binyan, himself a journalist in the industry section of the paper, sees her form of journalistic writing as closer to life, more truthful. "Inside News" thus makes a grand claim against the established authorities both in writing and in the political administration of writing.

Also in the opening paragraphs of the text, Huang takes on the factual situation prevailing in her paper. The paper is a *dangbao*, a Party paper of the leadership of a province. Within the text the name of the train station where she arrives is that of a station in Harbin, and the paper would thus be the *Harbin ribao*, confirmed by a later article by a journalist from this paper, as well as Liu Binyan's remark that this was the "worst paper of the nation."[3] The name of the paper here is changed

3. Huang Sha, "Expose the Reactionary Blabber" (p. 43 note 14).

to *Xinguang ribao* (New light daily), an ironic title, composed of two frequent components of PRC newspaper names; this enhances the generality of the story.

Having investigated the workers' complaints in the mine and supported their "strike" (refusal to attend meetings) against the leadership, Huang is suddenly recalled to her paper. Obviously, the mine's leadership complained to the editor. Her paper does not support her in this investigation, and, when she sits down to write up the results of her investigation, she ends up tearing the draft to pieces, since the conflict between the things she feels should be reported and the anticipated objections from the editors cannot be harmonized. The editor-in-chief holds the orthodox view that a Party paper should spread the Party's opinions and directives. Whatever he is given and told from higher levels he will print. *Linghui lingdaoshang de yitu* (to fathom the intentions of the leaders) is the technique he uses to decide what should be printed. Huang on the other hand, a 25-year-old female Youth League member who is not even in the Party, sets out to "express as forcefully as possible her own thoughts" in her articles, and her mentor in the paper, Cao Mengfei (Cao-with-the-Flying-Dreams), explicitly advises her "not to blindly follow [orders from above] . . . but to form a habit of independent thinking (*duli sikao*)." Because of this habit, and her penchant for "thinking and investigating," her articles are not printed even when she "blunts their points," reads *her* articles with "*their* eyes," and generally becomes more *xueguai* (skilled in the art of compromise).

The official realist literature is thus dominated by boring embellishers, and the papers' leaders refuse to publish investigative reporting about problems in the country. In this context a battle for the solution of one individual's problem or the publication of one article seems wasteful. The situation cries for fundamental reforms, and, since the party single-handedly manages the levers of power, Huang sets out to solve "the problem of greatest concern for her," namely "that she was not a Party member." She will enter the Party "without hiding her own opinions"; they should become those of the Party. The two specific problems depicted at the outset of the story—the workers' problems in the mine, and Huang's trouble with having her articles published—are thus quickly abandoned in the plot, and attention focuses on the broader conflict as well as the struggle for the general orientation of the Party and its power.

In the depiction of Huang Jiaying, the text evinces many signs of the stress under which it was written in mid-1956. First, Huang enters the story as an intellectual supporting the workers in the mine, not as a member of the intelligentsia in her own right. From her support of working-class demands, she derives some legitimacy. Nonetheless it is a great step from engineer Zeng with his immediate function in material production to Huang-the-Beautiful-Heroine in the newspaper.

Second, Huang, we are assured, is enraptured by the grand sights of progress and construction in new China. Liu Binyan forestalls his potential critics: "Exactly because there were so many good things which moved her, those which she felt were deficient upset her no end." Generally, Huang is not a depressed character; despite her "frustration" with her shredded article and ordered departure, she is impressed with the achievements visible from the train window where she sees "every village building bridges" which "sets her off thinking about many things. Sometimes, her thoughts were so happy, and then again they would roam far away." But altogether "how interesting life was." Liu Binyan defended her (and himself) against an ever-present charge of looking for the "dark aspects" of an otherwise glorious reality. While these passages stress the socialist idealism motivating Huang in her investigations, they also are part of the general scenario in which the conflict is set. The great things characterizing "spring 1956" given above as well as the constantly repeated metaphor of spring within the story itself depict a very favorable general situation with the emphasis being on the willingness and devotion of the workers and the intellectuals to contribute ever more to the rapid development of the country.

Compared to "Building Sites," the intellectuals and their realm have achieved greater prominence here. But from the very outset it is clear that these "newly born" and mostly youthful activist forces are running into an obstructive maze with their drive. In the mine, turners are kept "on reserve"; at present they are not needed there, but urgently needed in other plants. The Jiawang mine, however, hoards them for future use. In the midst of a great development of production these young turners are idle. The workers in the mine, furthermore, have to attend innumerable meetings with the effect that, after a long journey home, only four hours are left for sleeping. All remonstrations with the mine leadership have resulted in nothing, and eventually they wrote to the paper after an article had appeared there against the hoarding of skilled workers. In response, Huang went to the mine. Liu Binyan was careful to omit any reference to her being "sent" there; his journalists make their own decisions as does the authorial voice in "Building Sites."

Obviously, the immediate leadership in the factory, the managers, Party, and union personnel, form a unified body preventing the grievances of the "proletariat" from reaching the ears of the enlightened leadership at the top. The situation prevailing in the realm of material production is repeated in spiritual production. The innumerable readers' letters remain unread in the paper, just as the investigative articles on problems written by young journalists remain unpublished. The papers in fact don't fulfill their perceived potential function. Again, the paper's editor-in-chief prevents public grievances from being articulated in the press and being brought to the top leaders' attention. The leadership of the paper at this time can still rely on the provincial leadership for support, and on *Renmin ribao* for a model to emulate. Huang Jiaying, however, is convinced that the leaders at the very top would quickly move to change things if only they knew about them. "Several times already Huang Jiaying had thought of taking up her pen and writing to the Party's Central Committee to tell the Party of some of the bureaucratism, formulism, and workers' demands she had come across at base levels." In the situation prevailing in this June 1956 text, no substantial change seems possible in the paper for the time being.

Huang with her inclination to investigate things at base levels has a support cast with other prominent qualifications. Cao Mengfei (Cao-with-the-Flying-Dreams) is able to synthesize vast arrays of specific information to formulate bold suggestions for new policies at the Center; and Li Heqing with his satirical tongue tears apart the stylistic accoutrement of bureaucratism, *cadrese oder Kaderwelsch* in German, that is dull, formulaic language. With factual investigation, new theoretical propositions, and anti-bureaucratic satire the three represent the new features which came into the public sphere with the advent of the young activists. They are characterized by their positive names and good faces, a combination of good-heartedness and keen wit, and they enjoy the new leeway to dress up gorgeously, a feature carefully noted by Liu Binyan. Li sports a new "coffee colored Western-style suit," and Huang wears a "cherry-red jacket" to a rendezvous. They parade through the text in language, dress, and style of communication as the representatives of an urbane new youth culture for readers to emulate. Their lack of power finds symbolic expression in Huang Jiaying's gender, low rank in the paper, insecure political status, and youth. But they are in tune with the general political climate that comes in the guise of "spring."

They confront a diversified and formidable array of opponents. Neither the journalists on the paper nor the text itself dare to have a go at the editor-in-chief, Chen Lidong, Chen-who-Sets-Himself-Up-as-the-Ridgepole-of-the-Tent. It is a Party paper under the direct control of the provincial leadership, and thus Chen is well above the rank of the *xian* or city-district level. At this time cadres to be criticized for bureaucratism were not to be above this level, as Liu himself wrote in the story. Chen does not come on stage but is quoted with a comment about the activities of Huang and her crowd: "Ah! As far as I am concerned, some of our comrades here talk too much and do too little, with the effect that the entire paper smells too much, really too much, of intellectuals, in fact so much so that one does not find words for it. Whatever the subject under discussion, no one wastes time exploring the intentions of the leadership, but everybody comes up with his or her own seemingly plausible but in fact flawed views." From this note we know him to be an unrepentant opponent of the spring blossoming.

The text is focused on Ma Wenyuan, who heads the editorial office and is the first and most visible obstacle to the paper's reform in the eyes of the journalists. The son of a small office clerk, he has "the bookish honesty of an intellectual," which explains his personal name, *wenyuan* (literatus), although Liu Binyan spent no further time in fleshing out this aspect of Ma's character. Chen Lidong was a regiment commander and became used to receiving and giving orders, Ma worked in the underground Party organization, and had become used to receiving orders from his only Party contact. Both men, one from the "liberated" and one from the "white" areas, have kept their old attitudes after 1949:

Chen Lidong still can not listen to others; Ma Wenyuan still has not learned to speak out and run the paper as a collective effort. Both are calcified in their original postures although circumstances have radically changed. By 1954, Ma, then 33 years old, had accepted the leadership of Chen who had previously fired two other heads of the editorial office. Ma gets married, calmly calculates his advance with growing seniority and has settled in Chekhov's box. His attempts to regain his original fervor and to join up with the lively crowd around Huang Jiaying are repeatedly and successfully crushed by Chen Lidong. It is Ma who sends the telegram recalling Huang Jiaying from the mine. But he will decide on at best "one out of ten" controversial articles and defer decisions on the others to Chen Lidong. He cannot make up his mind where he belongs, and his age and opinions hover in the middle between the old and the young. In late 1955, the fever of the "socialist upsurge" catches up with him and he goes on an inspection trip to the countryside with Huang Jiaying, returning invigorated. The contact with the "mass movement," evident in his "sunburnt face," leaves him with two minds. Confronted with a controversial article, he reads it both with the eyes of potential readers from among the "people" and with the eyes of an editor, and then cannot decide. His "Chen Lidong mind" is "relatively authoritative, but very often out-of-date, and in some sense even wrong." His "Huang Jiaying mind" is "relatively new and original (*xin-ying*) but also not that solid and reliable." "What a wonderful thing to have views of one's own!" Although much younger than Chen, Ma has been pushed by his senior into senile rigidity, and consequently his face "seemed to sag a little more every day"; he is old-looking. The fundamental difference with Chen which is depicted through his "honesty" and intermediate age finds expression in the first part only in his internal ruminations. In terms of the techniques for expressing and limiting typicality, both Ma and Chen are broad types lacking features in their background which would limit their representative functions. Such limiting features are usually described through an unusual background such as growing up in a monastery or having a foreign mother. Chen stands for the older Party administrators with military background and ways rigid beyond salvation; Ma is intermediate in age and rank, from the "white areas," and ambivalent in his thinking, but as an "honest" person may be saved.

Liu Binyan did not classify all young people or Youth Leaguers in the progressive category. Developing the character of engineer Zhou-Protect-his-Own-Interests from "Building Sites," he here introduced Zhang Ye. Zhang Ye shares youth, education, and a penchant for fashionable clothes with the other young journalists, a similarity with them expressed in his being Huang's fiancé. But he has learned the craft of adapting his views to the exigencies of the situation. As Chen Lidong runs the paper, Zhang Ye toes Chen's line. When journalists in 1955 expressed dissatisfaction with the way in which Chen Lidong ran the paper, he skilfully deflected attention by charging Ma Wenyuan with handling his job badly. A smooth political operator, Zhang Ye's personal name *ye* stands for *yexin*, political careerist. Predictably, he and Huang Jiaying will not get along.

The point of contention is the role of a Party paper and the attitude of a Party member, two facets of the same problem. The reformers' demands for a change in the paper are not based on general considerations of freedom of the press. Rather, the problems Huang discovers in the factory, like hoarding of labor power, endless and numerous meetings, or exhaustion of the workers could not be addressed except in the press. The workers had made their complaints to the leadership with no result; the Party organization of the mine held a congress where none of these issues were discussed. The editorials in the national papers had already criticized all these things, but there was no channel through which the workers in their labor enthusiasm could communicate with their enlightened top leaders. For the benefit of the working class, the Party, and socialist construction it is thus necessary that the papers fulfill their crucial role. They must stand in the forefront of the battle against "bureaucratism and formulism" and must be the first to print the "demands of the workers." In fact, Huang charges, their paper lacks both "mass character and fighting spirit." It does not galvanize the masses' criticisms into a concentrated fighting force against bureaucratism. With a bristling new Thaw word, Liu Binyan said the paper lacked *minganxing* (sensitivity) for new issues, which is evident from the fact that readers' letters pile up unanswered and unprinted, while a simple telephone call from higher levels will fill an entire page with the pronouncements of some administrator.

Skillfully, Liu Binyan made some of his points by attaching them to seemingly innocuous passages. Cao Mengfei advises Huang that she should not try to become a social-welfare institution by supporting destitute letter writers with her own money, but should take action to bring about a situation where the responsible government organs take care of such matters. "You have to remember every moment," he adds, "that you are not an ordinary individual but a reporter on a paper; you should not through actions like this give people the impression that our paper is something like a government organ." The actual meaning of the statement of course goes far beyond the immediate issue.

Cao Mengfei generalizes the many letters and reports about the hoarding of workers and the poor care the personnel departments take of them by boldly suggesting what was suggested again thirty years later, that "people should be allowed to choose where they want to work; this would be more practical than the present system, and also would give more elbow-room (*huodong yudi*), and thus would be advantageous." If the control of the administrators over the workers were reduced, Liu argued, people would have more "room for movement" as the verbatim translation runs. This new word, which branded Liu Binyan with the charge of preaching "anarchism," seems to inspire the politics of the entire text and of its protagonists. In the paper, too, the journalists want more *huodong yudi*.

Both sides in the controversy can claim the authority of an ongoing campaign. The Sufan Campaign provides the factory administrators with the familiar word *individualistic* when the turners ask for work, and with *undisciplined and without organization spirit* when they eventually complain to the paper. The young worker Liu Shifu (Liu-Wealth-of-the-Age) who accompanies Huang to town to take his colleagues' cause to the provincial authorities, is suspended from "no-work" to write his self-criticism. The "all-too dense air of intellectual(ism)" in the paper, mentioned by Chen Lidong, again comes from this campaign as well as the implied charge of dissatisfaction with the leadership. Huang Jiaying and her friends, on the other hand, quote Mao's collectivization talk when they charge "Criticism in the paper develops only after the objective situation has already developed," or, the paper lags behind reality. They use the new slogans of "bureaucratism" and "formulism" against their superiors, and emphasize their own youth and independent thinking.

In terms of the actual power constellation, little has really changed in this first part of the story, but tension rises. Apart from one single editorial, written only after direct intervention by provincial leaders, no articles of the new kind envisaged by the journalists appear. Chen does not even have to come on stage to keep things under control. However, there is much movement at the base among the workers, among the journalists, and in the top leadership; Chen's paper is out of tune with the climate. Ma evolves from Chen's servant into a split and torn personality with much sympathy for Huang and her ways. Huang is ever more estranged from her fiancé, Zhang Ye. "The fact that the paper doesn't dare to bring up social problems is a social problem in itself," she says, and complains about "the many rules and regulations about what you can do and what not. Why shouldn't the paper let the Party Committees and the government hear the voice of the masses?" All this is *bu shiji* (unrealistic), her fiancé replies, and recommends that she not mention any of this at the Party meeting which will decide on her application for Party membership. This suggestion ends their relationship; she walks away with long strides without turning around, and the story ends. The division between the two camps on every level has become so deep that a love relationship between the two representatives is impossible. Huang Jiaying adds a defiant note from the new youth culture, telling herself, "If someone has kissed you once, does that mean you are his forever?"

The story, progressing to the very moment of its being written and published, has an odd structure. It takes up a great number of issues — hoarding of workers, the meeting craze, the unresponsiveness of the papers, the beginning changes in a middle-level bureaucrat (Ma), the question of Huang's Party membership, and so on — but, although changes are discussed and aspired to, none come about. The paper does not publish any other articles; Chen Lidong's control is unchallenged; no Party meeting discusses Huang's application.

The conflicts, however, deepen; both sides have their arsenal of words ready with which to denounce their opponents. Within the mine and the paper the challengers of the bureaucratic order are on the rise and well in tune with the general political spring climate, and it may be expected that an open conflict will soon erupt. At the time of the writing, in June 1956, both sides are just discovering who are their friends and who their enemies, and only in the most sensitive area, that of private relations, is the line actually drawn.

The technique is clearly taken from Ovechkin who ended his "At a Meeting" with a little postface stating that, at the time of the writing, things had not evolved further, and therefore he had stopped there, true to the principle of *texie*. Ovechkin had written sequels to "At a Meeting" later with the same protagonists, and it is not surprising that Liu Binyan took up the suggestion by Qin Zhaoyang to write a sequel to this story later. This sequel came in October. Since, in the meantime, Wang Meng's "Young Man" had been published, and, since the political situation had evolved dramatically, it is an altogether different piece. It will be discussed after Wang Meng's story.

TEN

The Challenge in Party Management: Wang Meng's "Newcomer"

Wang Meng's "A Young Man Who Only Recently Joined the Organization Department" is a short story written between May and July 1956, and published in *Renmin wenxue* in September, the month of the 8th Party Congress;[1] Wang Meng claimed in 1979, with some justice, that the piece was meant as a salute to the Party Congress.[2] Wang Meng was not a complete novice in the field of literature. Born in 1944, he had joined the Youth League in 1949 and had been sent to the Central Youth League School; his experience during these years had become the material for his first work, *Qingchun wansui* (Long live youth), serialized in part in the Shanghai *Wenhuibao* in 1956.[3] He had published two short stories in 1955 and 1956;[4] the latter, "Spring Festival" ("Chunjie")

1. Wang Meng, "Zuzhibu xinlai de qingnianren" (A young man who only recently joined the Organization Department), *Renmin wenxue* 9:29ff (September 1956). For a translation, cf. Wang Meng, "The Newcomer," tr. G. Barmé, in G. Barmé and Bennett Lee, *Fragrant Weeds* (Hongkong: Joint Publishing, 1983), pp. 71ff, and, in German, G. Will in W. Kubin, eds., *Hundert Blumen* (Frankfurt/M: Suhrkamp, 1982). For a Chinese recent interpretation, see Liu Wentian "'Zuzhibu xinlai de qingnianren' fenxi" (An analysis of "A Young Man Who Only Recently Joined the Organization Department"), in Shiliusuo gaodeng yuanxiao, ed., *Zhongguo dangdai wenxue zuopin xuanjiang* (Guilin: Guangxi Renmin, 1984) Vol. II, sect. *xiaoshuo*, pp. 138ff.

2. Wang Meng, "'Zuzhibu laile ge nianqingren' suotan" (Trifles concerning "A Young Man Who Only Recently Joined the Organization Department"), *Dushu* 1:81 (August 1979), originally written on 3 January 1979, immediately after the 3rd Plenum.

3. Wang Meng, *Qingchun wansui* (Long live youth; Beijing: Renmin Wenxue Press, 1979).

4. Wang Meng, "Xiao douer" (Little bean), *Wang Meng xuanji* (Tianjin: Baihua Wenyi Press, 1984), I, 367ff., and his "Chunjie" (Spring festival), *Wenyi xuexi* 3:36f (March 1956).

depicts a high-school student who returns for this festival to meet his girl-friend. She has abandoned the prospects of going to university, is a pri-mary-school teacher, and has found a purpose and fulfillment in this profession, as well as a boyfriend of equal sturdiness. The student leaves, distressed about his own queer values and lack of purpose in life. This was immediately read as an unfavorable depiction of university students and led to a stern article some months later in which a student claimed that, in fact, his peers were brimming with purpose.[5] Wang Meng had partic-ipated in the Congress of Young Literary Workers earlier in 1956 and was, with Liu Shaotang, Deng Youmei, and some others among the small group of young writers who had made a name for themselves and were now much sought after by editors. In summer 1956, when he wrote "New-comer," he had already become a Party member and worked in a district office of the Youth League in the capital. He was thus familiar with Youth League work in the big city, and with the problems encountered by the new crop of young intelligentsia called forth by recent Youth League poli-cies and moving into administration offices. There are two texts of the story, one Wang Meng's own text, the other the text edited by Qin Zhaoyang and published in *Renmin wenxue*. Since the public first read the latter text, and the discussion centered on that edition, we shall base our analysis on the public document. The changes wrought by Qin were made public in May 1957 in *Renmin ribao*, and the recent editions at the hands of Wang Meng himself restored the original text.[6] As the changes mark intentionality, they are indicative for Qin, and the study of the orig-inal version is vital for an understanding of Wang Meng himself.

The time of the story is March 1956; winter is nearly over, the air is thick with "something half rain half snow." The story is told by an omniscient narrator, his focus is on the "Young Man Who Only Recently Joined the Organization Department," as the published title went. Before, he had been a primary-school teacher. We are told a story about a young member of the intelligentsia who moves into a respon-

---

5. Ze Lu, "'Chunjie' shifou waiqule daxuesheng mianmao tanqi" (Does "Spring Festival" mis-represent the features of university students?), *Wenyi xuexi* 8:6 (August 1956).

6. Wang Meng, "Zuzhibu laile ge nianqingren," in *Wang Meng xiaoshuo baogao wenxue xuan* (Beijing: Beijing Chubanshe, 1981). The original passages changed by Qin Zhaoyang were pub-lished in *Renmin ribao*, 8 May 1957.

sible position in a Party office, a city district's Organization Department in charge of Party recruitment. The decisions taken in this place were not general appeals to public opinion but powerful institutional measures. The recruitment, promotion, and demotion of Party members is the main duty of this office as well as decisions on leadership personnel. The composition of the Party in the district depends on the decisions of this office as much as the composition of the "counterrevolution," as all personnel files are handled there. The Organization Department would set the criteria for Party recruitment and advancement. This is a much more important place than an industrial site, because the decisions made here have long-term effects on the composition of the leading bodies. Any advance made here will be multiplied through the department's discretionary powers, and any problems existing here will also be multiplied. The story never explicitly makes the point that the district is a district of the nation's capital, Beijing. But some familiar spots from Beijing are mentioned, and the "young man" has an article published in *Beijing ribao,* a paper for local distribution; thus the locale is set. Run by the powerful Beijing Party Committee under the leadership of Politburo member Peng Zhen, the city was, in principle, administered directly by the Center, and not by a provincial leadership. Wang Meng thus used a technique similar to Liu Binyan's in marking the "typicality" of the problems he addresses. This is a District Party Committee in the Capital directly administered by the Center, and the best forces are evidently assembled in such an important place. Whatever trouble will be found here is likely to haunt other areas much more severely.

The Young Man fits the description of the Youth League Propaganda Department, which recommended Galina Nikolayeva's novel to "students above upper-middle-school level and young cadres in (government and Party) organs with a relatively high educational level." The Young Man has done his homework and finished reading the book. He carries it in his pocket to his new job to "learn from Nastya," and act on her principles. His name, Lin Zhen, announces him as "Earthquake Lin."

When he arrives at the office, things look fine; the prestige of the District Party Committee of which the Organization Department is a part is so high that the driver of the tricycle transporting his things will accept no payment; the janitor helps him to unload his things, and calls Zhao Huiwen, who does secretarial work in the Department, to meet the newcomer, and she does so with a warm "We have been expecting you for so long." Zhao's facial expression, however, foreshadows problems in this idyllic and prestigious place. "In her beautiful white face, her large eyes shone with a friendly glimmer, but the skin under her eyes was blue with fatigue."

Lin Zhen, the Young Man, eventually meets his colleagues in the Organization Department and the District Party Committee; they all show similar signs of wariness and lassitude. The man who de facto runs the Department, Liu Shiwu, continuously smokes, a literary trope implying bureaucratic attitudes. He has a routine way of rattling out political phrases and principles, is *lengmo* (cold and indifferent) in his work, compares himself to a doctor, who, it is true, cures people, but it does not find the task pleasant, and eventually says that office workers inevitably are drained of their original fervor like cooks who lose their appetite because they are always handling food. He feels he has lost his *reqing* (enthusiasm) and is now *pijuan* (wary). Whatever Wang Meng's intentions with the name of this man might have been,[7] the public read the Shiwu (verbatim: "the-world-is-me") as the *shiwu* for "routine" which appears in the text itself and was a much discussed topic in the bureaucratism debate under the names of *shiwuzhuyi* or *shiguzhuyi*, "routinism."[8]

Under Liu and directly above Lin Zhen is Han Changxin, a young man with the air of a senior cadre whose eyes get drowsy when he hears about the problems in the district, trumps up glorious success reports, and has a marriage party which, for Lin Zhen, is so "suffocating" that he leaves. Han's personal name, Changxin, marks him as the opportunis-

7. Wang claimed in "Trifles" (note 2 above), p. 91, that he was unaware at the time of the possibility of using homophones for purposes of indirect allusion, claiming that this became a habit only in the early years of the Cultural Revolution. His critics in 1956 and 1957, however, were perfectly familiar with this possibility.

8. Wang Meng complains in "Trifles" (note 2 above) about critics reading Liu Shiwu as an allusion to *shiwu* or *shiwu zhuyi* "routinism," or even *shigu*, which also means "routined" in a negative sense. For such readings, see: Kang Zhuo, "Yipian chongman maodun de xiaoshuo" (A short story full of contradictions), *Wenyi xuexi* 3:20 (March 1957); Zeng Hui, "Yipian yanzhong waiqu xianshi de xiaoshuo" (A story that gravely distorts reality), *Wenyi xuexi* 12:9 (December 1956); Xin Gu, "Meiyou langhua de 'jilun'" (A rapid without "spray"), *Yanhe* 2:72 (1957); Yi Liang, "Bu jiankang de qingxiang" (An unhealthy tendency), *Wenyi xuexi* 1:18 (January 1957).

tic career-minded young cadre "ever-with-the-latest-wind" depicted by Liu Binyan in Zhang Ye. Above these two leaders there is the sickly head of the Department, whose physical decrepitude parallels his mental state, and the head of the Party District Committee, who loves to think in broad theoretical formulae and is bored with detailed facts. Finally there is the really bad egg, the factory manager, Wang Qing-quan, an ironic name "Wang-Pure-Source" for a womanizer who fell under the sweet temptations of "bourgeois lifestyle" when working as a Communist underground agent in the ranks of the Guomindang. These types represent the variations of bureaucratic transformation. One, the last, has a heroic past, but has been corrupted by the "other side" and is unwilling to change his ways. Others are in the wrong place given their qualifications and interests, like the head of the District Commit-tee; still others received sinecures in offices for earlier merits, or because they are related or married to someone in high office. The focus how-ever is on the most important representative, Liu-the-Routineer, who has a revolutionary past as a student leader, is a perceptive and capable administrator, and has fallen victim only to the professional disease of administrators.

The most dangerous group, however, are the young operators who lack past merits in the Revolution, like Han Changxin (Han-Ever-With-the-Latest-Wind). They smugly pursue their careers without any interest in the common good and lack any awareness of their dismal state. Alto-gether, the "bureaucrats" are referred to as "they," *tamen,* implying a cohesive "we," and general statements can be made about "them." "Their defects pervade the very achievements of our work as dust per-vades the beautiful air; you can smell it, but you cannot lay your hand on it; that is precisely the difficulty," Zhao Huiwen says to the Young Man, an image from the familiar stock of metaphors. Student readers, it was reported, found this a very apt description.

In an often-used image, the "Party" is described as the "heart of the people, of the class." Its work here is administered by the Organization Department and the "heart" is thus covered with layers of "dust," which threaten to suffocate it. The suffocating climate with smoke filling the air prevails in Liu Shiwu's office and at Han Changxin's marriage cere-mony, and it contrasts with the fresh spring air outside; but, as from Luo

Lizheng's office, this fresh political air of the socialist upsurge is kept out. "In April the east wind started blowing [i.e., this movement picked up steam]. . . . But business in the District Party Office was unaffected by this change in season."

Wang Meng traces the growth of the young forces opposing the bureaucratic degeneration with much the same technique as Liu Binyan, through a depiction of his hero's past. Lin Zhen became a teacher in fall 1953; he is thus a trainee and graduate of the "new society," no longer a product of "bourgeois education." Although older colleagues predicted that he would quickly succumb to the routine of his job, he has kept his exemplary devotion, and even received a citation. The further pedigree of the Young Man's attitude is much like the one depicted in Liu Binyan's story. The text was written after Lu Dingyi's elaboration on the Hundred Flowers policy had appeared, but it does not mention this document; by setting the action before the official beginning of the Hundred Flowers debate, Wang Meng claimed that the Young Man was not inspired by these statements from the leadership, but that the leaders' statements were in fact only the generalization of the individual experiences of the Lin Zhens, an implied argument already familiar from Nikolayeva and from Liu Binyan. However, while the argument carried much glory for the leadership for so truly following the mass line, in fact it established the claim that the young activists and not the leaders were in the forefront of this battle. Having no real-life model to follow, Lin Zhen writes into his copy of Nikolayeva's book his resolution "Live after the fashion of Nastya," that is, his resolution to live as a quotation. His name, Earthquake or Thunderstorm Lin defines his program. For readers who had overlooked this indication, Zhao Huiwen spells it out: "You . . . will whip up some wind and waves." Lin Zhen has inherited from Nastya and Zeng Gang the quality of being "like a child" who "loves to dream." In January, Lenin had been quoted in the press with a statement that revolutionaries had to be like children who love to dream about glorious things,[9] as a counter-quotation to the "steady and realistic" criterion upheld by the "conservatives."

<hr>

9. Yan Chen, "Rang women chashang huanxiang de chibang" (Let us rise on the wings of fantasy), *Zhongguo qingnian* 1:5 (1 January 1956).

Lin continues to be amazed that things are not as they should be. He is *danchun* (uncomplicated), resolves "absolutely not to tolerate evil things," and supports workers in voicing their criticism. When being invited for the first time to attend a meeting of the Standing Committee of the District Party Committee, he ponders whether he should speak up about the defects of the Organization Department. True to his original resolution, he encourages himself: "Taking part for the first time in a meeting of the Standing Committee, wouldn't it inevitably be too rash to come up with such an outspoken (*dadan*) speech. Don't be afraid! Don't be afraid! he encouraged himself."

He speaks up, using words of criticism like *apathy, procrastination,* and *irresponsibility* and speaking of a "crime against the masses" perpetrated by the colleagues in his Department. When the head of the Standing Committee lounges into an abstract consideration of the philosophical issues involved, Lin somehow gathers the "courage" (*yongqi*) to insist that this leader speak about the specific problem. In terms of action, Lin Zhen has come to the conclusion that it is wrong to wait until "conditions have matured," as Liu Shiwu recommends; he encourages the workers in a factory to voice their grievances to *Beijing ribao* without asking for directives from the Department. This amounts to a defiance of the procedure advocated by his superiors, and it is through this defiance that his great deed is eventually achieved, namely the dismissal of the factory head. Zeng Gang had defied orders from Luo Lizheng to move everyone off the work site, and had managed to keep ahead of the rising flood so that work could go on and his bridge was finished ahead of time. The "disobedient-hero" pattern established by Nastya, the doctor in the Heilongjiang forest, and the PLA film hero had become standard for fiction. Lin's characteristics are duplicated by Wei Heming in the factory, and they are in tune with the workers, who appear as an anonymous and unified mass aspiring for higher production without any further differentiation; it had been the same in Liu Binyan's story.

The confrontation in Liu Binyan's story is in the production realm; here, it moved one level higher into the administration itself, to which, since January 1956, a very substantial number of young intelligentsia had been transferred. The issue involved, however, remains the same. We are not dealing with "democracy" or "freedom." The workers in a factory are led by a "relative" of Zeng Gang's, Wei Heming, a man in charge of production management and Party work, originally put into this position by the now criticized general manager. The workers want to join in the general "upsurge of socialism" now thundering through the capital and increase production. The general manager, however, plays checkers and poker; quality is at its lowest, and, if complaints arise, he criticizes the workers for sloppy performance.

Lin Zhen achieves his legitimacy by supporting the workers' drive and their Wei Heming from within the Department. By fall 1956, things had evolved to a point in the universities that some students would publicly suggest that democracy was a "goal," a *mudi,* so that articles in the Youth League press had to remind them that, in socialism, democracy was not a *mudi* but a *gongju,* an instrument or a method (*fangfa*).[10] In a stunning turn, Mao would assert in his contradictions speech in February 1957, it was both,[11] but in the version published some months later he went back to stage one; it was only an "instrument" to be discarded when it proved ineffective. By subordinating the workers' assertion of the right of assembly (to discuss their grievances and formulate their letter) and of the right to publicly express their views (by writing an article for the press) to their desire to remove obstacles in the way of the production drive, Wang Meng maintains the *gongju* line. There is no abstract principle of democratic freedoms, but some of them are needed in emergency situations when internal avenues of solving problems are clogged.

The depiction of this clogging forms an important part of the text, as it does in Liu Binyan's *texie.* The reader joins Lin Zhen and Han Changxin in an investigative tour of the factory. The facts there tally with Lin Zhen's assessment. Han Changxin then produces a report quoted at length in the text; there, the problems have vanished, and the successes of a modest production increase are ascribed to the positive influence of the two newly recruited Party members, and, since Party

10. Jiang Ming, "Minzhu shi fangfa, er bushi mudi" (Democracy is a means, not an end), *Zhongguo qingnian* 23:34ff (1 December 1956). See also the "correction" for this important article, "Dui 'Minzhu shi fangfa er bushi mudi' yiwen de xiuzheng" (A correction to the article "Democracy Is a Means, Not an End"), *Zhongguo qingnian* 24:31 (16 December 1956).

11. Cf. Michael Schoenhals, "Original Contradictions—On the Unrevised Text of Mao Zedong's 'On the Correct Handling of Contradictions Among the People,'" *Australian Journal of Chinese Affairs* 16:102f (1986).

recruitment is the Department's work, the Department's efforts are credited. The leaders who get these reports cannot possibly understand what is in fact going on. On various occasions, the workers and Wei Heming have offered their opinions about the general manager. This has led to a formal rebuke of the manager, but not to lasting changes.

In this political contention, both sides again make use of the key terms present in the two simultaneous campaigns. This meant that the Sufan "hat factory" was still in full swing in 1956 and 1957. Surprisingly, there is neither in Liu Binyan's *texie* nor in Wang Meng's story a single "counterrevolutionary" against whom the vocabulary of the Sufan Movement might have been used with justice. This vocabulary is used exclusively by bureaucrats to defend themselves against critics. Within the structure of indications of typicality in Chinese texts, this does not mean that the *main* aspect of this movement was its use and abuse by bureaucrats, but that this was its *only* aspect. The general manager of the factory thus harangues that the workers and Wei Heming with Lin's support had "formed a small clique (*xiao jituan*) to oppose the leadership," both charges from the Hu Feng campaign, and that the "workers participating at the meeting presided over by Wei Heming all had a problematical past," the last again a charge from the Sufan Movement.

Wei Heming is suspected of "personal motives" in attacking his manager, and further meetings are banned. A meeting of the Department is convened to criticize Lin Zhen, and Han Changxin describes Lin's action with the terms familiar from Nastya and Zeng Gang, *wu zuzhi wu jilü* (lacking in organization spirit and discipline); Liu Shiwu praises Lin's "enthusiasm" and then echoes Luo Lizheng with the principle "Criticism from below must unfold in a guided manner." Lin, he continues is "idealizing life" in an unrealistic manner; he "overtaxes himself" and "takes on too many responsibilities" in the urge to "become a hero like Nastya," which is a laudable intention but *xuwang* (unrealistic), in its claim to have a monopoly on principled (*yuanzexing*) behavior. These grades of response to Lin Zhen's activities implied grades of punishment; the womanizing, poker-playing bureaucrat casts his opponents into the categories reserved for counterrevolutionaries. The sleek young careerist demands stern disciplinary measures which might go as far as expulsion from the Party; and Liu Shiwu, the best of this crowd, says Lin has good motives but is inexperienced and a bit unrealistic, but uses neither the words for "counterrevolutionary" charges nor those for "anti-Party" charges.

All the Young Man has going for him is the weather emanating from speeches and editorials of the Party leaders, and the aspirations of the "masses." This might seem a lot, and the text makes this point, but neither affects institutional power. However, the situation is not as desperate as in Liu Binyan's story, which deals with an earlier period. Lin Zhen stays in his office. The publication of the letter from the workers denouncing the general manager is eventually the way information gets by Han Changxin and reaches the district leaders. The press and literature operate as a two-way communication channel. The leaders reach the base with editorials; the base reaches the leaders with reportages and short stories. The administrators in the Department are experienced enough to know that "conditions are now ripe" and that they should act before exposing themselves to criticism.

The general manager is removed, and Lin Zhen criticized for the action which led to this removal. Both bases are covered. Within the Department itself, nothing substantial changes. The young man suddenly becomes aware of his essential weakness in this contest. "Only then did he [Lin Zhen] realize what a disparity in power there was between him and them [Liu Shiwu and Han Changxin]." True, with extreme efforts the worst and most visible exponents of bureaucratic misbehavior can be fired. But the dismissal of the general manager is counterbalanced within the Department by the promotion of Han Changxin to be assistant head of the Department—in the middle of the campaign against conservative thinking. The bureaucrats manage the campaign against bureaucratism, and get promoted for it.

The Soviet Union, already appearing as the land of spring, of doubling the norms, and of uninhibited freedom of speech in Liu's story, is here even more the realm of the ideal. Zhao Huiwen hangs an oil painting on her bare wall at home entitled "Spring," of course to signify the Thaw, and the theme is "Moscow—the sun comes out for the first time in spring, a mother and her child go into the street." When Zhao complains about her marriage, Liu Shiwu advises her that love is not "as in Soviet films" but as in Chinese reality. The novel Lin Zhen quotes as a model for his life is a Soviet novel. And when Lin Zhen and Zhao Huiwen sit together at night and alone in her apartment under the painting of Moscow "Spring," they listen to another "quotation." Nikolayeva used Tchaikovsky's waltz on "Mid the noisy stir of the ball. . . ." as a thematic foreshadowing of her novel. Lin and Zhao listen to Tchaikovsky's "Capriccio Italien," a sequence of popular themes from Italy, ranging from boisterous trumpets to melancholy violin solos.

> . . . a soft and beautiful dreamlike melody wafted in from the distance, and gradually became energetic and enthusiastic. The lyrical theme played by the violin suddenly gripped Lin Zhen's heart. His chin resting on his hand, he hardly breathed. It seemed that his youth, his hopes, and the rebuffs he had suffered could all be fused in this music.
>
> Zhao Huiwen was leaning with her hands behind her back against the wall, not caring that lime dust was soiling her clothes and, when the piece was finished, she said with a voice as melodious as the music itself: "This is Tchaikovsky's "Capriccio Italien." It makes you think of the south, of the sea, . . . When I was in the art troupe, I always listened to it and gradually came to feel that this melody was not played by others but broke forth from within my heart."

It is not Soviet socialism that enchants the fictional heroes in this story; Tchaikovsky lived long before the Revolution, and so did Turgenev whose *House of Gentlefolk* Liu Shiwu reads avidly, "crying for the old German" piano teacher. The feeling Nikolayeva's Chalikov has when listening to the Tchaikovsky waltz, that there is some great and exhilarating emotion lacking in his own life, and that he yearns for it, is the very feeling evoked by these Russian and Soviet works in China. Russia is the land of grand emotions, of lofty aspirations, of ideal love under the full moon, and enthusiastic production drives, of fiction that makes you weep, and eternal spring weather with buds of joy and energy sprouting all over the place. It is not a utopia where all houses are painted pink and all human relations are harmonious, but rather a place where one can live fully. This foreign land is so far out in space that we know of it only through films and novels, music scores and paintings; it exists as a work of art and can be appreciated only in this way.

Lin Zhen, Zhao Huiwen, and Liu Shiwu share this appreciation.

Describing his reading of Sholokhov and Turgenev, Liu Shiwu says: "Even now I still love reading them, and when I read them, I am enchanted, but when I am finished I don't feel anything special anymore, you know . . . when I read a good novel I imagine a pure, beautiful, and transparent life. I think of becoming a sailor, or of wearing a white coat and doing research on red blood cells or of becoming a gardener who specializes in raising variegated brocade-like patterns. . . ." The sailor tours the world, the scientist explores the wellspring of life in the red blood cells, the gardener deals with literature, and weaves it into a variegated rich pattern. All three examples symbolically explode the narrow factual confines of Liu's life, and these dreams are evoked by the Soviet novels as they were by the West after 1979. None of the three has ever been to the Soviet Union; they are talking about their own fiction, and their appreciation is to be read as indicating their frustrations and a breaking out, in fantasy, from their dull and narrow circumstances.

The fact that Liu has such dreams and appreciates these works shows that his former Communist enthusiasm is still alive in some recesses of his mind. After hours, Liu Shiwu retreats into this dreamland. But when talking to Zhao Huiwen about her marriage problems, he advises her "not to make unrealistic demands." Her husband has not left her, has not mistreated her, and no political problems have surfaced. Therefore, the situation is fine. "A lot of your opinions come from Soviet films; in reality, that's all there is to it." Her idea that there should be love in a relationship is but film fancy. Solid grounds for divorce are only those enumerated by Liu Shiwu.

In office matters, Liu takes the same stand. Lin Zhen's emulation of Nastya is charming but unrealistic. "A Party worker is not suited to reading novels." Liu maintains that the alternative options presented in Soviet fiction and the fictional Soviet Union should remain in the background as dream material, while Lin Zhen insists that they should be realized on Chinese soil by Chinese living persons. But he acknowledges, *Zhen nan a* (That's really difficult). Wang Meng further heightens the status of the Soviet/Russian/other alternative by having the real villain of the piece, Han Changxin, reject it. Han Changxin calls Nikolayeva's book "very interesting and perfectly absurd (*huangtang*). Being a writer you don't get hurt even if you fall; you can make flowers rain from heaven." For him the Soviet fiction is not the realm of the ideal but of the absurd. He maintains the same attitude with regard to the Youth League control stations and the shock brigades, both of which are imports from the Soviet Union. The attitude towards this distant Soviet dream becomes the yardstick with which to measure the ultimate revolutionary qualities of a cadre. This, needless to say, is a far cry from the very orthodox position in the socialist camp according to which all other interests had to be subordinated to those of the Soviet Union and its Party.

Liu Binyan had depicted bureaucratic degeneration as a more or less irreversible process in some cadres, leading to a situation where the problem was "not just a matter of conservative thinking." Wang Meng took a different tack. His bureaucrats start with the extreme of a former Communist underground agent corrupted by the sweet life he was forced to live by way of cover, to the old and disinterested leaders, who have no record of evil deeds but for reasons of health or personal interest are unfit for their job. But the attention is focused on the most "typical" of the bureaucrats, a former revolutionary who has lost his poise and enthusiasm. He, however, can be moved to positive action if conditions require it. Once the article has appeared in the paper, he moves quickly and efficiently. At the meeting to criticize Lin Zhen, Liu Shiwu starts by saying that Lin's motives are good, and after the meeting he turns out to have been so moved by Lin that his old self shines through for a moment.

This old self had once been like Lin Zhen. Liu Shiwu dreamed of turning fiction into reality, of bringing ideas from the parking orbit of dreams onto the Chinese ground of reality. But, just as Liu Shiwu once shared Lin Zhen's enthusiasm, Lin Zhen risks developing into a second Liu Shiwu. This is further emphasized by the introduction of an intermediate step in that transition, namely Zhao Huiwen. She, too, once shared the aspirations now driving Lin Zhen. But the assorted males in her office have worn her down, she is prematurely aged, and retains her old dreams only privately. When Lin Zhen meets with a rebuff from both Liu Shiwu and Han Changxin with regard to his cherished Nikolayeva novel, he buries his copy deep in his drawer. Eventually, when his obstinate attitude shows some results, he digs it up again, resolved now to abide by his emulation of Nastya, and knowing how difficult this will be. But the steps from his enthusiasm to Zhao Huiwen's retreat, and from there to Liu Shiwu's efficient cynicism are small. Wang Meng refused to imbue his hero with the aura of eternal youth and infallibility.

Liu Binyan had made a clear distinction between friends and enemies, although he did not advocate class struggle as the method to handle the conflict. Wang Meng presented not a fundamental conflict, but a continuum of bureaucratic affliction,[12] starting with Lin Zhen's wavering and ending with the general manager's engrossment in poker and chess and the complete dereliction of his duties. The "earthquake" operated by Lin Zhen in effect eliminates the most obvious and extreme bureaucrat, who has already been earmarked; it evokes in Liu Shiwu a stronger memory of the days of revolutionary fervor to the point where he admits, "Lin's criticism is right, and his spirit has somewhat aroused me." It does not fundamentally change Liu, however. Zhao Huiwen is rejuvenated by Lin's example to the point of writing down her criticisms and setting a new goal for her life.

While Liu Binyan saw the Luo Lizhengs as hopeless cases, who have become skilled, crafty, and ruthless operators in the preservation of their positions, Wang Meng, taking a more conciliatory stance, portrayed the main representative, Liu, as a man of great qualities and some knowledge as to what his problem is, a man furthermore who does not eliminate the Young Man from the Department, while of course promoting Han Changxin at the same time. This nevertheless leaves the Young Man the option of further exerting what little influence he might have, and instills in him confidence that he might be successful if only he perseveres. In the politically most important editorial change, Qin Zhaoyang wrote a new resolution for the Young Man in the end: "Whenever I see irrational things, things that cannot be condoned, I will not condone them and I will fight one time, a second time, and a third time to the very end until the things have been changed. Therefore I should absolutely not be completely disheartened. . . . I have to be more active and warmer, but I most definitely have to be more resolute."

12. A similar point is made by Liu Wentian, "An analysis of 'A Young Man'" (note 1 above), pp. 146f. It had first been suggested by Qin Zhaoyang, "Dadaode he meiyou dadaode" (Things achieved and things not achieved), *Wenyi xuexi* 3:8 (March 1957).

Nothing of this is in Wang Meng's original. There, the Young Man says, he has "to strive with all his might for the leadership to give guidance, this was now the most important thing." The formula here, *zhengqu lingdao de zhiyin*, might be consciously vague. In this form it seems to mean that the Young Man will urge that the leadership not wait until "conditions are ripe" but give guidance and show the way.

Far from "resolutely" imposing on the leadership his own views about what is "irrational" and "intolerable," the purpose of the Young Man now is to make the factual leaders into real guides through his own action, a political posture much more consistent with Wang Meng's generally accommodating attitude towards the Party then as now than is Qin Zhaoyang's daring editing. The story ends, in both versions, with the young man "resolutely and impatiently knocking at the office door of the leading comrade." The scene implies a political program; the Youth League Nastya heroes are knocking at the door of the leadership, demanding admission with their views and criticisms. The specific purposes of the two versions are, or course, different: Qin's Young Man wants to "struggle to the end" to eliminate irrational and unbearable things, whatever the obstacles might be; Wang Meng's Young Man is the loyal critic who wants to improve leadership style and is confident of his success. He has learned the lesson (from the discussions about Nastya) that "to rely on individual courage (*yongqi*) will not have any effect" in a large and important place like the District Office, and he therefore goes for the collective in his attempt to get the entire leadership of the office moving. In Wang Meng's version, the district head has "already thrice" sent word that he wants to see him when he eventually gets the message and knocks at his door. It is by invitation. Qin Zhaoyang eliminated the invitation; thus the knock is a challenge.

Lin certainly has not achieved much. With a bitter smile, he thinks, "And you think making a speech at the meeting of the Standing Committee would have quite an effect!" He opens his drawer, and takes out that Soviet novel so derided by Han Changxin; he opens the first page on which he had written: "Live according to Nastya's model!" He says to himself: "That's hard indeed." Wang Meng thus confirmed what Liu Binyan had suggested, that, in terms of power, the young newcomers were nobodies. Wang Meng was slightly more optimistic in his assessment by having a male hero instead of a "weak" woman. The newcomers could make speeches, get an article published in a daily paper, read an editorial, and express their feeling that the political climate corresponded to their aspirations, and even claim that the Chairman himself supported them, but all this was but weak clamor compared to the solid *liliang* (power) of the administrators.

Given this situation, and the rather depressed and gloomy prospects for change, the question is what would give Lin Zhen the strength and stamina to go on with this unequal battle, and what gives Zhao Huiwen the confidence to return to her original aspirations? The young emulators of Nastya had complained in readers' letters that they were ostracized by the administrators, by their parents, and by their peers, and had caved in or withdrawn. Their social isolation was complete and the development of personal ties with like-minded others was easily denounced as "small-clique" activity in the ongoing "purge of the counter-revolutionaries" campaign. Wang Meng entered new territory in this story, by rehabilitating close and warm personal ties as an essential condition for the stability and resilience of the young Nastyas in the relationship between Lin Zhen and Zhao Huiwen. Wang Meng's original text had only faintly indicated a love relationship between the two. True, it had been a friendship between the sexes, an unusual thing in China, Zhao Huiwen being married; they went to her apartment, her husband being away; they talked about their assessment of the leaders as Nastya had done it with the young mechanics; they found that they shared the same ideals for Chinese society; they listened to Tchaikovsky's "Capriccio Italien," and, in a gesture of untrammeled freedom, they threw the water-chestnut shells on the floor. What was in this manner written silently into the text was made much more explicit by Qin Zhaoyang, who had Zhao smile with "glistening teeth" at Lin, touch his shoulder "softly" with her hand; in the most dramatic changes, he eliminated Zhao Huiwen's mother from the apartment which changed the moral climate significantly. He had Lin ask "anxiously" whether Zhao's husband might return, and he added a long paragraph close to the end where Lin talks to himself about his ambivalent feelings for Zhao Huiwen, admits his love, and convinces himself to bury it and pursue a clean friendship with her. The scene of the young people sitting together in the young woman's apartment with the spring breeze outside, the Soviet Thaw painting hanging on the wall, Tchaikovsky's music of easy and untrammeled thoughts ("Sui-xiang qu," the Chinese translation of "Capriccio Italien") in their ears, and easy and untrammeled words in their mouths, discussing their hopes for the future, their frustrations, and their ambitions with the faint melancholy of the powerless but righteous young, and the sweet bitterness of love courageously unpursued—this finally was a Chinese text in which young readers could find themselves, their moods, and their hopes.

It has been mentioned that the Sufan Movement was depicted in the story as a cheap device in the hands of bureaucrats to get rid of their critics. In the realm of private relationships, Wang Meng went a step further by rehabilitating those forms of human relations specifically denounced as the devious inroads for counterrevolutionaries of the Hu Feng type. When Zhao Huiwen says: "I see you as if you were my younger brother. . . . Life must have the warmth of mutual support and of friendship, I have always abhorred coldness," she is using the very terms, *warmth* and *mutual support*, purportedly used by Hu Feng to lure dissatisfied cadres into the counterrevolutionary camp. Qin Zhaoyang added another line, more general in nature, about the "need for warmth (*reqing*) between human beings," a statement made against the backdrop of the dramatic cooling down of human relations during the preceding years. In the openness, support, and warmth of this relationship both will say things they might not say in public or at a Youth League or Party meeting, and they do establish a bond independent of the organizational ties dominated by the Party. This bond in turn becomes the very condition for their political effectiveness as critics of bureaucratism (Qin) or revitalizers of the bureaucrats (Wang Meng); it is an organic part of a lifestyle belonging to this new type of personality.

The time they meet is also important. They meet in the evenings, and not only on weekends. Written against a factual situation where most evenings of young League members or cadres were taken up by meetings, this constitutes a demand. There is no need for organized activity, they know quite well what to do with their evenings. They have a private life, and Zhao Huiwen, in both versions, puts on a red *qipao* for her guest, the long tight skirt slit at the sides, which came back with the "dress-elegantly" campaign in spring. This "spring," in this story, is thus a spring of the fullness of life; it is the time when the buds of anti-"conservative" criticism sprout as much as those of love. Liu Binyan and most of the *texie* dealt with the former, most *xiaoshuo* by young writers with the latter, Wang Meng dealt with both, with love, with politics, and with their interaction.

Liu Binyan had focused on Luo Lizheng and introduced Zeng Gang only from an oblique angle. Wang Meng focused on the Young Man and thus his purpose was not so much to set up a model bureaucrat for criticism, but a model hero for emulation in the Nastya tradition. By endowing his hero with the resolve to live as a quotation from a novel, Wang Meng agreed with the demand that literature should have an educative function, a rule which then forced him to craft Lin Zhen appropriately. While dismissing as ill-intentioned the Sufan charges against Lin Zhen and also rejecting Liu Shiwu's suggestion that Wei Heming might have personal motives in attacking the manager, Wang Meng had Lin Zhen accept appropriate criticism willingly. Lin concedes that he was "wrong in not consulting with my superiors beforehand" before encouraging the workers and Wei Heming to meet and air their grievances. And he takes Liu Shiwu's advice not to let the relationship with Zhao Huiwen get out of proper bounds. In both the private and political realm he modestly admits to a lack of experience and maturity, which frees Lin from the charge of setting himself up as the only purveyor of truth.

His orthodox aspirations notwithstanding, Wang Meng failed to keep the story entirely under his political control. Qin Zhaoyang's emendations jazzed up the text politically, but they merely gave sharper articulation to a mood prevailing in the original itself. In the blunt formulation of a critic, Wang Meng's "art has gone beyond his insight,"[13] a conflict between political intention and the internal dynamics of a story in spite of all intentions, which has since haunted Wang Meng both in his writing and in his theoretical statements. Describing his experience in 1957, Wang Meng wrote:

Characters in fiction have, in the same manner as persons in life, an "objective existence" vis-à-vis the author which does not change with the writer's subjec-

---

13. Kang Zhuo, "A Short Story" (note 8 above), p. 21.

tive intentions. They have their own thoughts, their own joys and sorrows, and their acts have their own logic. The moment a character is written up, he is written "into life," and the author discovers that he is powerless; he cannot at will change or improve his own character's fate, and the smallest deviation from life's reality can kill off the artistic value. . . . Once a character appears on paper, he will develop many contradictions with the writer. This character uses his own viewpoint and contradicts the writer, and influences him with his own feelings; inversely, the writer will debate with his character.[14]

Eventually, as will be seen later, Wang Meng solved the conflict between the inner logic of a text and the political intentions of the author through the device of self-pontification.[15] We shall deal with the tumultuous public reception of "Earthquake Lin" further below. It was less a reaction to the story itself than a battleground for the broader political contention of the last months of this year.

14. Wang Meng, "Guanyu xie renwu" (On depicting characters), *Beijing wenyi* 4:2 (April 1957).
15. Cf. infra, pp. 526ff.

ELEVEN

The Challenge of the Communist Personality: Liu Binyan's Sequel to "Inside News"

In the sequel to "Inside News," which came out in October 1956, Liu Binyan continued the conflict mapped out in the first part;[1] all lines, however, were carved deeper, itself evidence for the evolution of the conflict and the possibility of publicly articulating its issues.

The first part mentions that criticism of cadres afflicted with bureaucratism is restricted to those below the county (*xian*) and city district (*qu*) level. Wang Meng still adhered to this rule, but the first part of "Inside News" already began to circumvent it. The paper is a Party paper directly run by the provincial Party leaders, and thus the editor is certainly above the level mentioned; however, he remains in the background, a dragon in his cave or office, and the text deals with him by depicting the negative effects he has on the journalists and the paper itself. The sequel drags Chen Lidong on stage in the first line, and keeps him there. The level of criticism went up one considerable notch with this change. The text depicts Chen as a man with the best of intentions, and the worst of results. On two points, however, touches are added to this picture that change the entire physiognomy. In both cases these changes are due to interventions from Qin Zhaoyang.[2] Liu Binyan had originally written a phrase into Chen's inner musings, "If only one per-

---

1. Liu Binyan, "Inside News" (ch. 9 n 1).
2. Jia Ji, "Suo wei 'linghun' de 'wajue'" (What they call "digging out the soul"), *Renmin wenxue* 5:105ff (May 1958), gives some of the changes wrought by Qin Zhaoyang.

cent of the dissatisfaction would be reported by her [Huang Jiaying] to higher levels . . . ," the phrase breaking off here. Chen is aware of the dissatisfaction, and he is shaken by the dramatic drop in the paper's circulation when the provincial leaders cancel mandatory subscriptions for offices and officials. Chen even thinks—in the original version—of visiting the newly appointed provincial Party secretary at home. Qin cut this phrase. But when Zhang Ye comes to Chen Lidong with the bad news of general dissatisfaction and recommends the standard procedure of self-criticism, Chen originally only says, "I was afraid it was this way"; in the revised version eventually published, he thinks, "It's all because of the letter Huang Jiaying wrote to the Provincial Party Committee." He senses a conspiracy against him, involving Huang and the secretary of the Provincial Party Committee, aimed at toppling him. This quotation changes him from an arthritic blockhead to a cunning politician, and the transformation is made complete by the most important change wrought by Qin, which, as in Wang Meng's case, comes right at the end. Liu Binyan wrote there about the Party committee meeting which is to decide on Huang's application for Party membership:

> . . . but today such a flurry of opinions were proffered all at once. Whose criticisms were these? Chen Lidong went after this question with utmost energy, but he just could not figure out how much direct connection there was between the statements of these people here and the criticisms of the secretary of the Standing Committee of the Provincial Party Committee and of the various department heads.

His attempts to see a political link between his critics in the leadership and the journalists yield no result; these lines are but a flattering comment on the diversity presumably prevailing among the young reformers who did their "independent thinking." Qin substituted:

> What kind of assessment should he [Chen] make of these problems? If Huang Jiaying was a good comrade, was he, Chen, who always thought Huang Jiaying had many serious defects, by inversion not strong in his Party spirit? Did that mean that someone who worked as hard for the Party as Chen Lidong lacked enthusiasm? . . . And what position was he to take after all with regard to Huang Jiaying's admission into the Party? . . . It even seemed that the provincial Party secretary believed Huang Jiaying's "reports"! Today, when the two people sent by the Provincial Party Committee to familiarize themselves with the situation were about to leave, they just said hello to him, Chen Lidong, and walked off. . . .

The core information about a "report" by Huang, and the core words *Party spirit* and *enthusiasm* have all been newly inserted. After this, Liu's original simply stated: "In Chen Lidong's heart that question which was most painful to him came up again: What if I really was wrong?" Isolated above and below, Chen thus considers the possibility of his being on the wrong track, an essential condition for any further improvement of his attitude. Qin let the phrase stand, but then added a paragraph in which Chen finally comes out as a wily politician:

> Very fast, his mind went through some twists and turns; very fast he sized up the situation inside the paper and outside, and on the basis of this came very fast to a decision—true, it hurt, but he was quite pleased with his decisiveness on this occasion, and also thought of the effect his words were going to have. On his face appeared a faint smile. Slowly he got up and assumed a pose both conscientious and composed.

Then he speaks in support of Huang's admission. But, while this seems in Liu's original to be the consequence of his self-doubt resulting from his obedience to the Party leaders who seemed to appreciate Huang, it is here a tactical move, and we can expect him to lie low until a better opportunity to hit back presents itself. In view of the fact that this moment indeed came during the Anti-Rightist Campaign, one might argue that Qin, while tampering very substantially with the text, was shrewder in his assessment than Liu Binyan. In the recent re-editions of the text, the version originally published was reprinted. As opposed to Wang Meng who advocated printing his original more docile version, Liu Binyan seems to have accepted Qin's emendations.

This substantially changed political core of Chen Lidong has been then fleshed out by Liu with the traditional lore of anti-bureaucratic satire. The sequel starts with a confrontation of Chen and the general "climate" at the time:

> That evening, at 10:30. The opera *Fifteen Strings of Cash* [a Kunqu Opera directed against abuses of power that was much acclaimed in mid-1956] was almost over and the dance at the Friendship Hotel was probably at its hottest, but the editor-in-chief of the *New Light Daily*, Chen Lidong, dragged himself with his arthritic legs towards his office.

It was a time when the spring breeze blew into the world of Chinese culture. In a few spots, particularly in the (Sino-Soviet) Friendship Hotel, a niche of Soviet Thaw on Chinese soil, dancing in pairs was possible; some new plays caught the fancy of the public. But all these lively *kultur'nost* entertainments are beyond Chen Lidong's horizon. Afflicted with a symbolic arthritis which greatly reduces his flexibility, Chen is neither physically nor mentally able to participate. He never reads a book; he has removed the Russian oil painting originally in his office; and the raving of his visitors about the beautiful view from his office window over the river is beyond his understanding. To complete the picture, Liu has added, straight from Ovechkin's Borzov, whose Chinese equivalent Chen Lidong is, that Chen has no happy family life. He has five children, but has not been on an outing with his family for seven years, that is since 1949. When his wife complains, he scolds her for not doing so well in adult school. Needless to say, Chen does not join in the dress-up frenzy raging among his staff, although Liu refrained from dressing Chen in an old green Army uniform. (We are told, though, that he loves recently to reminisce about his wartime experience, the mental equivalent to wearing an Army uniform.)

Chen Lidong volunteers a statement about the most prominent features of his own character. "At the annual evaluation meeting each year Chen Lidong would, when assessing himself, first of all enunciate the following line with a solemn and self-effacing tone: 'I am loyal and faithful to the Party, and in everything follow the interest of the Party.'" Chen Lidong thus becomes an example, indeed a caricature of the already familiar *laolao shishi fucong dang de lingdao* cadre, the cadre who obediently and loyally follows Party leadership. The caricature is expanded through his recruits in whom this principle is replicated in the pure form of bureaucratic opportunism. The personality types recruited into the Party under Chen's direction and their assistants are represented by Qian Jiaxian, the young woman from the first part with her daring *qibao*, who is set up here as a contrast to Huang-the-Beautiful-Heroine. Contrasting the two, one of the journalists muses about Qian Jiaxian:

She writes an article, you tell her to change it a hundred times over and to turn each of the original thoughts on its head, she'll not object in the least, independent of whether your criticism was correct or not. . . . We have given a wrong meaning to the word "Party spirit." We think Party spirit means to be well behaved and never speak up, do things according to the regulations.

Her only interest, we learn, is her private comfort, and with this un-Communist attitude goes her interest in men, which lands her with the eponym of a "degenerate soul."

In the first part of "Inside News," only careerist Zhang sides with the editor-in-chief in order to promote his own career. Here in the sequel, Chen Lidong has built up through personal favors a support network among the young journalists and junior editors. There are now three to five people who report to him directly and have become his *zhixin xiaji*, intimates from lower ranks. They will speak up in the Party meeting against Huang's admission. Zhang Ye, interested in keeping Chen in place, provides him with public-opinion polls from the editorial offices, and with recommendations as to the public stance Chen should take. Careful not to throw in his lot with Chen alone, he gives an "objective" report for the Party group concerning Huang's application, balancing each positive statement with an expression or gesture undermining its impact.

Ma Wenyuan now moves to open rebellion against Chen and switches sides. He restates the description of his character in the first part by identifying his former self with what obviously was Liu Binyan's model, Chekhov's proverbial man in the box, whom we have already encountered. What is called his *pita* (indifference) in the first part now becomes the trope of his being in a "tightly sealed, small, black, box." "True, this was the way it had been during these last few years; he had manufactured for himself a rectangular thick-walled box, and had put himself into it. This box kept out noises [i.e. people's voices], provided protection against tides [*fanchao*, i.e. against the high tide, *gaochao*, of socialist transformation praised by Mao Zedong], and there was even no danger of shocks, but at the same time it kept the sunlight out."

These thoughts occur to him resting in the sunlight after a swim, and they mark the critical moment when he breaks out of this box. Ma's ever more open opposition to Chen's handling of the paper reflects the growing strength and self-confidence of the young journalists in Huang Jiaying's entourage. His growing ambivalence and eventual shift to a new orientation mark the potential and the limits of change in the administration's middle level. Ma is second-in-command, and Chen remains in charge, substantially unchanged.

The crowd around Huang Jiaying is, in the same manner as that around Chen, strengthened by other characters who come in only to say their little political line and are never mentioned again. Their function is mostly within the typicality scheme, confronting four speakers on Chen's side with five (and eventually, including Ma, six) speakers on the other. Considering the actual power of the editor-in-chief, this quantitative proportion still gives the "majority" to Chen; the defection of Ma, however, and, more important, the arrival of a new provincial Party secretary, seemingly supporting Huang's crowd, tips the balance for a time in the other direction.

Following the precedent of *Renmin ribao* in Beijing, which on 1 July 1956 suddenly declared that the articles it carried represented only the opinions of the writers (and no longer the Party's authoritative communication), the provincial leadership rescinds mandatory subscriptions from July on; since then, three different papers compete for the readers' attention. The paper's paid-up circulation drops from 30,000 copies to 12,000 in one day. The "masses" of readers are wary of being told by the paper to "unfold with all their strength," "resolutely implement," and "actively respond" to whatever the leadership suggests. It is difficult to "find out the date of publication" by reading the paper, since the content looks very much the same each day, while the "life" and the "demands" of the "masses" are missing. In the first part the paper has been called "dry" and "monotonous"; now the masses vote with their refusal to buy, and harmony reigns in the assessment of the paper among readers and leaders. "The criticisms this paper received from among the masses could also be heard each morning in the offices of the Provincial Party Committee"; consensus reigns among activist masses, enlightened leaders, and the Huang Jiayings in the middle. Chen Lidong's position is thus furthermore weakened by a popular vote of no-confidence. Now "he is afraid he [might have to] go."

In the afternoon of this shocking day, 2 July, the political weather suddenly clears, and the paper's staff promptly decides to have an outing and to immerse themselves in real life. This outing marks Ma Wenyuan's return to life from the reclusive existence in his sealed box. He exposes his body, which looks all whitish and sallow, as if it had "been in a medical liquid for quite some days," to the bright sun. After much trepidation, he swims across the river, a symbol familiar from "At the Building Sites" as the "real life" powered by the teeming masses. "Life during these few years was clean but empty," he muses; "true life is like this water, a bit muddy, but delicious, resounding, and colorful." In traditional Chinese political metaphor, the river water always represents the "people," and Ma's swim across shows that he has finally reimmersed himself among the masses. Consequently a "great many of his faculties and a great many of his hopes were coming back to life, the first among them being the capacity to think." And as this revival is that of a Communist, he does not "think" about God, DNA, or the causes for the fall of Han, but "what he most often thought about was the question what kind of persons members of the Communist Party should be."

With this thought he recarves Huang Jiaying's still flat decision in the first part to concentrate her attention on the "most important thing," to become a Party member. At that moment this is a positive resolve: She wants to become a Party member without going back on her views; the Party should accommodate persons like her with all her views and attitudes intact. With Ma's thought the text links up with the discussion in the Youth League papers referred to earlier about the values and goals that should dominate the upbringing of young people. As the thought occurs at the moment of his reform and revival, the discussion will not only be about traits to be accepted within the Party, but also about those which should not.

Ma Wenyuan outlines his own typicality:

> He thought of himself as neither a good Communist nor a bad one, neither an active nor a passive one, neither progressive nor backward. During these last years he had seen many Communists who were more or less like him . . . passable bureau chiefs, section heads, managers, and editors, but did they measure up to being Communists? . . . These people lacked something a Communist could under no conditions lack. . . . . He could find no words to

describe this, but he had a clear word for its opposite—indifference. . . . Being
a Party member was not the name of a profession.

Ma does not pursue this thought to the point of asking himself whether
they should be eliminated from the Party, and his own example shows
that, under pressing circumstances, they can revive. Combined, however,
with Chen's sudden fear that he might be forced to leave the paper, the
story suggests that institutional consequences might be called for where
calls for a voluntary revival fail. The frustration of the young reformists
about the institutional security of the bureaucrats energizes these lines.

The Party meeting about Huang Jiaying's application falls on the
very evening of this eventful day, and, in due order, the conflicting
views about what a Communist should be came out. Chen Lidong's re-
tainer Guo Ke maintains that Huang might say she is "loyal to the
Party" but "her deeds and words go counter to the Party's tenets. The
party needs people who are *laolao shishi* (obedient and honest), *qianxu
jinshen* (modest and prudent), while Huang Jiaying has her own views
on every single issue; she does not focus on the Party's policies. I cannot
help wondering whether for comrade Huang Jiaying the intentions of
the editorial board or her own views are more important." This familiar
line is substantiated by a woman editor who has calculated that over 20
of Huang's 50 items so far this year were of a "critical" nature, so that
she feels forced to conclude that, for Huang, "about half of our society
is all dark." "To handle things by relying on fire and intelligence alone
does not do. One also has to talk about standpoint [i.e. class stand-
point]. Doesn't it deserve thought why some of our journalists have
such an interest in the dark aspects?" The implied charge is that of the
Sufan Movement. These people are dissatisfied with the Party, and have
a bourgeois point of view. Guo Ke again intervenes to help the reader
understand this point: "I cannot help asking whether or not Huang Jiaying is dissatisfied with the Party," a formula excluding admission and
justiyfing persecution in Sufan terms.

Huang Jiaying's defenders come up with the opposite set of values.
"What's wrong with having one's own views?" asks one, and sets the
stage for Huangs' presentation of her principles:

Why should I hide my criticisms? I'll speak. What I am dissatisfied with is comrade Chen Lidong... and our paper. I think a paper should tell the truth, must tell the truth; then it will be forceful, and the masses will love to read it. Chairman Mao has often talked about adhering to truth [*laolao shishi*, i.e. the "original" meaning of that term is restored and its authority harnessed for this view] and seeking truth from facts [*shishi qiushi*, again a restoration of the "original" meaning, the term having sunk to the meaning of being "realistic"]. And our paper? It hedges and hides and fears the facts, and does not admit its own mistakes... Only a person fatally ill fears the doctor.

This is strong language. Huang Jiaying herself demands with these words that the Committee should decide between two types of personalities, Chen or her, and vote which of the two is most suited for Party membership.

What started in the first part as a "liberal" demand for the accommodation of different types within the Party turns now, as the political situation has evolved and the balance of power has shifted in some quarters, into the request to reject one type by accepting the other. Of course, it would be "unrealistic" to have the meeting actually vote on these alternatives, Chen being a powerful Party leader of twenty years standing, Huang but a novice.

Ma Wenyuan, who is to speak next, therefore confronts Huang not with Chen Lidong, but with Qian Jiaxian, the woman who was accepted into the Party at the age of 19 at a time when Chen held sway unchallenged. She represents his kind of Party member. After characterizing her as the docile creature at the beck and call of the leaders, Ma decides to withdraw his earlier consent to her membership, which comes as close to rejecting Chen's own qualification as he may "realistically" come. To make sure that he is not asking for a wholesale purge of Party members recruited earlier, Liu Binyan has Ma say that Qian is only one out of seven recently recruited members, and there are many positive characters in the Party like Cao Mengfei, although none in a senior position within the paper. We are far from a demand for a diversified Party. Both sides maintain the necessity for its exclusiveness and avant-garde role, but the young reformers claim to have the better definition of the proper Party member, and the better qualifications to meet it. Ma Wenyuan realizes "what was being discussed was not just whether Huang

Jiaying should join the Communist Party . . . He had to stand up against the counter-current." What had been the unimpeded mainstream a few months before, had now become a *niliu,* a counter-current, Chen Lidong's orientation:

> What sort of people does our Party need the most. For five years now, I did not have thoughts of my own, or perhaps I had them and hid them. Whatever Chen Lidong said, I did. And it did not bother me. But think, how dangerous this is. If everybody just acted on orders, we would depend in everything on Chairman Mao and the Central Committee to think for us. What would the end of this be? What kind of a Communist would he be who has no brain of his own? . . . Moreover, from the day we lose the habit of having our own thoughts, we also gradually lose our enthusiasm.

True, he says, there are people who "do their job, obey the rules, and are neither corrupt nor decadent," but this is not sufficient for Party membership. There, one needs *zhandouxing* (fighting spirit) and *chuangzaoxing* (creativity).

Journalists can do what only Party cadres can in China, move around, receive letters from readers, and conduct investigations. Their social experience is thus rather broad, and potentially they can act as a corrective to the clogged channels of communication within the Party. The quality of independent thinking is therefore of prime importance here, as is that of passion, or enthusiasm. They must feel "pain when they see the country in distress . . . and the people suffering."

In a radical turn, Liu Binyan finally introduces a new character at the very end for the single purpose of having him spell out without further embellishment what could and should be the function of the papers under the prevailing circumstances:

> I have been thinking for quite some days. As Party members, are we to do nothing but gather news, write it up, and make sure that the paper appears on time? At our Party meetings we have never discussed this kind of problem. When we do journalistic work, are we not bringing back some problems from each assignment? After our return our notebooks spill over with so many stories, so many thoughts have piled up in our brains; all of this is needed by the leading organs of the Party, but at Party meetings nothing about it is ever mentioned. When we report on our work nothing of it is mentioned, and we even don't know on what occasion we could bring these things to the atten-

tion of the higher levels. As this goes on ever longer one gets the impression that the Party has no need for us reporting about the problems persisting in the life below, and does not want us to offer our own opinions about those various problems. You are a Party member? Good, do your work obediently and without troubles (*laolao shishi gongzuo*), and that's sufficient. . . . However, now we all know that each Party member must *be the ears and eyes of the Party, must be the Party's brain.* [Emphasis added]

Evidently this broad statement mostly refers to journalists. The speaker does not say that the Party invested them with these crucial and critical functions of eye and ear and brain. The opposite is true; they were to be the cog and screw. But there is a categorical imperative that they "must" assume these functions, whether encouraged by the Party or not. In traditional China, the censors traveling through the country to check on abuses of power of officials were called the *ermuguan,* the eye-and-ear officials of the emperor. Their mandate was based on certain notions of public welfare and morality, not on the discretion of the emperor, and their mandate included criticism of the emperor himself. Liu Binyan assigned the same censorial role to journalists, and defended the urgency of their assuming this role with the presence of all too numerous "problems" which remained hidden and unsolved, and with the potential of the Party journalists as the Party's "brain" to contribute to their solution. Chen Lidong has "closed his pores" to society, and the paper has been run in his image.

Liu Binyan again left the end of the story open. No vote is taken on Huang Jiaying's application, and we do not learn about any effective changes in the paper. The misleading picture of a new harmony with everyone voting for Huang's admission is thus avoided. The concluding lines show Chen approving her application because the political constellation has turned against him since a new Party secretary took over. Careerist Zhang senses which way the wind is blowing, and, after assuring himself that "leadership, discipline, and organization are after all the most fundamental" and "reliable things," while "democracy and freedom are always tied up with individuals" who might be toppled, he resolves to stay with Chen Lidong, and at the same time to write some safe critical articles to tune in with the new wave. The coalition of old diehards and young careerists remains intact and waits for its time to come.

In the same issue where the sequel to "Inside News" was published, a short *xiangsheng*-type satire appeared. One of the two discussants is incensed that Liu Binyan would "criticize a Party paper" and have a "journalist support a strike against the leaders"; when asked what he would do in Chen Lidong's place, he argues that he would not only "criticize her, but punish her."[3] The little text served as an interpretive aid to the sequel of "Inside News," reminding readers that even Huang's limited leeway within the paper might be an exception.

All their differences notwithstanding, Liu Binyan and Wang Meng challenged what they saw as the bureaucrats' powers over the levers of social control, that is, the Party, and of public opinion, that is, the papers. They were not dealing with individuals any more but with institutional structures, and they proffered the new model Communist for the new society with its new problems. The youth and, in Liu Binyan's case, the sex of the chief protagonists epitomized the weakness, purity, and resolution of these heroes, which caused their melancholy and frustrated mood. Both authors were careful to point out in their stories that, while battle lines were more clearly drawn in late 1956, and some headway had been made by the young challengers, little had changed in terms of actual power.

Accompanying these literary texts, and the social commotion they reflected and promoted, the first long articles appeared which attempted to formulate a new literary policy designed to promote this new role of literature. The most important of these were Qin Zhaoyang's "Realism—the Broad Road,"[4] and Chen Yong's "Lu Xun, Fighter for Realism in Literature and the Arts."[5] Qin Zhaoyang's article appeared under his pen name, He Zhi, and came out in the same issue of *Remin wenxue* as Wang Meng's "Newcomer." Qin Zhaoyang argued as a Marxist, but referred to Marxism as an instrument of social analysis and not as the administrative code of a government; for the latter he reserved the epithets of dogmatism and formulism, and claimed for himself a critical Marxist tradition.

---

3. Jian Yu, "Richang tanhua lu" (Everyday chatter), *Renmin wenxue* 10:23f (October 1956).
4. He Zhi (Qin Zhaoyang), "Xianshizhuyi—guangkuo de daolu" (Realism—the broad road), *Renmin wenxue* 9 (September 1956).
5. Chen Yong, "Wei wenxue yishu de xianshizhuyi er douzheng de Lu Xun" (Lu Xun, fighter for realism in literature and the arts), *Renmin wenxue* 10 (October 1956).

His core notion was realism. With some finesse he pointed out that Engels's much-quoted letter to Margeret Harkness formulated the principle of realism (typical characters in typical circumstances) in a criticism of Harkness's overidealization of workers, and not in a criticism of "bourgeois idealism." Realism was thus a critical principle on which revolutionaries had to insist against the constant tendencies to embellish and turn to propaganda. This original critical stance, argued Qin, had been recently revived in the Soviet Union, when Simonov challenged the definition of socialist realism as partly "unscientific." Against the elements in that definition which are external to literature itself (like the education of the laboring classes in the spirit of socialism, and the revolutionary perspective works are supposed to have), he argued for internal criteria as essential for realism in his "broad" sense. These internal criteria were in fact the same as the external ones mentioned, but they originated within the writer's own realist craft, and could not be instruments in the hands of administrators to control fictional writing. The core notion of realism became "truthfulness" and, since Marxism was dedicated to truthful analysis, socialist spirit was already contained in this pursuit and so was "Party spirit." In order to get at the truth, the writer had to "actively intervene in life," the slogan thus receiving its theoretical justification; and the writer had to be independent of the day-to-day policies of the Party, as his commitment to its goals was a "long-term" commitment.

The institutional consequences were not spelled out, but they were obvious. The argumentative props for the institutional control of literature were being removed, and the time when these controls were in full vigor was referred to as the time when "some people have manufactured different kinds of hats according to the dominant fashions, which they put on people's heads to frighten them; until today these people have not completely lost their power." It will be recalled that, just three months before this article, in June, the Youth League paper had run an editorial against "the fashion to put hats on people" and branding them in the language of the Sufan Movement.[6] The expression *have not completely lost their power* is a euphemism. The text showed many signs of stress. The reincorporation of the external criteria of socialist realism into the inter-

6. Fang Qun, "This Habit of Putting Hats," (p. 175 note 20).

nal structure of realism evidently reacted to potential charges of separating literature from Marxist *Weltanschauung,* and advocating bourgeois literature. Later texts elaborating on Qin's line of thought constantly offered assurances of orthodoxy, well aware that there were silent but powerful opponents, and that their irritation was rapidly growing during these last months of 1956.

Accompanying Liu Binyan's sequel, *Renmin wenxue* in October carried Yang Xizhong's article on Lu Xun. His pen name was Chen Yong. Yang did to Lu Xun what Qin had done to Engles, namely made him into a fighter "against bourgeois idealism, but also against vulgar mechanistic understanding, and for realism." He detailed Lu Xun's opposition to Li Chuli's attempts in 1928 to make literature into conscious propaganda. Li had said: "All literature is propaganda. Generally speaking, and unquestionably, this is true; sometimes this is done unconsciously, mostly, however, consciously." Hu Feng had argued in the same manner as Yang Sizhong against the ultra-leftist reduction of literature to propaganda, an assumption, however, encoded into the very organizational structure of the new Chinese state, where literature fell into the area of responsibility of the Party's propaganda department. "Vulgar mechanicism and formulism were not fully eradicated in earlier times, and they have an extremely deep and longlasting influence in China," all of Lu Xun's and Mao Dun's efforts notwithstanding, wrote Yang. To claim the pedigree of Engels and Lu Xun for the reformers was no small feat, but neither man had run a state, and the opponents' authorities, Lenin and Mao Zedong, could easily match this challenge; they had not been talking ideas, but formulating policies.

The literary texts studied in the preceding pages together with their theoretical props greatly enhanced the general level of publicized discourse. Readers' letters and journalistic disquisitions were dominated by individual experiences and anecdotal events, while the editorial articles supporting the challengers dealt with social problems in vague, broad, general terms with appeals to persevere in the reform effort. As a medium, the literary texts united both elements through the instrument of typification. They helped to generalize the particular and anecdotal elements and to specify the general assessments and arguments.

TWELVE

The Open Counterattack

As has been shown, the texts implicitly contain a fairly elaborate description and analysis of the forces opposing each other, their background, lifestyle, and ideology, their respective justifications, the issues at stake, the strategies used by both sides to decide issues in their favor, and the actual state of the contention at the time of the writing. This close connection with the actual social contention is their "realism," and in this sense they are very "realistic." Such realism has no necessary link with the literary device of that name.

Realistically, Liu Binyan and Wang Meng showed that, after nearly a year of challenge, the stalwarts of the old order and their younger support cast were still firmly in place, at best driven into temporary retreat. They were in less danger than their opponents. The language they used against the young reformers was that of a *su*, a purge, while the reformers could only answer with verbal criticism and ridicule of bureaucratism, which carried no officially sanctioned institutional consequences. In fact, the few indications by Liu Binyan that institutional consequences might be necessary or unavoidable were so guarded and, as in "At the Building Sites," visible only in the violent conflict within the metaphor of the Yellow River that extreme external pressure is evident. The structural deformations, and constant unnecessary assertions of orthodoxy by the heroes in these texts show that the opponents might be silent in the media, but they were well entrenched in their positions, and maintained the latent threat that the young reformers might eventually be classified in Sufan terms.

Strangely enough, the 8th Party Congress in September 1956 defined bureaucratism (replacing the bourgeoisie and imperialism) as the main obstacle to further progress, but in social fact strengthened the bureaucrats' self-confidence. The new line came out most neatly in a small correction. Directly after the Congress, the Youth League paper, in an article on the (new) main contradiction, wrote that the contradiction with bureaucratism and corruption was "basically non-antagonistic."[1] This implied that it might become antagonistic under certain conditions, and would then have to be solved through violent means. The next issue printed a correction, saying it was simply "non-antagonistic."[2] That was reassuring. And so those attacked as "bureaucrats," too, started to bloom and contend in the fall of 1956.

The new semester, meanwhile, brought many reforms. Schools opened with a new curriculum which greatly alleviated the pressures on students by reducing mandatory courses from 30 to 24 hours a week, abolishing mandatory political classes, and eliminating most mandatory collective activities sponsored by the Youth League. Students had not only editorials and some short stories to draw on, but also had time to spend, and things quickly became more lively. People could choose for the first time among different courses, organize their own free time, were less 'stiff', and even more at ease in dealing with the other sex.[3]

All this was quickly read as a sign of bourgeois corrosion. With growing nervousness, the Youth League paper let an opinion dare to find its way into print from October on which had been unable to be publicly articulated before. In November, *Zhongguo qingnian* came out with a desperate defense against these articulations, quoting many of them:

1. Huang Nansen, "Wo dui dangqian guonei zhuyao maodun de yixie renshi," (Some personal opinions concerning the present main contradiction in our country), *Zhongguo qingnian* 21:9f (1 November 1956).

2. "Dui 'Wo dui dangqian guonei zhuyao maodun de yixie renshi' de buchong he gengzheng" (Additions and corrections to "Some Personal Opinions Concerning the Present Main Contradiction in Our Country"), *Zhongguo qingnian* 22:22 (15 November 1956).

3. Zheng Bijun, "Xin xuenian de xin qixiang" (The new climate in the new academic year), *Zhongguo qingnian* 22 (15 November 1956).

Since the beginning of the semester, a new situation has come about in many institutions of higher education, which has attracted much attention. Most recently quite a few papers have published articles on the matter. These articles all affirm that students have become more adventurous in their thinking compared to earlier times, that a climate of independent thinking and deeply probing issues is becoming more widespread, and that democratic life has expanded, all of which are good prospects. At the same time they point out that a course of persuasion by argument and of guidance by positive example should be pursued to solve habits among some students of laxness in discipline, non-adherence to the regulations, unwillingness to do social labor, disregard for political study, and so forth. Of course it is absolutely necessary that the papers pay attention to this. However, some papers give in their reportages and essays the impression that these habits of students' being undisciplined and not keeping the regulations have already become very grave, and that greatest priority should be given in the political work in the universities to the correction of these faults. An editorial in *Guangmin ribao*, for example, said on 29 October: "The development of these problems in the institutions of higher learning has already gone beyond the initial stage. It demands speedy suppression and correction. This cannot but cause people to be concerned." The criticisms leveled against the students by cadres ranged from "liberalism" and "individualism" to "propagating petty-bourgeois thinking." Many cadres and educators "are concerned that to let youths have relatively much freedom will only result in disturbances. Therefore they maintain that youths should be subjected to increasingly severe disciplinary measures of the old kind, and they use simple and crude means to suppress youths."

In fact, however, the problem was that, with all their eagerness, discipline, and hard work, the "capacity for independent thinking and independent work (among youths) was still insufficient," and thus the stress had to be on *fazhan gexing* (developing individuality) and not on strengthening discipline. The people who argued that the scattered recent disturbances were the "sudden explosion of pent-up frustrations" or "revealing petty bourgeois free-floating and undisciplined thinking and habits" had failed to notice that the young intelligentsia had recently changed status, were a part of the working population, and therefore to be "trusted."[4]

The article reveals in its desperate tone and its appeal that the propo-

4. Zhong Peizhang, "Shi qianjin, haishi houtui" (Is this progress or regress?), *Zhongguo qing-nian* 22:29 (15 November 1956).

nents of the "new personality" were very much on the defensive. From the then-unpublished speeches of Mao Zedong of this period we know that he was, too. He tried to bypass the high-level leadership and go directly to provincial leaders and intellectuals in order to generate some public pressure for his "anti-conservative" policies, which were seen by other leaders in the Center as voluntaristic and excessive. The year 1956 was the year of the "Leap Forward" with a dramatic speed-up in collectivization and industrial development. For Mao, the Hundred Flowers policy was not a goal but an instrument to weaken the opponents of this double "Leap Forward." He felt "nine out of ten" high-ranking cadres opposed this policy.[5]

At the end of August, the stalwarts of Party discipline were still on the defensive. They were only a "counter-current" in Liu Binyan's story, people who could be publicly satirized. *Wenyibao* reported a little incident in late August showing that both sides knew very well what they were talking about. The opera *Qin Xianglian* on the celebrated Song-dynasty Judge Bao Longtu was staged in a certain place. The plot was very well known. A scholar has left his wife to take part in the imperial examinations in the capital, comes out first, and, after claiming to be a bachelor, is married to a daughter of the emperor. The destitute first wife makes it to the capital, where her husband tries to have her assassinated. She brings the case before Judge Bao, just appointed. He has the husband arrested, and executed without asking, or waiting, for the Court's confirmation (which evidently would not be granted). At this moment, in the play, the head of a government or Party organ in the performance city jumped up and "loudly ordered the performance to be stopped, the reason: 'Judge Bao should not execute a person without asking the emperor's directives; this is making propaganda for undisciplined and unorganized behavior!'"[6] The official got the message of the opera quite correctly, translated Judge Bao's behavior into his own contemporary political language, and defined him in Sufan speak as a counterrevolutionary. But *Wenyibao* could recount his story in August as the bizarre act of a political lunatic. A few weeks later, this greatly changed.

5. Cf. note 15 below.

6. Jiang Jun, "Shi Bao Gong wuzuzhi wujilü ma" (Does indeed Judge Bao lack organization spirit and discipline?), *Wenyibao* 16:3 (30 August 1956).

The increasing resilience of these opponents after the Party Congress materialized in their growing willingness to speak up and to adopt institutional measures to discipline the students. They spoke of the "spiritual chaos"[7] resulting from the relaxing of controls, and proceeded to reestablish them. In December, the Youth League leadership itself started to warn students not to "reject everything" and to keep in line. The article gave an illustrative list of the issues most eagerly taken up by the young, with the Sufan Movement and bureaucracy reigning supreme:

> Today, there are some people who are very one-sided; wherever they go they see the trees and not the forest, and sometimes even make a few trees into a complete forest. . . . As an example, people see that some cadres have defects in their work style or make mistakes in their work, and then conclude that they are not worth a farthing, have nothing good about them, and therefore they "hate [these cadres] as one does enemies," to such a degree that they would love to beat them to death with a stick. Others see that in the work to eliminate counterrevolutionaries (Sufan) there are some slight deviations or they themselves have once been confronted a bit by comrades around them, and they conclude that the Sufan Movement is altogether unhealthy, and they hate the cadres engaged in this work. Others see that some socialist states acted improperly in some measures and thus evoked dissatisfaction among the people, and thus they doubt the superiority of the socialist system itself and lose faith in socialism.[8]

An editorial in late November suggested that the campaign "to educate youth in Communist morals and to reduce corruption by bourgeois thought" of the year 1954 through summer 1955 should be "permanentized" to counter the recent surge in "bourgeois" influence.[9]

The young activists were to push collectivization and rapid industrial development, but they were not to harbor doubt and resentment against the Party leadership and lose faith in socialism altogether. Their usefulness was in their spearheading Maoist policies; they were quickly out in the open, and without umbrellas, once they overstepped these

7. "Daxuesheng keyi ziyou chu qiangbao" (University students are allowed to freely hang up wall posters), *Zhongguo qingnian* 21:39 (1 November 1956).

8. Fang Qun, "Buyao fouding yiqie" (Don't negate everything), *Zhongguo qingnian* 23:15ff (1 December 1956).

9. "Jingchang zhuyi dui qingshaonian jinxing gongchanzhuyi daode jiaoyu" (Always pay attention to educate children and youths in Communist ethics), *Zhongguo qingnian* 22:7 (15 November 1956).

borders. The Youth League leadership thus tried to protect the socialist activist segment of the young by attacking those who would draw down a thunderstorm on the entire crowd with their uncalled-for doubts. In order to separate the wheat from the chaff, a big public debate was started in December about Wang Meng's story, which essentially dealt with transposing Nastya features promoted by the Youth League into a Chinese context.

The editors of *Wenyi xuexi*, the Youth League literary magazine, printed three types of articles—harsh attacks, fervent supports, and pieces with both praise and criticism—the editorial support obviously going to the middle position. As the greatest apprehensions against the new line were to be found in the Army, an Army politcommissar, Zeng Hui, could spell out this position. He saw the piece as a confrontation between young and old cadres, with the old leaders being denounced. He discovered that the piece, being situated in Beijing, by implication attacked the Center itself, and that the technique used was that of the late Qing critics like Wu Woyao in their battle against the corrupt feudal mandarins. The piece *waiqu* (distorted) reality, the title announces, and it, *waiqu* (distorted) "the image of the old cadres . . . killing them with the pen."[10] On the other end, a student from Qinghua University could come in with the assertion that he "loved Lin Zhen, although he has all the weaknesses young people commonly have. But he is in fact the genuine mainstream of our time"; he is so "familiar, yes, he is one of us." All this came under the headline "Lin Zhen Is Our Model."[11] The frenzy evoked among many young readers by Wang Meng's Lin Zhen was evident from the 1,300 letters flooding *Wenyi xuexi* after it started the discussion, and from statements by critics. Li Xifan who had, with Mao's support and guidance, attacked Yu Pingbo's interpretation of the *Dream of the Red Chamber* blasted the story; the "political effects" had to be considered, he argued on 9 February, "and what deserves pondering is the frenzied reaction Lin Zhen evoked among a part of the intellectual youth."[12] Ai Zhi, answering an unprinted letter

10. Zeng Hui, "A Story that Gravely Distorts" (ch. 10 note 8), pp. 8f.
11. Tang Dingguo, "Lin Zhen shi women de bangyang" (Lin Zhen is our model), *Wenyi xuexi* 12:13 (December 1956).
12. Li Xifan, "Ping 'Zuzhibu xinlai de qingnianren'" (On "A Young Man Who Only Recently Joined the Organization Department"), *Wenhuibao*, 9 February 1957.

from a student in March 1957, also claimed that the letter writer referred to Lin Zhen as the "Chinese Nastya" and "our model."[13] What was at stake was not Wang Meng any more, but the ideal type of a Communist personality; the leeway for public criticism of officials; the policy of the Youth League and its leader, Hu Yaobang; and, eventually, the course the Hundred Flowers policy was to take.

On 7 January 1957, *Renmin ribao* printed a public blast against the published opinion of the preceding year.[14] It came from four officials from the Propaganda Department of the Army, and they expressed their deep dissatisfaction with the negative portrayal of senior cadres, and with the emphasis given to depicting the "dark side" of society, bureaucratism in particular. They predicted a situation akin to that in Hungary and Poland. The article was justly seen by Mao Zedong and others as an expression of a very widespread resentment against his policies,[15] and the piece stood unopposed in *Renmin ribao* until March, while the Youth League continued to maintain guarded to glowing support for Wang Meng's story which, as everyone knew, was the battleground for this controversy.[16] Mao Zedong was incensed at the article by Chen Qitong and his colleagues from Army Propaganda; but not only was he unable to get his own opinion into print in *Renmin ribao;* even his statement on the article was quoted wrong. He had said: "These few comrades are loyal and devoted, they are for the Party's cause; but (their) article cannot be rated as good advice." In the protocol

13. Ai Zhi, "Lin Zhen, Zhao Huiwen ji qita" (Lin Zhen, Zhao Huiwen, etc.), *Zhongguo qingnian bao*, 14 March 1957.

14. Chen Qitong, Chen Yading, Ma Hanbing, and Lu Le, "Women dui muqian wenyi gong-zuo de jidian yijian" (Some of our criticisms concerning the present work in literature and the arts), *Renmin ribao*, 7 January 1957.

15. "Nine out of ten of the old cadres agree with the article by Chen Qitong and the other three," Mao said on 6 March 1957. Mao Zedong, "Zai jiushengshi xuanchuan wenjiao buzhang zuotanhuishang de tanhua" (Speech at the Conference of Heads of Departments of Propaganda and Education of nine provinces and cities), in *Mao Zedong sixiang wansui*, September 1967, edition in 337 pp., p. 45.

16. See the articles by Liu Binyan, Liu Shaotang, Qin Zhaoyang, and others in *Wenyi xuexi* 1–3 (1957), and the criticisms of Li Xifan's article by people associated with the reformers in Tang Zhi, "Shenme shi dianxing huanjing? Yu Li Xifan tongzhi shangquan," (What are typical circumstances? A controversy with Comrade Li Xifan), *Wenyibao*, 25 February 1957, and Zhou Peitong, Yang Tiancun, Zhang Baoshen, "'Dianxing huanjing' zhiyi" (A query about "typical circumstances"), *Guangming ribao*, 9 March 1957.

of this remark distributed to the provinces, the second clause was cut.[17]

Mao eventually came out in support of Wang Meng's article. On 9 February, Li Xifan had published his blast, specifying the general charge of Chen Qitong and others against this story, and claiming that it "had no educational value" in a Bolshevik sense.[18] On 16 February, Mao talked to a number of cultural leaders about the story. "The story exposes bureaucratism, very good, although the exposure is not penetrating; however, it's quite good. Liu Binyan's story also does not criticize the whole of bureaucratism. Wang Meng's story has its one-sidedness, the positive forces are not well enough taken; this has to be criticized. One has to criticize him, and to protect him, too. The positive character, Lin Zhen, is described without force, while the negative character sets the pace." Li Xifan, he said, was as "dogmatic" as the Army propaganda people.[19]

Mao thus came out in support of the Youth League position. It took another month until Lin Mohan could translate these remarks into a balanced article about Wang Meng's piece, published in *Renmin ribao.*[20] Wang Meng obliged, by coming out with a self-criticism in the same paper on 10 May,[21] and eventually the original text was made available. When the Anti-Rightist Movement started, Mao tried to protect Wang Meng; Peng Zhen, the Mayor of Beijing, which is described as a bureaucratic puddle in Wang's story, tried to get him a rightist hat. Wang's work unit was in Beijing, and institutionally he was under Peng's control; his possible protector, Hu Yaobang, was in Moscow during these crucial weeks in June/July 1957.[22] The complicated constellation produced a complicated result. Wang Meng was not publicly made into a rightist, and no such criticisms of him appeared. Peng Zhen then had

17. Mao Zedong, "Speech at the Conference" (note 15 above), p. 55.

18. Li Xifan, "On 'A Young Man'" (note 12 above). Ma Hanbing, one of the four authors of the January article (note 14 above), did the same in "Zhunquede biaoxian women shidai de renwu" (Accurately depict the characters of our time), *Wenyi xuexi* 2:16ff (February 1957).

19. Mao Zedong, "Zai Yiniantang de jianghua" (Talk in the Yinian Hall), 16 February 1957, in *Mao Zedong sixiang wansui,* pp. 34f.

20. Lin Mohan, "Yipian yingqi zhenglun de xiashuo" (A short story that evoked controversy), *Renmin ribao,* 12 March 1957.

21. Wang Meng, "Guanyu 'Zuzhibu xinlai de qingnianren'" (On "A Young Man Who Only Recently Joined the Organization Department"), *Renmin ribao,* 10 May 1957.

22. Cf. Yang Zhongmei, *Hu Yaobang, a Biography* (Armonk: M. E. Sharpe, 1987) p. 98.

his way by insisting on his leaving the capital and being denied the option for the publication of further slanders of the Beijing Party Committee (which in turn had ingratiated Wang with Mao). And Wang Meng obliged another time, by volunteering to go and live among the Uighurs in Xinjiang until 1979.

The Anti-Rightist drive, which started in June 1957, put an end to the challenge. The strong force overcame the weak challenge. The old values were reinstated, the challengers banned as rightists. The attempt to carve out space for a new personality more attuned to the demands of an industrializing society had failed, and so had the first major attempt at a generational change in post-revolutionary China. The innovative potential inherited from the old society had been crushed in the early years. With the Anti-Rightist drive, the Party now proceeded to crush its first generation of potential innovative successors which had grown up in the new society. This generation would have to wait another twenty years until its chance would come. Then, in 1979, their texts would be reprinted, and the survivors would be recalled into responsible positions.

THIRTEEN

Some Conclusions

It is time to break off this investigation. The methodological bases become overloaded. The analysis started out with the question whether and how a social history of segments of the Chinese population in the early 1950s could be written in view of the extreme homogeneity of the available material, and what the role of literature might be in this context. There is no necessity here to repeat the better-known history of the "hot phase" of the Hundred Flowers period for which more diversified sources are available.

From the inquiry, I believe the following conclusions might be suggested:

•The monopoly of thought and discretionary power claimed and arrogated by the Communist Party makes for a very dense structure of manifest behavior with all elements closely cohering. Factional struggles in the Politburo, female hairdos, ideological constructs, student course loads, political assassinations, and editorial techniques are all discussed in the same code, although they might have their origins in widely divergent causes. Given the enormous pressure for homogeneity, and the resulting expectation of the same, alternatives can be and are advocated, and lived, as often minute variations in a fringe area of the categorical universe, a reference to Balzac's royalist beliefs, a flowered blouse, a translation of a foreign text, the use of local dialect in a story, the absence of a class enemy in a story. Although often inconspicuous, they imply an entire set of assumptions alternative to the prevailing line. As this is well understood, the camouflage becomes ever more refined, and the themes more esoteric. By preference, such alternatives would be offered in either well-secured, or well-camouflaged realms. The former is the case with the Soviet model, evoked by the "reformists" in the early 1950s. There was the dominant role of the Soviet Party in the socialist world, recognized by the Chinese leadership; it was therefore possible to quote, translate, imitate, and emulate things from the Soviet Thaw in China, although the Thaw was certainly not the cause for the high prestige enjoyed by Stalin and his Party in China. In the post-1979 reform period, the economic opening to the West provided for a while the possibility to clothe the call for alternative values, lifestyles, and institutions in depictions of such things from the West. The "camouflaged" realms would include preferable forms of expression which do not compete with the official language on the same level, but operate with symbols; this is true for fiction, cartoons, and personal experiences expressed in readers' letters, but also "silent" statements like clothes, or non-action.

•The enforced cohesion of the most diverse social and political phenomena makes for a fairly uniform surface, but offers to the analyst the option of inference. A visible or discovered indicator in one area, like clothing styles, can be a guide to more elusive forms of alternative options in other realms. Proof for the correctness of the inference comes with the discovery of other indicators pointing in the same direction. The analysis is therefore justified in using the most diverse types of indicators, quite independent of the artificial divisions of academic fields which would advise the economist not to read short stories, and the Chinese literary scholar not to look at Russian texts.

•Objectively, the controversy might be described in terms of different generational experiences. The older leaders had found that a military command structure with personalities both obedient and willing to sacrifice themselves for the cause was the smoothest way to victory and success. The younger cadres did not share these experiences. Their sights were set on the modernization of the country, and the main problem they encountered was the bureaucratic foot-dragging of their elders. In a large society like China's there are always sufficient recruits of both types available to satisfy the Party's needs for new cadres from the store of either one. Thus, quite independent of the generational structure and the historical experience, the domination of a certain line will evoke the response of certain personality types of whatever age, and both sides will fight for the recruitment of their own replicas into the organization. At the same time, the conflict might be described in terms of problem definition; in this sense, strict military subordination and discipline were the guarantee of success until 1949, but then the emphasis had to shift to the development of the individual initiative with a concomitant reduction of the officials' discretionary powers. Finally, the element of interest might be introduced. In this sense, the older cadres with their generalist qualification had an interest to keep up the myth of the class enemies' threat after 1949 because it justified their remaining in power, and gave them the wherewithal to crush their challengers. The younger generation, on the other hand, with often better qualification was interested in defining the goal as modernization, in which leadership would quite naturally go to them. This problem definition also provided them with a well-trodden alley for criticizing their elders for "bureaucratism."

The material studied here is essentially polemical, whether it consists of readers' letters, cartoons, short stories, or Politburo decisions. As such, it rigorously follows a factional logic, where each case is closed and sealed; no opponent gets the benefit of the doubt. Inconsistencies within one's own position are blurred; as an example, the obvious link of Mao's anti-conservatism drive with his aim to accelerate the collectivization of agriculture and its concomitant drastic reduction in the peasants' leeway is inconsistent with Liu Binyan's emphasis on increasing the leeway, but he espouses both goals. Things are quoted and omitted in a tactical manner, so that Mao appears as the fountainhead of antibureaucratism; the fact that the Sufan language was also his creation remains unmentioned. While this form of tactical factional thinking and writing is certainly exacerbated in these literary manifestations, it also reflects the deep-seated animosity and vengeance within the Chinese political class, which precludes a mature and seasoned consideration of the issues at stake. However, the material stays close enough to the reality as perceived by at least one camp, and near enough in terms of time to permit guarded assessments of the actual state of the contention, and of the moods, and tactics, prevailing on both sides of the barrier. In fact, the literary texts studied here present the most elaborate, reasoned, and fact-based assessment of at least one social contention available for this time, certainly more so than the documents of the Center, or the extrapolations from just one set of data, be they economical, political, or social. By exploring the inner logic of their argumentation from a perspective outside the factional divide one is able to arrive at a fairly detailed understanding of the social and political process of a given period.

•Both sides in this controversy have at their disposal a complete canon of precedent and argument to justify their cause, and much ink is splashed over the pages to adduce ever stronger props in the form of quotations from Marxist-Leninist classics, or statements from prominent leaders. The one group relies on Sufan language, the other on the "anti-conservatism" drive, both with Mao's authority. In terms of their station and consequence, however, they are vastly different. The users of the Sufan language threatened their "young" opponents with the hats of being "counterrevolutionary," a term implying the necessity of being "purged" and even held legally accountable. Their challengers barked back with the "conservatism" charge, but there was never a Party policy to purge or dismiss conservatives and bureaucrats. The threats were thus unequal. And so was the power of the contenders. The "conservatives" have high rank and office, senior age, male gender, good connections, much routine, and time to wait for better climes. Their challengers are young and junior, naive, and often of the so-called weaker sex, have no connections, and no time, as they battle for their survival. What might seem to both sides a harsh social conflict—and this is the way it is presented in the literary texts—seems to the outside observer rather a social strategy mapped out by the leadership, perhaps as a compromise among diverging interests. It involved the use of the young and of the media—of two weak forces—to keep the bureaucrats moving, and to keep the bureaucrats secure in their positions in order to ensure stability and continuity—a calculated and limited social instability to handle the intrinsic inertia of autocratic rule without adopting democratic institutions. While objectively both sides might thus have been consciously locked into an antagonistic but overall stable structure, they operated like the heroes in the Iliad as antagonists with all the attendant bitterness and factionalism, with the effect that the situation got quickly out of bounds on both ends of the spectrum, the young becoming "irresponsible" in their demands, and the senior cadres brutal in their defense of the status quo ante.

•The battle for this ill-begotten piece of social technology lasted from 1953 through 1955. The strategies used to park its key concepts into a Chinese orbit, and gradually repatriate one after the other onto the soil and into reality reflect the closedness and density of the Chinese political culture at the time. Long before grand documents or speeches by the Chairman himself created some leeway for the Young Man's challenge, these concepts were already well in place, and some of the key personalities had made their appearance in the public sphere. While it would seem that Hu Yaobang had a decisive influence on each and every step in which the challenge was mounted, his public pronouncements give few clues in this respect. He verbally kept to the line, but in deed he created both institutional and ideological niches for a new type of cadre to emerge in the framework of the Youth League. At no time during 1956 did the challengers dominate more than some papers and journals, and, by mid-1956, the counterattack was already well under way. The reassuring statement that the contradictions with "conservatism and bureaucratism" were non-antagonistic, that is, not to be solved by purges and dismissals, prompted ever stronger measures by the senior cadres, who could also point to disturbing signs of unrest and independent action on the campuses and in the factories, until they eventually mounted the open counter-challenge in the article by Chen Qitong and associates in January 1957. Given the actual distribution of power, the "hot" phase of the Hundred Flowers movement would thus seem as a desperate last attempt to prevent the coming counterattack rather than the cause of it.

Needless to say, the events in Hungary and Poland had shown the enormous volatility of these young "socialist" societies in periods of reform. These societies have neither the political institutions nor the civic habits to soften and cushion the impact of the Center's antics. But the reverse is true, too. A situation can turn very unstable, within a matter of days and weeks, since there are no channels through which popular frustration could make itself felt in an orderly forceful and lasting way. Both sides have thus ample precedent to quote for justifying their own actions. The 1987 farcical replay of the Anti-Rightist Movement with the same protagonists, the same issues, and the same precedents shows to what degree even reform and restoration have become stylized exercises, with some minor adjustments to time and occasion. Deng Xiaoping in 1987 referred to the "necessary" harsh action of Jaruselski to establish law and order in Poland against some wild hooligans and Catholics in order to justify his own action, and the ousted scientist Fang Lizhi demanded a fast and radical democratization to prevent a recurrence not of "capitalism" but of the "Cultural Revolution." The events in China, the Soviet Union, and Eastern Europe since 1989 have, on the other hand, shown the fragility of the seemingly powerful socialist-state machinery once faced with a real challenge. What might have been read before as hysterical overreaction of some bureaucrats to a minor challenge turns out now to be based on a keen insight into the basic weakness of the socialist state.

Part Two
Liu Binyan, Ovechkin, Kisch, and the
Limping Devil—Archeological Explorations
of the Genre "Literary Reportage"

FOURTEEN

Top Layer: Texie *in the People's Republic of China*

INTRODUCTION

Few scholars would object to a proposition which maintained that, in contemporary (mainland) Chinese literature, theme, perspective, character, and plot of a work can often be meaningfully interpreted in a sociopolitical context, if not, as is sometimes the case, as outright political allegory and *ad personam innuendo*. In studies dealing with this context the literary genres to which the texts belong are rarely treated. They are assumed to be receptacles into which any kind of content might be poured.

To check this assumption, I propose to investigate the literary, social, and political code—if there be any—implied in the genre *texie*. Compared to the great genres like the long novel, few texts are written as *texie*, which makes for some economy in our research and presentation. At the same time, the detailed description of this fringe genre might offer insights about the larger genres to which it is adjacent; such insights might be hard to come by if one were to plunge into the middle of the huge mass of material assembled under their headings.

A genre typically is a silent but fairly detailed text. This text, which usually does not discuss the canon and rules it follows, might nevertheless determine the structure of the legible text and much more. What is dried and preserved in the appropriate Chinese and other textbooks as being the "characteristics" of each genre gives little insight into the kind of decision an author makes when opting for this or another genre. In their genesis and actual use, each of the genres has acquired a certain status, meaning, and role, and a writer using a genre not only opts for a structure, but also for these attendant qualities. Thus, apart from the internal characteristics of our genre, we shall have to explore the social role and history of the *texie*.

Finally, the different literary genres tend to be associated with different types of literati. The public stance and role of a poet is different from that of a novelist or a dramatist, and most authors affix themselves predominantly to one genre that they deem most appropriate for themselves and for the themes they treat. Thus, allowing for a wide margin of variation with regard to genre and theme, it will be meaningful at least to inquire whether to be a "*texie*-ist" involves a specific kind of personality and public posture.

With this triple set of questions in mind—dealing respectively with the internal structure, the genesis and social role, and the personality of the author—we might begin the exploration. It will be "archaeological" because archaeology as a rule deals with silent structures imbued with meaning, a meaning that might change with each new layer, while maintaining some continuity. A Christian church might be built onto the fundaments of a Roman temple, which again took the place of an earlier cult; the place remains, however, numinous. Also, much of the dead matter carried on in later transformations becomes understandable once the earlier layers are understood in their own light and logic.

LIU BINYAN'S TEXIE *AS A LITERARY GENRE*

Any list of those literary texts written in mainland China after 1949 that operated as "earthquakes" in Chinese public opinion evoked irritated rebuttals from one or the other faction in the Party, and landed their authors sequentially in the position of hero, villain, martyr, and again hero, would include among the first five no less than three texts by Liu Binyan: "At the Building Sites of the Bridges" (1956), "Inside News of Our Paper" (1956, in two parts), and "Between Human and Monster" (1979). All three are *texie*.[1] Liu Binyan has written other texts in this

1. Liu Binyan, "Zai qiaoliang gongdi shang" (At the building sites of the bridges), *Renmin wenxue* 4 (April 1956); "Benbao neibu xiaoxi" (Inside news of our paper) pt. I, *Renmin wenxue* 6 (June 1956), pt. II, *Renmin wenxue* 10 (October 1956); "Ren yao zhijian (Between human and monster)," *Renmin wenxue* 9 (September 1979), cf. the translation in Liu Binyan, *People or Mon-*

form, and also some short stories. The above mentioned are best known, however, and I shall use them as the starting point for this study. Although we are dealing with a fringe genre, the attention attracted by these pieces makes them core texts, which comfortably add relevance to the economy in this endeavor.

A list of the prominent characteristics of these texts might look as follows:

(1) TOPICALITY. All three texts deal with problems of the immediate present. "At the Building Sites" has a group of Youth Leaguers under engineer Zeng as heroes who have formed a youth shock team and want to "double the norms" as well as put a check on the waste of materials and manpower at their site. In early 1956 when the story came out, the Youth League indeed advocated the formation of such shock teams and the stopping of waste. The villain in the story is Brigadier Luo, the earliest "bureaucrat" in PRC literature. He obstructs the rapid progress for which the Youth Leaguers are fighting. Some months before the story appeared, Mao had criticized Party cadres for lagging behind the "masses" and the story explicitly refers to this statement. Conservativism was a prominent theme in the PRC press at the time. Thus the protagonists and their conflict are immediately tied in with debates going on in society at the time; *Zhongguo qingnianbao,* where Liu Binyan was then a member of the editorial board and head of the section responsible for industry, indicated that Youth Leaguers had troubles with their ossified elders in this campaign, but the story's criticism went further.

"Inside News" takes up several themes hotly discussed at the time: the problem of work assignment for young school graduates; the possi-

---

sters?, ed. P. Link (Bloomington: Indiana University Press, 1983), pp. 11ff. The collection of texts which were branded "rightist" in 1957 and have been restored, *Chongfang de xianhua* (Shanghai: Shanghai Wenyi Press, 1979), contains 20 texts without mentioning, however, whether they were *texie* or *xiaoshuo*. I could ascertain this for 11 texts, of which 5 were *texie*. The *xiaoshuo* texts seemed mostly to deal with love, the second most controversial theme, while the *texie* dealt with bureaucratism. There is little literature on reportage literature in China. See Jenny Tu-li Teng, "Liu Pin-yen. The Politics of Reportage Literature in Mainland China," *Issues and Studies* 9:28ff (1986); Noel Dutrait, "La Littérature de Reportage Chinoise," *Europe* 672:74–88 (April 1985); Dutrait, *Ici la vie respire aussi at autres textes de littérature de reportage, 1926–1982* (Aix-en-Provence: Alinea, 1986).

bility of strike meetings to get the bureaucrats to move; and, above all, greater leeway for the press if it was to criticize conservatism, which all too often was rampant among the papers' very leadership. The discussions of the last topic remained "inside" at the time, and came into the open some months later.

"Between Human and Monster" appeared in 1979, a few weeks after the scandal about Wang Shouxin had been reported in *Renmin ribao*, on which Liu was then a reporter. While the paper focused on Wang as a criminal and on her links with the "Gang of Four," and Liu Binyan shows that Wang was firmly tied into an "invisible machine" of cadre relationships, which survived her downfall unscathed. The story thus takes up a public and legitimate theme, pushing the analysis, however, far beyond the discursive norm at the time.

A check with Liu's other *texie* confirms this point. The texts react quickly to actual events and changes; none of them deals with earlier times or even recent history, although the genesis of a problem, or a character, will be given within a context geared towards explaining and describing the present. Thus we learn about Wang Shouxin's family background, Brigadier Luo's earlier revolutionary enthusiasm, and the origins of the editor-in-chief's way of running the paper as if he were commanding a platoon. We also learn about the slow growth of the illicit network of cadre relationships during the last decades; of the two stages in the conflict between the Youth Leaguers and the brigadier, and of the two stages in the conflict between the Youth League journalist and the ossified editor-in-chief. Yet the emphasis is always on the present.

(2) AUTHENTICITY. The texts, as a rule, do not have a plot in the sense of an invented action, like a *xiaoshuo* (short story or novel), with an introduction, a high point of conflict, and a denouement. The texts purport to present a vital problem in life as it is, and they go to great lengths in establishing the authenticity of both fact and structure of their narrative. Extensive use is made of dialogue; documents are quoted like the big-character posters in "Between Human and Monster" or Mao's statement in "At the Building Sites," and reference is made to factual historical events of PRC history like decisions of the Party (the 3rd Plenum 1979), the deposition of the "Gang of Four," or the establishment

of "special economic zones."[2] In some cases, real names are used like Wang Shouxin; in other cases, the names are changed, but the reader is to understand that the text refers to a real person. The geographic location is also sometimes changed, but again this is to protect the people there, or the author, and to indicate that similar things might occur elsewhere, but not to create typified literary figures as they appear in *xiaoshuo*. The stress on documentation with real facts, statements, and figures is part of the overall structure of the texts, which deal with "problems." A text will hunt for any information relevant for the understanding of the problem, but achieves economy by rigorously keeping out any information that does not directly pertain to its understanding. We learn nothing about Wang Shouxin's feeling for her son, or Luo's relationship with his wife, or the landscape flying by when Huang Jiaying travels back to her newspaper office. Thus a spotlight technique is used in terms of illumination, and the close-up in terms of observation.

The authenticity of the text is maintained by restricting it to phenomena that can be observed and proved. The emphasis is thus on surface phenomena, things that can be seen and independently observed by the reader. Even when the internal ruminations of bureaucrats are described, as in "Inside News," these are restricted to political tactics and to simple reflections on the irritating new phenomena. The characters remain "flat," and consciously so, the degree to which details are given being dictated by the "problem" reported. Similarly, the action remains "flat," and consciously so, with only those aspects immediately relevant to the understanding of the "problem" reported. The observations are sociological rather than psychological and literary.

(3) DISCOVERY. The texts catch the attention of the reader by inviting him to join in a discovery about the actual world around him. Like a travelogue of old, the texts enter a realm hidden to the eye of the reader. But here it is not distance that prevents direct inspection, but masking. Reality in its proclaimed eulogized socialist surface is only a verbal mask. Behind the glorious reports about the bridge's completion the bat-

---

2. Liu Binyan, "Yingshi longteng huyue shi" (This is a time when dragons should dance and tigers leap), *Dangdai* 5 (December 1982).

tles and frustrations of the Youth Leaguers are invisible. Reading through the pale pages of the Party papers, readers ignore what is going on inside the editorial room. Seeing the reports about the "criminal Wang Shouxin," which affirm that with her arrest and eventual execution the "problem" is solved, readers ignore the true story about the ongoing operation of the invisible machine. Even if they know a thing or two from their own experience, their insight and knowledge is confirmed, broadened, and deepened by the texts, and, once the texts are officially published, readers may ventilate their own views about the problem through open discussions. The text thus assumes a surface of officially described reality that is essentially a mask; but the surface has cracks that permit glimpses of the true surface of reality below, and the texts' investigation enters through these cracks. The texts do not go for the "essence." They do not argue that beyond the individualized and often irritating surface of social types and realities lies the blissful essence of socialism and of proletarian class-consciousness. Such texts do exist in great numbers in China, following the mandate of showing "typical characters in typical circumstances" as is required in the *xiao-shuo* genre. But Liu Binyan's *texie* go for the "truth" beyond the mask, refusing both the glitter of the official surface and the awe of the official essence.

The texts describe the process of discovery. Ideally, as in "At the Building Sites," the narrative voice belongs to an investigating journalist, the modern traveler into the entrails of socialism; or it may describe the discoveries made by characters within the text, as in "Between Human and Monster." "Inside News" here, as in some other features, is closer to the short story, as has been justly remarked,[3] and the picture of the narrator is blurred; nevertheless, there is no omniscient narrator. The investigation here proceeds on two levels, the factual and the analytical. The discovery is made on the first, and the sociological and political analysis on the second.

The texts borrow some elements from the detective novel and similar forms so as to let the reader join in the labors of unraveling the real situation and piecing together bits of information into a complete pointil-

3. Cf. *Zhongguo dangdai wenxueshi chugao* (Beijing: Renmin wenxue Press, 1981) II, 207.

list picture. The information is not for everyone to get; it takes daring, wit, and logical powers to probe what is really going on, and the texts are not reluctant to include constant references to the difficulties in getting access to the material. Already in "At the Building Sites" the journalist has trouble getting access to the young engineer Zeng, and is urged to talk to another engineer who is closer to the brigadier's views. The dramatic story of two individuals who go after Wang Shouxin and eventually undo her big conspiracy is told in detail in "Between Human and Monster." At the same time, the information remains fragmentary, and explicitly so. There is only so much the author discovers, and many things remain hidden even from his searching eyes, quite apart from the fact that many details are not of interest to him because they do not seem to be linked to the problem. Thus the texts reproduce the scattered and incomplete access to real information that humans in general have, and more definitely so in most socialist societies. By implication, they refute the underlying assumption of the omniscient narrator that he has such a grasp of the workings of the mind and of society that he can safely extrapolate the "typical" by means of his creative powers and describe it as the essential surface.

(4) "SOCIOLOGICAL" ANALYSIS. Liu Binyan's texts do not stop at providing fragments of factual information for the reader to digest. The authorial voice intervenes time and again with analytic commentary. This can be an extended sociological digression, as in "Between Human and Monster," when the authorial voice analyzes the list of extra-Party links forming the "invisible machine,"[4] or may take the form of characters within the story who discuss the "problem" at length, like the journalists in "Inside News."[5] The analysis extrapolates from the known data and tries to arrive at a broader conclusion about the inner workings and conflicts of society. The generalization contained in the text is of a logical and argumentative kind, and is based on an analysis of the information gathered. The sequence of the *texie* may be entirely determined by the explorative steps of the analytical voice as in "At the Building Sites"

4. "Between Human and Monster," p. 189. I quote the edition in *Liu Binyan baogao wenxue xuan* (Beijing: Beijing Press, 1981).
5. Liu Binyan, "Inside News" (note 1 above), pp. 9f.

and in "Between Human and Monster," or by the development of the conflict itself which brings out enough of the analytic elements to take over from the narrative voice as in "Inside News." Significantly, however, Liu Binyan's *texie* is dominated by the analytic motive (more specifically, the sociological motive), and not by the complex internal logic of interacting characters, interests, and institutions, that is, plot. The worker who does the analysis on which "Between Human and Monster" is based sets himself up as a branch of the Chinese Academy of Social Sciences and defines Wang Shouxin as a sociological research satellite in the sky of socialist states.[6] This sociological element has been noted by Leo Ou-fan Lee.[7]

(5) MODERNITY. Liu's *texie* all deal with variants of the same problem: the conflict between modernization-oriented, frequently highly qualified individuals of high moral calibre and those aspects and parts of the socialist state and Party machinery that obstruct their action. The point is consistently made that the institutional structure of socialist China in fact favors obstructionist activities by bureaucrats and corrupt cadres. Negatively defined, the emphasis on conflicts between modernizing individuals and bureaucratic state representatives excludes such other emphases as conflicts among or within individuals. The latter are mentioned only in the context of what Liu Binyan defines as the main problem of contemporary Chinese society. Liu Binyan is an industrial author, and his heroes are technicians, engineers, managers, and journalists, modernizing city-dwellers in the most advanced sector of material and cultural modernization. The latter element is of great importance; the daring, investigating, and arguing authorial voice finds its counterpart in the daring hero of the story with his or her independent thinking and unconventional personal habits. The bureaucrat and the innovator are opposed to each other, not just in terms of modernization and obstruction, but in terms of lifestyle. This is immediately obvious in the stories written in 1956, where the bureaucrat talks amidst suffocating dust ("At the Building Sites") and has

6. Liu Binyan, "Between Human and Monster" (note 1 above), pp. 198f.
7. See his "Introduction" to Liu Binyan, *People or Monsters?* (note 1 above), p. xv.

no feeling for the arts ("Inside News"), while the opponents are *kultur'nost,* like the young journalists on the paper. The point is not made in "Between Human and Monster" but taken up again in later *texie,* so that it may be considered a permanent fixture.

(6) MORALITY. The authorial voice has a sociological interest in understanding the inner dynamic of contemporary Chinese society, but in this analytical endeavor it always belongs to an *engagé* individual. This is evident in the frequent explicit authorial interventions and exclamations expressing the hope that the fresh wind from the Soviet Thaw might also blow into the brigadier's office ("At the Building Sites"), bemoaning the level to which "our Chinese working class" has sunk ("Between Human and Monster"), and warning the readers that "this is no time for triumph" (ibid.). It is even more evident in the telling names (Chen-Who-Sets-Himself-Up-as-the-Ridgepole-of-the-Tent, Luo-Who-Lays-Down-the-Official-Line) with their satirical twist, and in the often bitter irony of the description, as in the poetry competition organized by Wang Shouxin, or the grotesque image of the editor-in-chief with his mighty belly appearing as a shadow blocking the sun over his assistant editor who is taking a sunbath after having successfully thrown himself into the somewhat muddy and turbulent waters of life. In some cases this satirical element is developed in its own right, as in "Warning" in the conversations the ashes of some now dead adherents of the "Gang of Four" have on the garbage heap of the cemetery of history from within their urns, hoping for their posthumous restoration.[8] But this text is not called a *texie.*

The authorial voice thus does not belong to a bystander, but joins in the battle; it does so with the utmost self-righteousness and a high moral tone, which comes from the belief of representing all that is modern, advanced, and in the best interest of the people, while the opposite side is accorded the monopoly of all that is rotten, backward, and egotistical. The mask and the true surface of society are associated with different groups of people. The strong and mighty are self-serving and fabricate

8. Liu Binyan, "Jinggao" (Warning), *Zuopin* 1 (January 1980).

the mask in order to hide truth and preserve their interests. The realm of truth, however, the true surface, is the common people, and this in a two-fold sense. First, their actual life circumstances are the true and relevant reality of society; and second, it is only from them that information about the true surface can be gleaned. Thus the authorial voice, often a journalist, will visit the common people and interview them because their practical knowledge will give him access to the true, mostly ugly, face of the mighty. Liu Binyan pushed this principle to the extreme in "Between Human and Monster," where the entire network of Wang Shouxin is unraveled through interviewing and investigating two common laborers. Encoded into the literary genre *texie* is thus an idealization of the common people and a critical attitude towards those responsible for masking. At the same time, access to truth is open only to those who share the "people's" characteristics and therefore enjoy their confidence.

(7) IRONIC DISTANCE. The authorial voice keeps an ironic distance from the sombre social realities it details. This attitude rejects the wailing depiction of suffering as sheer propaganda and establishes the narrative voice as operating with intellectual coolness in its analysis. The ironic tone is a literary device designed to enhance the scholarly credibility of the authorial voice.

At the same time, the ironic distance separates the narrator from the phenomena described. It presupposes an attitude of great familiarity with the darker aspects of human greed and debauchery while ensuring the reader that, of course, neither the author nor the reader could possibly be afflicted with the same ills that the text describes. The ironic attitude does not extend to the authorial voice itself; it has no insight into its own weakness. The ironic distance thus establishes for the narrator and the reader a claim to moral superiority. It comes with a distinct bitterness, since the text incorporates only the knowledge of the evil doings of the mighty and not the power to prevent their continuation.

(8) MILITANCY. Militancy is often adduced as being the main feature of the *texie.* The active and daring intervention in life for the purpose of helping the new and progressive elements in their advance is the usual explanation for the term. Indeed, the term accurately describes a com-

mon feature of the *texie*, which is most clearly visible in their endings. They tend to end with the problem not solved; "At the Building Sites" has a negative ending, and only a hope remains that the spring wind might also blow into the office of Brigadier Luo. "Inside News" eschews a glorious end by not describing the Party meeting where a decision will be taken as to Huang Jiaying's admission into the Party. "Between Human and Monster" ends with a passionate appeal by the authorial voice: The reader should not be deceived by Wang Shouxin's arrest but must know that the invisible machine of which she is a part is still in place. This common feature of the *texie* endings thus marks the "intervening in life" in the sense that the readers are mobilized to see the obstacles still present in great numbers, and to join in the fight against them. The topicality of the texts with their emphasis on the present is to secure their effect on the readers' actual thinking and behavior, by helping them discern enemies and friends and the true surface from the mask.

(9) FUNCTIONALITY. The immediacy with which the texts react to developments in society attests to the urge to have literature "quickly" reflect real life. But, as we have seen, Liu did not stop there. His texts quite consistently take up an issue long before it has become a matter of permitted public debate. By subjecting an individual but representative case to literary and analytical scrutiny, and publishing the result with clear and unequivocal value judgments, the texts become potent instruments in the hands of real-life equivalents of the hidden heroes depicted in the texts for the promotion of their modernizing goals. This might be only the *intention* of the author in some cases, but in Liu Binyan's case there is ample evidence that the texts indeed really achieved this goal. "Inside News" was made mandatory reading material in a number of newspaper offices; "Between Human and Monster" was reprinted in many other periodicals and even in railway stations, as well as broadcast by various radio stations in China;[9] and the reports in *Zhongguo qingnianbao* in mid-1957 suggest how difficult the criticisms against Liu Binyan were in

---

9. Cf. A. Dolezelova, "Liu Binyan's Come-Back to the Contemporary Chinese Literary Scene," *Asian and African Studies* 20:92 (1984); *Wenyibao* 11–12:82 (December 1979).

view of the fact that his texts had informed the world-view and language of so many. Indeed, I think it is no exaggeration to say that the other elements that have been listed receive their place and value only insofar as they support the functionality of the texts, and the degree of their variation in different *texie* depends upon the leeway allotted to each element within this overarching category, which in Liu Binyan's own terms would be *ganyu shenghuo*, to intervene in life.

Within the context of the functionality of the texts, it is legitimate to ask for the implied reader and/or addressee. The texts maintain a clear idealizing stance towards some groups of people denouncing others, and it might be assumed that they address themselves to the members of this coalition of progress and modernity. In Liu Binyan and other authors using the genre in his sense, the coalition is, with some changes, stable, consisting of an enlightened small number of people at the very top of the country's hierarchy, of the honest common people with their modest demands for a decent life and for morality among the superiors, and of the intellectual intermediary, the journalist, the engineer, the manager. The bland glorifications prevalent in Liu's texts from the 1950s have not been maintained; both the top and the common people have lost much of their luster, while Liu has written many new *texie* about the intellectual group, in which they effectively turn up as the main props of the country's progress; they are appropriately idealized, while more complex characters appear in the other two groups. Given the structure of society and the reading public in China, we can assume that Liu's texts primarily address the group most embattled in all his texts, the progress-oriented, modernist intellectuals in the middle of the hierarchy, who have to face the bureaucrats directly, and who also form a large part of the reading public. This ties in well with Liu's longstanding association with the Youth League and the many intellectuals in its ranks who, even according to Deng Xiaoping in 1955, were to be in the forefront of the battle against conservatism and bureaucratism.

THE SOCIAL ROLE OF LIU BINYAN'S TEXIE

When Liu Binyan reentered the literary scene in early 1979, he published his program, neglecting no pitfalls, in two articles in *Shanghai wenxue.* The first was "Literature Must Discuss Politics, Discuss the Economy, and Discuss Culture" (January 1979).[10] Many new literary journals are appearing, Liu wrote, and they might contribute something useful by publishing, apart from literary works and literary criticism, "some things with more immediate links to life–like political essays (*zhenlun*), essays (*zawen*), *texie*, and even discussions about problems in real life. There are some intermediate stages between life and a literary work. Could one not put some of those materials, semi-finished products, some thoughts and depictions before the readers' eyes before they are finished?" The critical bite of this proposal is not hidden. "The topics of articles presently carried by the newspapers and periodicals are just too dull. They are either news or dispatches (and there are not enough of these either), or they are huge theoretical articles." On the issue of enforced multiple rice cropping, he wrote, "For a problem like this, which directly affects the Four Modernizations and the basic interests of a billion peasants, one could easily write a *texie* that would move people to the utmost." In view of rapid changes, society cannot wait until the writers have sat for years on their stories, but needs fast, accurate, and moving texts, the *texie* being the best vehicle. The second article, which came out in March 1979, is "On 'Depicting the Dark Side' and on 'Intervening in Life.'"[11] Liu argued that both slogans were developed to oppose a literature that evaded the treatment of contradictions and conflicts in life and did not pretend to constitute an encompassing program for literature. In the last years of his life, Lenin had described three main dangers for socialism: (1) the greatest danger, careerists and adventurers who, as self-appointed Communists, sneaked into the Party; (2) bureaucratic weeds, which poisoned the power of the Soviets; (3) our own mistakes.

All three have arisen in China, and, if literature does not independently examine and reveal these dangers, it in fact contributes to the damage. Under normal conditions, literature was to be the "most sensitive nerve" of the Party, and had to mobilize people to fight "under the

10. Liu Binyan, "Wenxue yao yi zheng, yi jing yi wen" (Literature must discuss politics, discuss the economy, and discuss culture), *Shanghai wenxue* 1:76 (January 1979).
11. Liu Binyan, "Guanyu 'xie yin'an mian' he 'ganyu shenghuo'" (On 'depicting the dark side' and on 'intervening in life'), *Shanghai wenxue* 3 (March 1973).

Party's leadership" against the dark forces, that is, to "intervene in life."
Lenin, Liu argued, had strongly advocated the development of sociology, but Stalin had eliminated it.[12] In his speech at the Writers' Congress
late in 1979, Liu returned to his plea for a sociological self-analysis of
Chinese society.[13] The transformation in China of the creative process
from "from life to artistic creation back to life" towards "from the intention of leading officials to artistic creation of life" was a dangerous thing,
because it deprived society and the Party of the capacity for self-
analysis.[14] Taking a sideswipe at Zhou Yang and others who had persecuted him and others during the Anti-Rightist Movement in 1957, Liu
added: "One must say that the successive criticisms in the past were all,
in a certain sense, the preconditions for Jiang Qing's climbing onto the
stage, for the appearance of the theory of the 'basic obligation (of literature)' [to serve politics], and for the hegemony of 'conspiracy literature'
over the literary stage."[15] Not only does literature have a power greater
than scholarly analyses to influence people's feelings; it might also have
greater analytic capacities. Liu quoted Engels's well-known statement
that he learned more from Balzac's *Comédie Humaine* about details of
the economy than from the assorted historians, economists, and statis-
ticians of the time.[16] The context of this quotation is highly unusual. In
the argumentative ecology of socialism, it is normally cited when a
writer is to be defended who is not a certified Marxist-Leninist. Balzac,
it then argued, was an outspoken royalist, but, nevertheless, he
described the demise of the French mobility, his own class, with extraordinary clairvoyance and insight. Thus realism itself forces the writer
into eventual agreement with Marxist tenets. Nothing of this appears
here. Liu Binyan is saying that literature in China should live up to
Balzac's great stature by turning out its own *Comédie Humaine* about all
aspects of socialist Chinese society. We shall return to this statement at
a later stage of this analysis.

12. Ibid., p. 55.
13. Cf. Howard Goldblatt, ed., *Chinese Literature for the 1980s* (Armonk: M. E. Sharpe,
1982) p. 116.
14. Ibid., p. 54.
15. Ibid., p. 55.
16. Ibid., pp. 50f.

For the post-1979 period we have thus solid grounds to assume that Liu Binyan made a very conscious decision to write *texie* and not other forms, a decision based on the inherent structure and potential of this form, while at the same time he engaged in polemics with the other literary genres. Turning to his writings in 1956, we quickly discover the same phenomenon. Liu Binyan was a personal friend of Valentin Ovechkin, who visited China in winter 1954 with a journalists' delegation from the Soviet Union. Ovechkin is known in Soviet literature as the most important *oçerkist* or *oçerk*-writer at the time, and he gave a talk on *oçerk* in Beijing, which appeared in March 1955 in *Wenyibao*.[17] The Chinese translation of *oçerk* is *texie;* the translator of the talk was Liu Binyan. Early 1955 was not exactly a stimulating time in Chinese literature; in the same issue, *Wenyibao* carried the material against Hu Feng, and during the next months the pages were filled with attacks against that writer. In this climate, the only way to publish broader views on literature which were in tune with the beginning Thaw in the socialist camp after Stalin's death was to stay under big brother's umbrella. One of Ovechkin's *texie* was already published in mid-1954, but no Chinese at the time could follow in his steps.[18] Once the political climate in China warmed up in late 1955 and early 1956, Ovechkin's text was discussed, and then Chinese *texie* could appear in the opening he had made. Ovechkin's talk on *oçerk* as well as the translation of his "Days in the Rayon" must thus be read as part of the Chinese literary scene, that is, as Chinese texts.

17. Cf. Gleb Zekulin, "Aspects of Peasant Life as Portrayed in Contemporary Soviet Literature," *Canadian Slavic Studies* 1.4:555ff (1967); and P. Carden, "Reassessing Ovechkin," in Richard Freeborn, R. R. Milner-Gulland, Charles A. Ward, eds., *Russian and Slavic Literature* (Columbus, Ohio: Slavica Publishers, 1976); W. Aoweiqijin (Ovechkin), "Tan texie" (On *oçerk*), *Wenyibao* 7 and 8 (1955), tr. Liu Binyan. Both issues came out in April.

18. Hualunting Aoweiqijin (Valentin Ovechkin), "Quli de richang shenghuo" (Days in the rayon), *Yiwen* 5 (May 1954). To this translation was appended a review of the work by the Soviet critic A. Petrosian, "Cong shenghuo chufa—ping Aoweiqijin de texie 'Quli de richang shenghuo'" (Taking life as the starting point—On Ovechkin's *oçerk* "Days in the rayon"), ibid. Petrosian saw the *texie* as a rejection of the "literature of no conflict," arguing that Ovechkin was well in tune with the Soviet leadership. Malenkov had said that "we need Soviet Gogols and Shchedrins, whose satires have like a fire burned off all putrid and rotten things which impede progress." Petrosian furthermore summarized the controversy in the Soviet Union about this *texie* and its surprising (because unresolved) end, a feature repeated by Liu Binyan in his *texie*.

The *texie*, said Ovechkin in Beijing, is a "militant literary form; it is simultaneously a form of artistic work and newspaper article."[19] The *texie* was thus introduced as a fringe genre "between" literature and reportage. Both Ovechkin and Liu Binyan were journalists and not full-time writers. The medium in which many of the *texie* appeared, the newspaper, reached a very wide public very rapidly. "I love the papers as a rostrum from which to face a broad audience. Only from newspapers that sell hundreds of thousands or millions of copies can a person appeal loudly to the broad public in order to make his own opinions/criticisms (*yijian*) known,"[20] said Ovechkin. The *texie* was described by him as a travelogue about things going on in other parts of such vast countries as the Soviet Union and China. Compared to the great novels it was a "comparatively small literary form. We call the *texie* a militant literary form. In order to write a *texie*, a writer does not have to spend five, seven, or ten years."[21] They were thus characterized by "maneuverability" and "agility" and were able to "help the Party" by "hastening to the most distant recesses of life and operating as an advance scout (*zhenchabing*)":

> A *texie* author, if he really closely observes life without turning his eyes away, if he has truly grasped the technique of *texie*, and if he is good at analyzing all things going on around him, will always be alert to an event or phenomenon that is just about to ferment. Whether it is a positive or negative event, a good or bad phenomenon, we have to discover it at the earliest possible time. If it is bad, we have to unfold a vigorous criticism of it all the earlier; but should it be good, we have to open a still broader avenue for it.[22]

The topicality and functionality of the *texie* as well as the other elements outlined above are thus a programmatic part of this genre in its social context:

> The *texie* is a very broad (*kuankuo*) and free form; thus a writer of a *texie* can express his own opinion as he pleases without any restriction and with all his enthusiasm, speaking openly in the first person; and with his full voice he can utter what he has to say about the phenomenon he has discovered. A texie-ist who has written a researched *texie* (*yanjiuxing texie*) can be compared to some-

19. V. Ovechkin, "Tan texie" (note 17 above), pt. 1, p. 36.
20. Ibid.
21. Ibid.
22. Ibid.

one who places his scouting report on the headquarters table, thus helping the leadership to take note of these phenomena. When we say that literature is a great army in the ideological struggle, this refers to attacks against the remnants of capitalism and to the battle for building socialism, and in this context we may say that the *texie*-ists form a small scouting contingent which can be sent far ahead of the front in order to scout.[23]

Ovechkin thus claimed for the *texie*-ist the responsible independence of the scout operating "behind enemy lines." The agility of the form enabled the *texie* to keep pace with the rapidly changing situation in socialism (however one might judge these changes), and thus the writers "quite naturally develop some urge to take our own artistic works in order to directly intervene in life (*ganyu shenghuo*), intervene in these transformations."[24]

The *texie* has also been used by the embellishers, Ovechkin continued. They have written documentary *texie* (*jilu texie*) or *texie* describing real persons and events (*xieshi texie*) depicting "new men" and "new things." Ovechkin's *texie* took issue with this "no-conflict" *texie*, and for himself proclaimed a different type:

> There is one kind of *texie* that focuses on presenting the problems in life; it generalizes certain social phenomena and militantly helps the people to discover and solve the contradictions and conflicts in life . . . This kind of *texie* is relatively large in form (*daxing*) and is called the pondered *texie* (*shensi de texie*) or the researched *texie*. It uses made-up names, and, although it starts out from phenomena of life, it is not reduced to this or that specific instance. Therefore, it permits the writer still greater possibilities for imagination (*xiangxiang*) and inventing things (*xugou*) and, while in formal terms remaining a *texie*, in terms of content it basically does not differ much from a short story.[25]

Ovechkin himself used this form in order not to be bound by the rules governing the short story, the latter promising the reader "an interesting plot, a story with complicated twists and turns, and an unexpected end."[26] The truthfulness of his *texie* did not lie in each character's hav-

---

23. Ibid., pp. 36f.
24. Ibid., p. 37.
25. Ibid.
26. Ibid.

ing "an address," but in its having "the truth of life. The Party calls on us to write the truth (*xie zhenshi*). This means writing about the things around us, and the taste of these things might be bitter and might not make people happy; they might be incorrect; but these, too, have to be described."[27] In fact, most of the *texie* written by Ovechkin use invented action put together from a variety of social materials at his disposal. The documentary element in the *texie* is part of a fictional claim at authenticity, involves the art of creating the authentic image in the readers' minds, but of course remains a purely literary device even when the event described actually happened. Ovechkin finally referred to Malenkov's statement that criticism and self-criticism were necessary even if "our foreign enemies gloat." "These words have given us Soviet writers additional strength, as if we had grown wings, and our strength is directed towards our daring to expose our own shortcomings and towards doing this well, to boldly admitting these things and overcoming them."[28] The editor of *Wenyibao* added a comment at the end of the first part: "This article gives a lucid analysis of the importance of *texie*, its peculiarities, and the question of the writer's deeply immersing himself in life; it deserves a great deal of attention from our Chinese literary workers."[29]

Opting for the form of *texie* thus involved a number of literary and political decisions. First, the use of *texie* implied the rejection of the two genres between which it is situated, the short story and the newspaper feuilleton. Both were at the time narrowly defined. The short story was under the strict mandate of typicality, the "essence" of classes and conflicts being determined by the Party. It was thus reduced to illuminating the Party line with appropriate literary means. It had wasted much of its prestige in the process, and had been the vehicle for most of the "literature of no conflict" against which both Ovechkin and Liu Binyan were rebelling. The newspaper *tongxun, baogao* (report) or *xiaopin* (feuilleton), on the other hand, were reduced to presenting "real people and real events" and thus were hard put to address general problems,

27. Ibid., p. 39.
28. Ibid.
29. Ibid.

especially as analytical comment was not a part of this genre. In the universe of highly defined categories set up by the socialist state as a reflection of its taking power in the superstructure and of the leading and determining role of Marxism-Leninism, the place of freedom was at the fringes "between" established categories.

Ovechkin's "pondered" or "researched" *texie* neatly placed itself "between" the short story and the reportage/feuilleton, claiming for itself the best of both worlds, the freedom to invent and generalize from the former; and the prestige of truthfulness, the actuality, and the wide distribution from the latter, being all the while "a work of art." It is in this categorical no-man's-land that Ovechkin (and Liu) found the *texie* to be a "very broad" and "free" form, which could be used speedily and "militantly" to "write the truth" and "intervene in life," discovering and unmasking the newly occurring problems and conflicts, and mobilizing people for their solution. Writing this kind of *texie* was a political program. From Ovechkin's texts we know that he described bureaucratism as the main obstacle to progress (not class enemies or foreign imperialists), and that he advocated all that was modern and advanced both in technology and behavior, equating, as did Liu Binyan, the modern with the morally good.

Writing *texie* did not only mean rejecting other forms, but also entering into a discussion with other texts of the same genre. Indeed the polemical note in Ovechkin's talk cannot be ignored when he says, "The *texie* is in no way restricted to the documentation of real people and events, and it is also not restricted to depicting so-called 'new men' and 'new things' coming to the fore in our life." Staying for the moment within the material printed in China, the writers and journalists present knew to whom he was referring, namely Boris Polewoi.

A wartime correspondent, Polewoi had written *The Story of a Real Man* (the "real" referring to the fact that it dealt with an actual person), of which there was a Chinese translation. Another collection of his *texie, Men of Stalin's Time,* appeared in China in 1954. Polewoi had entered the polemics against Ovechkin by demanding that the *texie* deal exclusively with "real men and real events," and that its purpose be to quickly sketch the tremendously exciting new heroes and feats of socialism for the emulation of readers. His talk "On *Texie*,' delivered at the Soviet Party School, appeared in Chinese in August 1953.[30] Polewoi restricted the *texie* themes to "successes of economic and cultural construction," "progressive Soviet men," and the "heroism of their ideologically rich life and labors."[31] "In *texie*," he maintained, "there can be no fictional elements."[32] In a most stunning contrast to the scout image used by Ovechkin, Polewoi wrote: "The success or failure of a *texie* primarily depends on theme selection and the socio-political meaning of the theme. If names of arms are given to the various types of newspaper writing, the *texie* would be the reserve artillery of general headquarters. These are the guns that shoot farthest, and, when the battle has entered a new phase or there is heavy work ahead, headquarters will put them into action."[33] The genre in this image becomes a direct and heavy instrument of "headquarters"; there is nothing of the nimble scout operating loyally but independently behind enemy lines to find out the real problems ahead.

China did not only create its Ovechkin in the person of Liu Binyan, but also had its Polewoi, perhaps best represented by reportage writers like Liu Baiyu and Xu Chi. For Polewoi the *texie* also "intervene in life,"[34] but they do so by being the "true annals of the struggle of the Stalin Five-Year Plans," immortalizing the progressive forces in agriculture and industry, the shock workers and Stachanovites.[35] The same arguments have been heralded throughout the socialist camp by Marietta Schaginian, another *texie* writer.[36] In China, this position was countered in the same month, August 1953, by a translation in *Renmin ribao* of "Some Criticisms of *Texie*" by D. Saslawski. "The odious 'theory of no conflict' has even done a lot of damage to our *texie*," Saslawski complained. "The Soviet *texie* must do away with the depiction of the sur-

---

30. Baolisi Boliefuyi (Boris Polewoi), "Lun texie" (On *očerk*), *Yiwen* 8 (August 1953). An earlier paper describing his views is "Bao Boliefuyi tan xie zhenren zhenshi" (Polewoi on describing real people and real events), *Yuwen xuexi* 9 (September 1952), tr. Ji Gao.
31. Polewoi, "On *Očerk*," p. 123.
32. Ibid., p. 139.
33. Ibid., pp. 141f.
34. Ibid., p. 128.
35. Ibid., p. 123.
36. M. Schaginian, *Auf des Fünfjahresplans Bahnen, Skizzen*, (Berlin [East], 1952), Chapter 1.

face. Most of our *texie* lack the elements of analysis and criticism . . .
The *texie* mostly reflected the current successes; they did not look at
tomorrow and also never point out the shortcomings of today. And this
is a shortcoming of our *texie* themselves." Proclaiming the "wide thematic range" of the *texie*, which has a "stylistic range like the musical
scale," Saslawski demanded that the *texie* become "more incisive
(*shenke*) and more richly embued with fighting spirit," and that they
had better contain "a bit of criticism."[37]

Read as a Chinese text, Saslawsi took issue with the wartime Chinese
texie, which shared the features of the Soviet *texie* as represented by Polewoi and Schaginian. Indeed, the *texie*, or, more generally, *baogao
wenxue*, had become the "main literary genre" in anti-Japanese circles
after 1937. Hu Feng, whose periodical *Qiyue* carried many of these *youjidui texie* (guerrilla *texie*) and who edited some collections, criticized
their crudeness and simplistic image of the world. Writing in December
1937 "On a militant literary form for the war period," Hu said that,
since July of that year, the literary supplements and periodicals carried
inordinate amounts of *baogao*, "80–90 percent of which are weak and
without force." They are unable to "see the entire world in a grain of
sand" and end up in trivia. Under the heading "One has to eulogize, and
also to criticize" he advocated a differentiated description, saying, "We
are living in the twentieth century, and we can hardly be of the opinion
that there are gods with ten thousand good character features, and devils
with ten thousand bad ones. They cannot be separated as easily as
dough with a knife."[38] In another article in May 1939, he again praised
the potential of the fast new forms like the *texie* in those hectic times,
but quoted people who oppugned these texts as "war-of-resistance ste-
reotypes" (*kangzhan baguwen*).[39] Hu Feng's articles were reprinted in
1950. By then, as He Qifang wrote a year later, "Chinese *baogao wenxue*
had died," the war being over and no need being felt for this kind of lit-

37. Sasilafusiji (Saslawski), "Guanyu texie de jidian yijian" (Some remarks on *oçerk*), *Renmin ribao*, 1 August 1953.
38. Hu Feng, "Lun zhanzhengqi de yige zhandou wenyi xingshi" (On a militant literary
form for the time of battle), in Hu Feng, *Jian, wenyi, renmin* (Swords, literature and art, people, Shanghai: Nitu Press, 1950), pp. 18ff. The text was written on 31 December 1937.
39. Hu Feng, "Minzu geming zhanzheng yu wenyi" (National revolutionary war and literature), in Hu Feng, *Jian, wenyi, renmin*, p. 104.

erature. The texts written in 1951 in this genre were of the kind "nice weather today, hahaha," but what was needed were *baogao wenxue* texts dealing with new problems.[40]

Hu Feng was not exactly an authority in late 1954 and early 1955 when the forces advocating a rapid modernization along Soviet (Krushchevian) lines, including a literature attacking bureaucratic obstacles, started to make their voices heard. Thus, at the same time when the campaign against Hu Feng reached its climax, some literary leaders and some writers with Youth League connections quietly put a Soviet-derived alternative option in the parking orbit–the Ovechkin-type *texie*. All the literary slogans which were to dominate during 1956 and 1957, as well as after 1979, "Writing the truth," "Intervening in life" (with the specific meaning of pointing out problems and mobilizing people to solve them), and the leeway of the "scout" came from Ovechkin's talk. The editorial comment, probably written by Kang Zhuo, did not dare to repeat these slogans, but strongly recommended this extraordinary document to Chinese literary workers. In 1955, Ovechkin's *Days in the Rayon* came out as a book, and in October a review in *Guangming ribao* affirmed "The Power of *Texie*."[41]

The article mentions that all too many such works appear in the papers which just deal with "real people and real events," eulogizing in Polewoi's manner, and expresses the hope that more *texie* of Ovechkin's type will appear, that is, "works with some criticism that can bring up problems," which are "analytical and critical." More specifically, the author maintained that the same types of characters as described in Ovechkin's *texie* "may be recognized among ourselves" in China.

Again some months later, in February 1956, the *xiaoshuo* group of the Writers' Union had a discussion, "Courageously unveil the contradictions and conflicts in life," which dealt with the translations of recent Soviet works, Ovechkin's *Days in the Rayon*, Galina Nikolayeva's *The*

---

40. He Qifang, "Baogao wenxue congheng tan" (Disquisitions about reportage literature), in He Qifang, *Guanyu xianshizhuyi* (On realism; Shanghai: Xinwen Press, 1951), pp. 233ff.

41. Tian Jing, "Texie de liliang–dule *Aoweiqijin texieji* hou" (The power of *texie*–after reading *Oçerki* by Ovechkin–a collection), *Guangming ribao*, 15 October 1955. The article explicitly links up with Saslawski's comments quoted above; cf. note 37.

Director of the MTS and the Woman Chief Agronomist, which had been made mandatory reading by the Chinese Youth League and provided the model for Wang Meng's "Newcomer," and the second part of Sholokhov's *Virgin Soil Upturned.* The discussion was published in *Wenyibao.*[42] It was stated that "present literary creation shirks struggle and is unable to truthfully depict life." Chinese works, Ma Feng argued, mostly showed "struggle with nature,"[43] while these Soviet works openly showed conflicts among men. Kang Zhuo agreed, deploring the "embellishment of life" in the Chinese works and taking up the slogan of "intervening in life."[44] Zhou Enlai's speech "On the Question of the Intellectuals" had by then been made, Mao's Hundred Flowers comment was to come a few weeks later, and a part of the Party leadership was bracing for the 8th Party Congress which would make the new concept of economic development a statute.

Within the political and literary world, there arose an expectation for Chinese works that would deal as courageously with the problems of bureaucratism and the "dark aspects" as Ovechkin had done. The challenge to write *texie* of the Ovechkin type was made all the more pressing by the publication of a collection of Chinese *texie* that rather resembled those of Polewoi. In February 1956, the Renmin Wenxue Press came out with a book compiled as a consquence of a decision of the Writers' Association, *Sanwen texie xuan (September 1953–December 1955),* collecting *texie* and other prose pieces from the period mentioned in parentheses. The preface by Wei Wei, written on 31 December 1955, bluntly denounced the very pieces collected in the volume.

> Our *sanwen* and *texie* are not now daring in bringing the contradictions and conflicts of life into the open, and that is indeed a great weakness. In the

42. "Yonggandi jielu shenghuozhong de maodun chongtu" (Courageously unveil the contradictions and conflicts in life), *Wenyibao* 3 (15 February 1956).

43. Ibid., p. 21.

44. Ibid. In February 1956, Liu Binyan wrote a reportage about the Third All-Soviet Youth Writers' Conference in Moscow, held early in January 1956. There, he wrote that "during the last few years quite a few of the young writers stood in the forefront of life, and brought up pressing and important problems in present life, and used their works to propel life forward." The first text mentioned by Liu in this context, was, of course, a *texie.* Liu Binyan, "Di sanci Quan Su Qingnian Zuojia Huiyi de qingkuang" (The situation at the Third All-Soviet Youth Writers' Conference), *Wenyi xuexi* 2:13 (1956).

Soviet Union this genre of *texie* is called "scout." This honorific is quite appropriate because it highlights the militant nature of this literary genre. But, alas, there are different kinds of scouts. First there is the exceedingly courageous scout, who is not at all afraid of enemies and dares to approach them closely, and thus he is able to understand thoroughly what they are after and to explore the way on which our Army will be advancing. But where do we find such scouts in China?

He then quoted Deng Xiaoping's talk at the meeting of Youth League activists for socialist construction, where Deng said, "You must combat laziness, corruption, bureaucratism and battle against all those evil persons who violate the laws and ruin discipline." The *texie* would be the optimal genre for this battle of the Youth League activists. But looking at the Chinese *texie*, one has "the impression that our construction proceeds smoothly without problems." The Chinese scouts don't see the problems, they "make their peace with all that is backward" which is due to "lack of experience" and "lack of courage" because writers are "afraid of losing their jobs. . . . If things go on like this the militant function of our scouts will be greatly impeded." Wei then recommended many of the Soviet *oçerki* as "excellent teaching material."[45] The *texie* were not the only victims of this devastating critique. Fiction writing came in for even harsher words; the *texie* was called upon to break the spell of the sugary no-conflict literature, to go ahead and clear the way for the "big guns" of literature who were to roll after them. A substantial and influential group of literary leaders who were politically linked with Deng Xiaoping and the Youth League (under Hu Yaobang) thus expressed their expectancy and hope for Chinese *oçerki* of the Ovechkin type, mirroring Soviet criticisms of Polewoi and Schaginian.

In socialism there is not an empty spot either in the sky of categories or on the earth of institutions. What is not specifically allowed is forbidden. Thus the *texie* had to find an institutional slot. The first was the periodical *Yiwen* (Translation literature). In January 1956, *Yiwen* opened a regular series, "*Texie* of our Time," where many of the *oçerki* of Ovechkin's friends were translated; furthermore, the impression was

45. Wei Wei, "Preface," in *Sanwen texie xuan (1953.9–1955.12)* (Prose and *texie*—a selection; Beijing: Renmin Wenxue Press, 1956).

given that progressive writers all over the world made ample use of this form.[46] There was some pressure for China to "mirror" the phenomenon. There was support from part of the leadership, and Qin Zhaoyang, editor of *Renmin wenxue* at the time, let it be known that he supported *texie* of the Ovechkin type. The offer was out, but who would dare to take it?

Liu Binyan dared. With one single story he established the form, the theme, and his person on the Chinese literary scene. Qin Zhaoyang was exuberant. *Renmin wenxue* had already earlier listed the *texie* among the genres to be published there, but had never received a *texie* of the Ovechkin type. Qin himself at this stage probably did not dare to write such a text himself. But when Liu Binyan's "At the Building Sites of the Bridges" reached his desk, he did everything he could to establish it as the model for other writers to follow. In the issue in which this text appeared (April 1956), the *texie* rose to the top genre in the table of contents, and the title for Liu Binyan's piece was set in boldface, a common technique to indicate the importance of a text. In a highly unusual step, Qin added two editorial comments to the story in this issue, one directly over Liu Binyan's text, the other in the "Editor's Comment" at the end of the issue. The first said:

> We have been waiting a very long time for just such a *texie,* with its incisive depiction of problems and its critical and satirical character, and we hope that, from the publication of "At the Building Sites of the Bridges" on, there will be a greater number of such works.[47]

In the second he wrote:

> In real life the battle between progress and retreat is eternally complicated and sharp, and therefore we need *texie* of the "scout" kind (*zhenchabingshi de texie*). Like scouts we have to courageously (*yonggandi*) explore the problems in real life, we have to lay them open, have to give the coup de grace to backward things in order to make way for the victorious emergence of the new. "At the Building Sites of the Bridges" in this issue is such a *texie*.

---

46. *Yiwen* had come out with translations of *texie* before, like that by Ovechkin, and another by Tendriakov (*Yiwen* 12 [1954]). As of January 1956, it made a special effort to import them into China as an umbrella for the development of Chinese *texie*.

47. *Renmin wenxue* 4:1 (April 1956).

Carefully, he added that the eulogizing *texie* published in the preceding issue were "of course . . . also good."[48] Qin evidently encouraged writers to follow in Ovechkin's and Liu Binyan's steps, using all the key terms now associated with this genre.

The reactions of the readers were enthusiastic indeed, but not of the writers. *Texie* manuscripts remained scarce. In the following issue Qin published, again with the title set in boldface, Geng Jian's (= Liu Xi's) "The Man Who Climbed up the Flagpole,"[49] a *texie* about a careerist cadre with the ironical name of Zhu Guang (Crimson Radiance) and his opponent, a rural base-level cadre with the problem (in Zhu's view) of "keeping to his own opinions" (which turn out to be quite correct), one of the few recent Chinese texts with a keen sense for the grotesque. Again, Qin Zhaoyang added a promotional comment:

> After our periodical published "At the Building Sites" we had some positive reactions showing that the broad masses of readers very much want this kind of *texie*. In this issue we publish "The Man Who Climbed up the Flagpole"; although it does not match "At the Building Sites" in "digging out the soul" of the characters, its satire is nevertheless rather spicy and the description of the hero is also well done. Besides, parasites who perch at the top of the pole are no rarity in our real life.[50]

Liu Binyan's "Inside News of Our Paper" appeared, again as the feature piece in the June 1956 issue of *Renmin wenxue*, the title set in boldface. Qin Zhaoyang noted that "at a time when everyone is already accustomed to find literary works opposing rightist conservative tendencies, this *texie* brings up a new question," pointing to the "scouting" function of the genre. Liu Binyan showed, according to Qin, that the bureaucratic villains are fairly complex in their inner structure, that they are not lazy, and that they have many good sides. And Liu Binyan started "digging out the soul" and analyzing the mental ruminations of these figures, of whom there are all too many around.[51] Writing

48. Ibid., p. 126.

49. Geng Jian, "Pa zai qiganshang de ren" (The man who climbed up the flagpole), *Renmin wenxue* 5 (May 1956); it is also contained in the collection mentioned in *Chongfang de xianhua*. Cf. S. Chan, "The Image of a 'Capitalist Roader'—Some Dissident Short Stories in the Hundred Flowers Period," *Australian Journal of Chinese Affairs* 2:81f (1979).

50. *Renmin wenxue* 5:126 (May 1956).

51. Ibid., p. 125.

under the pen name He Zhi, Qin included in the same issue an article "About the Truthfulness of *Texie*,"[52] which, as might be expected, refuted the Polewoi rule, saying that a *texie* might be true to life even if much were invented, and might be the opposite even if it described "real people and real events." The *texie* operated through the selection of real information. The journalists using this Polewoi variant "are only reporters of events in life, but do not intervene in life," Qin charged. This attitude of intervening was a crucial condition for a *texie*-ist. "A writer or a journalist with this attitude will still be able to write a moving *texie*, even with the same kind of material as others have, even if he describes real people and real events, and even if they are hard to describe in a lively way." Stating unequivocally that "our *texie* must courageously and openly intervene in life," he specified that "what we have to promote at present is the problem-oriented, critical, and satirical *texie*, because in this respect we have just begun the first attempts." The problem was that "there are journalists who think about writing a *texie* with the generalization of literature, and they think about laying open some problems in a moving way, but they don't dare to write. There is a traditional inhibition that blocks their initiative. It is time to change this situation in every respect."[53] Despite this appeal, he had to rely again on Liu Binyan, whom he encouraged to write a sequel to "Inside News," which came out in October 1956.

For Qin Zhaoyang, even the texts by Liu Binyan were not sufficiently bold. Consequently, he changed and edited them heavily to make the criticism even more pungent. He had done the same with Wang Meng's "Newcomer," which he published in the September issue of *Renmin wenxue*, and with Geng Jian's *texie*.[54] Qin continued to em-

52. He Zhi (Qin Zhaoyang), "Cong texie de zhenshixing tanqi" (About the truthfulness of *texie*), *Renmin wenxue* 6:59ff (June 1956).

53. Ibid., p. 61.

54. The editorial changes together with some of the original texts are described in Jia Ji, "Suowei 'linghun' de 'wajue'" (What they call "digging out the soul"), *Renmin wenxue* 5:105ff (May 1958). Qin had also "edited" Liu Xi's (Geng Jian's) story by "cutting off its bright ending"; cf. ibid., and Wang Meng's story, cf. "Renmin wenxue bianjibu dui 'zuzhibi xinlai de qingnianren' yuangao de xiugai qingkuang" (How the editorial department of *Renmin wenxue* changed the original draft of the "Newcomer to the Organization Department"), *Renmin ribao*, 9 May 1957. The original text by Wang Meng is now published in *Jianguo yilai duanpian xiaoshuo* (Short stories written after the founding of the PRC; Shanghai: Shanghai Renmin Press, 1980), Vol. III.

phasize the *texie* in the following issues. By fall 1956, the influence of the *texie* was felt in the short story.

Qin Zhaoyang, in a private letter to Liu Binyan written in August 1956, praised "Inside News" for "opening a new avenue for our literary creation," noting that the heroine of the piece is an intellectual, and not "one of those workers and peasants" who otherwise dominated among protagonists. He applauded Liu for "providing a model for others. This is of the utmost importance!" In October 1956, he encouraged Liu Binyan to write more such works, declaring himself willing to accept even works that did not match the high standard of "Inside News." "Your two *texie* are presently the 'top thing,'"[55] he quoted general opinion. The *texie* had intervened in life with two themes: the thinking and actions of the bureaucrat, and the aspirations of the enthusiastic socialist young intellectuals. Luo Lizheng had become a familiar type, as had Huang Jiaying.

Qin Zhaoyang then set out to change the editorial guidelines for *Renmin wenxue* to match his new aspirations. His 18-point draft for the reform of *Renmin wenxue* contained under point 4: "Set up the demand [for texts] to squarely face reality, daringly intervene in life, and have artistic quality." The terms used in this passage are all closely linked with Liu Binyan's *texie* and the tradition he had established. Zhang Guangnian, who in his polemic against Qin Zhaoyang during the Anti-Rightist Movement published Qin's program, was probably right in assuming that the specific example and model Qin had in mind when writing this program was Liu Binyan's work. Qin said in the second point, "Improving quality and establishing a specific style for the periodical will be the key problem in reform from now on." The "specific style" referred to was the one identified in point 4, to which we have already referred.[56] By late 1956, the flagship of national literature was thus beginning to move on the course charted by Liu Binyan's scouting

55. The letters, part of a collection internally published by the Writers' Association at the time of the Anti-Rightist Campaign, are quoted by Zhang Guangnian, "Yingdang laoshi xie" (A bit more honesty would be fine), in Zhang Guangnian, *Wenyi bianlun ji* (Essays on literature and the arts; Beijing: Zuojia Press, 1958), p. 143.

56. Zhang Guangnian, "Hao yige 'gaijin jihua'" (Quite a "reform plan"), in Zhang Guangnian, *Wenyi bianlun ji* (note 55 above), pp. 163ff.

texie. Qin could not publish his reform plan, there being strong opposition in the editorial board, to which he referred despondently in his correspondence with Liu Binyan, whom he admired not only as a writer but also as a daring human being. In March 1957, he wrote to Liu: "Since December of last year it was as though I have been in wind and rain," referring to the troubles with the Writers' Association's leadership and the members of his editorial board. He felt he was no match for Liu Binyan's daring. "I do not have much knowledge and courage; I am not 'pliable though strong like leather,'" he wrote. "I am ashamed for not having the strength to change the situation."[57] Qin Zhaoyang was not alone, however, and he still could make, and did make decisions as to the publication of specific works in his line.

At about the same time in late 1956 when Qin Zhaoyang wrote his program, the flagship of literary criticism in China, *Wenyibao,* publicly announced a "reform of content"; from now on, it said in bold print in December 1956, it would "actively intervene in life, encourage literary creation, unfold free discussion, and strengthen its guidance for belles lettres."[58] It had earlier published Ovechkin's "On *Texie,*" as well as Liu Binyan's "Days with Ovechkin," and it now incorporated the propositions of these texts into its own program.

Liu Binyan had not created the niche in which his *texie* appeared, although he had done his share. Basically, however, his works fitted into a social niche which had been established by powers higher than himself— the Youth League leadership and some literary and cultural leaders. The impact of his *texie* eventually was so dramatic that they became the guiding lights the nation's two most important literary periodicals used to chart their new course. No large number of *texie* of the Ovechkin type appeared as a result, but this small corpus had a disproportionally large effect. Of the 20 texts reissued in 1979 under the title of *Fragrant Flowers Abloom Again,* a volume that contains the most prominent texts of the 1956–1957 period that had been criticized, at least 8 were *texie.*[59] More important, apart from Wang Meng's text, which was under strong *texie* influence, all texts that dealt with bureaucratism were *texie,* while

57. Zhang Guangnian, "Yingdang" (note 55 above), p. 144.
58. *Wenyibao* 23: back page (1 December 1956).
59. *Chongfang de xianhua* (note 1 above).

the texts dealing with the second most controversial topic at the time, love, were all short stories, *xiaoshuo;* Wang Meng alone combined both themes. The *texie* is thus not only characterized by a certain status in the hierarchy of genres and its rejection of the options presented by the others, but also by a fixed set of themes. The *texie* of the Ovechkin type published after 1978 have remained loyal to this thematic canon.

The appearance of a bastard genre in a neatly ordered literary universe, which furthermore claimed the best of both worlds and refused to acknowledge the limits of either, led to strained efforts to reassert control in the superstructure through the creation of a neat category and the assignment of a proper place in the hierarchy of concepts. Even though the texts of the Ovechkin type were banned in mid-1957, they had made their impact on people's minds and created a latent public opinion to which the literary leadership had to react, even if that latent public opinion lacked an outlet for articulation. Thus, although no new texts of this genre appeared between 1957 and 1979, the textbooks on literary theory continued the debate. In this eerie sphere of theory the genre battled for two decades for its legitimate existence.

Liu Yanwen's *Wenxue gailun* (Outline of literature), which appeared early in 1957, took the broad view. He treated the *texie* as the core piece of *baogao wenxue,* the latter being "in terms of scholarship a social investigation (*shehui diaocha*) and, in artistic terms, realist literature." It emphasized the "complete freedom" of the form, where the author could directly intervene, as in a political essay, the "expression of ideological content in the *texie* being more direct and explicit."[60] The argument that the *texie* was a social investigation had entered the text from Timofeev's *Principles of Literature.*[61] In October 1956 the big and influential *Wenxue lilun xuexi cankao ziliao* (Reference materials for the study of literary theory) had appeared in Beijing. It was designed to present the texts to be studied by students of literature in the universities. It reprinted the articles by both Polewoi and Ovechkin in excerpts,

60. Liu Yanwen, *Wenxue gailun* (An outline of literature; Shanghai: Xin Wenyi Press, 1957), p. 263.

61. Cf. L. I. Timofejew (Timofeev), *Geschichte der Russischen Literatur vol. III, Geschichte der Sowjetliteratur,* (Berlin [East]: Kultur and Fortschritt, 1953), pp. 298f, 352ff.

as well as Hu Zhongchi's 1949 talk on *baogao wenxue,* which told something about the history and the key features of the genre.[62]

More than two years later, after many of the previous *texie* had been subjected to severe censure, Wu Diaogong stated in his *Wenxue fenlei de jiben zhishi* (Basics of literary genres) that a "small number" of *texie* of the Ovechkin type might be permitted, but that generally the Polewoi rule should be followed. Taking up an argument from Hu Zhongchi, which had been emphatically reinforced by Liu Baiyu,[63] Wu also argued that there had been reportage literature all through Chinese history, thus negating the modernist appeal of the foreign import.[64] Again two years later, in 1961, the *Cihai* defined the literary *texie* (*wenxue texie*) in similarly restrictive terms: "It demands fast and timely reflection of reality, prominent sketching of truthful (*zhenshi*) personalities and events with typical significance, a high degree of truthfulness. It has both the character of a political essay (*zhenglunxing*) and of a news report, but also needs depiction through images and a refined literary language."[65] The restrictions of "real person," "real event," and typicality did away with the leeway of the genre that Ovechkin and Liu Binyan had so eagerly sought to establish. Against these attempts to subject the genre to theoretical control, Yi Qun, who had written a history of the genre during the war of resistance,[66] came out with a spirited defense in "On the *Texie*'s Quickly Reflecting Reality." He referred to the *texie*'s being the "advance guard" or "scout," which he interpreted as indicating its "light and agile as well as capable and vigorous (*qingjie, jinghan*) form." "With regard to digging out new and great things in real life, investigating new contradictions and new problems in real life, reflecting new changes and developments in real life," Yi Qun continued, "It [the *texie*] is superior

62. Beijing Shifan Daxue Wenyi Lilun Zu, ed., *Wenxue lilun xuexi cankao ziliao* (Reference materials for a theory of literature; Beijing: Gaodeng Jiaoyu Press, October 1956), pp. 848ff.

63. Liu Baiyu, "Lun texie" (On *texie*), *Xinwen zhanxian* 1:10ff (January 1958).

64. Wu Diaogong, *Wenxue fenlei de jibenzhishi* (Basics of literary genres; Wuhan: Changjiang Wenyi Press, 1959), p. 187.

65. *Cihai* (Ocean of terms; Beijing: Zhonghua Shuju, 1965), under "*texie*."

66. Yi Qun, "Kangzhan yilai de baogao wenxue" (Reportage literature since the war of resistance), in *Zhongguo kangzhan wenyi shi*, quoted in Tian Zhongji, Preface, in Zhongguo Baogao Wenxue Congshu Bianji Weiyuanhui, ed., *Zhongguo baogao wenxue congshu* (Chinese reportage literature, a collection; Wuhan: Changjiang Wenyi Press, 1981), I, 1.

to all other literary genres; it first discovers situations, opens the battle first, and engages in battle, thus becoming a weapon that is helping to advance today's real life." After this measured introduction which put Polewoi and Ovechkin on the same level, Yi Qun mainly focused on the latter, emphasizing that the *texie* was "one of the lightest and sprightliest, most nimble and vivacious literary forms" which "gives the writer greatest freedom in its use." It required high "accuracy" and "concreteness." And each *texie* "has a specific object, and is directed against certain personalities and the relationships between them," acquiring, however, "a very broad general meaning." The key virtues of the genre were "reasoned selection of material, precision of language, and accuracy of description."[67]

The status of reportage literature during the early 1960s was high enough to prompt a plan for the publication of a very large collection of such texts with the purpose of lifting the standards and increasing the prestige of the form. The plan initially came to naught, however, eventually being realized nearly twenty years later, and then with the inclusion of Liu Binyan's works.[68] As though history had just made a full turn in the meantime, the protagonists of the early battles started the new phase after the 3rd Plenum of the Central Committee in December 1978 by restating their old positions. Huang Gang maintained the Polewoi rule, to be countered by Zou Xianmin.[69] Liu Binyan came out for "describing the dark side," "intervening in life," and "writing the truth,"[70] and Zhou Yang hinted that the last slogan had been created by Stalin, the one before that by another Russian — Ovechkin — and that describing "the dark side" was an altogether un-Chinese thing to do.[71]

---

67. Yu Gang, Guo Qizong, eds., *Wenxue gailun cankao ziliao* (Reference materials for the outline of literature; Xiamen: Xiamen Daxue, 1964), pp. 103ff. The article is by Prof. Wang Daoqian. On pp. 108ff, it incorporates the article by Yi Qun; the source for the latter is his *Wenxue wenti manlun* (Talks on literary problems; Beijing: Zuojia Press, 1959); the article has not been incorporated into the 1963 edition of this work.

68. Tian Zhongqi, "Preface" to *Zhongguo baogao wenxue congshu*, (note 66 above).

69. Huang Gang, "Baogao wenxue de shidai tezheng ji qi bixu yanshou zhenshi de dangxing yuanze" (The characteristic of timeliness in reportage literature and its obligation to strictly maintain the principle of party spirit), *Wenyi yanjiu* 1 (January 1980); Zuo Xianmin, "Tan baogao wenxue jian yu Huang Gang tongzhi shangque" (On reportage literature, being simultaneously a discussion with comrade Huang Gang), *Wenyi yanjiu* 1 (January 1980).

70. Cf. note 11 above.

71. Zhou Yang, "Jiefang sixiang, zhenshide biaoxian women de shidai" (Let us liberate our

The uneasy truce of the mid-1950s between the Ovechkin type and the Polewoi type thus restored, Liu Binyan conceded that the writings of Xu Chi, which praised the progressive intellectual and criticized the "Gang of Four," also had their good side, while Yi Junsheng suddenly and quite out of context stated that, since the *texie* of Liu Binyan had recently been rehabilitated, it was therefore safe to say that they were legitimate uses of the genre after all.[72] Neither side was strong enough to enforce its views administratively, and the leadership took pains to maintain an unstable balance. Few writers came to Liu Binyan's defense. There was a continued apprehension in literary circles about the intrusion of this bastard genre with its arrogant claim for being the avant-garde and its often shoddy descriptions of flat characters in flat circumstances. Ovechkin had already deplored that, "in the Soviet Union, there are still people who think lightly of this form. Like great lords they despise it and consider it vulgar (*diji*)."[73] The same attitude prevailed among writers in China. The authors of *texie* were often (like Liu Binyan) journalists, and the hard-hitting documentary style with its objectivity, or rather *Sachlichkeit* (a German term perhaps equivalent to "matter-of-factness"), was taken for simple crudeness (which it often was), with the result that the *texie* with their hot themes dragged the entire literary world into the very political troubles it so carefully tried to avoid. Thus, in January 1980, Liu Shaotang published a letter to Liu Binyan in which he expressed, somewhat awkwardly it seems, his amazement at Liu's capacity to "fly from one world to the other, from the newspaper world to the literary world." He then took him to task for his lack of attention to literary matters in "Between Human and Monster." The title "After You Have Now Transferred to the Literary World on a Full-Time Basis" (which Liu hadn't, since he remained a journalist)

---

thinking and truthfully depict our time), *Wenyibao* 4:10 (22 February 1981). For Stalin, cf. *Renmin ribao*, 8 October 1980, p. 5.

72. Yi Junsheng, "Gesong guangming, pouxi shibi, jili weilai, lun baogao wenxue de shehui zhineng" (Praise all that is shining, dissect the corruption of our time, urge forward into the future—about the social functions of reportage literature), in Yi Junsheng and Yang Rupeng, *Baogao wenxue zongheng tan* (Disquisitions about reportage literature; Chengdu: Sichuan Renmin Press, 1983), p. 51.

73. V. Ovechkin, "On Oçerk," p. 37 (note 17 above).

indicated that Liu should focus less on politics and more on style.[74] In the same month, Feng Mu came out with the demand that writers should be alert to the social consequences of their texts, at a time when preparations were under way for the prohibition of a number of film scripts and plays.[75] To focus more on style was, perhaps unconsciously, a plea to keep the literary world on the safe side.

This second part of the description of the surface layer of the *texie* in China focused on the social role of the genre, the themes associated with it, and the rejections of other forms as well as criticisms of other uses of the same form contained in the choice of the Ovechkin-type *texie*. Far from being a general receptacle for any sort of content, the pondered or researched *texie* was part of a political program, of which the key notions would be technological progress and anti-bureaucratism. The specific notions associated with the *texie* were contained in the vivid image of the scout with his fact orientation, nimbleness, astute powers of observation, independent decision making and investigation, and the freedom to choose any means necessary to get at the facts and convey them. With the bureaucrat Borzov, Ovechkin had created the literary counterpart of the real-life bureaucrat, and *Borzovian man* became a common term in Russian vernacular. Liu Binyan was not as successful; however, Luo Lizheng, Luo-Who-Lays-Down-the-Correct-Line, from "At the Building Sites" came close. In the 12th issue of *Xin guancha* in 1957, Shen Yan published his "Gei 'Luo Lizheng' de xin" (Letter to "Luo Lizheng"), taking him as the general symbol of the bureaucrat. An article signed Er Ying in *Wenyibao* late in July 1957[76] sternly took him to

74. Liu Shaotang, "Zhuanye dao wenyijie yihou—gei Liu Binyan de xin" (Since you have now transferred to the literary world—a letter to Liu Binyan), *Shanghai wenxue* 1 (January 1980). The *texie* is often described as an easy form which could serve as an entrance to the literary stage for young writers; cf. Shen Congwen, "Lun texie" (On *texie*), *Yishibao*, 13 January 1948 (in no. 76 of the literary supplement *Wenxue zhoukan*); and Wei Jinzhi, "Xian cong baogao texie rushou" (Starting first with reportage literature), *Wenyi yuebao*, March 1955. I am indebted to Jeffrey Kinkley for the reference to Shen Congwen's article.

75. Feng Mu, "Duiyu wenxue chuangzuode yige huigu he zhanwang" (A look back and a look ahead to our literary creation), *Wenyibao* 1 (January 1980).

76. Shen Yan, "Gei 'Luo Lizheng' de xin" (A letter to 'Luo Lizheng'), *Xin guancha* 12 (1957). Er Ying, "Guanyu 'Luo Lizheng' he 'huoran kailang de xiaorong,'" (On "Luo Lizheng" and his "smile of sudden understanding"), *Wenyibao* 17:8 (22 July 1957).

task for this. Luo Lizheng had caught the public fancy on both sides of the fence.

Within literary categories, the *texie* finds a nondescript niche in the space between *xiaoshuo* and newspaper reporting, a categorical no-man's-land, jurisdiction over which was not clear. Institutionally it found its medium in the prestigious journal *Renmin wenxue*, which supported at the time many authors linked to the Youth League (under Hu Yaobang) and provided practically the entire hero population of the texts, as well as shelter for Liu Binyan and others.

FIFTEEN

The Texie-*ist, or* Writer *of* Texie

As we have seen, writing a *texie* of the Ovechkin type communicates qua genre a highly loaded silent text, and takes a public stance among the other genres. But this is not all. Writing *texie* of this kind means becoming a *texiejia,* a *texie*-ist. The term is, of course, a translation from the Russian *oçerkist.* An *oçerkist* is not just someone writing *oçerki;* the term is something of an honorific (or, for others, denunciatory) description of an individual who realizes the values defended in his *texie* in his own public life. To write such *texie* is to adopt a public role. Ovechkin was regarded as the foremost *oçerkist* of the socialist camp at the time.[1] The qualities given to the heroes in the *texie* might give a clue as to the role the *texie*-ist set out to fulfil. Engineer Zeng[2] "dares to make decisions" and to "take responsibility for them." His team has a "maximum

---

1. The entire period of Soviet literature immediately after Stalin's death is often called the "era of Ovechkin"; see F. Kusnetsov, "Sud'by derevni v prose i kritike," *Novy Mir* 6:233 (1973). Cf. P. Carden, (page 259 note 17), p. 407. This is not a later judgment. Pomerantsev had singled out Ovechkin for the greatest praise in his important and controversial "Ob iskrennosti v literature" (On sincerity in literature), *Novy Mir* 12 (1953), as had K. Simonov in his 1955 article on problems of contemporary prose, which I quote from the German, "Einige Probleme der zeitgenössischen Prosa," *Sowjetliteratur* 5:168 (1955); see also Vadim Sokolov in "The 'Oçerk' in Contemporary Soviet Literature," *Soviet Literature* 6:148ff (1957). On p. 153: "The victor's crown in the Soviet Union goes today to Ovechkin, for he has brought out the most exciting and important social problems. Today his example is being followed and developed by scores of talented writers."

2. The young hero from "At the Building Sites."

innovative spirit (*xinshiqing*)," a "bold spirit (*dadan jingshen*)," and he does not direct work from an office, but personally takes charge in times of crisis, being closely linked with and greatly admired by the workers. He is, of course, young. As an engineer he belongs to the most qualified class; he works at the first steel bridge over the Huanghe built by new China, the very forefront of the nation's modern industry, and there he leads the top team. The work site of this team is exceedingly organized, and Zeng, who is a qualified manager, is even culturally alert, reading the *Hongloumeng*. All these qualities are reinforced through the confrontation with his negative counterparts, Brigadier Luo and engineer Zhou Weiben, Zhou-Who-Keeps-Himself-on-the-Safe-Side. Huang Jiaying in "Inside News" shows "creativity" and "initiative," demands more "latitude" for the workers, and "sensibility" from the journalists. She speaks out and refuses to compromise to gain admission into the Party. The other young journalists discuss the most daring proposals such as allowing workers to switch jobs or transforming the press into a "trumpet" for the people's voice. They think of themselves not just as the "eyes and ears" of Party leadership but even as its "brain," and they do a lot of independent thinking. Cultured lifestyle now includes fancy khaki suits and black leather shoes, and even a freer attitude towards love.[3]

The much-battered heroes described in Liu's post-1979 texts show the stress such attitudes put on these individuals. To be "outspoken" and "innovative" now requires a nearly sectarian stubbornness; the spring sun that shone into the newspaper office is gone. These new heroes, the engineer Zengs after twenty years of harsh persecution, are still *ken'gan* (people who "go at it with a will"); they still show *shiyexin* (devotion to their work); they are *gan shiqing de ren* ("people who get things done"). They are outspoken and refuse the soft murmur of intrigue and flattery.[4] They are most modern, concentrating on technology and management, making short phrases and fast decisions; the *texie* as a form

3. For a more complete analysis of the story, see R. Wagner, "The Cog and the Scout. Functional Concepts of Literature in Socialist Political Culture: The Chinese Debate in the Mid-Fifties," in W. Kubin, R. Wagner, eds., *Essays in Modern Chinese Literature and Literary Criticism* (Bochum: Brockmeyer, 1982), pp. 360ff.

4. Liu Binyan, "Yingshi longteng huyue shi" (p. 249 note 2), pp. 116, 130, 131; id., "Yige ren he ta de yingzi" (A man and his shadow), in *Liu Binyan baogao wenxue xuan* (ch. 14 note 4), pp. 207ff.

mimics their features—they are as important and isolated as the genre which describes them. The *texie*-ist is one of this crowd, sharing their ideals and fate, and being their advocate both in his writing and behavior.

Liu Binyan very consciously set out to play his public role as a *texie*-ist. After the translation of Ovechkin's talk on *texie* had created on Chinese soil the niche in which to place his own work, he used a lengthy article, "Days with Ovechkin," in April 1956[5] to create and fortify with his Soviet friend's prestige the social niche in which to perform his public role. The article's title was set in boldface, and appeared in *Wenyibao* in a series of articles under the heading "The *Texie*—a Sharp Weapon," where also an article by Su Ping on Liu Binyan's "At the Building Sites" appeared, which already in its title maintained, obviously against differing opinions, that this was "an excellent *texie*."[6]

Ovechkin was an independent investigator; although deeply committed to the ultimate goals of the Party, he was not characterized by *party'nost,* (Party spirit or the willingness to go along with everything the Party says and does), but by "Party conscience," that is, loyalty to its ultimate goals. "If he would not have this warm love for the Party and real socialist life, how could he. . . . for twenty years unswervingly and loyally revile and unmask bureaucratism?" The 20th Soviet Party Congress finally vindicated Ovechkin's aspirations. With an indirect reference to China, Liu quoted Ovechkin:

> One has to take exceedingly practical steps to battle against the after-effects of the cult of personality. In order to promote the people's initiative and creativity, one has to start by protecting the critic. It has to be strictly prohibited to suppress critics; one has to create an environment where the soil under the feet of those who suppress critics gets altogether too hot. We must get to a point where criticism becomes a habit, and people must see it proved with their own eyes that criticism is indeed a motive force for socialist society, and they must believe that we are not "frivolous critics" . . . otherwise it will be impossible to overcome the pervasive feelings of resignation that "nothing can be done about that kind of bureaucratism."

5. Liu Binyan, "He Aoweiqijin zai yiqi de rizi" (Days with Ovechkin), *Wenyibao* 8 (30 April 1956).

6. Su Ping "Zai giaoliang gongli shang'shi yipian chuse de texie" ("At the Building Sites of the Bridges" is an excellent *texie*), *Wenyibao* 8 (30 April 1956).

He added "Sadly, we time and again fail to foster the feeling among the masses that they are the masters."[7] The urgency of this battle against bureaucratism caused Ovechkin to defer his plans for a longer work and use his "militant" instrument, the *texie*.

It must be counted among the calculable professional risks faced by the *texie*-ist that he will encounter the bitter opposition of those he attacks. Ovechkin even made a principle out of this: "If a work does not run into some opposition, it means that it does not irritate anyone—and of what interest is it then?"[8] And Liu Binyan hinted that Ovechkin had been fighting bureaucrats "for twenty years," that is, even under Stalin, when the risks involved were certainly substantial. Quoting Ovechkin in order to deal with his Chinese colleagues, Liu Binyan had him say: "If you write about a touchy topic, go about it boldly; if you are cowardly, don't even write. If you ponder beforehand, 'Ai, there might be trouble when it is published,' then it is best to stop writing; don't torment yourself, and don't torment the topic. This cowardliness will certainly show up in your writing."[9]

Liu Binyan did not fail to invoke Ovechkin's authority for his own plan: "One should not be afraid of contradictions, should not be cowed by their muddled and confused outer appearance. One has to strip off their outer garments layer by layer, then one will always be able to discover the key issue. There is no other way. Were I, for example, to write about China without mentioning its difficulties and problems, how could I give a true picture of the Chinese people's struggle?"

The *texie*-ist is as outspoken in life as in his works. When a publisher wanted to exclude a *texie* by Ovechkin from a collection because it depicted "a complete gallery of people obstructing the newly born forces," Ovechkin bluntly replied: "No, one person is missing in this gallery, you!"[10]

In his article on the All-Soviet Youth Writers' Conference in Moscow, Liu Binyan had already given a first glimpse of Ovechkin the man. The frankness of the discussions at this meeting as a part of the emerg-

7. Ibid., p. 32.
8. Ibid., p. 30.
9. Ibid.
10. Ibid.

ing Thaw climate in the Soviet Union was held up by Liu Binyan for emulation by the Chinese Youth writers, who held their own conference immediately thereafter. At the Moscow meeting, Ovechkin bluntly and publicly contradicted the pontifications of the keynote speaker about the presentation of "positive heroes," being supported in this by Sholokhov, another stalwart of the early Thaw, who charged that this speaker had wasted much of his time taking individual works to task and had neglected many more pressing issues. Liu Binyan's own report about this meeting is a replica of its spirit, being factual, discriminating, critical, and utterly devoid of the mandatory verbiage usually embellishing such articles.[11]

The *texie*-ist confronts a formidable array of enemies, but his courageous stance also has its rewards. Ovechkin was a national figure; people from the entire country wrote to him, telling about their problems, finding the things that he attacked repeated in their own community, and pinning their hopes on him. As an individual and as a writer they saw him as a hero. Furthermore, after twenty years of "scouting" and pointing out the problems, finally a supreme body of the Party followed the path he had marked, accepting his description of the enemies and friends, and of the goals—"the people's initiative" and "creativity." The *texie*-ist is the ultimate critic, because he is not just harboring resentment, or making in-house reports; he publishes his views, condensing the multifarious social phenomena and subjecting them to a rigorous analysis, which not only reveals the forces of obstruction but also those of progress and the ways of achieving progress. The texts as well as his attitude thus become a matter of utmost public importance. Indeed, if really the "initiative" and "creativity" of the people are to be mobilized and the dictatorial say of the cadres restricted, the first step has to be the "protection of the critics," that is, primarily of their most outspoken and efficient subgroup, the *texie*-ists. Their treatment becomes the measure of the Party's sincerity, and the gauge of the latitude people can securely assume to be theirs in articulating criticism.

Liu Binyan certainly had no modest assessment of the public role of the *texie*-ist, and, as his article shows, he was fully aware of both the risks

11. Liu Binyan, "The Situation" (p. 267 note 44), pp. 13ff.

and the rewards such a role could offer, a role he was about to assume in China. Thus, his closing statement in "Days with Ovechkin" is both a description of this man and a daring program for his own life. "There is no separation, no difference, between what Ovechkin thinks, says, and writes." The literary genre, its content and role, and the public posture of the author are all intricately interwoven. They serve the people as a "surveyor's rod" for their assessment of persons and social phenomena, as one man wrote to Ovechkin.

Ovechkin proclaimed the *texie* to be the most important instrument to foster modern attitudes among the people in the critical period following Stalin's death, when the "new" forces were battling against the old bureaucrats. "Now is the time when one must make use of the effects of this literary form, the *texie*. One has to propagate among the people the spirit of the loyal and courageous citizen; and there are so many problems that need to be solved."[12] "In this manner," added Liu Binyan, "Ovechkin, with his own *texie*, helps people to bring about a new and better life, and it is here where the entire power of the *texie* resides."[13] We are back to Liang Qichao's dreams about the power of the political novel.

Becoming a *texie*-ist, Liu Binyan was thus not blindly courting disaster but opting for a highly conspicuous role in China's public sphere; having attached to this role the highest marks of legitimacy, both in terms of the Party and the people, he was willing to run the risk, having declared at the outset of his career that those who obstructed him could only be the very bureaucrats who rode roughshod over the people.

It is one thing to say that it is right to do something, another to adduce an example that this can be done elsewhere (Ovechkin), but a third to do it oneself. Liu Binyan has been remarkably consistent on this last issue, going about playing the role of the ultimately *modern texie*-ist on Chinese soil.

In the closed world of Chinese political culture, this means first of all to "think independently" and "boldly speak out" oneself. From his friendship with Ovechkin, his wide reading of Soviet Thaw literature in

12. Liu Binyan, "Days with Ovechkin" (note 5 above), p. 32.
13. Ibid.

the original, and his trip (together with Deng Tuo) to Poland and the Soviet Union in early 1956, Liu Binyan could talk with some authority about what was possible in socialist states after Stalin's death. In May 1956, he said in Harbin: "After the 20th Congress of the Soviet Communist Party, thinking in the various East European states opened up and free discussions sprang up; only we [in China] don't permit free discussion."[14] The Thaw still had to come to China. In the Soviet Union, he said, referring to Ovechkin, there is a *texie*-ist who became famous because he unearthed defects; he greatly praised this man and proposed to emulate his example.[15] He gave a detailed summary of Dudintsev's *Not By Bread Alone*, although it had not been translated and was controversial in the Soviet Union, calling it "excellent."[16] In Harbin, where he lived for many years, where he had many friends, and where his sister was a primary-school teacher, he not only gave a talk entitled "How To Write a *Texie*" (June 1956),[17] but made a public demonstration of how to go about it. In a factory for electrical machinery he hung up, "in the most conspicuous place," a notice that anyone who wanted to "appeal for redress of grievances and pour out his woes"[18] should come to see him. His credibility having been established by way of *xiaodao*, the small channel of rumor and information, "over a hundred workers"[19] came to see him under the wary eyes of management. A news story, "A Storehouse with Living Men" was the result;[20] the factory was hoarding

14. Pan Shishen, "Liu Binyan wumie woguo meiyou 'xinwen ziyou' deng miulun" (Liu Binyan's fallacies in defaming our country for not having "freedom of the press" and the like), *Zhongguo qingnianbao*, 20 July 1957.

15. Chen Xicheng, "Liu Binyan zai Harbin ganle xie shenma?" (What did Liu Binyan do in Harbin?), *Zhongguo qingnianbao*, 17 July 1957.

16. Gao Miaozheng, "Liu Binyan xiang *Beijing ribao* tuanyuan sanbu dusuo" (The poison spread by Liu Binyan among the Youth League members of the *Beijing Daily*), *Zhongguo qingnianbao*, 20 July 1957.

17. Cf. Pan Shishen, "Liu Binyan's Fallacies" (note 14 above).

18. Guo Yongze, "Liu Binyan zai Harbin de exing zhongzhong" (Assorted misdeeds by Liu Binyan in Harbin), *Zhongguo qingnianbao* 25 July 1957.

19. "Youpaifenzi Liu Binyan fandang fanshehuizhuyi de zhen mianmu" (The true face of the anti-Party anti-socialist attitude of the rightist Liu Binyan), *Zhongguo qingnianbao* 18 July 1957, p. 3 col. 3.

20. Rong Lianxiu, Pan Shishen, "'Huoren cangku'" (A "Storehouse with Living Men"), *Zhongguo qingnianbao*, 19 July 1956. Pan later claimed that Liu Binyan had directed the writing of this piece (which probably was true); cf. Pan Shishen, "Liu Binyan's Fallacies" (note 14 above). The story contains such alarming lines as: "The cadres are accustomed to regard the

manpower, letting skilled young workers idle around on miserable pay, playing poker at a time when other factories needed them badly. This material also made it into his "Inside Story" where the young journalist Huang Jiaying is investigating exactly this problem; there, the workers who complain to their superiors are accused of "individualism" and of "opposing leadership."

The *texie*-ist's duty does not stop at writing. Seeing long lines in front of the Labor Office in Harbin, which assigns jobs to youngsters who have finished school, Liu decided that the problem of job assignment could not be solved by further increases in official institutions.[21] He had the effrontery to compare the number of offices in Harbin in 1956 with those of the Manchukuo Administration. It turned out, as might be expected, that the number had greatly increased with the advent of socialism. Liu Binyan then stated publicly that the dramatic housing shortage in Harbin was due to the occupation of so much of the city's inhabitable space by government and party offices, in fact favorably comparing the level of bureaucratism in Manchukuo with that in New China.[22] Many of his studies and reports furthermore showed that the personnel offices developed exceedingly cynical attitudes towards the people over whose lives they had such tremendous power. Commenting on one especially gruesome case, he wrote: "Look to what degree professional cynicism can develop in Youth League work! Perhaps because the Youth League is doing personnel work every day, it is inevitable that it would become cynical with regard to all aspects of people's lives, including questions of life and death."[23] Thus he openly came out against the Party's "monopolistic control of everything" he supported in "Inside News"—the *bahui*, strike meetings of the disgruntled workers—as a means to bring pressure on the bureaucrats, and he ventured to give a talk in Harbin in front of the base-level Youth League secretaries advocating "free choice of

---

orders from higher levels as being ten times, a hundred times more important than the demands of the masses."

21. Chen Xicheng, "What Did Liu Binyan Do in Harbin?" (note 15 above).

22. Ibid.

23. Liu Binyan, "Leng" (Cynicism), unpublished, quoted in "The True Face" (note 19 above), col. 4.

profession" and of the working place,[24] a point also advocated in "Inside News." In the midst of a national debate about "rational distribution" of school graduates this put an enormous pressure on the Youth League as it articulated the demands of large parts of its constituency.[25]

His talk "How to Write a *Texie*" was attended by the entire staff and leadership of *Harbin ribao*, as well as by members of the Party and Youth League committees of the city. Liu Binyan was no longer just a young man who had written his first story. The story "At the Building Sites," was the first critical text after 1949;[26] it instantly made him *the texie*-ist of the nation, and his public exercises were appropriately advertised. The *xiaodao* of rumored information carried the word that he had not only the support and admiration of people like Qin Zhaoyang but also of the mighty new head of the Youth League, Hu Yaobang.[27] Zhou Enlai in person had asked him whether he wanted to go abroad; he had declined, thinking it more important to build up his public role as the nation's *texie*-ist in this critical time, but he did not fail to mention this flattering invitation in an aside.[28] Liu did not waste his time in talking about the generalities of the genre; he talked about the key issues under current conditions, namely, that it was a genre optimally qualified to help in the widening of latitude, initiative, independent thinking, and bold talk. His audience was mixed, but his talk was addressed exclusively to young journalists and perhaps some enlightened cadres. Don't accept things just because they come from higher levels. "Reserve your doubts," he told them. We get ahead not by eulogizing the successes, but by overcoming the defects, and the journalist-*texie*-ist has to "find those defects." And he does not find them by staring at the bland surface, but by finding "people who dare to speak out," as he was just doing in the Electrical Machinery Factory in that very city, which in fact gained him

24. Guo Yongze, "Assorted Misdeeds" (note 18 above), cols. 2f.

25. Cf. the directive of the State Council, "Heli fenpei rencai jiaqiang jiancha jiandu" (Rationally distribute manpower, strengthen inspection and supervision), *Zhongguo qingnianbao*, 2 August 1956, p. 1, as well as the editorial on the same page.

26. Liu was quite aware of this and remembers it well; cf. his statement in the interview with Lee Yee, "Liu Binyan he tade shidai" (Liu Binyan and his time), *Qishi niandai* 12:87 col. 2 (1982).

27. In the interview with Lee Yee, he mentions that a number of "high-ranking cadres felt it was very well written"; Lee Yee, "Liu Binyan" (note 26 above), p. 68, col. 3.

28. Cf. Chen Xicheng, "What Did Liu Binyan Do in Harbin?" (note 15 above).

a much better understanding of many problems of the city than the old hands in their offices could claim.[29] Ovechkin had already maintained that a good *texie*-ist must be able to see, in a very short time, problems that remain hidden to the habitués of the place.[30]

Liu Binyan as a *texie*-ist was credible enough. Even when he was being subjected to attacks after the beginning of the Anti-Rightist Movement, his critics were still conceding his public success. "When the speech was over, he had indeed bewitched a segment of the people present and drawn them over to his side. One journalist said: 'If Liu Binyan came to *Harbin ribao,* the editor-in-chief would probably break out in loud wailing.' Some people specifically sought out Liu Binyan in order to talk with him, and this is how he got the 'materials' he was looking for. The material for 'Inside News' is taken from our newspaper publishing house [*Harbin ribao*]"[31] This was quite a feat. He gave a talk to the entire staff of a paper which he was to call "the country's most disappointing newspaper,"[32] managing to encourage many of the probably younger journalists to talk to him and give him the "inside news" of the paper. His story, "Inside News," in turn articulated their resentment, and proposed that the newspapers be run much more independently vis-à-vis Party directives.[33] The effect of the article, his "militant intervening in life," was certainly felt, and one critic later complained that the workers' restiveness towards their management increased after the publication of the story.

It is an essential part of the *texie*-ist's public role that he speak out openly and confront his antagonists directly, not letting himself be

29. Ibid.

30. Liu Binyan, "Days with Ovechkin" (note 5 above), p. 31.

31. Chen Xicheng, "What Did Liu Binyan Do in Harbin?" (note 15 above).

32. Huang Sha, "Jielu Liu Binyan zai Shanghai Renmindiantai sanbu de fandong kuangyan" (Expose the reactionary blabber spread by Liu Binyan at the Shanghai People's Broadcasting Station), *Zhongguo qingnianbao,* 19 July 1957, col. 8.

33. Indeed, some "blooming and contending" articles appeared in the paper afterwards, like Wang Ti's "Ren yu ren zhi jian" (Between one human being and another), which deplored the cooling off of human relations as a consequence of the emphasis on class struggle; cf. *Harbin ribao,* 13 June 1957. A decision of the Harbin Party Committee from 25 June 1957 deplored the paper's lack of quality and "mass nature," that is, the inability to evoke interest among the readers, and then made the paper into an official *dangbao,* Party paper; cf. "Guanyu gaijin *Harbin ribao* de jueding" (Decision on the transformation of the *Harbin Daily*), *Harbin ribao,* 29 June 1957.

pushed into a sort of conspiratorial fringe. He is not only describing things, but proposes ways to solve the problems, this being the *zhenglun,* the "political essay," part of his work. And, as an individual, he combines loyalty to the ultimate goals of the Party and the people with daring independence in thinking, bold talk, and a free lifestyle in a compelling image for emulation by the young. Liu Binyan at the time was known as being exceedingly "elegant;"[34] he read Russian (and later Japanese and English) and was highly *wenming* ("cultured"). He had been traveling extensively in China, which gave him the experience necessary to find out "problems" of some general importance; he had been traveling to other socialist countries, which gave him a broader outlook regarding the problems of bureaucratism in such societies.[35] His urbane appearance coupled with his good looks made him the personification of the educated *kultur'nost* and daring young city intellectual who at the time was set up by Youth Leagues all over the socialist camp for emulation.[36]

Specificity and concreteness being the catchwords of the *texie*-ist, we may expect Liu to not to have restricted himself to talking about generalities of bureaucratism and the battle against it. The "sociologism" inherent in the life and labors of the *texie*-ist meant that he set out to develop a fairly complete view of the social structure of post-revolutionary China and the stress it was under. His views were surprisingly precocious and have received their fair share of glory many decades later in post-1979 pronouncements of Chinese political leaders.

The development of bureaucratic attitudes is nearly unavoidable among people who rise to official positions, even if they have the best

34. Cf. Liu Shaotang, "Since You Have Now Transferred" (p. 278 note 74), p. 85: "For twenty-one years we had not met; you had aged and I was shocked; the elegant and unrestrained Liu Binyan of the old days was gone."

35. Liu Binyan talked about his impressions in Poland 1956 in his interview with Lee Yee (note 26 above), pp. 67f. There, foreign papers could be openly bought, everyone had read Kruschev's "secret talk," and the Party paper reported factory strikes against the government.

36. Fang Ji, who later, in his "Laifangzhe" (The visitor), *Shouhuo* 3 (1958), made Liu Binyan and people like him into the negative hero, whose only merit is that he eventually turns himself in for labor reform, wrote about this role of Liu Binyan as a model for many young people. Fang argued that Liu Binyan managed to "intervene in life" by "giving to those people who were not satisfied with reality a boost and an example; they would always adduce him by way of proof. Look, are there not examples for intervening in life in 'At the Building Sites' and in 'Inside News'?" Fang Ji, "Liu Binyan chuangzuozhong sanbu shenme dusuo?" (What kind of poison is Liu Binyan spreading in his stories?), *Zhongguo qingnianbao,* 29 July 1957, p. 3 cols. 2f.

of intentions. Both Liu and Wang Meng used the term *professional disease*[37] to describe the phenomenon. Liu mentioned five types of bureaucrats among leading cadres in decreasing order of the danger they presented: "Conservatives [Chen Litong in "Inside News" is the model], people who don't try to achieve anything, but only try to avoid mistakes [Luo Lizheng in "At the Building Sites" fits this description], people who care only for their own department (*benweizhuyizhe*), people who are arrogant and pompous and have degenerated in their lives, and people who report encouraging news but nothing which could irritate."[38] On occasion he used less neutral terms like *quanruzhuyi* (cynic), *paxingzhuyi* (crawler), *shiseng* (city monk = petty bourgeois), *zhengke* (politico), or *geming zishen baoweizhe* (revolutionary protector of his self-interests).[39]

These leading cadres had for the most part no real grasp of the situation. The leaders in the center formed a new "nobility" or "privileged class," a "class of leaders," inside the Party, while the provincial leaders acted as "local gods."[40] Mao Zedong, who in 1956 and early 1957 advocated anti-conservativism and the Hundred Flowers policy, seems to

37. Wang Meng, "Zuzhibu xinlaide qingnianren" (A young man who only recently joined the Organization Department), *Renmin wenxue* 9:40 (September 1956); for Liu Binyan, cf. "The True Face," (note 19 above), p. 3, cols. 1 and 3.

38. Quoted from a letter to a *Zhongguo qingnianbao* correspondent in Tianjin in Wang Yushi and Ma Heqing, "Yanli pipan xinwenjie bailei Liu Binyan" (Severely chastise Liu Binyan, the scum of newspaper circles), *Zhongguo qingnianbao*, 22 July 1957, col. 5.

39. "The True Face" (note 19 above), col. 1.

40. Ibid.; cf. also Xing Yan, "Bo Liu Binyan de fandang miulun" (Against Liu Binyan's anti-Party slanders), *Zhongguo qingnianbao*, 20 July 1957, p. 3, col. 1; Huang Sha, "Expose the Reactionary Blabber" (note 32 above), cols. 3f; "Liu Binyan shi zichanjieji youpai zai dangnei de daiyanren" (Liu Binyan is the spokesman of the bourgeois rightists within the Party), *Renmin ribao*, 20 July 1957, p. 2, cols. 1f. In a reportage, Liu Binyan tried to describe how this separate class formed and behaved; Liu Binyan, "Gezhe yiceng" (Something in between), *Zhongguo qingnianbao*, 8 November, 1956. The theory of a specific bureaucratic class was widely discussed in China at the time, and some people were undoubtedly familiar with foreign writings on the topic. Prominent among the public figures upholding this theory was Prof. Zhou Dajue from the Aeronautics Institute in Beijing. He argued that one's station in production determined one's class, and thus there was a leading, administering, and commanding class in China. Cf. Zhao Jing, "Bo Zhou Dajue guanyu 'lingdaozhe jieji' de miulun" (Refutation of the slanders spread by Zhou Dajue about a "class of leaders"), *Beijing ribao*, 11 July 1957; cf. also the excerpts from his argument on the same page. The similarity of their views is noted in Shi Bing, "Bushi duli sikao, shi huangzi" (This is not independent thinking; it is a pretense), *Zhongguo qingnianbao*, 24 July 1957.

have been the only one in the Center who could be counted upon for progress. Asked how the decision about launching the *Zhengfeng* (Rectification) Movement was made in May 1957, Liu said publicly, "Chairman Mao is for it; as for the Center, one will have to wait and see," and the provincial leaders would be "most difficult to handle."[41]

Thus we have in both his stories and comments a bright top (Mao), a strong body of youthful activists at the base, and in the middle the ossified structures of bureaucratism. The same configuration seemed to be repeated everywhere. In the Youth League, he said, Hu Yaobang, the chairman, was "no conservative in his thinking, but, because he has no support from (Youth League) Central, his statements do not carry the day."[42] The middle level was bureaucratized, and the base cadres and common members of the Youth League were the reservoir from which he hoped those would emerge who would boldly speak out and storm ahead. In Harbin, Liu said (and described in "Inside News"): "The Center is progressive, the masses are progressive, but the middle level is very slow, very conservative, and very awkward."[43]

This already critical situation had been further worsened by the recruitment policies of the preceding years. The great potential of activist youths had not been tapped, and was even handled roughly. "In 1953, youths had a hundred-percent faith in the Party," Liu said, "and they stormed ahead. After the Three-Anti Movement they were somewhat depressed, but they did not dare to speak out. In 1954, youths intended to speak out but again were beaten down. Last year [1956] there was [Mao's description of] the upsurge [of socialism in the countryside] and the 8th Party Congress, and youths who thought about speaking out were again beaten down."[44] This went along with a marked "cooling down" of social relations. "Of course there is warmth between people, but not much," the cause being the constant emphasis on "class struggle." In Shanghai, he said: "After the New Three-Anti [Movement in 1955], human rights were trampled underfoot, the dignity of man was disregarded, and during the Sufan [Movement for the elimination of

41. Huang Sha, "Expose the Reactionary Blabber" (note 32 above), col. 3.
42. "Liu Binyan is the Spokesman," (note 40 above), col. 5.
43. Huang Sha, "Expose the Reactionary Blabber," (note 32 above), col. 4.
44. "The True Face," (note 19 above), col. 4.

counterrevolutionaries 1955], the mistakes were even greater. One did not know too well how to treat people with respect. The dignity of man was seen as a thing of no concern."[45] The effect was that Party bureaucrats managed to recruit their own replicas into the Party. Liu reveals this in his *texie* (as did Wang Meng), and simply stated that the new recruits were mostly "flatterers," "boot lickers," and "yes-men."[46] With these people, the Party was in danger of becoming but a "trade-unionist organization"[47] whose members went about preserving their own prerogatives. The reasons for this development were twofold: China entered socialism straight from feudalism; and the dictatorship of the proletariat itself breeds bureaucratism.[48] Liu Binyan did not operate with the concept of individual guilt or accusation, but with the concept of broader social developments where individuals played their role, and his role was to contribute to the modernization of China in all aspects, the most important immediate goal being to improve the conditions for those who wanted to battle the bureaucrats. This could best be done by increasing democracy and decreasing the prerogatives of the state and the Party.

To encourage other young writers to follow in his footsteps, he attacked Zhou Yang in person, saying that Zhou had no independent thought, but just regurgitated whatever Mao said, and that he suppressed criticism.[49] In the article that probably contributed most to his becoming a prominent target of the Anti-Rightist Campaign, "Shanghai Is Pondering," not only did he advocate the running of periodicals and papers by the professionals themselves (*tongren ban*), without their having to submit everything for approval, but wrote: "People think that the

---

45. Ibid. col. 2; cf. Liu Binyan, "Dao shi wuqing que youqing" (Where you claim there is no feeling, there is feeling), *Wenyi xuexi* 3:6f (March 1957). Cf. note 33 above. "Liu Binyan is the Spokesman," (note 40 above), col. 4; Huang Sha, "Expose the Reactionary Blabber" (note 32 above), col. 6.

46. "Liu Binyan Is the Spokesman" (note 40 above), cols. 1f. "The True Face," (note 19 above), col. 2.

47. Gao Miaozheng, "The Poison Spread by Liu Binyan," (note 16 above), col. 2.

48. "Chedi bodiao Liu Binyan de 'gexinzhe' waiyi" (Strip Liu Binyan completely of his cloak of being an 'innovator'), *Zhongguo qingnianbao*, 13 July 1957, col. 2. It seems that Lin Xiling had argued the first points strongly, and that Liu Binyan agreed; cf. "The True Face," (note 19 above), col. 7.

49. Xing Yan, "Against Liu Binyan's Anti-Party Slanders," (note 40 above), col. 4.

reason why there cannot be anyone today to oppose Zhou Yang, as Lu Xun had done some twenty years ago, is that the relationships between a writer and a head of Party propaganda [Zhou Yang's position at the time] are quite different [from what they were then]."⁵⁰ And he did not make himself popular with either the writers or the *baogao wenxue* specialists. He called many of his colleagues "chameleons" who would support the battle against conservativism today and turn their coats tomorrow,⁵¹ which implied a public commitment on his part to behave differently; and he would later write to a correspondent in Wuhan that he'd better write about problems there if he did not want to wait for people like Zhao Shuli or Yang Shuo to come up with their embellishments. He opined that the old writers stopped writing after 1949 "not because they are unfamiliar with the new life, but because they lack courage; they see the contradictions, but they don't dare to bring them up."⁵² He said that Zhou Erfu, in 1957 a member of the Shanghai Municipal Committee, was lukewarm towards the Hundred Flowers policy, and, after meeting with none other than Zhang Chunqiao, editor-in-chief of *Wenhuibao,* he added that some leaders were not just "conservative" but outright "dogmatic" [ultra-leftist], the worst category in his arsenal. He publicly stated that neither of them had any knowledge of literature, and both were a far cry from Chen Yi, who, when he was mayor of Shanghai, supported writers, gave them latitude, and read their works as a connoisseur.⁵³ It contributes to one's self-assurance and public posture to have such a remark on record twenty years before Zhang Chunqiao was deposed as a member of the "Gang of Four."

50. Liu Binyan, "Shanghai zai chensi zhong" (Shanghai is pondering), *Zhongguo qingnianbao* 13 May 1957; on the importance of this article for his further fate, see not only the various articles from the Anti-Rightist Campaign quoted above, but also Liu Binyan's interviews: Lei Shuyan, "Wo suo zhidaode Liu Binyan" (Liu Binyan as I knew him), *Wenhui yuekan* 8:37 (1984); Lee Yee, "Liu Binyan and His Time," (note 26 above), pp. 69f.

51. "The True Face" (note 19 above), col. 6.

52. Gou Yongze, "Assorted Misdeeds by Liu Binyan" (note 18 above), col. 3.

53. Ma Xinde et al., "Kangyi Liu Binyan wumie dang" (Protest against Liu Binyan's denigration of the Party), *Zhongguo qingnianbao,* 15 July 1957, cols. 2f. Liu Binyan also met Yao Wenyuan at this time (May 1957), and it seems that Yao had inside information that Liu Binyan was already singled out as the target of the next campaign. Cf. Lee Yee, "Liu Binyan and His Time" (note 26 above), p. 69.

Although, for Liu Binyan, the Soviet Union at the time stood for all that was modern and socialist, his interest and sympathy were with the writers of the Thaw and not necessarily with the government. In Shanghai in 1957, Liu made a speech in which he asked that tape recorders be turned off before he went into a description of what he felt were the problems in Poland and the Soviet Union at that time. To talk in this manner, and in public, about China's internal affairs, even naming high-ranking politicians, was in itself a sacrilege that must have made hearts swell in one part of his audience, and eyes bulge with rage in the other. To talk as an individual, publicly and critically, at this time about social-ist sister countries was such a sacrilege that later articles denouncing Liu Binyan had subheadings like "Liu Binyan Even Wantonly Slandered Some Policies of the Soviet Union and of Poland," but did not say a word about the content of those slanders.[54]

The dusty and dark figures of the bureaucrats in Liu's *texie* and in his public statements are in sharp contrast to the lively young crowd of intel-lectuals, especially in "Inside News." The warmth, ease, and openness with which the young people communicate is a respite from the cold cal-culations of the bureaucratic mind. Their dazzling clothes and free life-style are appropriately linked with a strong devotion to the people's interest, and in perfect harmony with the enlightened guidance from the very highest Party level, the Chairman being quoted. Huang Jiaying refuses to abandon her critical stance in order to gain entry into the Party. In real life, Liu Binyan tried to encourage young people to act in similar fashion.

Harbin was not an isolated case. He encouraged the correspondents of his paper to investigate and write critical reports, and not just tout the Party line, and he printed their stories. He helped in their education by joining in their practical work, and he has kept the habit of writing joint articles with younger colleagues throughout the 1980s. He person-ally supported Lin Xiling when she was attacked; in fact, she may have been one of the real-life models for Huang Jiaying. He advocated every measure that would help his heroes to get the leeway to speak out and give them responsibility. It is true, he said, "their political enthusiasm has

54. Huang Sha, "Expose the Reactionary Blabber" (note 32 above), col. 9.

waned recently," but "their political sophistication has increased," owing to their experiences,[55] a statement that certainly evokes the situation after the Cultural Revolution. He thought the Youth League should educate its members to consider the entire country their responsibility, and its paper should not reduce itself to dealing only with Youth League matters under Party guidance. The Youth League should take the initiative to deal with a number of problems and not wait for Party directives. Liu was later accused of wanting to transform the Youth League into "a second Party."[56]

The articles against Liu Binyan during the Anti-Rightist Campaign grudgingly conceded his success with this group of educated city youths. The example from Harbin has been quoted. On 6 December 1956, he gave a talk at a meeting at *Beijing ribao,* "where indeed he found a market among some of us young comrades, and some of the youths who were fond of literature and the arts were taken in by his statements about so-called 'independent thinking' and 'boldly intervening in life.'"[57] When he spoke to the journalists at the Shanghai radio station in May 1957, "A lot of comrades were taken in by false theories, and began to harbor doubts towards the Party; some relatively young (or naive, *youzhi*) comrades became his intellectual captives (*sixiang fulu*) and took his wild words to be 'profound knowledge and penetrating insight,' and 'original views'; some muddle-headed comrade even said, 'In my entire life I have heard only two good reports, the one by Chairman Mao and this one by Liu Binyan.'"[58] His immediate colleagues held him in great esteem, including the assistant editor of the paper, who, even during the Anti-Rightist Campaign, could not bring himself to attack his "friend with whom he went through thick and thin"; another member of the editorial committee confessed that he had come under Liu's influence, and so on.[59] Even Fang Ji, who in 1958, in his story "The Visitor," denounced Liu Binyan and young people akin

55. "Assorted Misdeeds by Liu Binyan" (note 18 above), col. 4.
56. Ibid., col. 3.
57. Gao Miaozheng, "The Poison Spread by Liu Binyan" (note 16 above), col. 3.
58. Huang Sha, "Expose the Reactionary Blabber" (note 32 above), col. 11.
59. Ma Heqing, "Youpai fenzi Liu Binyan chengren ziji youzui" (The rightist element Liu Binyan admits his guilt), *Zhongguo qingnianbao,* 18 July 1957, col. 2.

to him as "bourgeois decadents," admitted that Liu's two *texie,* "because of their stunning openness, had attracted much attention."[60] An interesting little article signed Yi Fu ("One Man") stated in July 1957: "It is said that Liu Binyan has quite some influence in four worlds: the world of youth, the world of news [as a newspaper journalist], the world of literature, and the world of translation [as he had translated some things, and the periodical *Yiwen* had carried large numbers of *texie*]. Of course," the article continued,

> one should not exaggerate the influence of this "innovator" (*gexinzhe*). Only during the last few years, Liu Binyan showed his talents in a great way in these "four worlds." . . . However, we should not underestimate Liu Binyan's effects in misleading people either. This he could do because he arrived on the scene under the trademark of the "newly rising forces." Don't you see that quite a few comrades in the newspaper world have made his "Inside News" a "mandatory document" for study? Don't you see that in the literary world quite a few people are of the opinion that Liu Binyan's *texie* are works "reverberating the sound of (our) time?" Don't you see that among young toilers [*gongzuozhe,* referring mostly to intellectual pursuits] indeed there are many who throw "all five parts of their body on the floor" in admiration of him?[61]

Lin Xiling, a student of journalism who worked for Liu's paper and was one of the most outspoken young Communists in 1957, gave the ultimate compliment to Liu Binyan, calling him "China's Ovechkin."[62]

One might argue with good reason that the link between Liu and this segment of the youth was not just one of idealism. Liu attacked the leading cadres as uneducated, uncultured, and lacking "qualification."[63] One article charged, and probably rightly so, that Liu wanted to "replace Party membership and Marxism-Leninism with a 'cultural niveau' [as key qualifying feature] for the guidance of China's revolution and construction."[64] In very practical terms, the avenues for many intel-

---

60. Fang Ji, "What Kind of Poison" (note 36 above), col. 1.

61. Yi Fu, "'Chensi' xiaoji" (A little collection of 'ponderings'), *Zhongguo qingnianbao,* 17 July 1957.

62. Guo Yongze, "Assorted Misdeeds by Liu Binyan" (note 18 above), col. 7; "Xiang Liu Binyan fandang fanshehuizhuyi yanxing kaizhan douzheng" (Unleash the battle against Liu Binyan's anti-Party anti-socialist activities), *Harbin ribao,* 13 July 1957.

63. Huang Sha, "Expose the Reactionary Blabber" (note 32 above), col. 5.

64. Ibid.

lectual youths into the leading stratum of new China were closed by that time, and even highly qualified youths with university educations had to accept lowly jobs; the hierarchy was clogged, filled with people many of whom had won their medals during the war, but not after. The standards advocated by Liu and his *texie*, with their emphasis on "modern" qualifications, certainly appealed to the educated young, and gave their very immediate needs and aspirations some higher purpose and glory.[65] There is an aspect of lobby literature to Liu's writings. Again, we are not dealing so much with Liu Binyan as an individual, but with a literary form, a social role, and a lifestyle all of which are linked by the term *texie*, all three of which Liu adopted. And it took a personality like his to do so. Liu himself feels that his family background with a father who had worked for several years in the Soviet Union as a translator for the railways, and the "frontier" climate among the immigrants in the northeast where "feudal" structures were less stable and entrenched, helped to foster his broad outlook, daring frankness, and free lifestyle.[66]

China's path to modernity, however, is a tortuous one, and to change habits and traditions takes time and a great many victims. Liu Binyan had no illusions on this point. China, he said, "did not pass through capitalism; therefore democratic rights are restricted, and even those one has one cannot use; one does not know them and one does not dare to put them into action."[67] The coalition of progress that Liu defended ran into trouble in May 1957. Internationally, Hungarian events had given potent ammunition to those who advocated a restriction on "blooming and contending," while the growing unrest among the laboring classes had the same effect nationally. Liu was in Shanghai when strikes and some other incidents occurred. The basis was weak; apart from *Wenhuibao* and *Xinminbao*, the other papers, his own included, did not take part in the "blooming and contending." He called his editor-in-chief,

65. Already in a very early article, Liu Binyan had eulogized youth for their daring and qualification as the main innovative force; Liu Binyan, "Xiang geng gaofeng qianjin" (Forward to still higher peaks), *Wenyibao* 18:6ff (30 September 1955); this is his speech at the grand meeting of youth activists for socialist construction.

66. Lee Yee, "Liu Binyan and His Time" (note 26 above), pp. 65f.

67. Huang Sha, "Expose the Reactionary Blabber" (note 32 above), cols. 6f.

Zhang Ligun, in order to convince him to join in the "blooming and contending" and was successful to the degree that his [Liu's] "Shanghai is Pondering" was published on 13 May. From his interviews in Shanghai, he sensed that things were taking a disastrous turn, with the "conservatives" and "dogmatists" preparing to hit back. On the night of 25 May, he decided to write a letter to the person he saw as the stalwart defender of the anti-bureaucratic movement, and whom he had never criticized, the Chairman himself. The Chairman, he wrote, should not listen to the suggestions of lower-level cadres, since the main problem at present was that certain party cadres resented the "blooming and contending." The letter was not published at the time, but the term *certain cadres* in the summary suggests that Liu was naming the leaders concerned.[68]

Less than two weeks later, the wind had turned. On 8 June, the editorial announcing the backlash appeared in *Renmin ribao*. In a last desperate effort, Liu, in his capacity as the secretary of one of the two Party branches in his paper, called a branch meeting on 14 June. The meeting upheld the policies of "blooming and contending" as well as the anti-bureaucratic stance that went with it, and the results of the discussions were made public among the paper's staff by means of a big-character poster. On 4 July, *Beijing ribao* came out with a long attack against Lin Xiling, and Liu agreed to meet with her on the 9th to find ways to defend her. On the night before that meeting was to take place, the attacks against Liu himself began.[69]

There followed the ultimate test: He knew and had said that there were only too few "bold" people in the country.[70] But it was still devastating to see one's friends cave in, those very few on whom one had set one's hopes. Qin Shi, his second-in-command in the industry section of the paper, who had earlier spoken out boldly for a greater independence of the paper from directives of the Youth League leadership, publicly

68. The strike was at the Yongda textile mill in Shanghai. Liu Shaoqi himself gave orders that it should be reported in the press. The purpose is not entirely clear; it might have been a step to legitimize a crackdown. Cf. Lee Yee, "Liu Binyan and His Time" (note 26 above), p.
69. The letter to Mao is reproduced in Liu Binyan, *A Higher Kind of Loyalty* (New York: Pantheon, 1990), p. 76ff.
69. "The True Face" (note 19 above), cols. 6f.
70. Guo Yongze, "Assorted Misdeeds by Liu Binyan" (note 18 above), col. 3. This article also outlines Liu Binyan's plan to write a *xiaoshuo* about bureaucratism in Harbin.

denounced him to get herself out of trouble: "Many comrades in the paper," she said, "have been concerned about me, concerned whether I would be able to take a stand in this struggle and return to the Party's contingent. Now I can tell them: 'Qin Shi has come back, has returned to the fold of the Party that nurtured and educated her like a mother; I have to take a firm stand and lead the battle against the rightist element Liu Binyan to the very end, and have to fundamentally reeducate myself through this battle.'"[71] A member of the editorial board of the paper put up a big-character poster detailing how he had fallen under Liu's spell. A young correspondent with whom Liu wrote "A Storehouse With Living Men" signed an article entitled "Liu Binyan Spread Slanders That There Is No 'Freedom of the Press' in China and the Like." He claimed that their joint article was written under Liu's directives.[72] Liu knew that each quotation and phrase in the long articles that profusely quoted his private and public statements represented the input of someone who had spied on him, or caved in and reported. Even his neighbor made a quick point by reporting that Liu had loudly asked his wife to turn off the radio because the gross propaganda was getting on his nerves.[73] And, during the few weeks of freedom restored in early 1966, the woman colleague working in the same office with him returned each evening after hours to copy out what he had written in his diary; the quotations were to haunt him through the next decade.[74]

His base had vanished from sight, and so had his umbrella. The Chairman himself had turned against the very movement he had initiated. Deng Xiaoping, who had engineered the changeover from class struggle to struggle for production at the 8th Party Congress, was in charge of the Anti-Rightist Movement, and Hu Yaobang was in Moscow.[75] Some

71. Ma Heqing, Wu Xuelin, "Liu Binyan de chou'e mianmu gengjia baolu" (Liu Binyan's repulsive face further revealed), *Zhongguo qingnianbao*, 25 July 1957, cols. 2f.

72. Pan Shishen, "Liu Binyan's Fallacies" (note 14 above); Pan co-authored the article "Huoren cangku" (note 20 above).

73. Lei Shuyan, "Liu Binyan as I Knew Him" (note 50 above).

74. Ibid., pp. 38f.

75. Hu Yaobang headed the delegation of the Youth League to the International Youth Festival in Moscow, according to *Harbin ribao*, 18 July 1957, reprinting a dispatch from Xinhua dated 16 July. At the crucial time of the public attacks against Liu Binyan, Hu Yaobang was not around. Liu mentioned this point in a discussion with Prof. Leo Oufan Lee. Personal communication.

years later, Wu Han would insert into his *Hai Rui Dismissed From Office* the wary line "When people are after the knights, they start by shooting the horses out from under them."[76] Hu remained in office, but he had to sustain heavy losses among his support cast, including people like Liu Binyan and Lin Xiling, who was the fiancée of Hu's private secretary. Only when Hu became head of Party propaganda at the 3rd Plenum in December 1978 could writers and journalists like Liu Binyan return to the literary stage.

Left alone and exposed, Liu's self-doubts arose. He maintained in his self-criticism that his motives were "good" but admitted that his stance had been in effect an "anti-Party crime." After his rehabilitation he wrote that he took these criticisms very seriously. After all, the prestige of the Party was still enormous, and he had been working for the Party since the late 1930s, actually joining in 1944. During his banishment to the countryside at the time of the Great Leap he saw the frenzy of the "Communist wind," with peasants who ate meat once a year being pushed to build a zoo for their village;[77] then his self-confidence returned and his understanding of the sociology of the Chinese Revolution was deepened.

But there was triumph even in distress. He had made his point, and had made it well and lastingly. The Youth League paper complained that "this struggle [against Liu] is rather complicated. The reason is that Liu Binyan for several years under the beautiful cloak of an 'innovator,' an 'anti-bureaucrat,' and 'a gifted author,' had spread many fallacies that seemed to be right but were not, and quite a few people were taken in by them, with the effect that these fallacies spread their poison among many without their even noticing it."[78] The "conservatives" and "bureaucrats" were forced to use the very terms with which Liu Binyan had been describing himself, and which others had used to characterize his most attractive feature, and had to turn these terms into slanders: "innovator," "pioneer," "anti-bureaucratic fighter," man rich in "spirit of the time" who dared "to think independently" and was, furthermore, a "young author" and a "celebrated journalist" who dared to "intervene in

76. Wu Han, "Hai Rui ba guan" (Hai Rui dismissed from office), *Beijing wenyi* 1:22 (January 1961).

77. Liu Binyan, *A Higher Kind of Loyalty* (note 68 above), p. 98.

78. Ma Heqing, "The Rightist Element Liu Binyan" (note 59 above).

life." *Renmin ribao* wrote up a long summary of the charges against Liu in July, and included in the title the two worst things they held against him—that he was an "innovator" (*gexinjia*), and that he was a "*texie*-ist" (*texiejia*).[79] They had a clear understanding of the public stance that went with the *texie*-ist, and they had to eat a lot of crow to handle these terms and the attitudes they described as something negative. Eventually they resorted to the ultimate antidote against the "poison spread by Liu Binyan," parading the "Man From Stalin's Time," Boris Polewoi himself, through China in fall 1957.

Read in hindsight, the articles denouncing Liu Binyan are excellent witnesses to the level of his sociological insight into the problems plaguing Chinese society and his familiarity with others in the socialist camp who thought along similar lines, like Djilas in Yugoslavia and, of course, Ovechkin. They were excellent witnesses to the public stance he took as a *texie*-ist and to the seriousness with which he went about "intervening in life." They showed him as a walking niche of exceedingly "modern" outlandish behavior on Chinese soil, willing to sacrifice himself in this oversized role for the benefit of the country's progress, a one-man civil society.

In the 1980s, he reemerged with all his roles intact. His sociological approach might have enabled him to see his own fate in the context of broader social developments where people are as much the makers as the victims of traditions that form them. Most of the heroes of his new texts have considered suicide at one moment or the other,[80] and they all rejected it, as did Liu himself. In an interview in 1982, he said:

> I cannot regret a thing, absolutely nothing. I have said, if by any chance the ultra-left should get power in China (this is just hypothetical, in fact it is impossible) and would drag me to the execution ground, I would be quite at ease. I have done what I had to do, and what I did exerted the influence it had to exert. I feel very fortunate that I am still alive; there were several occasions for me to die. I also thought about suicide, but then I thought about those who had died and that I should take up their baton. Isn't life like this?[81]

79. All the articles quoted above from the Anti-Rightist Campaigns turn these terms into slanders. "Liu Binyan is the Spokesman" (note 40 above).

80. Cf. Liu Binyan, "A Man and His Shadow" (note 4 above), and Liu Binyan, "Zai zuiren de beihou" (In the offender's background), in Liu Binyan, *Jiannan de qifei* (A difficult takeoff; Changsha: Hunan Renmin Press, 1982); in both stories the heroes ponder suicide.

81. Lee Yee, "Liu Binyan and His Time" (note 26 above), pp. 75f.

Liu Binyan felt that he had been right, and still was, and that the dynamics of the social process would eventually bring about a constellation where he might come back from that gruesome Chinese "parking orbit" to make his impact felt anew on earth. He was first assigned to the Philosophy Department of the Academy of Social Sciences in 1978, where he translated and read whatever he could find on the sociology of bureaucratism in socialism.[82]

When he returned to the literary scene, the form he used was the *texie;* he became again a journalist, this time with *Renmin ribao.* Although the basic parameters of his pre-1957 existence were again in place, there were also changes. His hair was grey, and his heroes had aged with him. Gone were the enthusiastic Youth Leaguers, now twenty years older; they had survived and remained committed to their old ideals, even under the most adverse circumstances. Whatever came about in terms of achievements in industry during the intervening years had been accomplished by them, Liu's new texts argue, sometimes running major enterprises with the hat of a rightist still on their heads and receiving a salary lower than that of the youngest apprentices. They were still his heroes and deserved to be the leaders of the Four Modernizations; their opponents, however, were also twenty years older and had learned about the superiority of the socialist system in their own way. They were no longer individuals with rigid orthodox minds formed during the war, but slick politicians who had formed networks of mutual protection and support—they had become the "invisible machine." The new class, the "nobility" that Liu had mentioned in his talks in 1956 and 1957 but not described as such in his *texie,* had now become the focus of his new "researched *texie*" like "Between Human and Monster" or "The Invisible Machine."[83] The leaders he supported then, like Hu Yaobang, were back, but again he kept his distance and his own council, making a public point of maintaining this independence, even as a much-heralded reporter for *Renmin ribao.* Rather than using the image of the Party's "scout," he depicted himself as the inde-

---

82. Xia Yan, "Xinde yidai, chengshang qixia" (A new epoch, inherit the old and begin the new), *Jingbao* 3:12 (March 1980).

83. Liu Binyan, Liu Guosheng, "Wuxing de jiqi" (The invisible machine), *Renmin ribao,* 8 February 1984.

pendent and committed sociologist whose loyalty was with the people, not with headquarters.[84] He supported the policies of the 3rd Plenum but did so for his own reasons: They increased the leeway of the individual and aided his modernizing heroes. The Plenum decided that there was no "bourgeoisie within the Party," a tactical statement designed to soothe the apprehensions of rehabilitated cadres regarding another Cultural Revolution, but not an analytical statement. Liu Binyan calmly pursued his investigation of the links within the "Invisible Machine," which indeed looks like something of a privileged class. Deng Xiaoping asked the writers to "look forward," and Liu focused on understanding the social and human dynamics underlying the chaotic history of socialist China.

He remained as outspoken as ever. When he met obstruction, he said so instantly and publicly. His informants were sometimes persecuted; when he interviewed people, the management sent spies to overhear what they said; he was fed wrong information so that he might later be criticized for sloppy research; and constant were the rumors that he was "in trouble." But with delight journalists told each other how he reacted.

When the Campaign against Spiritual Pollution got under way, directed mostly against Hu Yaobang, Liu Binyan of course was "sent down" to think about himself, and study the tremendous successes in the countryside instead of publishing further morose studies about bureaucrats. After several weeks, his paper wrote him to ask how things were; Liu took a sheet of paper, scrawled a very large *hao* (great) on it, folded it, and sent it back. Twenty years "out" have hardened his bones. And his influence in the "four worlds" as the model of a modern man was greater than ever, it seems.

An article written after the Writers' Congress in 1985 might stand as the ultimate commentary on his *kultur'nost* modernism. It will be recalled that he had attacked Zhou Yang in 1957; Zhou Yang had responded by comparing Liu to Wang Shiwei, who had been executed, in fact demanding a similar treatment of Liu Binyan.[85] When Liu came

84. Cf. my "Liu Binyan, der Autor als wandelnde Nische," in W. Kubin, ed., *Moderne Chinesische Literatur* (Frankfurt: Suhrkamp, 1985), p. 434.

85. The allusion to Wang Shiwei was already made in January; before a discussion of Wang

back in 1979 he explicitly referred to this incident without, however, mentioning Zhou Yang.[86] Later in 1979, Liu Binyan demanded the rehabilitation of the man who had been the model for engineer Zeng and who had to suffer for this by being capped a "rightist" for the next twenty-two years. In the same speech, he requested that the student leader Lin Xiling be rehabilitated, who was not just capped as a rightist but had sustained criminal charges. By then, Zhou Yang had again taken over the leadership of the cultural establishment. As Zhou Yang had been one of the most active persecutors during the Anti-Rightist Movement, these demands most certainly cut him to the quick with the implied charge that Zhou seemed to be willing to rehabilitate those associates who were dismissed with him during the Cultural Revolution but failed to do the same honor to his own former victims. Although, in Liu Binyan's *texie*, there is only a single bureaucrat who is able to change for the better (Ma in "Inside News"), Liu Binyan was willing to accept Zhou Yang's change of mind. By 1985, Zhou Yang had come out for much greater latitude for writers and had done much to protect them from the fallout from the internal political struggles in the Center.

Zhou Yang was unable to attend the 1985 Writers' Congress which listened with amazement and exhilaration to a long statement by Hu Yaobang's spokesman that literature should indeed be free from political interference. Zhou Yang sent a telegram from the hospital congratulating the Congress. The same man who had formulated Mao's thoughts on the revolutionary duties of literature in 1958,[87] who had relentlessly purged and persecuted any writer and critic who was in his way, and who had been capped a "bourgeois" during the Cultural Revolution and had returned without a word of self-criticism to the literary leadership in 1979, now received, *in absentia*, a five-minute ovation from the assem-

---

Meng's "Newcomer," the participants were handed a copy of Wang Shiwei's "Wild Lilies" to help them understand what was the issue; cf. Lee Yee, "Liu Binyan and His Time" (note 26 above), p. 69. Zhou Yang had compared Liu Binyan directly to Wang Shiwei; Zhou Yang, "Wenyi zhanxianshang de yicheng da bianlun" (A great debate on the literary front), *Wenyibao* 5:11 (11 March 1958).

86. Liu Binyan, "On 'Depicting the Dark Side,'" (p. 257 note 11), p. 50.

87. Zhou Yang, "Xin minge kaituole shige de xin daolu" (New folksong opens a new way for poetry and songs), *Hongqi* 1 (1 June 1958).

bled writers. Liu Binyan sat down to write an article about this applause for a Hong Kong journal. In a culture where vengeance for past misdeeds is such a dominant and poisoning factor, Liu Binyan's change of mind about Zhou Yang must have cost him some pain.[88] But he had made up his mind to be a *texie*-ist, possibly a style of life and thinking which at times is self-righteous, but which always implies a commitment to be modern and free from the feudal relics of both loyalty and vengeance.

In his search for a segment of the political class that had the prestige, experience, and the legitimacy to take over the leadership in the big reforms after 1978, Liu Binyan quite naturally turned to the old "rightists." They provided the heroes in his stories, and they provide the personality traits Liu Binyan felt were necessary to get China out of its feudal morass. In a radicalization of the old confrontation of 1955 through 1957 between two personality types described earlier, Liu Binyan eventually contrasted his bold, outspoken, and committed heroes with their idealized opponent, namely Lei Feng.

Lei Feng was a young man who, during the early 1960s, had been set up as the ultimate model of self-denial in the service of Party orders and the people. Lei Feng had facilitated his transition to a role model by being killed early in an accident.[89] He had graciously left behind a diary recording his saintly life, and was then set up as a behavioral model of blind obedience and devotion by none other than the Youth League under Hu Yaobang. Millions of copies of little tracts on Lei Feng were distributed among the youths, and learning from Lei Feng was a cornerstone of the edifice of Party education.

For the rehabilitated older generation of leaders after 1978 Lei Feng was the daydream of youthful behavior. Liu Binyan took on this ideal figure in his 1986 "A Second Kind of Loyalty," confronting the slavish obedience of Lei Feng with the independent thinking and critical approach of his heroes.[90] They, he said, had made a much greater contri-

---

88. Liu Binyan, "Zhenxi delai buyi de chuangzuo ziyou" (A treasure hard to come by—freedom of artistic creation), *Jingbao* 2:7 (February 1985).

89. For a short depiction of this hero, cf. David and Nancy Milton, *The Wind Will Not Subside* (New York: Pantheon Books, 1976), pp. 62ff.

90. Liu Binyan, "Di er zhong zhongcheng" (A second kind of loyalty), *Kaituo* 1 (January 1985); many reprints, among others *Zhongguo zhi chun* 4 (April 1986).

bution with their "second kind of loyalty," namely to the people and nation. The heroes of that story are individuals who investigate the ills of the country, much like the *texie*-ist himself, and write straight to the Chairman, only to be branded counterrevolutionaries and criminals. Tactically speaking, the elevation of the rightists to the status of heroes was a challenge to Deng Xiaoping, Peng Zhen, and the military leaders of the older generation. They had been the persecutors during the Anti-Rightist drive, and in the *Resolution on Some Questions Concerning the History of our Party* (1981) they still maintained that the Anti-Rightist drive had been "absolutely" correct, although too many people had eventually been affected.[91]

As the summer of 1987 brought the 30th anniversary of the beginning of this drive, Liu Binyan and others began a big project to collect the life histories of those rightists, and to have them published on the anniversary in a 3-volume set. If he had been looking for a political constellation which would work for his demise, Liu Binyan surely had found it. He attacked Lei Feng with the implication of reminding his own mentor, Hu Yaobang, of his blunder. He attacked Lei Feng as a man with slavish mentality, denouncing the strongly held beliefs of the older military leaders in strict obedience and devotion to orders. He came out in favor of the rightists as the true heroes of the PRC, reminding Deng Xiaoping and Peng Zhen of the fact that they themselves had cut down this promising crop and now failed to clear the way for those people who alone would be able to run the reform program. And eventually he ran afoul of a mighty political machine with a local focus in Shaanxi province, centered around the old general Xi Zhongxun, whose son held a high rank there. In an article on another rightist's fate in Xi'an, published in *Renmin ribao,* he inserted a phrase about that "infamous clique from Shaanxi," which was correctly interpreted by that clique as referring to them.[92]

When Hu Yaobang was ousted as Party Chairman in January 1987,

---

91. "Resolution on Certain Questions in the History of Our Party since the Founding of the People's Republic of China," here quoted from Harold Hinton, ed., *The People's Republic of China 1979–1984* (Wilmington, Scholarly Resources, 1986), I, 95.

92. Liu Binyan, "Meishang yinmu de gushi" (A story that was not put on screen), *Renmin ribao,* 7 August 1986.

Liu Binyan was for the second time thrown out of the Party.[93] A guard was stationed in front of his door, he was dismissed from *Renmin ribao,* and members of the Party and the mass organizations across the country were given dossiers with his statements which they were to denounce publicly.[94] Liu Binyan refused self-criticism, and, for the first time in PRC history, people not only privately felt sympathy for him, but publicly showed it. Deng Xiaoping was flooded with letters from overseas Chinese; writers flocked to Liu Binyan's home for the Spring Festival; foreign newspapers reported his fate in great detail. China's foremost *texie*-ist had become a force to be reckoned with.

Late in 1986, the overseas edition of *Renmin ribao* had printed a statement by an overseas Chinese who described Liu Binyan's fate as a political *wendubiao,* thermometer, for China.[95] If Liu's fate was endangered, things were looking bad for the country, and vice versa. When the 13th Party Congress late in 1987 eventually looked at the damage done, the leadership was quick to reestablish some international credibility by dramatically upgrading Liu Binyan's status. He was allowed to publish again, and has been permitted the ultimate privilege—to spend a year at Harvard as a Nieman Fellow.[96] Due to the political crackdown after June 1989, he was unable to return. Finally confronted with a broader challenge to its aristocratic rule, the Communist government resorted again to the same strategy that had already done so much harm to the country over the past decades: suppression of the critical intelligentsia.

93. "Jianchi sixiang jiben yuanze, jianjue zhixing dang de jilü" (Firmly hold on to the four basic principles, resolutely keep Party discipline), *Renmin ribao* (Overseas ed.), 25 January 1987.

94. Personal communication from Liu Binyan, January 1987.

95. Kang Lin, "Yige huaqiao kan zuguo 3, Qing shang yinmu" (An overseas Chinese observes the fatherland 3, Please put that on screen), *Renmin ribao* (Overseas ed.), 18 August 1956.

96. "Chinese Journalist Liu Binyan Named 1988–89 Nieman Fellow," *Harvard University Gazette,* 26 February 1988, p. 1.

SIXTEEN

The Oçerk *in the Socialist Camp*

Liu Binyan made use of the *texie* as an established literary form, as a genre tied to certain themes as well as political and social attitudes, and as a mode of expression of the *texie*-ist, who in his own words and deeds has to be the first protagonist of the attitudes and values advocated by the genre. It turned out that neither of the three elements had been created or invented by Liu Binyan, but rather adapted from other, in this case directly Soviet, sources to the Chinese ambience.

The adaptation was highly successful; in literary terms, Liu's *texie* exerted a strong and lasting influence on other authors dealing, in the form of *xiaoshuo*, with social problems, such as Wang Meng. In terms of status, the researched *texie* had become a recognized literary pioneer with respect to themes, speed, and effectiveness, although in terms of style it was still regarded as being slightly "vulgar" because the fascination with the "documentary," with "raw life," had not found its way to China. In terms of the *texie*-ist, Liu Binyan set up a behavioral model for young intellectuals. To them it appealed in its decided modernism, in its high moral pitch of social responsibility, and in its boldness, freedom, and promise of warm human relationships with like-minded peers.

In tactical terms the *texie* tries to establish the space "between" fixed categories as the place of openness and freedom. This is true for the genre, situated as it is "between" the news report and the *xiaoshuo*; it is true for the themes, situated as they are "between" literature and politics, artistic depiction and sociological analysis. And it is true for the *texie*-ist with his amphibious existence as both a writer and a journalist. The *texie* thus occupies a potentially innovative niche in an otherwise overdefined and overhomogenized political culture.

"Three shoemakers combined match a Zhuge Liang," as the saying goes. Liu Binyan had asked that literature, and above all *texie* and texts under *texie* influence become for contemporary China what Balzac had been for nineteenth-century France, where the level of empirical social and economic research by scientists was about the same as in China today. Looking back at the texts written during the last few years, Liu opines that there is not any one Balzac, but that these texts together might become his match in China. Writing in a Hong Kong periodical after the Writers' Congress in early 1985, he said that, in terms of social analysis, "compared to philosophy, the social sciences and reading matter spread among the masses, literature is far, far ahead and in big strides has topped the levels arrived at by 1956. In order to understand China, the best method is to read China's *xiaoshuo* and reportage literature."[1]

The foundations on which Liu Binyan erected this *texie* construct, which has been explored above, were well in place before him. Their structure determined the Chinese *texie* to a high degree. In this first stage of my analysis, the emphasis was on describing the inner logic and stress of the Chinese *texie* construct. Each part of its foundations, however, was fraught with meaning, and pointed back to earlier structures. To explore the full meaning of the Chinese *texie* we shall have to move from the analysis of inner logic to that of historical genesis. The next layer to be investigated will be that pointed out by Liu Binyan himself, that is, the tradition of the *oçerk* within the socialist camp and, further back, the leftist movement of the 1920s and 1930s. Beyond this lie the depths of European literary social physiology.

SECOND LAYER

MAPPING THE FOUNDATIONS IN THE SOCIALIST CAMP. From the Russian translations and the travels between the Soviet Union and China in matters

---

1. Liu Binyan, "A Treasure Hard to Come By," (p. 307 note 88), p. 6.

of *texie/oçerk* during the years 1953 through 1957, it is evident that support for this genre was part of the political program of the socialist camp at the time; accordingly, our exploration will have to take the measure of this wider area in investigating the foundations on which the Chinese edifice rested.

The *texie* itself was ambivalent. There were authors praising the "new men," "new things," and "new achievements," like Polewoi and Schaginian in the USSR, and Liu Baiyu and Xu Chi in China; and there was the *texie* of the Ovechkin kind, with its emphasis on "uncovering the dark side" and "intervening in life" and "writing the truth." The fact that the same genre gave shelter, after Stalin's death, to writers of the two factions opposing each other in the Soviet Union made for a lively debate about its essential characteristics in which the underlying political issues were rarely spelled out, as neither side in the USSR or elsewhere was then strong enough to dominate the entire field.

A cursory glance at the other socialist countries confirms the pattern visible in the Soviet Union and China. In East Germany and in Czechoslovakia, the same Russian texts were translated as in China,[2] local authors relating to the different types took up the challenge, discovering their own traditions on the way. The Youth Leagues organized a literary contest in 1956 where *texie* figured prominently,[3] and since 1955 an international conference of *texie*-ists was developed, eventually held in Bucharest in 1958.[4] Neither of the two variants dominated official policy between 1953 and 1957; both branches coexisted in a tense and uneasy relationship. The public attention, however, was drawn towards the *texie* of the Ovechkin kind, and a number of young intellectual critics started to explore the potential of the genre. Rainer Kunze, some years later to become one of East Germany's foremost poets, who soon found his works banned, wrote a dissertation on the "Essence and Functions of the Reportage,"[5] Stefan

---

2. Cf. Marietta Schaginian, *Auf des Fünfjahrenplans Bahnen*, (p. 264 note 36), Chapter 1, "Von der Sowjetskizze," Boris Polewoi, *Skizzen in der Zeitung* (Berlin, 1953).

3. Yuan Shuipai, "Ji guoji texie jizhe huiyi" (A report on the international meeting of *texie* writers), *Xinwen zhanxian* 7:54ff (1958).

4. Ibid.

5. Reiner Kunze, *Wesen und Bedeutung der Reportage* (Berlin, 1960) Beiträge zur Gegenwartsliteratur 17.

Heym, who had gone to East Germany from his emigration in the United States, used the genre in his *Five Days in June,* the proverbial "black manuscript"–it being bound in black–which dealt with the upheaval in East Berlin and other cities in June 1953 in the form of a slightly fictionalized reportage with much political intervention of the authorial voice, and was collecting dust on one editor's desk after another in East Germany until it was finally published in West Germany and in the United States.[6]

The movement for *oçerk/texie/reportage* of the Ovechkin type received its official sanctification within the post-Stalin reforms, probably from Smirnov's report to the Soviet Writers' Congress in November 1955:

> If, with regard to literary works of the past few years, we talk about their bringing up problems and offering solutions, the genre *oçerk* can be viewed as having the greatest achievements. And this is quite natural as well as according to rule because the genre *oçerk* is the most agile, and is richest in fighting spirit, so that it is not surprising that we call it the scout . . . The content of the *oçerki* is of the most diverse kinds. But they all do have a point in common, namely that they fervently wish to "get at the root of things," fervently wish to fully understand the colossal material present in the life of today's kolkhozes with their sudden high tide, and, furthermore, that they, among the complexity of contradictions and difficulties, understand the broad vistas of a great future. We think the glorious contingent of oçerkists which is marching in the forefront is about to open a way for the "heavy guns" of literature, the long and middle-length novel, the epic poem, and the drama.[7]

He mentioned Ovechkin, Kalinin, Smuul, Tendriakov, Troepolski, Zalygin, and others as good oçerkists. With this statement the *texie* was destined to become the avant-garde and scouting contingent of the reformists against the old guard, opening the way for the rest of literature.

In such movements it is customary in the socialist camp to recall the acceptable heroes of the past in order to increase the standing and historical legitimacy of the matter in question. Egon Erwin Kisch, a Prague journalist of Jewish origin, writing mostly in German, had pio-

---

6. Stephan Heym, *Five Days in June* (London: Hodder and Staughton, 1977).

7. Huaxili Simiernuofu (Wassili Smirnov), "Miaoxie jiti nongzhuang shenghuo de wenxue" (A literature depicting life in the kolkhozes), *Yiwen* 1:152 (January 1956).

neered the *literarische Reportage* as a new literary genre in the 1920s, and had, with the tremendous international success of his works, contributed to make this new genre acceptable, at least among the literati on the left. Returning to Prague from his Mexican exile, he died in 1948. East Berlin put together a *Kisch Kalender* in 1955, when Kisch would have reached the age of 70.[8] Together with the homage to Kisch, which included a piece by Mao Dun writing as chairman of the Chinese Writers' Association and spokesman for literary circles of his country,[9] East Germany put out a Kisch edition. As Kisch had been born in Prague, Czechoslovakia translated the entire volume and also published a Kisch edition, adding another reportage writer from the left, Fuçik, to the pedigree of the genre.[10] The Soviet Union put out, in 1956, a huge collection of pre-revolutionary *oçerki;*[11] in China, various collections of *texie* were published[12] as well as the strongly edited version of G. E. Miller's *Shanghai–Paradise of Adventurers* (1938), a work using the methods of fictionalized reportage.[13]

The heavy restrictions imposed on the Ovechkin type *texie* since 1957 were part of a backlash against the Thaw/Hundred Flowers literature which was felt throughout the socialist camp. Khrushchev demanded, in late 1957, "closer links between literature and the masses" and asked that more space be given to idealizing the feats of workers and peasants and more efforts be made to recruit writers from these classes; their healthy outlook and vigorous spirit would be the best antidote against the nihilism pervading the intellectuals' minds.[14] Early in 1958, Mao Zedong demanded, in his Chengdu speech, the combination of "revolutionary realism with revolutionary romanticism," in other words,

8. F. C. Weisskopf, ed., *Kisch-Kalender* (Berlin, (East): Aufbau Verlag, 1955). See also *Egon Erwin Kisch zum 60 Geburtstag* (London: Verlag der Einheit, 1945).

9. In ibid., p. 96, the Chinese letter is reproduced, on p. 77, in translation.

10. *Kalendar E. E. Kische* (Prague, 1955).

11. B. Kostelanets, ed., *Russkie Oçerki*, 3 vols. (Moscow, 1956).

12. *Sanwen texie xuan, September 1953–December 1955* (A collection of prose and *texie*; Beijing: Renmin Wenxue Press, 1956).

13. Mile (G. E. Miller), *Shanghai, maoxianjia de leyuan*, (Beijing, 1956). The English edition is G. E. Miller, *Shanghai, the Paradise of Adventurers* (New York: Orsay, 1937).

14. N. S. Khrushchev, "For Close Links Between Literature and Art and Life of the People," originally given as a series of speeches on 13 May 1957 and 19 May 1957, in N. S. Khrushchev, *The Great Mission of Literature and Art* (Moscow, 1964).

severe restrictions on depicting the "dark side" and describing the lives and problems of intellectuals, initiating at the same time a mass poetry and folksong movement from which a new crop of writers was to be recruited.[15] A year later, Walter Ulbricht seconded the two big leaders in his Bitterfelder Weg speech, in which he advocated a literature written in direct contact with and about workers, who also should be the readers and eventually become the writers.[16] As in the Chinese case, we may expect individual *texie* writers and their works to play an extremely influential part, since the unique combination of personal characteristics and literary/journalistic skills required of the *texie*-ist is only rarely achieved, and since governments within the socialist camp were unwilling to tolerate more than one or two individuals to play this important national role.

Liu Binyan's *texie*, their themes, and his role as a *texie*-ist were thus part of a familiar pattern in the socialist world at the time that might be called a period of mirroring. Certain social, political, and historical features of the Soviet Union were mirrored in the other socialist countries. Thus Lu Xun would have to fill the historical slot established by Mayakovsky; Goethe and Cao Xuegin would match Dostojevsky's contribution when the latter was reinstalled in the early 1950s. In the same manner, Ovechkin and his *texie* opened the possibility and even created some pressure to match and mirror his writing and role in the sister countries. Mirroring was of course most prominent in the role assigned to the supreme leader, where the Stalinist pattern was to be repeated in the other states, and where, after Stalin's death and Krushchev's criticism of him, his local replicas had to be removed as well, which happened in most cases except for China and East Germany. Mirroring operated throughout the hierarchy in the socialist camp as a whole, as well as within the individual socialist countries, where the pattern of the Center was repeated at each lower level. In the case of the *texie*, mirroring involved the simultaneous presence of Ovechkin and Polewoi,

15. See p. 73 note 2.
16. Walter Ulbricht, "Fragen der Entwicklung der Sozialistischen Kultur," in *Greif zur Feder, Kumpel. Protokoll der Autorenkonferenz des Mitteldeutschen Verlags, Halle (Saale) am 24 April 1959 im Kulturpalast des Elektrochemischen Kombinats Bitterfeld* (Halle/Saale: Mitteldeutscher Verlag, 1959).

Liu Binyan and Xu Chi,[17] but also the specific relationship of the *texie* to the short story.

In the Soviet Union, Galina Nikolayeva's *The Director of the MTS and the Woman Chief Agronomist,* a novella,[18] deals with the countryside after Khrushchev took over, and was, at the time, Ovechkin's main competitor in the field of rural themes. Ovechkin singled out this work for criticism at the conference on the treatment of rural themes in November 1955, where he made the main speech, charging Nikolayeva with having over-simplified the complexity of the problems of Soviet agriculture,[19] especially the problems of the "fight between the old and new." As the secretary of the Soviet Writers' Union, Smirnov, remarked: "Its author has taken the path of least resistance."[20] In China, Liu Binyan/Ovechkin thus found his counterpart in Wang Meng/Nikolayeva. Wang Meng, like Nikolayeva, wrote a *xiaoshuo,*[21] and not a *texie*; he included the theme of love, as did Nikolayeva, and in his original draft he took a much more conciliatory attitude than Liu Binyan towards the problem of bureaucratism in the leadership. Given the strong evidence for mirroring within the socialist camp (with the "original" normally provided by the Soviet Union), it seems a sound methodological principle to assume hypothetically such mirroring to occur wherever new patterns emerge which cannot be accounted for solely by internal factors. In terms of its social effects, mirroring, while based on a hegemonial structure, may operate in different directions. It may mean the imposition of Stalinist rule, and it may open the option for a Thaw where all local conditions are against it; in any case, it considerably enlarges the potential for legitimate action for all members of the political class. We have to deal, then, with Ovechkin.

17. Even the *Zhongguo dangdai wenxueshi chugao* (p. 250 note 3), written under Chen Huangmei's spiritual guidance, which is exceedingly appreciative of Liu Binyan, pairs him with Xu Chi to maintain the balance between the two variants; II, 202ff., 385ff.

18. Jialinna Nigulayewa (Galina Nikolayeva), "Tuolajizhan zhenzhang he zongnong yishi" (The director of the Machine Tractor Station and the [woman] chief agronomist), *Zhongguo qingnian* 23–24 (December 1955). For this work see p. 91 of this book.

19. Ovechkin's comments in "Guanyu 'Tuolajizhan zhanzhang he zongnong yishi' de tao-lun" (Discussion on *The Director of the Machine Tractor Station and the [Woman] Chief Agronomist"),* *Yiwen* 1:144f (1956). Cf. "The Rural Theme in Literature," *Soviet Literature* 3:185ff (March 1956).

20. Smirnov, "A literature depicting life in the kolkhozes" (note 7 above), p. 152.

21. Cf. p. 193ff.

OVECHKIN'S OÇERK. Although Ovechkin had written some short stories, as has Liu Binyan, he found the form of *oçerk* most suitable for his purposes. After some years as a kolkhoz chairman, he turned journalist and remained in the double role of journalist and writer for the rest of his career, a standard feature for most *oçerk*ists. The figure of Martynov, the opponent of the bureaucrat Borzov in "Daily Life," repeats Ovechkin's own career, significantly ending up as a second secretary of the rayon with a specific capacity to discover problems and to handle them.

Functionality seems to be the key characteristic of Ovechkin's *oçerk*. "Daily Life," on which our attention will focus, was written in the context of the sweeping reforms in agriculture announced by Khrushchev at the September Plenum in 1953. The reforms included the opening up of virgin lands, the transfer of large numbers of qualified young agronomists and technicians to the countryside, and, above all, the downward transfer of qualified leaders to become managers of the kolkhozes.[22]

Ovechkin fully supported this line, and even anticipated some of the proposals in stories written before the Plenum. However, he was not focusing on propagating its wisdom or glorifying its success, but on depicting the problems in terms of organization and the human attitudes that prevented its being enacted. The themes of his stories thus deal with the immediate present, and the enormous public attention the texts received was due to the immediacy and outspokenness with which they treated actual problems. "Daily life" has much of a *zhenglun*, a political essay. The description of Borzov, the chief bureaucrat, who is interested only in having the numbers right so that higher levels will have a high opinion of him, but does not care about the actual situation and the life of people, is mostly presented through a discussion between Martynov and Borzov's wife (who earlier had been a model tractor driver), not through a plot showing Borzov in action, or through probing his psychology. Borzov is evaluated by what he does; the purpose is not so much to understand the motives for his behavior, but to assess his behavior in the context of the grand goals of socialist progress, and to identify

22. V. Ovechkin, "Days in the Rayon" (p. 259 note 18). An English translation in V. Ovechkin, "Short Stories," *Soviet Literature* 10:40 (October 1954). For details on this text, cf. p. 80ff.

the structural conditions that let such characters thrive. Within the story, Martynov is not simply right because he is in agreement with the Plenum's decision; he replicates the essential features of the *oçerk*ist, *Sachlichkeit* (matter-of-factness), analytical impetus, and frankness.

Ovechkin succeeded with a few *oçerki* to establish this form, which had become the main panegyric genre during the preceding decades, as the "scout" exploring the formal and thematic avenues along which the heavier big guns would advance some years later. He actively sought and found a considerable number of young writers who emulated him and his form—for example, Tendriakov, Troepolski, Kalinin, Zalygin, Voronin, Zhestev, and Dorosh. The years between 1953 and 1956 were the years of the triumph of the *oçerk* of Ovechkin's type. Literary historians later spoke of the "Ovechkin era"; Pomerantsev singled Ovechkin out for praise in his "On Sincerity in Literature."[23] During these times of hectic changes in the post-Stalin period, Ovechkin's *oçerk* responded fast and efficiently.

Galina Nikolayeva, in late 1955, defined what she saw as Ovechkin's weakness. "The realm of literature," she said, answering a letter criticizing her *The Director of the MTS*, "is man's soul, and a writer must above all concentrate his attention on this feature," and not on the surface of social, political, and organizational problems. And, talking directly to Ovechkin:

> Everyone knows that his "Greetings to the Front" is a very remarkable novella as far as the documentary side is concerned, but why does it not make very moving reading? Why can't it become a novella the masses love to read? This cannot be explained by a lack of familiarity with life. But perhaps is it because he lacks talent? No, Ovechkin has talent. Or does he lack daring? No, he also has daring. What then is he lacking? [His writing] lacks a correct and principled orientation. It lacks human soul. This is what detracts from Ovechkin's works. In view of the fact that a great many young writers go along with him, I am very much concerned that they might become lax in their observation, might reduce their attention to life's experiences and move towards reportages that leave the main duty of literature aside.[24]

---

23. Cf. p. 281 note 1.
24. Nikolayeva's comments are in "Discussion on 'The Director,'" (note 19 above), p. 147.

Zalygin concurred on this point: "In Ovechkin's works time and again the same thing occurs: The problems (of society) are there, but no characters."[25] In the same manner as Wang Meng had to deal with the criticisms of Galina Nikolayeva when he wrote his "A Young Man," Liu Binyan reacted to the apprehensions concerning Ovechkin's work. Already in "At the Building Sites," Liu Binyan had tried to develop his protagonists through their actions rather than to describe them in authorial political commentary. In "Inside News," he went a step further. He gave up the direct link of the *texie* with the problems of modern production management, and focused instead on intellectuals; he furthermore expanded the depiction of the characters' surface by including their lifestyles, clothes, and various opinions on culture, life, and love. And, most important, he set out to explore their "soul," their inner ruminations. True, they are mostly political and tactical in nature and thus remain tied to the genre, but all three characters which are thus treated, Huang Jiaying (the young heroine herself), Ma Wenyuan (who eventually exposes himself to the turbid waters of life and enjoys it), and Chen Lidong (the editor-in-chief), gain considerably in depth. The point was not lost on the editor of *Renmin wenxue*, Qin Zhaoyang, who also was familiar with the Soviet debate to which Liu Binyan was reacting. Qin wrote in a private letter to Liu Binyan that has already been quoted in another context: "I think your 'Inside News' has, to say the least, started to open a new way for our literary creation, has started to have writers pay attention and describe the *depth of the soul* [my emphasis] of people in life around us, and does not pay attention only to workers and peasants."[26] Liu Binyan had thus moved closer to what Galina Nikolayeva had called the true "realm of literature."

As mentioned earlier, the choice of a genre implies the rejection of other genres and a critical reflection on works written in the same genre.[27]

---

25. Ibid.
26. The letters were published in a still inaccessible collection for the Anti-Rightist Movement put together by the Writers' Union in 1957. I quote from Zhang Guangnian, "A Bit More Honesty Would Be Fine," (p. 272 note 55), p. 143.
27. Cf. B. Eichenbaum, *Aufsätze zur Theorie und Geschichte der Literatur* (Frankfurt/Main: Suhrkamp, 1965), p. 27. Eichenbaum there quotes Shklovski. Cf. G. Hess, ed., Hans Robert Jauss, *Literaturgeschichte als Provokation der Literaturwissenschaft* (Konstanz: Konstanzer Universitätsreden, 1967), pp. 22–25.

There have been various ways, both in the Soviet Union and China, to domesticate the *oçerk/texie*. Its agility, it was said, enabled it to keep pace with rapid social change. Its closeness to the newspaper report made it an ideal form for the literary beginner to gain some experience with collecting material and with writing. Even the honorary title of "scout," while acknowledging the importance of the genre, continued to define literature in terms of the "big guns."

Although we have, to my knowledge, no statements from either Ovechkin or Liu Binyan claiming a superiority for the *texie/oçerk* for socialism, the twentieth century, or the modern age in general, there are some indications that the true *oçerk*ists are far from seeing their genre merely as a transition or even training genre. At the Soviet conference on rural themes in November 1955, the *oçerk*ists defended their claim of describing the true face of the countryside against the competition of Galina Nikolayeva's novella *The Director of the MTS,* which they strongly criticized for "harmonizing conflicts." Greatly irritated at the *oçerk*ists' claim to have the monopoly of describing the truth, Nikola-yeva defended the novel: "Each genre has its own rules, and one cannot reduce the entire literature to this one genre, *oçerk*," which obviously was the claim of her opponents.[28] They argued that the cause of her fail-ure to describe accurately the problems in the countryside was her "mak-ing up" things. In the context of a literature which for decades had consisted in things "made up," sincerity as Pomerantsev demanded it, required now to stick to the facts and analyze them with what is called *xin xieshizhuyi,* in works dealing with critical texts after 1979, the term being but a translation of the German *neue Sachlichkeit* to which we shall return.[29] Literary invention was associated by the young *oçerk*ists

28. Nikolayeva's talk is excerpted in "Sulian zhaokai zuojia huiyi taolun jiti nongzhuang ticai wenti" (The Soviet Union convened a writers' conference to discuss problems of the kolk-hoz theme), *Yiwen* 12:236 (December 1955).

29. The volume edited by Li Yi (Lee Yee) and Bi Hua from the periodical *Qishi niandai* in Hong Kong, containing some of the more revealing new texts from the post-1978 period, is en-titled *Zhongguo xin xieshizhuyi wenyi zuopin xuan.* Xin xieshizhuyi is a technical term which ver-batim translates the German *Neue Sachlichkeit.* Cf. Yang Rupeng, "Guoji baogao wenxue de qiyuan, xingcheng he fazhan" (Origin, formation, and development of international reportage literature), in Yi Junsheng, Yang Rupeng, *Disquisitions about Reportage Literature,* (p. 277 note 72), p. 130. Yang there describes the German current of *Neue Sachlichkeit,* using the Chinese term *xin xieshizhuyi.*

with political opportunism which, according to Liu Binyan, reduced creative writing to the sequence "directive by leading cadre–creative work–life," that is, reduced literature to making up realities to fit the political directives. The revaluation of the factual was a literary, a political, and a moral issue at that time. The *oçerk*ist rejected "creative" writing, and "at the center of the discussions" at the said conference on the rural theme in literature there was only the question of "how to develop the *oçerk*" further.[30]

In his critical discussion of other uses of the genre *oçerk*, Ovechkin not only rejected the *oçerki* of Polewoi, Schaginian, and others, but also adduced what he considered the proper pedigree for the genre. In terms of real history, he could refer to two phases of popularity of the *oçerk*—the time of the 1st Five-Year Plan for the Soviet Union, and Russian literature in the nineteenth century. He thus referred to Uspenski, Turgenev, and Chekhov on the one hand, and to the *oçerki* written during the 1st Five-Year Plan on the other, where Gorki promoted the form.[31]

In terms of themes, Ovechkin's emphasis on the problems of agriculture does not seem to match Liu Binyan's treatment of industry. Outlining Ovechkin's "program," Patricia Carden mentioned as the first point "devotion to efficiency, modern technology, and practical knowledge in the organization of work."[32] Indeed, Ovechkin dealt with the problems of an "industrialized" agriculture, bureaucratism in the management being the main problem. Liu Binyan, in the same vein, did not deal with the wonders and advances of industrial technology but with the social organization, institutional behavior, and political conflicts in enterprise management. They left the edifying descriptions of great heroes and scientific advancement to the "embellishers" or "varnishers" in whatever genre. Ovechkin's personality as an *oçerk*ist was well in tune with the heroes of his stories, with Martynov who gives the full depiction of Borzov's character to none other than the latter's wife, or with Grandfather Oshibka who constantly starts rows in public about poor work done in the collective farm until he is expelled (and reinstated

30. Cf. "The Soviet Union" (note 28 above), p. 237a.
31. V. Ovechkin, "On Oçerk" (p. 259 note 17), p. 36.
32. P. Carden, "Reassessing Ovechkin" (p. 259 note 17), p. 412.

after the intervention of the political commissar).[33] In 1937, Ovechkin was expelled from the Party because he intervened with Sholokhov for a friend who he felt was unjustly accused as an enemy of the people. In 1940, back in Moscow, he intervened for another friend. These were, as Ehrenburg mentions, times when survival depended on luck, and such interventions required much courage.[34] At the end of the war, he did not indulge in describing the glories of victory but attacked the conceit and negligence of the cadres towards the people who had suffered through that war.[35] After the September Plenum, he did not reduce the problems of the enactment of its Resolution to sending down technically qualified and strong-willed persons to the countryside, as had Galina Nikolayeva, but, together with his young friends, set out to attack the bureaucrats who repeated the Resolution verbatim and failed to act on it. In 1961, "at the height of his influence and popularity . . . he took exception, in a talk at the Kursk Party Congress, to the official line which placed the blame for a disastrous harvest on the weather," whereupon he was driven from his native province. He found shelter in Tashkent with the Uzbek writers. Mikhail Kolosov wrote about him: "He couldn't tolerate unprincipled people, vacillators, double-dealers, time-servers, 'maneuverers.' He absolutely broke off all relations with them, broke off completely, abruptly, at times even rudely, although not without regret."[36]

The polemic implicit in Ovechkin's choice of genre, theme, and behavior, as well as the explicit polemics in his *oçerki*, articles and public speeches, together with his unshaken belief in the eventual glories of socialism, made him the foremost *oçerk*ist at the time. He did not live long enough to see himself turn from a scout into a sociologist, and the bureaucratic individuals into an experienced political class united in the wish to secure their rank and privileges, as Liu Binyan has described it in his post-1978 works.

---

33. V. Ovechkin, *Gosti v Stukachakh* (Moscow, 1972), p. 29; cf. P. Carden, "Reassessing Ovechkin" (p. 259 note 17), pp. 410f.

34. Nikolai Atarov as quoted by P. Carden, "Reassessing Ovechkin" (p. 259 note 17), p. 409.

35. V. Ovechkin, *S frontym privetom* (Moscow: Sovietskii pisateli, 1946); an English translation by B. Issacs, *Greetings from the Front* (Moscow: Foreign Language Publishing House, 1947).

36. Cf. P. Carden, "Reassessing Ovechkin" (p. 259 note 17), pp. 409f.

While Liu Binyan indeed established the social role of the *texie*-ist in China, his edifice rested on foundations already in place within the socialist world. While Ovechkin must be credited with making the *oçerk* the most important literary genre of the early Thaw period and with establishing a new kind of *oçerk*ist in his critical role of a roaming scout, he nonetheless seems to have operated within a framework of literary and social rules already in place before him, and encoded into the genre *oçerk*. This is evident not only from the core features of his *oçerk*, but also from some elements that survive as dead matter or in a hardly recognizable form. The latter point to earlier stages of the genre of which some features survived without being properly integrated into the new uses to which they were put. An example may be offered. Given the high moral pitch of the anti-bureaucratic attitude present in these *oçerk*, the occasional lightness and satirical casualness of the narrating voice is surprising. It had not been introduced into China by Ovechkin, who did not use satire, but by Troepolski and Tendriakov, who also pioneered in elements of the grotesque. The texts want to be entertaining, not just edifying and polemical, and they use satirical language and anecdotal material for this purpose, although the narrative voice itself rather tends to choke with anger. Liu Binyan thus used grotesque situations like the reporter's car ride with Brigadier Luo in the suffocating dust emanating from his mind, the outing of the editorial board in "Inside News," or the poetry contest in "Between Human and Monster." He painstakingly explained the obvious superiority of socialism over capitalism as far as embezzlers were concerned, because they could exchange benefits with secure profits for all sides without the financial risk a capitalist would have to take. Or he started a lyrical description of the moderate sunny climate of a town in China's northeast only to end on the second page with the suicide of a woman whose apartment has been appropriated by the son of one of the secretaries of the city committee, the last examples being in effect black humor otherwise rare in contemporary Chinese literature.[37] There is an incongruency and a change in functions of earlier patterns which will have to be explained.

37. Liu Binyan, "Haoren a, ni bugai zheyang ruanruo" (Good men, don't be so feeble), in Liu Binyan, *Jiannan de qifei* (p. 303 note 80), p. 319.

SEVENTEEN

Literary Reportage in the Left-Wing Movement of the 1920s and 1930s

EGON ERWIN KISCH

As we have seen, Ovechkin referred back to the *oçerk* of the 1st Five-Year Plan, but without mentioning how he assessed its achievements. During the 1st Five-Year Plan, a large number of gigantic industrial projects were undertaken in great haste, attracting international attention and numerous tourists from inside the country and from abroad.[1] There was little infrastructure to support these projects, and even less experience, and the natural conditions were mostly adverse. The enthusiasm instilled by the Revolution among many city dwellers had not yet been washed away by the show trials and mass persecutions. Things seemed to be moving as indicated by the title of a popular *oçerk* (with the length of a novel) by Katayev which came out in 1930, *Time, Forward.*[2] To describe, support, and propel this unique industrial movement forward, many avant-garde Soviet writers, filmmakers, and artists felt that only the documentary form was adequate. The Revolution finally had something to show, new men and new developments; its essence was shining forth at the surface.

---

1. The best treatment of the *oçerki* of this time I have found in H. Borland, *Soviet Literary Theory and Practice during the First Five-Year Plan 1928–1932* (New York: King's Crown Press, 1950), pp. 38ff.
2. Valentin Katayev, . . . *Time, Forward!*, tr. Charles Malamoth (New York: Farrar and Rinehart, 1933).

Thus, from Sergei Tretiakov's "bio-documentaries,"[3] to Dzig Vertov's documentary films, *The Man With the Camera* and *Enthusiasm – Symphony of the Don-Bass*,[4] to the montage technique used by avant-garde artists to the flood of *očerki* about the new gigantic projects, Soviet cultural circles entered into a frenzy of *Sachlichkeit.* The *očerki* at the time, while holding forth on achievements, admitted that organizational and personal problems existed that had to be overcome by battle, but these battles always ended successfully. The *očerki* were to be, as Marietta Schaginian later claimed, the chronicles of the Stalin Five-Year Plans.

The authors of the *očerki* were mostly professional writers, but their genre was close to reportage and could claim some of its popularity. Since the mid-1920s, reportage was greatly promoted within the Rabkor, the Workers Correspondents Movement, designed to provide first-hand accounts form the workshops, written by and for workers. The *očerk* thus shared the glory of being part of a new "proletarian" literature. Gorki did his share to promote the *očerk* by founding the first journal for reportage literature and *očerki* called *Our Achievements*, a title that set the tone for the contents. Polewoi with his *očerki* on Soviet heroes and Soviet achievements was thus strictly in Gorki's post-revolutionary tradition, and Ovechkin rejected this tradition. The Soviet *očerk* at the time seems to have contributed little towards making the *očerk* a recognized genre in the international fields of literature; by the time the genre became internationally accepted, it already had a secure place in Russia.

The person most instrumental in establishing this genre among "progressive circles" at the time, was Egon Erwin Kisch. To soothe the minds of strictly Sinological readers who might at this point feel they are being dragged too far from their realm of knowledge and interest, a quotation from Xiao Qian, the eminent Chinese journalist, should be inserted here. He reminisced in 1979 about the history of the *texie* in China: "How our *texie* eventually developed I cannot say exactly. I only remember that, during the 1930s, the Czech writer Kisch came to

---

3. Sergei Tretiakov, *Den-shi-chua, Ein Junger Chinese Erzählt Sein Leben, Bio-Interview* (Berlin: Malik Verlag, 1932).

4. Cf. Bertand J. L. Sauzier, "Dziga Vertov and 'Man With the Movie Camera'" (PhD dissertation, Harvard University, 1982).

China, and he promoted this literary form of *texie* in our country."[5] Xiao Qian referred to Kisch's *Secret China,* translated by none other than Zhou Libo; some chapters were printed in periodicals in 1936, and the book *Mimi de Zhongguo* eventually appeared in 1938.[6] Mao Dun wrote in the posthumous festschrift for Kisch in 1955: "Kisch . . . created his own specific style and developed reportage literature so that it was transformed into a modern new literary form and a small but superb weapon in battle. Kisch's collection of reportages, *Secret China,* is not only unconventional in terms of form, but also rich in content, incisively depicting semi-feudal and semi-colonial old China while evincing unbounded sympathy for the Chinese people."[7]

These judgments do not stand alone. The German edition of the literary periodical edited by the International Union of Proletarian Revolutionary Writers, *Internationale Literatur,* devoted one of its 1935 issues to a veritable homage to Kisch. Henri Barbusse and Michael Gold, Sergei Tretiakov and Emi Siao (Xiao San), Leon Feuchtwanger and Bert Brecht, Detlev Kantorowicz and Georg Lukács, Bruno Frei and Andor Gabor, and the secretariat of the International Association of Revolutionary Writers itself praised Kisch's contribution in this unique tribute.[8] He, they all maintained, had made literary reportage into a work of art, neither forfeiting its militancy nor relinquishing artistic standards.[9] Kisch was the ultimate "scout." Tretiakov praised him for "pitilessly investigating the empire of the bourgeoisie," calling

5. "Shang'ai xinwen gongzuo, ji Xiao Qian tongzhi dui Zhongguo shehuikexueyuan xinwen yanjiusheng de yici jianghua" (Beloved newspaper work, comrade Xiao Qian's talk to researchers in journalism at the Chinese Academy of Social Sciences), *Xinwen yanjiu ziliao* 4:74 (1979).

6. Egon Erwin Kisch, *Egon Erwin Kisch berichtet: China geheim* (Berlin: E. Reiss Publikationen, 1933). The English version is Egon Erwin Kisch, *Secret China,* tr. Michael Davidson (London: John Lane, 1935). From this translation Zhou Libo's translation is made: Ji Xi (Kisch), *Mimi de Zhongguo* (Tianjin, 1938), individual chapters in *Wenxuejie* 1.1–1.3 (1936), and in *Shenbao meizhou zengkan* 1.13 (1936).

7. Mao Dun, "Letter to F. C. Weiskopf," facsimile in Kisch-Kalender (p. 315 note 8), p. 96. It should be mentioned here that D. Saslavski, whom we have quoted above, p. 265 note 37, with his "Some remarks on *oçerk*" criticizing the work of Polewoi and others in 1953, was a friend of Kisch's. Cf. D. Saslawskij (D. Saslavski), "Wir kannten ihn," in F. C. Weiskopf, ed., *Kisch-Kalender,* pp. 91ff.

8. *Internationale Literatur* 4 (1935).

9. This is stated by Michael Gold in *Internationale Literatur* 4 (1935), p. 5; Michael Kolzow, p. 6; the secretariat, p. 8; L. Feuchtwanger, p. 9; Bert Brecht, p. 9; Hans Gunther, p. 15; Otto Heller, p. 15; D. Kantorowicz, p. 17; Bruno Frei, p. 24.

him a "fearless scout of the unbeatable proletarian armies, sharp-eyed and of pungent language . . . Kisch is agile, resourceful, and without pity . . . He is courageous, straightforward, and funny."[10] Others repeated the term.[11] The Soviet *Literaturnaya Entsiklopedia* of the early 1930s featured Kisch as "reporter-*oçerkist*."[12] It seems that the genre developed in this century mainly through exceptional individuals; we are not artificially limiting our field of vision when we now deal with Kisch as the next segment within the socialist layer.

Kisch, like Liu Binyan and Ovechkin, had started out as a journalist; eventually he moved, like his two successors, into a position where he could choose his own topics. And finally, like Ovechkin and Liu Binyan, he published his literary reportages in book form. Since the end of World War I, he had been associated with the newly forming Communist Parties in Europe, eventually moving to Berlin, where he became a member of the Bund Proletarisch-Revolutionärer Schriftsteller, the German equivalent of the League of Left-Wing Writers in China. He had earlier written a highly acclaimed novel, *Mädchenhirt*, but eventually moved to writing only his peculiar literary reportages. They were published in the big publishing houses, not the left-wing press, and they were enormously successful. His *Secret China*, the German edition of which was burnt in 1933, ran through 8 printings within one year in France.[13] His book on the United States went through over 20 printings in two years. A sociological study of reading habits of employed city dwellers in Germany showed that their preferred genre was reportage.[14] What is today called New Journalism had established itself. We shall now briefly review the features already described for Liu Binyan's *texie* and Ovechkin's *oçerki*, to see how they relate to Kisch's literary reportage.

10. S. Tretiakov in *Internationale Literatur* 4 (1935), pp. 5f.

11. The term was used for Kisch by Kolzow and Schückle, while Anna Seghers called him a "detective," p. 11.

12. *Literaturnaya Entsiklopedia* (Moscow, 1930–1939), IX, 268.

13. E. E. Kisch, *La Chine Secrète*, tr. Jeanne Stern (Paris: Gallimard, 1935). In this year at least 8 printings came out. The tremendous success of this book outside Germany is mentioned in the congratulatory message of the IURW, quoted in note 9 above.

14. S. Kracauer, *Die Angestellten. Aus dem neuesten Deutschland* (Berlin, 1930), p. 20.

(1) TOPICALITY. Kisch's reportages dealt with the immediate present. It was argued, and Kisch agreed, that the fast development of industry, but especially the hectic times after World War I, did not lend themselves to other literary forms. Theodor Balk, whose 1935 article on Kisch's reportage became the main source on Kisch's theories in China after 1938, wrote:

> Upheavals, revolts, and revolutions had come. One of them was victorious. . . . Reality became more fantastic than all poetic fantasy, Jules Verne's novels fell into oblivion—reality had left them far behind. The time had come to bring the naked sober report into a consciously planned and stirring form, the time for writers who report swiftly about a world where the today and the tomorrow change the face of the world with the speed of a film.[15]

Here we have an argument instead of a blunt fact: Under the new conditions, the visible reality itself had become the harbinger of truth, and, in the fast pace of such changes, only reportage could keep track.

Kisch operated, however, as a free journalist. He was a CP member and shared that general outlook, but seems to have retained for himself the right to define the problems. Liu Binyan makes a fine point when saying that Ovechkin had "Party consciousness," which means a loyalty towards the ultimate goals of socialism, by implication denying that he had "Party spirit" or was *party'nost,* meaning following the directives of the Party in all he did. Kisch agreed with most of the Communist left at the time that the Soviet Union was described in the West with vituperative slander, and he wrote two books of his reportages defending the Soviet Union. He also agreed that the Guomindang should focus on the Japanese instead of diverting its troops to fight the Jiangxi Soviet, and he wrote his *Secret China* in this context. But he did his own interviewing, selected the topics and focus himself, and thus established the image of the loyal but independent scout.

15. Theodor Balk, "Egon Erwin Kisch und die Reportage," in *Internationale Literatur* 3 (1935), then in Egon Erwin Kisch, *Abenteuer in Fünf Kontinenten* (Moscow: Verlagsgenossenschaft ausländischer Arbeiter in der UdSSR, 1936); then as "Ji Xi ji qi baogaowenxue," *Qiyue* 4.4 (1939), which I have not seen. Hu Feng, who edited *Qiyue,* mentioned in "Minzu zhanzheng yu xin wenyi chuantong" (National war and the traditions of new literature and art), written in 1939 and included in his *Jian, wenyi, renmin* (p. 265 note 38), on p. 253, that this article by then had already been "known (in China) for a long time." The article by Balk is again reprinted in *Lun baogao wenxue* (On reportage literature; Shanghai: Nitu Press, 1953). The above quotation is on p. 12 of the edition in *Abenteuer in Fünf Kontinenten.*

(2) AUTHENTICITY. Kisch battled on two fronts, against the bourgeois novel on one side, and against Party propaganda writers on the other, again a constellation familiar from the Soviet and Chinese examples. In 1929, the heat was on in the debate among leftist writers whether the novel still had a future, or whether it should not be replaced by reportage. Kisch's successes seemed to point the way. Answering a request to state his opinion on the topic, Kisch wrote:

> Novel? No. Reportage! What do I think of the reportage? I think it is the literary nourishment of the future. But only the reportage of high quality. The novel has no future. There will be no novels, meaning books with invented plots. The novel is the literature of the past century. . . . What is left of French nineteenth-century literature? Practically nothing but Zola and Balzac. And why these two? Only because they described their century in the manner of reporters, because they used reportage technique in writing their novels. . . . After the war all novel plots have dissolved into nothingness, compared to the overwhelming impressions we have received during the World War. . . . In short, each and everyone experienced his own novel, and sometimes even a series of them. Thus, a very particular kind of reportage work has arisen, which I would call the pure reportage, the reportage per se. After the war this reportage became the general fashion. . . . I believe there will be a time when people will want to read nothing about the world but the truth! Psychological novels? No! Reportages! The future belongs to the truthful and daring, far-seeing reportage.[16]

Literary reportage is thus not only in a tactical collision with the novel; it challenges its very principle, literary creation, as a "lie," as propaganda, or intellectual introspection.[17] The circumstances may change; the battle lines remain the same.

---

16. Quoted from the Czech leftist periodical *Cin* 1929 by the former editor, Marie Majerova, in her "Als Egonek den Roman zum Tode verurteilte," in *Kisch Kalender* (p. 315 note 8), pp. 185f.

17. Kisch used the term *lie* directly for fictional writing when pondering how to match the attraction of fictional writing with factual reportage through the introduction of artistic elements: "Can the depiction of truth do without fantasy? It is true, fantasy cannot unfold here according to her whims, only on the small plank leading from fact to fact is she permitted to dance, and her movements have to accord with the rhythm of the facts. And even on this narrow dancing plank, fantasy is not alone. It has to engage in a round dance with a complete corps de ballet of artistic forms so that the driest raw material—reality—would not in any way fall short of the most elastic matter, the *lie*." Kisch, "Von der Reportage" (About reportage), in E. E. Kisch, *Marktplatz der Sensationen* (Mexico City: Das Freie Buch, 1942), pp. 250f.

At the same time Kisch argued and operated against the mandate of "tendentiousness" or *party'nost,* which was present in many reportages written by his colleagues in the Bund Proletarisch-Revolutionärer Schriftsteller, and led Lukács into a drawn-out battle against the new genre. Kisch wrote in 1924, and did not change it in later editions:

> The reporter does not have an inclination, he has nothing to justify, he has no standpoint. He has to witness without prejudice, and has to bear witness without prejudice. . . . He depends on the facts, and has to acquire knowledge of these facts by personal inspection, an interview, an observation, a piece of information. . . . The places and phenomena he describes, the experiments he sets up, history of which he is a witness, and the sources he discovers do not have to be so far away, so rare, and so difficult to reach, as long as he has, in a world monstrously inundated with lies, in a world that wants to forget itself and therefore is only after the untruth, the dedication to his object. Nothing is more stunning than simple truth, nothing more exotic than our immediate environs, nothing more full of fantasy than *Sachlichkeit.* And there is nothing more sensational in the world than the time in which one lives oneself.[18]

Insight into social processes, Kisch maintained, can achieve its political effectiveness only if the work of the author is not a "pathetic outcry," but when "only the facts do the work, the facts he explores because he loves them, and which he loves because he explores them." There is no place for plaintiveness in this work, which Kisch felt had crept even into Gorki's writing.[19]

Authenticity, *Sachlichkeit,* truthfulness are thus the hallmarks of his genre. "I detest empty phrases, I am a fanatic of *Sachlichkeit"* proclaimed Kisch,[20] and *Neue Sachlichkeit* was the intellectual category with which he is justly associated. His new literary genre belonged to the new factual genres developing during the 1920s—literary reportage, film, and photography. Dziga Vertov, Soviet avant-garde filmmaker of the 1920s, objected to the introduction of literary and lyrical elements into film; like Tretiakov, he belonged to the LEF, the Leftist Front, and his film group was called Kinoki (Film-eye). His film *The Man with the Camera,*

18. E. E. Kisch, *Der Rasende Reporter* (Berlin: Erich Reiss Verlag, 1924), Introduction.
19. Kisch as quoted by Christian Ernst Siegel, *Reportage und Politischer Journalismus* (Bremen: Studien zur Publizistik, Bremer Reihe. Deutsche Presseforschung. Hg. Elger Bluehm) XVIII, 102ff.
20. E. E. Kisch, *Der Rasende Reporter* (note 18 above), p. 78.

which had great influence on such modern filmmakers as Godard and Antonioni, radically avoided those elements and tried to capture the pure and true surface. Kisch noticed the similarity to his own approach and said that Vertov's film, *Enthusiasm – Symphony of the Don-Bass*, had impressed him most. In his book on reportage and political journalism, Christian Siegel justly stressed the links between Kisch's writing technique and the films of Vertov, Pabst, and even Chaplin, with whom Kisch was friends.[21] The abandonment of the all-knowing narrator and his replacement by the investigating and analyzing reporter who makes a montage of fragments without hiding the seams, would correspond to the procedure of the cameraman. "Vertov," Siegel wrote, "wants to decipher the most common objects in a new way; Kisch explores areas that are so close by that his researches seem sensational . . . Both use the fact, but not as a building block for an integrative and psychologizing form of narrative, but restored the meaning of the fact itself by revealing – in the condensed form of film and reportage – its demonstrative character."[22] We are thus dealing with a claim for truth not based on the factuality of the events described, but on the writing technique of authenticity. This is as much a fictional technique as is realism, or symbolism. Of course, the most incisively "realistic" depictions of social reality can be presented through symbolism, while the dullest propaganda might be confined tightly within a corset of authentic portrayal.

For Kisch himself, as much as for Ovechkin and Liu Binyan, there was no difference between their literary technique of suggesting authenticity and their claim to be truthful and authentic in their writing. As shown by a compatriot of Kisch's, his standard example for reportage, a piece about the fire in a mill in Prague, was in fact written much later and without Kisch's ever having seen the conflagration.[23] It was an

21. C. E. Siegel, *Reportage* (note 19 above), pp. 69ff, 99. The point was made earlier by Balk, "Kisch und die Reportage" (note 15 above), p. 12, and, in 1934, in an article in the *Neue Deutsche Blätter* 5.2:258 (1934/5), the issue being mostly devoted to homage to Kisch. Yi Junsheng even maintained that "Kisch was the first writer to transfer film techniques into literature." Yi Junsheng, "Baogaowenxue – xinxingde dulide wenxue yangshi" (Reportage literature – an independent literary form with a new shape), in *Disquisitions About Reportage Literature* (p. 277 note 72), p. 13.

22. C. E. Siegel, *Reportage*, (note 19 above), p. 99.

23. D. Schlenstedt, *Egon Erwin Kisch, Leben und Werk* (Berlin [East]: Volk und Wissen, 1968), p. 77.

authentic piece of fiction (although the event happened), and could lay claim only to fictional authenticity. But, of course, it reads as if Kisch had written at the scene of the fire.

There are more than just parallels between literary reportage and film. Even the Chinese term for the genre is taken from film language. *Texie* is the close-up, a technique used in critical moments of a film where a single detail, a glance, a gesture, an object, will reveal the true meaning of an entire sequence or the plot itself. Kisch (like many authors of novels since the time) extensively used techniques adapted from film. Theodor Balk noted in his essay: "Reportage and film are young, very young artistic genres. In their dynamism they have much in common. The close-up, the shutter, the parsimony of gesture, the montage." Kisch's reportages, Ovechkin's * oçerki*, and Liu Binyan's *texie* all emphasize things that are visible and audible, selecting anecdotal material of heightened specificity as part of a broader mosaic. Thoughts and arguments are proffered in the form of dialogue, bureaucrats have flabby bodies, the section of the bridge where Luo Lizheng is in command is submerged by the spring waters, the section where the daring engineer Zeng is in charge is finished fast enough to remain above the tide. The human eye and ear are the sensors.

Kisch's introduction to a chapter in *Secret China* describing his visit to a farm outside Beijing is classical:

It was one of those summery walks in the neighborhood of Peking which seem to have nothing whatever to do with Peking and its neighborhood. Our brains were crammed with impressions, our eyes dazzled. Here there was a pagoda, fourteen stories high; the roofs floated in the ether like fourteen malachite-green, parallel waves with golden crests . . . [This chance excursion with some idle talk eventually ends at a wall.] We, possessed by the obstinacy of the aimless, followed the wall along in order to find a place where it would leave our path free again. After a hundred paces, we came upon a wide opening; it was the gate of a dairy farm, through which—our direction, our direction—we had to go. Dogs leapt at us yelping; with cowardly aggressiveness they chased round us, at three paces' distance; at three paces' distance they stopped, waiting, when we stopped. Such an escort was not exactly agreeable. "One ought never go walking without a stick," we said. All the same, we soon forgot the dogs. The people coming towards us resembled each other in such a peculiar manner that with each fresh encounter this similarity became more and more striking, until finally it was uncanny.

They were all elderly women, evidently women working on the farm; some were leading cattle on a rope, others carried sacks pickaback, or walked past with rakes and hayforks. They wore dark-blue trousers, as is the custom with working women in this country; nevertheless, contrary to all convention, the upper part of their bodies was naked—their breasts hung down unblushingly.

These matrons were chattering together, and although they were not talking loudly, their voices rang shrill—or, more correctly, each sound they uttered was accompanied by a shrill secondary note . . . [Still the visitors' eyes were looking for a clue to this mystery.] And then a little incident occurred that gave us a clue: One of the old ladies turned away to perform a perfectly natural function—but in an essentially masculine posture.[24]

The text, then, in a flashback, narrates something about the history of the eunuchs in imperial China, and how the present establishment was set up by the old eunuchs in case they were to fall from favor. The entire text is a close-up on one very minute detail—eunuchs in the early 1930s; it is used to illustrate something about the functioning of politics in imperial China. Together these 23 texts, like a pointillist painting, give a highly complex picture of many of China's problems at the time. Within each close-up, further close-ups are used as clues like the bare-breasted lady "performing a natural function in an essentially masculine posture" above. The camera eye does not pretend to know; it observes reality. Its observation would catch an advertisement for a bordello touting the assurance that the ladies employed there have a weekly checkup by Dr. R. Halpern, M.D.; monitor details of the exchange market between gold, silver taels, US dollars, and copper cash; register the execution of a criminal, the burial of a prominent gang leader, and glimpses from a mental ward in Beijing; and all this to support certain conclusions suggested by the authorial voice. The authenticity is thus achieved by factual documentation and explicit inductive reasoning.

In many of the texts of all three authors, the focus is on something sensational. "The reporter is in the service of sensations" wrote Kisch.[25] Wang Shouxin's gigantic embezzlement, the suicide in Dandong,[26] the appearance of a bureaucratic *first* secretary in "Everyday Life" before

---

24. I have followed the translation in E. E. Kisch, *Secret China* (note 6 above).
25. E. E. Kisch, *Der Rasende Reporter* (note 18 above), Introduction.
26. See Liu Binyan, "Between Human and Monster" (p. 246 note 1).

Stalin's death, and the bizarre collection that constitutes Kisch's *Secret China* all show the traces of this sensationalism. But, although the genre in this respect shows some of its journalistic origin, as a genre it is not primarily interested in sensationalism. Liu Binyan was not interested in the sensational case of Wang Shouxin but in digging out the social and institutional roots of her existence and actions. Kisch was not interested in eunuchs, prostitutes, criminals, madmen, or riksha coolies per se but in the Chinese social and political fabric. Both writers balance their use of sensationalist topics by describing persons and incidents far below the threshold of newspapers' headlines and by inserting analytical statements. The sensation of the small detail was already dominant in *Secret China*, and most of the texts written in this tradition followed the example. Still, much of the language was taken from the sensational report, and served to draw the reader into the text. In our search for the origins of the artistry of authenticity we have again reached the level where this specific feature shows its reasoned fundament and logic, and stops being dead factual matter.

All the continuity notwithstanding, the use of this set of devices by Ovechkin and Liu Binyan took place under quite different circumstances, which changed the import of these devices. Kisch could easily argue that the mask was put over society's reality by "them," the bourgeoisie and imperialists. True, he also opposed the flat propaganda on the left and demanded that the difficulties of the Soviet "giant enterprise . . . [should be described] without embellishment and in the form of a factual record,"[27] but the polemics encoded in his *Neue Sachlichkeit* were directed against the bourgeoisie. By transferring the artistry of authenticity to socialist society, Ovechkin and Liu Binyan argued that masking was now done by bureaucrats in power, that is, members, even leading members, of the Communist Party. The falsification of reality through misreporting, dressing up of facts and figures, failure to report problems, difficulties, and tragedies, as well as suppression of fact-based criticism are constant themes in both Liu and Ovechkin. The official press and even the inside reports to the higher levels are but a mask imposed on reality. Reality will shine forth in its authenticity only in

27. Kisch, quoted in C. E. Siegel, *Reportage* (note 19 above), p. 113.

the works of the *očerk*ist/*texie*-ist. The historical continuity claimed by
Ovechkin and Liu Binyan implied to a certain degree the continuity of
the problem across the revolutionary divide, an implication that did not
help make the genre popular among the new leaders.

(3) *DISCOVERY.* According to Kisch, the detective story and the *India-
nergeschichte* (a series of novels by the German Karl May featuring an
American Indian hero [Winnetou] and a white hero [Old Shatterhand]
confounding all kinds of evil schemes) animate the reader to *Denksport*,
to exercise his mental faculties. In both genres "identification of clues
and their interpretation based on experience and skillful combination"
dominate the action; the reader follows the "equation full of unknown
quantities" with "suspense." For purposes of an operative "social insight" these devices, which make for the mass success of the detective
story and Karl May's books, are "not to be discarded." Social insight has
to be promoted by using the successful devices from the entertaining
genres.[28]

At the same time, the discovery of the true surface involves a struggle, because such powerful interests keep the masks firmly glued in
place. Furthermore, discovery often involves personal risks of going
into the abysses of society or into the headquarters of the Japanese chief
of staff. The readers, who come from the middle levels of society, might
not dare to confront these powers and dangers, but they rejoice in the
vicarious daring and dangers when following the investigative reporter's
camera into the darkest corners, and they rejoice in the exercise of their
mental faculties when forming their own thoughts about topics, in spite
of the pressure to keep to what pertains only to the official social mask.

Kisch adduced as evidence for the social and moral pitch of this detective work Diderot, who sneaked into factories to gather material for the
Grande Encyclopedie; Voltaire's undoing of the judicial murder of Jean
Calas; Beaumarchais's memoranda, and the descriptions given by the
convict Languet of life in the Bastille. The facts themselves were social
dynamite.[29]

---

28. Kisch, quoted in ibid., p. 103.
29. E. E. Kisch, "Soziale Aufgaben der Reportage," *Die Bücherschau* 4:163 (1926).

The realm of Kisch's discovery was much larger than that of his successors, who limited themselves to the conflict between the modernization-minded coalition and the bureaucrats. Kisch was interested in society as a whole, and there was no topic too lowly for him, including the history of certain commodities or a puppet show in Beijing. He was operating in a social framework where he could, with some daring and wit, get access to the most amazing situations, information, and personalities, even if he had to use a false passport, or jump from a ship onto the quay (and break his ankle), as he did in Australia when the government did not grant him permission to land. Within a free world, he made use of his freedom to the utmost. His readers were tied into their narrow social patterns; their power to exercise their freedoms seemed futile in view of the numerous restrictions that state, modern industry, and they themselves imposed on their lives. Kisch's discovery thus became the daydream of the reader who otherwise did not move very much.

This element was much more pronounced in the case of Kisch's successors. Their realm of operations was more restricted, and they were operating in societies where access to information and independent deliberation was immeasurably more controlled than in bourgeois societies. Kisch had mass success with his work. His successors managed to shake up their entire countries for years with only one or two narrowly targeted texts.

Although some of the literary devices associated with the feature "discovery" were introduced by Kisch, his inheritance of the travelogue and the elements encoded into this form of writing, suggests earlier fundaments.

(4) "SOCIOLOGICAL" ANALYSIS. Kisch's texts are not political in the sense of attacking a specific individual or a specific institution. They are sociological in their attempt to understand social forces and their dynamics. The same is true for his successors. One of the reasons why the *literary reportage/oçerk/texie* changes the names of persons and places is to reduce the *ad hominem* elements and indicate that the same or similar things could happen anywhere in the country, that the insight gleaned from one close-up could well be substantiated from a dozen others.

The sociological drive inherent in Kisch has been noted by contemporaries. In a review of Kisch's *Der Rasende Reporter,* a collection of reportages, the master of German criticism at the time, Karl Korn, wrote that Kisch had "added sociological depth" to his descriptions.[30] Kisch himself wrote that "fact is only the magnetic compass of [the reporter's] journey; he also needs a telescope: 'logical fantasy.' The autopsy of the scene of an action or of a place, the utterings of participants and witnesses caught at random, and conjectures which have been suggested to him could never give a picture of the actual situation without gaps. He had to create for himself the pragmatics of the event and the transitions that led to the results of his investigations, only making sure that the line of his presentation led exactly through the facts known to him (the given points in that line)."[31] Underlying this argument was the assumption of a comprehensible structure of reality which had only to be revealed from the fragments of the true surface that became accessible. Underlying the argument was also the assumption of a homogeneity of reality, which permitted a transfer of the results of one social investigation to another, and the logical combination of several such pieces into a higher concept of "social insight," *soziale Erkenntnis.* "Any reporter," wrote Kisch, "that is, any writer or journalist who strives to describe from personal inspection truthfully and for its own sake circumstances and events will, in this empirical endeavor, eventually come to the same final conclusion. By far the greatest part of all events in their seeming heterogeneity and the interest evoked by them is resting on the same base. The level of this social insight is indeed the gauge for measuring whether a reporter with intelligence and instinct has truly exerted his love of truth."

Kisch described this as the way "from the simple registration of facts to socialism" which "the reportage has pursued from the very beginning."[32] The facts of society, his argument ran, forced the author of the literary reportage into the "social insight" contained in socialism. Ovechkin and Liu Binyan did not deny this, both never having abandoned Marxist-Leninist tenets. However, they were not looking forward to

---

30. Karl Korn is quoted in C. E. Siegel, *Reportage* (note 19 above), p. 182.
31. E. E. Kisch, "Wesen des Reporters," *Das Literarische Echo,* 15 January 1919, p. 1.
32. E. E. Kisch, "Soziale Aufgaben" (note 29 above), p. 163.

socialism, but living within it, and, while they remained committed socialists, the facts of society forced them to help remove the main obstacle to further progress, the bureaucrats. While Kisch could arrive, after much racy description of the surface, at conclusions well in tune with the CP's general line, his successors operated in contested lands; there was no accepted "class analysis" of socialism, and even to demand that there be such an analysis (which implies that there were still classes) meant risking one's existence as a writer and even as a human being. Liu and Ovechkin thus in fact expanded the sociology inherent in the genre beyond Kisch's limits, setting the *texie*-ist/*očerk*ist up not only as the "eyes and ears" but as the "brain" of the Party, developing new social insight from investigative scanning and logical inference.

While Kisch seems to be at the root of the theory of the literary reportage as a vehicle for *soziale Erkenntnis,* the inherent sociologism of the genre seems to be inherited matter and will have to be further pursued. The sociology of his reportage differs from other social investigations by its consistent inclusion of the historic-genetic element. Typically, Kisch started, as in the chapter on eunuchs, at the level of the immediately visible, even accidentally visible. Having interested the reader in the unraveling of the mystery, he proceeded to detail some of the historical background of the eunuchs, their role in the imperial court, and their eventual demise. These descriptions again use the verbatim quotation, the anecdote, the telling detail of the surface. The exploration of the roots and genesis of a phenomenon add to the analytical character and dominate the plot of most texts. Ovechkin and Liu Binyan adopted this feature. Martynov explored the origins of Borzov's careerism to the point that Borzov's wife asks herself whether he married her only because she was a Stachanovite. Liu Binyan traced the history of Luo Lizheng and Chen Lidong in detail, suggesting the historical experiences on which their present attitude rests. In his later pieces, Liu detailed the dynamics inherent in the growth of the cancerous network of unofficial relationships of mutual protection within the Party. In the leanness inherent in the genre, the history is explored only for the problem itself, and there only for that aspect that makes it a social problem. Johannes Schellenberger has described the absolute dominance of "the problem" for Ovechkin's texts, and his words hold true for other pieces of the genre: "Ovechkin freely creates his characters, but this does not mean that he intends to write a story; the characters are developed only to the point needed to show the psychological aspect of a problem. But the latter is not the center of his work. He is primarily and mainly concerned with the problem itself."[33]

Three elements are thus combined under the heading of "sociological analysis"–the sociological, the historical, and the analytical. The combination of the first two under the heading of the third implies an assumption that a phenomenon can be understood only from its genesis; its structural relationship with other phenomena on the screen of the present is by itself meaningless. This assumption ties in with the Marxist credo of the three authors studied above.

The sociology of the genre presupposes a simple and rational structure of those elements of reality that are observed. Indeed the truth is hidden, but understandable and simple. The complexities of human behavior and interaction can be reduced to a few easily definable motives.

The final problem of sociological analysis is the representativeness of the surface material. Kisch himself demanded that his work sustain "scholarly scrutiny" (*wissenschaftliche Uberprüfbarkeit*).[34] In terms of contemporary sociology, his method would be subsumed under qualitative as opposed to quantitative analysis. He and his contemporaries spelled out the methodological principle underlying this approach, a principle again based on the assumption of a coherently logical reality— *maxima in minimis*. Leonard Frank, himself an author of reportages, maintained in his response to the questionnaire on reportage and poetry in 1926, "In each square centimeter of matter in Berlin the entire world is contained."[35] In an article about John Reed, Kisch himself

33. Schellenberger's analysis of Ovechkin is quoted from *Beiträge zur Gegenwartsliteratur* 16 by Reiner Kunze, *Wesen und Bedeutung* (p. 313 note 5), p. 51.
34. E. E. Kisch, "Reportage als Kunstform und Kampfform," talk at the Congress for the Defense of Culture, Paris 1935, quoted in "Die literarische Reportage–ihre Tradition, ihre Technik" (Literary reportage–its tradition, its technique), *Neue Deutsche Literatur* 8:18 (1954). This series of articles in the East German periodical was written in preparation for the Writers' Congress in 1954, where a discussion about "hitherto neglected genres" was sponsored, which "first of all refers to reportage." This was part of the East German mirroring of the Soviet Ovechkin phenomenon.
35. Quoted from his answer to the inquiry about reportage and fiction in *Die literarische Welt* 26.2 (1926).

argued that Reed's and Larissa Reissner's books would survive millions of other books "because these two have understood that journalistic actuality can be handled only under the aspect of eternity, and that in each individual fate and in each episode the grand fate of mankind is reflected."[36] Thus, each individual, seemingly anecdotal element is fraught with broader meaning.[37] Again the parallels to film come to mind. Kurt Pinthus said that Eisenstein's film *Strike*, with its daring montage of short shots, used *pointillistische Nahaufnahme-Sachlichkeits-technik*, a linguistic monster which in English would read "pointillist technique of close-up/*Sachlichkeit*."[38] The term *pointillism* was used for Kisch's technique by Thomas Balk in 1935: "The impressionist Kisch draws life point for point, with the thoroughness of a pointillist."[39] While Kisch's collections of reportages originally were just that, his later works grouped points together so as to give a fairly complete picture of the country or problem in question through detailed and thorough explorations of individual aspects.

Ovechkin used the same technique in his collection of *očerki*. In Liu Binyan's case, the cohesion of the individual pieces was fairly loose—their common theme notwithstanding. He did not establish coherence through the invention of stock characters (Borzov and Martynov) or a single narrator.

The use of the meaningful detail for qualitative sociological analysis implies the homogeneity of society and the world, where each detail is part of a logically structured universe and can therefore open the door to the understanding of this entire universe. None of the authors hitherto treated seem to have explicitly reflected upon this point; it is thus a carry-over from an earlier layer which became encoded into the genre itself.

36. E. E. Kisch, "Our Own Correspondent, John Reed," *Die Neue Bücherschau* 7/8:375 (1928). Cf. D. Schlenstedt, *Egon Erwin Kisch, Leben und Werk*, pp. 92f.

37. Bruno Frei wrote, in his homage to Kisch in *Internationale Literatur* 3:24 (1935), "To show in the small the big, always with documentary proof—that is the reportage. You need for it love for truth, Marxism, and industry."

38. Pinthus is quoted by C. E. Siegel, *Reportage* (note 19 above), p. 138.

39. Th. Balk, "Egon Erwin Kisch" (note 15 above), p. 14.

(5) MODERNITY. The modernity of the genre is linked to the media in which its products appear, and to the modernity of its brother genres like film and photography. It is present in the analytical attitude of the author-ial voice with its daring inquisitiveness, unsentimental irony, and sharp big-city wit; it is present even in the authors' socialist commentaries, socialism at the time being still very young and seemingly less tainted by massive infusions from traditional and new bureaucratism. Kisch occa-sionally ventured into rural areas, but his heartland was the city with the worker, the banker, the madhouse and the whorehouse, the newspaper, the political parties and factions. Even when he wrote about Soviet Asia, he wrote about its modernization and the obstacles it had to overcome. The reportage does not deal with love, nature, gothic horror, heroes of olden times, or the mutterings of what Marx called rural idiocy. It is urbane, cosmopolitan, rationalistic in the extreme, and, while driven by a fever of social engagement, it uses the cool, hard language of *Neue Sach-lichkeit*, like Georg Grosz in his paintings.

(6) MORALITY. Like his successors, Kisch identified the "backward" with the bad, and the progressive with the "good." The *Sachlichkeit* style of literary reportage prevents sloganeering denunciations, but uses telling surface phenomena and cool information to evoke the appropri-ate moral judgment in the reader, sparing him the pain of being exhorted and lectured to. The morality is thus a function of the modernity of the genre. The implied moral standard is based on the assumption that soci-ety should be run by incorrupt, upright, just, honest, truth-loving, progress-oriented, democratically and egalitarian-minded individuals; in fact, however, this is rarely the case, although the individuals running society like to see themselves presented in this benign guise. The possi-bility that the purest motives may lead to the most disastrous conse-quences; that, as Liu E maintained in his *Laocan youji*, the honest officials are the worst, because they can vent their uprightness only on powerless common folk but never on the mighty; that the relationship of these rigid moral standards to the dynamics of a modern mass society is a very complex one—nothing of this is admitted in the genre. The genre thus reproduces the abstract standards the essentially powerless educated city dwellers like to apply to their superiors. As the common

folk and their heroic scout, the authorial voice of the reporter, are presented as being imbued with exactly this morality, the implied standards are reinforced for the reader by the material presented in the reportage. As much, however, as the freedom and daring of the reporter is the surrogate for the confined existence of the reader, the high moral pitch of the authorial voice might be seen as the surrogate for the reader's incapacity to live up to the standards he applies to his superiors.

Within the texts, morality, like truth, is invested in the lower orders. This becomes more pronounced in Kisch's later, more socialistic texts.

(7) IRONIC DISTANCE. The ironic distance in Kisch's work comes in two forms. First, through the grotesque deformation of the realities described. His *Secret China* sums up the political and social situation of the country through a depiction of freak extremes, like eunuch farms, Shanghai brothels, the Temple of Hell in Beijing, and the hysterics at the Shanghai gold market. All this evokes in the reader the image of a country weighed down by the dregs of the feudal past and colonial present, to be confronted by the proverbial riksha coolie. He tells about their glorious strike and provides perspective and hope in this morass. The polemical deformation of reality through the selection of freaks on both ends provides the reader with an orderly universe where right and wrong are well defined, and reality has lost all its irritating ambiguity. He can side with the coolie, for it is only "reality" that has been shown to him, and in this reality no other reaction is meaningful.

The second device is ironic language. This in most cases consists in a mock-adoption of the position of the villain, either by spelling out his inner ruminations neutrally without comment or by letting him hold forth to the narrator in the most outrageous fashion on his real motives and goals. In both cases he reveals himself through his own "real" words and thoughts, giving the reader at the same time the satisfaction of joining in outwitting the powerful villain. Either his thoughts are put in perspective so as to give away his most secret motives, or he is too stupid to recognize in the innocent appearance of the journalist the scout of the "people." The villain's failure in the intellectual battle exposes his real power to very satisfactory ridicule.

(8) MILITANCY. Kisch started out as a reporter whose inquisitiveness was stimulated by sensational events. Gradually he moved towards attributing a politically and socially militant role to his craft. It seems that the standard attribute of the genre as being "militant" actually originated with Kisch, who entitled his great speech at the Paris "Congress for the Salvation of Culture" in 1935, convened as a broad anti-fascist forum, "Die Reportage als Kunstform und Kampfform" (Reportage as an artistic and militant form).[40]

The power of reportage quickly to reach a very broad public and to help in forming public opinion was a prime motive for Kisch's holding onto this form. What was later called "intervening in life" was not meant in a narrow political sense of interfering in the handling of a specific case, but in the broader meaning of helping the public to articulate thoughts on pressing issues on the basis of factual analyses. In this sense, Kisch's books about the United States, Germany, the Soviet Union, and China, as well as numerous individual reportages, showed "militancy" by implicitly urging the reader to take sides in the big issues of national and world affairs. His earlier texts had their starting point in the inquisitiveness of the reporter, and later, in his Mexican exile, he resumed this attitude with some disillusionment about the revolutionary cause. During the "militant" phase, which became most important for his image in the leftist world, his texts kept within the broad guidelines of Communist opinion at the time, while refusing to subordinate artistic to political demands, even in extreme situations. In his 1935 speech in Paris he said:

> The double tactics the socially conscious writer has to live up to, those of the battle and those of art, would fall apart in their unity and would become ineffective and worthless on both sides, were the writer to yield in either art or battle. . . . For a socially conscious person, it would seem natural simply to register such facts [of brutality mentioned before], to enumerate the horrors, to be really banal. And it is equally tempting to cry out in the face of this misery, and thus be suspected of demagogy. And, again, there is the temptation to let these accumulated facts speak for themselves. All these temptations the true writer, that is, the writer of truth, has to avoid; he is not allowed to lose

40. There does not seem to be a complete text of this talk. Long quotations appear in the article quoted in note 34 above.

the sense of his being an artist, he has to depict the gruesome model with judicious selection of color and perspective as an accusatory work of art, he has to relate the past and the future to the present—this is logical fantasy, the evasion of banality, and of demagogy. And with all his artistry he has to give the truth, nothing but the truth, because it is the claim for a truth that is verifiable by scholarly means that makes the work of the reporter so dangerous, dangerous not only for the usufructuaries of this world, but also for himself, and more dangerous than the work of the poet, who does not have to fear being disavowed or contradicted.

Kisch thus defended his genre in two directions, against those who wanted to subject it completely to the mandate of militancy which would land it in demagogy, and against the poets who did not dare to enter the dangerous realm of truth. The attitude Kisch evolved during these middle years became encoded into the genre among the leftists.

(9) FUNCTIONALITY. Functionality, or operativity as it sometimes is called, again is the overarching category characterizing Kisch's work between the two wars. He was outspoken about it. From the "masters" of reportage whose works he compiled in *Meister der Reportage* one has to "learn the honest striving for *Sachlichkeit* and truth," so that the publicist may "led by social feeling, . . . be of use and help, through his unvarnished testimony, to those who are suppressed and deprived of their rights."[41] Functionality would thus be best achieved through a complete absence of tendentiousness in the presentation. The power of immediately influencing broad sectors of public opinion had attracted leftist writers to this genre quite apart from the "frenzy for the documentary" prevailing during the 1920s. Kisch took issue with these tactical considerations. The truth was not to be deduced from the decisions of the CP leaders; inductive reasoning from the facts was the only avenue, and if this yielded result similar to those evinced by the CP leaders, he would agree with them. The functionality of the work explicitly rejects the idea of a literature written to order. For Kisch, Ovechkin, and Liu Binyan, socialism was not a matter of belief and authority, but a result of social investigation.

The periodical *Internationale Literatur,* the central organ of the

41. E. E. Kisch, "Mein Leben für die Zeitung" *Schuenemans Monatshefte* 7:926 (1928).

International Association of Revolutionary Writers, published a series of congratulatory articles on the occasion of Kisch's birthday in 1935. The common metaphor used for Kisch by his colleagues was that of the scout, the very same term used by Ovechkin and Liu Binyan to describe their own activities. Tretiakov called Kisch the "fearless scout of the invincible proletarian armies." Michael Kolzow, a journalist, called him the "relentless scout of the working class in the darkest jungles of capitalist society, the brilliant satirist." And Bruno Frei claimed that Kisch showed "the whole in the detail." Karl Schmückle said: "Kisch has elevated reportage to the level of art. He has incorporated those qualities into it that characterize the scout and discoverer. Our movement needs such wonderful scouts and discoverers."[42]

The success of Kisch's work with its huge print runs and wide circulation outside the immediate influence of the leftist organizations in Germany and abroad confirmed him in his assumptions. The existence of an organized political body like the CP seemed accidental to the functionality of the genre, because even the authors who operated within the framework of a CP owed their loyalty in their own minds primarily to the facts of social reality, not to the political line of Party leadership.

The Rise of Reportage Literature and the Role of Kisch's Literary Reportage

Reportage literature became the fashion after World War I, and the fashion prevailed among the left. The rapid changes, the (transitory) visibility of "truth," the need to provide avenues for reports directly from the workshops, the need to provide stepping stones for an aspiring contingent of writers of working-class origin towards the higher genres, and the insight that the revolution had failed in Europe in 1918 and that the battle was now on for the Communists to conquer the minds of the people to gain hegemony in the superstructure, as Gramsci said, all contributed to the rise of reportage literature. It started in Germany in the wake of Kisch's successes, became integrated into the worker-correspondent movements in Germany and the Soviet Union, and, by the late

---

42. *Internationale Literatur* 4:5f, 24, 27 (1935).

1920s, aspired to full literary status, the first truly proletarian genre available. A conference of leftist writers in Charkov in November 1930 made reportage literature one of the pillars of proletarian and revolutionary writing. Kisch attended, trying to establish, as he said, "literary reportage as an independent literary genre," with some success. Indeed the actual role of this genre was such that a questionnaire circulated in 1926, asking what writers thought about the relationship between reportage and fiction, found few answers that would not admit reportage to have had a very strong influence on fiction. In 1930 the German Association of Proletarian-Revolutionary writers resolved to promote reportage literature above everything else; its Soviet counterpart made the same decision; the Japanese and Chinese leagues quickly followed, the Chinese resolution dated November 1931.

After outlining in point 5 the themes and methods, this latter concluded the passage about genres, after some exhortation to use the simple language of the masses, with the proposal: "Furthermore, the genres of the works have to be simplified and clarified, the principle being that they must be easily understandable by the masses of workers and peasants. Now we have to study and critically make use of the genres of China's own mass literature, of West European reportage literature, of propaganda art, wall stories, and popular recitative poetry."[43] In January 1932, Xia Yan translated an article by Kawaguchi Ko "On Reportage Literature," which detailed the mostly German discussion on the genre and, maintaining a clear distinction between workers' correspondences and literary reportage, quoted Kisch's opinions at length, giving Kisch his due as the "first writer to make *reportage* his special metier and to write his reportages about everyday life independent of his personal attitude," the latter referring to Kisch's opposition to tendentiousness.[44]

43. "Zhongguo wuchanjieji geming wenxue de xin renwu" (New talks of proletarian revolutionary literature in China), *Wenxue daobao* 1.8:6 (15 November 1931).

44. Chuankou Hao (Kawaguchi Ko), "Baogao wenxue lun" (On reportage literature), tr. Shen Duanxian (Xia Yan) in *Beidou* 1.2:240ff (1932). The article was originally published in the Japanese left-wing writers' periodical *Senki* (Battle flag), and took issue with the periodical's lack of discrimination between writings of the worker correspondents and literary reportage in the manner of Kisch. Xia Yan translated it into Chinese with the obvious intent to clarify the same matter, and established literary reportage as a distinct genre, which he himself was to use shortly thereafter. The worker correspondence, the article said, quoting the authority of similar discussions in Germany and the Soviet Union, is "not literature, while reportage literature is pure literature"; p. 241.

Kisch's emphasis on "literary reportage" as a literary genre excluded the workers' correspondence from this honor.

The term used in China at the time for the reportage of the Kisch type was *baogao wenxue* if not "reportage" in Roman spelling.[45] In China, however, there was little to go by at the time. The first major collection of writings of this type, which were still very much newspaper reportages, was put together by A Ying after 28 January 1932 under the title *The Shanghai Incident and Reportage Literature*.[46] There had been some such texts before, and as early as 1930 Huang Tianpeng had summarized what he had learned in Tokyo about journalism, mentioning that, since Liang Qichao, there had been something like *baozhang wenxue*, periodical literature, which was functional, but also "contained quite some aesthetic literary quality." He even said that Wang Tao's eyewitness account of the Franco-Prussian War was written "as if he were a novelist."[47]

What was taught in Tokyo most likely came from Germany and the United States. In China itself, Edgar Snow, probably in 1934, taught at Yanjing University a course which, according to his student Xiao Qian, was "on *texie*," although the term was not common at the time.[48] The dictionaries of the time refer to *texie* as the close-up in film.[49] The

45. As Yang Rupeng pointed out, the term *baogao wenxue* had already appeared in another article by Kawaguchi Ko, "Deguo de xinxing wenxue" (A newly emerging literature in Germany), tr. Feng Xuanzhang in *Tuohuangzhe* 1.2 (February 1930), where he said that Kisch "from a long life of a journalist created a new literary form, which is the so-called *Lieboerdazhiai* [transliteration of 'reportage']. This literary form has expanded the realm of literature" (p. 732); in March 1930, *Dazhong wenyi* carried another Japanese article on the same matter. Cf. Yang Rupeng, "Baogao wenxue jige lishi wenti de kaozheng" (Investigating some historical problems of reportage literature), in *Disquisitions on Reportage Literature* (p. 321 note 29), p. 190.

46. Qian Xingcun (A Ying), *Shanghai shibian yu baogao wenxue* (The Shanghai Incident and reportage literature; Shanghai, 1932). In 1936, Mao Dun, following the precedent of Gorki's *One Day of Our World*, which purported to collect reportages on one single day from all over the world, compiled *Zhongguo de yiri* (One day in China; Shanghai, 1936); a partial translation of the latter by Sherman Cochran and Andrew C. K. Hsieh with Janis Cochran is *One Day in China: May 21, 1936* (New Haven: Yale University Press, 1983).

47. Huang Tianpeng, *Xinwen wenxue gailun* (An outline of newspaper literature; Shanghai: Guanghua Press, 1930). The quotations are on pp. 2, 6.

48. Xiao Qian, "Wei dai ditu de lüren" (Traveler without a map), in *Xiao Qian sanwen texie xuan* (Beijing: Remin Press, 1980), p. 6. The date, 1934, is inferred from Helen Snow, *My China Years* (New York: William Morrow, 1984), p. 129.

49. Huang Shifu and Jiang Tie, *A Comprehensive English-Chinese Dictionary* (Shanghai: Commercial Press, 1937), describes *close-up* as a film term, *tejing, tezhao,* and *texie,* but does not

earliest reference to the term *texie* I have been able to locate is in an article by Xie Liuyi in 1935, "What Is Reportage Literature?" Each of the subcategories of reportage literature is illustrated with an example. After quoting at length an article on the Japanese advance on Shanghai from the *Shanghai Times*, originally, of course, written in English, the author identifies this as a *texie de xinwen jishi*, for which he gives the English "Feature News Story," the *texie* standing for the "feature" part, the feature also being an important ingredient in the New Journalism of the 1920s and 1930s.[50] Xiao Qian remembered that Snow time and again had stressed that *xinwen* (news) and *wenxue* (literature) were not two different things, and Snow offered the examples of Dickens and Shaw, both of whom were journalists and writers at the same time. Although the term *texie* was occasionally used at the time, the common term throughout the war was *baogao wenxue*, reportage literature, in China; only because the Russian *očerk* was translated as *texie* did this term eventually come to prominence.

Kisch's literary reportage was thus a specific variant within the broader current of leftist literature towards which he retained a critical distance by emphasizing artistic quality and truthful investigation and

---

mention a use of the last term in the literary world. Dai Shuqing's *Wenxue shuyu cidian* (A dictionary of literary technical terms; Shanghai: Wenyi Shuju, 1932) mentions on p. 101 *sanwen* (prose) as a general term for "the newly emerging literature" but does not refer to *texie*. Even in the early 1950s, *texie* was not really fixed. Chen Changhuo et al., *E Hua cidian Russko kitaiski slovar* (Russian-Chinese Dictionary; Beijing: Xinhua, 1953), does not give *texie* as an equivalent for *očerk*, but gives *gailun, duanping, mantan*, and *suibi*. The same is true for the *E Hua jingji jishu cidian* (Russian-Chinese economical and technical dictionary; Dalian, 1950), which gives only the technical equivalents for *očerk*, i.e. "sketch" or "blue-print drawing." The *E Hua da cidian* (Chinese-Russian dictionary; Beijing, 1956) gives a second explicitly literary meaning of *očerk*, and has as the first equivalent *texie*. It is said to be a revised edition of a work that appeared in 1953, but I have not seen the original. The Japanese sources I have checked indicate no Japanese precedent for the term.

50. Xie Liuyi, "Shenme shi baozhang wenxue?" (What is newspaper literature?), in Cai Yuanpei, ed., Fu Donghua, comp., *Wenxue baiti* (A hundred literary topics; Shanghai: Zhongji Shenghuo Shudian, 1935), pp. 250f., the term is on p. 253. Tian Zhongji, who, under the name of Lan Hai, published a *Zhongguo kangzhan wenyi shi* (History of Chinese literature of the War of Resistance; n.pl.: Xiandai, 1947) and has worked for many years on the genre, says that the term *texie* came into use in the mid-1930s as a conscious adaptation from film. Cf. Tian Zhongqi, "Texie baogao fazhan de yige lunguo" (A sketch of the development of *texie* and reportage), in Tian Zhongqi, *Wenxue pinglun ji* (A collection of literary criticism; Jinan: Shandong Renmin, 1980).

never mentioning it as something like a "proletarian" genre. Within this general emphasis on reportage literature, however, his own works as well as works by writers imitating his approach were also published. His *Secret China* was translated by Zhou Libo, who wrote much reportage literature on his own, and whose writing seems to be greatly informed by the two authors whom he translated at the time, Sholokhov and Kisch. From the latter he took much of the film technique.[51]

In a 1936 article on reportage literature, Zhou Libo, who had access to the discussions in Moscow and introduced the term *literature of national defense* from thence into the Chinese debate, summarized the issue of *Internationale Literatur* in 1935 which had become something like a festschrift for Kisch. "Kisch's work," he wrote, "is without question a kind of model for reportage literature." He especially emphasized Kisch's capacity to get at the conflicts inherent in things that, "in terms of scholarship, [Kisch's reportages] can be called a kind of very detailed social investigation," while at the same time he had "poetic fantasy," a "correct worldview" and was, in short, able accurately to describe the true state of society. While Zhou maintained that, by 1936, this type of literature had already "very great importance," he felt at the same time that the texts were still in their "fledgling stage," they were written too "fast" and "lacked three-dimensional studies and analyses about real incidents."[52] His translation of Kisch's book must thus be read as a critical comment on the Chinese reportage writers. A foreigner who did not

51. For an analysis of Zhou Libo's best known work, *Baofeng zouyu*, in this context see my "Der moderne chinesische Untersuchungsroman," in Jost Hermand, ed., *Neues Handbuch der Literaturwissenschaft, Literatur nach 1945. I* (Wiesbaden: Athenaion Publ., 1979), p. 380, and, in greater detail, my "The Chinese Writer in His Own Mirror," in Merle Goldman, ed., *Chinese Intellectuals and the State: The Search for a New Relationship* (Cambridge: Council on East Asian Studies, Harvard University, 1987), pp. 192f. See also Wu Tiaogong, *Wenxue fenlei de jiben zhishi* (Basic knowledge of literary genres; Wuhan: Changjiang Wenyi Press, 1959), pp. 198f. There Wu describes how Mao Dun used techniques carried over from film in his "Tibilisi de 'dixia yinshuasuo'" (The "underground print shop" in Tbilisi).

52. Zhou Libo, "Tantan baogao wenxue" (On reportage literature), *Dushu shenghuo* 3.12 (1936), reprinted in Wang Yongsheng, ed., *Zhongguo xiandai wenlun xuan* (Guiyang: Guizhou Renmin, 1982), I, 610. The importance of Kisch's book is well attested for China; it sometimes is mentioned together with the book by G. E. Miller (p. 315 note 13). Cf. Tian Zhongqi, "A Sketch of the Development" (note 50 above), pp. 66f, where the concreteness of the material and the "great influence" of the work are stressed; Lan Hai, *History* (note 50 above), p. 83; He Qifang, "Baogao wenxue zongheng tan" (Deliberations on reportage literature), in He Qifang, *Guanyu xianshizhuyi* (On realism; Shanghai: Xinwen Press, 1951), p. 239: "Kisch's *Secret China*

speak a word of Chinese would come up after a few weeks in Shanghai, Nanjing, and Beijing with a more incisive description and analysis of Chinese society than his Chinese colleagues were able to write.

Partly under the influence of the Soviet *očerk* of the 2nd Five-Year Plan and the war period, the *očerk* of the Polewoi type, with its flat propaganda and crude black-and-white depictions, dominated in China. Given the high moral pitch of these texts with their patriotic tone, it was difficult to criticize them directly. Kisch thus became the password for those who opted for higher standards. Hu Feng complained as early as 1938 about *kangzhan baguwen*, resistance literature which was as dried up and dead as the stale 8-legged examination essays of the nineteenth-century. He published, also in 1938, Balk's long article on Kisch and his reportage in his journal *Qiyue* which published reportage literature and thus reached many writers of the genre, indirectly admonishing them to live up to this model instead of confronting rarefied heroes with equally rarefied devils on the battlefield. Although Hu Feng's criticism was reprinted in 1950, and Balk's article in 1953,[53] in both cases with critical intentions concerning the then contemporary *texie*, the revival of the analytical and critical *texie* did not come through Kisch, whose *Secret China* does not seem to have been reissued in the 1950s, but through Ovechkin, who had adapted Kisch's heritage to socialist conditions.

Throughout this historical phase, *baogao wenxue* of all sorts, whether *kangzhan baguwen* or more Kischean works like Xia Yan's "Baoshengong" (Indentured laborers, 1936),[54] or Fan Changjiang's reportages,[55] had to endure the scorn of the true literati, who considered

---

is good indeed. But the best point is that he writes about some Chinese 'secrets,' 'secrets' about which even many of us Chinese are in no way clear. In other words, he convinces through content. To speak frankly about his formal embellishments, they show some affectedness and traces of showing off."

53. Cf. note 15 above.

54. Xia Yan had not only translated the article by Kawaguchi Ko, but also Gorki's *Mother* and an American reportage. Tian Zhongqi stated that Xia's text, unanimously described as the peak of Chinese *texie* literature before 1949, used the same technique as Kisch and directly copied Kisch's chapter on the Riksha-Kulis. Tian Zhongqi, "A Sketch of the Development" (note 50 above), p. 74. Cf. Tian Zhongji, "Preface," in *Zhongguo baogao wenxue congshu* (p. 275 note 66), I.1:6ff.

55. Fan Changjiang, dean of Chinese journalism during the 1930s, reiterated some of the emphatically critical statements on the state of the art of his time, demanding careful investi-

all this vulgar. The battle *with* Kisch in China, which for obvious reasons has been told more in detail, was led *by* Kisch himself in Europe.

Within the leftist movement, he refused to join the debates in the journal of the Association of Proletarian-Revolutionary Writers (*Linkskurve*) about proletarian literature and reportage. He admitted to the "social duty" (*soziale Aufgabe*) of reportage, but, even at the Paris Congress in 1935, he spoke about reportage as an "artistic and militant form" mentioning the artistic feature first, and maintaining it even under the pressing circumstances of his exile.

His reportage being neither short story nor news story, Kisch took full liberty with the genre form. In his *Secret China* alone, there are reportages written as travelogues, others as dramatic sketches, one in the form of a letter to his son, and still another with the look of a puppet play. Balk called the form of this genre the "wild west of literature";[56] the formality of the old literary world had no place there, it was the genre of the pioneer and scout. It might be remembered that Liu Binyan, from quite another angle, attributed his own capacity to live up to the role of the *texie* scout to his coming from the Chinese northeast, which he likened to the American west in its untraditional lifestyle. The later definitions of the * oçerk/texie* as a "broad" and "free" form have their origin here.

The critics of the new genre refused to see a qualitative difference between crude propaganda reportage and Kisch's work. Max Hermann-Neisse, one of the editors of the *Neue Büchershau*, in 1929 sang the praise of Gottfried Benn's poems while charging Kisch and his ilk with "churning out political propaganda material," for being, in short, "functionaries holding forth on the markets with cheap slogans, drawing-room Tyroleans of the colored propaganda print."[57] (Tyroleans in local costume are considered uncouth villagers who don't fit into a drawing room but are invited there as something chic and authentic.) While these attacks were directed against the political attitude of the reportage

---

gation based on personal observation in order to move the reader by facts. Cf. Ren Zhong, "Liangshi yiyou" (Excellent teacher, beneficial friend), *Xinwen yanjiu ziliao* 1:98 (January 1979).

56. Th. Balk, "Egon Erwin Kisch" (note 15 above), p. 26.

57. Quoted in C. E. Siegel, *Reportage* (note 19 above), pp. 106f.

writers, the more formidable opposition came from Georg Lukács himself, the leftist theoretician of the novel, as well as from many fiction writers. Lukács acknowledged Kisch's skills but saw reportage as an operative genre (*Gebrauchsgenre*) without artistic value. But there was a more fundamental criticism.

In the Marxist world, the surface has continuously had a very bad status. Marx himself had associated the "fetish character" of commodity with its illusory outward appearance. According to this, the true character of commodity was hidden from the eyes of its producers precisely by this illusory outward appearance. The same argument holds true for social phenomena in general. Their immediately visible form is characterized as the screen that hides their true nature from view. Reportage, Lukács charged, made the surface into the typical and objective, and thus unconsciously reproduced the fetishist illusion.[58] Ernst Bloch concurred, arguing that "the overexposed foreground only veils the true background a second time over."[59] The political and social motives in this debate are not quite clear. However, whatever they may have originally been, the structural change in the status of literature after the advent of socialism made for important consequences. First, from the early 1930s, literary criticism in the Soviet Union developed the apotheosis of the argument proposed in a more scholarly fashion by Lukács and Bloch. The visible surface, the average daily reality of socialism, they argued, did indeed hide the true essence of this new social formation; the daily reality was plagued with problems, while the essence of socialism was Communist wealth and happiness. Thus, factual descriptions of the ongoing everyday problems would just reproduce the fetishist illusion of the surface, while the essential surface was in those few heroic persons and events also appearing at the visible surface in whom

---

58. G. Lukács, "Reportage oder Gestaltung," in *Linkskurve* 4.7/8 (1932). Lukács there took issue with Ottwalt's *Denn Sie Wissen Nicht Was Sie Tun*. He admitted that "reportage is a perfectly legitimate indispensable form of journalism" (p. 25), which he linked to the works of Victor Hugo, George Sand, and Eugene Sue, but the lack of the elements of conscious creative activity (*Gestaltung*) excludes it from the realm of literature. In his contribution to the homage for Kisch in *Internationale Literatur* 3:18 (1935), Lukács maintained that he "had always fought against the transfer of the creative method of reportage to the novel, the drama, or the novella," but that this had been misunderstood as being an opposition to reportage itself. The latter article is reprinted in the *Kisch-Kalender* (p. 315 note 8).

59. Bloch is quoted in C. E. Siegel, *Reportage* (note 19 above), p. 137.

and in which the glories of the future were already fully apparent. While Lukács and Bloch originally intended to come out against propaganda writers like Marchwitza, their argument eventually ended up by imposing the ultimate propaganda line even on reportage literature.

Second, the overpowering authority of Lukács in literary circles in Eastern Europe during the 1950s prevented literary reportage from becoming a truly recognized literary genre at a time when it could have been (as in the Soviet Union and China) the important medium of a sober self-assessment of the polity after the Stalin years. Kisch reacted in his own way by dissociating his later work from the immediate political environment, and returning to earlier forms of reportage. Ovechkin, and after him Liu Binyan, took up a greater challenge. Ovechkin's *Rayonnie budni* (Days in the rayon) was quite accurately translated into the Chinese *Quli de richang shenghuo* (Everyday life in the district). The title already contains the program. Against titles at the time which inevitably contained big words like *hero, flames,* or *victory,* titles which brought out the "essence" of the new society, he offered a banal *everyday life* with everyday problems and such shocking revelations as that a peasant in a collective farm might earn only a few kopeks a day. The rehabilitation of the surface in the name of "truth" by Ovechkin and Liu Binyan by implication repeated Kisch's charges against the big lie of the novel of his time. The emphasis on the true surface, encoded in the Kischean variant of the genre, thus offered a potential for descriptions based on the tenets of *Neue Sachlichkeit* which did not have to be mediated with Marxist assumptions, because they were written into the silent structure of the genre itself, and were not spelled out by the authors using it. The charges coming from the opponents of Ovechkin and Liu Binyan as well as their personal fates, however, attested clearly to the stringency with which substantial factions in the leadership adhered to the theory of the essential surface, which they found denounced as nothing but masking in the texts of these authors.

Kisch's use of the genre was the result of a conscious decision, based on certain assumptions about the character of the time, the duties and the potential of literature, the specific contribution his genre could make in this context, and a polemical rejection of both fictional literature and propaganda reportage. From Kisch's edition of the classics of journalism, from his own double role as a writer and a reporter, and from his many theoretical writings as well as his reportages it is clear that he saw himself in a good and unbroken tradition, as did Ovechkin, a tradition that had already written some of the key assumptions into the genre which Kisch inherited and used only because they fitted his purpose. Wherever Kisch did not consciously alter structural features to imbue them with new meaning, but inherited the silent structure inscribed into the genre, we shall have to probe further.

DER RASENDE REPORTER (THE ROVING REPORTER)

In Liu Binyan and Ovechkin we found that the genre went with a certain type of public role and a personality able to play it. It was Kisch, however, who cast the mold into which his successors fitted themselves. Kisch was very much aware of the uniqueness of his role as the daring explorer of truth and of the charms this role had for a public which followed his forays into the entrails of modern society as it had more than a century earlier followed the explorations of travelers in unknown foreign lands. Kisch often combined these assets by writing about modern society in foreign lands. His awareness of his role is indicated by the titles of his books. *Schreib das auf, Kisch*[60] (Write this down, Kisch) is a series of reportages about World War I; Kisch, according to the title becomes the chronicler of the life and insight of the inarticulate but honest common people. *Der Rasende Reporter*[61] (The roving reporter) is another collection of his reportages. The title indicates that the hero of the book is the reporter himself, Kisch. The book ran through dozens of editions in a short time, and its title became proverbial, describing the daring reporter who would probe into the abysses of society, and report back to his readers. *Abenteuer in Fünf Kontinenten*[62] (Adventures in five continents) again has the investigation as its main theme, namely the adventures of the journalist hunting for the hidden truth. Other

60. Egon Erwin Kisch, *Schreib das auf, Kisch* (Berlin: E. Reiss Verlag, 1930).
61. Egon Erwin Kisch, *Der Rasende Reporter* (note 18 above).
62. E. E. Kisch, *Abenteuer in fünf Kontinenten* (note 15 above).

books would carry something like a serial title *Egon Erwin Kisch reports:* . . . and then came *Secret China* or *Czars, Popes, and Bolsheviks.* Kisch's role acquired the quality of a brand name.

He was mostly concerned with uncovering the hidden truths of bourgeois society; thus we do not have the production and management enthusiasts in his texts whom we find in Ovechkin and Liu Binyan, and whose attitude is a replica of that sported by the authorial voice. In Kisch, the authorial voice is the hero, and, on occasion, when Kisch himself becomes a cause célèbre, authorial voice and object of description merge; this is the case in his *Landing in Australia.*[63] After the government there refused to issue him a visa in order to prevent his participation in a Communist-sponsored anti-fascist congress, Kisch, by then a mature 54, jumped from the ship onto the quay, broke his ankle, and from his hospital bed caused the government unending embarrassment, until a court decided in his favor.

The ultimate modern man in Kisch's reportage is thus the reporter himself. He is without respect for great words, is sharp-eyed, inquisitive, turning up in the most unexpected quarters; he is *sachlich,* relentlessly pursuing his investigation; and he retains a cool distance, when he spells out the most gruesome truths about the abysmal life of the common people.

His literary posture was matched by his public posture. Indeed, his credibility was such that much information reached him because people trusted him and felt that with him information was in proper hands. His unconventional appearance, even evident from the photograph accompanying the article on him in the *Literaturnaia Entsiklopedia,* where he has his hat drawn to one side and a cigarette between his lips, was but the counterpart to the wealth of anecdotes circulating about him. The author of the literary reportage/*očerk*/*texie* did not only collect the bizarre detail on the surface which gave access to truth, but also in his life produced the incidents and statements to show him in all his essential modernity, commitment, and inquisitive wit;[64] and with what

63. E. E. Kisch, *Landung in Australien* (Amsterdam: A. de Lange, 1937).

64. The *Kisch-Kalender* attests to this as well as the issue of *Internationale Literatur* and the 1945 festschrift devoted to Kisch, all containing anecdotes about him. Franz Werfel introduced Kisch into one of his novels. In Franz Werfel, *Barbara oder die Frömmigkeit* (Leipzig, 1929), Kisch is portrayed in the figure of the journalist Ronald Weiss "who has acquired his reputation

Kisch saw as the most important quality, *Sensibilität*, sensitivity, followed in this by Liu Binyan's journalistic heroine Huang Jiaying.

His social engagement led Kisch to come out strongly for the Soviet Union, but his commitment as a reporter seems to have helped him to keep his eyes open even there. The liberal Paul Marcus, talking about a conversation he had with Kisch in 1945, said that "Kisch was the only Communist with whom one could really talk; he did not make a show of his convictions." Similar statements have been made about Ovechkin and Liu Binyan. In his Mexican exile Kisch said towards the end of the war, "Woe to us once we have won."[65] He did not expect the sun to shine from dawn to dusk.

Kisch, however, was a reporter before he became socialist. In his own life he negotiated the transition from inquisitive, slightly ironical big-city *flâneur*, who picked up bizarre and interesting stories here and there, to engagé journalist, who used the skills of his craft to make "social investigations" within the medium of reportage. Well into the 1920s, his collections still retained the air of casualness, while later they became more organized to form a coherent image of a given society. In this transition from the *neusachlichen Flaneur*, as Siegel called it, to literary reportage as a part of the social investigation along Marxist lines, Kisch, in his use of the genre, in the selection of its theme and social role, and in his personality, was the link between Ovechkin and Liu Binyan on the one side, and the tradition of nineteenth-century literature in Western Europe and Russia on the other.

---

through some brilliant adventures in the American sense . . . and can claim for himself the merit of being the creator of this journalistic variant which today is so much en vogue" (i.e. literary reportage), p. 216; cf. C. E. Siegel, *Reportage* (note 19 above) p. 17.

65. Quoted in C. E. Siegel, *Reportage* (note 19 above) p. 19.

EIGHTEEN

Third Layer: Oçerk, Physiologie *and* The Limping Devil

Both Kisch and Ovechkin saw themselves in the tradition of the Russian *oçerk*. For Kisch, the *oçerki* of the young Gorki were a revelation,[1] and Ovechkin mentioned, besides Gorki's work, the *oçerki* by Dal and Uspenski, including even Turgenev's *A Sportsman's Sketches* in the genre, although formally it was not called an *oçerk*. In China, Lu Xun had translated some of Gorki's *oçerki*,[2] Turgenev's sketches had been available since the late Qing,[3] and Qu Qiubai had translated some of the new German reportage works.[4] Before the genre appeared with its full name and garb, some works were already in place. Liu Binyan did not fail to refer directly to the attitude and daring of Lu Xun and Qu Qiubai as his own models.[5]

---

1. Egon Erwin Kisch, "Bekanntschaft mit Maxim Gorki," *Die Rote Fahne*, 22 March 1928: "For our entire generation, Gorki had been the decisive experience. We who turned from boys to young men around 1900 jumped directly from the classics into the reading of Gorki's novellas." Cf. also Kirsch's contribution to the special issue on Gorki, *International Literatur* 9.6:45 (1936).

2. Gorki's "9 January" is an *oçerk* on this bloody day in 1905. It was translated by Lu Xun in May 1933. In his preface to the translation, "Yiben Gaoerji 'Yiyue jiuri' xiaoyin" (An introductory note to Gorki's "9 January"), Lu Xun wrote that Turgenev and Chekhov had already been well received in China, but Gorki was still unknown because he represented the "lower classes." Cf. *Lu Xun quanji* (Beijing: Renmin Wenxue Press, 1961), VII, 637.

3. *Zhongguo baike quanshu, Waiguo Wenxue* (The Chinese encyclopedia: Foreign literature; Beijing: Zhongguo Baike Quanshu Press, 1982) Vol. II, under "Tugeniefu."

4. During the early 1930s, Qu Qiubai translated Hans Marchwitza's *Sturm auf Essen*, noting in the postface that "its description has not only full artistic force, but also a very correct consciousness." Cf. Yang Rupeng, "Origin, Development and Formation" (p. 321 note 29), p. 131.

5. In his talk about *texie* in Harbin in 1956, Liu Binyan said: "The independent reflection

In nineteenth-century Russia, the *oçerk* had become the most important vehicle of literary expression of the naturalist school,[6] attracting
many important authors. The *oçerki*, or "physiological" *oçerki* as they
were sometimes called, made forays into the geographically and socially
unknown realms of society, enriching the old Russian travelogue with
the element of social analysis, and, to a moderate degree, of humor. The
authors were mostly from well-to-do families. In their growing social
engagement, they used the genre to give analytical reports to their peers
and a broader city reading public about the hidden true face of society.
The authors would, like social investigators, dive into the squalor of run-
down bars, visit the huts of lowly serfs, detail the life of actors in the theater of or the players of the *orgues de Barbarie.*

Their tone tried to be casual and objective, as if their attention just
happened to be arrested by one intriguing thing or the other. Turgenev's
A Sportman's Sketches might serve as an example. The narrative voice
belongs to the sportsman, a nobleman who seemingly is just after fine
game but happens to see a thing or two, and talks about them in a light
tone. In fact, Turgenev gave the first detailed description of the consequences of serfdom, confronting free peasants with their stately behavior, energy, and meticulous care for their work with the downtrodden
serfs who had even given up repairing their fences. His work is said to
have made the idea of the abolition of the serf system acceptable to the
younger generation of landed gentry in Russia, and to have had a strong
impact on Czar Alexander himself.

In the *Fiziologia Peterburga,* a collection of *oçerki* edited by Nekrasov
in 1845 with a preface by Belinski, we find the narrator often acciden-

---

of the journalist is the most precious thing; whatever kind of article one writes, they all have
to embody one's own opinions and point of view. In life one has to have a militant attitude
towards life, a daring spirit against the enemy like Lu Xun and Qu Qiubai—they are the models
we have to learn from today." Quoted in Liu Shusheng, "Liu Binyan waiqule Lu Xun de zhandou jingshen" (Liu Binyan has distorted Lu Xun's fighting spirit), *Harbin ribao,* 4 August 1957,
p. 3.

6. Cf. L. I. Timofejew, *Geschichte der Russischen Literatur* (Berlin [East]: Kultur and Fortschritt, 1953), II, 427. A. G. Tseitlin, *Stanovlenie realizma v russkoi literature. Russkii fizioloce-
skii oçerk* (Moscow 1965), the most extensive treatment of the "physiological sketch" in
19th-century Russia, calls them the most important genre of the naturalist school; cf. Johanna
R. Döring, *Literaturwissenschaftliches Seminar zur Analyse dreier Erzählungen von Vl. I. Dal,
Modellierung eines Lebensweges* (München: Otto Sagner Verlag, 1975), p. 156.

tally confronted with some phenomenon of the city where he and his readers live without being aware that such things exist. The bizarre things described in travelogues can be found right next door.[7] Some of the key features of the genre were already in place—the actuality; the authenticity of direct observation and quotation,[8] often enhanced by illustrations;[9] the discovery of the hidden truth;[10] the sociological analysis of social types and typical social problems;[11] the modernity of the city; and the progressive, objectivized morality as well as the functionality of the texts, given the political purposes they were to serve. The philosophical assumptions about the true surface behind the mask were there, and there were polemics against the untruthfulness of the "romantic" fiction which had dominated the decade of the 1830s.[12] The social engagement was present, although the wish to entertain and inform still

7. N. A. Nekrasov, *Fiziologia Peterburga, sostavlenaja iz trubov russkich literatorov* (St. Petersburg, 1845). For this work, see the excellent MA thesis by Elisabeth Berres, "Strategien der Leserbeeinflussung in der 'Fiziologija Peterburga' (1845)," (University of Munich, 1973). I am indebted to Prof. Holthusen who has kindly made a copy available to me. An excerpt of the work is published in *Literaturwissenschaftliches Seminar* (note 6 above), pp. 160ff. Cf. also Ann W. Perkins, "Nekrasov's Prose and Russian Popular Fiction of the 1840s" (PhD dissertation, Harvard University, 1979), Chapter 12, "The Physiological Sketch."

8. In "Zisn Aleksandy Ivanovny" (1841), Nekrasov announced being bound by "the duty of the conscientious reporter who reports a true event." Cf. J. Döring, *Literaturwissenschaftliches Seminar* (note 6 above), p. 200.

9. Nekrasov's work is illustrated. Turgenev wanted to have all his *Sportsman's Sketches* illustrated, but the censor banned all illustrations but 3; cf. Edmund Heier, "Elements of Physiognomy and Pathognomy in the Works of I. S. Turgenev (Turgenev and Lavater)," in *Beiträge und Skizzen zum Werk Ivan Turgenevs* (Slavistische Beiträge 116; Munich: Otto Sagner Verlag, 1977).

10. Nekrasov himself wrote in a review of his own book about the purpose of the collection: "To unmask all the mysteries of our social life, all the pleasant and sad aspects of our domestic life, the origin of all incidents in our streets, the development and orientation of our civilization, the character and form of our pleasures, the typical singularities of each class of our population, and finally all particularities of St. Petersburg as a city, port and capital." Quoted in Dimitri Stremooukhoff, "Les Physiologies Russes," in *Etudes de Presse* 9.17:79 (1957).

11. Tseitlin wrote of Dal that he, "even more than the other Russian "physiologists," made efforts to select a protagonist who would be completely typical for his milieu, and includes all characteristic features of an entire segment [of the population]." Quoted in E. Berres, "Dal's physiologische Skizze: Peterburgskij dvornik," in J. R. Döring, *Literaturwissenschaftliches Seminar* (note 6 above), p. 167.

12. Belinski scoffed that the "threadbare definition of poetry as 'nature beautified' may be applied at a stretch to the works of any of the Russian poets; but this cannot be done in regard to the works of Gogol. Another definition of art fits these—art as the representation of reality in all its fidelity. Here the crux of the matter is *types*, the *ideal* being understood not as an adornment (consequently a falsehood) but as the relations in which the author places the types he creates in conformity with the idea which his work is intended to develop." The latter definition and description pertains to the *očerki* by Dostojevsky, Luganski (Dal), and others treated

prevailed over the social message in many pieces, as it had done in the early pieces by Kisch. The texts are centered on the narrator with his keen observation and enlightened attitude; there is no plot to speak of. The focus is on the exploration of the high and low strata of society; and the different levels of society are associated with different levels of morality. The authors were of the new breed of amphibious journalists/ writers, trying to carve out the new existence of the independent city intellectual who was writing for the papers, and they imitated in their lighthearted tone the most fashionable type in Paris at the time, the *flâneur*.

Nekrasov's collection *Petersburg Physiology* (1845) in which his own *oçerk*, "Petersburgski Ugly," figures most prominently, was the beginning of a veritable frenzy of physiological *oçerki*, mostly published in periodicals. Tseitlin, who wrote the history of these sketches, estimated that there appeared between 1839 and 1848 over 700 such sketches in Russia. They helped establish a firm tradition for the *oçerk* which remained an acceptable form for writers of high standard throughout the rest of the century up to Chekhov and Gorki. The *oçerk* was not considered a high artistic form, but a preliminary sketch. The relative place of the *oçerk* in the literary hierarchy had been indicated by Belinski in his Preface to Nekrasov's collection. Belinksi complained that "we have no literary works" about Russia that "are genuine *oçerki*." Although Russia's cities and provinces could be a great "nourishment for an observant pen, for a humorous pen," the Russian *oçerk* "does not take a serious look at what the situation really is. "Consequently," he argued, "what we need is many ordinary talents," not just one Gogol. These ordinary talents only need powers of observation and some knowledge so that they "are

---

in this article. Referring to the criticisms made of the *oçerki* of the natural school, Belinksi said, and this passage has been quoted much as will be immediately evident: "The natural school is impugned for a striving to depict everything in a bad light. As usual, with some men this accusation is deliberate calumny, with others sincere complaint . . . But even if its prevailing negative trend were really its one-sided extreme, this too has its uses and its good: the habit of faithfully rendering the negative aspects of life will enable the same men and their followers, when the time comes, to faithfully render the positive aspects of life without placing them on stilts, without exaggerating, in short without rhetorically idealizing them." The first quotation is from "A View of Russian Literature in 1847," p. 413, the second from "A View of Russian Literature in 1846," p. 357, both in V. G. Belinski, *Selected Philosophical Works* (Moscow, 1948).

true to life." Sadly, the collection put together by Nekrasov is still unsatisfactory, but "literature is a reflection of society, and the fact that literature is insufficient only reflects the insufficiency of our society." The book, he said, sets out "to give the moral physiognomy [of Petersburg] with artistic fullness" but as there were no talents like Gogol participating, "it is completely without pretense of poetic or artistic talent, it has a modest goal. Its goal is to create a book like the French works." The *oçerk* was the vehicle for the modest talents to do what was needed, write a "moral physiognomy" of Russia "true to life."[13] According to Belinski, during the 1930s and 1940s, a new group of readers had appeared, the *razučincy*, the *intelligent* and some educated people of lower social origins, whose tastes might also be best served by *oçerki*.

A year before Nekrasov's collection, a translation of Dickens's *Sketches by Boz* had come out in Russian, social sketches with Cruikshank's illustrations which gave something of the social physiognomy of a part of London inhabited by its humbler citizens. The immediate model, however, that Nekrasov and the other authors of the new "physiological" sketches had before their eyes, was French, and they tried to live up to the French. Since the 1820s, Paris had seen the rise of a new type of mass literature, the *physiologies* or *esquisses physiologiques*.[14] They took their name from the new popular books of a medical-philosophical analysis, like Cabanis's *Traité du physique et du moral de l'homme* (1798–1799), or Demangeon's *Physiologie intellectuelle* (1808). They described psychic processes and factors by means of the physiological, that is, what is invisible, difficult to grasp by means

13. V. G. Belinski, "Preface," in N. A. Nekrasov, *Fiziologia* (note 7 above), p. 9. I am greatly indebted to Dr. Robin Feuer-Miller for this translation. Belinski said two years later that "full recognition" had been granted to the "so-called 'phisiologies,' character sketches of various aspects of social life." Cf. V. G. Belinski, "A View of Russian Literature in 1847" (note 12 above), p. 437. Three pages later he pointed out that art is no "intellectual China, cleanly walled off by precise boundaries from everything that is not art in the strict sense of the word."

14. There are amazingly few treatments of these popular texts, written by the greatest writers of their time. Cf. Jean Prinet, "Avant-Propos. Les Physiologies, la Presse et l'Estampe"; Andree Lheritier, "Les Physiologies"; Claude Pichois, "Le Succes de Physiologies"; Antoinette Huon, "Ch. Philippon et la Maison Aubert"; all in *Etudes de Presse* 9.17 (1957); Peter Schon, "Naturwissenschaft und "Les Physiologies" im 19. Jahrhundert in Frankreich," in *Alma Mater Aquensis* 6. (1968); most extensively they are treated in Hans-Rüdiger van Biesbrock, *Die literarische Mode der Physiologie in Frankreich (1840-1842)*; H. J. Lope, ed., *Studien und Dokumente zur Geschichte der Romanischen Literaturen*, Vol. III; Frankfurt: Peter Lang Verlag, 1978).

of that which is accessible, easy to understand. They operated through classification, grouping diverse elements into one type, and by means of induction, extracting the hidden from the visible.

In the same manner, another branch of what was then considered real science evolved, namely the study of physiognomy as heralded by Lavater. Lavater's *Physiognomische Fragmente* were the most prestigious volumes in German, English, French, or Russian since the late-eighteenth century, and many of the important writers down to the latter half of the nineteenth century, like Goethe and Dickens, Balzac and Turgenev, were avid Lavaterians.[15] Physiognomy, said Lavater, "is the capacity to perceive the inner qualities of a person by means of his outer appearance." The body, Lavater said, referring especially to the face, was "the image of the soul, or rather is the soul itself, made visible." Lavater himself expanded this notion: "Each country, each province, and each village has its specific physiognomy and special character, and a character to which this physiognomy is evidently adapted."[16]

The young journalist/writers thus set out to describe the physiognomy/physiology, or, to use the modern term, sociology, of human society.[17] Balzac was one of the earliest with his *Physiologie du Mariage* (1929).[18] Later he wrote more physiological texts; his *Comédie Humaine* intends to be a scholarly *étude des moeurs*, analyzing society as the big *physiologies* of the animal kingdom had done with the non-human

15. For Lavater's influence on European society and literature, see F. Baldensperger, "Les Theories de Lavater dans la Littérature Francaise," in his *Etudes d'Histoire Littéraire*, 2e série (Paris: Hachette, 1910); John Graham, *Lavater's Essay on Physiognomy, A study in the History of Ideas* (European University Studies, Series XVIII, Comparative Literature, Vol. XVIII; Frankfurt: Peter Lang Verlag, 1979); Edmund Heier, "Elements" (note 3 above); and Graeme Tytler, *Physiognomy in the European Novel, Faces and Fortunes* (Princeton: Princeton University Press, 1982). For Lavater's intellectual background as to the mask and the true face, see Ernst Benz, "Swedenborg und Lavater. Über die religiösen Grundlagen de Physiognomik," in *Zeitschrift für Kirchengeschichte*, Dritte Folge VIII, Vol. LVII. 1/2, 1938.

16. Johann Caspar Lavater, *Physiognomische Fragmente, zur Beförderung der Menschenkenntnis und der Menschenliebe* (Winterthur: Weidmanns Erben und Reich, 1775), I, 13, 28; IV, 321.

17. The notion of the *physiologie sociale* was used by Sainte Beuve in 1833; cf. *Oeuvres* (Paris, 1956), I, 542, for social investigations. Y. Guyot was still using the term as an equivalent for sociology in the 1880s; cf. his *Etudes de physiologie sociale* (Paris, 1882–1885).

18. Stendhal's *De l'amour*, which came out in 1822, is called a *"physiologie"* in the author's preface.

world. The fashion of the *physiologies* rose to a frenzy for the short years of 1840–1842, when well over 1,000 little volumes appeared in Paris, promising to describe with scholarly precision every social type and phenomenon, from the *Physiology of the Smoker* to the *Physiology of the Deputy,* from the *Physiology of the Kept Woman* to the *Physiology of the Bois du Boulogne,* from the (earlier) *Physiology of the Pear* (which was a pun on Louis Bonaparte) to the *Physiology of Physiologies* (which made fun of the *physiologies* themselves).[19]

The new genre quickly became collections, the best known being *Les Français Peints par Eux-memes,* which was imitated in Russia, the Anglo-Saxon world, and, some years later, even by a Chinese military attaché in France, who wrote his *Les Chinois Peints par Eux-memes* in 1883;[20] other well-known collections, which linked up with the popular works on the customs of Paris compiled by Mercier and Jouy decades before, were *Le Livre des Cent-et-Un* and *Le Diable à Paris.*[21] To underline the physiological/physiognomical character, the texts were richly illustrated. And, as among the authors of the *physiologies* everyone who had a name in literary circles at the time, be it Balzac, George Sand, or Alphonse Karr, Nerval, Gautier, de Musset, or Soulié, we find among the illustrators Daumier, Gavarni, and other celebrities.[22] The genre had tremendous influence on fiction, and not only on Eugène Sue with his *Les Mystères de Paris,* which contained in fictionalized form all his researches into the entrails of this "capital of the nineteenth century"

19. A microfilm edition of them has recently been published under the direction of Andrée Lheritier, *Les Physiologies* (Paris, Série internationale des microfilms, 1966).

20. Tcheng-ki-tong (Chen Jitong, 1851–1907), *Les Chinois Peints par Eux-mêmes* (Paris: Calman Lévi, 1884); with this and his other books he was tremendously successful. *Les Chinois* was in the 3rd printing in 1884, and in the 10th by 1886. An English translation is *The Chinese Painted by Themselves* (London, 1885). Chen later returned to China with his French wife and became the teacher of Zeng Pu, author of *Niehaihua,* whom he initiated into the latest trends of French literature. Little work has been done on this; for a short notice see Peter Li, "Tseng P'u: A Literary Journey" (PhD dissertation, University of Chicago, 1972).

21. *Paris, ou le Livre des Cent-et-Un* (Paris, 1831); *Le Diable à Paris—Paris et les Parisiens* (Paris: Hetzel, 1845).

22. The cartoon, in fact, is part of the surface arts spreading at the time, being based on Lavaterian principles. Cf. Michel Melot, *Die Karikaturen* (a translation of his *L'oeil qui rit*; Stuttgart: Kohlhammer, 1975), p. 70 note 2, where he says "the caricaturists of the 19th century have systematized the teachings of the physiognomists."

(Benjamin), but also on Stendhal, Hugo, and Zola. *Littérature* like the Russian equivalent and Chinese *wenxue* included any writing with esthetically refined style, while the Anglo-Saxon and Germanic terms were more restricted, and the prejudices more firmly rooted. The new genre did not rank high on the scale of literary seriousness, but very high among readers, and the new crop of writers who made a living from writing made ample use of this option to get into a literary mass market.

As might be expected, the *physiologies* as a rule had no plot; the narrative advanced through the argumentative and documenting activity of the narrator, who was otherwise quite free in the formal handling of his text. They were concerned with the present, but explored the history of their topics. They took the reader on a tour of discovery, mostly in his own town; they were very scientific in the sense of being physiological and physiognomical, which were the old names for what later was called sociology, dissecting their topic into types and subgroups, talking like zoologists about "dissection," "analysis," and "dissecting" their topic "with most stringent exactitude"; they were light, humorous, and self-ironic, constantly poking fun at their own scientism and promising ultimately the exact description of the devil himself; however, with all their lightness, most of them showed some social engagement, bringing the practices of usurers or businessmen to the knowledge of the world.

The authorial voice, which at times dons the title of a *naturaliste*, a nature researcher, pursues the type in question into all its social ramifications, maintaining the *flâneur*-like ironic distance and cursory tone. The voice does not belong to a revolutionary or social activist who also tries to be funny and entertaining, but to a light-footed big city sharp wit who knows the world inside out, and with mock-seriousness communicates some of his bizarre observations to the reader. There is no self-righteous pontification in the French *physiologies;* rather the authorial voice knows so much about the less pleasant aspects of Paris because its owner happens to be one of them.

On their way through the next century the *physiologies* and their authors changed somewhat. The ironic distance of the *flâneur* from his city and from his reader and the ensuing humor were already mostly lost when the genre remolded the Russian *oçerk*. There was still some light verbiage, and it survived through Kisch,[23] Ovechkin, and Liu Binyan, becoming more and more a bitter caricature. The ironic distance was transformed into a more ponderous scholarly objectivity with its heavy and very serious analytical endeavor, *neue Sachlichkeit*, and sociology. The entertainment was legitimate only if it was instructive, and, instead of contributing primarily to the understanding of society, the later texts wanted to "intervene in life." On its way to becoming a minor world literary genre, literary reportage joined with local traditions; the translated French and English texts resonated with the traditional travelogue and *oçerk*. The translations from Turgenev, Gorki, and others into Chinese, as well as the oral instructions of the first Chinese physiology writer, Chen Jitong (1851–1907), to his Chinese disciple in Shanghai (none other than Zeng Pu), interacted with the *Rulin waishi* and translations from Japan in the formation of some of the late Qing novels. However, although some of the original features are recognizable only as relics or dead matter in the modern texts, the stability of the genre as a whole is surprising. The same is true for the type of personality who made use of this genre.

In a last dig, we shall therefore search for the logical ground for the two most stable elements—the implied theory of the mask and the true surface, and the social role of the reporter. The collection *Le Livre des Cent-et-Un* (1831) with 101 authors ranging from Eugene Delacroix to Jules Janin, from Paul de Kock to Balzac and Hugo, was originally to be called *Le Diable Boîteux a Paris, ou Paris et les Moeurs comme Elles Sont*. Paris being too complex a topic, one single author could not manage it; therefore 101 of them united for the project, and the title was changed to the above, the reader now having, according to the preface "the Limping Devil made up of all people who write, think, bite, praise, observe, and write either prose or verse."[24] The writers thus formed a composite Limping Devil. With this image they referred back to a book by Lesage,

---

23. Stremooukhoff, "Les Physiologies," (note 10 above), p. 79, makes this point: "Les études physiologiques russes. . . . cessent d'être des oeuvres légères, des bagatelles, pour prendre, chez les écrivains de l'école naturelle, un ton plus sérieux destiné à éveiller la pitié sociale."
24. *Paris, ou le Livre des Cent-et-Un* (note 21 above), pp. vi ff.

written about a hundred years earlier, and just reissued, *Le Diable Boiteux*.[25]

Lesage, the first French writer to make his living as a writer, in this work adapted from the Spanish of Velez de Guevara, *El Diablo Cojuelo*, written between 1636 and 1640, and having the subtitle *novela de la otra vida, traducida a esta* (news from the other world, translated into this [world]).[26] The "other world" is nothing but the true surface of Madrid itself. The "news" items are held together by a frame story. A student who was the 22nd to enjoy the carnal favors of a virgin, is trapped by her other lovers and flees over the roofs of Madrid, finding refuge in the small study of an astrologer who is absent. In a bottle on a shelf the Limping Devil is corked up, "the wittiest spirit of the nether worlds, who certainly had no calling for higher things, but stuck his nose into everything and embodies all the vermin of the nether world, the gossip, the intrigues, usury, and default" and has taught mankind dancing and other pleasures.[27] The student sets him free, and in gratitude the little *diablo cojuelo* leads him to the tower of San Salvador above Madrid to show him what happens at night in this *Babilonia española*. In order to make the true surface of Madrid visible to the student, the devil, by means of diabolical arts, lifts the roofs of the houses of the city like puff pastry covers (*lo hojaldro*) in order to have him see "the meat inside the Madrid pastry." In rapid succession he then shows the student social scenes, mostly of the darker variety of greed, with scholars, clergy, gambling-house owners, duped husbands, nobles, elderly galants, coquettes, servants, cardsharps, pharmacists, doctors, and so forth. The emphasis is on unmediated direct documentary evidence, with the narrator/devil intervening with sarcastic, analytical, and moral comments. The descriptive technique is characterized by scholars as *distanciamento*, objectivizing and ironic distance; the purpose is evidently *disengagno*, to help the mildly educated reader (in the person of the stu-

---

25. Alain Rene Lesage, *Le Diable Boiteux* (1707), ed. R. Laufer (Paris: Mouton, 1970). Cf. Uwe Holtz, *Der Hinkende Teufel von Velez de Guevara und Lesage* (Wuppertal: A. Henn Verlag, 1970), pp. 83f.

26. Velez de Guevara, *El Diablo Cojuelo, Novelas de la otra vida, traducida a esta* (written between 1636 and 1640), ed. E. P. Cepeda and E. Rull (Madrid: Ediciones Alcala, 1968).

27. Cepeda/Rull (note 26 above), Introduction, p. 34.

dent) to overcome his naive belief in the truth of the mask and to show him the true surface of reality. There is no plot to speak of; the characters are flat, and stand for social types.

Velez de Guevara by implication rejected the bucolic novel of his time as a lie. The image is powerful. The reader finds his peer in the person of the honest but naive student, initiated to the sombre mysteries of the big city by the writer who is but an underling of the devil, being himself a part of the jungle of the big city. The student sets the devil free or actually helps him to materialize. The readers enable the independent little city writer to exist, but for a price; the writer has to show them the true surface of society, and remove the puff-pastry mask covering it. The reader gets a panorama of social reality in fast, short scenes, is entertained—although with some bitter aftertaste—is instructed, and is reinforced in his moral principles.

We have to stop digging further at this point. However a single question may still arise: Why the devil? The devil and his underlings had generally not been looked upon favorably by authorities during the centuries preceding Velez de Guevara. But there was good evidence that only diabolical forces could provide access to the truth. The Christian churches had identified the serpent in Paradise as an agent of the devil or the devil himself. From the recently discovered texts of the Gnostic Christians, we know that they saw in the serpent an ally of Sophia, highest wisdom. It was the serpent which opened the way of Gnosis to man, whom the demiurge Jahve tried to keep ignorant and subdued.[28] The serpent, in this reading, represents a protest against the rigorous control over the intellectual world exerted by Jahve, and his representative on earth, the Church. Popular tradition, while accepting the identification of the serpent with the devil, proceeded to endow the devils Asmodée, Belphegor, Flammèche, and Limping Devils with most endearing traits. Under the pompous masks sold by church and state as reality, they showed, with a cunning grin, the true surface to the new city readers, the new bourgeois classes. The living incarnation of these *diabolicos* was the journalist/writer, and the earliest role model for his own behavior and public attitude seems to have been cast by Velez de Guevara's Limping Devil.

28. Cf. "On the Origin of the World," tr. P. G. Bethge and O. S. Wintermute, in *The Nag Hammadi Library* (Leiden: E. J. Brill, 1977), pp. 161ff.

Lesage, writing his adaptation in 1707, unfolded some of the latent traits of the genre. His text might have been part of reaction against the frenzy for the bucolic engendered by Honore d'Urfé's *L'Astrée* during the seventeenth century. The student in one passage comments on the "nature of the novel where people are painted as they should be rather than as they are." Velez witnessed the demise of the Spanish empire, Lesage the end of the glories of Louis XIV. Lesage began the social engagement which later came to dominate the entire genre, not by praising the lower orders, but by sparing them his satire. All have to suffer the whip of his satire and the tear of his unmasking but the ones who alone obviously can be considered morally acceptable and true in their face, the craftsmen and laboring classes.[29]

The structural model for the new genre, its writers, and readers had thus been developed long before the number of works, writers, and readers became a significant phenomenon in the literary and social world during the first third of the nineteenth century. Then, the image of the journalist/writer as the underling of the devil taking off the puff pastry from the meat of the big city quickly became a matter of routine. In 1823, a journal with the title *Diable Boiteux* appeared.[30] In the *physiologies*, the Limping Devil would guide the reader through the dark corners of Paris,[31] and the associated crowd of journalist/writers appears as the composite Limping Devil in *Le Livre des Cent-et-Un*. The idea was again taken up some years later, in 1845, in the grand collection *Le Diable à Paris*.

29. Cf. U. Holtz, *Der Hinkende Teufel* (note 25 above), p. 162.

30. Horace Raisson, a friend of Balzac's and journalist like him, was instrumental in its founding; cf. A. Lheritier, "Les Physiologies, Introduction" (note 19 above), p. 15.

31. This happens in the *Physiologie des Quartiers de Paris*. It should be added that the devil and his underlings became a great theme at the time; cf. Claudius Grillet, *Le Diable dans la Littérature au XIXe siècle* (Lyon/Paris: Amm. Vitte, 1935). Grillet traced the changes in the devil image up to the "diabolisme louis-philippin," when Frederic Soulié came out with his volumes of *The Memoirs of the Devil*, where the devil not only lets the air out of his pompous interlocutors but also pokes fun at himself. The image of the devil as characterized here has not been lost in socialist literature. M. Bulgakov's *Master and Margerita*, tr. M. Glenny (New York: Harper and Row, 1967), has the devil come to the Soviet Union. All kinds of problems are laid at his door; but in the structure of the narrative he is not responsible for these things, but only makes them visible. In Tertz's *The Trial Begins* (New York: Vintage Russian Library, 1960, tr. Max Hayward), the Master (Stalin) lifts the roof for the writer, showing him with this powerful device of Marxist-Leninist dialectics the true inside of society, and ordering him to write the paean for the public prosecutor. The use of the devil as reporter here satirizes the Communist use of this traditional topic and the arrogation of the insight of the devil by the leadership.

It has, as is customary, some loose frame to hold the individual texts together. The Devil is bored in his empire. After a tour through the various hells, he arrives at the sub-hell of earth where his speech is interrupted by the rumpus of people from Paris next door. Intrigued about their stories, but concerned that his personal appearance in Paris would cause too much of an uproar, the Devil sends Flammèche, his under-devil, to Paris to report to him about this city. Flammèche, upon arrival, instantly falls in love; being too preoccupied, he has no time for researching and writing his reports; whereupon he hires all the journalist/writer scribblers from Paris like Balzac, Sand, Nodier, and de Musset, as well as the best illustrators and caricaturists, like Gavarni. He installs a mailbox with a direct link to hell, pays the scribblers well, and then concentrates on his more interesting pursuits. The book is thus made up of reports to the Devil about "Paris and Parisians, the mores and customs, characters and portraits of the inhabitants, a complete picture of their private, public, political, artistic, literary, industrial life," and so forth. The reader is no longer an innocent young student coming to the big city, but the devil himself.

The Paris reading public was bored, lusting for entertainment; it paid its scribblers and writers to come up with interesting matter and was liberal enough to accept George Sand's bitter revelations next to an amusing piece about the "True History of the Canard" by Nerval. The principle of homogeneity was by then well established. Flammèche himself spelled it out: The entire world could be understood according to the principle *maxima in minimis*.[32] The scientific attitude was attributed to the Devil himself, who started out by "considering Paris . . . with the banal curiosity of an entomologist examining some ant under his lens"[33] and is shown in a full page illustration doing exactly that.[34] His magnifying lens was the precursor of the "microscope and telescope" the writer of the literary reportage needed according to Kisch. The archaeological exploration can be terminated at this point. Neither in the foundations nor in the structure itself do there seem to be further important supporting elements that have not been accounted for and placed in their own light and logic.

32. *Le Diable à Paris* (note 21 above), I, 74.
33. Ibid., "Flammèche et Baptiste."
34. Ibid. Illustration by Brugnot, at beginning of the book, reproduced here on the preceding page.

NINETEEN

Some Conclusions

The genre of *physiologie/očerk/literarische Reportage/texie* evolved as the documentary counterpart of the fictionalized novel into a minor genre of world literature. The basic logic of the genre is easily described. By fiat of authority and for ulterior motives reality is masked. The common city *intelligent* as well as the lower orders of working people have no stake in this masking, but, being themselves invested with honesty and love of truth, they rely on the writer/journalist to help them in their *disengagno* by showing them the true surface of society. The characters are described in flat fashion, not because the writer knows no better, but because they are intrinsically flat. Their motives are money and power, if they are bad; honesty and progress, if they are good. In the same manner, events are flat, not because the writer cannot describe them in a more complex manner, but because the genre assumes all events to be determined and understood by means of simple logic, based on straightforward rational (if not necessary moral) considerations. The physiology of society is not more complicated than that of nature; truth is essentially sociological and simple, and needs only uncovering through the investigative and analytical efforts of the writer/journalist. Thematically, the genre sets out to take off the roofs under which the darker sights of society are hidden, excluding from its realm the description of things as "they should be" as well as those things not amenable to its rigid rationalism, like love, gothic horror, mass psychology, or politics. It rejects the fictional character and plot of the novel as a part of the masking, and rejects social propaganda as a mistrust of truth, which, if only it is adhered to, will *prove* those things that propaganda merely *asserts*. The rationalism underlying the genre lies most clearly in its representational principle, *maxima in minimis,* which presupposes a homogeneous, rationally structured social world parallel to that of nature, allowing for the establishment of types and typical actions representative of great cohorts of persons and their relationships.

The drive of the text comes from the pursuance of the problem, not from the unfolding of a plot. The suspense is not created by the reader's ignorance about the further development but by the thrill accompanying the documented and analytical unveiling of tabooed truth. Formally the writer is as free in the presentation of his problem as he is strictly bound by the compository principle. As long as he effectively develops the problem and its causes, he may write verse, quote numbers, recite documents, write theater sketches, or use the form of the letter or the diary, the first or the third person.

The morality that drives the narrative voice (even that of the Limping Devil) represents and reinforces the values of the city-*intelligent* reader. This reader finds his idealized counterpart in the narrative voice, having himself been left out of the text after Lesage. The implied criteria of the narrative voice are his: The free and daring exploration of the dark side of society is his daydream, and the frank, slightly ironical and always relatively light language of the narrator is what he aspires to. The narrative voice thus vicariously satisfies the reader's aspirations. Morality is primarily invested in the narrative voice, but it sympathizes with the plight of the honest laboring masses. They remain mostly anonymous even in Liu Binyan's texts, but the narrative voice takes much of its legitimacy from speaking and investigating in their interests, and it spares them the scornful dissection it pursues with the powers that be.

The core elements of the genre have survived a turbulent history of several centuries; the transfer into different literary traditions like Russia's and China's; the merger with the specific literary traditions of these cultures; the rule of a great variety of philosophies, including some of the most rigorous schools, like Marxism; and the radical changes of the French Revolution, the October Revolution, the Industrial Revolution, two World Wars and the Chinese Revolution. The genre is thus remarkably stable. Its stability, however, does not reside in a canon of rules laid down anywhere. In fact, the individual works written in the genre, its history, and constitutive elements have not attracted much scholarly attention, nor have writers cared to lay down rules as they have tried to do for the novel, the short story, or the various forms of poetry. Although everything seems possible in this untidy mélange of literary genres, the assumptions encoded into the genre have survived without much, indeed without any, theoretical support. The most diverse philosophies and literary theories have rather tried to bring these writings under their control, most visibly in the socialist world. The genre rejects the variant developed by Polewoi, Schaginian, Liu Baiyu, and Xu Chi in the same way that it rejects the tendentiousness of Ottwalt or Marchwitza, the response of readers being the form this rejection takes.

The ever-stronger social engagement in which the genre has been used has led to increasing tensions. The authorial figure of the journalist/writer was originally identified in a self-ironic manner as a little underling of the Devil himself, that is, in the shape in which the authorities saw those writers. The self-ironic element indicated that the writer could write so knowledgeably about these things only because he was all too familiar with them; the Limping Devil himself has taught many of the evils he later uncovers for the readers' eyes. The easygoing Paris *flâneur* is so familiar with big-city types because he is one of them, and knows it. The self-irony of the narrator vanished with Kisch. The authorial voice became ever more righteous, identifying itself not with the Devil or the *flâneur* but with the idealized lower classes. In Ovechkin and Liu Binyan, the self-irony is completely washed out of the authorial voice; the scout-cum-sociologist becomes a national and nationally essential figure, the eye, ear, brain, and nerve without which socialist society can neither see, hear, nor understand and sense itself. In the same process, the entertaining lightness and analytical wit has withered. In Troepolsky, Tendriakov, Liu Binyan, and Geng Jian, the elements of social satire and of the grotesque serve only to increase the moral and emotional impact of the story without recourse to outright moralizing. Entertainment comes with the thrill of treading on politically dangerous ground and the satisfaction of getting at the true essence of things, but without the ironic insight into the essential triviality of all things human.

The inordinate success of these texts in the socialist world, however, shows that the genre has retained its attractiveness under certain social circumstances, and it has at times even acquired a dominant position among the literary genres on the attention scale of the city *intelligent*, who have remained its most loyal and devoted readers. The authors furthermore have kept in their lifestyle the fading memory of the old *flâneur*, their narrators are on independent scouting missions without anybody's orders, and they still purport to lift the mask from the social scene to show the mess inside to gasping readers.

It might be assumed that, with the advent of democratic societies with their often (as in the United States) extremely open access to information and well-established publication channels, the genre would lose its interest and luster for both writers and readers. The facts do not bear this out. From *The Ugly American* to *In Cold Blood* and many other works, literary reportage, now called "new journalism," has held the public's attention, rising on the same foundations as the works studied here.

Part Three
Three Post-Mao Stories

TWENTY

The Manager Takes Over—
On Jiang Zilong's "Qiao changzhang shangren ji"

INTRODUCTION*

Jiang Zilong's "Qiao changzhang shangren ji" (Director Qiao takes over) was written in April or May 1979,[1] and published in the *Renmin wenxue* issue of July 1979.[2] There, it was the lead story, its title printed in boldface in the table of contents, two indications that the editors intended it as a key piece. It received the first prize in the national short-story competition for 1979, organized by *Renmin wenxue*. Readers were asked to note their preferred story on a ballot sheet; the ranking within those stories receiving the largest numbers of votes was made by a selec-

---

*My thanks to Nancy Hearst, the librarian at the John K. Fairbank Center for East Asian Research, for her patient help in locating data and sources for this chapter.

1. Jiang Zilong, "'Qiao changzhang shangren ji' de shenghuozhang" (A pedigree of "Director Qiao Takes Over"), *Shiyue* 4 (December 1979), here quoted from the edition in Mou Zhongxiu, ed., *Huojiang duanpian xiaoshuo chuangzuo tan 1978–1980* (On the creation of the award-winning short stories 1978–1980; Beijing: Wenhua Yishu Press, 1982), p. 45.

2. Jiang Zilong, "Qiao changzhang shangren ji" (Director Qiao takes over), *Renmin wenxue* 7 (1979). Sadly, the translations are very inadequate, eliminating most of the interesting details. "Manager Qiao Assumes Office," tr. Wang Mingjie, in Jiang Zilong, *All the Colors of the Rainbow* (Beijing: Panda Books, 1983); this edition reprints the translation in *Chinese Literature* 2 (1982). With minor editorial emendations but without attribution it is reprinted in Lee Yee, ed., *The New Realism* (New York: Hippocrene Books, 1983); a German translation with commentary will be found in my *Literatur und Politik in der Volksrepublik China* (Frankfurt: Suhrkamp, 1983). To indicate to readers of the English translation the context if not the text of my quotations, I shall refer to Wang Mingjie with the initial W plus page, and to Lee Yee with L plus page. All translations, however, are my own. The Chinese text is quoted J from the *Renmin wenxue* edition.

tion committee dominated by leaders close to the group around Deng Xiaoping.[3] The story has been frequently reprinted, was made into a TV feature, and received much praise in reviews and readers' letters; it was, however, far from uncontroversial. The press in Tianjin, where the author lives, criticized the piece, and the mayor of that city called it a "poisonous weed."[4]

Jiang Zilong was born in 1941 in Hebei province. His first story was published in 1965 when he was with the Navy. During the Cultural Revolution, he was much heralded as a spare-time writer of working-class origin;[5] from 1972 some of his stories were published, and by 1976 he had made it onto the national literary flagship, *Renmin wenxue.*[6] At the time of the publication of "Director Qiao," he was still working on the administrative staff of a heavy-machinery plant in Tianjin; he became a full time writer owing to the success of this story.

The story has been translated into English by the Peking Foreign Languages Press; the translation has been variously reprinted.[7] Sadly, most elements of literary interest have been lost in the process; witness the excerpts from Director Qiao's speech at the beginning of the story, and, more important, the frequent allusions to Peking operas in the text, which provide substantial clues for the unraveling of the story.

A SHORT SUMMARY OF THE STORY

The story has three parts, each with its own title. In the first, "Coming out from the Mountains," Qiao Guangpu, director of a company com-

---

3. *1979 nian quanguo youxiu duanpian xiaoshuo pingxuan huojiang zuopin ji* (Award-winning works from the national short-story competition 1979; Shanghai: Shanghai Wenyi Press, 1980), pp. 1–48. The sequence in this publication indicated the rank in the first-prize category. Jiang's story was first. Cf. my "Rewriting the PRC's Foundation Myth: Gao Xiaosheng's 'Li Shunda Builds His House,'" p. 437, for the composition of this committee.

4. J, p. 6; W, p. 135; L, p. 59.

5. For his biography, see his autobiographical sketch—Jiang Zilong, "How I Became a Writer," in Jiang Zilong, *All the Colors of the Rainbow* (note 2 above), p. 255ff; and W. Locks, "Jiang Zilong" (MA thesis, Berkeley, University of California, 1985), pp. 1ff.

6. For a bibliography of his pre-1976 works published in *Tianjin wenyi,* see W. Locks, "Jiang Zilong," pp. 11ff. Jiang Zilong, "Jidianjuzhang de yitian" (A day in the life of the head of the Bureau for Electromechanics), *Renmin wenxue* 1 (January 1976).

7. Cf. note 2 above.

posed of many small factories for electrical appliances, volunteers to "go down" and become the manager of a big heavy-electrical-machinery plant. He is supported by Huo Dadao, who heads the Bureau for Electrical Equipment of the town, and who is thus in charge of this entire industrial branch of the city. Qiao's step is surprising because no one among the leading cadres is willing to work on a lower-ranking job. The plant has not fulfilled its plan for two and a half years, and is run by a coterie of seemingly inept cadres. Qiao had been manager of the plant before the Cultural Revolution. He now demands that Shi Gan, who at that time had been his Party secretary, should be reinstalled with him. Shi Gan, he says, can "give me guidance and help me in critical moments in a manner unmatched by anyone else," and, second, can "convince the masses to subordinate themselves to me." Shi Gan, who had been criticized during the Cultural Revolution as had Qiao, has retreated to a cadre school where he rules as a "general over three armies," namely, chickens, ducks, and sheep. In an accident during the Cultural Revolution, he had bitten off half his tongue, leaving him with a permanent speech defect. Qiao cajoles and forces Shi to accept the assignment.

The second part, "Taking Over," has Qiao taking over a wife and the factory. Qiao studied in the Soviet Union during the 1950s. There, he met Tong Zhen, then an engineering student. She fell in love with him, but he, being married to a woman in charge of propaganda in the local university, treated her as a brother would treat his younger sister, although his real feelings went further. Upon their return, he became the manager and she an engineer at the heavy-electrical-machinery plant. Tong's nephew, Xi Wangbei, who had grown up in her household, suspected Qiao had designs on his aunt. After the beginning of the Cultural Revolution, he spread rumors attacking Qiao as a lecher. His rebel friends blew up the story, and Tong Zhen, who admired Qiao for his managerial capacities and also loved him, attempted suicide, being saved, however, by none other than her nephew. Qiao's wife died under unclear circumstances during this period. Now, Qiao's last child has just left for university, and he has just accepted the new assignment as a manager. He has not seen Tong Zhen for a decade. He calls her up, and proposes marriage to her. Like Shi Gan, she has aged, but Qiao's ardent advances revive some of her earlier fire.

Together, they inspect the factory on the eve of Qiao's official take-over. The workers, it turns out, are "ideologically confused, for the most part having lost all faith after the loss of the idol they had earlier adored . . . all had degenerated, both physically and mentally." This is epitomized in Du Bing, a young worker with a Hong Kong hit song on his lips who produces rejects and, after six years of working at his lathe, still ignores the functions of the lever which has to be pressed every morning to oil the machine. As a sole contrast, a young West German technician is introduced who works with evident skill and energy through the night shift to repair a machine after having amused himself for some unaccounted days in Japan.

Meanwhile, the leadership of the factory under Ji Shen has an emergency meeting after the news of Qiao's appointment has leaked. Ji Shen had been subjected to some criticism during the Cultural Revolution, but ended up as the vice-principal of a cadre school, a position that gave him the opportunity to alleviate the fate of some high-ranking cadres who were out of favor, but who have now been reinstalled. In their turn, they now protect Ji Shen. Ji Shen had cleverly anticipated the impending change from class struggle to the Four Modernizations as the main occupation of the Party, and had himself assigned to become manager of this factory in 1976, bringing his coterie along. To make things difficult for his successor, he now dismisses Tong Zhen's nephew, Xi Wangbei, from his position in the factory leadership to which he had risen during the Cultural Revolution, the charge being that Xi had been a rebel leader during that time. In a second move, Ji Shen prepares a "mass campaign" to raise production. Shi Gan, who also had gone to the factory to explore, undoes Ji Shen's plot by suddenly appearing at the meeting together with Qiao and Tong.

The third part, "Playing the Lead," shows Qiao Guangpu running the plant. At first, he does nothing but investigate each stage of the production process, leaving the factory to buzz around like a "beheaded fly." He prepares for "major surgery." This eventually comes in the form of a general examination for all, workers and cadres alike, on strictly professional matters. Qiao refuses automatic reinstallation of the cadres who had been deposed during the Cultural Revolution but offers the chance of promotion to old cadres and Cultural Revolution rebels alike on the basis of their examination results and their performance. He disregards his old enmity with Xi Wangbei, since the latter shows both acumen and managerial capacity, and installs this former rebel as his assistant-manager. The former manager, Ji Shen, ends up leading the "service brigade" of personnel who failed in both job and examination. With his rigid standards recklessly applied to both friend and foe, Qiao Guangpu manages to alienate nearly everyone in the factory, but production rises to the set norms.

Qiao comes acropper, however, in "foreign relations" with other factories from whom he needs parts. With his uncompromising ways he blocks the way for the fulfillment of his ambitious production plans. It is Xi Wangbei who then takes over the job of mediating between Qiao's grand ideals and the complex realities of Chinese economic bureaucracy. In the process, Jiang Zilong gives vivid sketches of the actual practices and "deals" oiling the unwieldy machinery, practices that on the surface appear as the functioning of the "plan." Although in the end the old cadres and the disgruntled young workers band together to write wall posters and anonymous letters against him, Manager Qiao is vindicated through the support of Hu Dadao, the Bureau chief, and finally the Minister himself. Content, he sings his favorite Peking-opera tune: "Bao Longtu Sat in Judgment in Kaifengfu," linking himself to the legendary Judge Bao.

THE THEME

The theme of the story is the takeover of the commanding heights of industry by the manager, Qiao Guangpu, the hero. Manager fiction, short stories, novellas, or novels, is a rarity in China. During the industrial and literary reforms in the wake of the 8th Party Congress of 1956, the theme emerged with Ai Wu's *Steeled and Tempered* (1958),[8] which includes some lively scenes. In the socialist order of things, the manager is a *zhishi fenzi*, an intellectual; within the worker-peasant-soldier orientation of literature there was no place for intellectual heroes. Thus, we find them only during the Hundred Flowers period (when Ai Wu's text

8. Ai Wu, *Bailian chenggang* (Beijing: Zuojia Press, 1958); an English translation is Ai Wu, *Steeled and Tempered* (Beijing: Foreign Languages Press, 1958).

was written), occasionally in the early 1960s, and after 1977. Then, industry and agriculture vanished from the literary scene, and the *shanghen wenxue*, or Literature of Scars, put exclusive emphasis on intellectuals' sufferings during the Cultural Revolution. With the formulation of the policy of the Four Modernizations at the 3rd Plenum in late 1978, industrial management became a legitimate issue again.

Manager literature, however, is a well-established genre in socialist literature, at least since Stalin's introduction of the one-man leadership principle in industry. Through the manager novel/story/play, a variety of societal problems were discussed:

- The personality a socialist manager should have, his background and education, his psyche, latitude, and social life;
- The relationship the manager should have with the Party, which is usually represented within these texts by the Party secretary; their separate decisional powers;
- His relationship with the other specialists in the factory, the engineers and accountants;
- His relationship with the workers, that of an inspiring military commander rushing into battle ahead of his men, or that of a cool manager who translates the "objective laws" of the economy into decisions, with or without the consent of the "proletariat" of the plant;
- The rigorous demands of "scientific management" vis-à-vis the social realities of a bureaucratic state and the human element in industrial relations.

The manager stories belong to a time when the emphasis was on technical and professional expertise, be it in war or industrial management. They provided status and prestige for managers as legitimate heroes. They gave guidelines for this new class both in their personal actions, and their crucial relationship with the Party. And they gave glimpses of the fascinating exclusive life of this new class to the general public.

The first substantial batch of such texts appeared in the Soviet Union during and directly after World War II. As Vera Dunham has pointed out in *In Stalin's Time*, the texts were part of a "New Deal" offered by the Party to the technically proficient middle classes, providing much latitude in personal behavior as long as submission to the Party was guaranteed.[9] During the early phase of the Soviet Thaw, the theme became an important element in the propaganda for the replacement of old Stalinist bureaucrats with new Khruschevian industrial heroes. When the prerogatives of the Soviet managers became more firmly established after the new law on socialist enterprises in October 1965, the manager novel became even more topical.[10] With the emphasis on the "scientific-technical revolution" and the idea of social technology as a set of devices applicable to the government of socialist society as it was articulated in the Soviet Union and East Germany, a new and more self-righteous type of manager appeared in the texts.

The manager story developed its modern form as the inversion of the worker novel. The latter would paint the leadership as easily corruptible, while the workers were idealized. In the manager novel, the managers were the heroes, and the workers were assigned the more sombre roles. Two texts, both with impact in China, may be taken as representative of the Soviet writings, Vil Lipatov's novel *The Tale of Director Pronchatov* (1969)[11] and Ignatij Dvorekij's play *The Man from Outside* (1972).[12] Both have been much heralded, translated within the socialist camp, and have

---

9. V. Dunham, *In Stalin's Time, Middleclass Values in Soviet Fiction* (Cambridge: Cambridge University Press, 1976), especially pp. 5–23, 137ff. Cf. also G. Gibian, "The Factory Manager in Soviet Fiction," *Problems of Communism* 8.2 (1959).

10. "Regulations for the socialist state enterprise, confirmed by a decree of the Council of Ministers of the USSR 4 October 1965," *Ekonomiceskaya Gazeta*, 20 October 1965, the German translation in *Die wichtigsten Gesetzgebungsakte in den Ländern Ost–, Südost–Europas und den ostasiatischen Volksdemokratieen* I (1966), p. 50. These regulations neatly fit the setup described in Jiang's story. According to #90, "The director of the enterprise is appointed and dismissed by the higher organ" and "The director organizes the entire work of the enterprise and has full responsibility for its condition and activity . . . Within the framework of his competence, he gives directives to the enterprise; in accordance with labor laws he hires and dismisses workers and employees, takes measures to give labor incentives, and disciplines the work force of the enterprise."

11. Vil Lipatov, *Skazanie o direktore Proncatove, Zamja* 1, 2 (1969). German translation, *Die Mär vom Direktor P.*, (Berlin (East): Verlag Volk und Welt, 1973). See the Chinese summary in *Suxiu wenyi pipanji* (A collection of criticisms of Soviet revisionist literature; Shanghai: Shanghai Renmin Chubanshe, 1975), pp. 125ff.

12. Ignatij Dvoreckij, *Celorek so storony*, in *Teatr* 10 (1972). A German translation with a substantial "toning down" of the aggressive pitch, Ignatij Dworjetzkij, *Der Aussenseiter*, ed. F. Hitzer (Munich 1973). Chinese summary in *A Collection of Criticisms* (note 11 above), pp. 139ff.

been the topic of published discussions among managers, planners, scholars, workers, and literary men. Both deal in programmatic fashion with the takeover around 1960 of the commanding heights of big industrial enterprises in the Soviet Union by the new manager type.

Pronchatov is described as a skilled young manager fighting for the post of general manager of a huge wood-cutting and shipping enterprise near lake Baikal after the death of the former director in 1961. (The date refers to the sweeping industrial reforms of that year which greatly strengthened the hands of managers.) The Party secretary of the rayon under whose leadership the plant operates wants to appoint one of his friends, an inept "conservative" bureaucrat, against whom Pronchatov builds a formidable alliance. He wins over the alcoholic old engineer who is afraid of any new person threatening to wreck his well-cushioned life; the head of the planning office, who has appropriated substantial amounts of wood and is afraid of a new director; the young chief engineer who had earlier once worked under the proposed new director, had been fired for making an innovative proposal, and now hopes for improvements of the situation; and the district Party secretary who had proposed Pronchatov in the first place to become the successor of the deceased director. Pronchatov's fight for power is perfectly unabashed; he sees the plant as his private domain. With pleasure he recalls how his little son called the huge area under his administration "Pronchatov country," and complacently remarks that his area is larger than France. The Party plays a positive role only at the higher levels, who support Pronchatov while the lower levels consist mostly of bureaucrats specializing in personal relations and/or leftist phrases about the necessity to lend an ear to "the workers."

These workers, however, are a sorry lot. They are lazy drunkards with a criminal bent, hardly a bright figure among them, a rejection of the glorifying efforts bestowed on this class in the worker novel. Their stature is epitomized by a group of workers dispatched to Pronchatov's plant from a labor camp. They have mutinied on the ship that brought them, confining the guards in fetters to the lower quarters. Their bodies tattooed, they engage in drinking, knifing, whoring, swearing, and gambling, a far cry from the glorious proletarian in socialism.

Pronchatov subdues them with a ruse, risking his own life on the way. He has the ship towed out into the middle of the river, and cuts off supplies. The workers have to signal their submission individually by swimming to the shore through icy water. The measures are hard, necessary, and effective. Within the text, Pronchatov may not be much loved, but objectively he is doing the right and necessary thing. This justifies the leadership's tolerance for his personal antics.

Dvoreckij's play develops this line of thinking further. When Pronchatov becomes manager, he is 36 years old; Dvoreckij's Cheshkov is only 32. The new managers are both competent and young. Cheshkov is bored in his factory which he has led to optimum performance. Risking censure by his own Party committee, he applies for the manager's job in another factory which has new machines but is not well managed. He has clear demands regarding his salary, his apartment, and a job for his wife, insisting on instant satisfaction. He enters a factory that had been evacuated during the war so that some camaraderie had sprung up between managers and workers, which in turn slackened discipline. Cheshkov explodes this casual mood with his conception of "scientific management." During the first ten days, he only looks around, commenting on the old age of the secretaries on the way, who should be sent to kindergartens where their old brains will not be taxed with shorthand. He eventually comes up with his two "knives," disciplinary supervision ("get them at their throat") and financial punishment ("hit them with the rubel"), to solve the problems of absenteeism and alcoholism. Against those opposing this style of work, he proudly proclaims: "We lead, and don't do a thing with our hands; we use language and brain for our work." He is a "man from outside" in the sense that he forces on this factory modern methods mostly taken from the West, and that he is and remains a stranger to those working in this factory. A lot of workers and engineers leave the plant after his takeover, his original Party committee utters a stern censure against him, and his only support within the factory is from the woman in charge of finances, with whom he is having an affair which symbolizes their close alliance. There is some self-pity in this character. In a discussion about the play, Dvoreckij himself said: "Without pity, he immediately demands discipline; otherwise the cause would die. For the benefit of general welfare, he dares not play the nice fellow, although personally he would like this better."[13] We thus get a tragic tinge to the manager-hero. For the good of the whole he has to blow himself up to the proportions of a super-human giant who ruthlessly enacts what is necessitated by the "objective laws"; he is a lonely creature, hated by many, and willing to pay this price for the gratification of playing the lead.

The East German manager novels since the 8th party Congress of the Sozialistische Einheitspartei share most of the features of these texts, which have been translated into German. Scholars have been constrained by a tradition of nineteenth-century scholarship which read literature as codeterminate with national boundaries. This approach already failed to give an accurate description at the time but has become a major obstacle in the twentieth century. The "socialist camp" was the first to include the development of a common literature among its goals and plans. There is, accordingly, such a thing as a common manager literature in this camp. No piece of this can meaningfully be studied without reference to the other pieces, most of which have been written in other languages, particularly in Russian.[14] Before returning to the Chinese texts, some key features of this genre may be listed:

(1) The new socialist manager is portrayed as a new human type—daring, strong, even eccentric, ruthless, but a hero nonetheless.

(2) His legitimacy is provided not by popular consent or Party confirmation but by his enactment of the "objective laws of economy" in the context of the specific plant or trust.

(3) While he is idealized, his environment is not. His way to power has to be secured through alliances with weak and shady characters, to whom, however, he will not feel bound and obligated afterwards. Hard-hitting descriptions of the actual state of the enterprises are the rule in the portrayal of both the hero's support cast and his enemies.

(4) The Party is, at best, reduced to a supporting role. In general, the

13. Dvoreckij quoted in the German edition (note 12 above), p. 135.
14. See Jochen Staadt, *Konfliktbewusstsein und sozialistischer Anspruch in der DDR-Literatur, zur Darstellung gesellschaftlicher Widersprüche in Romanen nach dem VIII Parteitag der SED 1971* (Berlin: Verlag Volker Spiess, 1977), Chapters 1 and 3; both deal with the East German manager novels by Kant, Jakobs, Steinberg, Werner, and Neutsch without any reference to the Soviet models.

Party leadership is described as being in support of the modern manager, while the lower levels are passive or even obstructive. Within the enterprise, the technical and financial specialists tend to support the management specialist.

(5) The workers, in an ironic inversion of the way relationships were portrayed in more radical phases, like the 1st Five-Year Plan in the Soviet Union or the Cultural Revolution in China, never appear in the heroic garb of the Marxian proletariat, but as a degenerate, crestfallen and numb class, to be awakened only by harsh discipline and material incentives. They tend to resist the new manager for the worst possible motives, but eventually come to see the virtues of his harsh rule.

(6) The texts take pains to describe the new latitude allowed the manager in terms of his private comfort, his personal habits, and his moral stature.

Evidently, the type of social relations described in the socialist-manager novel was anathema to social relations as envisaged by the leaders of the Cultural Revolution. Mao himself had railed against the one-man leadership which had been abolished in China by the late 1950s. And numerous were the old directors who were attacked as "capitalist roaders" during the Cultural Revolution, accused of exactly the opinions and behavioral patterns described as ideals in the manager novel. After a fundamental change in government line in 1972, Deng Xiaoping was called back into power in 1975 and instantly proceeded to develop plans for science, education, and industrial reorganization; these included an abrogation of the system of having factories run by revolutionary committees, which at this time already included managers, engineers, and accounting specialists.[15] The faction associated with the "Gang of Four" fought back. It resorted to the well-established method of attacking things Chinese by calling them "Soviet revisionist." This line of attack combined the targets of revisionism as treason to Marxism and Soviet imperialism as a threat to the Chinese motherland. In June 1975,

15. Deng Xiaoping, "On the General Program for All Work of the Whole Party and the Whole Country," in *Issues and Studies* 8.8 (1977); and his "Some Problems in Speeding Up Industrial Development," in *Issues and Studies* 8.7 (1977); also his "Several Questions Concerning the Work of Science and Technology," in *Issues and Studies* 8.9 (1977).

the Shanghai People's Press printed an edition of 100,000 copies of *Suxiu wenyi pipan ji* (Collection of criticisms of Soviet revisionist literature), 23 articles that had appeared individually during the previous months in the Shanghai journals *Xuexi yu pipan* (Study and criticism) and *Zhaoxia* (Rosy dawn). Both were considered to be directly associated with the faction around Mao's wife, Jiang Qing, and were immediately closed down after the arrest of this group. The articles deal with Soviet works from the preceding years that were considered illustrative of certain aspects of Soviet social reality and of the Soviet government's attitude towards them. The clear purpose of the articles is to provide "excellent negative teaching material" (*henhaode fanmian jiaocai*) to the Chinese about Soviet revisionism and evidence for the "restoration of capitalism" in this country.[16]

Among the works selected for denunciation we find both manager pieces described above. However, in the strictly controlled market of available thoughts in China at the time, readers and writers seem to have developed their own technique of reading *fanmian* or against the grain. If one looks backward from the industrial and managerial reforms spelled out since 1979 and the literary texts exploring them, like Jiang Zilong's story about director Qiao, it is probable that the forces opposed to the line of industrial management prevailing during the Cultural Revolution found their own aspirations quite accurately presented in the summaries of the Soviet texts about managers. And, once they had the chance to spell out these aspirations openly, they clearly adopted the key features of the Soviet manager stories summarized in the collection of criticisms of "Soviet revisionist" works. There is some oral testimony that many people read these 1975 Soviet texts (which might have been published internally in full translation) as a truthful depiction of their industrial manager-heroes, and read the leftist analyses in that book as the true *fanmian jiaocai* or negative teaching material.[17]

But there is more. Jiang Zilong himself introduced the manager

16. Cf. *A Collection of Criticisms* (note 11), Postface, p. 336.

17. I am most grateful to Wendy Locks, then a graduate student at the University of California, Berkeley, for a stimulating discussion in 1984 about Jiang's story. She specifically pointed out that Chinese friends had mentioned in talks with her that they had read the Soviet stories in 1975 in the way suggested here. This was instrumental in suggesting a further exploration of the links between Jiang's manager stories and those of the socialist camp, which I had studied earlier.

theme into Chinese literature at the time by publishing a story, "A Day in the Life of the Head of the Bureau for Electromechanics," in the January 1976 issue of *Renmin wenxue,* just before the open attacks against Deng Xiaoping began.[18] Although this story appeared during the "bad time" of the Cultural Revolution, the links between this text and the present story are explicit. A highly laudatory article in *Renmin ribao* in early September 1979 referred to the "excellent short story, 'A Day in the Life' which was madly criticized by the "Gang of Four" and their literary henchmen as supporting the 'theory of production only'" and supporting the "capitalist roader" Deng Xiaoping. The article thus links the 1976 and 1979 texts in a positive way and identifies the earlier story as some kind of pro-Deng resistance literature.[19] Jiang Zilong himself also makes this link. The hero of the earlier story is Huo Dadao, who in our story reappears with his old name and in the same function as earlier. Xu Jinting, too, the former vice-head of the Bureau, is still in office. Jiang thus claims a continuity in his writings during and after the Cultural Revolution, refuting allegations that he was a writer protected by the "Gang of Four."

Thus, before entering our story, we have to introduce another text into the background, namely "A Day." The story forms an intricate web of new manager-oriented propositions and political concessions. It describes one day in the life of Huo Dadao: Production is behind in one important factory; meetings have to be attended; the vice-head, Xu Jinting, does not do his work; and during the night a cloudburst threatens to put the factories the Bureau manages under water.

Under all these pressures, the head of the office, Huo Dadao, collapses and is brought to the hospital, unconscious. He has joined in productive labor, and, after six hours of heavy work, his already feeble heart stalled. From the rest of the story, which portrays Huo as an indomitable hero, the reader is led to wonder about the wisdom of having aging leading cadres of such unquestionably high commitment participate in physical labor. They have more pressing things to do. Huo Dadao, whose name means Big-Knife Huo, is contrasted with the vice-

18. Jiang Zilong, "A Day in the Life," (note 6 above).

19. *Renmin ribao,* 3 September 1979; see the polemics against this appreciation in Zhao Ke, "Ping xiaoshuo 'Qiao changzhang shangrenji,'" (On the story "Director Qiao Takes Over"), *Tianjin ribao,* 12 September 1979, at the end of the article.

head of the Bureau, Xu Jinting, whose name betrays him as Mr. Slow-Who-Has-Stopped-Progressing. Huo has been steeled by the Cultural Revolution to become a better manager; he is respected and loved by both workers and activists and responds quickly to their suggestions and criticisms. Xu Jinting, on the other hand, bides his time, cares more for political connections and personal comfort than for hard data and taxing work, and retreats to the hospital when things go awry. However, Huo's main emphasis is on getting out good-quality products in time and on solving the practical problems associated with this task; he does not see Xu as the main obstacle, and consequently does not engage in "class struggle" as the "main link" for the solution of the problem. The criticism of the workers and young cadres, the education by the Party secretary, and the great model provided by Huo Dadao eventually achieve Xu's compliance.

This plot structure implies a rebuttal of the key proposition of the Cultural Revolution according to which production problems were mostly caused by class antagonisms and could be solved by class struggle. The favorable statements on the Cultural Revolution were purged by Jiang in his new edition of the story in 1980,[20] but they are an integral part of the old plot, because the Cultural Revolution produced a new brand of youthful enthusiastic managers like Jiang Yongtu, "one of the young new cadres springing up during the Cultural Revolution." Her achievements are described in the following puzzling way: "Everyone says that, when ginger gets old, it becomes hot [her family name Jiang means 'ginger'], but our Jiang, though young, is already quite formidable. She has been forged by the Cultural Revolution, *and grasps production with enthusiasm and energy as well as having a keen sense of realities. In their water-pump factory they have set up two automatic assembly lines and have fulfilled their plan targets for the year in five months* [my emphasis]."[21] Thus, even when following the language of the Cultural Revolution as well as its literary forms in the extremely exaggerated portrayal of "Big-Knife" Huo, Jiang Zilong adhered to the new emphasis on production demanded by Zhou Enlai and then Deng Xiaoping at the time, adding: "Cadres who grasp only production but not management are the wastrels of socialism."[22] With his stress on production and deemphasis of class struggle, Huo emulates the example set by the Soviet texts, without, of course, Jiang Zilong's saying so. Huo's name, "Big-Knife," looks like a direct quote from Dvoreckij's "two knives" (money and discipline), but, in this early story, the name announces more than the character does. Huo has no time to really run the factories, and with indirect criticism Jiang Zilong indicates that Huo is wasting most of his energy trotting through the rain and working on a machine, although both elements are glorified in the surface text of the story.

When after the Tiannanmen events in April 1976 and the dismissal of Deng Xiaoping, the struggle against the "capitalist roaders" was intensified, Jiang Zilong recanted with a rewriting of the text, a self-criticism and a new story. The rewriting focused on "class struggle" against Xu Jinting. Unhappily, the first three installments of the longer version "Jidian juzhang" (The head of the Electrical Equipment Bureau) had already appeared in *Tianjin wenyi* when Jiang was overpowered by his new insights, so that he changed only the last part.[23] In his self-criticism, Jiang Zilong accused himself in a manner that was later to become an important defense for him since he could claim to have followed Deng Xiaoping's lead. (He would later say that he was forced to sign this text.) It said, "Last year [1975], when I wrote this short story, I was under the influence of Deng Xiaoping's 'Take the Three Directives as the Key Link.'" A self-criticism of the editorial board of *Renmin wenxue* in the same issue took a moderate line toward Jiang Zilong because he was "of the proletariat."[24] The issue also contained his new story, "Tiexian zhuan" (Biography of Miss Iron Shovel),[25] about a young woman fighting the capitalist trends represented by the Party secretary,

---

22. Ibid., p. 54.

23. Jiang Zilong, "Jidian juzhang" (A day in the life), *Tianjin wenyi* 4–8 (April-August 1976).

24. Jiang Zilong, "Nuli fanying wuchanjieji tong zouzipai de douzheng" (Eagerly reflect the struggle between the proletariat and the capitalist roaders), *Renmin wenxue* 4:92ff (April 1976); and "Bianzhe de hua" (Editor's comment) in the same issue, pp. 95f.

25. Jiang Zilong, "Tiexian zhuan" (Biography of Miss Iron Shovel), *Renmin wenxue* 4:39ff (April 1976).

an adherent of Liu Shaoqi. This man had pushed Liu Shaoqi's line in 1961, and was now, like Deng Xiaoping, rehabilitated, but "unrepentant." The facility acquired in rewriting texts to fit changing political lines was to stay with Jiang Zilong in later years.

The reemergence of the manager-hero thus carried important implications. It announced a fundamental change in the political and industrial system, in the legitimation of the powers of decision making, and in the status of the various groups engaged in industrial pursuits. It brought back, although hardly recognizable in this early story, the familiar manager-hero from the Hundred Flowers period, a period lingering in memory as one of rapid and sustained economic growth and optimism. Jiang's earlier story made its political statement by bluntly introducing the manager as a legitimate hero, and then making him acceptable with many "proletarian" accoutrements. "Director Qiao Takes Over" (or "assumes command") announces with the title a more fundamental change. Before, others, and not qualified managers at that, had been in charge of industry. Now, the manager takes over. Jiang Zilong announced a fundamental shift in the power relations of the PRC. This is a familiar situation in the Soviet stories. They all emulate the taking of power by the new managerial elite, and focus on their struggle in achieving the transfer. Pronchatov fights for the post of the top manager, and he gets it by replacing a "conservative" opponent. Cheshkov replaces the old-style director and his moldy camaraderie. Indeed, one critic remarked in a discussion of Dvoreckij's piece: "Literature got stuck in a preparatory phase of the formation of the contemporary heroic character. For fifteen years now it has demonstrated in the examples of Bachirev, Lobanov, Krylov, and their countless epigones, as well, ultimately, in Cheshkov himself, how an engineer is transformed into a fighter. But there is not a single case where it has shown the next step—literature has not shown him after victory, in a collective which is already functioning and has been transformed by him."[26]

These words by the sociologist Janov do seem to miss the point. It is

---

26. A. Janov, "Das 'Produktionsstück' und der literarische Held der 70er Jahre," in I. Dworjetzkij, *Der Aussenseiter* (note 12 above), p. 83.

not the purpose of these texts to describe the actual functioning of a collective transformed by the new manager. The battle for control is still going on, and the texts still go about emulating the new managers and substantiating their claim for power against the "old," "Stalinist," "Cultural Revolution" leaders. In neither case, it should be noted, is the issue democracy. The old guard based its legitimacy on the "leading role" of the Party; the new guard bases it on the "objective laws" of the economy. Neither of the two seriously require worker consent. In fact, literature sets greater store by describing fervent worker consent in the case of the old-style leaders who stress the adjective *proletarian*. The "manager-takes-command" theme is thus traditionally the vehicle to describe the takeover of the commanding heights of industry by a new technocratically-minded leadership.

Jiang Zilong directly integrated bits from Dvoreckij's play, like the two-week investigation period, the death of the wife and entrance into a new love relationship, and even, as Wendy Locks pointed out, his voluntary downward transfer. He thus squarely fits into this tradition. His programmatic title "Manager Qiao Takes Over" refers to the ascension to power of Deng Xiaoping and his associates in the crucial year 1978/79, when Hua Guofeng was still in office, but Deng Xiaoping already laid down the political line. The Literature of Scars, written after the dethronement of Jiang Qing and her associates during the years 1977 and 1978, was highly critical, but only of the past, of the Cultural Revolution. The 3rd Plenum in December 1978 declared that the struggle against the Gang of Four was basically over, and that the focus of attention should now be on the Four Modernizations. This implied new duties and possibilities for literature—to describe the progress in the realization of the Four Modernizations, and to point out obstacles in their way. The proportions of propaganda for the Modernizations and of criticism of bureaucratism and other impediments varied with each writer. Jiang Zilong found the ideal mix with this programmatic story, which earned him unequivocal support from Deng Xiaoping's faction and hence an umbrella large enough to weather the storms unleashed against him by those opposed to the "takeover" of the managers. He could justly pride himself on having changed the focus of social criticism from the past to the immediate present.[27] Having outlined the theme, we now turn to the protagonists of the story.

THE PROTAGONISTS

THE MANAGER. Qiao Guangpu is an altogether new type in contemporary Chinese literature. He has shed the extreme heroism of Huo Dadao, who fights through the rainstorm in the middle of the night while his pain-relieving pills are dissolved by the waters. Qiao also has shed Huo's earlier mass appeal. The form has become purer. Jiang Zilong introduces his hero through a speech he gives to the workers of the factory. The excerpt stands as a preface to the story. In this prominent position, it is a program. Qiao Guangpu says:

> Time and numbers are cold and pitiless, like two whips they hang over our backs.

> Talking about time first. If there are twenty-three years in which to modernize the entire country, factories like ours, which provide the electro-mechanical equipment for the rest of the country, have to complete their own modernization by the end of the 1980s. Otherwise, it is like the kitchen personnel arriving at the canteen at the same time as the workers. They'll never have the food ready in time. Now about numbers. The Japanese electro-mechanical plant Hitachi employs 5,500 people, and produces equipment with a total capacity of 12 million kw. per year; our factory with its 8,900 people reaches 1.2 million kw. What does this mean? What do we have to do?

> The day before yesterday, there was a Japanese called Takashima; when he heard me mention our annual production, he shook his head and said I was hiding something! My face turned red like a monkey's ass, my fists sweated water. Not that I wanted to hit somebody else, I could have hit myself. And you still laugh! If I would have seen you laughing there, I would have beaten you up!

> In fact, time and numbers have life, and feeling, you just have to make up your mind to go after them, and they will be yours.[28]

The past of the Cultural Revolution is forgotten, only the future exists. There is no word about socialism and the proletariat, there are

27. Jiang Zilong, "A Pedigree" (note 1 above), p. 46.
28. J, p. 4; W, p. 130; L, p. 56.

only the objective laws, time and numbers. There is nothing of the end-less pontification of the leaders on such occasions, but short bursts of language, deft in both grammar and imagery. The circumspect wooing of the top leaders and the broad masses has vanished. He, Qiao Guangpu, lays down the line, and he does so in the most advanced sec-tor of the nation's industry. Jiang Zilong does not mince words when it comes to introducing the physiognomy of the man after these extracts from his language and ideas. His physiognomy presents the living image of painfully repressed explosive energy. His face "had the color of iron and the rough traits of a hunter: brows rising steep like a cliff over deep-set eyes of a hungry tiger; the cheeks with somewhat high cheekbones, the broad and muscular face; in short, the very image of strength."[29] The dark complexion is iconographically linked to the honest strength of poor peasants working the fields. The images of a "hunter," a "hun-gry tiger," and of the cliff show an internal dynamism that is quite inde-pendent of a benign social motivation. We know nothing of Qiao's "class background," and are thus informed that it is unimportant com-pared to his actual attitude. Qiao grinds his teeth when deep in thought or agitated, showing his efforts to control himself. But, when anony-mous letters attack him, this is too much. "Suddenly there was a crack and a piece of a molar broke off. Without a word he spat out that cor-ner of the tooth."[30] His lips are closed "like steel floodgates," his eyes fix his opposite's pupils "like gun barrels," being at the same time like a "mirror pitilessly reflecting" the other's "soul." His language is explo-sive, and to the point. Xu Jinting comments on Qiao Guangpu's state-ments at the meeting of the Bureau: "Heavens! A moment ago you pulled that hand grenade, and now you add an atomic bomb; are you perhaps going to follow this up by a neutron bomb?"[31]

Qiao handles women with the same vitality as industrial production. He has not seen Tong Zhen for more than a decade, and now proposes marriage to her in his third sentence. Qiao Guangpu comes on stage with a bag full of new values and attitudes. Qiao is said to be *dadan*, "dar-ing" and "outspoken." Nearly a dozen times Jiang Zilong repeats this

29. J, p. 4.
30. J, p. 26; W, p. 176; L, p. 84.
31. J, p. 5; W, p. 131; L, p. 57.

Hundred Flowers term. Qiao "dispenses with formalities," rules "with an iron fist," he is "quick in making decisions" and willing to take the responsibility for them. He is willing to "risk experiments" and has no problems with his own authority. If he is on stage, he "plays the lead whether a tragedy or a comedy is given" and he transforms the assistant managers into his simple "assistants." He seethes with "energy" and enthusiasm. His name, significant like that of the other protagonists, says he is *guangpu,* "brilliant uncouthness," the "uncouth" being in the *Laozi* the term for a primordial and vital simplicity and strength. His family name might refer to *jiao* (written with the horse to the left) with the meaning both of "arrogant" and "the pride," making him both haughty and the pride of the nation.

The sources of Qiao's "energy" and "enthusiasm" are not quite clear. Jiang Zilong does not talk about any "class feeling" of his hero or his devotion to the betterment of the lot of his compatriots, or even his patriotism. We get only a weak echo of the unabashed careerism of his Soviet colleagues, when Qiao Guangpu says: "In the past the war had to be fought, and now we have to run industries. I have not the slightest wish to sit in the wing and play the drums which accompany [the singers on stage in the Peking opera]; I want to play the lead, whether we give a comedy or a tragedy."[32]

Qiao's gratification, accordingly, is not dependent on the workers' or cadres' agreeing with his measures. Huo Dadao explicitly formulates from what source Qiao and his coalition get their self-confidence, gratification, and legitimacy: "Modernization is really not just a technical question; one will also have to step on some people's toes . . . We need time and we need data in order to realize modernization, because in *modernization resides the essential and long-term interest of the people."* [my emphasis][33] Within the text, as in the Soviet models, the manager as the torch-bearer towards the achievement of these "essential and long-term interests of the people" is justified and obliged to use a heavy hand, an "iron fist"[34] to achieve this goal. Qiao, in short, is an orgy of

---

32. J, p. 10; W, p. 143; L, p. 64.
33. J, p. 26; W, p. 178; L, p. 85.
34. J, p. 24; W, p. 173; L, p. 82. Cf. J, p. 25; W, p. 174; L, p. 83. In both cases the term is used by Xi Wangbei with regard to Qiao with Xi spelling out the limits of its application.

new or restored values and words, physiogonomical traits and attitudes. In substance, however, he is a quotation; his biography admits this by having him study in the Soviet Union. His traits come straight from the Soviet manager novel. In him, the Soviet-trained specialists from the 1950s are elevated to the national reserve for the top leadership of the modernization drive, and through him the readers are told that "Soviet revisionism" might be the real thing for Chinese industry.

Qiao, in a strange way, interacts with another hero of China's modernization, Lin Zhen from Wang Meng's "The Young Man Who Only Recently Joined the Organization Department," written in 1956. "Earthquake" Lin enters the story with a Soviet novel in his pocket, determined to emulate Nastya, the young heroine. He adapts a Soviet text to a Chinese personality and Chinese surroundings. Qiao Guangpu enters the story as an outlandish being, and the text anxiously explores the question of how he and the Chinese environment can accommodate each other. But, even though in his essential traits Qiao remains unchanged, Jiang Zilong took pains to make him at least culturally compatible.

Qiao, with his over 50 years of age, is substantially older than his Soviet literary parallels. In 1979, his group of Soviet-trained specialists was being actively recruited by the Deng Xiaoping leadership as replacements for people who rose during the Cultural Revolution or, more important, were retainers of Hua Guofeng.[35] The most important adaptation of Qiao Guangpu to a Chinese environment occurs in his *kulturnost'* lifestyle, so important in the Soviet precedents and their Chinese adaptations from the 1950s. These *kulturnost'* traits might be crude, like the perfume wafting around director Pronchatov's body; they might be expressed in symbols of petty-bourgeois culture, a music room, or a diamond brooch on the evening dress of the manager's wife. In the Chinese Hundred Flowers texts, the military hero in Wu Qiang's *Red Sun* would sport a fancy fur coat, and write love letters to his wife amidst heated fighting.[36] Ai Wu's director has a "cultured" home complete with a nanny for the children in the Soviet fashion.[37] Wang Meng's young heroes dress elegantly, as do those of Liu Binyan, who included a devas-

---

35. *Gongren ribao*, 25 August 1979, editorial note.
36. Wu Qiang, *Hongri* (Red sun; Beijing: Zhongguo qingnian Press, 1958).
37. Ai Wu, *Steeled and Tempered* (note 8 above).

tating critique of the cultural desert surrounding the workaholic leading cadre in his "Inside News of Our Paper."[38] At the outset of the story, Qiao is alone; his home is not "comfortable" because there is no woman; and he is deprived of culture, never going alone to a Peking opera, of which he is both a connoisseur and a devotee. Jiang Zilong takes pains to describe Qiao's rejection of the role of the work robot, which takes the form of his instant marriage with Tong Zhen. She is the very essence of *kulturnost,* arranging a party for his birthday, and buying tickets for the opera. Jiang is still uneasy about the limits of the acceptable hero. Each time Qiao engages in *kulturnost'* activity, the political battles for the control of the plant prevent him from enjoying them. The reader is led to sympathize with this man who cannot enjoy even the modest pleasures of life.

The purpose of describing the *kulturnost'* life in the manager novel is twofold: first, a public recognition that these rough-hewn characters will live out their vitality whether in their managerial jobs, or in their private lives; second, to define limits to the leeway of this new group or class. The Soviet texts show their heroes drunk, having affairs, bragging. Jiang probes this area in Qiao's relationship with Tong Zhen. Tong Zhen's "daring" and "longing" glances notwithstanding, Qiao had remained faithful to his wife. But he had himself photographed in Moscow with Tong and had "bitterly accused himself, and had once confessed in front of a picture of his dead wife that Tong Zhens' fervent words had made him waver, and that there were times when, deep inside, he loved her dearly."[39] As Jiang Zilong wrote elsewhere, many of the male specialists who went to the Soviet Union during the 1950s started affairs with Chinese woman students; often they divorced their wives upon their return and married these much younger students.

In his story, Jiang does not go so far, but only dimly indicates that a man of Qiao's stature cannot be expected to be a suave modest citizen in his private life. As the nervous reactions of friend and foe to the eventual marriage between Qiao Guangpu and Tong Zhen in the text show, Jiang Zilong assumed he could not let his hero have a Soviet affair with-

38. Cf. p. 216.
39. J, p. 8; W, p. 138; L, p. 62.

out endangering his status as a modernizer. The new class at the time was not now conscious enough of its having become a class to push its claims as far as the Soviet texts did.

Although it might seem somewhat far-fetched to have the ultra-modern hero Qiao be a devotee of the Peking opera, this provided Jiang with an elegant device to portray Qiao's perception of his own role. In the story, various operas are quoted verbatim by Qiao, and he identifies himself with the characters he is quoting and sees his situation as similar to theirs. When Qiao is attacked during the Cultural Revolution and stands on the platform, he does not listen to the charges but sings arias to himself. "From the tower of the city wall, I listen to the noise beyond."[40] The line is from *Kongcheng ji* (The ruse of the empty city)[41] and is there sung by the famous strategist Zhuge Liang. Zhuge Liang is outnumbered five to one by his opponent Sima Yi. To prevent his defeat, Zhuge Liang resorts to a ruse. He has the city evacuated by his best troops, opens the doors, and has a drinking party on the tower of the city wall when Sima Yi arrives with his army. Zhuge Liang takes his lute and invites Sima Yi with a song to enter the city, promising that it is no trick. In this song, the quoted verse is the opening line. As Zhuge Liang is known as a wily strategist, Sima Yi beats a hasty retreat fearing a trap. But the retreat goes through a narrow path, where Zhuge Liang has laid an ambush, and Sima Yi's troops are abysmally defeated. Qiao Guangpu sings the line while he is on stage for public criticism. He is as helpless vis-à-vis his opponents as is Zhuge Liang. But Zhuge Liang's plot will fail if he does not convey to Sima Yi his utmost nonchalance. And Zhuge Liang can have this self-assurance because he knows that, if he succeeds in not knuckling under, his enemies will soon be cut to pieces in an ambush. Qiao is thus depicting himself in the figure of Zhuge Liang; the masses are on his opponents' side, but the strategic genius and long-term victory are his, Zhuge Liang's, and he draws the stamina to survive the present plight from this reassurance.

It is surprising that this quotation depicts the Cultural Revolution as a simple battle for power without much right or wrong. Xi Wangbei

---

40. J, p. 6; W, p. 134; L, p. 58.

41. *Kongcheng ji* (The ruse of the empty city; Shanghai: Shanghai Wenhua Chubanshe, 1956), p. 14.

makes this point within the story, equating the purge of the old guard during the Cultural Revolution with the purge under way after 1976 of the *bangsi ren*, of those (suspected of being) associated with the "Gang of Four."[42] Jiang defused this point in changing the line in an edition made a year later, in 1980. There, Qiao sings: "For the hills and rivers of my country, I drove the battle-proven horse to its exhaustion," a key line from *Jingde Feigns Illness*, (*Jingde zhuangfeng*), another opera.[43] Wei Jingde was a man with great merits in the Tang dynasty establishment. When his friend Xue Rengui is later attacked by prince Li Daozong, Wei Jingde opposes Li, whereupon he is dismissed from office and made a commoner. Later, the Liao attack the Tang, and Xue Rengui is asked to organize the defense. Being no specialist in military matters, he feels he is no match for the fierce enemy warriors. Upon his request, the Court then decides to put Wei Jingde in command; upon hearing of this plan, Wei feigns illness. But the emissary is his friend Xue Rengui himself; Wei Jingde is soon overcome by patriotic feeling and accepts. With the words quoted above he hurries to serve his country again, although he has been so shamefully wronged.

By identifying himself with Wei Jingde, Qiao anticipates a situation where the fatherland will end in a crisis due to the policies pursued by his present detractors. Singing the line, he holds himself ready to serve the country again, regardless of his present duress. Qiao thus changes from a wily strategist, a Zhuge Liang, into a fervent patriot overcoming all his misgivings in the interest of the fatherland. This change considerably heightens his moral pitch. Another quotation from a Peking opera, contained in both versions, emphasizes another quality of Qiao's—his fearless righteousness. In the very last line of the story, he sings, after having been confronted with anonymous letters criticizing him: "Bao Longtu sat in judgment in Kaifengfu."

This line is taken from the opera *Qin Xianglian* attended by him in the story, commonly translated as *The Forsaken Wife*.[44] Qin Xianglian's

---

42. J p. 19; W p. 163; L pp. 76f.

43. I have not located the exact edition from which this quotation is taken, but the context is clear. *Jingde zhuang feng* (Jingde feigns illness) in *Jingju da guan* (Beijing: Beijing Baowentang Shudian, 1954), Vol. VIII.

44. Again the line does not exactly occur in the editions at my disposal, but again the con-

husband goes for the examinations to the capital, finishes first and, without informing his wife who, by her labor, has made his studies possible, accepts the emperor's offer to marry his majesty's daughter. When, after three years, Qin Xianglian seeks him out, he refuses to recognize her, eventually sending a hireling to kill her and their two children. Qin Xianglian manages to appeal to Judge Bao, the celebrated figure whose unmitigated (and as a result quite brutal) righteousness has made him the hero of many tales and operas. Bao is on his way to be chief judge in the Song dynasty capital, Kaifeng, when confronted with the case. The pressures of the emperor's daughter and of the empress herself notwithstanding, he opens court on the spot and has the unfaithful husband beheaded. The opening of the court in this instance is the supreme act of defiance towards illegitimate pressures to bend the law for the mighty. Assuming Bao's role, Qiao poses as the champion of righteousness and virtue in defiance of those in power bent on twisting the law to their own purposes. The outlandish manager is thus the true heir to the best that Chinese tradition has to offer—uprightness and patriotism—and these always go with iron fists. The identification with these heroes gives Qiao the stamina to sustain the tribulations of the Cultural Revolution and those of his rise to power. The vital role of his link with Chinese cultural traditions for his spiritual survival is emphasized through the confrontation with his Party secretary, who is neither in love nor a devotee of the opera, and thus succumbs.

It is a common strategy in Chinese novels and short stories to delineate the typicality of a character. If no quantitative or qualitative delineation appears, it is to be assumed that the character stands for his class. Qiao Guangpu is not a common social type or the typical representative of a social class. He is a rarity, and Xi Wangbei spells this out: "Qiao is a good manager, and presently we have not many like him in the country. . . . His style of work was no exception among managers before 1958, but today it is a rare treasure."[45] Within the story there are only two persons of his kind; first, Huo Dadao, "Big-Knife" Huo with

---

text is unambiguous. *Qin Xianglian* (Qin Xianglian; Shanghai: Wenhua Shenguo Chubanshe, 1954), p. 93.

45. J, p. 25; W, p. 174; L, p. 83.

eyes "like needles" "piercing into men's hearts," who says bluntly, "When I am on stage, I play the lead, and each one has to do what I say," which is the very attitude of Qiao himself. Huo understands and supports Qiao,[46] with whom he shares the key physiognomical traits in the illustration accompanying the story. The similarity between the two men is so strong that one commentator felt they lacked individuality.[47]

The physiognomy of the new manager. To the left Huo and Qiao, nearly identical, to the right, suave, lax, and smoking Xu Jinting, the leader who is "slow and stopped progressing."[48]

Beyond the two, and still further up, is the Minister who appreciates Qiao's "big surgery" and probably is of the same type. The protagonists of the managerial revolution are at the very top of their respective levels, and they recognize each other. Their revolution starts from the top. Their first assistants are bad eggs. On a political level, Jiang Zilong dealt in this set-up with the structure of Deng Xiaoping's takeover. The new leaders are exceptions, but, being exceptions, they all deviate from the common men in the same direction, and form the exceptionally qualified leadership.

Qiao Guangpu as the hero is supposed to provide a behavioral model

46. One enthusiastic critic stated that, within the story, only Huo could understand Qiao. Huang Guiyuan, "Zhuo you chengxiao de tansuo, du duanpian xiaoshuo 'Qiao changzhang shangren ji'" (A search yielding quite some results. Reading the short story "Director Qiao Takes Over"), *Tianjin ribao*, 25 August 1979.

47. Cf. Teng Yun, "Yuan you gengduo de Qiao changzhang shangren" (If there only were more Director Qiaos to take over), *Gongren ribao*, 10 September 1979.

48. J, p. 4. The illustrations are not reprinted in the translations.

for the growing managerial elite. Within the story this is exactly what happens. Xi Wangbei says after eulogizing Qiao: "Don't you see that a lot of the cadres in our factory copy something from him and imitate his iron fist and even the way he talks." Commentators have stressed this point, saying that this form of behavior was certainly not common in China, but that the "realism" of the story lay in the fact that the people aspired and hoped to have such leaders.[49]

Thus Jiang created a rare character, recommending that his readers obey those like him and imitate him, thereby maintaining the educational functions of literature, which served him in good stead with the nominating committee for the short-story awards. However, the strength of the strong is sympathetic only if it fails him in crisis and has to be replaced by will power, showing his strength to be the utmost exertion of a human being, and not the easy power of a superman. Thus a long tradition has evolved since Fadejev showed, in *The Rout*, the leader Levinson turning away in the moment of crisis and desperation to both shed and hide his tears. After returning from his defeat in the area of the factory's "foreign relations," after seen his "enemy" Ji Shen triumphantly strut about in the opera house, and after being informed of various attempts to topple him, Qiao leaves *The Forsaken Wife* prematurely. "Tong Zhen followed her husband's departure with feeling; his bearing had not changed, his step was firm and forceful. She knew that he often hid his pain and weakness; alone and quietly he would go about curing them, even in front of her he would not reveal that he was depressed and helpless. Some men's strength is forced on them by their self-respect, but on Qiao it was forced by the load on his shoulders."[50]

Iconographically speaking, the image of the manager is indebted not to the Western idea of a manager as the leader of a management team with a highly diversified command and responsibility structure, but to the military commander and his ways. The language of human relations,

---

49. This is said by commentators praising the story. Cf. Liu Xicheng, "Qiao Guangpu shi yige dianxing" (Qiao Guangpu is a model), *Wenyibao* 11/12:86 (December 1979). Liu also indicates that Jiang describes his ideal state, his utopia, ibid. p. 89. Teng Yun, "If There Only Were More" (note 47 above) says that Qiao is what people wish to have as manager, not what they in fact have. Huang Guiyuan, "A Search" (note 46 above) also points to the rarity of persons like Qiao.

50. A. Fadejev, *Die Neunzehn* tr. A. Boettcher (Frankfurt: Röderberg Verlag, 1977), p. 173.

accordingly, has nothing of the easy informality presumably dominating in team work, but is military, with its bombs, knives, and guns.

THE PARTY SECRETARY, WHO HAS "LOST (ALL) DARING." Qiao occupies the center of the stage throughout; the other protagonists are defined in their relationship to him and his project. Shi Gan represents the good elements in the Party. A "witty and knowledgeable agitator" before the Cultural Revolution, he has now lost all acumen after a long ordeal during that time. His face is marked by deep wrinkles like "a peach stone"; he calls himself "a cripple" whose "thinking has been crippled" and who "is completely worn out."[51] This is epitomized by his bitten-off tongue. Shi has an oscillating name; its original meaning is Stone-hard Daring, Shi Gan, but meanwhile the *shi* for stone-hard has changed into the *shi* meaning "to lose"; thus he is now one who has Lost (All) Daring, but his name still carries the promise contained in the original writing, and in the end his old self reappears. Within the text he keeps to his assigned role of politically mediating Qiao's "big surgery." Qiao is the specialist for the organization of production; Shi Gan does not seem to have any technical or administrative know-how. He is the specialist for politics. He finds out about the mental state of the workers, he discovers the secret plottings of Ji Shen with his emergency meeting of the Party Committee, he mediates between Qiao and the Party authorities; and through his hands anonymous letters are filtered before they reach Qiao.

The notion of politics within the story has radically changed from earlier descriptions. Shi has nothing to do with "the masses"; he does not give stirring speeches and leads no mass campaigns. He never quotes the "classics" and does not remind Qiao of some "principles." He simply is an honest man with a nose for politics and a sense for the feasible. Jiang Zilong probably reacts with his figure to the new concept of *shehui gongcheng* (social technology), heatedly discussed in the papers since late 1978.[52] Within this concept, state affairs are to be run by "specialists"

51. J, p. 24; W, p. 174; L, p. 83.
52. The first article on this topic seems to be "Zuzhi guanli de jishu—xitong gongcheng" (The technique of organization management—systems engineering), *Wenhuibao*, 27 September 1978; in the first issue of the periodical *Jingji guanli* (Economic management), the very first article was Qian Xuesen and Wu Jiapei, "Zuzhi guanli shehuizhuyi de jishu—shehui de gong-

for management, technology, finance, propaganda, politics, education, and so on. None of them rely on beliefs, but their authority rests on their mastering the "objective" and therefore unpolitical "laws" of their respective realms. Shi Gan's modest authority thus rests on his, as he calls them, "utterly abominable political feelers," and on Qiao Guangpu's hope that he "can convince the masses to subordinate themselves" to the new manager. Shi's energies are entirely infused into him by Qiao. In the story, the Party draws its energy, hope, and renewed prestige from the new technocrat managers and their performance in power.

THE WOMAN ENGINEER "BITTER DEVOTION." Within the coalition led by Qiao Guangpu we next have Tong Zhen. She is presented in the role of a highly qualified Soviet-trained woman engineer. Jiang Zilong was not too successful in handling this combination, equipping her with two full sets of sensory faculties (an "engineer's heart" and a "woman's heart"), but the intentions are clear.

Tong Zhen is the only engineer in the piece and stands for the technical intelligentsia of the country. Although still "in her best years," she is afflicted with "that disease rampant today—political decrepitude." She does not want to go back into the factory with Qiao, having suffered there from much calumny; she does not dare to state her opinions openly ("I have made it a rule not to meddle with things that don't concern me") and is generally "intimidated." This contrasts with her buoyant spirit in the 1950s when she wanted to design "giant generators. . . . and even the first Chinese nuclear power plant with a capacity of one million kw.," as Qiao reminds her.

Revived by Qiao, like Shi Gan, she reimposes rigid technical standards on the production of the plant. Tong Zhen is instantly promoted to become a member of the Permanent Committee of the factory's Party Committee, and thus, together with Shi Gan and Qiao Guangpu,

---

cheng" (The technology of managing socialist construction—social engineering), *Jingji guanli* 1:5ff (15 January 1979). Qian Xuesen in 1980 summarized the ongoing discussions on social engineering with a radical proposal, "Cong she hui kexue dao shehui jishu" (From social science to social technology), *Wenhuibao*, 29 September 1980. I am indebted to Dr. David Kelly (Canberra) for drawing my attention to this discussion and for pointing out the last-named references.

has joined the highest governing body of the factory. This reflects the reorganization of factory management promoted by a CCP decision "On some questions concerning the acceleration of industrial development (draft)" dated July 1978, incidentally the date when Qiao takes over in the factory. According to this draft, "The factory director takes charge of production and administration under the unified leadership of the Party Committee" and there will be a "system of responsibility for the chief engineer, the chief accountant."[53] The eventual setup described by Jiang Zilong for this plant, but officially proclaimed only later, is described by two economists for the year 1980: "The system of responsibility with the factory director responsible for the entire enterprise at the core was strengthened [in 1980]. The factory director was now to take full charge of organizing and directing the production of the enterprise; the general engineer was to take charge of the technical work of production; and the general accountant was to take charge of financial work."[54] Tong Zhen's career thus fits nicely into the official policies mapped out by the new leadership, which used the new management set-up to get its own forces into the leading positions at factory levels. The technical intelligentsia are brought back into the leadership after many hard years, and are restored from political senility and decrepitude by the new manager.

Tong Zhen directly descends from a similar character in Dvoreckij's play (where she is the financial analyst). In her life as a woman she is reduced to being in love with Qiao Guangpu. Her name *tong* (child) for *tong* (pain or sadness) and *zhen* (faithful devotion) expresses her attitude towards and her experience with Qiao. She has loved the manager since the 1950s, attempts suicide during the Cultural Revolution when he is persecuted, is now revived in her feelings for him, and marries him. She

53. The draft resolution "On Some Questions Concerning the Acceleration of Industrial Development (draft)" is quoted in full in Xue Muqiao, ed., *Almanac of China's Economy 1981* (Hong Kong: Modern Cultural Company, 1982), pp. 178f.

54. Wang Haibo, Wu Jiajun, "China's Industry in 1980," in Xue Muqiao, *Almanac of China's Economy*, p. 451. On one occasion, Jiang Zilong's story in turn served as the main source for problems of industrial management in China in 1979; cf. Andrew Walder, "Industrial Reform in China: The Human Dimension," in East Asia Program, The Wilson Center, Conference Report, *The Limits of Reform in China*, 3 May 1982 (Washington DC.: The Wilson Center, 1982).

does not marry the Party secretary. Marriage is one of the convenient symbols used in the tradition of the political novel, indicating close and permanent alliance between the groups or classes represented by the protagonists. The easiest example is in Disraeli's *Coningsby*, where the young descendant of the landed gentry, Coningsby, marries Miss Millbanks, whose name indicates the two sources of wealth of the new industrial barons from Manchester—mills and banks—both the property of her father. The coalition is presided over by the elderly and wise Jew, Sidonia, a fanciful image of young Disraeli himself, who set up his program for Young England with this novel.[55] Tong Zhen's feelings and hopes lie with the managerial hero, not with the Party; she marries Manger Qiao as an engineer, indicating the alliance of two segments of the technocratic elite to emerge with the Four Modernizations program. Originally, industrial management was tied to Party propaganda. The latter died a mysterious death in Qiao's wife, making room for the new alignment. But Tong is also a woman, innocent, devoted, sad, and helpless in the context of the story; Jiang Zilong seems to play on the traditional image of the "nation" as the young, pure, and helpless female, looking to the (male) hero for salvation from the hands of the villains, a literary convention I have tried to describe elsewhere.[56]

Qiao has not only to be obeyed and admired; he can even be loved. We shall mention only in passing Li Gan whose name is a pun meaning Mr. Energetic-Getting-Things-Done. He is in charge of financial matters and loyal to Qiao Guangpu. At the time when the story was published, the financial latitude allowed factories was still small, and Jiang Zilong did not envisage much development. In the sequel to the Director Qiao story, which appeared in *Renmin wenxue* in February 1980, Li Gan's role is more prominent. He owes his literary existence to the July 1978 decision, which mentions the general accountant.

THE "GENERATION OF HOPE." The most interesting and controversial character in Qiao Guangpu's alliance is Tong Zhen's nephew, Xi Wangbei. Having grown up in the house of Tong Zhen's parents, he is "one

---

55. B. Disraeli, *Coningsby, or the New Generation* (Oxford: Oxford University Press, 1982).

56. See "women, symbolic use of" in the index to my *The Contemporary Chinese Historical Drama, Four Studies* (Berkeley: University of California Press, 1990).

of the family" and thus predestined for the new leadership. He became a "rebel chieftain" during the Cultural Revolution. This feature brings in the fact that a substantial portion of the Cultural Revolution rebels came from the families of the political class. They have, in the view of today's values, gravely erred, but this does not prevent their being part of the elite and from hopefully aspiring to top jobs under the new dispensation.

Xi Wangbei's motive in attacking Qiao Guangpu is not the latter's management style and emphasis on boosting production, but the defense of Tong Zhen, Xi Wangbei's aunt. This curious motive cries for analysis because Xi Wangbei's character is not described as imbued with traditional moral norms. When Tong Zhen refuses other suitors, Xi Wangbei is "firmly convinced that Qiao Guangpu has a knack with women, even to the same degree as with production."[57] There is no question that Xi Wangbei acknowledges Qiao Guangpu's capacities with regard to production, but the brutality of imposing one's will in industrial production is, according to Xi Wangbei, inappropriate for handling China's human dimension; Qiao Guangpu, Xi feels, "has ruined his aunt's whole life." Later when he has become a part of the new management group set up by Qiao, he still lectures him on this point: "Even the foreign capitalists have understood how complex human relations are and how difficult to handle; and, since their industries have reached a certain level of development, they automate and use robots. The most important advantage of robots is that they have no flesh and blood, no feelings, but only iron rules and laws."[58] It seems that Jiang Zilong is making a fairly complex and sophisticated argument. The criticism leveled by the young rebels against the Qiao Guangpus during the Cultural Revolution was directed at their reckless handling of China's human dimension, which might end up in utter destruction. Qiao Guangpu is badly adapted to the Chinese environment. This is epitomized by his admiration for the young German worker, who has notions of time and number engraved on his habits and expects the fair price of freedom in his personal life as a reward for efficiency in his work life. But he shares with Qiao Guangpu an essential foreignness to the Chinese environment.

---

57. J, p. 9; W, pp. 140f; L, p. 62.
58. J, p. 24; W, pp. 173; L, p. 82.

Qiao Guangpu knows nothing of the importance of *guanxixue,* the art of making social connections. Jiang Zilong is realistic enough not to simply denounce *guanxixue* as an unhealthy phenomenon and leave it at that. The modernization effort has to be made on Chinese soil, Qiao Guangpu has to run his plant successfully in China, and this effort has to be adapted to the realities of the country. Shi Gan protects Qiao Guangpu against possible ill winds from the Party and the "masses" of workers. But Xi Wangbei has learned the lesson that Qiao Guangpu does not have to be overthrown, but that his efforts have to be adapted to Chinese human realities, and that it is his, the former rebel chieftain's duty, to achieve this adaptation. It is not enough to be a fanatic for time and numbers like Qiao Guangpu.

Xi Wangbei displays a slightly cynical intimacy with the political and economic realities of China. Knowing of Qiao's outlandish ways, he takes it upon himself to negotiate the conflict between Qiao and China by taking over the "foreign relations" of the enterprise with peer and lower-level units, trying to transform Qiao's potentially destructive (and self-destructive) energy into motive power. The story here inverts the order of Wang Meng's "Newcomer"; there, the older generation (through Liu Shiwu) brings the young Soviet-oriented idealists back to Chinese realities. Here, the former youngsters have grown into older die-hard figures like Qiao, and are integrated into the Chinese environment by the technically and politically experienced "old Red Guards" like Xi Wangbei. Within the story, Xi Wangbei unites in his person the qualities of both Qiao Guangpu and Shi Gan, and represents the next generation of technical-managerial reformers.

Jiang Zilong had presented similar characters in 1975 with Miss Ginger in "A Day in the Life," and in 1981 in the two young protagonists, Xie Jing and Liu Sijia, in "All the Colors of the Rainbow."[59] All are "new cadres" who started their careers during the Cultural Revolution. Jiang Zilong belonged to this generation, and through them pleaded the case of his cohort; in them he invested the best mixture of qualities.

59. Jiang Zilong, "Chi cheng huang lü qing lan zi," (All the colors of the rainbow), in *Jiang Zilong zhongpian xiaoshuo ji* (Middle-length stories by Jiang Zilong; Changsha: Hunan Renmin Chubanshe, 1982), pp. 1ff.

In the Chinese context of 1979 this role of Xi Wangbei was seen by many as outrageous. The very document of July 1978 that initiated the management reform and paved the way for Qiao Guangpu's takeover, said: "It is imperative [in the shake-up of the enterprises] to take the struggle to expose and criticize the Gang of Four as the key link."[60] True to this passage, Ji Shen dismisses Xi Wangbei from his post on the very eve of Qiao's takeover. But not only is this described as being but a political ploy to make things difficult for his successor, Jiang Zilong goes to great lengths to give Xi Wangbei a positive stature. Xi Wangbei has worked his way up from below, has no share in criminal acts, nor personal links with the Gang of Four. True, he has criticized Qiao Guangpu as a capitalist roader, but his motives, the protection of Tong's "virgin purity" (*zhen*) against the outlandish brutal onslaught of this expert in production and among women, are honorable. As family links (next to marriage and friendship) are the traditional symbolic device to describe alliance, Xi Wangbei actually belongs to the "family" of the new leading class.

Most stunning, however, is his name, Xi Wangbei, a pun on *xiwang bei*, "generation of hope"; an enraged critic assisted this identification by writing the name out with its real characters.[61] Jiang bluntly rejected the common name given in 1979 to the generation of youths who had grown up during the Cultural Revolution, that is, "lost generation." The "old Red Guards," who have acquired technical and managerial skills, and have a sober and knowledgeable view of the realities within and against which the modernization drive has to operate, became the "generation of hope," combining the skills separated in the older generation in the persons of Qiao and Shi. Still in his early thirties, Xi Wangbei is made an assistant manager in charge of relations with other factories, and in the sequel he takes over the leadership of the factory's production. Theirs is the future.

---

60. Cf. note 53.

61. Zhao Ke, "On the Story" (note 19 above), col. 4. Xi's name in the story is *xi wang bei*. The characters mean "*xi* (a surname) looking north." Zhao refers to this as *zhiyou ta cai shi xiwangde yibei*, "he alone is the generation of hope," indicating a reading for the name with identical phonetic writing but different Chinese characters, namely *xiwang bei*, "generation of hope."

THE FOE WHO "CARES ONLY FOR HIMSELF" Qiao's top "foe" is Ji Shen.[62] As critics were quick to point out, his name is a pun on *ji shen,*"caring only for himself."[63] Ji has had some problems during the Cultural Revolution but managed to use this time to build up a close network of connections with high-ranking cadres who were at the time sent down to cadre schools. They are now back in office and in a position to repay his services. He rises to the leadership of the factory in 1976. This is quite a surprise, since the story takes a positive attitude towards the "rebel chief," Xi Wangbei, but harshly attacks the transition cadre, Ji Shen, who obviously came to power sometime in early 1976. Ji has no experience in economic management, but calculates that some years as a manager will stand him in good stead once the focus shifts to economic construction. However, his main skill is that of a cunning politician. "He was great at solving riddles; between the lines of the papers and circulars he was able to read quite different meanings ... He decided where to put the emphasis in his work in accordance with his assessment of the time and the power relations ... This had to impede his work, and, when he met with a difficult problem, he reacted with dissimulation and by uttering empty phrases."[64] Dissimulation is the prominent feature of his physiognomy: "His bony haggard face showed exceeding friendliness, but, like a map of a complicated territory, it showed ten thousand dislocations so that it was difficult to find one's way through it ... His bearing had routine, he was relaxed and calm ... He got along well with people."

In 1978, the Center under Hua Guofeng tried to push for another Great Leap Forward on the basis of a renewed mass movement. The management reforms of that year defined the "class struggle" against the

62. Commentators who justly sensed an attack against Hua Guofeng through the character of Ji Shen were quick to point out that Ji Shen was only following the Central Committee's directives when dismissing Xi. Cf. Zhao Ke, "On the Story" (note 19); Song Naiqian, "Qiao changzhang neng lingdao gong ren shixian sihua ma?" (Is Director Qiao capable of leading the workers to achieve the Four Modernizations?), *Tianjin ribao,* 19 September 1979; Liu Zhiwu, "Wenxue yingshi shenghuo, shidai de yimian jingzi" (Literature must be a mirror of life and times), *Tianjin ribao,* 5 October 1979.

63. The pun with Ji Shen's name is revealed by a commentator praising the story, who reads the Ji Shen as *ji shen.* Zhou Jintian, "Ji Shen de chuxian shuomingle sheme?" (What does Ji Shen's appearance signify?), *Tianjin ribao,* 5 October 1979.

64. J, p. 14; W, p. 152; L, p. 70.

"Gang of Four" as the "key" link—not time and quantities of production. Both policies were personally initiated and supported by Hua Guofeng, who indeed had come to power in early 1976, and had been censured during the early phase of the Cultural Revolution. Ji Shen, the transition cadre, thus replicates Hua Guofeng on the lower level in the same manner in which Qiao Guangpu replicates Deng Xiaoping. Like Qiao Guangpu who is linked to a chain of similar characters in the higher levels of the hierarchy, Ji Shen is part of a network of mutual help and protection. In his case, this network is not promoting the modernization of the country but the personal advancement of its own members. In the city's bureau, Ji Shen can rely on Xu Jinting, Mr. Slow-Who-Has-Stopped-Progressing, whose conversion in "One Day" does not seem to have lasted. Beyond Xu Jinting is the City Party Committee, which legalizes Ji Shen's rapid upward flight out of the plant into high office, and above this Committee is the bureau in the Ministry that is in favor of increasing foreign imports instead of supporting the development of China's own potential, another reference to Hua Guofeng's gigantic import plans for 1978. On lower levels, Ji Shen finds support in the young lathe worker, Du Bing, and his colleagues in the "service brigade," where the unqualified and unfit congregate, among them a number of cadres who were criticized and demoted during the Cultural Revolution, and indeed lack any qualification. As Ji Shen is the kingpin of this alliance, his reckless egotism becomes their common hallmark. Bureaucratism is rampant in this network and forms the main obstacle to modernization in the story.

Jiang Zilong clung to a conservative Marxist notion of bureaucratism. Most other texts in 1979 focused on corruption, back-door deals, and tyrannical behavior as the most repulsive aspects of the Chinese bureaucrat, and hardly ever on his incapacity to handle his duties efficiently. Jiang Zilong's Ji Shen is slick, but not corrupt; he wants personal bureaucratic leverage, not private petty gains. In this line of criticizing bureaucratism, Jiang Zilong harked back to the Soviet texts, and their early Chinese adaptations during the Hundred Flowers, when Wang Meng's and Liu Binyan's bureaucrats looked like Ji Shen.

THE "CRITICALLY ILL" WORKING CLASS. One single worker is introduced into the text as an individual with a name and a character, Du Bing. There is nothing in the text marking him as an exceptional case, so he has to bear the burden of typicality. The reader is not left to speculate about this. Tong Zhen warns Qiao Guangpu that Du Bing is certainly not the "worst worker in the factory." Shi Gan volunteers the generalization that Du Bing's state of mind stands for the entire proletarian crew at the time: "The workers in the factory were ideologically confused. Most of them had lost all faith after having lost the idol they had worshiped before [Mao Zedong]; even national pride and pride in socialism had ceased to exist. Was there something worse than people who ideologically were but loose sand? During these years [of the Cultural Revolution], the workers had been fooled, stultified and berated, and they had all degenerated both physically and mentally."[65] Even the "twelve sharp knives," model workers originally trained by Qiao Guangpu before the Cultural Revolution, degenerated and retreated to comfortable sinecures. The summary of this sad state of proletarian affairs is Du Bing's name, a pun on the inverse *bing du* "critically or terminally ill." He works "sloppily," producing nothing but rejects, and sings a popular slushy tune from Hong Kong "Aiya Mama, please don't get angry at me, young people just don't see any light." The illustration gives him the features of the *chou* (ridiculous figure) in the Peking opera.

As mentioned earlier, the manager novel operates on the principle of inverting its opposite, the worker novel. There, the proletarians are glorified, and the managers are afflicted with the deadly disease of bourgeois thought. Thus, to be saved, the managers have to submit to proletarian reeducation. Here, things are the other way round; the workers have degenerated, and need managerial reeducation to be saved. Both sides give no quarter to their opposites. Du Bing will be saved in the sequel of the story where Qiao discovers his talents as an artist (of a cartoon of Qiao himself), and transfers him to the design and advertisement office, where he does great work.

Du Bing actively opposed Qiao Guangpu. He hangs up big-character posters, and threatens to go on a hunger strike, linking up with other

65. J, p. 13; W, pp. 149f.; L, pp. 69f.

The "critically ill" working class (left) confronting the technical-managerial alliance.[66]

malcontents in the city. The year 1979 saw many demonstrations and hunger strikes, as well as a flood of big-character posters from people who felt they had been unjustly treated. These democratic rumors don't find favor with Jiang Zilong, who summarily dismisses them as complaints of people like Du Bing. "Scum. Bad eggs," says Qiao.

THE BALD "OLD CADRES." Du Bing is incited in his opposition to Qiao Guangpu by Baldy Wang, who in turn claims Ji Shen's support. Wang is an "old cadre" who had been removed from his post during the Cultural Revolution. When Jiang Zilong wrote the story, the leadership

66. J, p. 12.

defined the Cultural Revolution as a "social fascist dictatorship" exercised by the "Gang of Four" and decided to have the cadres who had been dismissed reinstated. When Baldy Wang and his friends come to claim their reinstatement, Qiao Guangpu bluntly refuses. They will have to prove their skills in an examination. There, they mostly fail. This somewhat explosive detail contains the silent argument that most of the "old cadres" were dismissed with good reason during the preceding years, since they lacked qualification. The Cultural Revolution has thus done away with bureaucratic debris, and even fostered the new manager crowd, the "generation of hope." Jiang Zilong was careful to avoid the impression that it was his purpose to reevaluate the Cultural Revolution. Xi Wangbei is not preferred *because* he was a rebel leader, but *although* he was one; the old cadres are not rejected because they were criticized during the Cultural Revolution but because they are professionally unqualified. For Qiao Guangpu, the measuring rod is the examination, not the past.

The cast consists of two sets of protagonists grouped around Qiao and Ji Shen respectively. The first contains all the positive characters, the second all the negative ones. The story describes the takeover of power by the positives from the negatives. From the details given for the lead roles it is clear that the story deals, on another level, with the battle against the transition cadres around Hua Guofeng, who made their careers between the end of the Cultural Revolution and the advent to power of Deng Xiaoping and his group.

THE PLOT

The plot describes the formation of the alliance around Qiao Guangpu, his takeover of power, and the continuing problems thereafter. His relationships with his own group deserve close scrutiny. The July 1978 draft resolution had put the new manager under the "unified leadership of the Party Committee." In the story, however, it is Qiao who "demands" that Shi Gan should become his Party secretary, and, anticipating approval, has already sent for him. Without consultation, Qiao decides on transfers of leading personnel, sets up the examinations, and forms a "service brigade" of "superfluous" people. His discretionary powers are those commonly associated with one-man leadership. Indeed, since early 1979 articles had appeared extolling one-man leadership of factories as having been developed "by Lenin," and unjustly slighted by the "Gang of Four."[67] Jiang Zilong went to some lengths in describing how necessary a benevolent dictatorship of Qiao's kind is for a "Party" which has "lost its daring" and is "physically and mentally crippled." Evidently, Qiao Guangpu is not "under the guidance of the Party" but is, instead, cajoling that decrepit body back into life. After his takeover, no further meetings of the Party in the factory are reported, and they are not needed. Qiao Guangpu is "friends" with Shi Gan, but "marries" Tong; the alliance with the technical specialists is closer. She, too, has to be dragged back into life by Qiao, who is also the savior of the afflicted working class, subjecting all to his invigorating discipline. The "workers' congresses" proposed by Deng Xiaoping in 1978 to supervise management and discuss problems are treated with benign neglect in this and the later stories.[68] The Party, the engineers, and the workers have no claim to any say, given the state to which they have fallen.

The main conflict is with the "transition cadres" around Ji Shen. The

67. Cf. Wang Mengkui and Jia Chunfeng, "Responsibility System Is a Basic Management Principle," originally in *Guangming ribao*, 27 January 1979, here from the translation in *JPRS* 19 July 1979, p. 13. They refer to Lenin saying that "the basic management principle is one person assuming full responsibility for the whole management" and that, in factories, "particular attention must be paid to uniting responsibility with power." An article in *Jingji guanli* in December 1979 by Wu Jiajun refers to Engels's statements on one-man leadership, the advantages this had brought the Soviet Union in "promoting the rapid maturing of specialists proficient in technology and business," but still refrains from openly advocating the introduction of this system. Cf. *JPRS* China Report, Econ. Affairs no. 46, 28 February 1980. In August 1979, Xue Muqiao himself advocated one-man leadership under the direction of the Party committee in "Jingji guanli tizhi gaige wenti" (Problems of the reform of the system of economic management), *Hongqi* 8 (1979), pp. 16ff, *JPRS* 74294, 2 October 1979, pp. 34f. Liu Xicheng, "Qiao Guangpu is a Model," (note 49 above) p. 89, explicitly makes the point that Qiao represents the one-man leadership system advocated by Lenin. The examinations for the personnel already installed in the factory had also been envisioned by the Draft Resolution which said: "Leading cadres at all levels in the enterprises and technical and professional personnel shall be examined and assessed once every year. The good ones shall be recommended and the bad ones criticized. Those who neglect their duties or are incompetent shall be removed or readjusted" (note 53 above), p. 178.

68. Deng Xiaoping, speech at the 9th National Congress of the All China Federation of Trade Unions, cited in Stephan Feuchtwang, Athar Hussein, eds., *The Chinese Economic Reforms* (New York: St. Martin's Press, 1983), p. 233. First attempts with such a system came only in the second half of 1980.

mutterings of unqualified old cadres, the big-character posters and rallies, the cynical attitude of young workers, the extreme reliance on technology imports of products that could for the most part be produced in
China and, if not, are too complicated for the Chinese work force to
handle, the political maneuvering of Party generalists trying to keep
their posts, the numerous grey-market deals accompanying the exchange
of goods within the planned economy, the irregular transfers of cadres
to other units while their salary had to be underwritten by their old
units, the underutilization of labor power—in short every economic,
political, and social ill discussed in 1979 is caused by Ji Shen and his ilk,
and, if it has not disappeared after his replacement, this is because he
still has functions, power, and links and goes on to sabotage production
where he can.

The story is open-ended. Ji Shen transfers, but is not dismissed. The
factory has fulfilled its quota, and Qiao Guangpu is committed to persevere, now with the active support of his wife, the engineer, the Party
man who has again "stone-hard daring," the generation of hope, and
even the workers. The focus of the text is on "taking command" and
only dimly the perspective of a truly modern and productive enterprise
comes into sight.

Jiang Zilong took care to delineate the degree of typicality of this success. Qiao Guangpu's plant is at the cutting edge of the modernization
drive; its generators are to produce the energy for industrial development. It is a big factory in a city [Tianjin] directly under the central government (no provincial authorities are mentioned) and it has links
directly to the top. The minister phones in person to transmit his congratulations to Qiao Guangpu. But just as Qiao Guangpu is an outlandish utopian character, so is the factory a utopian island, where people
submit to an examination and act on it, where discipline is restored by
infusion of "energy" and "enthusiasm," where the workers quickly "find
that Qiao's expressive eyes are full of experience," and where they have
already "become accustomed to obeying him; he just had to open his
mouth, and everything was instantly executed."

The technique of describing the pure form of one's political ideal in
some kind of "liberated island" is not new. It was used by the opposing
faction during the last phase of the Cultural Revolution. An example is

the film *Juelie* (Breaking with old ideas, 1975), which described one single pure "Maoist" university branch in Guangxi province, amidst a sea of "bourgeois" education, which is shown to the spectator during a trip of the school's director to China's big universities.[69] The "bourgeoisie" even has its agent in this school in the figure of the assistant director, while only the director has "the correct line." Jiang Zilong does not draw the line in terms of "bourgeois" and "proletarian" as does this film, but Qiao Guangpu's unsuccessful trip to the "brother factories" shows that Chinese industry as a whole is operating on principles quite different from those subscribed to by Qiao, and that mutual destruction will follow if no mutual adaptation is achieved.

Jiang thus shows an enclave of outlandish industrial modernism in China, protected by the highest leadership, but which stands out as an utopian ideal in the real waters of the Chinese economy, which—the times of class struggle being over—he describes as bureaucracy country but not as being under a class of foes. Within this idealized island there is benevolent dictatorship under Qiao's "iron fist" in the "essential and long-term interests of the people." Democracy is not an issue. The hopes of the text lie in Xi Wangbei, just over 30, who combines in his person the virtues of both Qiao and Shi Gan. They will spend their last strength in "taking control" and in the "big surgery" against the obstructions of Hua Guofeng and his smaller clones. The business of actually managing modern enterprises will be Xi Wangbei's.

Handling the Text

Given the reproduction of the conflict in the Center between Hua Guofeng and Deng Xiaoping at the factory level of the story, and the highly controversial handling of many issues in the text, a battle ensued about its standing. The stress of dealing with such a weighty topic is already felt in the text itself. Ji Shen only "seems" to be at the root of the problems, and Baldy Wang only "claims" to have his support. Ji Shen is not corrupt, and keeps to the written word of the regulations. The stress was stronger still in the discussions of the text in the papers. Supporters

69. Chun Chao, Zhou Jie, *Juelie* (Breaking with old ideas), *Renmin dianying* 1:60ff (January 1976).

praisingly restated the story in its surface aspects. They could not spell out its actual content because Hua Guofeng was, after all, chairman of the Party. Critics had to restrict themselves to non-controversial charges: Qiao Guangpu installs a Cultural Revolution rebel in a high position, runs the plant in a dictatorial manner, and denounces protests against his person as coming from "rotten eggs, scum," although the protesters are only taking their democratic rights seriously. And Jiang Zilong slandered Ji Shen, who in fact keeps to Party regulations.[70]

The stress was most severely felt by Jiang Zilong himself. One month after the story was published in *Renmin wenxue*, the union paper *Gongren ribao* published the story which had "now been revised again by the author."[71] At that time no published criticism had appeared, but the revisions were substantial, and literary only incidentally. A year later, the Youth Press published a collection of Jiang Zilong's stories.[72] The text printed there in substance returned to the *Renmin wenxue* text, and retained only the strictly stylistic changes of the *Gongren ribao* text. This enables us to identify and study the purely political changes. This rewriting offers a fine insight into the craft of a Chinese writer of highly politicized stories, and into the different levels of political sensibility associated with media of differing distribution patterns. *Renmin wenxue* mostly reaches members of the political class with higher educational levels. *Gongren ribao* is a mass-circulation newspaper addressed to workers at large.

First, in the revised edition, the status of the Party is substantially improved. All generalized critical remarks about Party cadres have been eliminated. Shi Gan is freed from his passive position: He has not bitten off "half" his tongue but only "a bit" and thus he now speaks understandably; he is no "child" anymore, nor a "cripple." Ji Shen now has only "some" friends among Party leaders, not "very many," and Qiao Guangpu politely asks the Party Committee to ratify his proposals, where in the earlier text he "demands" and makes decisions on his own. When Huo Dadao asks Qiao: "Do you have other demands?" Qiao

---

70. This point was not missed by the critics, who referred to Qiao's "dictatorial," "feudal" methods; cf. Zhao Ke, "On the Story" (note 19 above).

71. See note 35 above.

72. Jiang Zilong, *A Collection* (note 20 above).

answers in the original text: "Yes, I want to take Shi Gan along; he will go as the secretary of the Party Committee, I as the director of the factory." The new version reads: "I propose that I may go together with Shi Gan, he becoming Party secretary and I director; I would ask the Party Committee to deliberate and decide on this." The text was thus brought in line with the demand that the manager should be under the "unified leadership of the Party Committee." But the change is rather cosmetic; no change in plot occurs, and the Party Committee of the factory still fails to meet.

Second, Qiao Guangpu's explosive features are toned down. His physiognomy flattens: Gone are the "eyes of a hungry tiger" and the brows "rising steep like a cliff"; Qiao fails to gnash off a piece of his molar, and all the bombs he throws have disappeared. He has also abandoned wanting "to play the lead," but only "wants to storm forward." Qiao's "iron fist" is gently replaced by his "heart's blood." The reduction of Qiao's pitch matches the heightening of the stature of the people around him.

Third, the Chinese working class is enhanced. Young Mr. Tell from Siemens in Germany vanishes without trace as the model to be emulated by the Chinese workers. Qiao is much nicer to Du Bing, and instantly finds "serious assent" from the workers for his measures. The tough remarks about the sorry state of the working class have therefore become obsolete, the workers have neither physically nor mentally regressed, and the number of people relegated to the "service brigade" is dramatically reduced. Xi Wangbei stops volunteering the remark that Qiao would be at his best in cooperating with robots.

Fourth, the edges are taken off Xi Wangbei. He ceases to have been a "rebel leader." Instead of "He became the chieftain of a rebel organization that focused its attacks on Qiao Guangpu" we now read "He made up some calumnies about Qiao's work style," and the blame for the campaign against Qiao Guangpu is put on Xi Wangbei's associates, further toning down his "problem."

Fifth, Tong Zhen is purified and promoted. She now is more restrained in her love for Qiao. They have their photograph taken in a large group of 50 tourists and not as a pair. Tong does not attempt suicide, because things were never that desperate, and she actually gets ahead of Xi Wangbei by becoming assistant director in charge of production, the only plot change.

Ji Shen, however, remains "the foe," although some of the hardest phrases about him have disappeared such as "His temples with the thin blue veins and his eyes which attacked from an ambush, seemed to become the root and source of all problems in the factory."

Finally, the barriers between the factory-island and the surrounding Chinese economy have been lowered. Qiao does not return "defeated" from his excursion to the "brother factories" but he has not been "entirely victorious."

Three things can be gleaned from these changes.

First, Jiang Zilong was highly conscious of the political implications of each detail of his text. When changing, as an example, the relationship between the manager and the Party, he changed everything, including physiognomy, metaphor, and dialogue. The close political reading given to these details in my analysis would seem to be supported by Jiang Zilong's own handling of his text. The polemics around his story are a further illustration of the fact that this indeed was the reading technique applied to such matters by China's political class. (This does not in any way exclude the possibility that other Chinese readers were stalled at the surface meaning.)

Second, Jiang Zilong changed those elements that might have displeased critics supporting the thrust of his attack, for example, his own faction. This mostly refers to the role of the Party and to Xi Wangbei, both having been mentioned as "problems" in positive reviews of the story.[73] Thus the changes mainly purport to reduce friction within the camp; however, Jiang Zilong held his ground in substance with regard to his own generation by keeping Xi Wangbei in a positive role. That Jiang Zilong's revision mostly reacted to criticisms from within his camp would seem to be confirmed by the fact that the series of attacks against the story in *Tianjin ribao* appeared only a little more than a month after the *Gongren ribao* edition. As the *Renmin ribao* edition had gone substantially further, critics referred to this text only, and never mentioned the revision. In a way, they were right, because Jiang Zilong returned to his original text in 1980 when he could be sure of

---

73. These criticisms were indeed made in articles praising the story; cf. Teng Yun, "If There Were Only" (note 47 above). But the figure of Xi Wangbei also found acclaim here; cf. Jin Mei, "Xin shiqi de yingxiong xingxiang" (Heroic images of the new period), *Wenyibao* 9:22f (September 1979).

more active official support, especially from the then protectors of the "new" literature, Chen Huangmei and Feng Mu, both of whom came out personally to defend him.[74]

Third, and finally, Jiang Zilong, all revisions notwithstanding, retained the original thrust of the text and the political alignment proposed in the original version.

PEKING OPERA

The "model operas" promoted during the Cultural Revolution were not just to be the model for other local opera forms, but also for other media like the film and the *xiaoshuo*, the novel and the short story. Consequently much opera language entered the text, the heroes with striking gestures and performing as if on stage; their emotions were expressed in the stylized manner familiar in the opera, and they were made emphatic by appropriate environmental arrangement. In the other media, the weather mostly stood in for the music in the Peking opera. Jiang Zilong, who had written much during this period, also used this imagery.[75] The strong resonances of the Director Qiao story with the Peking opera thus indicate a continuity rather than a literary innovation. However, in the Director Qiao story the literary potential of the resonance between Peking opera and a socialist-realist manager story is explored much more systematically.

Qiao and Huo Dadao see their own work in terms of Peking opera role playing. Both insist on "playing the lead" and see the historical action in operatic terms. Huo encourages Qiao at the end of the story: "Modernization certainly is not only a technical question; one also has to step on some people's feet. It is always safest not to do a thing, but that is precisely the real crime. To all those misunderstandings, complaints, calumnies, insults, and jokes listen unperturbed. As long as I am on stage, I play the lead, and everyone has to do as I say. We need time, and we need numbers to achieve modernization, because there lies the

---

74. Huangmei (Chen Huangmei), "Dui shenghuo de renshi he tansuo" (An understanding and an investigation of life), *Wenyibao* 8 (August 1980).

75. Cf. W. Locks, "Jiang Zilong" (note 5), p. 19.

essential and long-term interest of the people. The curtain has just gone up; the beautiful opera is only about to begin."[76]

This is not only superficial metaphor but vital for maintaining the hero's stamina. Qiao interprets his own situation through comparable situations in operas. He comes out as the patriot (Jingde), strategist (Zhuge Liang, eliminated in the later version), and upright judge (Bao Longtu), and his opponents become identified with well-known villains, Chen Shimei and his imperial protectresses, as well as the Tang prince Li Daozong. The historical backdrop gives an aura of legitimacy to his actions—even the promise of eventual success and popularity. He does not choose heroes who are executed for their righteous action. The knowledge that he is part of this venerable tradition of upright heroes, and the firm belief that his opponents reenact the old villains' roles lets him survive the Cultural Revolution unscathed. "Only the weak think of revenge," he says. Shi Gan lacks this link with tradition, and goes under. The protagonists see themselves reenacting historical roles and conflicts. Qiao describes his own takeover as that of a qualified director replacing a hack in an opera company:

> During the past few years, I have scarcely seen any really good plays; I don't know whether the reason for this is the lack of first-class directors in our theaters and studios. But in industry, that much I know, quite a group of political directors came to the fore. Each unit has some of them; if a campaign comes or work runs into trouble, they instantly call a mass meeting, pep talks are given, rallies are organized, and slogans are shouted like "Down with So-and-So" or "Knock the head off So-and-So"—directed now against this one, then against someone else. The factory becomes the stage, the workers turn into actors, arbitrarily shuffled from one role to another.[77]

Qiao will not only play the lead but will also be the director.

The text, however, goes much further than this. The authorial voice organizes the story on the pattern of a Peking opera. The title "Qiao changzhang shangren ji," literally "The Story of Director Qiao's Take-over," is crafted in its slightly archaic language on opera titles like *Kong-*

---

76. J, p. 26; W, pp. 177f.; L, p. 85.
77. J, p. 16; W, pp. 155f.; L, p. 72.

cheng ji, Xixiang ji, and so forth. The play comes in three acts, each using opera terminology. The first, *chushan* (coming out from the mountains), is an opera phrase, the full version of which is given elsewhere by Jiang Zilong himself as *qingzhan chushan,* "asking for battle [I] come out from the mountains." "Going into the mountains" refers to the upright scholar-officials' retreat from official service due to the low moral stature of the court. "Coming out from the mountains" refers to a situation when things have come to a point where improvement seems possible, and the battle against the villains may be successfully waged. Within the metaphor, the period when Qiao and Shi were "in the mountains" refers to the Cultural Revolution. Now they come forth, and "look for battle" against the villains in power, Ji Shen and his ilk. The second, *shangren,* "taking over," or "taking office," refers to reinstatement in a leadership position, akin to Wei Jingde who was reinstated as a military specialist after having been dismissed earlier. The third, *zhujiao,* "playing the lead," is no longer from Peking opera, but about it. History becomes the stage, and Qiao finally plays the lead again.

The quotations from the operas introduced through Qiao Guangpu provide an economical and effective means of textual enrichment. With a single allusion the story's plot is linked to the plot and characters of an opera familiar to the readers, which adds both depth and perspective.

The language of the narrator borrows imagery from the opera. Jiang Zilong begins the third section with the following words: "Just imagine, the big curtain in front of the stage has been raised; with a frantic rolling of drums and gongs the music starts; the lead character enters the stage with majesty and awe; but he neither says a word nor sings—what a scene that would cause in the opera house!" This refers to Qiao's imitation of Dvoreckij's Cheshkov, who, during the first two weeks, familiarizes himself with the plant and refuses to make any decisions.

The text is organized in scenes, where the protagonists act out their roles in a highly stylized manner. There is no even flow as in a prose narrative. Each scene has its own dramatic momentum, and is linked to the next not by plot development but by the continuous presence of the protagonists. The words, facial expressions, and actions of the protagonists correspond to the rules of the opera. There are no prose feelings, words, or actions with their potential for diffuseness and ambivalence.

Du Bing is ignorant to the point of not knowing that the machine on which he works has to be greased. To bring out his degenerate attitude, his cap sits askance, and he sings a Hong Kong tune. Qiao takes a handkerchief to wipe the machine, and it is instantly black. He has Du Bing attach it to his machine as a public sign of his being a sloppy worker. Of course, even the most meticulously cleaned lathe would dirty a handkerchief, but we are dealing with stylized opera gestures. Even among themselves, the protagonists communicate in an operatic manner. Ji Shen dismisses Xi Wangbei just before Qiao's takeover. Then he fumbles around lighting his cigarette "as if he wanted to indicate something by it."[78] In fact, he indicates that he has just lit the "fuse" under Qiao's chair, which he hopes will blow up his successor in due time.

Finally, the protagonists themselves are crafted after Peking opera types. Therefore it is easy for Qiao to see himself in the image of a Wei Jingde or a Judge Bao. Their telling names replace the masks; their facial expressions and gestures modulate their basic nature to the exigencies of the given moment in a symbolic fashion. One might even explore how far the individual protagonists correspond to Peking opera types. Qiao gives his own pedigree through his quotations; he would play the *honglian* ("red face"), daring, upright, but irascible male hero of the Judge Bao type. Ji Shen would correspond to Chen Shimei, and play the *bailian*, white face, with his customary cunning. Shi Gan would then be the *laosheng*, and Xi Wangbei the *xiaosheng*. Tong Zhen would, as an engineer, certainly wear pants, but would be neither "old" nor "military," so that her role would be the *huadan*. While for the last three this can only be a suggestion, we are on firmer ground with Du Bing. His physiognomy, action, and his likeness given above clearly show him in the role of the *chou* (clown).

What appears here in the cloak of Peking opera tradition is, however, quite familiar in cruder examples of contemporary prose writing: the telling names of the protagonists; the stylized physiognomies with their specific message about the characters of those who wear them; the overdrawn words, gestures, and actions with their symbolic load; the remarkable coincidence between the protagonists and the "classes" in society

78. J, p. 16; W, pp. 155f.; L, p. 72.

for which they are made to stand (corresponding to the match between the exigencies of the plot and the fixed set of established types in Peking opera); the use of loosely connected scenes to bring out the essence of character and conflict; the thunderous, and fully symbolic, use of the environment (music) to enhance the stature of the action at the stage's foreground; and, of course, the heavy moral message always seeping through the lines.

The conscious interweaving, however, in Jiang's story, of this set of fairly stale devices from socialist realist lore with the Peking opera gives them a certain freshness and even originality. It does away with the implied *pretense* in socialist realism of being "realist," and frankly goes about using the same devices as before, but now as a part of the traditional and familiar Peking opera, as a traditional narrative technique with no further claim to the laurels of following the civilized world's "most advanced" way to represent reality. There is no hint of self-irony in Jiang Zilong's use of Peking opera technique. But recast into the mold of the Peking opera, his text loses its presumptions and becomes, within limits, readable.

POLITICS

While many stories at the time aroused considerable public and leadership interest, Jiang Zilong capitalized on more points than anyone else.

First, he did not deal with the problems of the Cultural Revolution; his hero, who had suffered then, shows his vitality and strength by even installing his former rebel-enemy into the rank of an assistant director. What many in the leadership and some critics regarded as the morose sulking, in literature, about past wounds, is not only absent from the story, but liberally denounced in both the secondary heroes (Tong Zhen and Shi Gan) and the secondary villain (Du Bing).

Second, the story is fully oriented towards the Four Modernizations, and shows problems only insofar as they prevent the early achievement of this campaign. Many other writers like Liu Binyan, Ru Zhijuan, Ye Wenfu, or Sha Yexin had maintained that there was a continuity in bureaucratism which Deng Xiaoping's faction did not escape.[79] Jiang

79. See the stories and their analysis in my *Literatur und Politik* (note 2 above).

neatly deposited all problems plaguing Chinese industry at the time before the door of the transition crowd around Hua Guofeng. The other authors had been focusing on describing the problems of bureaucratism as such. At the Writers' Congress in autumn 1979, Deng Xiaoping reacted by asking the writers to *xiang qian kan,* "look ahead." This is what Jiang had already done in July, and it helped him win the first prize.

Third, the story with its title, hero, and conflict was programmatic for the takeover by Deng Xiaoping's group, which was still to come. It announced the "manager" as the new hero, defined Ji Shen as the main problem, and eulogized Qiao's "taking command." It became the programmatic literary rendering of the view Deng and his associates had of themselves, the problems of industry in the country, the problems they confronted, and the solutions they would bring. "The Manager Takes Over" was the program for the political and institutional changes in industry after 1979.

The story has not remained unscathed, Jiang's own juggling with the text notwithstanding. While many a reader might overlook the quotations from the operas as literary garnish—to be sure they are all left out in the available English translations—a Tianjin critic found there the real key. Zhao Ke wrote: "At the very end of the story, Qiao Guangpu sings 'Bao Longtu sat in judgment in Kaifengfu' which, as one might say, puts the dot into the dragon's eye. He poses as Qiao Blue Sky [blue sky, *qingtian,* was a honorific given Bao] and returns to the factory to save Xi Wangbei from water and fire and to beat down the cadres who persevere in the campaign to 'discover, criticize, and investigate' [the followers of the 'Gang of Four']."[80] Zhao Ke sees Xi Wangbei as the incarnation of Qin Xianglian, the forsaken wife. Within the text, there is no evidence for this identification. True, Chen Shimei is Ji Shen, but the woman saved is the nation, which has been forsaken and betrayed by

---

80. Zhao Ke, "On the Story" (note 19 above). Song Naiqian, "Is Director Qiao Capable?" (note 62 above); Wang Changding, "Rang zhengming kongqi geng nong yixie" (The atmosphere of blooming and contending should be still stronger), *Tianjin ribao,* 10 October 1979; these articles reacted sharply to this point. Further attacks on the story are in Gao Tongnian, "Zheyang de 'minganxing' you he buhao?" (What is wrong with this type of "sensitivity"?), *Tianjin ribao,* 10 October 1979.

Chen's egotism and thirst for power. Nevertheless, Zhao Ke, even in his mistaken polemics, does have a point. Xi Wangbei is depicted as the generation of hope, combining political realism with professional qualification. He might play a secondary role in this story, but the future is his, in Jiang's depiction. The story thus is taken to task for supporting the "rebels" and slandering the group around Hua which came to power in 1976.

Jiang did not fare much better in the criticisms of some literary colleagues, who like him supported the new line of Deng. At the Writers' Congress, Liu Binyan came out most bluntly in what seems to be a reference to the Director Qiao story:

> To another group of comrades, those writers and critics who hold that it is the responsibility of literature to introduce modernization and construction, I should like to offer a different observation. The modernization of industry and agriculture is by no means simply a matter of new machinery. Human beings are still the mainstay of all productive forces, and the enthusiasm of people today still suffers many artificial constraints. This question deserves notice and additional study.
>
> Methods of enterprise management that are modeled after the patriarchal family system, or after medieval practices or the ways of Genghis Khan, cannot possibly sustain a lasting rise in production. Militaristic methods and political incentives can, it is true, motivate workers over the short term; but as time wears on, this approach is also doomed to failure. It is simply incompatible with the nature of modern industry. In history, the birth and development of modern industry has gone hand in hand with the liberation of human beings . . . Management principles modeled on the feudal patriarchal system are a step backward from capitalism; they constrict people, inhibit them, and block their abilities and potential. It should go without saying that socialist modernization gains nothing from this.[81]

Against Jiang Zilong, Liu Binyan, who was also an industry author, argued, that industrial modernization could not do without democracy.

81. Liu Binyan, "Listen Carefully to the Voice of the People," in P. Link, ed., Liu Binyan, *People or Monsters?* (Bloomington: Indiana University Press, 1983), pp. 7f.

TWENTY-ONE

Rewriting the Republic's Foundation Myth: Gao Xiaosheng's "Li Shunda zaowu" (Li Shinda Builds His House)

THE STORY

"Li Shunda zaowu" is a short story by Gao Xiaosheng which appeared in July 1979.[1] It ranked fifth in the first-prize category of the national short-story competition for that year,[2] has been reprinted widely, and is regarded as a first major attempt to capture the psychology of the Chinese peasantry in the spirit and tradition of Lu Xun's "Ah Q zheng-zhuan" (Official biography of Ah Q).[3]

The story follows the efforts of Li Shunda to build a house with three rooms for himself and his family after the Revolution. Before, his family had lived on a ramshackle boat in the waters south of the Yangtse,

1. Gao Xiaosheng, "Li Shunda zaowu" (Li Shunda builds his house), *Yuhua* 7 (July 1979). There are many reprints. See *1979 nian quanguo youxiu duanpian xiaoshuo pingxuan huojiang zuopin ji* (Award-winning works from the national short-story competition 1979; Shanghai: Shanghai Wenyi Press, 1980). Translations have appeared in: Lee Yee, ed., *The New Realism* (New York: Hippocrene Books, 1983), tr. Ellen Klempner; Ellen Klempner and Mason Wang, eds., *Perspectives in Contemporary Chinese Literature* (Michigan: Green River Press, 1981), tr. M. Ross; the translation by Ms. Kempner originally appeared in *Monsoon* 3.8 (September 1980). A German translation is in A. Donath, ed., *Die Drachenschnur* (Frankfurt: Luchterhand, 1981). I use my own translation throughout. For an extensive study on Gao Xiaosheng's work, see M. Decker, "The Vicissitudes of Satire in Contemporary Chinese Fiction: Gao Xiaosheng" (PhD dissertation, Stanford University, 1987).

2. Cf. the table of contents in *1979 nian quanguo*, (note 1 above).

3. Li Oufan, "Gao Xiaosheng de 'Li Shunda zaowu' yu fanfeng yiyi" (Gao Xiaosheng's "Li Shunda Builds His House" and the significance of irony), *Dangdai* 4:4ff (December 1980).

some members fishing, others scouring about for salvage. Eventually, heavy snows had submerged the boat on a winter night when Li Shunda and his sister were away, and the parents, strangers to the bandit-infested place, were unable to find shelter with local peasants. They died. Li used half the boat for coffins, the other half to make a hut. Being a stranger, he had no local protection against Guomindang press gangs. He was forced to sell himself as a stand-in for the son of a local strongman. But, by making the "little detour" twice, that is, by absconding from the Army, he managed to sell himself thrice. While Li Shunda was away, his sister took in a refugee woman for company and protection. Li Shunda married the woman, and they had a son.

At that time "not even in their dreams could they buy an ox," let alone build a house. Since their parents' death and the dismantling of the boat, however, not to have a house was seen by Li Shunda as the ultimate deprivation. Land reform gave him land but no house, yet his hopes were kindled, and he started his grand project to save up for a dwelling.

He worked as a peddler. He sold old clothes, shoes, and scraps of metal, for which he paid with self-made candy, to a state-run buying agency, saving every penny. To help him, the sister deferred her marriage until late in 1957, when Li had finally amassed the necessary building materials. Just before he planned to start building, however, in late 1958, he woke up one night to hear that the Great Commonweal had broken out under Heaven; there was no further difference between mine and thine. His timber was taken for push carts, his bricks for a small smelter, and his tiles were used to cover the collective pigsty. Tears rose in his eyes as he saw his materials being carried away, but the tears were mixed with joyous expectation. Why carry one's own house on the back like a snail; soon, he would get a two-tiered house from the People's Commune. His thinking was "profoundly liberated." His wife had more wit. She prevented their frying pan from becoming raw material for the steel drive and did not have to buy a new one when the collective kitchens were closed down. "When eventually all money was spent and the play was over, there was a return to building socialism. The blunder had been committed by our own people; there was no use in talking about it any further." There were no government or Commune funds to make repayment for the material. The district Party secretary, Liu Qing, in person came to visit Li Shunda and "raised his political consciousness" to such a degree that Li Shunda did not ask for the restitution of his surviving building materials, but was content with getting two sections of the communal pigsty as a dwelling in lieu of his new house. The secretary also made sure that Li Shunda got the sugar needed for his trade.

Li had bought the building materials because money had been unstable in the "old society." Now, it seemed, the building materials had become unstable, and, in his second attempt, he proceeded to save cash.

By 1965, due to the economic opportunities provided by the Sixty Points in Agriculture, his object was again in sight. Then the Cultural Revolution began. He had been a *gengenpai*, a "follower" of the Party through the years, but now he was at a loss about which of the many factions to follow. Also, his building plans ran into trouble, because now no building materials were to be had. Eventually, the "rebel" leader of a commune-owned brick factory cajoled him into handing over his savings for some future delivery of bricks. He then had Li Shunda jailed because of his past in the Guomindang Army, his unclear "class status," and his odd utterings. Li was severely beaten and eventually rescued and released by the "rebel" against the promise not to mention the money anymore.

Li Shunda became afraid of turning into a "revisionist" in the manner described in the old stories when they said "and then he changed into a. . . ." He was especially concerned with the danger of such a mutation when his limbs hurt, and he could not sleep. In his long nights, old stories and ditties came back to him, and found their way into his *xiqi de erge*, his "strange, strange" nursery rhyme, which he sang on his long walks. One day, he met Party secretary Liu Qing, who now underwent reeducation through labor as a "bourgeois authority" and had been dismissed from his functions. Li sang his song to the secretary, and the two men wept.

Eventually, Li Shunda starts on his third attempt, afraid that, without a house, his son would find no wife. Building materials are available only for people with *guanxi*, with connections. After years of scouring for materials, Li secures only some lime, helped by a salesman at the building-materials store who takes pity on this obstinate character, and who even refuses a pack of cigarettes by way of recompense. The son's girl-friend is willing to marry, pigsty or not, but her father objects. He himself has managed to build a house, and Li Shunda obviously is a good-for-nothing. Then, however, the rivulet winding its way through the fields is straightened out, and this new houses happens to be in the way. His daughter advises him to "learn from uncle Li Shunda" who has been wise enough not to build a house, and the father has to agree to her marriage.

On his long tours to get material, Li Shunda witnesses bizarre events. Houses just built are being torn down; tiles that have not seen their first rain are being "emancipated." "New villages" are built. Li Shunda again meets Liu Qing, whose reeducation is still in progress. Liu Qing claims that only the formal frame of the socialist People's Commune has survived while its content and meaning have been changed into their opposite. Liu Qing prods his granddaughter to "say hello to the uncle," an honor for poor Li Shunda that makes him Liu Qing's "friend" for the rest of his life.

In spring 1977, Liu Qing is restored to his post, and Li Shunda asks him for help to get building materials through his connections. The secretary calls on him to be the first to abandon such unwholesome ways, and to help him not ever to begin them. Liu Qing pressures the rebel leader finally to deliver the bricks, other building materials become available, and Li finally builds his house, not without qualms for having given some cigarettes to the transport workers by way of bribe.

THE BACKGROUND

INTRODUCTION. The Chinese reader does not read a short story with his mind a blank sheet of paper but within an established set of categories with which the author (and censor/editor) is familiar—a horizon of expectations. This is made up of the general categories for the genre, the specific demands made on literature in the People's Republic at a given time, and earlier or contemporary treatments of similar plots and characters. Given the strong institutional constraints of literature in the People's Republic even during its "liberal" phases, Boris Eichenbaum's "Each text is written against another" must be supplemented here by "and in the context of institutional and political constraints."

THE FUNCTIONS OF THE SHORT STORY. "Li Shunda zaowu" is a "short story." According to the accepted definition, the short story can, being short, "react quickly" to changes in life and politics. It is therefore described as the "light cavalry" of the literary army, the heavier guns being provided by the long novel.[4] Like other works of cultural endeavor, the short story was to "serve politics" (*wei zhengzhi fuwu*); it was the common understanding that "politics" here referred to the specific political measures and campaigns proclaimed by the Party leadership. The definition had been further narrowed by Mao Zedong's interpretation that literature was to "serve the workers, peasants, and soldiers" (*wei gongnongbing fuwu*). This had the effect of eliminating segments of the population from the ranks of candidates of literary heroes, especially the intellectuals. Heroes had to come from the three groups mentioned, and the Party was their avant-garde. With the death of Mao Zedong and the demise of the faction upholding his narrow definition, it lost its institutional standing. The first wave of new writing in 1977 and 1978, *shanghen wenxue* (the Literature of Scars), dealt mostly with intellectuals and their sufferings during the Cultural Revolution. In this, however it remained true to the more general slogan to "serve politics," as the new leadership under Hua Guofeng engaged in a campaign to criticize "Lin Biao and the Gang of Four."

In tune with the official line, the stories did not describe the Cultural Revolution as a phase in the continuum of Chinese political and social history, but as a conspirational effort of the "Gang of Four" to take over Party and government and to hurt people. Only in 1980, the general slogan "Literature and the arts are to serve politics" was officially changed so that they had, more broadly, to "serve the people and socialism," and did not have to illustrate day-to-day politics.[5] When the story was

4. Such definitions are most easily and succinctly found in the PRC *Cihai* (Ocean of terms; Beijing: 1963) under *xiaoshuo*.

5. The slogan was first announced by Zhou Yang in his talk on 11 February 1980 at the Drama Conference. The talk was published only in 1981 as "Jiefang sixiang zhenshi di biaoxian women de shidai" (Let us liberate our thinking and truthfully present our time), *Xiju luncong* 1 (January 1980), and then reprinted in *Wenyibao* 4 (12 April 1980), where the details are on p. 10. The new line is developed more in detail (and with more restriction) in Zheng Wen, "Jianchi wenyi wei renmin fuwu, wei shehuizhuyi fuwu" (Persist in serving the people, serving socialism), *Wenyibao* 10:16ff (12 October 1980).

written, the old rule was still in force. The "politics" in mid-1979, however, were far from unified. There was bitter contention at the top between Hua Guofeng, still the government and Party Leader, and Deng Xiaoping's group, which had managed to impose its political line on the 3rd Plenum of the 11th Congress of the CCP in December 1978, a line that later led to the dramatic changes in industry, countryside, and administration witnessed during the 1980s. At the Plenum, Hu Yaobang, later to become Secretary General of the Party, had been installed as the head of the Party's Propaganda Department, which directs the Ministry of Culture and the Association of Cultural and Art Workers, of which the Writer's Union is a subgroup. Hu was a close associate of Deng Xiaoping and Zhao Ziyang. Hu's appointment engendered a fundamental change in the literary climate of the country.

GAO XIAOSHENG'S POLITICAL AFFILIATION. The Chinese public studies with connoisseurship and appreciation the links of prominent intellectuals to individuals in the highest leadership, sure that only on this level umbrellas are wide enough to protect people out in the open fields of public spiritual contention. It is assumed, and usually with good reason, that a writer, historian, or philosopher would sympathize with a given leader's view, and support the leader through his or her work. Gao Xiaosheng has a long history linking him to Hu Yaobang and his politics.

In July 1955, he had written "Jieyue" (Breaking off the engagement), a short story distributed in the countryside as a small separate volume for its educational meaning.[6] It tells how two Youth Leaguers in the countryside—a rarity at the time—break off their old-style engagement arranged by their parents before 1949 and through some struggle overcome the feudal ideas lingering in the heads of the older generation and of the young man.

For the city readers, Wang Meng and Liu Binyan had emulated Youth League heroes in stories treated elsewhere in this volume.[7] Within these texts, the hope of China's future lies in the idealized Youth Leaguers who dare to defy the feudalistic or bureaucratic elders. Gao, who was 27

---

6. Gao Xiaosheng, *Jieyue* (Breaking off the engagement; Nanjing: Jiangsu Renmin Press, 1955); a translation is in *Chinese Literature* 4 (1956).
7. Cf. Part One.

years old at the time, might still have been a Youth League member.
The texts are part of what may be called a lobby literature (in a strictly
technical sense) for the League.[8] At the time, the head of the Party's
Youth Work Committee, and shortly after head of the Youth League
itself, was Hu Yaobang. He strongly supported the stance taken by the
8th Party Congress in 1956 under Deng Xiaoping's aegis, which
switched the main focus of the Party from politics to economic construction, at least for some months, until in mid-1957 their opponents
ushered in the "Anti-Rightist Campaign" and later its economic accoutrement, the Great Leap Forward. Hu Yaobang's wings were clipped
and the writers who were seen as his political retainers, among them
Liu Binyan, Wang Meng, and Gao Xiaosheng, disappeared into state
farms or Uighur villages until Hu became head of Party Propaganda
late in 1978, after which all of them were instantly rehabilitated and
started to write again.

The 3rd Plenum again shifted the focus from "class struggle" to "economic construction." There are, thus, reasons to assume that Hu saw
Gao Xiaosheng as a supporter, and that the political views of the two
had much in common. This hypothesis receives support from the fact
that "Li Shunda zaowu" was given one of the top awards in the new
national short-story competition. The committee for the awards was
composed of such prestigious but aged writers as Ba Jin, Ai Wu, Sha
Ding, Cao Ming, and Bingxin, and of political leaders in cultural affairs
like Zhou Yang, Feng Mu, Chen Huangmei, and Kong Luosun.[9] The
selection was made on the basis of a poll taken among readers of literary
journals, who were asked to send in their ballots listing their preferences, and of political criteria taking into account the politics of the
writer and of the text. Perhaps it is appropriate to say that for this year
inclusion in the top list depended mostly on popular vote, while the
place within the list depended mostly on political criteria. Gao Xiao-

8. For this concept, see my "Lobby Literature: The Archaeology and Present Functions of
Science Fiction in China," in *After Mao: Chinese Literature and Society 1978–1981*, ed. J. Kinkley (Cambridge: Council on East Asian Studies, Harvard University, 1985), pp. 59ff.

9. Cf. the photograph in the beginning of *1979 nian quanguo* (note 1 above) and Ba Jin,
"Zai 1979 nian quanguo youxiu duanpian xiaoshuo pingxuan fajiang dahuishang de jianghua"
(Talk at the meeting to give popular appreciation awards for the best short stories of the coun-
try for the year 1979), ibid., pp. 1f.

Xiaosheng's inclusion and rank would thus indicate a considerable popularity of the text and a high political value of its content in the eyes of the leadership. The political leaders represented in the selection committee were all associated with the political and cultural line represented by Hu Yaobang; and the texts selected bear witness to their preferences. Thus we have good reasons to assume that the cultural leaders saw Gao's story as beneficial in the context of their own priorities.

GAO XIAOSHENG'S POLITICAL AND ARTISTIC VIEWS. It would not do justice to Gao Xiaosheng (or Wang Meng, or Liu Binyan) to portray them as simple literary spokesmen for one faction or the other, although they might have strongly and consistently supported the political philosophy of such a faction. At the same time, it would not do justice to Party leaders like Hu Yaobang to impute a serious commitment to the freedom (or the suppression) of literary creation to them. There prevails at best an uneasy and tactical alliance, where Hu Yaobang would personally intervene to have plays banned, if he thought it politically necessary,[10] and Gao Xiaosheng and his literary colleagues wrote texts and made statements presenting their particular interpretation of the issues at stake without even a hope that men like Hu would agree.

A curious and unique document will help us to explore Gao's more personal views. He was attacked during the Anti-Rightist Campaign in late 1957 for his role in the founding of an independent literary magazine, *Tanqiuzhe* (The explorer). The journal never saw the light of day, but regulations and a public announcement were drawn up during the last days of the Hundred Flowers period in June 1957. In October, they were published as evidence of the crimes of the prospective founders, who were charged with setting up a Chinese Petöfi Club (and trying to bring down the Revolution).[11] Besides Gao Xiaosheng, the list of found-

10. Hu Yaobang, "Zai juben chuangzuo zuotanhuishang de jianghua" (Talk at the Conference on Creative Work in Drama), *Wenyibao* 1 (1980). The original unedited text has been published in the Hong Kong journal *Guangjiaojing* 5 (1980).

11. Their statute and proclamation were published as black material, "'Tanqiuzhe' wenxue yuekanshe de zhangcheng yu qishi" (Regulations and announcement of the society to publish the literary journal *The Explorer*), *Yuhua* 10:13ff (October 1957). I have published a translation of the material, "Documents Concerning *Tanqiuzhe* [*The Explorer*], an Independent Literary Journal Planned during the Hundred Flowers Period," *Modern Chinese Literature* 3.1/2:137ff (1987).

ing fathers included Chen Chunnian, from the editioral board of *Yuhua*, the official literary magazine of Jiangsu province; Fang Zhi, who also (but posthumously) received a first prize in 1979; and Lu Wenfu.

They were all young writers then, had all published in *Yuhua*, and dared to propose founding a literary monthly not controlled by Party Propaganda (and the agencies under its directive) but "by fellow-members for the purpose of propagating our political views and artistic tenets" as the "Regulations" stated. This *tongren ban* (fellow-member-managed) journal was not going in for art for art's sake. It seems to have taken its inspiration from the Soviet Thaw literature, and perhaps publications like the *Literaturnaia Moskva*.[12] For the latter, the selection had been made by the editors, and it had not gone through official channels. Reports about this circulated in China. The journal was to help in developing a "literary current" of its own:

> The periodical will not publish empty theoretical articles, nor works that varnish reality. It will courageously intervene in life, and make known its own views about the present situation in literature and the arts. It will not flatter the mighty, nor make a principle of opposing them; it will not follow the trend, and will not make criticisms replete with calumny; in everything, from cover to layout, it must have its own distinctive style.[13]

The public announcement gave a clear-cut outline of the political and artistic views of the fellow members. The official literary journals were "unable to live up to the militant role of literature. Although these journals also explicitly state that literature is to serve politics, their editorial departments are devoid of independent views, and evidently unable to search out the spirit of human life."[14] The fellow members in no way rejected the notion of serving politics with literature, but they interpreted it in their own specific way:

> We are of the opinion that the socialist system is the best system in the present world, and that it has great vitality. We wish to contribute all our strength to the victory of this system. At present, the socialist system has been established in China for only a short while. When it is said that the way for

12. M. Aliger, ed., *Literaturnaia Moskva* (2 vols., Moscow, 1956).
13. *"Tanqiuzhe"* (note 11 above), Regulations #6.c, p. 14.
14. Ibid.

the full establishment of socialism is still under exploration and in need of constant accumulation of experience and of absorbing lessons, then the way of man's life in the process of this full establishment of socialism is even more intricate and needs to be probed from even more angles. When the social relations of production have changed, the consciousness of people will as a consequence also change. However, generally speaking, the latter remains far behind the former. Thus it is a most urgent task to press forward ideology and consciousness so that it may more quickly meet the demands of our age. And literature must join in this huge enterprise.

The transformation of [people's] ideology and consciousness is an arduous process. Among the ideology and consciousness left behind from the old times, there are bad [parts], but there are also good parts. The differentiation between the two must be strengthened. The bad elements must be rooted out, the good ones inherited and strengthened. This is an exceedingly complicated affair. In the process of the establishment of a new ideology and a new consciousness, the beneficial and the noxious, the correct and the faulty always appear at the same time, and are woven together in an intricate manner, and thus their differentiation needs strengthening. The beneficial and correct elements need propping up and have to be nurtured in their growth. The noxious and faulty elements must be criticized and corrected. This is an even more intricate affair. During the last years, all old things have been considered bad and all new things good, a dogmatic point of view which has already caused serious damage, and has obstructed the healthy development of ideology and consciousness, and especially the growth of the younger generation. Dogmatism has also reduced the vast and unified social life to fragments, and has ossified people's normal lives. Furthermore, we have, during the long class struggles, based on the necessities of these times, in the past made the political attitude the main standard by which to evaluate a person's qualification, and have time and again neglected the development of a multi-faceted social and moral life. Class struggle has its historical inevitability and necessity, but, after class struggle has been basically concluded, the main contradiction in society is now manifesting itself among the people itself, and we perceive that many kinds of flaws still exist in the morals of the people. Human relations have become insipid, and this is felt by everyone.[15]

Things were difficult, complex, and diffuse, the assertions about "scientific socialism" notwithstanding. The intellectual endeavor in such a period must focus on exploration, not on pontification. Thus the title of the journal, *The Explorer*, became an anti-dogmatic program. Quite in

15. Ibid., pp. 14f.

tune with traditional Marxist assumptions, the editors stated that consciousness lagged behind reality's development. But then they introduced a new note. In Koestler's *Darkness at Noon*, Rubashov convinces himself that, due to this "lag," dictatorial and terrorist methods of government are objectively necessary to prevent the backward peasantry from destroying the progressive socialist system.[16] Gao Xiaosheng and his colleagues, however, did not confront a backward consciousness with a progressive set of social relations of production. Ambivalence reigned in both realms, traditional consciousness contained much that should be preserved and should become part of the interior decoration of the new man, and the bitter class struggles which did not end in 1949, together with dogmatism, fragmented social life, and established the mouthing of official verbiage as the standard for social behavior. "Human relations have become insipid."

The young intellectual writers from the big city of Nanjing set out on the grand project to explore the subjective side of the dramatic changes in China with the ultimate aim to help in the self-exploration of society as a necessary accompaniment to its progress, "so that ideology and consciousness may more quickly meet the demands of our age." The central theme of their exploration was fixed in this manner, and so was the purpose to which they would bend their efforts. The spiritual situation of the country and the bane that comes with political power prevented the official journals from engaging in this "most urgent task," and therefore they had to do it on their own. They were not dissidents and hoped the government might give them a credit to bridge over the first issues.[17] Their proclamation resonates with much of what Wang Meng said through his "Newcomer," and what Liu Binyan would say through his stories and political talks, analyzed elsewhere in this book.[18] In a mixture of loyalty to and independence from the line advocated by the 8th Party Congress, *The Explorer* founders argued that, within the government-controlled literary press, they could not go about their urgent project. They were loyal to their faction or what they saw as the politics of this faction at the time, but demanded independence in the pursuit of their common political goals.

16. A. Koestler, *Darkness at Noon* (New York: Macmillan, 1941), tr. Daphne Hardy.
17. "*Tanqiuzhe,*" (note 11 above), p. 15.
18. Cf. Parts One and Two.

In literary terms, they were as explicit:

> In view of the above, we will exert ourselves to make use of this militant weapon that is literature to beat down dogmatic constraints, to courageously intervene in life, to seriously probe life, and to further socialism. Literary creation has a very long history and has accumulated a great variety of methods of creation. Seen today, much as for a battle one might use all kinds of weapons, all sorts of creative methods may be used as long as they are beneficial to socialism. We are not of the opinion that socialist realism is the best method nor do we think that it is the only method.

They espoused "realism" as their mode of exploration writing, and wanted to "use the creative method of realism under the guidance of the world view of dialectical materialism." They decried "socialist realism" as some kind of assignment literature managed by the government, and held against this their own goal of a truly realistic literature which used dialectical materialism as an instrument of analysis. To enrich their realist writing experience, they set out to study the great works of this mode. "The grandiloquent statements floundering about on abstractions and meaninglessly talking about socialist realism we consider bereft of any reasonable point."[19] They were evidently referring to the Balzac debate. Marx had greatly praised Balzac for his exhaustive exploration of French society of his time. Balzac, however, had been a royalist in his political beliefs. But adhering to his realist mode, he came up with the truth nonetheless. Liu Binyan explicitly formulated the goal, in 1979, that the new literature written after 1979 should eventually come up with the *Comédie Humaine* of contemporary China.[20]

They ended their proclamation by stating their intention to use *The Explorer* to help in the "formation of a literary current."[21] The journal was to publish only texts committed to the above political and literary values; it was to be "one among a hundred flowers" but not the entire garden, but the editors would not be a "small sectarian clique."[22]

In late 1957, Gao and his friends were acidly attacked for their program, and later their literary texts were similarly treated. Gao is said to

---

19. *"Tanqiuzhe"* (note 11 above), p. 15.
20. Cf. p. 258.
21. *"Tanqiuzhe"* (note 11 above), p. 15.
22. Ibid., Regulations #2, p. 13.

have written the programmatic literary text of the school.[23] Critic Su Juan started his attack with a quotation from an Engels aside against the historian Ranke: "In any kind of movement, any kind of ideological struggle, there are always some mudworms who will feel perfectly comfortable only when they are entirely engulfed in the sewers," which he felt was an appropriate description of *The Explorer* group.[24] Yao Wenyuan blasted the proclamation as an "anti-socialist program."[25] Only in March 1979, the hat *counterrevolutionary* was removed from *The Explorer*, and its founders were restored to their memberships in the the Writers' Union and Party.[26] This detour to Gao's earlier political and artistic views yields several parameters for the reading of his "Li Shunda Builds His House"; they will not determine our approach, but give guidance to the development of hypotheses about the workings of the story.

(1) Gao was writing as a sophisticated city intellectual of long standing, trying to explore the peasantry, not as a peasant writer coming from popular tradition.

(2) He was committed to the political line dominating the 8th Party Congress and again prevailing since the 3rd Plenum of the 11th Congress, which was, in terms of leadership personalities, represented by Deng Xiaoping, Hu Yaobang, and now Zhao Ziyang and younger leaders, although in other circumstances they supported other policies; witness Deng Xiaoping in the Anti-Rightist Campaign. Gao stressed the political and artistic integrity of the writer, assuming a pose both of loyalty and independence.

(3) His literary craft adhered to the program inherent in the notion of realism in the sense of Balzac, but with "dialectical materialism" as the instrument of investigation.

(4) His investigation focused on the "lag" between consciousness and

23. Gao Xiaosheng, "Buxing" (Adversity), *Yuhua* 6 (June 1957). The story deals with the assistant director of a theater company.

24. Su Juan "Qitushang de tansuo—ping 'Tanqiuzhe' de 'yishu zhuzhang'" (Investigation going astray—on the artistic tenets of *The Explorer*), *Yuhua* 10:9 (October 1957).

25. Yao Wenyuan, "Lun *Tanqiuzhe* jituan fanshehuizhuyi gangling" (On the anti-socialist program of *The Explorer* clique), *Wenyi yuebao* 10:47 (October 1957).

26. Cf. *Prize-Winning Stories from China 1978–1981* (Beijing: Foreign Languages Press, 1981), p. 527. For Gao's fate after 1957, see his "Xiwang nuli wei nongmin xiezuo" (I hope that all efforts are made to write for the peasants), *Wenyibao* 5:12 (May 1980).

reality in a situation where both were characterized by diffusion and ambiguity. There was no simple equation between the "old" and the "bad."

(5) He saw his realist exploration as a contribution to the urgent task of furthering the interaction between the subjective and the objective, and thus to the advancement of socialism.

(6) It may be surmised, that, if anything, the developments in China in the twenty-five years since Gao's becoming a "Rightist" have increased the fuzziness prevailing both in people's consciousness and in reality; our story can be expected to react to this experience.

CULTURAL POLICIES DURING THE FIRST HALF OF 1979. Although the 3rd Plenum marked a decisive change, the development in the field of literature was in no way smooth during the next months. In January, February, and March of 1979, some daring essays and new texts were published, among them a very outspoken demand by Liu Binyan that literature should now "discuss politics, discuss economics, discuss culture" and proceed to the social exploration of the country's experience, which the Party was unwilling or unable to undertake.[27] By April, the new line was under attack. Liu Binyan described the climate in editorial offices and among writers during the following weeks:

> It was now early May. Those political winds that blew counter to the liberal spirit of the 3rd Party Plenum were at their height. No one, probably, was more alert to this shift than people at the newspaper [where the hero of this story works after his rehabilitation following the 3rd Plenum]. Editors rushed around to revise plans, rearrange layouts, solicit new manuscripts. Writers tried to recall manuscripts they had already submitted, or—badgered by panic-stricken families—to submit quick recantations of those articles. Readers, on the other hand, were bewildered. They wondered what kind of major upset had suddenly befallen this country of theirs. All the slogans like "Liberate your thought," "Break down the enclosures," etc. which only yesterday had been parroted up and down the hierarchy, had in the twinkling of an eye become flagrant heterodoxy. The remnants of the Gang of Four popped up with new truculence: "What's this about false charges and wrong verdicts? We are more wrongly accused than anybody."[28]

27. Cf. p. 258.
28. Liu Binyan, "The Fifth Man in the Overcoat," in P. Link, ed., *Liu Binyan, People or Monsters* (Bloomington: Indiana University Press, 1984), p. 91.

In June, the periodical *Hebei wenyi* published a scathing attack on the "detractors of our achievements," the *quede*, and demanded that literature should praise the virtues of socialism, *gede*.[29] The institutional change in December 1978, however, had been substantial enough to permit a rapid and powerful counterattack. In July, August, and September the rehabilitated writers like Gao Xiaosheng, Wang Meng, Ru Zhijuan, Deng Youmei, Liu Binyan filled the national and provincial periodicals with what was to be the most impressive harvest of new and "exploratory" writing hitherto in the People's Republic. All their texts contained a sharp critical note, rejecting the *gede* demand. Gao's text was thus read in the context of this battle. Describing the sad fate of an honest rural peddler during the last decades, it was both a polemic against the *gede* faction, and an exploration of the new Party line, which was still prevented from being spelled out in open discourse by the fact that Hua Guofeng, whose policies it undid, went on to chair the Party. The literary story used a different code, and could go much further in exploring what the new leadership might have in store.

THE RURAL THEME AND THE PEDDLER. "Li Shunda Builds His House" is set in the countryside, and the actors are engaged in rural pursuits. It has been mentioned that, after 1976, the *gongnongbing*, workers, peasants, and soldiers, who had monopolized the stage of literature for a time, had virtually disappeared in the Literature of Scars. And, indeed, the new writing in 1979 and 1980 also dealt mostly with cadres and intellectuals. The realm of production, both rural and industrial, and of the people engaged in these tasks, remained outside the interest of most writers. With the announcement, however, of the 3rd Plenum, that all attention would now be fixed on the Four Modernizations—industry, agriculture, science, and defense—one would have expected a large slate of texts dealing with these productive endeavors. The proletarian and rural theme, however, had an unsavory immediate past. The literature of the preceding period of the Cultural Revolution, and indeed of most of PRC history, had extensively dealt with peasants. The most jubilantly acclaimed literary creations of that period had "poor-peasant" and "lower-middle-

29. "'Gede' yu 'Quede'" ("Praising achievements" and "denouncing achievements"), *Hebei wenyi* 6 (June 1979); cf. Ye Yun "Zhonggong wentan you qi zhenglun" (A controversy erupts on the Chinese Communist literary scene), *Qishi niandai* 9:31ff (September 1979).

peasant" heroes, to mention only Hao Ran's multi-volume novels.[30] The "peasants" had had their day in literature, and, although many writers had now lived for decades exiled to the countryside, they shunned the theme, and focused on cadres and intellectuals. Gao was battling on two fronts, against the earlier treatment of the rural theme, and the exclusion of the theme from recent writing. He had focused on the rural theme since his earliest texts, and was trying to establish its legitimacy in the context of the new policies. The award given his story signaled a modest success, and he was to pursue the rehabilitation of the rural theme throughout the next years in conference and articles.[31]

To reestablish the legitimacy of the theme, he had to reestablish its credibility in terms of the political and literary values of what may be called the "literature of the 3rd Plenum." The "poor and lower-middle" peasant heroes of the preceding years were great activists both in class and in production struggle; they put "collective" interests first, and supported the "true revolutionaries" within the Party. Their inner life had been fully revolutionized; their thinking conformed fully to the rationalist and materialist categories of popularized Marxism with a striking absence of "feudal" thinking such as superstition, or garbled thought due to an unsure grasp of the foreign words of Marxism or a lack of coherent information. Even their dreams were streamlined. Their opponents had some blood-links with the former exploiting classes, if they were not themselves former landlords. They provided the negative replica of the poor peasants' values and behavior, and they went to any length in pursuance of their dark plans to undermine the Revolution. In the depiction of both villains and heroes, Gao's text was written against this earlier type of treatment, and, for the readers who approached his text with a long training in the earlier variant, the contrast could not have been more striking.

More specifically, Li Shunda is a peddler. Gao's readers could not fail

---

30. Hao Ran, *Jinguang dadao* (The golden road; Beijing: Renmin Press, 1972).

31. Gao Xiaosheng, "I Hope" (note 26 above); Sun Wuchen, "Wenxue, yao guanzhu bayi nongmin—ji benkan zhaokai de nongcun ticai wenxue chuangzuo zuotanhui" (Literature, care for the 800 million peasants—on the conference convened by our periodical *Literary Creation on Rural Themes*), *Wenyibao* 5 (May 1980); Liu Xicheng, "Xiangzhe nongmin, jizhe nongmin" (Thinking of the peasants, keeping the peasants in mind), *Wenyibao* 5 (May 1980); Ed. Dept. of *Fenshui*, "Zhongshi nongcun ticai" (Pay attention to the rural theme), *Wenyibao* 5 (May 1980).

to remember the specific place allotted the rural peddler in the political ecology of the Cultural Revolution. To give a theoretical generalization to their political assumptions about the dangers of capitalist restoration in China, Yao Wenyuan and Zhang Chunqiao had both come out with long articles in the first half of 1975, Yao with "The Social Base of the Lin Biao Anti-Party Clique" and Zhang with "On All-Out Dictatorship over the Bourgeoisie";[32] in these articles they attempted a new class analysis for China. Both articles became mandatory reading for Party and mass organizations. Zhang quoted Mao:

> In a word, China is a socialist country. Before Liberation she was much the same as a capitalist country. Even now she practices an eight-grade wage system, distribution according to work, and exchange through money, and in all this differs very little from the old society. What is different is that the system of ownership has changed.[33]

Zhang now listed the changes in the system of ownership in industry, agriculture, and commerce, ending the enumeration with the words: "Then commerce. State commerce accounted for 92.5 percent of the total volume of retail sales, commercial enterprises under collective ownership for 7.3 percent, and individual peddlers for 0.2 percent. . . . The above figures show that socialist ownership by the whole people and socialist collective ownership by working people have won a great victory in China."

Readers of political texts in China are aware that the important argument commonly follows the word *however*. Further down, Zhang continued: "However, we must see that the issue has not entirely been settled with respect to the system of ownership . . . Neither in theory nor in practice should we overlook the very arduous tasks that lie ahead for the dictatorship of the proletariat in this respect." Mao had said that the great difference between capitalist and socialist China lay in the realm of ownership; Zhang here is arguing that, even in this realm, things are in no way settled, due to the "private traders," to which the existence of small private plots in the countryside must be added, point-

---

32. Zhang Chunqiao, "Lun dui zichanjieji de quanmian zhuanzheng" (On all-out dictatorship over the bourgeoisie), *Hongqi* 4 (April 1975); cf. *Peking Review* 14 (1975).
33. Ibid. (Chin. ed.), p. 5.

ing ominously to the "very arduous tasks" lying ahead in this area. The full dimensions of the "very arduous tasks" became clear from a Lenin quotation which Zhang adduces: "Unfortunately, small production is still very, very widespread in the world, and small production engenders capitalism and the bourgeoisie, daily, hourly, spontaneously, and on a mass scale. For all these reasons the dictatorship of the proletariat is essential."[34]

Zhang might be accused of argumentative hyperbole in seeing "capitalism" and "the bourgeoisie" as rising from the paltry 0.2 percent of rural trade in the hands of individual peddlers, and the small private plots. However, the strong emphasis on the collective in the context of the campaign to "Learn from Dazhai" (Dazhai had even abolished private plots) created a dearth of many commodities sought after by rural families, from building materials, which were allotted to the collective projects, to many other products of private use. This dearth gave rise to a black market in the countryside, interpreted by Zhang as a political resistance to socialist goals and the means for their achievement. The condition for this black and uncontrolled market was the persistence of private ownership, and the network operating this market consisted, in this view, of the petty rural traders. Within the story, the existence of this black market during the mid-1970s is also acknowledged, but, predictably, the blame is distributed differently.

Given Zhang Chunqiao's political standing at the time and the importance attached to the text in the media, the literary community quickly took up the implied assignment to show the true face of these wellsprings of capitalism—the petty rural traders. Their texts were not lacking in realism, because black markets in fact existed. Their interpretation of this reality was Zhang's. A few weeks after Zhang's article, the first stories by Hao Ran and others appeared. An illustrated journal with a mass readership, *Lianhuan huabao*, started a new series of cartoons to the theme *Pi "zi" xinpian* (New works criticizing "capital"[ist sprouts]). All the stories of the series deal with the countryside.[35] There is the black marketeer who has "procured" building materials (!) and

---

34. Ibid.
35. *Lianhuan huabao* 6 (June 1975) and following.

tries to bribe a military truck driver into transporting them. The driver notes that such materials are all under "unified planning" and wonders how the man got hold of them.[36]

Hao Ran had a man appropriate a commune-owned rowboat to transport people over the river for money, and also do some private grain smuggling.[37] "Bad elements" in another story drain badly needed water from the communal irrigation system to their private plots, damaging the collective economy.[38] In another, someone sells fish that he privately caught,[39] and another again deals with the black market in building materials, the villain being appropriately called by the telling name Qian Laifu (Money-to-Get-Rich).[40] The private trader usually operates over a wider area, moving from one place to the next with his goods. He thus defies the ban on horizontal communication institutionalized in China, being able to pick up news here and there, spread rumors, and organize informal communication among the "bad elements," even being on occasion a Taiwan spy.[41]

Among the various "sprouts of capitalism," the peddler was considered to be by far the most obnoxious. First, he was a part of commerce, a branch of human activity with a low status in the Marxist hierarchy of values; commerce, as opposed to industry and agriculture, is not considered to be productive, but merely as serving the circulation of produced goods. Under capitalist circumstances commerce is described as the seat of the most rapacious exploiters, since the merchants do not even organize production as the capitalist entrepreneurs do. Second, being bereft of the direct contact with the producing laborers and the iron logic of modern production, trade and commerce were seen as the most ideologically retrograde and reactionary of the professions. And, third, worse even than the farmer caring only for his private plot, the

36. Genggeng, "Dache" (Hitching a ride), *Lianhuan huabao* 6:30ff (July 1975).

37. Hao Ran, "Xiaguang qu" (Song of dawn), *Lianhuan huabao* 7:21ff (July 1975).

38. Tang Zefu, "Tiantou fengyu" (Trials and hardships at the head of the field), *Lianhuan huabao* 8:32ff (August 1975).

39. Wu Jun, "Qin 'yu' ji" (Catching a "fish"), *Lianhuan huabao* 10 (October 1975).

40. "Fangxiang pan" (Steering wheel), *Lianhuan huabao* 10 (October 1975). It should be added that texts against black marketeering had appeared during the 1950s, but they would refer to the necessity of state control over grain markets. The political emphasis here is quite different.

41. Yu Songyan (text) and Chen Yanming (drawings), *Hai Hua* (Beijing: Foreign Languages Publishing House, 1975). I use their German edition.

peddler moved and communicated. He was the transmission belt for black rumors and reactionary ideas.

Against this background of general Marxist doctrine and specific attacks with regard to the rural peddler, one can imagine the violent shock generated by Gao Xiaosheng's story, which brazenly presented the black core of the "capitalist sprouts" in the countryside, the individual rural peddler, as the hero. And the deep purpose of the political leaders became evident when they promoted this story from a provincial literary magazine into the top ranks of the nation's award-winning short stories, thus putting their stamp of approval on this strange new protagonist.

BUILDING A HOUSE. As the title announces, "Li Shunda Builds His House." The title announcement, that the story deals with his effort to build a house, might not seem impressive, but a glance over the countryside at the time the story was written quickly reveals the relevance of this title: As has been mentioned, all house-building material was under "unified planning" during the Cultural Revolution. Only after the "needs of the collective" and of households with strong backdoor connections had been met would material become available. Rural harvests, and, in the richer areas, rural incomes had been rising; and the population had grown, so that the need for new housing as well as the ability to finance it had greatly increased.[42] The national model at the time, Dazhai, had built collective housing and this only after all investment had gone for years into rural construction. This decreased the political legitimacy of private house building, and set a time frame according to which collective housing would be built only after other building projects had been completed. After 1976, the ideological climate for private housing construction improved only slowly. But a steep rise in state purchasing prices for rural products and a relaxing of controls over the sale of building materials to private households in winter 1977 led to a veritable boom of house building in the countryside. During 1978 and 1979, about 20 million peasant families built new houses or rebuilt

---

42. Cf. Gao Xiaosheng's own comments in Gao Xiaosheng, "'Li Shunda zaowu' shimo" ("Li Shunda Builds His House"–the background) in Mou Zhongxiu, *Huojiang duanpian xiaoshuo chuangzuo tan 1978–1980* (On the creation of the award-winning short stories 1978–1980; Beijing: Wenhua Yishu Press, 1982), pp. 70f.

their old ones, which corresponded to about 11 percent of the entire rural population.⁴³ The fever struck entire areas, especially the wealthier districts. People were in a frenzy to use the opportunity as long as it lasted. Li Shunda lives in the Yangtse valley between Shanghai and Nanjing near the railroad line, decidedly one of those districts.

Defined in terms of the Cultural Revolution, Li's great endeavor is the building of a private house, a "dead investment" for private comfort, which moreover withholds important materials from collective projects. The progress or stagnation of his project is the standard by which the different historical phases are measured. The title of the story announces both in the figure of the peddler hero, and in his main concern—house building, a challenge to the treatment of the rural theme during the preceding years.

ANALYSIS

THE HERO, LI SHUNDA. Class Background. Class background is a category in Chinese identity papers, the list of recognized classes being taken from Mao's analysis of Chinese society. This administrative measure had led to a standardization of the political discourse, and of literary characters. The reader is informed about the class status (and consequently political status) of each protagonist either by direct reference, or through genealogy (status of the parents). Persons with no clear class status or a shady past are suspect, and tend to reveal themselves as bad elements. Ambivalence in the case of intellectuals, said to vacillate between the exploiting and the exploited classes, is often expressed by a class split in the parent generation, for example, landlord father and "poor peasant" mother. Gao Xiaosheng rejected this traditional framework by not giving Li's class status, and endowing him with a past for which the rigorous legal categories were evidently unsuitable. Li is neither a peasant, nor a worker, not a landlord, nor a bourgeois. During the Cultural Revolution, class status was vital for the status of a character in the scale of values.⁴⁴ Gao implied

43. Xue Muqiao, ed., *Almanac of China's Economy 1981* (Hong Kong: Modern Cultural Company, 1982), pp. 383, 394.

44. Within the story, Li is accused of being a Guomindang spy of uncertain class background during the Cultural Revolution, exactly the charges against peddlers at the time.

that it is of no analytical value for understanding his hero. This is in tune with government policy after the 3rd Plenum—to emphasize actual attitude and performance, not descent. Li, however, comes from a "poor" family, which is no administrative category at all.

Physiognomy and Iconography of the Peddler: His Political Face. Classes in contemporary literature are directly associated with physiognomies, and with the moral values inscribed into them. Gao described Li:

> At the time [of the founding of the People's Republic] Li Shunda was 28 years old. With his short-cropped, coarse, black hair, his dark complexion, his middle-sized stature, his broad shoulders and thick neck, he stood just like an iron pagoda ... He felt with the energy stored in his body he would be a match even for heaven. ... His steady but not particularly bright eyes and his regular ample nose which pressed down on his thick lips like a stinging-tiger fish, showed his stubborn and strong determination.

This little piece of modern Lavaterianism is matched by an illustration accompanying the text:

Li Shunda, Summer 1979[45]

To sharpen our vision, the picture of Li Shunda might be confronted
with depictions of the rural peddler in 1975.

45. Illustration in *Yuhua* 7 (July 1979).

The man depicted here is a Taiwan spy, carrying messages among the scrap.[46] Iconographically, he is the same type as the black marketeer, as the following illustrations show.

A rural black marketeer caught by Red Guards. 1975.[47]

In the car on the left, another black marketeer. 1975.[48]

46. Yu Songyan, *Hai Hua* (note 41 above), p. 22.
47. *Lianhuan huabao* 6:28 (June 1975).
48. *Lianhuan huabao* 12:32 (December 1975).

A private fish seller on the left.[49]

This iconographic type goes back to the image of the "puppet officer" in cartoons from the Anti-Japanese War. The general elements of villainous physiognomy and "bad class" are linked with the idea of slimy weakness.

The iconographic model for Li Shunda's physiognomy is that of the rural or proletarian hero; by implication the earlier depictions are rejected as calumny. Li's dark skin marks him as a person of lowly ("good") origin against the fair skin of the rural "capitalist." His strong build symbolizes devotion to physical work, the stout posture "like an iron pagoda" contrasts with the cringing crook. The stubborn and straightforward determination stands out against the sly and wily faces of his "ancestors." His honest lack of intellectual powers negates their cunning and craft. Gao thus gives to his pedlar a high moral pitch with symbols that are taken from the "good" classes. At the same time, he rejects the operatic postures of the earlier proletarian heroes. Li does not go on stage to give flaming speeches, and does not smash counterrevolutionary plots with his iron fist. From the posture in the illustration which shows him standing in front of the rehabilitated Party secretary it is clear that he is a much humbler character, and much more "traditional" in his attitude towards authority. He completely lacks the glories of a revolutionary rebel. However, he retains the "good class" marks,

49. *Lianhuan huabao* 10:37 (October 1975).

and this pedigree indicates that, in Gao's story, the rural peddler has shed the "reactionary" physiognomy and moves into the hero's slot vacated by Mr. Eminent Great-Perfect, Gao Daquan, the hero of Hao Ran's novel.

The Telling Name. Telling names are frequent in traditional Chinese literature, and they are in good standing in socialist realist lore, both Soviet and Chinese. In most cases, the personal name indicates the special modulation the protagonist gives to the general features of his or her class. As a rule, the family name is not informative. There are exceptions. A hero could not have the family name Qian (money), but reactionaries might, like the peddler Qian Laifu (Money-To-Get-Rich). The family name Tang is a frequent pun on *dang,* the Party, so that it is mostly reserved for Party cadres. Some writers, however, regularly used the entire name for characterization, like Jiang Zilong who is studied elsewhere in this volume.[50] Only rarely is a name in satirical contrast to the character, probably because of the fear that this would overtax the intellectual powers of readers.

Li's personal name is Shunda. It is not a pun (to be read with homophonous but differently written Chinese characters) but comes on straight. It means "following the great" or "adapting to the great." Li Shunda is thus a "small" man, not a leader, and he is content to "follow" the directions given by the "great." Two statements in the story confirm this reading: "However, Li Shunda after all was not a revolutionary, he was only a follower. He listened to the words of Chairman Mao, went along with the Communist Party, whatever was within his abilities to resolutely achieve and entirely fulfill—one single sentence from whatever Party member always counted as a command for him."[51]

The Chinese term for "follower" is *gengenpai,* denoting the faction of those who go along. Later on, Gao Xiaosheng tells us that Li Shunda himself sees his role as that of a *gengenpai:* "Under normal conditions, Li Shunda thought of himself as a *gengenpai,* and he followed fully convinced, honestly and seriously, without any emotional reserve."[52] Li

50. Cf. pp. 406ff.
51. "Li Shunda" (note 1 above), p. 130.
52. Ibid., p. 134.

Shunda cuts an awkward figure in the large space reserved for the "revolutionary hero." That Gao Xiaosheng puts him there rejected the notions implied for filling that role. True, Mr. Eminent-Great-Perfect is a positive character, but, the story argues, in terms of reality, the Mr. Gao Daquans are fantasy fiction. Sadly, the only character who can be a serious candidate for the hero's slot is a *gengenpai*. Historical experience has to be accounted for. If indeed the mania of the Great Leap Forward reigned as described in the story, why did not the peasants rebel? If the villains and bullies took over during the Cultural Revolution, why were they not overthrown by the peasants?[53] True, Li stops being a *gengenpai* at the beginning of the Cultural Revolution because things are getting just too confused, and really bad people are suddenly in power with glowing rhetoric on their lips. But even then he does not go further than mutter his "strange, how strange" comment.

With the humble figure of a hero as a *gengenpai*, Gao Xiaosheng challenged socialist realism with realism in the manner announced in *The Explorer* proclamation. The structural irony implied in putting humble Li into the big hero slot was made explicit in the ironic distance the authorial voice keeps from its hero, a feature to which we shall return.

The hero of the story, to sum up, is a lowly man of diffuse class background going about his private trade with the purpose of building himself a house, rejecting in each feature a core assumption of the preceding literature, which emphasized "good class" background, collective labor, and collective goals. In the fate of this man the history of the People's Republic is reflected, and each phase is judged according to the contribution it makes towards his completing his grand project. This leads to a complete rewriting of PRC history in the story.

THE NEW HISTORY. If the political definition of the story emphasizes its capacity to serve politics "quickly," its literary definition says that it deals with one event and a short time span. On occasion, the two definitions come into conflict. The year 1979 was a year of dramatic changes. The 3rd Plenum, in both personnel and line, seemed to have started a

53. Gao Xiaosheng was pondering these questions himself in the article on his story quoted in note 42 above, pp. 75f, even speaking of the "responsibility" people like Li had to take for past events.

new epoch but had failed to spell out in detail new correct views about the past, the present, and the future. The new agricultural policies with an ever-growing emphasis on the private household as the basic economic unit were detailed only in 1980,[54] and only in June 1981, after Hua Guofeng had been removed from the leadership, was a brand new past presented to the public.[55] The typical form of dealing with long stretches of the past would have been the novel, the *changpian xiaoshuo,* which in China has developed into an epic chronicle. In the hectic battles of 1979, there was no time for writing novels. Most writers associated with Hu Yaobang were furthermore specialized on the "fast" *duanpian xiaoshao,* short story, and the social documentary form of the *texie.* The challenge to review the history of the PRC in the light of the Resolution of the 3rd Plenum and thus to strengthen those views and leaders associated with the "correct-line" periods was too great to be foregone. For a while, the short story took over from the novel, the political purpose broke through the genre barriers. Wang Meng's barber, Liu Binyan's Wang Shouxin, Jiang Zilong's Director Qiao, and Gao Xiaosheng's Li Shunda are all living through decades of PRC history in the 1979 short stories and provide opportunities to reevaluate the stages of the past. The writers tried to explore the still unwritten text of the new history.

History, however, was no unmapped terrain. Two "histories" were available, the version of the Cultural Revolution, and the version proposed by Hua Guofeng, which, however, never made it into a full text. During the Cultural Revolution, the Party press had maintained that the entire period before this Revolution had been dominated by a "black" bourgeois and revisionist line. Only the Great Leap Forward was recognized as an attempt to shake off the domination of the "bourgeoisie within the Party," which was said to consist of leaders and members at all levels who had been active during this period, especially the

---

54. The new policies were fixed by the *Zhongfa* 75 of 1980 in September of that year. Publicly, *Renmin ribao* began to refer to the reform in early November 1980. Cf. "Yin di zhi yi fenlei zhi dao" (Give directions according to local conditions), *Renmin ribao*, 1 November 1980, editorial.

55. "Resolution on Certain Questions in the History of Our Party Since the Founding of the PRC, 27 June 1981," in *Resolutions on CPC History* (Beijing: Foreign Languages Press, 1981).

older generation. They had joined the Party, it was charged, before 1949 as patriots and bourgeois democrats, but had never made it to become socialists. According to this concept, even the leaders who had led the Anti-Rightist Movement and the Great Leap Forward, and had sent several hundred thousand people to "labor reform" were subjected to attack, as many of them had come out in 1961 in favor of more moderate policies; witness Deng Xiaoping and, in the field of culture, Zhou Yang. After 1976, Hua Guofeng and his supporters sketched a new history. It retained the glory of the Cultural Revolution and proclaimed its victory over all sorts of "revisionists," lumping Liu Shaoqi and Jiang Qing into one category in order to legitimize the "continuation of the criticism of Deng Xiaoping," whose star was rapidly rising. The Cultural Revolution thus was the "first" of its order with more to follow, and Hua tried to engage the country in a "new Great Leap Forward" to achieve the basic mechanization of the country by 1980. The Tiananmen Incident, which led to Deng Xiaoping's dismissal and Hua's rise, remained a "counterrevolutionary" affair.

By the end of 1978, this construct lost its political bearings, first with the public clamor for the reevaluation of the Tiananmen Incident as a "revolutionary" action, then with the demise of the Old Great Leap subsequent to that of the New Great Leap at the 3rd Plenum. The fates, careers, and lives of millions of people depended on these historical evaluations. Stating his case through Li Shunda, Gao Xiaosheng established a new criterion for evaluation and mapped out a new history.

The new criterion is the progress of Li's grand project of building a house for himself, not the development of agriculture into ever higher degrees of "collective" ownership, nor the progress in the ever new battles against the "reactionaries," nor even the economic development in general. Warding off the charge that he said peasants were as bad as or worse off than before after the founding of the People's Republic, Gao made it clear that Li could not even dream of building a house before 1949. Within the story, Li needs about three to five years of extreme parsimony to accumulate the funds necessary for his three-room house. Had things followed a straight course, he could have built three or even four houses during the time span of the story. However, until 1978, he built none. In principle, we learn, socialism is superior to the old society,

while in fact the political troubles on the socialist surface have prevented this superiority from showing itself. Gao stayed true to the position spelled out in his 1957 proclamation.

There were three "good" phases in post 1949 Chinese history: land
reform to 1957, 1961 to the Cultural Revolution, and 1978 and thereafter.
During these periods Li's project makes progress. Two phases undo his
efforts—the Great Leap and the Cultural Revolution. In this view of history, all danger is coming from the "left," which rejects the earlier assumptions that all danger came from the "revisionist" right. Gao managed to
anticipate correctly the evaluations to be issued in June 1981.

There was a problem, however. The leaders who rose to new prominence at the 3rd Plenum had actively supported the Great Leap; Deng
Xiaoping himself had been the Party's Secretary General at the time. In
literature, Zhou Yang had run a harsh campaign at that time against the
very group to which Gao belonged, and now he was again in charge of
cultural matters. As far as Li Shunda was concerned, he lost all his funds
in 1959, and was cheated out of only a part of them during the Cultural
Revolution, where, however, he was also beaten and jailed. In Gao Xiaosheng's story, though, there is a fundamental difference between the two
events. The disaster of the Great Leap had been committed by *zijiaren,*
"our own people" and "what is the use of talking about it any further."
The Party Secretary Liu-the-Pure, Liu Qing, authenticated by his name
to be a thoroughly positive character in the *qingguan* "pure official" category, drives the point home: "His [Li Shunda's] property had not been
embezzled, nor had it been carried off out of personal ill will. The original intention of Party and government had been very good; they had
just attempted to accelerate socialist construction in order to help everyone to have a happy life even earlier."[56]

One might suspect that Gao Xiaosheng's "realism" turns to direct lobbying at this point. Recent demographic evidence shows that the hunger-
related increased death toll of the Great Leap was about 30 million lives,
with a concomitant drop in the fertility rate corresponding to about 30
million non-births.[57] The generation which at the time was under 5

56. "Li Shunda" (note 1 above), p. 132.
57. B. Ashton, K. Hill, A Piazza, R. Zeitz, "Famine in China 1958–1961," *Population and
Development Review* 10. 4:614 (1984).

years of age still bears the imprint of the Great Leap in the form of severely stunted growth.[58] There were stories in 1979 that addressed the unknown human history of this period.[59] Perhaps Gao felt that a more realistic description of this time would not contribute to the political purpose of the story.

That he was all too aware of this problem is shown through the figure of Liu-the-Pure. He is in charge during the Great Leap, ousted during the Cultural Revolution, and reinstated in 1977, closely matching the career of Deng Xiaoping and many of his new associates. The Great Leap was a mistake made by "our own" good-intentioned people. The Cultural Revolution was run by "them," certified villains, brutes, and embezzlers. The rebel leader is after Li's savings: "One day, in broad daylight, a chieftain of a rebel faction, a pistol on his belt and the precious red book in a sash over his shoulders, accompanied by the head of the production team, paid a visit to Li Shunda."[60] The pistol, the book, and the company of the team head are all designed to intimidate Li, and, though he hands over the money, he is arrested shortly after in a move of plain extortion. There is as little finesse and penetration in this description as in the portrayal of the role of the Party during the Great Leap. The text falls back into the depiction of emblematic "scenes," the typicality of which is to support the educative lesson. But then writers felt relief in 1979 to bombard their Cultural Revolution critics and jailers with the worst invective printable in the official discourse, such as "social-fascist dictatorship" and the like. Wang Meng elevated a heap of human feces (with roundworms complete) to the supreme literary symbol for what was left behind by this period, the roundworms subtly alluding, for the knowledgeable, to Engels's "mudworms" quoted above, today's Cultural Revolution villains who rejoiced in this steaming smelly matter. Factional stress can thus be felt in the didacticism of Gao's new history, which is more of a legitimation pedigree for the new leadership.

58. D. Jamison, J. Evans, T. King, I. Porter, N. Prescott, A. Prost, *China, the Health Sector* (Washington D.C.: The World Bank, 1984), pp. 29ff.

59. Cf. Ru Zhijuan, "Jianji cuole de gushi" (A badly edited story), *Renmin wenxue* 2 (February 1979), and Ru, "Heiqi" (Black flag), *Shanghai wenxue* 2 (February 1979).

60. "Li Shunda" (note 1 above), p. 134.

THE FOLLOWER AND THE PARTY. In 1979, the relationship between various segments of the population and "the Party" was a frequent theme. The unified meaning of Party had given way during the Cultural Revolution when even "the bourgeoisie" was included, and many of the Party leadership had been dismissed. The new leadership and its literary supporters had to claim that the dismissal of the "Gang of Four" and later of Hua Guofeng corresponded to the deep aspirations of the masses in the same manner their opponents had claimed when they were dismissed. There was one option, to ascribe the merit of politically toppling the "Gang of Four" to the hundred thousands who had congregated on Tiananmen Square on 5 April 1976, and perhaps to the criticism made by people like the Li Yi Zhe group in Guangzhou.[61] But even after the Tiananmen action was declared to have been "revolutionary" and the participants were released from prison in late 1978, this option was considered inopportune on political as well as ideological grounds. It would have given too large a role to the young, who had been the great majority on Tiananmen; where, then, was the broad popular support from the productive classes? There had been no revolution, but the recent change amounted nearly to that. One could hardly have ascribed this to a coup d'état, since the planning of such a coup was the main charge against the "Gang of Four." Most writers would thus simply mention the change in 1976 as one would refer to an earthquake. Some, like Wang Meng in his story analyzed in this book, as well as Gao Xiaosheng went on to portray the ongoing loyalty of their humble heroes to the "true Party." In both cases they used the symbol of a personal friendship based on human respect, which continued after the restoration of the cadre to his former high position.

The district Party secretary Liu-the-Pure and Li-Who-Follows-the-Great meet at the end of the Great Leap. Liu talks Li out of asking for a reimbursement of his losses. With skill, Gao Xiaosheng used the modulation of the authorial voice in this scene.

The government's reimbursement policy was undoubtedly welcomed by the people. However, Li Shunda's building materials had not been used up by the

61. Cf. A. Chan and J. Unger, eds., *The Case of Li I-che, Chinese Law and Government*, 10.3 (1977).

state but by the collective. Of course, this collective, too, would have been obliged to reimburse him. However, the collective was impoverished and had neither materials to return nor money to pay, and so the cadres had no other means left but to go about ideological work with all their might, lift the political consciousness of people like Li Shunda, and ask them to sustain a sacrifice on their own in order to handle the reimbursement at the lowest possible rate. Li Shunda's losses were really not small, but his political consciousness was greatly lifted, because, before this time, nobody ever had given him such conscientious and meticulous ideological education.

Then follows the argumentation of Liu Qing as quoted above. Finally Liu makes sure that Li Shunda will get the raw material for his candy, essential for his trade, so that he may get started on another attempt to build his house. Gao goes on: "Li Shunda was so easily carried away with emotions, and when he had received comrade Liu Qing's guidance and concrete help, his eyes soon flowed over with tears and without demur he sighed his consent."

Liu Qing then proposes that they take two of the seven sections of the pigsty (which had been covered with his tiles) as his new abode, arguing:

> The pigsty was a more solid structure than Li's straw hut; the two rooms together measured 10 paces and provided space enough; in addition, the ceiling was well over 10 feet high; true, it slanted, and at the back end was lower than a man's height, but there was no reason why the new owner would have to strut about the rooms with his chest thrown out, so there was no great harm in that. Li Shunda had been accustomed since his early youth to the low shed on the boat, and of course he wouldn't be troubled by this.[62]

The authorial voice does not identify with Liu Qing. It keeps a critical distance by satirizing the terminology and the argument of the cadre. "Ideological education" comes only to convince Li to give up his rightful claim, and the argumentative structure is that of a salesman trying to fool a dimwit, with the difference that Liu is *qing*, not out for personal gain, but trying to get the collective out of the red.

The authorial voice at the same time keeps its distance from Li Shunda. There is an ironic tone in the description of Li's being so impressed by the visit of such a high official and by the fact that Liu Qing

---

62. "Li Shunda" (note 1 above), p. 133.

takes him so seriously as to argue with him at all, that Li Shunda quickly gives in. Not a word of criticism comes over Li Shunda's lips during this grotesque scene.

Gao Xiaosheng kept his distance from the Great Leap past of the new leaders of 1979, although he accepted and repeated the central argument that these were mistakes by "good people." We now turn to the Cultural Revolution. Texts written in earlier years (and not just during the Cultural Revolution) had made efforts to show how their heroes supported the "true" revolutionaries in the Party, and not the bad eggs. Gao had the same problem, if from the opposite side. The hero of the Cultural Revolution story would support the "true" Party during the reign of "Liu Shaoqi's black line" in the early 1960s to prove that the best among the people supported the faction that came to power with the Cultural Revolution. Gao proceeded in two steps: First, Li Shunda dissociates himself from being a general *gengenpai* of "the Party" and becomes ever more critical of the new leaders; second, he befriends the "true Party" in Liu Qing. First, then his breaking away: "Under normal conditions, Li Shunda thought of himself as a *gengenpai* . . . But, after the beginning of the Cultural Revolution, he would no longer 'go along.' Even if he had wanted to go along, he would not have known with whom; everywhere, east, south, west, and north someone screamed: 'Only I am correct!'"[63]

Gao did not claim any great theoretical insight for his hero. The honest simple rural dweller, we learn, did not go along with the Cultural Revolution. There was some kind of spontaneous (and unarticulated) dislike among these people for the new rebels: "Li Shunda was somewhat depressed. This had much to do with his intention to build a house. He felt that the [present] hectic time was different from 1958; then, many material things had come to naught, this time men were ruined; each gesture became a matter of life and death."[64]

After he is imprisoned and beaten, again without any attempt to protest and fight back, his slow brain sets to work to process his new experiences. In the year when the story was written, Kafka's "Metamorphosis" had come out in translation.[65] As has often been the case during this

63. Ibid., p. 134.
64. Ibid.
65. Kafuka (Kafka), "Bianxing ji" (The metamorphosis), tr. Li Wenjun, *Shijie wenxue* 1 (January 1979).

century, a modern foreign import would suddenly shed new light on the potential of traditional Chinese lore. Kafka's piece resonated with the innumerable stories about people who woke up as "something else." The language of the Cultural Revolution with its rich vocabulary of "ox" and "snake spirits," "monsters" and "spectres" for various members of the human race provided the immediate impulse to use this imagery.[66] "Revisionism," the Cultural Revolution's common identifier of any kind of monster, becomes in Li's mind a "cauldron." When his body still hurts many months after his release from prison, he wonders in one of Gao's stronger passages:

> He hadn't changed into a "revisionist," had he? This gave him quite a start. It was all right with him to change into an ox or a horse, but absolutely not into a "revisionist." "Revisionist"—what kind of a thing was that? It was a black cauldron, a decoration, however, you could not cook with but could only wear on your back; it was a "family treasure" to be handed down from generation to generation, which had no life and therefore could not die. The son was now 19; if he [Li Shunda] would wear that cauldron on his back, how would he [the son] ever find a wife? Also, he hadn't built the house, so that he fulfilled none of the conditions for a marriage.
>
> When Li Shunda thought about this, his heart filled with terror and superstition. As a child, he had heard many old stories, and there had been some where people changed into all kinds of other things. The person telling the story would then say: "And when the night was over, he had changed into this or into that." And before this metamorphosis one always had some strange feeling; as an example all of one's bones would hurt, or the feverish skin cracked, and similar things. For this reason Li Shunda feared the black night when he did not feel well, and was afraid of falling asleep. He always kept his eyes wide open to prevent himself from unconsciously changing into a black cauldron during sleep. He really was very much on his guard, and so he hasn't changed once until this day.[67]

The first part is of course easy political allegory. All kinds of people could indeed wake up one morning to find themselves changed into a "revisionist," which was indeed a "family treasure" because their chil-

---

66. One story described a Peking University professor who had changed into a snake monster wallowing through the mud to reach the pond near the university to drown himself; see Zong Pu, "Wo shi shei?" (Who am I?), Changchun 12 (1979), repr. in Xiaoshuo yuebao 3:49ff (1980).

67. "Li Shunda" (note 1 above), p. 136.

dren would quickly receive the same "ornament." And to marry someone whose father was such a "revisionist" was exceedingly unwise. In
the second part, the metaphor comes into its own, and Li borrows
freely from Kafka and traditional ghost stories to weave these phrases.
The ironic confrontation of "revisionism," about which billions of
words have been written and spoken using the entire arsenal of the
Marxist doctrine, with the "black cauldron" satirizes both Li's low level
of understanding and the big words about "revisionism," which in substance were but slander glued on people's backs by way of "ornamenta-
tion." In fact, we are told in this passage that Li, with his dull head,
understood well the substance of this elusive concept. In the long nights
when he is keeping watch to prevent his metamorphosis, Li puts together his song, a unique piece in PRC literature. It is the main evidence
of Li Shunda's thoughts about society and the government given to the
reader. It runs:

> *Strange, strange, really strange,*
> *Grandpa's dozing in the cradle;*
> *Strange, strange, really strange,*
> *The Eight-Immortals-Table is in the pocket;*
> *Strange, Strange, really strange,*
> *The rats are tearing open the cat's belly;*
> *Strange, strange, really strange,*
> *The lion's ever cowed by jumping fleas;*
> *Strange, strange, really strange,*
> *The dog sends weasels to guard chickens;*
> *Strange, strange, really strange,*
> *Swan's meat's entering toads' snouts;*
> *Strange, strange, really strange,*
> *The great ship capsizes in the gutter;*
> *Strange, strange, really strange,*
> *The giants act as the dwarfs' ladder.*
>
> *Ayaya, grindy head wears melon rind,*
> *The clam is full of piss,*
> *The ball's belly's filled with fart,*
> *The long-cloaked evil god is all of clay.*

Strange ya, strange, ya, really strange,
The fire-red tempered one passes winter in the Bodhisattva's belly,
smelling the incense, she puts on airs.[68]

This "popular song" (*lige*) or "children's song" (*erge*), as Gao Xiaosheng called it, belongs to the category of *tongyao*, boys' songs, familiar from Chinese tradition. These consisted of (usually rhymed) ditties which were understood as referring to the character and eventual fate of political leaders of the time. They were not seen as conscious products of agitation but unconscious articulations of Heaven's will, much like heavenly portents or natural disasters. The *tong* being the spirit media in Chinese religion, the *tongyao* were communications from the higher spheres. They were collected and many of them have been transmitted in the dynastic histories, as they had been preserved in the imperial archives. They were duly reported under the *wuxing zhi*, the chapter dealing with heavenly portents.[69] Together with people's songs these *tongyao* were, theoretically at least, unreproachable forms of articulating public opinion about the higher-ups. People's songs have accordingly been highly regarded by the Communist government, especially during the Great Leap; popular proverbs, sayings, and adages are common genres in PRC literature to express "the people's" opinion. The Great Leap songs have, however, been purified and edited to conform to the presumably essential thoughts of the "good classes." They express jubilation for socialism, and hatred for its enemies, and are linked to their earlier variants only through some deft rhyme or earthy metaphor. The traditional form of the *tongyao*, however, has not received such a place of honor in the categorical household of the PRC. They are in "heavenly" language and therefore inevitably cryptic in their meaning; they would as a rule allude to a high-ranking official and the prospects awaiting him. Often they are predictions of downfall and doom. The allusion often is contained in characters used in the *tongyao* which, when put together in a certain form, will give the name of the person alluded to. A boy could thus sing a *tongyao* in the street, but the mean-

68. Ibid., pp. 136f.
69. Cf. my "The Structure of the Public Sphere in Traditional China," unpublished manuscript.

ing became evident only if it were written down and the indirect allusions deciphered. They constituted a form of communication among the lowly dealing with their judgment of those higher up, and difficult to discern by government spies. In Communist analysis, they are linked to times of oppression, when no other avenues of talk are open.

Using this form here, Gao Xiaosheng was communicating to his readers several things. First, the period of the Cultural Revolution experienced such a heavy-handed repression of public opinion that people had to take refuge in "feudal" forms of expression, speaking indirectly and in dark language. Second, there existed during that period popular resentment and resistance, which used these dark forms of communication. And with the text of the "Strange" song he hinted that many true insights were hidden in these bizarre popular observations. Without claiming to be able to explain each line, I feel confident that appropriate interpretations for most of them can be found.

The text comes in three parts, each one separated from the next by a full stop. The first long piece deals with general strange things, while the second and third pieces, distinguished by a change in rhythm, seem to deal with specific individuals.

The gist of the first pericope is readily evident; the regular order of things political is inverted. Line for line: The grandpa dozing in the cradle might refer to Mao having lost control; the cradle occurs in the familiar term "cradle of the Revolution" (*geming yaolan*); the meaning would be that Mao, being old, rests on the merits and methods of the old times. The Eight-Immortals-Table is always well laid for the great worthies, but now, with corruption rampaging, every (unworthy) leader's pockets have grown to accommodate such splendid banquets. The cat is there to catch the rats, the Party exercises the dictatorship over the rat-like being of capitalism; but now these very rats, in the form of Gang of Four adherents, have managed to tear the Party apart. The lion being afraid of fleas might again refer to Mao not daring to get at his flea-like opponents from the "left" faction. The dog is there to guard the chickens like the army is there to guard the people; the weasel sent to guard the chickens probably refers to the role of the militia, implicitly denounced as feeding off the people by killing its members. Swan's meat counts as the most precious of viands, while the toad is the most abominable of creatures; thus the highest ideals and functions of Chinese socialism have become the verbiage of toad-like people. The great ship would normally be a metaphor for the state, but it might here refer to the great enterprise of Party and Revolution, capsizing in the gutters of lewd individuals' narrow, shallow, and stinking interests. The giants refer to those high up in the hierarchy, serving as the dwarfs' ladder by providing careers to these undeserving persons. I do not discover a specific system in the sequence of these dark charges.

The next section directly alludes to Lin Biao. He wears the long coat special to the Chinese military, and the "grindy head" is an unceremonial reference to his being bald, while the melon rind always covering his baldness nicely conveys the image of the bulging cap in the Mao style, always worn by Lin. The clam and the ball are both images of the head, piss and fart being definitions of its presumable content. Lin Biao is a *xieshen*, a heterodox god, but, although he might look imposing in his long overcoat, having control over the Army and being Mao's chosen successor, there is neither valuable substance nor strength in him; he is but of clay.

As might be expected, the last part refers to Jiang Qing. The "fire-red tempered one" is the name of a snake. Jiang Qing's constant reference to the red-hot tempering of the Cultural Revolution undergone by herself and her retainers marks her as the "fire-red tempered" snake. When cooler winds blow, which are inimical to her hot nature, she crawls into the Bodhisattva's belly to hide there and find shelter, the Bodhisattva referring to Mao Zedong. Sitting inside him, she takes the incense burned in his honor as being devoted to her, and "puts on airs"; the last expression, *shenqi*, could also be translated verbatim, "puts on the airs of a god(dess)."

Li Shunda volunteers one more remark on the politics of the time. When his not building a house suddenly becomes the result of astute political calculation from which others should "learn" (subsequent to the demolition of the new house of his son's prospective father-in-law), and when his son finally marries, Li is quite content. He gets drunk and transmits the following "unfathomable insight" to the son's father-in-law: "Today the earth(card) eats the heaven(card), the rotten two becomes the king." The reference is to the card game *paijiu*. The heaven-card is the highest, the earth-card comes next. The "two" in the second part refers to the earth, which now becomes the highest. That reference is to Lin Biao's presumed attempt on Mao's life and position.

By its unusual form, the description of Li Shunda's thinking during the Cultural Revolution held the promise of a more individualized content. Sadly, Gao Xiaosheng restricted himself to formal innovation. What is described as the spontaneous insight of Li Shunda's humble brain during the Cultural Revolution is but the government's very official line after the 3rd Plenum.

With his "strange" song, Li Shunda joins some kind of underground dissent. Liu Xinwu's new heroes read banned books during the time, a working woman in another story falls in love with a man wearing spectacles and thus being for everyone to see a "stinking number nine," an intellectual.[70] Li Shunda does exactly what the anti-peddler literature in 1975 claimed the peddler did: He goes from place to place and offers Gao Xiaosheng opportunities to quote bizarre events from here and there; he observes and hears many things, which lead to his surprisingly "correct" insight; and he sings his "strange" song which, not surprisingly, brings him into close contact with Liu Qing, who is still undergoing labor reform. This brings us to the second step of Gao's treatment of Li Shunda's attitude towards the Party:

> One day when Li Shunda was in a neighboring village trading candy against scrap and sang his song, chance willed him to run into that capitalist-roader who was undergoing labor reform there—the old secretary of the Party's District Committee, Liu Qing; mixed were their feelings of grief and joy, and for a long time they could not part from each other; and, when finally Liu Qing pressed him to sing his "strange" song again, Li Shunda started singing without the slightest hesitation. Grief, sadness, and outrage in his voice shook the air, and tears streamed from the eyes of the two men.[71]

The former party secretary is trusted by Li Shunda, who sang "without the slightest hesitation," and we see him nodding at each line, translating it into his own language, his tears streaming. The secretary expresses himself in Party language, Li Shunda in his strange observations, but in substance they agree. Liu Qing is now the underdog; he

---

70. Liu Xinwu, "Banzhuren" (The form master), *Renmin wenxue* 11 (November 1977).
71. "Li Shunda" (note 1 above), p. 138.

talks with this simple man, and even asks his granddaughter to say hello to uncle. He dispenses much wisdom; when Li wonders about the necessity of tearing down new houses to build entirely new villages, he would "not contradict, yes he even nodded with his head and answered solemnly":

> You are right with your question "Why was that necessary?" Let me tell you, some people want to use this as a ladder to heaven. As you know too, collectivization is after all the basis of the new village, but, if people are out for restoration, they can also use this organization form of the people's commune. You have to open your eyes still wider. Just look, the poor and lower-middle peasants have suffered twenty and more years of hardship to build a house, and on one command—"tear down"—they have to tear it down. Who cares about people's life and death? And is not the people's commune still the same as before?[72]

The ironic distance from the Party secretary characteristic of the attitude of the authorial voice in its description of the Great Leap has disappeared. It should be remembered that, at the time the story was written, the charge against the "Gang of Four" was still that they had tried to "restore capitalism." Only when Deng Xiaoping's reforms, which looked much like the "restoration of capitalism," got under way was this charge deemed inappropriate; and the leadership decided that the "Gang of Four" had made a leftist deviation. In its depiction of Liu Qing during the Cultural Revolution, the text offers to the new leadership a platform to popularize its goals and assessments. The text turns to pontification.

Li Shunda and Liu Qing are now "friends." The honest common folk and the "pure" officials form their secret alliance during this time. We are assured by Liu Qing that, although he has "labored and labored," he still has "not reformed" in the sense expected during the Cultural Revolution. He is still his "clean" old self. And, while Liu Qing has not changed into a rebel, Li Shunda has not changed into a "revisionist" either. History is arrested until the nightmare is over. After the restoration of the Party secretary to his old position, the two friends battle together against the bad habits of backdoor dealing and corruption, which have become widespread during the new dark years.

72. Ibid., pp. 143f.

THE NEW MYTH: LI SHUNDA AS THE FOOLISH OLD MAN. When Li Shunda announces after land reform that he intends to build a house with three rooms, the neighbors are skeptical about the feasibility of this ambitious plan. "In the many discussions of this kind [dealing with his plan], Li Shunda used to say laughingly: 'It can't be more difficult than it was for the Foolish Old Man to remove the mountain.' When he spoke, his thick lips made his large, heavy nose move, which evidently was quite an exertion, and therefore the simple words he uttered gave others the impression that they were of great weight."

Li's plan to build his house is his version of the "Yugong yishan" story. There are two more references to the "Foolish Old Man" in the text. The title, "Li Shunda zaowu," read in this context reveals itself to be patterned on the title of that other story, "Yugong yishan," (The foolish old man removes the mountains). Li sees himself in the image of the foolish old man. The story about the foolish old man was first reported in the *Zhuangzi*, but, more important, it is one of the *lao sanpian* the three articles by Mao Zedong which had to be read time and again, embodying his message in simple and specific form for broadest popular consumption. It is known to everyone in China, and thus this reference instantly evoked that text and its Maoist interpretation in the minds of the readers. Mao had used this story at the 7th Party Congress in July 1945 immediately after the Japanese defeat.[73]

The foolish old man together with his sons decides to remove two mountains blocking the sun from his house. The old man is defined by Mao as the Communist Party, the two mountains as imperialism and feudalism. A neighbor, the Wise Old Man, derides them for the impossible task they are about to undertake, but the Foolish Old Man replies that, after his death, his sons and grandsons will continue the work, and, while they persist, the mountain can not grow higher. "God was moved, and he sent down two angels, who carried the mountains away on their backs," God being, according to Mao's interpretation, "none other than the masses of the Chinese people. If they stand up and dig together with us, why can't these two mountains be cleared away?"

---

73. Mao Tse-tung, "The Foolish Old Man Who Removed the Mountains," in Mao Tse-tung, *Selected Works* (Beijing: Foreign Languages Press), III, 322ff.

This heroic myth in lofty words is commented on by Gao's story in the most pedestrian manner. Instead of removing two mountains, Li Shunda wants to build a house with three rooms. The main obstacles are not "feudalism and imperialism" but activities of the Communist Party and its members, that is, the Great Leap, and the Cultural Revolution. God in all his majesty reappears in the form of Li Shunda's future daughter-in-law, who marries his son although the house has not been built and Li is still living in two sections of the communal pigsty. The woman's father and Li's neighbors represent the "Wise Old Man" of the Yugong story, deriding Li as an illusionist, blockhead, and weakling, who is unable to get things done. But the house of the woman's father is pulled down because "he had not borne in mind that the Old Man in Heaven liked to poke fun at people, especially those who bragged too much." The two angels reappear in the salesman of the building-material store and in Liu Qing, who restores Li Shunda's tiles to him. Indeed, in the end Li Shunda does build his house.

The change of dimensions (mountain–house; God–daughter-in-law) and of protagonists makes for a lively and ironic interplay between the two texts. Most important, the role of the heroic Foolish Old Man goes to Li Shunda himself, who thus becomes the symbol of the best in the Chinese people. His stubborn adherence to his plan, the great sacrifices he makes for its realization, the orthodoxy of his political affiliation with the Deng Xiaoping line, and his physiognomy, which expresses the traits of the "best elements" of China's rural population, make him into the new symbol of the people; the blurring of his "class background" turns out to be a conscious device to prevent his identification with any one sector of the rural population. We have moved into a different dimension. Gao Xiaosheng took on the text which could be considered the foundation myth of the People's Republic, and he rewrote that myth.

We have identified Li Shunda. What does this embodiment of the best forces of China's countryside want from the new society? "In his opinion, socialism was 'first floor plus second floor, electric light, and telephone,'" a popular slogan of the 1950s. (The second floor and the telephone might be dispensed with, in his opinion.) The original version of the founding myth had defined as the goal the removal of the two mountains through the common endeavor of the Party and the people. During most of the history of the People's Republic, the common endeavor was translated into the development of state industries and collective agriculture. Here, the functions of socialism are pointedly reduced to providing better personal living conditions for the rural populace, the private house being the symbol. While this might seem quite a normal goal, during most phases of PRC history it was considered reactionary.

While Li has received some land, and while we may assume that he joins in agricultural labor, there is a pointed absence of a single word mentioning his working in the field or with "the collective." The money for building his house is coming from his activities as a private peddler. This is a dramatic shift in emphasis. Socialism here is that political structure that enables the rural populace to achieve personal comfort through private economic activities. The collective appears only twice—when Li's building materials are taken away by the people's commune in 1958, and when the rebel leader from the collective brick factory appropriates the money Li has saved for his next attempt. Read against the background of Cultural Revolution writing, Li presents what amounts to a "specialized household" engaging in private economic activity for private purposes as the embodiment of the virtues of the common people in the Chinese countryside. The Party's personnel and politics are measured against Li Shunda's person and goals, and pass for acceptable only if they conform. Long before the Party leadership decided in October 1979 on the new agricultural policies permitting "specialized households" that do not take part in collective labor and operate for their private accounts, Gao Xiaosheng, true to the functions of the short story as the "light cavalry" dashing ahead to the hottest points of contest, explored the new, and dramatically reduced, Yugong.

THE HAPLESS IRONIST. In this last section we shall return to the major literary innovation of the story, the ironic tone of the narrative voice, a topic earlier broached by Leo Oufan Lee.[74] The ironic mode enables the narrative voice to keep a critical distance. This is a consciously used device. Party secretary Liu Qing is described with ironic distance for the period of the Great Leap, and, when the narrative voice turns to

74. Cf. Li Oufan, "Gao Xiaosheng" (note 3 above).

express its support for Liu during the Cultural Revolution, the irony disappears. In a similar manner, the treatment of Li Shunda changes. Through the change in the ironic pitch the narrative voice presents its own views vis-à-vis the protagonists.

The narrative voice makes it clear that it is not part of the world in which Li moves and has trouble understanding his garbled thoughts. While it is critical of Party policies during the Great Leap, it eventually identifies with Liu Qing, the image of the new government leader. The intended reader is not the rural population for whom the ironic distance would be irritating and condescending. The text is addressed to the intelligentsia and the educated cadres who follow the ironic voice in its attempts to understand the dark mutterings of the rural mind. The narrative voice, through this distance, claims to have a clear and analytic grasp of the realities of the country, while both (at least for the pre-Cultural Revolution phase) Li Shunda and the Party stumble around within this world without any clear notion of its laws of operation. When Li plans to build a house for himself after land reform, the narrative voice exclaims: "Ai, this honest fellow is really aiming somewhat high, setting his mind on building a brick house with three rooms—that is easier said than done!" The slogan handed out by the Party at the time describing how houses would look in socialism said "A first floor and a second, electric light and telephone." For the reader who read this slogan from the early 1950s the realities of some thirty years later (in 1979) would make this sound definitely lunatic. Compared to the Party's promises, Li Shunda has already greatly scaled down the dimension of his own project, but, as the story bears out, he is still far off the mark.

It will be recalled that *The Explorer* set out to probe the "lag" between consciousness and reality in a rapidly changing world. Within their Marxist assumptions, the lag was doubtlessly greatest for the peasant mind. Gao thus set out to explore peasant consciousness. In the framework set up by *The Explorer* group, Gao's ironic mode was most appropriate. They were to use the sophisticated instrument of "dialectical materialism" to explore the consciousness lag; they retained the base-superstructure assumptions of Marxism so that the "problem" lay in bringing consciousness as rapidly as possible up to date with the new structure of the "social relations of production." They were aware that the rapid adaptation of consciousness to these new relations was hampered by the dogmatic fragmentation of life, and the fact that "human relations have turned insipid" after decades of class struggle. Nevertheless, they still defined the problem as the adaptation of a irrationally tainted (rural) mind to the progressive rationality of the new relations of production.

To describe the desperate attempts of rural logic to come to grips with new realities, and the surprising conclusions drawn from partial and badly digested information in the peasants' desperate attempts to understand what was going on and get some control over their lives, is topical in socialist literature, and was known to Gao from his reading of Russian translations during the 1950s. Here is an example. In 1933, a Soviet government team comes into a village and declares its intention to register all children. Being city bureaucrats, they don't feel the need to explain for what purpose this is to be done. The villagers in the newly founded kolkhoz remember that the last count was that of cattle, and that their cattle had then been driven off. Now they know how to handle the situation. In a frenzy, they hide their children. Only one dull-witted female, overburdened with household chores and her many children, fails to notice what goes on. The officials descend on her, and her children are promptly registered—to some dreadful end, according to the unanimous opinion of the villagers. But this time, the officials were sent to disburse subsidies to families with many children. The villagers change their opinion about the woman and regard her now as a sharp-witted person who has the "knack" to understand a situation. From her one can learn a lot. Similar situations are frequent in Sholochov's novels, the major literary source for Chinese writers dealing with rural themes.

Gao Xiaosheng used the same descriptive technique with his all-knowing, ironic, but sympathetic narrative voice. Li Shunda concludes from the inflation of the 1940s that it is better immediately to use whatever money one has saved to buy building materials. When his building materials are taken away from him during the Great Leap, and when he sees that prices have remained stable for several years, he saves in cash. But again social reality pokes fun at him; there are no building materials on the market. He stumbles around in a maze. When eventually many houses are torn down to make way for the "new village" or other projects, his inability to calculate reality so as to be able to complete his project turns into a shrewd assessment of the direction developments would take, and turns him into a man who has the "knack." From him one can learn a lot.

Gao Xiaosheng thus set out on a well-trodden path. However, he wrote in 1979, not in 1957, and in the meantime the assumptions on which his original project was founded and with which the ironic voice justified its superiority had all but foundered. The maze is not just Li Shunda's perception of reality; it is the very structure of reality itself, and the narrator is quite unable to come up with the "analysis" and "perspective" promised by his ironic distance. He stays glued to the factual development of PRC history. The basic structure of the new "social relations of production" is so inextricably entangled with the "superstructure" of the new institutions and the political battles going on within them that the basic paradigm of the consciousness lag collapses. The Party secretary even spells this out: "Collectivization is after all the basis for the new village, but, if people are out for capitalist restoration, they can also use the organizational form of the people's commune." The narrative voice is no stranger to the consequences resulting from this insight. Its big city "dialectical-materialist" irony capitulates before Li Shunda's rural logic. True, Li Shunda has failed to predict accurately the development of building-materials futures, but who has not? More important, he comes up with the essential insight that the new leadership, Liu Qing, consists of good people, "our people," and is disgusted with the rebel leaders locally, and Lin Biao and Jiang Qing nationally. Awkwardly the narrative voice wonders about these orthodox insights which the writer had put into Li's head in the first place: "'A sense for right and wrong everyone has'—this sounds grandiloquent, and in fact if there had not been the Great Cultural Revolution, one would [have thought it] to be all too naive. It is never sufficient to just observe what people are singing on stage; one also has to observe what they [actually] do back stage. 'A sense for good and bad everyone has'—that is also quite true." The text then spells out Li's spontaneous insights into the bad character of the Cultural Revolution leaders.

The conflict between the implications of the ironic tone and the admission of Li's insights is not just one between the analytic and the propaganda purpose of the text. It is more genuine. The young explorers have come to trust simple common sense and human values even more than sophisticated rationalizations. The text abandons its ironic tone, and retains it for Li Shunda only as a stylistic ornament.

We are left in the end with the new coalition of the Party and, broadly speaking, "the people." Li Shunda is no revolutionary and no rebel, he follows the great. This might be deplorable, but it is a fact. The people did not overthrow the "Gang of Four," although they muttered their imprecations. In principle, they tried to accommodate to a situation. This, in the context of the text, is due to their consciousness, not due to the political structure of a Leninist state (or the interaction of their consciousness and the Leninist state structure with tradition). Thus they need a "great" one to follow. The only one around is "the Communist Party." The narrative voice does not idealize the representative of that organization too much. His key feature is expressed in his name, he is "clean," not corrupt; the rehabilitated best elements of the Party match this standard while others are mentioned in the end of the text who do not. *Qing* is a very traditional virtue, and Li Shunda is a traditional character. We know nothing about the analytical, administrative, or political capacities of Liu Qing but that he corresponds to the *qingguan*, honest official, ideal, and that is the best the text can hope for. In the demise of the ironic mode, Gao Xiaosheng thus deconstructed his own earlier assumptions.

Since the publication of the text, history itself seems to have taken on an ironic look and has started to play with the assumptions of the story. Liu-the-Pure, who charged the Cultural Revolution rebels with the intention to *fupi*, restore [capitalism] or even "feudalism,"[75] promotes the development of the specialized households (anticipated in the modest activities of Li) along lines one might well consider "capitalistic." Li Shunda has merged with his rejected forerunner, Money-To-Get-Rich, Qian Laifu. The people's commune, for Liu Qing still the unques-

---

75. Gao himself reads the *fupi* as restoration of feudalism; cf. Gao Xiaosheng, "'Lin Shunda Builds His House'—the Background" (note 42 above), p. 72.

tionable basis for the "new village," has all but disappeared under his aegis. And in the bustling development of the economy since the early 1980s, the *qingguan* seems to have become a rarity, if there ever was much wisdom in promoting *qing* as a minimal and sufficient virtue for a political leader.

TWENTY-TWO

A Lonely Barber in China's Literary Shop: Wang Meng's "Youyou cuncaoxin" (The Loyal Heart)

BACKGROUND: LITERARY LIBERALIZATION

The 3rd Plenum of the 11th Central Committee in December 1978 marked the return to power of the group around Deng Xiaoping and the beginning of their reform program. The new policies were to take up from where the Party's line had left the "correct" path, namely, at the 8th Party Congress in 1956.[1] That Congress had envisaged a rapid economic development based on technical and administrative modernization managed by specialists and a concomitant liberalization of the intellectual sphere that promoted criticism in the press and literature of bureaucratic obstacles to modernization.

In 1956 the emphasis was on shifting from "class struggle" for the socialist transformation of industry and agriculture to "production." In 1978, after years of "class struggle," a similar shift was again set in motion. In terms of literature, this shift had important consequences down to the details of plot structure and character portrayal. The times were now over when the key adversaries in class struggle were the "capitalist roaders" (of the Cultural Revolution) or the "Gang of Four" (of the years subsequent to 1977). Literature was now to contribute to the

---

1. *Guanyu Zhongguo gongchandang lishi de jueyi* (Beijing: Renmin Press, 1981), available in English translation as *Resolution on CPC History 1949–1981* (Beijing: Foreign Languages Press, 1981).

Four Modernizations by writing about heroes who criticized the bureaucrats and propelled production forward. The 1956 slogan, "Let a hundred flowers bloom and a hundred schools contend," was reinstated, and a cultural environment developed that allowed for greater latitude in the choice of literary topics and forms.

The writers of the Hundred Flowers period returned with Deng Xiaoping's group and their pre-Great Leap policies. Among them were Liu Binyan, Wang Meng, Liu Shaotang, Deng Youmei, and Gao Xiao-sheng. They had been more or less uniformly capped as "rightists" in mid-1957. They had lived through twenty harsh years, mostly banned to distant rural areas with perhaps a short respite during the early 1960s. They did not escape these experiences unscathed nor was their view of the Party and of their own station in society left unchanged. Their Hun-dred Flowers texts which had been banned were *chongfang*, released again.[2] While the new leadership called on them to forget about their past and, as Deng Xiaoping asked, to "look ahead,"[3] the writers of this generation felt compelled to redefine their own role and purpose in the light of their experience and of the new social situation.

They were troubled by two problems, one old, one new. The old problem was their credibility. According to the official definition in Mao's Yan'an talks, literature was a "weapon for education" and thus an educational device wielded by the leadership. Once the credibility of the leadership and its policies declined, so did that of literature. It lost its readers. At the same time, as in other socialist states, the symbolic lan-guage of literature had often been used for critical innuendo and attacks on government policies, or had been accused of being so used. The rela-tively independent discursive universe of a fictional text made literature into one of the very few public expressions of dissident opinions, with the effect that it lost its reliability for the leaders. As has been argued elsewhere, this is a common phenomenon in the socialist world and has

2. The most criticized Hundred Flowers texts were republished in 1979 under the collective title *Chongfang de xianhua* (Fresh flowers released a second time; Shanghai: Shanghai Wenyi Press, 1979).

3. Deng Xiaoping, "Zai Zhongguo wenxue yishu gongzuozhe disici daibiaodahui shang de zhuci" (Congratulatory speech at the 4th Congress of Chinese Literary and Art Workers), *Wen-yibao* 11/12:5 (December 1979).

forced writers into a defense on both fronts.[4] There is no easy way out of this predicament. Reestablishing credibility with the leadership of the time through docile literary reproduction of the leadership's goals and assessments would only exacerbate the loss of credibility with the readers, who are only too aware when they are reading official dispensations. Reestablishing credibility with the readers through a more truthful depiction of experiences and views would have a detrimental effect on the writers' standing with the authorities.

While this predicament is the very fate of the socialist author, the situation after the Cultural Revolution marked a high point in that respect. During the preceding decades since 1957, the educational weapon of literature had been wielded quite mercilessly and people had become used to a very cynical attitude towards the contents of officially printed matter. With the hectic changes, and the equally hectic adaptation of literature to these changes, literature's credibility had hit its lowest point. On the other hand, the main avenue of criticism of the political structure and the economic and social measures of the country during that period had been through fictional texts, mostly the "new historical drama." It was the criticism of these texts which set the stage for the Cultural Revolution, and Mao was even credited with stating that people used "novels to make counterrevolution."[5] All members of the leadership thus saw literature as a weapon in class struggle used by both sides, and this to a degree that literature was reduced to such a combative purpose.

The new problem faced by writers was experience. The young writers of the Hundred Flowers period had broken with the pattern established by their elders of comparing the "old society" with the "new society" and showing how bright the latter was compared to the former. For the young writers, the main problems the country faced in 1956 were new problems, and homespun ones at that, with bureaucratism of party cadres leading the field. They saw this as a brand new phenome-

4. See Rudolf G. Wagner, "The Chinese Writer in His Own Mirror," in Merle Goldman et al., eds., *Chinese Intellectuals and the State, In Search of a New Relationship*, (Cambridge: Council on East Asian Studies, Harvard University, 1988).

5. See Rudolf G. Wagner, *The Contemporary Chinese Historical Drama: Four Studies* (Berkeley: University of California Press, 1990), p. 318.

non which had just emerged, and they envisaged a broad coalition of progressive forces to deal with it. In 1979, after their rehabilitation, these formerly young and now matured writers had to ask more probing questions. History had taken its own chaotic course and they had been down under for many years; the new leaders were old men whom they knew well and who had their solid share in the making of that history, having sent their critics down first before becoming victims themselves. There was no set of established and tested categories with which to describe the mechanics of this society, and the logic of their own fate, but evidently this haunting experience of the nation had to be explored. Otherwise there was no hope of forestalling the advent of further cataclysms should the country continue to throw itself blindly into the next campaign, that of the Four Modernizations.

Similar experiences have been endured by writers in other socialist countries, the closest parallel perhaps being East Germany, where the collective and official forgetting of the past both before and after the establishment of the GDR has been decried and counteracted by authors as diverse as Stefan Heym and Christa Wolf.[6]

Since an official discourse had been established by the 3rd Plenum, we may expect writers to adhere to it in texts falling into the category of official language, such as articles and speeches. Not that there is no diversity in these texts, but they deal with policy questions and use the essentially flat discourse of argumentative reasoning. The craft of a literary writer, however, is writing fiction, and both the potential of this mode of expression and the writer's familiarity with and control of the fictional discursive universe are used to deal with these pressing problems. As shown in other studies, the self-depiction of the writer's role and the establishment of his credibility through fictional works with symbolic representatives of the writer have a solid tradition in China as well as in other socialist countries.[7] We may thus expect to find such texts written by writers of the Hundred Flowers generation. It is my contention that Wang Meng's "The Loyal Heart" ("Youyou cuncaoxin") is such a text.

6. See Rudolf G. Wagner, "On Christa Wolf's *Cassandra*," in M. D. Birnbaum and R. Trager-Verchovsky, eds., *History: Another Text* (Ann Arbor: Michigan Studies in the Humanities 7, University of Michigan, 1988).

7. See Wagner, "The Chinese Writer in his Own Mirror" (note 4 above).

It was published in September 1979. That it was a "typical story" of that year which marked such a dramatic turning point in Chinese writing is evident from Deng Xiaoping's urgent plea in the Writers' Congress of that year to "look ahead," implying that the writers weren't looking ahead but should. That it was an "orthodox" story is evident from the fact that it received one of the 25 first prizes for short stories in the national short-story competition of that year, and was ranked 10th in the series.[8]

Wang Meng is a skilled craftsman and an eager politician. (In 1986, he became Minister of Cultural Affairs, a post from which he was removed in 1990.) The tension between these two poles—literature and politics—is evident in the text.

A SHORT SUMMARY

The narrative "I" belongs to a barber. Looking back from "now" (1979), he ponders his life since Liberation, when he entered the barbershop of the Guest House of the Provincial Party Committee as an apprentice. Promoted to master in due order, his job has brought him into contact with many high-ranking leaders. During the first six or seven years, the social climate is healthy; the leaders are close to the people. He joins the Party and becomes secretary in the "service-trade" branch. Rousing news about some achievement gradually changes to inflated news and the general exhilaration is strangely accompanied by the sudden disappearance of one or the other of the leading heads he used to trim; they had become targets of political campaigns.

With the onset of the Cultural Revolution, the Guest House is occu-

---

8. Wang Meng, "Youyou cuncaoxin" (The loyal heart), originally in *Shanghai wenxue* 9 (September 1979), then included in the volume collecting the award-winning stories, *1979 nian quanguo youxiu duanpian xiaoshuo pingxuan huojiang zuopinji* (Award-winning works from the national short-story competition, 1979; Shanghai: Shanghai Wenyi Press, 1980). There it is ranked 10th. Various translations have appeared. English: "The Barber's Tale," *Chinese Literature* 7 (1980); in Wang Meng, *The Butterfly and Other Stories* (Beijing: Panda Books, 1983), pp. 113ff; and as "A Fervent Wish," in *Prize-Winning Stories from China 1978–1979*, (Beijing: Foreign Languages Press, 1981). German: "Das Treue Herz," in Rudolf G. Wagner, ed., *Literatur und Politik in der Volksrepublik China* (Frankfurt: Suhrkamp, 1983). The very useful bibliography of works and essays by and on Wang Meng appended to Xu Jiming and Wu Yihua, eds., *Wang Meng zhuanji* (Guilin: Guizhou Renmin Press, 1984), contains some articles on "Youyou cuncaoxin" on pp. 523f. These, however, do not seem to contribute more than a few general observations.

pied by a Red Guard faction, and the barbershop becomes a guard post, complete with loudspeaker and submachine gun mounted on the roof. The barber withdraws.

In 1974, "the new red political power" is consolidated, new leaders move in, and the barber returns to find the mirrors and lamps in the barbershop broken, clubs and cartridges on the ground, and human feces complete with worms in the device once used for sterilizing combs and brushes. Much money is spent to refurbish the place with especially comfortable rooms for the proletarian leaders, and a fence with two guards now encloses the compound. The Guest House is renamed Worker-Peasant-Soldier Guest House, but no worker, peasant, or soldier has access any longer.

Shortly thereafter, an elderly couple moves into a storage room on the top floor of the Guest House. Their sober and modest attitude impresses the barber, who also notices that they receive no visitors except a young man in worker's clothes on Saturdays. One morning, the barber finds the elderly man collapsed on the ground in the courtyard from an attack of Ménière's disease. He carries the man to the car-pool office, but, when he tries to have him transported to the hospital, young Bu, who is on duty, tells him that this is the "counterrevolutionary" Tang Jiuyuan, formerly of the Party leadership in this provincial capital. The barber insists on humane treatment even for such a man, and Tang Jiuyuan is brought to the hospital where he soon recovers. He comes to officially express his thanks to the barber, and over dinner tells him his story. While imprisoned during the Cultural Revolution, he pondered his own acts as a leader and discovered that he himself had done unto others many of the things which were now done unto him, and that he in fact had helped prepare the ground for the present situation. He propounds a reform program in the event of his being restored to office. It includes the resolve not to put tags on people, to improve the treatment of prisoners, and never again to give employment to the ultra-leftists as presently in power. After Zhou Enlai's death, Tang Jiuyuan and the barber share the general grief, and Tang, much like the commander he had earlier been, becomes active in the memorial activities on Tiananmen Square in April 1976.

Even during this time when Tang Jiuyuan is out of power, however, the barber is slightly irritated at the life and thought habits of the couple.

He registers the high prices of the delicacies they offer him for dinner, wonders at their unwillingness to accept assignments below their original level, is shocked when Tang suddenly warns him of "liberal attitudes" after Deng Xiaoping's being ousted subsequent to the Tiananmen Incident, and is dismayed at Tang's request to arrange a meeting between him and the provincial leader of the leftist faction. Tang's more problematic features appear exacerbated in his wife.

After the deposition of the group around Jiang Qing in September 1976, Tang is quickly restored to power and becomes the head of the city of S, which is under direct provincial administration. After repeated invitations, the barber decides to visit his powerful friend. On the eve of his trip, the young chauffeur Bu, who had initially refused to drive Tang to the hospital, comes with presents to the barber, hoping to persuade him to use his influence with Tang to gain some advantage for the chauffeur's girlfriend. The barber's son throws the man out, and the trip is canceled.

Later, the barber hears from some colleagues not only about the achievements of Tang in S, but also of his securing privileges for his children, and of the offensive, arrogant behavior of Tang's wife. He decides to bring these things to Tang's attention. He finds Tang in the Guest House of S. Before being admitted into the compound, the barber has to pass a policeman, a soldier, and eventually the man guarding the door. They treat him with arrogance, and he is admitted only because Tang's wife happens to come by. Tang is busy preparing the stage for a conference and has no time for the barber, whose name he does not remember accurately. When the barber wants to proffer his criticism about the rare goods at bargain prices offered to the leaders participating in the conference in the compound, Tang misunderstands and, thinking the barber wants a share in the bargain, gives him a voucher so that he too may buy things there. In dismay, the barber leaves, scoffed at by his son and criticized by his colleagues for being too impatient. He convinces himself that it is his duty to proffer the people's criticism to his mighty friend and to defend his friend among the people as a basically good official.

THE NARRATIVE VOICE

The story starts with a programmatic *wo*, "I," the narrating voice belonging to a modest man, a barber, a *qiong gongren* (lowly worker).[9] The use of first-person narrative is not frequent, even in post-1978 texts. As a rule, the socialist-realist writer would adopt the position of the omniscient narrator, who is at the same time the organizer and analyst of the material, creating a universe of hermetic structure and definite meanings. A frequent device to break the monotony of this type of narration and to lend some earthy flavor to the narrative is the introduction of a first-person narrator as a side character (a journalist or writer) who witnesses the events and intervenes with some personal observations. Starting with "Gongkai de qingshu" (Open love letters, 1971),[10] the first-person voice was often used for love stories. Among the award-winning short stories of 1979, most first-person narratives fall into these two categories.[11] Wang Meng's "Loyal Heart" uses the intimacy and authenticity of the first-person love narrative for a highly political text.

The first-person narrator is subjective. In "Loyal Heart" we are told only what the barber himself experienced, did, or thought. We are explicitly informed about his limited knowledge and insight, and the narrator is often reduced to offering only a statement of what happened without being able to offer an explanation. The early years after 1949, we are told, were "bright like the Heavenly Hall," with leaders and led "on equal footing" and "close like relatives." This idyllic state changes: "Then came the years of the great slogans, the great calls, and the great deeds. . . . The city

9. Wang Meng, "Youyou cuncaoxin" (note 8 above), p. 262.

10. Jin Fan, "Gongkai de qingshu" (Open love letters), *Women zazhi* (Hangzhou) 1 and 2 (1979); later reedited in *Shouhuo*.

11. The use of a secondary character to describe, in a first-person narrative, the main protagonist is found in Fan Tiansheng, "Azha yu Hali" (Azha and Hali); Ye Weilin, "Lanlan de mulanxi" (Blue Magnolia Creek); and Liu Xinwu, "Wo ai meiyipian lüye" (I love every green leaf). In Chen Guoji, "Wo yingai zenme ban?" (What shall I do?), Zhang Chang, "Gonggu lan" (Valley orchid), and Kong Jiesheng, "Yinwei youle ta" (Because there was she), the first-person narrative is used for love stories. Only Mu Guozheng, "Women jia de chuishiyuan" (Our family cook), Zhong Jieying, "Luofushan xuelei ji" (A sacrifice of blood and tears at Mt. Luofu), and Zhou Jiajun, "Dute de xuanlü" (A special melody) use the first-person narrative to deal with broader issues, although none as broad as Wang Meng's. All texts in *Award-Winning Works* (note 8 above).

and our Guest House became ever greater and swelled as if air was inflating them. At the same time we heard today that a certain high-ranking personality was but a wolf in sheep's clothing, and tomorrow that a quarter of the country's arable land was to be transformed into flower beds." The "I" works in his "little barbershop" unable to check these reports. The hair colors of the leaders coming to the shop give no clues about the dark contents of their minds. Nonetheless, the barber joins heartily in the general outcries, "Having heard of XXX's crimes, our lungs burst with anger." When reality gets out of joint and things turn positively parodoxical, the narrative "I" even fails to understand his own spontaneous reactions. In what certainly is a dialectical but definitely not a "materialist" statement, he says:

> To this day I have not quite fathomed why I suddenly felt so much sympathy with a "counterrevolutionary" with whom I was not at all acquainted. Anyhow, the outcome of many things is the very opposite of what had been intended. During these years the result of emphasizing the necessity to draw clear class lines was the blurring of these "class lines"; the emphasis on struggle, struggle, and more struggle resulted in people's cherishing the value of friendship, personal loyalty, and connections.

The narrative "I" is a Party member, and as such expected to explain things in the discourse appropriate to this affiliation. Indeed, in earlier years, he had been much taken in by the new society and the leaders whose pictures were paraded in the rally on May 1st, and had believed every word of the official press. Confronted after many years of the Cultural Revolution with a bleeding old man of yet unknown identity, the barber is moved by a humanitarian impulse and takes little Bu, the chauffeur, to task: "I don't know why, but suddenly I became enraged. 'You dimwit,' I blurted out, scolding him, 'how can you refuse help when someone is dying? Even if he is a counterrevolutionary, he still has to be brought to the hospital. Can't you get that into your head?'" Again, the voice "does not know" the causes for its own reaction, but, rather, the reaction is depicted as spontaneous and emotional, not reasoned and pondered as would be expected of a Party member of long standing.

By this time, the value system to which the narrator adhered in the 1950s has already been ground down, and he feels that, at a time when "revolutionaries" soil his barbershop with feces, a person accused of being a "counterrevolutionary" might not be altogether "hateful and repulsive." The narrator returns to a set of more traditional values, looking for "good people" who "speak humanely," are "trustworthy," "truthful," "seek truth from facts," and have *tongqing dali,* (common sense).

It had been an important message of the stories of the Hundred Flowers period to spell out new values and attitudes for the young intellectuals. "Daringness," "outspokenness," "greater latitude," "independent thinking," and "intervening in life" were the positive catchwords,[12] while the negative side was occupied by the various attributes of bureaucratism. The new values spelled out by the narrative voice now, in 1979, have nothing of the fresh vigor of that earlier time; they are more modest and conservative, pointing to the unviability of revolutionary ethics as well as the insight that traditional values might be more reliable criteria to assess Tang Jiuyuan. Tang is the barber's "friend," and he supports this friend. At the same time he does not deny the great gulf separating them nor his being "appalled" by his friend's arrogance of power and insistence upon special privileges.

The narrative voice belongs to a "lowly worker," but he is a trained and skilled craftsman, which makes for both a certain narrow and confined world, and a certain self-assurance. We are told by the narrative voice that "of course, even a small barbershop mirrors the ocean-blue and field-green of life," and, in the traditional symbolic arrangements of socialist realism, the barber himself plays in this miniature replica of the great world the role of "the common people." Supposedly, his values are theirs. Like Gao Xiaosheng's Li Shunda, Wang Meng's barber is a *gengenpai,* a follower of the Party leadership, or rather of the true Party leadership, and does not himself become a leader or aspire to become one. We shall return to the fact that the "people's" representative in the story is neither proletarian nor peasant, but a barber.

The barber's modest plea is for a humane, trustworthy, and halfway clean government. In tune with his symbolic role, he is neither especially intelligent and perspicacious, nor well-informed, but *laolao shishi* (honest and decent), the authentic image of "the people."

An "I" narrative presents the writer with a limited number of options.

12. See Chapters 6 and 7.

As a rule, the language will essentially be spoken language with its characteristic rhythm, looseness of grammatical structure, interruptions, colloquialisms, and, above all, personal touches in trivial information and detail. We hear an individual speaking. The language of the first phrases of "Loyal Heart" sets the mode for the rest of the text. The English language does not seem to permit a translation that retains the order of words, however. "I have worked in the barbershop of the Provincial Committee's Number 1 Guest House for already close to thirty years." In the Chinese after "I have worked in the Provincial Party Committee's Number 1 Guest House" (the reader does not know that this is a genitive to be determined later by "barbershop"), a clause follows "in the beginning it was officially called Radiant China Restaurant." In the spoken language, such independent explaining clauses are frequent and can be modulated by voice; our text is read properly only when read as a spoken narrative. "In that year of liberation I was barely 16 and had not even finished my apprenticeship when I came here. And now (*xianzai ne*, the *ne* being a colloquial additive) . . ." The narrative voice may relate some experiences and then suddenly change direction and offer a thought about them. "The new heads who came here for a trim not only never brought eye medicine or rebound the broom; they also rarely smiled . . . Men, the climate, the manners—did they change? I was at a loss and felt ever alone and without purpose." This shift from narrator to an expression of feeling again is a technique from the spoken narrative.

The emotional pitch of the narrative voice rises and falls with the feelings experienced during the events narrated. When the barber tries to visit Tang in the Guest House of S, his voice changes from factual narrative to the grotesque description of his helplessness vis-à-vis the door guardian, to a direct enmity towards this man, and, after he is admitted through the services of Mrs. Tang, to an ironic superiority over this little bureaucratic frog with his obsequious smile for his leader's wife:

> When I arrived at the gate, the guard permitted me to address myself to the guardian's lodge. The door of this lodge was firmly locked, and even the glass on the windowpane had been completely pasted over with white paper; you couldn't get in, nor could you see a thing. How was one to get the guardians? Actually, a little square opening had been cut into the thick wall of the lodge, and people requesting admission had to report their identity and purpose

through this opening, let themselves be examined, and wait for approval.

The opening had been cut rather high up on the wall, as might be appropriate for a basketball team center with a height of over 2 meters. The opening was small to begin with, and a wooden board closed off another third. Standing on tiptoe and stretching my neck, I called, "Comrade!"

Although my neck was already so extended that it hurt, I managed to get only a glance at the fat fleshy back of a broad-shouldered paunchy man. In fact, the man in charge of the door guardian's lodge sat with his back towards the window.

"Comrade! Comrade! Comrade!" After I had called the fourth time with my neck all stretched out, the attendant with the broad shoulders, the paunchy body, and the fat back turned his head, shot a glance at me, and then turned away again.

"Comrade!" I now started to yell.

"You know the language, can't you speak?" came darting back from the lodge, hitting my nose, face, and heart like a bullet.

What did he mean by "Can't you speak?" Was I dumb? Wasn't I Chinese? My face got red to the ears.

"I am looking for Old Tang! For Tang Jiuyuan!" My shouting alarmed the sentry and earned me a warning: "Don't shout!" Tang's name and the fact that I had called him by his name and not by his title did produce some effect; the guardian turned his head, came close to the opening and sized me up from head to foot and again from foot to head. His stare made me tremble. Heavens, I'd rather have endured the gaze of an enemy's bloodshot eyes full of hatred than suffered the stare of this comrade.

The barber is not admitted; but then, a sudden change occurs:

> "No visitors." His voice grew faint as he answered, he turned his head away, and again there was this fat back. But at this very moment, he heard a female voice calling at the door, and he jumped up to open the door. Indeed, from the second he heard this voice the muscles and the skin, the wrinkles and the furrows, the posture and the expression of his entire body evinced a nearly miraculous transformation, as if Bodhisattva Guanyin's poplar purification water had been sprinkled on a lump of wood [and made it come to life] or as if the prince's love had transformed the toad into beautiful Wassilissa, in such a honeysweet, delightful, civilized, polite, dextrous, cute, nimble, and affable manner did he turn the bolt and open the door.

Using this spoken language, the narrative "I" may engage in a soliloquy, an inner monologue, or dialogue, following the barber's stream of consciousness; or it may talk to an ever-present, but not necessarily mentioned, interlocutor. As we have seen, the narrative voice tries to establish its credibility through devices signaling authenticity and truthfulness. This signal is directed towards an audience. The text itself deals with highly political matters; the entire history of the People's Republic is reevaluated, and the leadership reinstalled after the end of the Cultural Revolution appears in the figure of Tang Jiuyuan. In short, the text is talking back to the implied assumptions of an audience, establishing its own credibility and coming forth with its own assessments. Although the text is in the form of an internal monologue, it has a dialogue structure as it engages in a silent debate with the audience.

In East German literature, writers across the political spectrum from Hermann Kant, who tends to take the leadership's line, to Christa Wolf, who has moved towards defining her own assumptions, have used a similar writing technique since the early 1970s. Kant's novel *Der Aufenthalt*[13] is an "I" narrative of a political and cultural leader of the older generation explaining and defending his life and labors to members of the young generation. They are present as the addressee; the text reacts to their opinions, prejudices, and criticisms, but they don't enter the text proper. In the same manner, Christa Wolf's *Kassandra*[14] is an "I" narrative in the spoken language, engaging in an implied dialogue with a variety of social forces from the East German government to the feminist movement, defending and describing her own political and human development as a "prophetess" of the modern world, a writer.

In a perceptive study of this new phenomenon, Hans Richter termed this narrative structure "monologic dialogue."[15] Our interest here is less in catchy terminology than in the methodological implications, which Richter himself does not develop. The use of monologic dialogue by Wang Meng forces us into a duplication of our material. He is not only saying what he says, but reacting in both form and content to his dialogic environment. The specifics of that environment will have to be

---

13. Hermann Kant, *Der Aufenthalt* (Berlin: Ruetten and Loehning, 1977).

14. Christa Wolf, *Kassandra, eine Erzählung* (Darmstadt: Luchterhand, 1983). An English edition is Christa Wolf, *Cassandra*, tr. Jan van Heurck (New York: Farrar, Straus, Giroux, 1984).

15. Hans Richter, "Gegenwartsprosa der Deutschen Demokratischen Republik in gattungs–und stiltheoretischer Hinsicht," *Sinn und Form* 3:587ff (1984). See my "On Christa Wolf's *Cassandra* (note 6 above), page 99.

extrapolated from the signs of stress within the text itself. A simile may be introduced to illustrate the point. In training for a fight (shadow boxing) a boxer will have mock exchanges "in the air" with his opponent, reacting in his defense blocks to the opponent's presumed attacks and with his own attacks to the other's weaknesses. Although the opponent is not present in fact, he is so in the boxer's mind, all of whose movements explain themselves in terms of interaction with the opponent. The role of the analyst is to identify from the boxer's visible movements the features and actions of the (quite real) phantom to which he is reacting and to identify the phantom in the real world.

To apply this insight directly: The great efforts of the text to establish the authenticity and credibility of the narrative voice in class, moral, and political terms are in reaction to a dramatic loss in the credibility of fiction among readers in the People's Republic. The experience of several decades of a fiction more or less and very quickly reasserting the latest government assessments, a trend only (if greatly) exacerbated during the Cultural Revolution, has reduced the writer in the reader's mind to a propagandist telling the same story in a (sometimes) more pleasant, appreciable, and concrete form. The cynical attitude prevalent among substantial parts of the fiction-reading public (younger literate city dwellers for the most part) towards "the politicians" included writers in that category.

Wang Meng's narrative voice shows the stress of reacting to that attitude. It forfeits the great claims of "revolution," "class analysis," and "objective truth" written into the tradition of the omniscient Chinese narrator; it even joins in the audience's ironic sneer at the bureaucratic symptoms apparent among the new leadership; it concedes that reality has lost its categorical bearings, its definiteness, and the absolute validity of its evaluation; it proposes that access to this ever more complex reality can be gained only through a subject with all its limitations, but as long as the subject is authentic in its voice and truthful within its powers, the outcome will at least approach truth and not be just smoke and mirrors like many great slogans and claims. Neither the narrative voice nor its "friend" are beyond reproach; nevertheless, all these concessions notwithstanding, the narrative voice defends a cause in this silent dialogue with the audience; it does not sink into silence or cynicism. In order to establish or reestablish some trust with the audience, it retreats to the authentic pose of the man of the people with traditional values and limited knowledge and understanding, who is driven, however, to contribute to the establishment of a viable polity and talks to the public about his personal opinions, experiences, and actions.

SYMBOLIC INSTITUTIONS

The choice of a barber for the narrative voice and main character is unusual in several respects. The standard Chinese "I" narrator is a journalist on assignment from his or her paper. The standard main protagonist is a worker, peasant, soldier, or low-level Party secretary. Only during the Hundred Flowers period could intellectuals be the main protagonists, but there were, to my knowledge, no "I" narratives by intellectuals. Technically speaking, the barber is in a *fuwu hangye*, in a "service trade" as the story mentions. Given the low priority of this sector in traditional socialist economy, the status of the people working there hardly made them into worthy literary protagonists. Yet, within the symbolic structure of the barbershop as a mirror of the entire country, the narrative voice claims to speak for the "common people"; this was quite a daring proposal for someone outside of both production and proletarian dictatorship as the government was defined in the Constitution valid in 1979. In class terms, barbers are hard to define as intellectuals, and the barber's perspective is hardly "proletarian." His profession thus indicates a rejection of a "revolutionary," "proletarian," and "class analytical" approach in his narrative, and the content of his narrative corroborates this rejection quite explicitly by associating all these terms with negative past experiences.

Some features of the barber and his surroundings indicate further symbolic meaning. The barbershop with its "great brilliant mirrors on all sides" evokes the standard formulation for literature's purpose in socialist countries, to "mirror reality." During the Cultural Revolution, the mirrors in the shop were smashed and literature lost its functions. Instead, Red Guards mounted a loudspeaker and a submachine gun on the roof, the first a reference to the propaganda functions of literature, the second to its being a "weapon in class struggle." To fill out the picture, the barber finds "clubs and cartridges" in the salon when he returns, the "big clubs," *da gunzi*, being frequently mentioned in post-Cultural Revolution criticism and cartoons as the preferred instruments of literary and intellectual "criticism" during that period, and glorified as the magic weapon of Sun Wukong, the Monkey King.[16] Some cartoons may illustrate this.

Jiang Qing, wielding the big stick of criticism[17]

Yao Wenyuan as the "golden cudgel," the honorary title alluding to Sun Wukong's weapon, and inscribed by Jiang Qing[18]

16. Cf. Rudolf G. Wagner, "Sun Wukung Subdues the White-Bone-Demon, a Study in PRC Mythology," in Wagner, *The Contemporary Chinese Historical Drama: Four Studies* (Berkeley: University of California Press, 1990), pp. 141, 210f.

17. The title of the cartoon is "The witch ascends the mountain." It was published in 1977, reproduced in J. Erling, V. Graeve, *Tigermaske und Knochengespenst, die neue chinesische Karikatur* (Köln: Prometh Verlag, 1978), p. 102.

18. Taken from a series of cartoons entitled "Yao Wenpi yingji" (Photographic collection of Yao the Literary Riffraff [a pun on Yao Wenyuan's name]), reproduced in *Tigermaske und Knochengespenst* (note 17 above), p. 81.

Articles of criticism operating as a big stick[19]

I suggest, as an hypothesis to be substantiated, that the barber's salon refers to the literary salon or world, and the barber himself is the image which Wang Meng draws of his own person as the writer within it. It remains to be seen, how far this hypothesis carries.

The work of the barber also carries some symbolic potential. *Titi tou* (to trim or shave the head) is a common metaphorical expression for subjecting someone to strong criticism. The barber's profession has the metaphorical potential of men engaged in clipping away the "natural outgrowth" on their customers' heads with the shears of the criticism and in restoring a proper and clean appearance. This understood, the barber could appear in cartoon and metaphorical political language, and did.

Wang Meng's story is not addressed to an insider circle of cognoscenti as was the historical drama of the late 1950s and early 1960s. While I would contend that the interpretation given above of the symbolic meaning of the barbershop and its institutional place as well as of the barber himself is so strongly substantiated by textual evidence as to be a conscious symbol, it might still be argued that the average reader saw the text as a story about a barber. While the "average reader" is a fairly vague entity, we might try to find out whether in the public imagery the barber and the writer/critic were identified. The best evidence for this would have to come from cartoons, since they draw on a shared

19. Cartoon reproduced in ibid., p. 97.

canon of metaphorical clichés to communicate with the public.

In early 1957, Hua Junwu drew a cartoon of a cadre who comes to a barbershop with the question "Who'll do a hair-trimming?"

The expression *titou* alludes to the critical potential of the barber's job. It is important that the cadre himself, recognizable as such by his dress, asks for a trimming. The barber is busy with other things. When the customer comes again, now with a substantial beard, the barber wants to rest, and refuses. In this manner the "problem" grows, as the following pictures show.

"Shui gan titou de"[20]

None of the different barbers is willing to do the job. It seems that the different barbers would allude to the different potential institutions of criticism and problem solving. The "barber" in picture 5 actually carries a brush, identifying him as the writer. The inscription "Who'll do a hair-trimming" contains a pun. The *gan*, to do, is homophonous with the *gan* to dare, thus "Who'll dare to do a hair-trimming." Nobody dares, and the problems grow unchecked.

In mid-1957, a person denounced as a "rightist" for criticisms of the Party leadership was quoted as having said, "Helping the Party in (its) Rectification [Movement] is like trimming somebody's hair and tidying up his appearance." The Rectification Movement beginning in May 1957 called on people outside the Party to come forth with their criticisms of cadres. A cartoon from this time shows (Fig. 1) the barber at his work, well-liked by his customer, and in Fig. 2 the transformation of his instrument of "criticism" into a weapon with which to hurt his customer. The inscription on top reads: "That is [what they mean by acting as] 'barber,'" while the explanation below reads: "Helping the Party with rectification is [they say] like grooming someone's hair to tidy up his appearance, however. . . ." Both text and cartoon presuppose a metaphorical code common to cartoonist and reader that enables the images to be understood.

20. Bu Hua Junwu, in *Hua Junwu manhua xuan* (Shanghai: Shanghai Wenyi, 1980).

"Ruci 'lifashi'"[21]

From these two cartoons it emerges that the Hundred Flowers critics, who often but not exclusively used literature as their vehicle, claimed the role of barbers for themselves; they claimed to perform a necessary and useful public function in trimming away the natural and disgraceful outgrowth of their clients' heads, and did this with the consent of these clients. They criticized their own peers for not being "daring" enough in this endeavor. Although the Party called (during the Hundred Flowers period) for such criticisms, those who had the instruments for criticism refused to perform this duty. During the Anti-Rightist Campaign, the critics were taken at their word. As Figure 2

21. Bu Gao Mingan, *Harbin ribao*, 14 June 1957.

makes clear, their claim to be the benevolent barbers of the leadership was but a hoax. In fact, they had murderous ambitions.

During the "small" Hundred flowers revival in 1961–1962, the metaphor was revived, and a new element emerged. The barber metaphor could potentially suggest the embellisher, the flatterer. Instead of laying on with the scissors of sharp criticism, he would use only the "44776 Snow Flake Cream," ironically alluded to by Wang Meng. Again, the cartoonist Hua Junwu might illustrate this point:

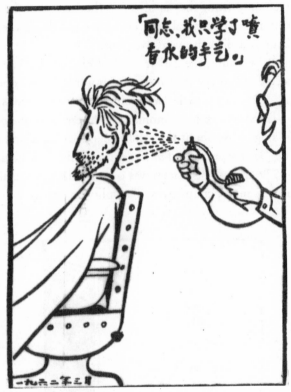

"Excessive Praise"[22]

A customer comes to the barber's. His hair needs trimming and his beard shaving. The barber, however, does not do his job but merely

---

22. Bu Hua Junwu, "Guoyu de pinglun," in *Hua Junwu* (note 20 above), p. 32.

sprays some eau de Cologne on the customer, saying "Comrade, I've only learned the arts of spraying *chunshui,* eau de Cologne." the cartoon, dated March 1962, charges that the people whose duty it would have been to criticize have not learned this craft. They only know how to flatter. The customers' "problems" are not solved. The barber is marked as an "intellectual" by his glasses. The lesson is driven home by the text: "Comments containing excessive praise." The cartoon directly compares the work of the barber and the critic who uses his pen. The fragrant air coming from the vaporizer is the metaphor for the word and then for writing in general. The critics are not doing their job, the cartoons claim, but dispense excessive praise.

After the 3rd Plenum, the barber too had his comeback, as might in fact be expected, given the revival of the Hundred Flowers policies.

In April 1979, an article criticizing the new trends of anti-bureaucratic literature created a momentary freeze. It claimed literature should *gede,* sing praise about the achievements of socialism, instead of depicting the "dark aspects" and *quede,* denouncing these achievements. By August 1979, a spate of articles was out criticizing in turn the *gede-pai,* faction of achievement-praisers. The following cartoon appeared in *Renmin ribao.*

"歌 德" 理 发 馆

——我们这儿只有吹风，没有镜子！

王乐天 画

"'Gede' lifaguan'"[23]

---

23. Bu Wang Letian, *Renmin ribao,* 13 August 1979.

The cartoon shows the "Praise-the-Achievements Barbershop," a pun on the *gedepai*. The hairdryer is inscribed *gesong*, praise. Out of its "mouth" comes only wind of praise. The face of the customer, however, is dirty, and the stubbles of his beard stand out. These "problems" remain unreflected, because the mirror is gone, all broken. On a small fragment in the upper left corner of the mirror stands the word "criticism," *piping*, to inform the reader, that this mirror is the mirror of criticism, the mirror which, in reflection theory, shows the true face of things. This mirror is broken in this barbershop; that is, the potential critical function of literature does not exist for the achievement-praisers. The text repeats the symbolic message. The barber says: "Here we have only a hairdryer; we don't have a mirror." The warm winds of praise coming from the hairdryer solve no problems. Again, the barber does not do his job, but the cartoon clearly implies what the barber should in fact be doing.

In the same vein, Fang Cheng satirized the writer/critics who only praised the leaders in 1980:

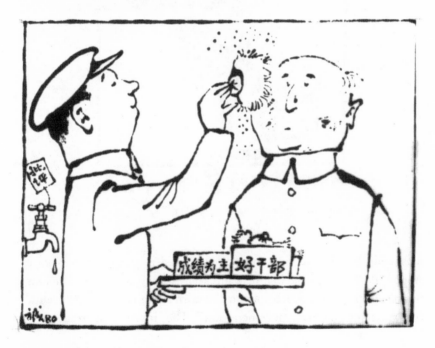

"Dry Wash"[24]

24. Fang Cheng, "Ganxi" in *Fang Cheng manhua xuan* (Shanghai: Shanghai Wenyi, 1982), no. 14.

The customer here is a leading cadre. His role has changed; he is no longer interested in real criticism, but only wants to hear flattery and is happy to have found a writer/critic who is willing to powder his face with fragrance. The barber has turned off the faucet of "criticism" on the left corner. He does not wash the man's dirty chair, not clip his outgrowth. The powder he puts on the cadre's face comes from pots inscribed "Excellent cadre" and "The successes are the main thing." The cartoon is entitled "Dry wash," and contains a pun on "cadre whitewash."

The last cartoon we shall consider here directly identifies the "problems" of the country when the hair grows naturally and is not clipped:

"Not worthy of the name of 'barber'"[25]

It is again by Hua Junwu, and was published in the *Renmin ribao* in August 1979, some time before Wang Meng's story came out. The long-haired and long-bearded beings in the corner are entitled "problems," the snoozing barber "bureaucratism." The inscription reads "The

25. Hua Junwu, "Bu chengzhi de lifashi," drawn in July 1979, published in *Renmin ribao*, 16 August 1979.

barber who lacks competence for his job." In this cartoon, the image of the barber has become even broader. In line with the new government policy of "seeking truth in facts," all cadres were called upon to have a realistic and critical assessment of the problems of the country, and they were to tackle them. The duty to point them out to the leadership was not only to be shouldered by professional writers/critics.

The image of the barber is thus a well-established part of the metaphors of Hundred Flowers politics. By writing a story about a barber, Wang Meng could communicate with a readership already familiar with its connotations. His text could rely upon implications of a familiar metaphor to convey his criticism.

Wang Meng's story takes up many of the elements of the cartoons. The barber as the critic, the mirror as the literary instrument to reflect bluntly reality's problems, the customer as the Party leadership, and the potential of the barbershop's being turned into a place of praise and flattery for the leaders. At the same time, he explores further aspects, such as the potential of the "salon," the institutional framework within which the shop is set up, and the limits imposed on the barber by this institutional affiliation.

His barber is the hero of the story. His barbershop is attached to the provincial Party leadership, and thus all the customers mentioned in the text are high Party and military leaders. Wang Meng is a cadre author. The great majority of his texts have dealt with cadres and confronted bureaucratic leaders with criticism. In the barber metaphor, the "customers" of his texts are the leading heads, and the interaction between barber and customers is a peaceful one. There is no guilt involved in the fact that hair "naturally" grows, and the barber has no bitterness in his heart when cutting off this outgrowth and restoring a proper, trim appearance.

This mild metaphorical relationship between the barber/critic and customer/cadre enters into a dialogue or even polemic with many other depictions of this relationship. It seems that the aggression already evoked during the 1950s in the popular mind by bureaucratic foot dragging and more recently by the enormous spread of backdoor dealing and corruption, implies a substantial guilt on the part of the bureaucrats and calls for their punishment and dismissal. Liu Binyan, for one, has cast the bureaucrats in the role of villains. He too portrayed the degeneration of the revolutionaries in his earlier stories; but in his more recent texts, the bureaucrats form a class of leaders ruthlessly fighting for their personal power, privilege, and security. The battle against them becomes much more militant and so do their measures against the "progressive protagonists." In fact, much of the appeal of the Cultural Revolution in the early years lay in the burgeoning resentment among youths and junior cadres at the bureaucratic arrogance displayed by many leaders. And the forms of battle adopted there were certainly a far cry from the barber's mild activities.

Wang Meng had already taken his much milder stance in 1956 with his "Newcomer."[26] There, the leading bureaucratic cadre, Liu Shiwu, describes his affliction, uncontradicted, as a "professional disease" similar to that of a cook who loses his appetite for food after years in the kitchen. Wang Meng's new story casts the relationship between leader and critic, at least during the 1950s, in the metaphor of the customer and this barber. This depiction rejects the others named above (and their ensuing consequences in terms of treatment) as inappropriate. In Wang Meng's eyes, the "customers" in those glorious days of old were very happy and content to undergo the treatment with its fine combination of "criticism" and "embellishment," *fali* and *zhengrong*. The autobiographical element in the barber, which has also been mentioned by Qin Zhaoyang,[27] is furthermore visible in the man's age. Around 1949, he was about 16; Wang Meng was born in 1934. The protagonist in the "Newcomer" in 1956 was a *nianqingren*, a "young man"; now the protagonist is in his fifties.

There were three generations of writers present in 1979; the old writers, whose careers peaked before 1949; the middle-aged writers, who came to the fore as youths during the Hundred Flowers period; and the young writers who started writing during the Cultural Revolution, in some cases privately and for private circulation, like the authors of the piece which became the pioneer of the new youth style, the "Open Love Letters." Within the logic of "Loyal Heart," we may expect the

---

26. For a detailed analysis of this story, see Chapter 10.

27. Qin Zhaoyang says in "The Writer Wang Meng," *Chinese Literature* 7:7 (1980), "In 'The Barber's Tale,' Wang Meng seems to identify with the narrator."

text to deal with the relationship among the still active generations, that is, the middle-aged and the young. Wang Meng's own relationship with his own cohort would be treated through the barber's relationship with his colleagues, and his relationship with the younger generation through that with his son.

As the institutional place of his work, the barber's salon is thus a metaphor for the "salon" of the *wenxue shijie*, the "literary circles." In a loving description with a touch of irony, the barber describes the environment where he works "in the glow of the great bright mirrors all around and of the fluorescent and other lamps at the ceiling," both of which hark back to the standard socialist theory according to which literature is to "reflect" reality; the "manifold perfumes of pomade, shampoo, almond and pineapple essences, and the 44776 Snow Flake Cream (!)" play on the literary flavors and embellishments while the "symphonic accompaniment of clicking shears, humming hairdryers, buzzing electrical clippers, and the water rushing from the faucets" mimics the busy chatter and hum in the literary world. The symbolic indicators of the changes brought about during the Cultural Revolution, like the breaking of the mirrors and lamps and the replacement of the trade's paraphernalia with clubs and cartridges, have been mentioned and support the symbolic interpretation given here.

The place of literature or, more broadly, of literature and the arts, in society is treated through the institutional affiliation of the barbershop. As the "barbershop of the No. 1 Guest House of the Provincial Committee," it is physically located within the premises of the leadership and under its direct control. The barber describes his own work as a *fuwu hangye*, a service trade. The expression plays on the standard definition of literature's duties, *wei zhengzhi fuwu*, "to serve politics," that is to propagate the policies promoted by the Center. Some years after "Loyal Heart" was published, the formula was broadened in the sense that literature was to "serve socialism and the people," but it still was to "serve," *fuwu*.[28]

28. The original formula was gradually changed. Deng Xiaoping in his speech at the Writers' Congress in September 1979 (note 3 above) explicitly abandoned the old formula, as did Zhou Yang at the same congress; see Zhou Yang, "Xuwang kailai, fanrong shehuizhuyi xinshiqi de wenyi" (Carry forward the cause and surge ahead—literature and the arts are enriching

In most Western states, a writer would hardly feel prompted to describe the institutional place of his trade. Authors in socialist countries, however, are keenly aware of the importance of institutional positions in an environment of bureaucratic and exceedingly rigorous organization and control. Other metaphors for literature's station would be the Temple of Apollo outside Troy's city walls but under the direct control of King Priam (with his "daughter" Cassandra as the nationally prominent writer) in Christa Wolf's *Cassandra,* or King Solomon's Royal Commission for the Writing of the King David Report, with the King presiding and laying down the line and Ethan the historian as the writer who has no vote in the Commission but is to research and write the text, in Stefan Heym's *King David Report.*[29]

Owing to the location of his barbershop, the barber might look to outsiders like a member of the leadership, and in fact many people see prominent writers like Wang Meng in that category. Wang Meng has rejected this assumption by depicting his persona as a humble barber and simple Party member and his shop as only a "minute little barbershop." It is true, however, that he enjoys a unique position and is one of the very few persons in this rigorously hierarchical society of China who is able to communicate with both high and low. Being a humble laborer, he knows the feelings and mumblings of his peers; working in the barbershop of the Center, he is familiar with the highest leaders.

Other authors have used other images to handle this amazing social mobility of the writer in socialism. In China, the image is often that of the doctor who treats high and low (as in *Guan Hanqing*[30]) or the

---

the new period of socialism), *Wenyibao* 11–12:17 (December 1979). In his speech at the Playwrights' Conference, 12 and 13 February 1980, Hu Yaobang explicitly referred to this statement, "Zai juben chuangzuo zuotanhuishang di jianghua" (Talk at the Conference on Creative Work in Drama), *Wenyibao* 1:20 (January 1981), but the new formula that literature was to "serve the people and to serve socialism" became standard only in September 1981; cf. Zhou Weizhi, "Nongcun ticai dayou zuowei" (The rural theme has great importance), *Renmin ribao,* 16 September 1981, and Ma Weian, "Zuojia yingdang duo tingting qunzhong yijian" (Writers must listen more to the criticism of the masses), ibid.

29. Stefan Heym, *Der König David Bericht* (Frankfurt/M: Kindler Verlag, 1972). An English edition is Stefan Heym, *The King David Report* (London: Hodder and Stoughton, 1972).

30. Cf. R. Wagner, "A Guide for the Perplexed and a Call to the Wavering: Tian Han's *Guan Hanqing* (1958)," in Wagner, *The Contemporary Chinese Historical Drama* (note 5 above), pp. 62ff.

patriotic poet who is also a kind of minister of foreign affairs (*Qu Yuan*).[31] In *Cassandra*, it is the King's daughter who as a woman also gains access to the humble milieu of the people living on the banks of the Skamandros and on Mount Ida with all their uncensored knowledge of history and contemporary events. Wang Meng thus treated the writer's role in socialism and took issue with the frequent portrayal of the writer as a member of the Center (albeit with little institutional power) in other Chinese texts. The humble station of the barber thus becomes a polemical statement against other portrayals, as well as a *captatio benevolentiae* for the readers by depicting the writer as "one of them."

The only important character left before we turn to the plot's analysis is Tang Jiuyuan. His biography evinces much similarity to that of the leadership coming to power after the 3rd Plenum in December 1978, namely, Deng Xiaoping and his associates. Tang was released from prison and sent to the Guest House in 1974 to await further decisions. This was the time of Deng's first return. In 1975 he was to get new employment but then a campaign started (the criticism of Deng in late 1975), so that things came to nothing. After the Tiananmen Incident, Tang tries to save his skin by toeing the new line. He is eventually reinstalled in power at about the same time as Deng. Tang is also the only protagonist whose full name is given. Wang Meng has used telling names since the 1950s, and Tang Jiuyuan fits this mold. The Jiuyuan might either be read at face value (as in most of Wang's telling names) as "long-lasting and far-reaching" or, with the aspiration of the *jiu* into *qiu* (a common technique), as he "who strives for far-reaching (or long-term) results." More important, the family name Tang, as in Tang dynasty, is a common pun on *dang*, "the Party." The historical dramas of the early 1960s often played on this pun, and in the Shaoxing opera *Sun Wukong Three Times Beats the White-Boned Demon*, Tang Seng (from the *Xiyou ji*) becomes the general name for "the Party," *dang*, while *seng*, meaning "the monk," defines him as a man who has *chujia*, "left his family," and joined the closed Buddhist community as a Communist is supposed to do when entering the Party. It is thus a meaningful

31. Cf. my "The Chinese Writer in His Own Mirror" (note 4 above), pp. 62ff.

hypothesis to read the evolving friendship between the barber and Tang Jiuyuan as a treatment of the relationship of a writer of Wang Meng's stature with the new leadership. We have encountered this theme in Gao Xiaosheng's story about Li Shunda.

HISTORY

As mentioned previously in this volume, the short story is supposed to focus on a single conflict concentrated within a very short time span. In times of rapid political changes, the long novel, however, is too slow to spell out the new orthodox epic of the past; the short story, *duanpian xiaoshuo*, has to stand in. "Loyal Heart" covers thirty years of history, and spells out the new evaluations of the different periods long before the official new view on history was spelled out in a Party document. During the Cultural Revolution, the good periods had been those of the war against Japan, the Civil War, the Great Leap Forward, and the Cultural Revolution itself, with the last two being the proper pedigree of a correct socialist line. In Wang Meng's story, the measuring rod for evaluating the different periods is the barber himself with his triple qualification as the honest man from the people, the writer as the representative of the people's best aspirations, and the writer as the man familiar with the lives and values of the leaders due to his unique access to the top echelon.

To the barber, the time before the Great Leap appears as the Golden Age when leaders and led were on an equal footing. With the Anti-Rightist Movement and the Great Leap, things go from bad to worse and reach their nadir during the Cultural Revolution and the occupation of the barber's salon by Red Guards. All the paraphernalia of the barber's craft are smashed and replaced by crude instruments of "class struggle" and propaganda. More important, the barber's link with "the Party" is attenuated. Neither the Red Guards nor the "newly born red political power" established in 1974 can command the barber's loyalty as a Party member. The Party of which he has been a member seems to have vanished from sight.

Wang Meng (and Gao Xiaosheng) were addressing a dilemma. In 1979, two years of sharp denunciation of the Cultural Revolution had passed. At the same time, the Party leadership under both Hua and Deng maintained that "the Party" certainly was not responsible for the turmoil of those ten years. In late 1978, the judgment on the Tiananmen Incident had been reversed; it was turned from a "counterrevolutionary incident" to the glorious "April 4th Movement." But who, if not "the Party," had led the Cultural Revolution, and who, if not common people, had resisted and protested at Tiananmen? There had been earlier criticisms of the leadership's policies, as the huge poster hung up in Canton by the Li-Yi-Zhe group in 1974.[32] The participants in the Tiananmen rally proudly maintained that it had been a spontaneous action of the people, and one member of the Li-Yi-Zhe group, Wang Xizhe, came out with an article arguing that the "people" had shown more political maturity in seeing through the facade of the Cultural Revolution leadership than "the Party" and that therefore much more democratic latitude should be accorded to the people.[33] The new leaders, he said, could not have staged their successful bid for power in September 1976 against the "Gang of Four" had not popular resentment against this group been evident since the Tiananmen Incident. Against this line of argument, the new leaders maintained in good tradition that "the Party" had smashed the "Gang of Four" and seen through them, so that "the Party's" legitimacy in monopolizing all levers of power was, in principle, unquestionable.

Writers tackling this complicated problem came up with a variety of plot-encoded explanations. Liu Binyan maintained that, since the mid-1950s, an invisible machine had established itself within the Party and as the Party in all too many realms, a machine consisting of bureaucrats devoted to their privilege, power, and self-preservation. The Cultural Revolution dramatically enhanced the potential and the cohesiveness of this machine, and all the reforms thereafter had hardly touched its core. Closer to Wang Meng, Gao Xiaosheng had his popular representative Li Shunda strike up a friendship with a Party leader who was deposed dur-

---

32. Cf. A. Chan and J. Unger, eds., *The Case of Li I-che, Chinese Law and Government* 10.3 (1977).

33. Wang Xizhe, "Wei wuchanjieji de jiejizhuangzheng er nuli" (Striving for the class dictatorship of the proletariat), *Qishi niandai* 116:30 (1979). Originally in *Renmin zhi sheng* (Guangzhou, 1978).

ing the Cultural Revolution and later reinstated, much as the new leadership. They become friends in distress, the Party man undergoing "reform through labor," Li Shunda being branded a Guomindang man of uncertain class status. The basis for this "friendship" between high and low is humanitarian concern, respect for human values, and empathy; and, on this basis, common political opposition to the Cultural Revolution leadership and their policies. Gao made it clear that these leaders were not "Party" leaders; their titles are "rebel chiefs" and the like. The true Party is invested in the momentarily deposed Party secretary.

Wang Meng adopted the same explanatory model of the true "underground" Party. The Red Guards and the "newly established Red Power" cannot claim and are not given the title of the Party; the name of his friend already indicates where the true Party is with its pun on Tang/*dang*. Tang Jiuyuan is the man with the long perspective, he has learned from his earlier mistakes as has Li Shunda's friend. Reacting to demands for greater democratic leeway, Wang Meng supported the charge made in April 1976 that the Tiananmen Incident had been engineered by Deng Xiaoping. Naturally, Wang Meng changed the evaluation. Both the barber and Tang Jiuyuan mourn for Zhou Enlai, the union of "true Party" and "the people," but it is Tang Jiuyuan who is organizing the manifestations like a "commander on the field."

> In January 1976, we and the Tangs sank into bitter mourning for Premier Zhou; together we shed tears, together we clenched our fists. From morning till night the Tangs took part in the memorial activities on the Place of the People. "This is mourning, and a demonstration, too!" said Old Tang, agitated, his eyes shining with the fire they had when he had been the commander of an artillery battalion. I had the vague feeling that he was engaged in planning a battle.

In 1979, the Party leadership claimed that many common Party members had taken part in these manifestations and had in effect led the movement. According to Wang Meng, the movement had in fact been "planned" like a "battle" by the later-to-be-restored old Party leaders. At the time when the text was published, the man who had come to power in 1976 in the wake of Deng's demise, Hua Guofeng, was still in office as the highest Party and government leader. In the story by Jiang Zilong studied elsewhere in this volume, Hua's transition government forms the main obstacle to rapid progress in the country's modernization. Wang Meng was more careful. His "newborn red political power" enters in 1974, and its representative is dismissed by February 1977 for having had close links with the "Gang of Four." In March, Tang is restored to a high leadership position. His biography closely matches the pattern of a large group of cadres who were criticized and often dismissed during the Cultural Revolution, tentatively reassigned for leadership work in 1975 with the official return of Deng to the highest government and Party leadership, again cast aside when Deng was dismissed from all Party and government offices in April 1976, and eventually restored after 1977 so that they could make their bid for power at the 3rd Plenum in December 1978.

The plot structure in Wang Meng's text solves a number of problems. It vaguely links Hua Guofeng with the "newborn red political power" made up of profiteers of the Cultural Revolution who should be dismissed for slandering the leaders of the true Party (Hua had led the campaign against Deng Xiaoping); it maintains the legitimacy of the Tiananmen demonstrations and links them with policies pursued by Zhou Enlai who had recalled Deng Xiaoping; and it boldly accepts the old claim made in 1976 by Mao and his cohorts that the Tiananmen demonstrations had been staged by Deng and his supporters and had been anything but outbursts of spontaneous popular feelings; it denies, on the way, the claim of "the people" for more rights and latitude and fortifies the new leadership's claim for the traditional role of the Party leadership as legitimately monopolizing all levers of power. In his rejection of the popular claims, Wang Meng went so far as to have the Tangs alone join in the rallies, while the barber, although sympathetic, stays home. In terms of factional struggle, Wang Meng assigned the merit of toppling the "Gang of Four" to Deng Xiaoping and his faction who mobilized public opinion, not to Hua Guofeng and his associates, who eventually arrested their fellow members in the Politburo. The political pedigree of both the Tangs and the barber is described by juxtaposing in the text an elaborate description of their mourning for Zhou Enali with the thundering silence about Mao's death, which is only indirectly evoked in the reference to the demise of the "Gang of Four." The implication is that only Mao's death made these arrests possible.

Wang Meng's description of the Cultural Revolution is not elaborate. The recurring image of human feces as the substantive leftover from this period is more a scatological denunciation than a sophisticated and probing analysis. The same pattern is repeated in the ironic comments about the renovation of the Guest House after 1974. "In the 'Worker-Peasant-Soldier Guest House' special-class rooms were furnished for the benefit of the powerful in the provincial and military top echelons who were not going the capitalist road, so as to improve conditions for their sleep, their personal hygiene, their nutrition, and their bowel movements so that, refreshed in both body and mind, they could lead the masses of workers and peasants in their fight against corrosion by revisionism and capitalism."

The most elaborate and interesting reflection on this mixture of leftist slogans and privilege is given only to insider readers through two book titles. The barber's son works in a bookstore, and thus is able to lay his hands on two much coveted books published in 1975, which the barber presents to Tang Jiuyuan. These books are to evoke some association in the reader's minds, and the barber certainly would not present his high friend with books running counter to his political beliefs and supporting the "newborn red political power." The first book is *Dong Zhou lieguo zhi* (Chronicle of the Eastern Zhou States).[34] The work had been compiled by Feng Menglong in the early Qing. Although little known in comparison to the great novels, it conveys a clear message, describing what happens if the founding virtues of the dynasty fall into disrepute and the state dissolves into warring states (factions), each vying for control. The second work, *Zhanzheng fengyun*, is the translation of Herman Wouk's *The Winds of War*.[35] The text deals with the events leading up to World War II, mostly with developments in Europe. It contains a poignant description of the radical leftist verbiage of the National Socialists and their intense borrowing from Leninism,

---

34. Feng Menglong, ed., *Dong Zhou lieguo zhi* (A chronicle of the Eastern Zhou states; Beijing: Zuojia Press, 1955). I assume that the 1975 edition is a reprint of this, but I have seen no copy.

35. Herman Wouk, *Zhanzheng fengyun* (The winds of war), tr. Shiren (standing for *shi ren*, "ten people," who cooperated in the translation). I have not seen the Chinese edition. The English edition is Herman Wouk, *The Winds of War* (Boston: Little, Brown, 1971).

gives elaborate portrayals of the pompous luxury and wealth amassed by Nazi leaders, and brings out their peculiar combination of gross lies, reckless atrocities, and personal affability.

Shortly before Wouk's book, Shirer's *Rise and Fall of the Third Reich*[36] had been published in Chinese translation for a public yearning for reading material and accustomed to reading any printed matter as a coded text. When Wang Meng introduced Wouk's title into his story, the identification of the "Gang of Four" as a "social-fascist" clique, using leftist vocabulary and pursuing "fascist" goals, had already become the line of the government. Cartoons showed the skeleton of Goebbels laughingly holding up his baby Yao Wenyuan:[37]

36. William Shirer, *The Rise and Fall of the Third Reich, a History of Nazi Germany* (New York: Simon & Shuster, 1960).

37. The illustration is taken from *Tigermaske und Knochengespenst* (note 17 above), p. 77.

The leadership could trust in 1979 that the public would be able to savor this identification of the "Gang of Four" with the Nazis through its familiarity with Shirer's and Wouk's books. Heinrich Böll has written a well-known article on German "ruin literature," "Trümmerliteratur," arguing that German literature after the war started out as such *Trümmerliteratur* since it had been cut off from world literature for a long time.[38] In 1979, this article was translated into Chinese, and Wang Meng as well as other writers began to describe their own writing efforts as being similar to those of young German authors after 1945.[39] In this manner, Wang Meng established the books appearing during the Cultural Revolution about the German Nazis as a subtle underground literature critical of the pseudo-leftism of the "Gang of Four," well in tune with the "left in form, right in essence" definition of the Party leadership which had not yet come to the conclusion that a truly "leftist" deviation (without quotation marks and not "rightist" in "essence") was even possible. The barber and Tang thus silently agreed in 1975 that the Gang of Four were Nazis in disguise.

Sadly, the sophisticated and open-minded probing of Wouk in his effort to understand the dynamics of German politics and personalities in this period finds no counterpart in Wang Meng's own text. By writing into Tang's "program" the resolution never again to employ "these leftists," Wang Meng deftly supported a rigorous purge of all cadres who "made it" during the Cultural Revolution, as opposed, for an example, to Jiang Zilong, who describes the former Red Guard rebel leader in the name of Xi Wangbei, "Generation-of-Hope." In the story, the provincial

38. Heinrich Böll's "Trümmerliteratur" appeared in a Chinese translation by Cheng Jianli, "Tan feixu wenxue" (On the literature of ruins), *Zhongbao yuekan* 5:108f (May 1980). Wu Meng suggests the term "literature of ruins" as appropriate for some recent Chinese works, most of which had appeared in the unofficial (*minban*) press like Shi Mo's (Zhao Zhenkai), who also writes as Bei Dao, "Zai feixu shang" (Among the ruins) and other works mostly from the journals *Jintian* (Today) and *Zhi yidai* (This generation); see Wu Meng, "Feixu shang de huhuan, lun dalu 'feixu wenxue'" (A call from the ruins—on the "literature of ruins" on the mainland), *Zhongbao yuekan* 5 (May 1980). In this and three later issues, this periodical reprinted some examples of this literature.

39. Arguing about the same parallel between Nazi Germany and the Cultural Revolution, Liu Binyan reported on his visit to Germany in late 1985, searching for the German handling of the "spiritual ruins" after the removal of most of the material ruins of the Nazi period; see Liu Binyan, "Tamen buken yiwang . . . —Lianbang Deguo sanji zhi yi" (They refuse to forget—notes on the Federal Republic of Germany 1), *Baogao wenxue* 1:3ff (January 1986).

leader who is said to have been affiliated with the Gang of Four is promptly dismissed. This seems like a solution of the problems plaguing the country. Wang Meng did not agree with the assumptions written into Liu Binyan's "Between Human and Monster," according to which the old networks of backdoor cadre links that had grown during the last twenty (not just ten) years remained unscathed by the post-Cultural Revolution purges.

The evaluation of the various phases of PRC history in the narrative of the humble barber is in happy coincidence with the official view elaborated by the new leadership in December 1978, and eventually congealed into the new ONE AND ONLY AUTHORITATIVE AND CORRECT VIEW OF THE PARTY'S HISTORY DURING THE LAST FORTY YEARS, the new Party resolution on history. Woven into this fairly orthodox warp for Wang's story, however, is the woof of the plot. Twenty years have passed since the "Golden Age" of the pre-1957 days, too long for them to be restored, and much of the spoken and silent text deals with and reacts to the intervening changes.

CHANGED EXPECTATIONS, ALTERED ROLES

The young generation, represented by the barber's son and the young chauffeur, a cadre's son, did not live during the "Golden Age." They go by their own experiences during the Cultural Revolution. They go with the latest flow like chauffeur Bu, or lump all politicians old and new together and cynically refuse any contact with them like the barber's son. The barber, like Wang Meng himself, has grown older; his enthusiasm of the 1950s, visible even in Wang Meng's "Newcomer," has gone, but he has found in traditional political values some stability and in the restored political leaders like Tang Jiuyuan some officialdom in which "my hopes for the future of the country, the Party, and myself rested," as he blandly states. His colleagues in the same age group have turned in another direction, repeating the little chauffeur's attitude and caring mostly about getting a proper share in the goods handed out through the backdoor by the new leaders.

Tang Jiuyuan has learned during his years in prison that his own policies certainly have contributed to the contempt for human beings and to the leftist radicalism of the Cultural Revolution, and that fundamental reforms in the personal structure and the prison system are a necessity. Tang again is not alone; his own weaknesses of privilege hunting, his arrogation of first-class apartments for his son, his ease with the offering of special services to the leading cadres are concentrated in his wife, a veritable dragon. She is spiteful, arrogant, and factitious with no visible commitment to the future of the nation. Wouk's *Winds of War* alludes to her in the figure of Captain Victor Henry's wife Rhoda. While the family name "Henry" is explained by Wouk as the condensation of all of the all-American qualities, and "Victor" foreshadows the eventual triumph of this character, Rhoda is the preserve of the more problematic aspects. She is somewhat taken in by the Germans, has some anti-Semitic leanings, is somewhat disgruntled with being only a Navy officer's wife, drinks somewhat too much, falls somewhat in love with another man, but eventually rejoins her husband in the worst crisis of his life. In the same manner, all weaknesses are concentrated in Madame Tang, who, needless to say, is also a high-ranking cadre. While these weaknesses are also present in her husband, the positive elements dominate in the leading male; the status of political women was low enough in 1979, some years after Jiang Qing's demise, to make them an easy repository for all that was problematic in the Chinese land.

Compared to the "Newcomer," the face of bureaucratism has changed. Routineer Liu in the "Newcomer" is afflicted with the bureaucratic disease of foot-dragging; he has lost his revolutionary zeal. There is no indication whatever that he does back-door deals with other cadres, feathers his own nest, is corrupt, or the like. He is a bureaucrat in the Leninist definition of a bureaucratic obstacle to the progress of the productive forces. In Tang Jiuyuan's case, this aspect is no longer mentioned; quite the opposite is true for him. Somewhat awkwardly he is described as an efficient organizer in the handling of a leadership conference in his city. This organizing includes the setting up of stores with first-class goods and prices reduced under a variety of disguises, all of which are listed by the barber, like "factory price," "introductory price," "sale price," and the like. The goods are available to the participant leaders only. The new leaders do feather their nests a bit, but the city has become much cleaner after Tang's takeover, and, like a Confucian magistrate of old, he occasionally dons common clothes to inspect a food store in this disguise, rooting out back-door dealings.

Wang Meng had, in 1956, conceded many weaknesses in the leadership he supported, but had written a text which at least in the explicit verbiage defended this leadership and expressed confidence that the young generation of "Newcomers" would "win the orientation of the leadership." Against the much harsher depiction of the bureaucrats as die-hard tyrants and obstacles to any progress in Liu Binyan's and others' writings, Wang had in fact defended the leadership. He claimed to have done so, and he did so. He maintained a similar attitude under the changed circumstances in 1979. He conceded the truth of much that has been written in other literary and journalistic texts, and added his bit of sociological observation. His own role and assessment, however, is vested in the barber, as it had been in the Young Man in the "Newcomer." Given the new circumstances, the barber will have to define his new role and with it that of his craft. The colleagues from the "service trades" have gone into the business of securing their spoils from the new dispensation.

The barber concedes to a wary readership that his powerful friend Tang did not attack the Cultural Revolution leadership (a charge leveled against him) because he did not dare; that, after the Tiananmen Incident, Tang became tight-lipped and even claimed to support the sharp attacks against Deng Xiaoping; that he was arrogant and haughty; that he was tied to and under the influence of Mrs. Tang, who pursued careerism and privilege hunting quite unabashedly; that he let the walls around the Guest House of S. be as high as those around the barber's Guest House; that he feathered his own nest and that of his relatives through backdoor deals; that he closed most of the city's good restaurants, theaters, and ice-cream shops to have the personnel serve the leaders assembled in the Guest House; that he set up special stores where they can buy rare goods at bargain prices; that, although grateful to the barber for his life-saving help, he even forgot the name of his benefactor. In short, the Tangs "naturally were no living gods, they ate the five kinds of grain, had the seven feelings and the six desires."

The resentment felt among the lower orders at the doings of the recently restored old cadres has no outlet, and the leaders don't even know about it. The walls around the Guest House have been fortified by the "newborn red political power" but the restored cadres have done nothing to tear them down; rather they have walled themselves up even more. The image is a familiar one from other texts of this time. Liu Binyan described in the opening paragraph of his "Between Human and Monster" how already in the 1960s "the walls around the building [of the Bin County Committee] seemed to grow higher and higher." Bai Hua went into loving details in his "A Sheaf of Letters" in the description of the walls, fierce dogs, and guards warding off any commoner from the plush living quarters of the rehabilitated officers and their families, and Sha Yexin and his colleagues present the audience in "If I Were Truly" with a veritable sightseeing tour through the house of the Party secretary of S, accompanied by ironic comments about the seclusion of the leaders from public view.[40]

This combination of growing resentment and barred avenues of remonstrance produces a situation of social crisis which might quickly become explosive. Using his unique social mobility across the dividing line between the rulers and the ruled, the barber sets out to prevent the social cataclysm and to carve out his own role. He muses,

> What was wrong with her [Mrs. Tang]? What was wrong with them [the Tangs]? They had suffered so much bitterness, and people had sympathized with them. Perhaps [Mrs. Tang] felt they had the right to "grab" back the losses inflicted on them by the Gang of Four. But they couldn't "grab" in such a fashion! No, they did not have the right, they did not have the right to do so. People set their eager hopes on them . . . If they were to get divorced from the masses . . . Heaven!

The scene of the barber's saving Tang in his distress marks the turning point in the barber's life. He helps and befriends Tang/dang at a time when the latter is powerless. "This blood, this moaning, this limp body, the waxen face, and the closed eyes" are what the barber recalls of the moment when he carried Tang to the car. In this, Tang's most crit-

---

40. Liu Binyan, "Renyao zhijian" (Between human and monster), *Renmin wenxue* 9 (September 1979); Bai Hua, "Yishu xinzha" (A sheaf of letters), *Renmin wenxue* 1 (January 1980); Sha Yexin, Li Shoucheng, Yao Mingde, *Jiaru woshi zhendi* (If I were truly), *Qishi niandai* 1 (1980); the first and the last text have been translated and commented upon in my *Literatur und Politik in der Volksrepublik China* (note 8 above).

ical moment, the "people" in the person of the barber stand by Tang. "If it had not been for Master Lu [the barber], you would not have survived it," says Tang's wife.

It is important that this scene is not related to the barber's professional activities as a barber. It does not take place in the barbershop, and the barber pays for Tang's transport to the hospital with his private money. Since the "newborn red political power" has fenced in the Guest House and has stationed guards at the door, the barber's salon, too, has been fenced in, and the "masses," that is, the non-Party people, have been walled out so that the place has lost the function of a place of communication between high and low that it enjoyed during the Golden Age. The barber remains in his trade and stays in the Party, but the motivation of his subsequent actions comes from a personal friendship with Tang, established without ulterior motives and pursued in his spare time without mandate or institutional requirement at his own cost and risk. When he visits Tang after the latter's restoration to power, we are explicitly informed that this visit is not part of his activities as a participant in the conference of the service trades, but his private affair. Nonetheless, his professional affiliation still serves some purpose; his participant's pass from that conference secures access at least to the outer wall around the Guest House complex of the city of S, a slightly ironic allusion to the access to "social reality" presumably coming with the writ from the Writers' Union.

The barber's activities are private and outside his social institution as much as his values are now private and independent of the mental counterpart to his *danwei*, the Party. As has been mentioned, the text does not establish the image of the barber as the writer/critic, but explores an already established image. The story argues that the institutions of social criticism that have been set up by the Party leadership, the barbershops of the nation, in fact cannot serve their purpose anymore. In order to do his job as the writer/critic, the barber now has to act as a committed individual in his "spare" time and with his spare values. This depiction of Wang Meng's own role reacts to a double credibility gap.

The credibilty of the analytical and evaluative instruments of Marxism-Leninism-Mao Zedong Thought was at its lowest in the aftermath of the Cultural Revolution, when it had eventually dawned on about everyone that the bane of power had reduced these doctrines to bland post facto justifications for factional pursuits. Furthermore, literature as an institution had been so ostentatiously reduced to being "a weapon in class struggle" a feature it had assumed all along since the founding of the People's Republic or the Yan'an days, that its credibility in terms of simple truthfulness and authenticity was also at its lowest.

Wang Meng's barber neither leaves the Party nor his job. Through first-person narrative, through dissociation of his present political activities from traditional Party and professional pursuits, and by claiming a humanitarian, common-sense, and highly personal motivation for the barber, Wang Meng attempted to reestablish his own authenticity and hence his credibility with a wary readership. By having his barber stay in the Party and in his job, Wang Meng rejected the option very much present in society in 1979, namely to operate completely outside the established power structure, an option alluded to in the figure of his son. There is no need to be a dissident and outcast if one wants to be an honest writer, Wang Meng argued, and had his barber speak out frankly as a putative member of the laboring classes.

When the barber learns who the man he saved is, and becomes familiar with that man's past experiences and future plans, he sets the hopes for the country and for his own future on him. True, he is appalled by the way the Tangs deal with their career, and especially by Mrs. Tang, but, confronted with the choice between human feces and Tang/*dang*, he opts for the latter.

THE LONELY BARBER'S BURDEN

The barber as the people's iconographic representative has "saved" Tang/*dang*, when the latter was out of power and in the dust with Ménière's disease. The disease seems as metaphorical as the barber's attitude is symbolic. The depiction of the writer as the medical doctor treating the body politic or parts thereof has been a familiar metaphor since Liu E's *Laocan youji* in the late Qing; it has been kept alive in the PRC through pieces like Tian Han's *Guan Hanqing* (1958). Among the many connotations adhering to this simile, most prominent are the humanitarianism of the doctor who treats high and low and his great mobility across the social scale. In Wang Meng's story, the barber is not a doctor, but he helps the sick Tang/*dang* out of a strictly humanitarian motive, and, expressed through other means, he also shares the doctor's access to all layers of society. Wang Meng thus alluded, by way of reinforcement, to another, and related, simile for the writer's role. Tang/*dang* is sick. Ménière's disease is an ailment accompanied by dizziness, nausea, and partial loss of hearing. The immediate cause is excess pressure on the inner-ear's fluid, but, according to Chinese as well as Western medical encyclopedias, no definite cause has yet been determined. Within the story, Tang indicates that the occurrence of attacks is linked to stress. Wang Meng did not use the current name of the disease, *Meinier shi bing,* Ménière's disease, but *Meinier shi zonghebing,* verbatim for Ménière's syndrome. Tang/*dang* is not suffering from some clearly definable disease but from a "complex of symptoms" the specific causes of which are not known. He is not "mortally ill" like Jiang Zilong's Du Bing, but he is chronically ill, and constantly threatened. No link is made between his disease and his treatment during the Cultural Revolution. The standard descriptions of the effects of the disease read like a metaphorical description of Tang's reaction to the reality around him; in his view, there is a Communist Party in power, but it is a CP only in name; revolutionary slogans abound, but they serve only to hide the reactionary "essence" of the leaders, and he himself, an old Communist, lands in "the prison of our Communist Party." This seems enough to explain the causes of dizziness and nausea.

The new leader, the barber's personal friend, runs the danger of drawing upon himself the same sort of aggression that secured so much support for the Cultural Revolution in the beginning. The danger and threat of such a renewed onslaught was keenly felt in 1979 when bureaucratic privilege-hunting of the restored cadres angered all too many. Writers other than Wang Meng had taken up this issue, Liu Binyan, Sha Yexin, and Ru Zhijuan, to name but a few. They often described the bureaucratic abuses of the restored cadres in much harsher terms.

The barber sees it as his responsibility to prevent the breakdown of communication between high and low which could lead only to a renewed breakdown of orderly government. Wang Meng's writing thus set out to be the meeting point between these two social spheres separated by ever thicker walls. The barber resolves to visit his high friend to tell him about the criticisms those below utter with hushed voices and which Tang/*dang* would never hear if not through his, the barber's, mediation. At the same time, he sets out to defend his powerful friend against the cynical rejection all too common among the people.

The story does not claim that this is a popular enterprise. When the barber visits his powerful friend, his colleagues see him as someone who has gotten the "knack" of getting contacts to high leaders. They take it for granted that the barber will use this link to his own advantage, and they proceed to give him cash to buy some rare goods for them inside the leadership compound. At the other extreme, the barber's son scoffs at his father for being so "naive" as to think normal associations with such leaders are possible, and pressures the barber to break off all contacts. As the barber's "son," he is closely linked to him, albeit as the younger generation; working in a Xinhua bookstore indicates that he, too, has some relationship with the literary world. Many of the younger writers indeed refused to operate through the official channels in 1979; they set up literary and political magazines of their own, or just distributed their stories and poems among friends.

The son's counterpart in that generation, the young chauffeur, also assumes that the barber is a wily and astute politician to have befriended Tang/*dang* when he was out of power. The motives of the barber in visiting Tang are thus not in doubt; they are perfectly clear to his peers. They see him as a wily opportunist. The barber does not fare better with Tang. When he has finally made it into the Guest House compound and meets his old friend, he wants to proffer his criticism of the small shop where all the bargain goods are offered. He starts, "That shop . . . ," but old Tang has urgent business to attend to and enough experience to know that the barber also wants to buy things there. He has him handed a voucher. Misunderstood and misjudged in his pure intentions by the people and his colleagues on the one hand, and Tang/*dang* on the other, the barber flees the Guest House. In literary terms, the story ends here, although, in fact, it is followed by two pages of political discourse.

When read against the backdrop of the "Newcomer," the barber's complete isolation is most striking. In the "Newcomer," the Young Man could feel safely bound in with a coalition of progress made up of the workers at the base and the top Party leadership, both of whom loathed bureaucratism and relied on young writers and journalists to establish a link between them so that pressure might be brought to bear on the bureaucrats in the middle. Now, in 1979, both top and bottom have lost their luster and their drive, and the intellectual middleman, twenty years older and with ideals much toned down, is left alone in his motivation and his actions, looked on by his former supporters with a mixture of envy, distrust, gratitude, and self-interested admiration. The Young Man's socialist idealism has ceded to the barber's Confucian morality; order has replaced swift "progress" as the best attainable end.

Although the social climate and the coalition structures have fundamentally changed, the barber's social position and role show a strong continuity with the Young Man. He is still the mediator articulating the "people's" grievances for those above to hear and defending those above to "the people." As before, the publicly available literary texts become the form of this mediation. Told now as a first person narrative, however, "Loyal Heart" claims the authenticity of personal honesty, no longer the orthodoxy of socialist tenets. In the depiction of the loneliness of the barber, there is self-pity for being burdened with such a misunderstood and ill-recognized role, as well as the assurance to the reader that the writer is truly driven only by motives of public interest.

The literary text, however, is more than a construct of the writer and the reader. Already in writing the "Newcomer," Wang Meng had encountered the problem that a literary text takes on an energy of its own in the process of the plot's unfolding, and limits the discretionary powers of the writer to an ever greater degree. A text might move in a direction not only unforeseen, but unwanted. In his self-critical article about the "Newcomer," Wang Meng described in 1957 this dilemma between a writer who lets the inner logic of a text unfold, and the political believer or politician who intends to convey a certain message.[41] In the version originally submitted, the "Newcomer" indicated the rather gloomy view the young people took of their leaders and their capacity

---

41. Wang Meng, "Guanyu 'Zuzhibu xinlaide qingnianren'" (On "A Young Man Who Only Recently Joined the Organization Department"), *Renmin ribao*, 10 May 1957.

to change their attitude. These scenes attracted most of the attention, both critical and supportive, and Liao Mosha's final verdict referred to this gloominess pervading the text as its main fault. However, in the text itself, Wang Meng had already tried to get control of the plot by having the Young Man engage in what may be called "self-pontification." After all his discouraging experiences, Lin Zhen is suddenly convinced that "he will win the orientation of the leadership." This upbeat note flatly contradicts the text itself, and, as it has no place within the text (and Wang Meng is too good a writer not to have noticed this), it is appended at the end. The Young Man proceeds in this manner to talk to himself and convince himself that his own experience and subsequent attitude is wrong. He lectures himself on the right principles and thus permits the author to end his story on an upbeat note. Read against other contemporary texts and against much of the popular attitude at the time, the text actually came out in support of the very bureaucrats so harshly denounced by Liu Binyan and others. They needed only a little fresh enthusiasm from their younger colleagues. In a movement of criticism of the bureaucrats, Wang Meng, while conceding many of the charges against them, in fact defended them, at least in the conscious thrust of the text, while the piece as a literary work calmly pointed in the opposite direction.

"Loyal Heart" evinces the same stress. The Cultural Revolution leadership is dismissed in scatological verbiage as privilege hunting and aloof from the masses. The two last features are in fact shared by Tang, and the difference is simply that the barber has him as a "friend." This friendship seems to be more a factional alliance than one based on politics or principle or even actual policies, because Tang's reform program has not been acted upon by the end of the story. It is to the benefit of the text that the author's political intervention, his attempt to get control over its development, again does not come before the last two pages of the text; it certainly contributed to the acceptance of the text. In the last part, the barber proceeds to convince himself of his thankless political duty as a writer in a voice which curiously mixes self-pity for his isolation and the misreading of his motives by all concerned with a lengthy stroke of self-pontification:

Musing about this last unfortunate visit, I was also angry with myself. How could one be so rash, and so one-sided and superficial in looking at a problem? Too much work, was that his [Tang's] fault? Taking care of the drivers who had brought the leaders also was nothing bad. True, his wife tends to lose her temper—but that's her problem. All told, I could hold against him only things like the low price for the ice cream [in the store at the Guest House]— and I had even eaten that ice cream myself. What's more, the Center had just published a document establishing discipline commissions on all levels, so that they would hardly again sell this kind of ice cream for 6 pennies in the Guest House of S.

In short, the barber convinces himself of the triviality and irrelevance of his own experiences with the new leadership. The first part of the story details many of the things most irritating to the public at the time and establishes the claim of the author's truthfulness; through the identification with the barber the reader is to share in the self-pontification and to accompany the barber into his final vindication of the new leadership. This vindication is not based so much on the innate qualities of the new leaders as on the necessity of preventing another social cataclysm like the Cultural Revolution. In a final statement, the barber addresses himself and his audience:

> I thought a society could not do without "officials"; to topple the "officials" altogether would only lead to human feces and roundworms. But who should be the officials? I was against those Zhaos [the Cultural Revolution leader of the province] and against those "commanders" and "servants of the people" who destroyed everything, and I myself was not and certainly did not intend to become an "official." I supported old Tang. One should make allowances for people. For the realization of his three-point "political program" one had to give him some time. I should not persecute the "officials" as these "commanders" had done, nor should I simply make use of them like [the chauffeur] little Bu and my colleagues. I should not blindly submit to the "officials" as some delegates in S had suggested, but I should also not keep a distance from the "officials" and regard them as enemies as my son did. Blood had flown in torrents, white bones had piled up in mountains, the price had been too high. It had been difficult enough to topple the Guomindang "officials" and then to beat down the "officials" of the Gang of Four, difficult enough to reestablish our own old comrades again as "officials," but, if no one keeps contact with them and tells them what is on his mind, what shall become of our state, what of our beloved Party?

The barber, an emotional man, is quite moved by this address to himself. "When my thoughts reached this point, tears dripped from my eyes," he ends his soliloquy. His modest purpose is stability, and he is willing to give his life and energy to the prevention of chaos and to the support of the new leadership by keeping open a small line of critical communication between high and low. When returning to the literary scene in 1978, Wang Meng first wrote "Buli," a "Bolshevik Salute" to the Party. In the title of the present text, the barber's attitude is defined as *youyou cuncaoxin, youyou* meaning "patient," and *cuncaoxin* a "heartfelt (gratitude), no taller than grass." This latter term denotes a child's gratitude for the unending care of the parents, this gratitude being, in comparison, at best as minute as an inch-long blade of grass. The illustrations of the text bring out this aspect of the barber's attitude towards the Party in his modest and devout body posture.

The barber listening to Tang Jiuyuan explaining his "political program."

It may be added that Wang Meng's political career tends to bear out this interpretation. In 1980, he became the editor of the most official national literary periodical, *Renmin wenxue;* he was elected an alternate and in 1987 a full member of the Central Committee after having been made Minister of Culture in early 1986. He had come out in support of the Campaign against Spiritual Pollution, had sharply (if indirectly) attacked Liu Binyan in the pages of *Renmin ribao* in early 1986, and had otherwise paid his dues as the head of various writers' delegations abroad. As a Chinese delegate to the PEN club's meeting in 1985 in New York he maintained, amidst the incredulous stares of his colleagues, that the Chinese government did not interfere at all in literary affairs. He kept his post after the government crackdown on 4 June 1989, but did not demonstrate support publicly thereafter. Late in 1989, he was first stripped of his post of Party secretary within the Ministry, and was eventually replaced by He Jingzhi as both minister and secretary. As the above analysis has shown, he is well aware of the isolation and distrust his attitude might bring him. In his own logic, however, any criticism too acrimonious and any literary topic or form too much out of the mainstream might endanger the social fabric altogether and bring back factional strife and bloodshed. The barber defends Wang Meng against the charge of being an opportunist; he is only being responsible.

SIGNS OF STRESS

Everything in a literary text is fiction, is artifice, and all the more so if it claims to be just truthful depiction of reality. "Loyal Heart" reacts to a wide variety of environmental pressures and lures, not the least among them being Wang Meng's attitudes as a politician. Read as a construct, the effort is visible to regain credibility and authenticity for the narrative voice through a variety of literary devices. The implied readers are the vague and anonymous "honest people" who share the barber's values but might be strongly enough influenced by the attitudes visible among this colleagues or the younger generation to warrant explicit criticism of these attitudes. The addressee, especially of the last part, is the political leadership which is, without a trace of irony, assured of the barber's unfailing support.

When "Loyal Heart" is held against Gao Xiaosheng's story, which operates through the artifact of a muddle-headed uneducated rural inhabitant, it becomes quickly evident that the barber and the pedlar in their simple and honest minds incidentally agree with the Party leadership's new view of history. Spontaneously they manage to come up with the latest insights of their leaders, most strikingly in their view of the Great Leap. The new leaders like Deng Xiaoping had been in charge of the country's politics during the Great Leap, and they had been dismissed during the Cultural Revolution. From this it follows that the Great Leap was not as bad as the Cultural Revolution. Demographic data, and reports about widespread famine during the Great Leap indicate the possibility of seeing things quite differently. In the efforts of East German writers like Christa Wolf, who also tried to reestablish "subjective authenticity" as the key criterion for literary works against socialist-realist typicality, the "authentic voice" there indicated a far more serious effort to probe, in a self-critical manner, the very foundations of the writers' own former beliefs and of the underlying stresses and tensions of their society and its collective psyche. By contrast, having the "authentic voice" reiterate in other words the official line, Wang Meng reduced what might have been the beginning of a serious probe to a tactical device. Needless to say, even the depiction of bureaucratic privileges in the text follows the directives of the 3rd Plenum, which called for a criticism of such phenomena. Against a very popular anger at these abuses, the text offers a defense of the leaders, and its thrust is thus exactly opposite that of Liu Binyan's texts.

Within "Loyal Heart," Wang Meng did not introduce the "implied readers" in force to show their eager support for the barber's position. The credibility of the barber within the text is low with both the leaders and his peers, his honest and authentic intentions notwithstanding. When he leaves the Guest House of S, shocked and trembling, his efforts have come to naught, and he can claim some sympathy from the reader. In view of the plot and the realities it depicts, this would have been the logical conclusion. In literary terms, both text and plot dissociate themselves from the matter appended by the politician Wang Meng at the end.

In this manner, "Loyal Heart" in its entirety evinces the tension between a skilled literary craftsman and a politician trying to convince himself and others of certain necessities. True to the traditional self-perception of the Chinese writer in this century, "Loyal Heart" shows an overpowering self-righteousness in the barber's voice. There is self-aggrandizement in the depiction of the ultimately crucial role of the writer's vital deeds for the conservation of social peace while he assumes the modest pose of the barber in a small barbershop; there is self-pity for the slanders and doubts he has to endure in his solitary role; and there is a complete absence of a self-ironic insight into the narrative voice's own weakness. Thus, there is little wisdom in this text.

Glossary

A Ying 阿英
Ah Q zhengzhuan 阿 Q 正傳
Ai Nan 愛南
Ai Wu 艾蕪
Ai Zhi 艾之
an yu xianzhuang 安於現狀
An Ziwen 安子文
Anhui Wenxue 安徽文學
Aoweiqijin 奧維奇金
Azha yu Hali 阿扎與哈利

Ba Jin 巴金
ba jiti tuanjie fushi
　　把集體團結腐蝕
Ba Ren 巴人
bahui 罷會
Bai Hua 白樺
baichi 白痴
baifen zhi jiushi ji 百分之九十幾
bailian 白臉
Bailian chenggang 百煉成鋼
bangsi ren 幫四人
Banzhuren 班主人
Bao Longtu 包龍圖
baochi yituan heqi 保持一團和氣
Baofeng zouyu 暴風驟雨
baogao wenxue 報告文學
baogao 報告
Baoshengong 包身工

baoshou 保守
baozhang wenxue 報章文學
Bei Dao 北島
Beidou 北斗
Beijing ribao 北京日報
Beijing Shifan Daxue Wenyi Lilun
　　zu 北京師範大學文藝理論組
Benbao neibu xiaoxi 本報內部消息
benweizhuyizhe 本位主義者
Bianxing ji 變形記
Bianzhe an 編者按
Bideluoxiang, A. 彼得羅相
bing du 病篤
Bingxin 冰心
biran 必然
Boliefuyi 波列伏依
bu da hui chu shenme maobing
　　不大會出甚末毛病
bu gan shuohua 不敢說話
bu gao bu di 不高不底
bu he ren chaojia 不和人吵架
bu qiu chenggong 不求成功
bu qiu shangjin 不求上進
bu shiji 不實際
bu xihuan zhudong zuanyan
　　不喜歡主動鑽研
bufu zeren 不負責任
bugou shiji 不夠實際
Buxing 不幸

buxue wushu 不學無術

cai 才
Cai Yuanpei 蔡元培
cankui 慚愧
Cao Lifu 曹力夫
Cao Mengfei 草夢飛
Cao Ming 草明
Cao Xueqin 曹雪芹
Changchun 長春
changpian xiaoshuo 長篇小說
Changxin 常新
chaoshui 潮水
Chen Boda 陳伯達
Chen Changhuo 陳昌活
Chen Chunnian 陳椿年
Chen Guoji 陳國飢
Chen Huangmei 陳荒煤
Chen Jinyan 陳今言
Chen Jitong 陳季同
Chen Lidong 陳立棟
Chen Qitong 陳其通
Chen Shimei 陳世美
Chen Xiaoyu 陳笑雨
Chen Xicheng 陳希成
Chen Yading 陳亞丁
Chen Yanning 陳衍寧
Chen Yi 陳毅
Chen Yong 陳涌
Cheng Hai 程海
Chi cheng huan lü qing lan zi
    赤澄黃綠青藍紫
chongfang 重放
Chongfang de xianhua 重放的鮮花
chou 丑
chu fengtou 出風頭
chuangzaoxing 創造性
Chuankou Hao 川口好
chujia 出家
Chun Chao 春潮
Chunjie 春節
chunshui 春水

chushan 出山
Cihai 辭海
cuncaoxin 寸草心

da gunzi 大棍子
dadan jingshen 大膽精神
dadan 大膽
dadandi ganyu shenghuo
    大膽地干預生活
dadandi sixiang 大膽地思想
Dai Shuqing 戴叔清
dan qiu wuguo 單求無過
Dan Tong 丹彤
dan'gan 膽敢
danchun 單純
dandiao 單調
dang 黨
dangbao 黨報
dangxing 黨性
danwei 單位
danxiao pashi 膽小怕事
Dao shi wuqing que youqing
    道是無情卻有情
daoli 道理
daxing 大形
Dazhong wenyi 大眾文藝
de 德
Deng Xiaoping 鄧小平
Deng Youmei 鄧友梅
Di er zhong zhongcheng
    第二種忠誠
diji 低級
dimei shunmu 低眉順目
Ding Cong 丁聰
Ding Ling 丁玲
Ding Panshi 丁磐石
Dong Cunrui 董存瑞
Dong Xin 董昕
Dong Zhou lieguozhi 東周列國志
Du Bing 杜兵
du chu xincai 獨出心裁
duanpian hsiaoshuo 短篇小說

duanping 短評
ducu 督促
dui bu heli xianxiang he buliang qingxiang ye bu jiji douzheng 對不合理現象和不良傾向也不積極鬥爭
dui gongchandang buman de ren 對共產黨不滿的人
duli de jianjie 獨立的見解
duli sikao 獨立思考
duoguan xianshi 多管現實
Dute de xuanlü 獨特的旋律

Er Ying 爾英
ermuguan 耳目官

fali 髮理
Fan Changjiang 範長江
fan diao 反掉
Fan Tiansheng 樊天勝
fanchao 反潮
Fang Cheng 方成
Fang Ji 方紀
Fang Lizhi 方勵之
Fang Qun 方群
Fang Zhi 方之
fangfa 方法
fangxiale bigan 放下了筆桿
fanmian 反面
fanshi houtui 凡是後退
fazhan gexin 發展個性
feili wudong 非禮無動
feili wuyan 非禮無言
Feng Menglong 馮夢龍
Feng Mu 馮牧
Feng Xuefeng 馮雪峰
fengming weijin 奉命唯謹
Fenshui 汾水
Fu Donghua 傅東華
Funiqie, Ai.Li., 艾. 麗. 伏尼契
fupi 復辟
fushou tie'er 俯首貼耳

fuwu hangye 服務行業

gailun 概論
gaizao 改造
gan 干
gan 敢
gan shiqing de ren 敢事情的人
gangyi 剛毅
Gansu 甘肅
ganyu shenghuo 干預生活
gao chao 高潮
Gao Daquan 高大全
Gao Gang 高崗
Gao Ming'an 高明安
Gao Tongnian 高桐年
Gao Xiaosheng 高曉聲
gaochao 高潮
gaogao guaqi 高高掛起
Ge Defu 葛德夫
Ge Yi 戈一
gede 歌德
gedepai 歌德派
geming de jinquxin 革命的進取心
geming yaolan 革命搖籃
geming zishen baoweizhe 革命自身保衛者
Geng Jian 耿簡
gengenpai 跟跟派
Genggeng 更更
gesong 歌誦
gexin 革新
gexinzhe 革新者
Gezhe yiceng 隔著一層
gongju 工具
Gongkai de qingshu 公開的情書
gongnongbing 工農兵
Gongren ribao 工人日報
gongzuo bu qijin 不作不起勁
gongzuozhe 工作者
guaihua 怪話
Guan Hanqing 關漢卿
guangpu 光樸

guanshangle zuiba 關上了嘴巴
guanxi 關係
guanxixue 關係學
Guanyu "xie yin'an mian" he
  "ganyu shenghuo"
  關於"寫陰暗面"和
  "干預生活"
guiju 規矩
guniangmen 姑娘們
Guo Ke 郭珂
Guo Moruo 郭沫若
Guo Qizong 郭啟宗
Guo Xiaochuan 郭小川
Guo Yongze 郭永澤
Guomindang 國民黨
guoyu jinzhang 過于緊張

Hai Feng 海楓
Hai Hua 海花
Hairui ba guan 海瑞罷官
Han Changxin 漢常新
hao hao xiansheng 好好先生
Hao Ran 浩然
hao 好
Haoren a, ni bugai zheyang ruanruo
  好人阿，你不該這樣軟弱
Harbin ribao 哈爾濱日報
He Aoweiqijin zai yiqi de rizi
  合奧維奇金在一起的日子
He Fei 何非
He Jingzhi 賀敬之
He Qifang 何其芳
He Zhi 何直
Hebei Wenyi 河北文藝
henhaode fanmian jiaocai
  很好的反面教材
Hong Yiping 洪一平
honglian 紅臉
Honglou meng 紅樓夢
Hongri 紅日
Hu Bowei 胡伯威
Hu Feng 胡風

Hu Keshi 胡克實
Hu Shi 胡適
Hu Yaobang 胡耀邦
Hu Zhongchi 胡仲持
Hua Junwu 華君武
huadan 花旦
huafei 花費
Huang Gang 黃鋼
Huang Guiyuan 黃桂元
Huang Jiaying 黃佳英
Huang Nansen 黃枏森
Huang Sha 荒砂
Huang Sha 黃砂
Huang Shifu 黃士復
Huang Tianpeng 黃天鵬
Huang Zhuanmou 黃傳謀
Huangmei 荒煤
huangtang 荒唐
Huo Dadao 霍大道
huodong yudi 活動餘地

ji shen 寄身
Ji Shen 冀申
Ji Xi 基希
Jia Ji 賈霽
Jian Yu 鑒余
jianfeng shichuan 見風使船
Jiang Jun 江軍
Jiang Meng 江萌
Jiang Ming 江明
Jiang Ming 江鳴
Jiang Tie 江鐵
Jiang Yousheng 江有生
Jiang Zilong 蔣子龍
Jiannan de qifei 艱難的起飛
jiaoao qingxu keneng shengzhang
  驕傲情緒可能生長
jiaoao 驕傲
Jiaru wo shi zhendi 假如我是真的
Jidianjuzhang de yitian
  機電局長的一天
Jidianjuzhang 機電局長

Jieyue 解約

jilu texie 記錄特寫

jilü 紀律

Jin Fan 靳凡

Jin Mei 金梅

Jin Zhendu 金振都

Jingbao 鏡報

Jingde zhuangfeng 敬德裝瘋

Jinggao 報告

jinghan 精悍

Jinguang dadao 金光大道

jinshen 謹慎

Jintian 今天

jinxiao shenwei 謹小慎微

jitizhuyi 集體主義

jituan 集團

jiu 久

Juelie 決裂

juju shushu 拘拘束束

jun 駿

Kafuka 卡夫卡

Kaituo 開拓

Kalining, A. 卡里寧, 安

kan wenti bu quanmian
看問題不全面

kan yanse shuohua 看顏色說話

Kang Lin 康林

Kang Zhuo 康濯

kangzhan baguwen 抗戰八股文

Kawaguchi Ko 川口好

ken'gan 肯干

kenzhi 懇摯

kesuxing 可塑性

Kong Jiesheng 孔捷生

Kong Luosun 孔羅蓀

Kongcheng ji 空城計

Konggu lan 空谷蘭

kuangwang 狂妄

kuankuo 寬闊

kuzao wuwei 枯燥無味

kuzao 枯燥

Lai Ruyu 賴如愚

Laifangzhe 來訪者

Lajiao 辣椒

Lan Hai 籃海

Lanlan de mulanxi 籃籃的木蘭溪

Lanzhou 蘭州

lao sanpian 老三篇

Laocan youji 老殘游記

Laodong bao 勞動報

laolao shishi 老老實實

laolao shishi gongzuo
老老實實工做

laolian 老練

laosheng 老生

laoshi ren 老實人

laoshi taidu 老實態度

laoshi 老實

laoshitou 老實頭

Lee Yee 李怡

Lei Shuyan 雷抒雁

lengjiao 棱角

lengmo 冷漠

Li Binsheng 李濱聲

Li Chuli 李楚離

Li Daozong 李道宗

Li Gan 力干

Li Helin 李何林

Li Heqing 李鶴青

Li Oufan 李歐梵

Li Shengliang 李盛亮

Li Shiwen 李士文

Li Shoucheng 李守成

Li Shunda zaowu 李順大造屋

Li Xifan 李希凡

Li Yi Zhe 李一哲

Liang Qichao 梁啟超

Lianhuan huabao 連環畫報

lige 俚歌

liliang 力量

Lin Biao 林彪

Lin Liu 林流

Lin Manshu 林曼叔

Lin Mohan 林默涵
Lin Wei 林為
Lin Xiling 林希翎
Lin Zhen 林震
linghui 領會
linghui lingdaoshang de yitu
　領會領導上的意圖
lishishang you wenti de ren
　歷史上有問題的人
Liu Baiyu 劉白羽
Liu Binyan 劉賓雁
Liu E 劉鶚
Liu Guosheng 劉國勝
Liu Qing 劉清
Liu Shaotang 劉紹堂
Liu Shifu 劉世福
Liu Xi 柳溪
Liu Xicheng 劉錫誠
Liu Xinwu 劉心武
Liu Yanwen 劉衍文
Liu Zheng 劉諍
Liu Zhiwu 劉志武
liumang 流氓
liushengji 留聲機
lixiang 理想
lizheng 立正
Lu Dingyi 陸定一
Lu Fei 逯斐
Lu Jindong 路金棟
Lu Le 魯勒
Lu Shiqing 陸士清
Lu Wenfu 陸文夫
Lu Xun 魯迅
luan 亂
lumang 魯莽
Lun texie 論特寫
Luo Lizheng 羅立正
Luo Ren 洛人
Luo Ruiqing 羅瑞卿
Luo Yuanzheng 羅元錚
Luofushan xuelei ji 羅浮山血淚祭
luohou fenzi 落後分子

Ma Feng 馬烽
Ma Hanbing 馬寒冰
Ma Heqing 馬鶴青
Ma Tieding 馬鐵丁
Ma Weian 馬畏安
Ma Wenyuan 馬文元
Ma Xinde 馬信德
mangcongzhe 盲從者
mangmuxing 盲目性
mantan 漫談
Mao Dun 茅盾
Mao Zedong 毛澤東
maoshi 冒失
maoxian 冒險
maozhe shibai de weixian
　冒著失敗的危險
mei ya, taimeile 美呀, 太美了
Mei Zu 梅械
Meinier shi bing 每尼爾氏病
Meinier shi zonghebing
　每尼爾氏綜合病
Meishang yinmu de gushi
　沒上銀幕的故事
meiyou chuangzao jingshen
　沒有創造精神
meiyou quedian 沒有缺點
meiyou yongqi 沒有勇氣
Mimi de Zhongguo 秘密的中國
minban 民班
min'ganxing 敏感性
mingzhi bu dui 明知不對
Minoru Takeuchi 竹內實
mo shou chenggui 末守成規
Mou Zhongxiu 牟鍾秀
Mu Guozheng 木國政
mudi 目的

Nanfang ribao 南方日報
Nasijia de xingxiang guwu women
　qianjin 娜斯嘉的形象鼓舞我門
　前進
nianqingren 年青人

Niehaihua 孽海花
Nigulayewa 尼古拉耶娃
niliu 逆流
Ningxia 寧夏
nisu mudiao de huo siren
　泥塑木雕的活死人
Niumang 牛氓
nuoruo de ren 懦弱的人

Pa zai qiganshang de ren
　爬在旗杆上的人
paijiu 牌九
Pan Hannian 潘漢年
Pan Shishen 潘士申
paxing zhuyi 爬行主義
peiyang yonggan jingshen
　培養勇敢精神
Peng Zhen 彭真
Pi "zi" xinpian 批"資"新篇
pijuan 疲倦
pingchang 平常
pipi tata 疲疲塌塌
piping 批評
pita 皮塌

Qian Laifu 錢來富
Qian Xingcun 錢杏邨
Qian Xuesen 錢學森
qianxu jinshen 謙虛謹慎
qianxu 謙虛
Qiao changzhang shangren ji
　橋廠長上任記
Qiao Guangpu 橋光樸
Qin Chuan 秦川
Qin Shi 秦式
Qin Xianglian 秦香蓮
Qin Zhaoyang 秦兆陽
Qingchun wansui 青春萬歲
qingguan 清官
qinggui jielü 清規戒律
Qinghai 青海

qingjie 輕捷
qingnian tujidui 青年突擊隊
qingsong 輕松
qingtian 青天
qingxu kunao 情緒苦惱
qingxu xiaochen 情緒消沉
qingzhan chushan 請戰出山
qiong gongren 窮工人
qipao 旗袍
Qishi niandai 七十年代
qitu xiangle 企圖享樂
qiu 求
Qiyue 七月
qu 區
Qu Qiubai 瞿秋白
Qu Yuan 屈原
quanmian 勸勉
quanru zhuyi 犬儒主義
quede 缺德
Quli de richang shenghuo
　區裡的日常生活

Rao Shushi 饒漱石
Ren yao zhi jian 人妖之間
Ren yu ren zhi jian 人與人之間
ren yun yi yun 人云亦云
Ren Zhong 任重
rennai 忍耐
reqing 熱情
Rong Lianxiu 榮蓮秀
Ru Zhijuan 茹志絹
Rulin waishi 儒林外史

sangshi jingtixing de ren
　喪失警惕性的人
Sanwen texie xuan 散文特寫選
sanwen 散文
Sasilafusiji 薩斯拉夫斯基
seng 僧
Senki 戰旗
Sha Ding 沙汀

Sha Yexin 沙葉新

Shanghai zai chensi zhong
上海在沉思中

shanghen wenxue 傷痕文學

shangren 上任

Shao Quanlin 邵全麟

Shao Yanxiang 邵燕祥

shaonian laocheng 少年老成

shaoshuo weijia 少說爲佳

shehui diaocha 社會調察

shehui gongcheng 社會工程

Shen Congwen 沈從文

Shen Duanxian 沈端先

Shen Tongheng 沈同衡

Shen Yan 沈雁

Shenbao meizhou zengkan
申報每周增刊

shengdong huopo de zuofeng
生動活潑的作風

shenke 深刻

shenqi 神氣

shensi de texie 深思的特寫

Shi Bing 石冰

shi buguan ji 事不關己

Shi Gan 石敢

shi ren 十人

shiguzhyi 世故主義

shiji 實際

Shijie wenxue 世界文學

shikuai 市儈

shishi qiushi 實事求是

shiwu 事務

shiwuzhuyi 事務主義

shiyexin 事業心

shiyong 實用

shouchuang jingshen 首創精神

Shouhuo 收獲

shoujiu 守舊

shun da 順大

shushou shujiao 束手束腳

Sima Yi 司馬懿

Simiernuofu 斯米爾諾夫

sishi er fei 似是而非

siwenren 斯文人

sixiang fulu 思想俘虜

sixiang you wenti 思想有問題

su 肅

Su Hui 蘇慧

Su Juan 蘇雋

Su Ping 蘇平

Suerkefu 蘇爾科夫

Sufan 肅反

suibi 隨筆

Suixiang qu 隨想曲

Sun Wuchen 孫武臣

suoshou suojiao 縮手縮腳

suqing fangeming yundong
肅清反革命運動

Suxiu wenyi pipanji
蘇修文藝批判集

tai dadan 太大膽

taidu buhao 態度不好

Tamen buken yiwang . . .-Lianbang
Deguo sanji zhi yi 他們不肯逸忘
聯邦德國散記之一

tamen 他門

Tan texie 談特寫

tanbai 坦白

Tang 唐

Tang Dingguo 唐定國

Tang Jiuyuan 唐久遠

Tang Zefu 唐則夫

Tang Zhi 唐摯

Tanqiuzhe 探求者

tedian 特點

tejing 特景

Teng Yun 騰云

texie 特寫

texiejia 特寫家

tezhao 特照

ti yijian 提意見

Tian Jing 田靜

Tian Zhongqi 田仲濟

Tiandeliyakefu 田德里亞柯夫
Tianjin wenyi 天津文藝
tiaopi gui 調皮鬼
Tieshui benliu 鐵水奔流
Tiexian zhuan 鐵鍁傳
Titi tou 剃剃頭
titou 剃頭
Tong Zhen 童真
tong 痛
tong 童
tongqing dali 通情達理
tongren ban 同人班
tongxun 通訊
tongyao 童謠
tou 頭
tuji liliang 突擊力量
Tuohuangzhe 拓荒者
Tuolajizhan zhanzhang he
   zongnongyishi
   拖拉機站站長和總農藝師

waiqu 歪曲
Wang Changding 王昌定
Wang Letian 王樂天
Wang Meng 王蒙
Wang Qingquan 王清泉
Wang Ruowang 王若望
Wang Shiwei 王實味
Wang Shouxin 王守心
Wang Ti 王倜
Wang Xizhe 王希哲
Wang Yongsheng 王永生
Wang Yushi 王禹時
Wang Zekun 王則昆
wanyir 玩意儿
wei (xinzhuyi) 唯(心主義)
Wei Heming 魏鶴鳴
Wei Jingde 尉敬德
Wei Jinzhi 魏金枝
Wei Junyi 為君宜
Wei Qimei 韋啟美
Wei Wei 魏巍

wei zhengzhi fuwu 為政治服務
weishou weiwei 畏首畏尾
weiwei nuonuo 唯唯諾諾
wendang 穩當
wendubiao 溫度表
wenming 文明
wenxue 文學
Wenxue fenlei de jiben zhishi
   文學分類的基本知識
Wenxue gailun 文學概論
Wenxue lilun xuexi cankao ziliao
   文學理論學習參考資料
wenxue texie 文學特寫
Wenxue yao yi zheng, yi jing, yi wen
   文學要議政議經議文
Wenxuejie 文學界
Wenyi xuexi 文藝學習
Wenyibao 文藝報
wenyuan 文員
wenzhong 穩重
wo 我
Wo ai meiyipian lü ye
   我愛每一片綠葉
Wo shi shei 我是誰
Wo yinggai zenme ban
   我應該怎麼班
Women jia de chuishiyuan
   我們家的炊事員
Women zazhi 我們雜誌
Wu Diaogong 吳調公
Wu Han 吳晗
Wu Jiapei 烏家培
wu jilü 無紀律
Wu Jun 吳俊
Wu Meng 吳蒙
Wu Qiang 吳強
wu suo yongxin 無所用心
Wu Tiaogong 吳調公
Wu Woyao 吳沃堯
Wu Xuelin 吳學林
Wu Yihua 吳毅華
Wu Yun 吳耘

Wu Yuzhang 吳玉章
wu zuzhi 無組織
wu zuzhi wu jilü 無組織無紀律
Wuxing de jiqi 無形的機器
wuxing zhi 五行志

Xi Wangbei 希望北
Xi Zhongxun 習仲勳
Xia Yan 夏衍
xian qian kan 先前看
xian 縣
Xiang geng gaofeng qianjin
　向更高峰前進
Xiang Nasijia xuexi 向娜斯嘉學習
xiangsheng 相聲
xiangxiang 想象
xianzai ne 現在呢
Xiao douer 小豆爾
xiao jituan 小集團
Xiao Jun 蕭軍
Xiao Li 肖里
Xiao Qian 蕭乾
xiaodao 小道
xiaopin 小品
xiaopinwen 小品文
xiaosheng 小生
xiaoshuo 小說
Xie Liuyi 謝六逸
xie zhenshi 寫真實
xieshen 邪神
xieshi texie 寫實特寫
Ximengnuofu 西蒙諾夫
Xin Guancha 新觀察
Xin xieshizhuyi 新寫實主義
Xing Fangqun 邢方群
Xing Yan 邢雁
Xinguang ribao 新光日報
Xingjiang 新疆
Xinminbao 新民報
xinshiqing 新式情
xinwen 新聞
xinwen jishi 新聞紀事

Xinwen yanjiu ziliao 新聞研究資料
Xinwen zhanxian 新聞戰線
xinying 新穎
Xin yulin 新語林
Xin yusi 新語絲
xiqi de erge 希奇的兒歌
xiwang bei 希望輩
Xixiang ji 西廂記
xixin 細心
Xiyou ji 西遊記
Xu Chi 徐遲
Xu Jiming 徐級明
Xu Jinding 徐進亭
Xue Rengui 薛仁貴
xueguai 學乖
Xuexi yu pipan 學習與批判
Xuexi 學習
xugou 虛構
xuwang 虛望

Yan Chen 嚴辰
Yan Xue 晏學
Yan'an 延安
Yang Rupeng 楊如鵬
Yang Shuo 楊朔
Yang Tiancun 楊田村
Yang Xizhong 楊熹中
Yang Zhongmei 楊中美
yanguang duanxiao 顏光短小
Yanhe 延河
yanjiuxing texie 研究性特寫
Yao Mingde 姚明德
Yao Wenpi yingji 姚文痞影集
Yao Wenyuan 姚文元
Yao Yuanfang 姚遠方
ye 野
Ye Weilin 葉蔚林
Ye Wenfu 葉文夫
Ye Yuming 葉煜明
Ye Yun 野云
yexin 野心
Yi Fu 一夫

Yi Junsheng 尹均生
Yi Qun 以群
Yige ren he ta de yingzi
　一個人和他的影子
yijian 意見
yingshengchong 應聲虫
Yingshi longteng huyue shi
　應是龍騰虎躍時
yingwu xueshe 鸚鵡學舌
Yinwei youle ta 因為有了她
Yishu xinzha 一束信扎
yitu 意圖
yituan heqi 一團和氣
Yiwen 藝文
Yongda 永大
yonggan 勇敢
yonggandi 勇敢地
yongqi 勇氣
yongyong lulu 庸庸碌碌
you cuowu de ren 有錯誤的人
youjidui texie 游擊隊特寫
youyou 悠悠
Youyou cuncaoxin 悠悠寸草心
youzhi 幼稚
Yu Gang 余綱
Yu Guo 于果
Yu Kun 于昆
Yu Pingbo 俞平伯
Yu Songyan 余松岩
Yuan Shuibo 袁水拍
yuanda de lixiang 遠大的理想
yuanzexing 原則性
yuchun 愚蠢
Yugong yishan 愚公移山
Yuhua 雨花
Yuwen xuexi 語文學習

Zai feixu shang 在廢墟上
Zai qiaoliang gongdi shang
　在橋梁工地上
Zai zuiren de beihou 在罪人的背後
zao yundong 造運動

Ze Lu 澤路
zekun 則綑
Zeng Delin 曾德林
Zeng Gang 曾剛
Zeng Hui 增輝
Zeng Pu 曾朴
Zeng Xisan 曾習三
Zhancheng fengyun 戰爭風雲
zhandouxing 戰斗性
Zhang Baoshen 張葆莘
Zhang Chang 張長
Zhang Chunqiao 張春橋
Zhang Guangnian 張光年
Zhang Jun 張駿
Zhang Liqun 張黎群
Zhang Tailai 張太來
Zhang Wenyuan 張文元
Zhang Ye 張野
Zhang Zhengti 張正偫
Zhang Zhong 張鐘
Zhang Zhongxiao 張中曉
zhanqian guhou 瞻前顧後
zhanzhan zixi 沾沾自喜
Zhao Huiwen 趙慧文
Zhao Jing 趙靖
Zhao Ke 召珂
Zhao Shuli 趙樹理
Zhao Zhenkai 趙振開
Zhaoxia 朝霞
Zhe yidai 這一代
zhen 真
zhen nan a 真難阿
zhenchabing 偵察兵
zhenchabingshi de texie
　偵察兵式的特寫
Zhenfan 鎮反
zheng 靜
Zheng Bijun 鄭匕俊
Zheng Wen 鄭汶
Zhengfeng 整風
zhengke 政客
zhenglun 爭論

zhenglunxing 爭論性

zhengqu lingdao de zhiyin
　爭取領導的指引

zhengrong 整容

zhengzhi renwu 政治任務

zhengzhi reqing shuaitui
　政治熱情衰退

zhenshi 真實

Zhenxi delai buyi de chuangzuo
　ziyou 珍惜得來不易的創造自由

Zhi Guang 之光

zhiqi 志氣

zhishi fenzi 知識分子

zhishi xia'ai 知識狹隘

zhishuai de xingge 直率的性格

zhishuai 直率

zhixiang 志向

zhixin xiaji 知心下級

zhiyou ta cai shi xiwangde yibei
　只有他才是希望的一輩

zhiyuan 志願

Zhong Jieying 中杰英

Zhong Peizhang 鐘沛璋

Zhong Qun 鐘群

zhongcheng laoshi 忠誠老實

Zhongguo de yiri 中國的一日

Zhongguo qingnian 中國青年

Zhongguo qingnianbao 中國青年報

Zhongguo zhi chun 中國之春

Zhou Dajue 周大覺

Zhou Enlai 周恩來

Zhou Erfu 周而復

Zhou Jiajun 周嘉俊

Zhou Jie 周杰

Zhou Libo 周立波

Zhou Peitong 周培桐

Zhou Weiben 周維本

Zhou Weizhi 周巍峙

Zhou Yang 周揚

Zhu Guang 朱光

Zhu Guangqian 朱光潛

Zhuangzi 莊子

zhudong jingshen 主動精神

zhudong zuanjiu 主動鑽究

zhudongxin 主動心

Zhuge Liang 諸葛亮

zhujiao 主角

Zi Gang 子岡

zigan pingyong 自甘平庸

zigao zida 自高自大

zijiaren 自家人

zijue 自覺

Zong Pu 宗樸

Zou Shumin 鄒樹民

Zou Xianmin 鄒賢敏

zuofeng shengying 作風生硬

zuofeng shi culu ... bu neng
　rongxudi 作風是粗魯...不能容
　許地

Zuzhibu xinlaide qingnianren
　組織部新來的青年人

Index